NEW ENGLAND

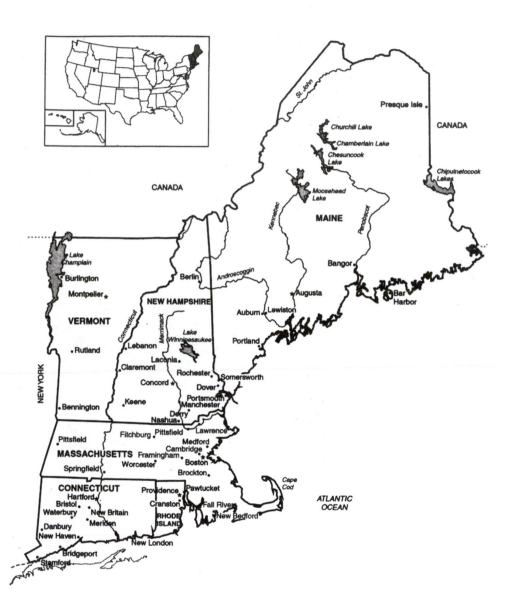

NEW ENGLAND

The Greenwood Encyclopedia of American Regional Cultures

Edited by
Michael Sletcher

Foreword by William Ferris, Consulting Editor

Paul S. Piper, Librarian Advisor

GREENWOOD PRESS
Westport, Connecticut • London

Library of Congress Cataloging-in-Publication Data

New England : the Greenwood encyclopedia of American regional cultures / edited by
Michael Sletcher ; foreword by William Ferris, consulting editor.
    p. cm.
  Includes bibliographical references and index.
  ISBN 0–313–33266–5 (set: alk. paper)—ISBN 0–313–32753–X (alk. paper)
  1. New England—Civilization—Encyclopedias. 2. New
England—History—Encyclopedias. 3. New England—Social life and
customs—Encyclopedias. 4. Popular culture—New England—Encyclopedias.
5. Regionalism—New England—Encyclopedias. I. Sletcher, Michael. II. Series.
F4.N47 2004
974'.003—dc22   2004056058

British Library Cataloguing in Publication Data is available.

Library of Congress Catalog Card Number: 2004056058
ISBN: 0–313–33266–5 (set)
       0–313–32733–5 (The Great Plains Region)
       0–313–32954–0 (The Mid-Atlantic Region)
       0–313–32493–X (The Midwest)
       0–313–32753–X (New England)
       0–313–33043–3 (The Pacific Region)
       0–313–32817–X (The Rocky Mountain Region)
       0–313–32734–3 (The South)
       0–313–32805–6 (The Southwest)

First published in 2004

Greenwood Press, 88 Post Road West, Westport, CT 06881
An imprint of Greenwood Publishing Group, Inc.
www.greenwood.com

Printed in the United States of America

The paper used in this book complies with the
Permanent Paper Standard issued by the National
Information Standards Organization (Z39.48–1984).

10 9 8 7 6 5 4 3 2 1

Copyright Acknowledgments

The editor and publisher gratefully acknowledge permission for use of the following material:

Excerpts from N. S. Shaler, "Environment and Man in New England," *The North American Review*,
vol. 162 (June 1896), 725–740. Courtesy of Cornell University Library, Making of America Digital
Collection.

CONTENTS

Contents

FOREWORD

Region inspires and grounds the American experience. Whether we are drawn to them or flee from them, the places in which we live etch themselves into our memory in powerful, enduring ways. For over three centuries Americans have crafted a collective memory of places that constitute our nation's distinctive regions. These regions are embedded in every aspect of American history and culture.

American places have inspired poets and writers from Walt Whitman and Henry David Thoreau to Mark Twain and William Faulkner. These writers grounded their work in the places where they lived. When asked why he never traveled, Thoreau replied, "I have traveled widely in Concord."

William Faulkner remarked that early in his career as a writer he realized that he could devote a lifetime to writing and never fully exhaust his "little postage stamp of native soil."

In each region American writers have framed their work with what Eudora Welty calls "sense of place." Through their writing we encounter the diverse, richly detailed regions of our nation.

In his ballads Woody Guthrie chronicles American places that stretch from "the great Atlantic Ocean to the wide Pacific shore," while Muddy Waters anchors his blues in the Mississippi Delta and his home on Stovall's Plantation.

American corporate worlds like the Bell system neatly organize their divisions by region. And government commissions like the Appalachian Regional Commission, the Mississippi River Commission, and the Delta Development Commission define their mission in terms of geographic places.

When we consider that artists and writers are inspired by place and that government and corporate worlds are similarly grounded in place, it is hardly surprising that we also identify political leaders in terms of their regional culture. We think of John Kennedy as a New Englander, of Ann Richards as a Texan, and of Jimmy Carter as a Georgian.

Because Americans are so deeply immersed in their sense of place, we use region like a compass to provide direction as we negotiate our lives. Through sense of place we find our bearings, our true north. When we meet people for the first time, we ask that familiar American question, "Where are you from?" By identifying others through a region, a city, a community, we frame them with a place and find the bearings with which we can engage them.

Sense of place operates at all levels of our society—from personal to corporate and government worlds. While the power of place has long been understood and integrated in meaningful ways with our institutions, Americans have been slow to seriously study their regions in a focused, thoughtful way. As a young nation, we have been reluctant to confront the places we are "from." As we mature as a nation, Americans are more engaged with the places in which they live and increasingly seek to understand the history and culture of their regions.

The growing importance of regional studies within the academy is an understandable and appropriate response to the need Americans feel to understand the places in which they live. Such study empowers the individual, their community, and their region through a deeper engagement with the American experience. Americans resent that their regions are considered "overfly zones" in America, and through regional studies they ground themselves in their community's history and culture.

The Greenwood Encyclopedia of American Regional Cultures provides an exciting, comprehensive view of our nation's regions. The set devotes volumes to New England, the Mid-Atlantic, the South, the Midwest, the Southwest, the Great Plains, the Rocky Mountains, and the Pacific. Together these volumes offer a refreshing new view of America's regions as they stretch from the Atlantic to the Pacific.

The sheer size of our nation makes it difficult to imagine its diverse worlds as a single country with a shared culture. Our landscapes, our speech patterns, and our foodways all change sharply from region to region. The synergy of different regional worlds bound together within a single nation is what defines the American character. These diverse worlds coexist with the knowledge that America will always be defined by its distinctly different places.

American Regional Cultures explores in exciting ways the history and culture of each American region. Its volumes allow us to savor individual regional traditions and to compare these traditions with those of other regions. Each volume features chapters on architecture, art, ecology and environment, ethnicity, fashion, film and theater, folklore, food, language, literature, music, religion, and sports and recreation. Together these chapters offer a rich portrait of each region. The series is an important teaching resource that will significantly enrich learning at secondary, college, and university levels.

Over the past forty years a growing number of colleges and universities have launched regional studies programs that today offer exciting courses and degrees for both American and international students. During this time the National Endowment for the Humanities (NEH) has funded regional studies initiatives that range from new curricula to the creation of museum exhibits, films, and encyclopedias that focus on American regions. Throughout the nation, universities with regional studies programs recently received NEH support to assist with the programs that they are building.

The National Endowment for the Arts (NEA) has similarly encouraged regional initiatives within the art world. NEA's state arts councils work together within regional organizations to fund arts projects that impact their region.

The growing study of region helps Americans see themselves and the places they come from in insightful ways. As we understand the places that nurture us, we build a stronger foundation for our life. When speaking of how she raised her children, my mother often uses the phrase "Give them their roots, and they will find their wings." Thanks to *American Regional Cultures,* these roots are now far more accessible for all Americans. This impressive set significantly advances our understanding of American regions and the mythic power these places hold for our nation.

William Ferris
University of North Carolina
at Chapel Hill

PREFACE

We are pleased to present *The Greenwood Encyclopedia of American Regional Cultures*, the first book project of any kind, reference or otherwise, to examine cultural regionalism throughout the United States.

The sense of place has an intrinsic role in American consciousness. Across its vast expanses, the United States varies dramatically in its geography and its people. Americans seem especially cognizant of the regions from which they hail. Whether one considers the indigenous American Indian tribes and their relationships to the land, the many waves of immigrants who settled in particular regions of the nation, or the subsequent generations who came to identify themselves as New Englanders or Southerners or Midwesterners, and so forth, the connection of American culture to the sense of regionalism has been a consistent pattern throughout the nation's history.

It can be said that behind every travelogue on television, behind every road novel, behind every cross-country journey, is the desire to grasp the identity of other regions. This project was conceived to fill a surprising gap in publishing on American regionalism and on the many vernacular expressions of culture that one finds throughout the country.

This reference set is designed so that it will be useful to high school and college researchers alike, as well as to the general reader and scholar. Toward this goal, we consulted several members of Greenwood's Library Advisory Board as we determined both the content and the format of this encyclopedia project. Furthermore, we used the *National Standards: United States History* and also the *Curriculum Standards for Social Studies* as guides in choosing a wealth of content that would help researchers gain historical comprehension of how people in, and from, all regions have helped shape American cultures.

American Regional Cultures is divided geographically into eight volumes: *The Great Plains Region, The Mid-Atlantic Region, The Midwest, New England, The Pacific Region, The Rocky Mountain Region, The South,* and *The Southwest*. To ensure that cultural elements from each state would be discussed, we assigned each state to a particular region as follows:

The Great Plains Region: Kansas, Nebraska, North Dakota, Oklahoma, South Dakota
The Mid-Atlantic Region: Delaware, District of Columbia, Maryland, New Jersey, New York, Pennsylvania, West Virginia
The Midwest: Illinois, Indiana, Iowa, Michigan, Minnesota, Missouri, Ohio, Wisconsin
New England: Connecticut, Maine, Massachusetts, New Hampshire, Rhode Island, Vermont
The Pacific Region: Alaska, California, Hawai'i, Oregon, Washington
The Rocky Mountain Region: Colorado, Idaho, Montana, Utah, Wyoming
The South: Alabama, Arkansas, Florida, Georgia, Kentucky, Louisiana, Mississippi, North Carolina, South Carolina, Tennessee, Virginia
The Southwest: Arizona, Nevada, New Mexico, Texas

Each regional volume consists of rigorous, detailed overviews on all elements of culture, with chapters on the following topics: architecture, art, ecology and environment, ethnicity, fashion, film and theater, folklore, food, language, literature, music, religion, and sports and recreation. These chapters examine the many significant elements of those particular aspects of regional culture as they have evolved over time, through the beginning of the twenty-first century. Each chapter seeks not to impose a homogenized identity upon each region but, rather, to develop a synthesis or thematically arranged discussion of the diverse elements of each region. For example, in turning to the chapter on music in *The Pacific Region*, a reader will discover information on Pacific regional music as it has manifested itself in such wide-ranging genres as American Indian tribal performances, Hawaiian stylings, Hispanic and Asian traditions, West Coast jazz, surf rock, folk scenes, San Francisco psychedelia, country rock, the L.A. hard-rock scene, Northwest "grunge" rock, West Coast hip-hop, and Northern California ska-punk. Multiply this by thirteen chapters and again by eight volumes, and you get a sense of the enormous wealth of information covered in this landmark set.

In addition, each chapter concludes with helpful references to further resources, including, in most cases, printed resources, Web sites, films or videos, recordings, festivals or events, organizations, and special collections. Photos, drawings, and maps illustrate each volume. A timeline of major events for the region provides context for understanding the cultural development of the region. A bibliography, primarily of general sources about the region, precedes the index.

We would not have been able to publish such an enormous reference set without the work of our volume editors and the more than one hundred contributors that they recruited for this project. It is their efforts that have made *American Regional Cultures* come to life. We also would like to single out two people for their help: William Ferris, former chairman of the National Endowment for the Humanities and currently Distinguished Professor of History and senior associate director for the Center for the Study of the American South, University of North Carolina at Chapel Hill, who served as consulting editor for and was instrumental in the planning of this set and in the recruitment of its volume editors; and Paul S. Piper, Reference Librarian at Western Washington University, who in his role as librarian advisor, helped shape both content and format, with a particular focus on helping improve reader interface.

With their help, we present *The Greenwood Encyclopedia of American Regional Cultures*.

Rob Kirkpatrick, Senior Acquisitions Editor
Anne Thompson, Senior Development Editor
Greenwood Publishing Group

INTRODUCTION

For many the name "New England" conjures up images of Puritans, white church steeples, quaint towns, and intimate farms nestled in the forested hills of the American Northeast. As a region, New England comprises six states and extends from New York's eastern border to the Atlantic coast. There has often been a romantic vision of New England's cultural landscape. Such images, however, tend to be static and monolithic, ignoring the diversity and dynamism of the region and its past. The development of New England, in other words, was by no means a monocultural progression from Puritan discipline and godliness to Yankee industry and ingenuity across a single region, but rather a complex and multifaceted evolution of diverse cultures over many centuries and geographical spaces. As Edward L. Ayers and Peter S. Onuf have pointed out in their introduction to *All Over the Map: Rethinking American Regions*, "Regions may be in danger not only from malls and cable television but also from attempts to freeze places in time or to define some particular component of a region as its essence, leading regionalists to despair when that essence seems to be disappearing. It is better, we think, to recognize that regions have *always* been complex and unstable constructions, generated by constant evolving systems of government, economy, migration, event, and culture."[1] In the chapters that follow, Ayers and Onuf's words serve as the best model, for, as the reader will soon discover, New England is not a stable, unified region in the American Northeast, but rather a complex, evolving series of regions with many cultural identities.

New England's cultural origins predate the arrival of the Puritans and even the name "New England," which Captain John Smith gave to the coastline in 1614. Portuguese, Basque, Irish, and English sailors had discovered the rich fishing grounds off the coast of New England as early as the late fifteenth century, and the Popham colonists arrived at Sagadahoc, Maine, in 1607, predating the arrival of the Pilgrims at Plymouth Rock. In the chapter on Language, Bruce F. Murphy remarks on this early development: "The image of the landing of the Pilgrims as a new beginning is in some ways erroneous. When the Pilgrims met Samoset, he spoke to them in English—probably a pidgin form learned from sailors in his native Maine. Pidgins are trading languages with a root stock but often incorporating terms taken from several different tongues. Sailors, as a multinational group, were early developers of pidgins and brought them to the New England coast, where they used them to trade with the native peoples." New England's multicultural past, therefore, was a precursor of Puritanism and the European migrations in the nineteenth century. European involvement in the region, including the French, had existed as early as the late fifteenth century.

Other cultural groups predated the arrival of the Puritans. Native American groups, for example, arrived in the region millennia before the first Europeans set foot on the shores of New England and developed a variety of cultures within the region. They shared the same Algonquian language but were by no means a homogenous group. As Enrique Morales-Díaz, Gabriel Aquino, and Michael Sletcher point out in the chapter on Ethnicity, "although many of these tribes belonged to the same family of language they differed in terms of their customs, beliefs, traditions, and locations." Europeans, however, used "uniformity in order to classify them" and solidified later attitudes toward natives in the region. In northern New England, the Eastern Abenaki inhabited the coast of Maine while the Western Abenaki (or Sokoki) inhabited the mountainous range of New Hampshire and northern Vermont as far as Lake Champlain. They lived in individual tribes, sharing certain traditions, customs, and beliefs, and moved seasonally. In southern New England, where the climate and land were less hostile for later European settlement, the Pocumuck, Massachusetts, Nauset, Niantic, Wampanoag, Nipmuc, Narragansett, Pennacook, Mattabesic, and Pequot/Mohegan inhabited the lands from Massachusetts and parts of southern New Hampshire and southeastern Maine to Rhode Island and Connecticut. They too were semi-sedentary and moved with the seasons.

The arrival of these peoples in the region was a long and gradual process, extending over millennia and geological periods. Between 30,000 and 11,000 B.C.E., the first human inhabitants crossed the Bering Strait and entered North America via Alaska and Canada, migrating eastward and southward. They established a variety of cultural and linguistic groups through the Americas, but the settlement of the New England region itself was at the tail end of this great transpacific migration. The last glacier, known as the Wisconsin glaciation, did not begin to recede until about 18,500 B.C.E., and New England was covered by glaciation and arctic-like tundra until about 11,000 B.C.E. During much of this period, the region was uninhabitable, and although the first inhabitants began to arrive in southern and northern New England at the end of or shortly after the Bering Strait migration, they encountered a hostile terrain. Glaciation still covered northern Maine and, as Lisa Krissoff Boehm points out in the chapter on Ecology and Environment, the region was not only covered by glaciation but was also partly submerged under water and sea: "Glaciations caused a variety of lakes to be scattered across New England, although many have become dried out over time and have left only their tell-tale shapes and soils behind. For example, a lake later named Lake Hitchcock was once located in the Connecticut Valley. Thousands of these ancient bodies of water remain. Vermont's Lake Champlain is the remaining component of the former Champlain Sea, and much of coastal Maine and New Hampshire was formerly underwater."

The environment, in many ways, shaped the beginning of human settlement in the region and later the first European settlements in the seventeenth century. The Puritans, after all, had read favorable reports of the land in Captain John Smith's *Description of New England* (1616), *New England Trials* (1620), and *Advertisements for the Unexperienced Planters of New England* (1631). Smith's promotional view of New England as a barren yet earthly paradise exaggerated the real climate and terrain of the region and contradicted other Elizabethan and Jacobean literature at the time, but as John Conforti has explained in *Imagining New England* (2001), "Smith imaginatively assimilated the landscape of his New England to the geography of the homeland, he represented the region as a primitive England, and he exemplified the convention of overstatement that was the staple of promotional literature."[2]

This Anglocentric vision of the region's geography was not all that the Puritans brought with them to the New World. They transplanted many aspects of their English culture, anticipating "that they would be able to live much as they had done in England, in an artisanal and farming community with work rhythms, class relations, and a social order similar to the one they had left behind—the only difference being their own improved stature in society."[3] They transplanted an English "city upon a hill," and in most of the chapters, the reader will find examples of this as well as occasional adaptations to native culture in the face of unexpected challenges during the early years of settlement. In the chapter on Fashion, for example, Linda Welters tells us that Puritan clothing reflected the styles worn by the middling classes in England. In the chapter on Architecture, Blanche Linden mentions English forms of architecture that the first settlers transplanted to Massachusetts and then to other parts of New England. In the chapter on Sports and Recreation, Martin J. Manning refers to sports and recreations, like bowling, card playing, dice throwing, billiards, shuffleboard, angling, hunting, and horse racing, that were played in colonial New England despite the Puritan suspicion of "unlawful" games and leisurely pursuits.

But clearly the most important cultural feature that the early settlers transplanted to the New World was religion. Puritans brought and imposed a strict form of Calvinism on the region, which shaped the cultural landscape for over two hundred years. In the chapter on Religion, Jeremy Bonner and Anthony George tell us that these early Protestants came from East Anglia, Lincolnshire, the West Riding, the Midlands, and the Southwest, as well as London: They "represented those who increasingly questioned the long-term commitment of the English crown to the Protestant Reformation, particularly after the accession of James VI of Scotland to the English throne in 1603 and his subsequent refusal to tolerate Protestant religious dissent." Their migration to New England, therefore, was an attempt to establish godly commonwealths in the New World. Variant forms of congregationalism evolved in different regions, as Bonner and George also observe. The plantations of Rhode Island, for example, were more tolerant than those of Massachusetts, Connecticut, and New Haven, but overall they maintained the basic tenets of Calvinism, namely, the belief in predestination and original sin. Religion influenced every aspect of life in early New England, including music, as Barry Marshall and Suzanne Cope point out in the chapter on Music. For Puritans music was an extension of their religious beliefs. They sang psalms, a form of music that had been transplanted from England and sung at the end of the church service, "if singing is the word to describe the strange cacophony that rose from a Puritan congregation," as David Hackett Fischer has noted in *Albion's Seed* (1989). They emphasized the words rather than the music. By the later part of the colonial period, observers "were astounded by the noise, which carried miles across the quiet countryside. But New Englanders were deeply moved by this 'rote singing' as it was called, and strenuously resisted efforts to improve it."[4] By the mid-eighteenth century, there was a movement to "reform" this crude, unsophisticated manner of singing. Progressives, as we learn in the Music chapter, introduced note reading as a way for Congregationalists to counter this old style of rote singing or what reformers called the "Usual Way."

If Puritans imposed their Anglocentric vision of the world on the New England region, they also had to be flexible at times and adapted themselves to new challenges. During the first winter in Plymouth, for example, the Pilgrims found themselves on the verge of starvation and without the means of completing their permanent shelters. The local Native Americans provided them with the means of making temporary shelters as well as introducing them to new foodways. The Puritans embraced these foreign elements, including the introduction of new foods, like squash, corn, and maple syrup, adding them to their diet. They also accepted Native American methods of cooking. The clambake, for example, was a popular Native American method of cooking clams. In the chapter on Food, Robert F. Moss explains this process of what has become not only a method of cooking but also one of New England's most popular forms of social gathering: "A large pit is dug in the sand and its inside lined with stones. A wood fire is built in the pit and allowed to burn down to coals, which are then raked out and removed. The white-hot rocks are covered with wet seaweed, which creates steam for cooking, then clams, lobsters, and corn are placed into the pit. A variety of other ingredients are sometimes added to the clambake, including crabs, mussels, fish, chicken, sausage, potatoes, and other vegetables. Then, the pit is covered with a heavy tarp, and the food steamed." Baked beans also came from the Native Americans, and although Puritans were familiar with this method of cooking in England, they adopted, as Moss explains, a Native American "version of baked beans, which were cooked in the ground in an ember-filled 'beanhole.' British colonists adopted this recipe readily, for it was very similar to pease porridge, a staple of English cooking. Today, the dish is best known outside the region as 'Boston baked beans,' but it is prepared throughout New England, with the ingredients varying from state to state." Puritans also borrowed Native American techniques of building temporary shelters. The first settlers of Salem (1626) and the Massachusetts Bay Colony (1630), as Linden tells us in the chapter on Architecture, built curvilinear wigwams, "better than tents with crude openings, fireplaces, and walls of bark over branch supports, a form [they] copied from natives who migrated seasonally." And although the Puritans were selective about their sports and recreations, the Indian game of lacrosse (baggataway), as Manning illustrates in the chapter on Sports and Recreation, became a popular New England sport after the Civil War.

Puritans, like other colonists in North America, however, tended to see the world through their own cultural prism and imposed that vision on the environment and people living in the New World. They set out to convert Native Americans to their Protestant brand of Christianity, as Bonner and George explain in the chapter on Religion, establishing Indian "praying villages," like the one in Natick, Massachusetts, and founding Harvard College as a seminary for the training of a Native American as well as a white ministry. They also did irreparable harm to the environment, as Boehm tells us in the chapter on Ecology and Environment. As Calvinists adhering to the scriptural tenet of man's dominion over nature, Puritans were clearing forests at an unprecedented rate, creating an ecological imbalance and disaster for many native and later communities. Thus, Peter Kalm, a Swedish naturalist visiting New England, complained about New England's deforestation in 1749 when he wrote, "We can hardly be more hostile toward our woods in Sweden and Finland than they are here: their eyes are fixed upon the present gain, and they are blind to the future."[5]

New England's future, although unknown to Puritans at the time, was a shift from an agricultural to industrial economy. By the middle of the nineteenth century, the region had become the most urban and industrialized part of the nation. In the chapter on the Environment and Ecology, Boehm points out that in 1800, "6.8 percent of the residents of Massachusetts lived in towns of more than ten thousand. By 1840, 22 percent did, and by 1870, almost one-half of the state lived in towns of over ten thousand. As the United States considered a location to be urban if it contained 2,500 people or more, and because by this standard the United States would not become an urban nation (more than one-half of the population living in places of 2,500 or more until 1920), we can see that the urbanization of New England precedes that of the United States as a whole." The gritty mixture of clay, sand, and rocky soil, making farming difficult, and the region's many natural rivers, providing waterpower before the introduction of steampower, contributed equally to this process of urbanization. Indeed, as Welters explains in the chapter on Fashion, textile manufacturing led the way toward industrialization in New England: "Every state in New England was involved in textiles, thanks to the region's many rivers, which provided waterpower."

The view of New England as a quaint, small-town region emerged around this time. With urbanization and the growth of industry, rural areas increasingly turned to tourism rather than farming. At the same time, the American public associated them with a healthy escape from the city rather than agricultural labor and idealized the image of the old New England town. A revival in everything colonial resulted in new architecture and art mimicking the colonial past. Ironically, there was an absence of historical accuracy in much of the detail. The white wooden steeple of the New England church, for example, was largely a feature of the nineteenth century and not the colonial period. By the early republic, however, Federal-style wooden churches with tower and spire, as Linden points out in the chapter on Architecture, "were so widespread that they characterized the New England town." Nor was white paint a feature of the New England town until the early nineteenth century, and it certainly was not a "typical" feature until much later. Often homes in early New England were painted in bright reds, greens, or blues, in contrast to our perception of Puritans as a dark and somber people. In the chapter on Art, Herbert R. Hartel, Jr., and Michael Sletcher show further signs of this nineteenth-century invention of New England colonial life. Despite views to the contrary, New England women were not quilting or holding quilting bees until after 1750. The idealization of New England women quilting by the fire or participating in quilting bees was largely a nineteenth-century invention, a romantic vision of the colonial past. With the trend toward tourism by the second half of the nineteenth century, the New England town increasingly became an American symbol of an idealized colonial past, an escape from the disturbances and discords of a fast-paced, new industrialized age. Unsurprisingly, large rural resorts also became fashionable. New Hampshire's Crawford Hotel (1859), Montpelier's Pavilion Hotel (1876), and the Mount Washington Hotel (1902) in Bretton Woods, New Hampshire, all appeared around this time as another form of escape from the city or as a playground for the wealthy.

The idealization of rural New England also reinforced the creation and perpetuation of the Yankee character-type. The precursor of this character was "Brother Jonathan," a rural figure who possessed qualities associated with rural simplicity and honesty. He first appeared, as Bruce F. Murphy explains in the chapter on Film and Theater, in Royall Tyler's comedy, *The Contrast* (1787). Jonathan, a "plain-spoken Yankee of dry wit and hard sense, often comical but also wise," is one of the central figures in the play. Although his rural simplicity serves as a "contrast" to city sophistication and urbane New York society, allowing for many episodes of humor at the Yankee's expense, it also serves as a contrast between the honest and simple values of the new American republic vis-à-vis the corrupt and decadent values of old Europe. This theatrical representation of the Yankee character became popular throughout the country in the nineteenth century. He "was a looming figure," as Constance Rourke has described him in *American Humor* (1931). "He might be a peddler, a sailor, a Vermont wool-dealer, or merely a Green Mountain boy who traded and drawled and upset calculations."[6] He represented rural simplicity and, as Michael Hoberman points out in the chapter on Folklore, he was a new kind of cultural hero across America: "If the Yankee, on stage and in real life, was known for anything it was his understated quick-wittedness, his ability to out-talk and out-trade anyone while seeming all the while, in his ill-fitting clothes and stranger colloquialisms, to have been born yesterday." Hoberman demonstrates this simple quick-wittedness of the Yankee character in a folk tale from the *Saturday Rambler* (1848), in which a New Englander outwits a group of western New York farmers. The popularity of this character in the nineteenth century perpetuated another cultural myth about the region, but perception is equally important to understanding cultural identities as is reality and manifests itself in the present as well as the past.

The popularity of the Yankee character also extended to the sphere of womanhood. As Luca Prono tells us in the chapter on Literature, Lydia Maria Child of Medford, Massachusetts, wrote domestic manuals creating the female countertype of the male Yankee character. The Yankee woman, as Child portrayed her, was a domesticated woman who transported Yankeeness into the household and protected American values from antirepublican excesses. She sheltered members of the family from corruptions in the public sphere and installed republican virtue by example. Similar matriarchal types of this figure appear in Harriet Beecher Stowe's writings, but her characters are more ambiguous about their gender roles. In *Imagining New England*, John Conforti has remarked that Stowe's "Yankee women are often strong, assertive, even masculine, their mission to domesticate the character and behavior of their men requiring a New England androgyny. Stowe herself, while fulfilling the responsibilities of domesticity and motherhood, became through her writing the principal breadwinner for her family. A republican mother who peddled domesticity in the literary marketplace, she found in the mirror of her own life elements of the cross-gender model of the Yankee character that she examined in her fiction."[7] Such ambiguity of gender is present not only in *Uncle Tom's Cabin* in the character of Miss Ophelia, but also in Stowe's letters and in her New England historical novels, *The Minister's Wooing* (1859), *The Pearl of Orr's Island* (1862), and *Oldtown Folks* (1869).

With industrialization and mass immigration in the late nineteenth and early twentieth centuries, New Englanders, like other Americans, developed a sense of nostalgia for the colonial past. Colonial Revival architecture, for example, became fashionable, and during the Great Depression years of the 1930s, Cape Cod–style homes, known for their simplicity and strength, were middle America's favorite architectural style when it came to buying a home. In Thornton Wilder's play *Our Town* (1938), the characters of Grover's Corners, an imaginary New Hampshire town, are white Protestant Yankees. In the opening monologue, the playwright makes a brief allusion to Polish and French Canadian immigrants living on the other side of town, but they are never part of the drama itself. "Their absence suggests a tacit meaning of Wilder's title," as Stephen Nissenbaum has said, "and makes it clear that the phrase 'Our Town' is to be pronounced with the stress on the first word: '*Our* Town.'"[8] The Depression years also reinvigorated the idealization of the old Yankee when Robb Sagendorph launched the New Hampshire magazine *Yankee* (1935), which is still in circulation today. The object was an exploration of New England's customs and traditions; it was, as the editor explained it at the time, "the expression and perhaps, indirectly, the preservation of that great culture in which every Yankee was born and by which every Yank must live." This purpose was all the more urgent, as Prono mentions in the chapter on Literature, because "of the impending 'sea of chain stores, national releases, and nation wide hookups,' which, together with 'mass production, mass distribution, mass advertising, and mass almost-everything-you-can-think-of,' were destroying the New England Yankee's typical 'individuality, initiative, and natural ingenuity.'" The twentieth-century nostalgia for something more stable and familiar in the American past was partly a reaction to this fast-paced and technologically evolving world, but it was also a reaction to something else, the loss of a white Protestant identity in regions dominated by almost three centuries of white Anglo Protestantism.

Indeed, if the Yankee was the prototype of individuality, simplicity, and honesty, among other attributes, he was also Protestant and white. The process of industrialization, however, brought many new immigrants to the region in search of jobs or as an escape from political and social conditions in their home country. The Irish Potato Famine during the 1840s resulted in the first wave of mass immigration from Europe. The Irish, arriving in large numbers in the port cities of Boston or New York, moved to other urban centers, like New Haven, or to smaller towns, like Lowell, Lawrence, and Fall River, Massachusetts, where they worked in the factories or as unskilled laborers. To understand the magnitude of this first wave of Catholic Irish immigration, Morales-Díaz and Aquino point out in the chapter on Ethnicity that the Irish made up less than 1 percent of the entire population in New England by the end of the colonial period; by 1870, however, they accounted for 11 percent of the population, and 55 percent of all foreign-born in the region. The British, including Scottish and Welsh, accounted for about 98.5 percent of the population in the census of 1790, but today they are just over 10 percent of the population—with the English being the fourth largest ethnic category, behind the Irish and Italians as well as the first category, those with no recorded ethnic identity. The Irish were soon followed by smaller groups of Germans, Poles, and Russian Jews, and by the turn of the century, large numbers of Italians were coming to New England and settling in cities like Boston, Providence, and New Haven. White Protestant Yankees for the first time found themselves no longer the majority in certain regions, fostering a conservative reaction against non-Protestant, nonwhite immigrants—"undesirables," as the Boston Immigration Restriction League, established in 1894, called them.

Other ethnic groups arrived in the region both before and after the great migrations of the nineteenth century. African Americans, for example, had arrived in smaller numbers with the first settlers as slaves or servants. Contrary to popular belief, slavery was present in parts of New England after the colonial period. Although Vermont and Massachusetts had abolished slavery by the end of the colonial period, Connecticut did not completely abolish slavery until the year 1848, even though it did pass the Gradual Abolition Act of 1784. The issue of slavery was more complicated in other New England states, except for Maine, which became a state in 1820. Slavery simply withered away after the states passed gradual emancipation acts or received a formal declaration of abolition with Congress' ratification of the Thirteenth Amendment to the Constitution. After the Civil War brought an end to slavery in the South, African Americans began to migrate to New England, but it was not a widespread and noticeable trend until the early and later twentieth century when black migrant workers moved to northern urban centers to find work in factories and the service sector.

Franco-Americans also arrived in small numbers during the colonial period after they refused to take a loyalty oath to the British crown in the mid-1700s and were expelled from Nova Scotia. These French-speaking migrants were "Acadians," some of whom fled south to Louisiana. Larger groups of French Canadians arrived in the nineteenth and twentieth centuries, mainly between 1840 and 1930, when nine hundred thousand French-speaking people came to the United States, most settling in textile mill towns and villages in northern New England. Their continuing influence in the northern part of New England is evident in states like Maine, where nearly a quarter of the population, as Bruce F. Murphy points out in the chapter on Language, is of French origin, and where many families speak French as a first or second language in the household.

At the beginning of the nineteenth century, Portuguese immigrants settled along the coast of New England, namely in New Bedford, Fall River, and Martha's Vineyard, Massachusetts. This first wave of Portuguese settlers, as Morales-Díaz and Aquino point out, came from Portugal to work in the New England whaling industry, but as jobs became less plentiful, they became fishermen and worked in the textile mills and the shoe industry. They introduced the musical form of the *fado*, described by Marshall and Cope in the chapter on Music as a mournful solo that resonated "with people of all cultures who relied on whaling or fishing to support their families" and reflected on the "pain and uncertainty, often associated with sorrow over those who did not come back from boating disasters." The Portuguese have maintained their communities and are still a presence in New England. In the last thirty years, they have accounted for 14 percent of new immigrants in Massachusetts, and have large communities in Connecticut and Rhode Island, though it should be remembered that the Portuguese community is made up not only of immigrants from Portugal, but also of immigrants from the Azores, the Madeira and Cape Verde islands, and Brazil.

One of the most salient features of these new immigrants was their religion. They were by and large Catholics. Their arrival in the region, as Bonner and George explain in the chapter on Religion, "was anything but welcome to many in the Protestant community, but they proved unable to stem either the tide of newcomers or their high birth rates, and by the early twentieth century Catholic majorities in Massachusetts and Rhode Island promised a new outlook for New England." Unitarianism and Methodism had replaced the old brand of Protestant Calvinism in the early part of the nineteenth century, but by the twentieth century, migration patterns and high birth rates had made Catholicism the dominant religion of New England. The fact that Connecticut chapters of the Ku Klux Klan had over twenty thousand members by 1920 was more a reflection of antipathy toward this Catholic majority than toward the smaller black migrations from the South.

New England also had a significant Jewish presence in its urban areas and more recently has seen the arrival of Muslims, Hindus, and Buddhists, but with the growth of religious pluralism in the post-1960s, New England has continued to maintain a large Catholic identity. This is more interesting when we consider, as Bonner and George also point out, that "almost three-quarters of New England church goers (73.4 percent) claim to be Catholic, a figure thirty points above the national average and which exceeds that of both the Mid-Atlantic (63.0 percent) and the Pacific (59.3 percent)." Such numbers have translated into political representation and power in key New England regions, including important cities like Boston, Massachusetts; Hartford and New Haven, Connecticut; Providence, Rhode Island; and Manchester, New Hampshire.

Twentieth-century immigration has seen a wider assortment of ethnic groups coming to New England, including Puerto Ricans who arrived after the Jones Act of 1917 (granting them American citizenship) and, more recently, Asians from Vietnam, China, the Philippines, and India. In the chapter on Film and Theater, Murphy points to the growing representation of immigrants and cultures in New England film and theater. By the end of the nineteenth century, there were several Italian theaters in Boston, New Haven, and Vermont. There were also Polish, Greek, and Latvian theaters, and more recently immigrants are finding themselves represented in modern cinema, in films like *Mermaids* (1990), about a Jewish couple living in Massachusetts; *The Inkwell* (1994), about African Americans on Martha's Vineyard; *Mystic Pizza* (1988), which deals in part with Portuguese living in Connecticut; *The Blue Diner* (2001), about a Puerto Rican woman who moves to Boston and the troubles she faces; and *Passionada* (2002), a romantic story about the Portuguese community of New Bedford and the widow of a fisherman who finds love again. Multicultural representations in both film and theater have corrected some of the myths of the region, including the popular stereotype of New Englanders as stoic descendants of the Puritan tradition. As Murphy explains with regard to the evolution of New England theater in the twentieth century, "It was farcical to continue to present nationalistic plays that asserted that America had left backward Europe behind and realized human freedom. Somehow, the sincere if flawed spiritual vision of the first colonists had devolved into the fatuous projection of a myth. The 'city on a hill' that John Winthrop had exhorted the faithful to build in the Massachusetts Bay Colony had turned out otherwise."

Today New England is a variety of regions. It has grown into a complex series of cultures, as indicated by the 2000 Census in the Ethnicity chapter, in which the largest ancestry group recorded was "Not Reported." A growing number of New Englanders, in other words, are not familiar with their ancestry or simply find it too complex and intertwined to provide an individual category for race. New England is more cosmopolitan than it ever has been; it is an evolving multicultural landscape, though myths like the New England town and the Yankee character persist and are still important to understanding the region in both the present and the past. In the chapters that follow, the reader will come into contact with these cultural evolutions and find, as Andrew Delbanco has summarized it in *Writing New England* (2001), that New England "is more than merely a geographical term." It is the history of diverse cultural memories, of continuity and change, of confrontation and accommodation, of the past, present, and future. It is, to use different words, more than a list of reverential symbols alluding to "Pilgrims, Puritans, Boston Tea Party, Paul Revere, City on the Hill, Underground Railway, Massachusetts alone for McGovern, etc."[9] It is a vibrant region that continues to thrive in many forms by looking to its past, present, and future.

ARCHITECTURE

Blanche Linden

Understanding New England architecture goes beyond scrutinizing buildings to knowing their place in the landscape. Styles borrowed and adapted persisted through four centuries of innovation, declension, and revival. Despite so much having been lost, preservationists have refurbished and recycled the worn-out for a palpable sense of place, the past living in the present while modern styles intrude in whole districts of recent urban design.

NATIVE AMERICANS

The earliest forms of New England architecture emerged with the first inhabitants, the native tribes of the Algonquian family, who migrated seasonally from sheltered inland valleys in the winter to camps and fields near the coast or in river valleys from spring through summer. They built circular or oval *wetus* (12' × 14') or *neesquttows* ("houses with two fires," 12' × 20') with frames of saplings or poles bent sunken in the soil, bent to the top, and covered with rain-proof bark or woven mats held in place with hemp. Skins covered chimney holes, doorways, and floors. When migrating, extended family groups carried exterior matting along for reinstallation in another camp, periodically shifting summer sites to let fields for corn, beans, and squash lie fallow to regain fertility. They stored dried produce in grass sacks or baskets buried in deep holes. *Puttuckakuans* ("round houses" or longhouses up to 30' × 100') served for communal wintering, often surrounded by a circular stockade of upright logs up to twelve feet high, gaps filled by branches, with narrow entrances on two sides that could be filled with brush in case of attacks by rival tribes. Other than a few modern re-creations of the form and unlike in other regions, none of the portable and biodegradable originals remain.

The native population of New England, estimated at sixty-five thousand in 1610, was devastated by epidemics in 1619, 1633, and 1637, while English settlements displaced many more natives from their old coastal sites. At the outbreak of King

A Pequot *wetus*. Photo by Nancy Walker.

Philip's War in 1675, Native Americans numbered under ten thousand in the whole region and lost even more of their number when about half of them attacked Anglo settlements during the war. By then, Puritans had converted and acculturated a number of Native Americans in fourteen "praying towns" in eastern Massachusetts that replicated the English village. The war reduced "praying towns" to four, including Natick, and many natives were forcibly relocated to Deer Island and adjacent Boston Harbor islands.

THE PURITANS

A priority of the Pilgrims after they landed in 1620 was the digging of sawpits to cut timbers for Plymouth's fort, "a large square house of thick sawn planks stayed with oak beams." Given English law, wood was also cut for the deforested Mother Country. The first settlers in Plymouth, in Salem (1626), and in the Massachusetts Bay Colony (1630) built curvilinear English "wigwams," little better than tents with crude openings, fireplaces, and walls of bark over branch supports, a form copied from natives who migrated seasonally. Wampanoags and southeastern tribes built *wetus*, *neesquttows*, or *puttuckakuans* with frames of saplings or poles bent to the top and covered with rain-proof bark. Mats or skins covered chimney holes, doorways, and floors. Settlers also used caves or "dugouts." Then came crude houses with one room and a sleeping loft. The General Court forbade thatching as a fire hazard. It awarded America's first patent for a Saugus sawmill in 1646. Sawmills spread in the Piscataqua frontier near virgin forests in New Hampshire and Maine.

The Massachusetts Bay Colony towns allotted land to freeholders by merit close to the meetinghouse. Houses on narrow lots fronted the road for winter access. "Out-livers" (those living outside of the town) were frowned upon. When land ran out, new generations and newcomers "hived off" (broke away) and settled new, adjoining towns. Puritan Boston reserved fifty acres as a militia "trayning field," cattle pasture, and execution place peripheral to harbor-centered life. The common had a granary, burial ground, almshouse, workhouse, and combined prison and insane asylum. Towns had secular graveyards given the Puritans' desire to get rid of "Papist churchyards." John Brockett's plans for New Haven (1638) and Hartford (1640) were formal grids around multifunctional "market places," later "greens."

"First Period" houses mimicked the late-Tudor architecture of Essex and East Anglia. Carpenters built half-timber mortise-and-tenon frames. Chimney girts bolstered the middle with side "summer beams." Vertical studs held internal walls;

joists held floors; and high-gabled roofs prevailed until about 1750 when the pitch lowered. Daub and wattle (straw mixed with clay or lime) insulated walls as in Dedham's Fairbanks House (1636), the oldest surviving timber frame structure in North America. Clapboard with pine-shingled roofs covered most early structures, while low ceilings with exposed beams and central chimneys conserved heat. Hearths occupied a wall in a great room or "hall," doubling for cooking as in Portsmouth's Jackson House (1664). Later houses covered ceiling beams with paneling or plaster as in the Arnold House (1678) in Lincoln, Rhode Island, and the nearby Clemence House (1680), examples of that area's "stone-enders" with two fieldstone sides.

More illustrious houses had two floors with multiple "fire rooms" containing small fireplaces and rear kitchens under lean-tos (extended roofs), like Saugus' Boardman (1667), Andover's Abbot (1685), Watertown's Browne (1698), Ipswich's Whipple (1639) and Paine (1694) and Salem's Ward House (1684) and Corwin (1678), all in Massachusetts. Fishermen built one-and-a-half-story cottages with lean-tos in Cape Cod dunes, a chimney between two rooms with a sleeping loft. The "half-Cape" had one room and an end chimney, and was ready for expansions, as the enlarged weathered-gray Hoxie House (1637), a shingled saltbox in Sandwich, Massachusetts.

Wooden meetinghouses, which were built in the town center for town meetings and worship, reflected Puritan rejection of Papist ceremony and symbolism. Noncruciform in shape and detail, they were rectangular structures and had one large room with a pulpit and benches. The oldest surviving is the Old Ship Meeting House (1681) in Hingham, Massachusetts. Originally 45' × 55', additions by 1775 enlarged it to 75' × 55'. A modest steepled belfry tops the hipped roof. "Nooning" or "Sabba-day" houses with one or two rooms often existed behind for those who could not walk home between services.

The architectural simplicity of meetinghouses extended to the frontier towns of Danville (1760) and Sandown (1774), New Hampshire, and Rockingham (1787), Vermont. Carpenter Timothy Palmer built Amesbury's Rocky Hill Meeting House (1785), a spartan structure resembling Judah Woodruff's meetinghouse in Farmington, Connecticut (1771). St. Paul's Church (1707) in Narragansett (later moved to Wickford) and Trinity Church (1771) in Brooklyn, Connecticut, although Anglican, had the four-square Puritan form, which makes the Round Church (1813) in Richmond, Vermont, a New England curiosity.

The introduction of the round form in New England architecture has an association with the Shakers, who maintained the austerity and simplicity of Puritan architecture. The round, rough-hewn stone barn (1827) they built in Hancock, Massachusetts, epitomizes functionality, topped by a wooden clerestory and lantern for light and ventilation. Shakers built a meetinghouse and sexually segregated "family houses," believing in celibacy. Their Meetinghouse (1794) survives in Sabbathday Lake, Maine. Shaker style may also have inspired the Southwick family's round barn in East Calais, Vermont (1900).

MERCANTILE PROSPERITY

With the rise of the merchant class in the early eighteenth century, New England builders soon looked to Georgian styles of architecture, and inspired by Sir

Christopher Wren's and Andrea Palladio's designs, they emulated the British fashion for detached "town houses." The Wren-Baroque minimized regional differences in the colonies. Portsmouth's brick MacPhaedris House (1723) was Georgian, its central door with a segmental pediment atop fluted Corinthian pilasters, its balustraded gambrel roof punctuated by dormers and topped by a cupola and twin chimneys. Medford's Royall House (1723) began with two and a half stories, expanded by 1737 to three, two rooms deep with side chimneys, its wooden facade painted to mimic stone, with quoining (decorative detailing on the corners of the structure) and fluted Doric pilasters. The Thomas Hancock residence (destroyed in 1740) on Boston's Beacon Hill by master mason Joshua Blanchard had similar elements, its grandeur from granite trimmed with sandstone.

Emulation of Palladianism grew from James Gibbs' *Book of Architecture* (London, 1728). The Hunter House (1748), a three-story gambreled mansion, reflects the prosperity of one of Newport's "merchant princes." Gibbsian formalism is seen in the Vassall House (1759) in Cambridge, built for a leading Tory by Newport architect Peter Harrison (1716–1775), and later enlarged by Henry Wadsworth Longfellow. Pilasters embellish its two-story symmetrical clapboard facade. A balustrade and two chimneys top a low-hipped roof with a central pedimented pavilion flanked by dormers. Harrison used such elements for the Lady Pepperell House (1760) in Kittery Point; for the Malbone House (1760) in Newport; and for the first Apthorp House (1760) and the second (1763) for the minister's father in nearby Brighton.

Georgian taste migrated to Connecticut River towns in the Webb, Deane, and Stevens houses in Wethersfield. The Cowles family of Farmington, Connecticut, having acquired their wealth from imports to country stores, hired master builder William Sprats for a gambrel-roofed house (1780) with quoining, Ionic pilasters, fluted columns, and Palladian windows. Importer Julius Deming in nearby Litchfield had Sprats build a hipped-roofed residence, "The Lindens" (1793), with detailing like that of the Boardman House (1796) in New Milford. Sprats also remodeled Sheldon's Tavern (1760) across from Senator Uriah Tracy's residence.

Solidity: Brick and Stone

Use of brick and stone increased, while wood remained popular farther from the coast. Salem had a brickyard in 1629. Other brickyards opened on clay deposits as in Cambridge. Creating a sense of permanency and the urbane mattered, but necessity demanded brick because fires endangered towns built of wood.

After Boston's Great Fire of 1711 destroyed his house, apothecary Thomas Crease built his brick shop and family quarters (1718, now Old Corner Bookstore) under a gambrel roof. The fire also ruined the Town House (1657), and the royal province, county, and town financed a four-story brick state house with room for the elders' meeting, library, arsenal, and arcaded market for "Country people that come with theire provisions to sitt dry and warme." Reconstructed after another fire in 1747, a three-tiered tower rises above the slate gambrel roof, its ends stepped as perches for lion and unicorn symbols of monarchy. The New Town House, Province House, or Court House (now the Old State House) had a second-floor "seat of the Vice-Regal State of Governors," court chamber, and assembly chamber plus a fire station, wine cave, and warehouse in the half-cellar. A post office, merchants' exchange, and records offices occupied the first floor. The structure served as a center for revolutionary activity, and from its balcony John Hancock read the Declaration of Independence to a Boston crowd.

Boston's oldest religious structure is the Anglican Christ Church or "Old North" (1723). British officials hired print seller William Price and draftsman Anthony Blount, who used designs of Wren's London churches. Of Medford brick, its tower, topped by a spire, holds the colonies' first bells (1744). The rectangular nave has high-sided family pews to curb winter drafts. A semicircular apse frames the altar. Two ranges of piers support balconies under archways. The Second Church was a two-story, cedar structure large enough for town meetings but inadequate when master builder Joshua Blanchard built the brick South Meeting House (1729) with a tower and wooden steeple on a colonnaded belfry using plans by Robert Twelves. It had the largest capacity of any Boston building, and standing-room-only crowds of five thousand convened amid its box pews during the Revolution.

Newport's Anglicans commissioned Richard Munday for Trinity, its nave completed in 1726, a rectangular wooden core with cruciform aisle bays. Emulating Boston's Old North but in clapboard, a spire rose above a two-tiered front tower in 1741. Munday designed Newport's "Old Colony House" (1739) for the provincial assembly, a Wren-

Reconstructed after a fire in 1747, Boston Old State House served as a center for revolutionary activity. Courtesy of Massachusetts Office of Travel and Tourism.

Baroque, three-story brick building topped by a truncated central gable in the gambrel roof with balustrade and cupola, one of the first brick structures there with red sandstone quoins and rusticated trim with white woodwork. Munday placed a balcony over the entrance flanked by Corinthian pilasters. A truncated pediment with a clock breaks the roof's front line, flanked by dormers. Newport was then the fifth largest colonial seaport.

The hated Governor Edmund Andros had put an Anglican chapel on the corner of Boston's first burial ground in 1684, after the revocation of the Massachusetts charter by Charles II. Boston Anglicans hired Newport merchant Peter Harrison in 1741 to design a larger King's Chapel influenced by Wren and Gibbs with a hipped roof. With four-foot-thick walls, it was America's first stone church and the first using Quincy granite, hard to quarry and move. Work proceeded slowly, displacing "bodies of bones." Workers removed the wooden structure through new windows in 1754. The Ionic wooden portico added in 1785 under a squat tower, never topped by a steeple as planned, was painted to resemble stone.

Some deem Harrison America's first professional architect, using his library of Georgian architecture for derivative designs, yet transitional to the Greek Revival. He designed the Roxbury rural mansion for Massachusetts governor William

Shirley (1746). His work includes Newport's Doric colonnaded Abraham Redwood Library and Athenaeum (1750), the first drawing upon Palladio, and the nation's oldest library with wooden Doric colonnade. Harrison also designed Cambridge's wooden Anglican Christ Church (1761), and he designed Newport's Touro Synagogue (1763) for the colonies' first Sephardic Jewish congregation. Newport's Brick Market (1761–1772) has an open-air, arcaded ground floor with two above, embellished with white wooden pilasters and a full entablature.

In 1742, Boston merchant Peter Faneuil erected at his "own cost and charge" as a public bequest a two-story Georgian brick market, 140 feet wide, designed by painter John Smibert at the docks' end. Faneuil Hall replaced market functions beneath the State House and had second-floor space for public meetings. When it succumbed to fire in 1761, the Ancient and Honorable Artillery Company, America's oldest militia headquartered there, raised lottery funds for reconstruction. As Boston's population surged from seventeen thousand to twenty-five thousand in the last quarter of the eighteenth century, Charles Bulfinch renovated Faneuil Hall (1805), doubling its size with four bays and a story, making its second-floor meeting room grander with gallery seating. Ionic pilasters and fine detailing gave the "Cradle of Liberty" fitting grandeur.

New England boasts many examples of this eighteenth-century studied symmetrical rationalism. During this period, Harvard College (1636) began its era of brick when president John Leverett and Benjamin Wadsworth designed Massachusetts Hall (1720) and Governor Sir Francis Bernard built Harvard Hall (1765). Yale built Connecticut Hall (1752). Charles Bulfinch (1763–1844) added Harvard's University Hall (1814) and two buildings to the Phillips Academy at Andover by 1819.

THE FEDERAL STYLE: THE EIGHTEENTH AND NINETEENTH CENTURIES

After the Revolution, builders drew upon the English Adams brothers' work with low-pitched, hipped, or flat roofs and balustrades atop third stories. Dark external shutters came into fashion. Restrained exteriors flanked by quoins or pilasters surmounted by cornices and with Palladian windows belie interior elegance—staircases with carved balusters, mantels with low-relief festoons, delicate cornices with dentils and modillions, rinceau borders, rosette motifs on architraves, and raised dadoes—a new design idiom.

"Gentleman-amateur" Joseph Brown (1733–1785), a Rhode Island College professor (of what is now Brown University) and brother of the mill developer, designed the first College Edifice (1770), four stories built in brick by James Sumner; and Providence's First Baptist Meetinghouse (1775), combining the best Gibbsian elements with clapboard and quoining. College Hill acquired fine mansions with four rooms and five front windows per floor as Brown designed brick houses in imitation of his own (1774) and that of his brother John (1786). Carpenter Caleb Ormsbee built Colonel Nightingale's mansion (1792). The Ives House (1806), set back and elevated above the street, has a brick façade with white woodwork—a Palladian window over a curved, colonnaded portico. John Holden Green designed dozens of fine houses. A carpenter added a Corinthian porch to Edward Carrington's house in 1812. Architect Russell Warren brought grandeur to nearby Bristol with George De Wolfe's "Linden Place" (1810), a three-story portico with Corinthian columns.

Carver and master builder Samuel McIntire (1757–1811) used Adamesque elements for Salem houses—the Peirce (1782), Cook (1804), Waters (1805), and Pickman (1810) Houses. The Gardiner House (1805) has an elliptical porch with slender Corinthian columns, its facade softened by horizontal marble bands and window heads plus a balustraded parapet. Ornate wooden or cast iron fences fronted many set back from the street. McIntire adapted Bulfinch's design for Elias H. Derby's Peabody summer house (1799). McIntire designed Salem's Federal Style Assembly Hall (1782). Mercantile prosperity is also seen in the Custom House (1819) overlooking Derby Wharf, the imposing brick structure made famous by Nathaniel Hawthorne. It boasts a Palladian window above an Ionic portico, round-headed windows, balustraded parapet, and cupola.

Merchants from Rhode Island to Maine built Federal houses with end chimneys like the Nickels House (1807) in Wiscasset, Maine, but they were more modest inland. Litchfield's Collins House (1782) was wood painted red to suggest brick until 1815, when it was redone in white. Williamstown's Sloane House (1801) is a rectangle covered with clapboard but decorated with elements carved in Boston. The Aubin House (c. 1810) in Vergennes, Vermont, is of brick with modest details. Northern New England made "continuous" buildings, houses joined to sheds and barns, to eliminate the need to go out in winter. One visitor remarked, "The farms are like little attached villages," a kitchen wing connected or "jined" between house and barn.

Federal-style wooden churches with tower and spire were so widespread that they characterized the New England town. The Congregational Meetinghouse (1771) in Farmington, Connecticut, inspired by Wren, has a Greek Doric portico on the side added later. The First Congregational (1806) in Old Bennington, Vermont, is typical with details from pattern books. Daniel Wadsworth used the Federal idiom for Hartford's Center Church (1807). Asher Benjamin (1773–1845), a carpenter from Greenfield, Massachusetts, designed New Haven's Center Church (1812), and his assistant Ithiel Town built it. Samuel Belcher built Old Lyme's Congregational Church (1817) with an Ionic portico.

Charles Bulfinch, educated at Harvard, studied the architecture of Robert Adam and William Chambers in England. Back home in 1787, he combined practice as one of the first "professional" architects with service as Boston's chief of police and "Great Selectman," developing his own designs rather than cribbing from pattern books. He gave the dilapidated town a coherent character, transforming and upgrading Boston's urban fabric first with his Tontine or Franklin Crescent (1794, demolished in 1858), a 480-foot curved block of sixteen connected houses overlooking gardens. Its brick facade with central pedimented pavilion harmonized with the adjacent Federal Street Theater and detached houses he designed. Boasting a Corinthian colonnade, pilasters, and Palladian windows, the Federal Street Theater was revolutionary in introducing theater to Boston, where Puritans had once banned it. His Holy Cross, the city's first Catholic church, was built behind the Crescent and consecrated in 1803.

The Old State House seemed an antiquated symbol of the colonial period. The idea of moving the capital from Boston led to planning a new one in 1787, the town contributing building costs to retain the seat of government. Bulfinch selected a

Beacon Hill site overlooking the Common owned by John Hancock. Governor Samuel Adams laid the cornerstone on July 4, 1795, with Paul Revere as grand master of Masonic ceremonies. Bulfinch's neoclassical, colonnaded, brick State House epitomized the power and permanency of the new republican government with a large representatives chamber under the dome. The "Great and General Court," legislature, and governor occupied the building in 1798. White shingles covered the dome until 1802 when Revere's new Canton foundry produced copper sheathing. The lantern, 220 feet above sea level, remained the town's highest point for decades, a landmark above the steeples, symbolizing the triumph of secular government and the city as the "Athens of America." State House additions by Isaiah Rogers (1831) and Gridley J.F. Bryant (1856) are hidden by extensions from 1889 to 1895 that made the capitol six times its original size. Revere's copper was replaced with 23-carat gold leaf in 1874. William Chapman, R. Clipston Sturgis, and Robert D. Andrews added large granite wings in the rear (1914–1917).

A Boston town meeting in 1803 asked the general court to require that all buildings over ten feet high be of brick or stone and roofed with noncombustible slate or tile. That same year Harrison Gray Otis and Samuel Cabot purchased fifteen acres on Beacon Hill from Hancock's widow and painter John Singleton Copley. Their Mount Vernon Proprietors removed fifty feet off the top as workers dumped the infill into the Mill Pond (1803–1811). Bulfinch laid out Park Street in 1804 as a fine approach to the State House with a row of eight attached houses. Mayor Josiah Quincy beautified the Common, removing the almshouse and workhouse and planting trees to make a promenade, the first park on the Back Bay's tidal waters. Bulfinch created his famed Colonnade Row of nineteen row houses on the Common's south side in 1811.

Mount Vernon Proprietors developed a dense but elite neighborhood of brick townhouses and a few detached mansions on Beacon Hill's south slope with more modest residences and stables on the north slope. Bulfinch designed three houses for Harrison Gray Otis and the joined Swan Houses at 13, 15, and 17 Chestnut Street. Other Beacon Hill architects included Alexander Parris and Ephraim Marsh. Benjamin used the Federal style for his Old West Church (1806) and Charles Street Church (1807), and may have designed the brick African Meeting House (1806).

Benjamin's pattern books inspired emulation from the Georgian to the Adamesque and Grecian "adapted to the republican habits of this country"—*The Country Builder's Assistant* (1798), the first American architectural treatise; *The Builder's Assistant* (1800); *The American Builder's Companion* (1806); *The Rudiments of Architecture* (1820); *The Practical House Carpenter* (1830); and *The Practice of Architecture* (1833), all running into over forty editions. Benjamin may have designed the three-story brick West College (1790) in Williamstown, a classroom, chapel, and dormitory. He used Federal elements in the Old South Church (1798) in Windsor, Vermont. Bennington's First Congregational Church (1806) and Middlebury's First Church (1809) show how carpenter Lavius Fillmore drew upon his patterns, as did a builder for the First Church (1811) in Templeton, Massachusetts. David Hoadley, New Haven's leading architect, made his United Church (1812–1815) grander, its white pedimented portico atop Ionic columns with matching cupola on a tower above the brick structure with two levels of Palladian windows.

Of Bulfinch's Boston churches, only the New North (1814, now St. Stephen's) is still standing. Bulfinch won the competition to design the Massachusetts General Hospital (1820), and Alexander Parris prepared drawings for construction in granite. Bulfinch also designed the Connecticut State House (1793–1796) and the Maine State House (1829). The First Church of Christ in Lancaster (1817), one of his masterpieces, was constructed by master builder Thomas Hearsey. It has a white domed cupola with Ionic columns resting atop a pitched roof behind the portico, which has white Doric pilasters between three brick arches.

Nantucket Quaker Joseph Starbuck, rich from whaling, blended Georgian and Federal elements for three adjacent brick houses he designed for his sons. Master mason Christopher Capen and master carpenter James Childs built the trio (1837–1840) atop the Main Street hill on lots sixty feet wide and three hundred feet deep. Each has eighteen rooms with fourteen-foot ceilings, green shutters, five chimneys, pillared porticos, white balustrades, and large cupola. By then, many sea-captain neighbors chose the Greek Revival, like the two white wooden houses William Hadwen built in 1846. Georgian and Federal elements lingered in vernacular hinterland buildings. The brick Larkin House (1815) in Portsmouth is austere. Aaron Sherman designed the Judge Ruggles House (1818) with delicate detailing in Columbia Falls, Maine, for a major lumber dealer. David and Zephaniah Ordway employed the Federal style in Vermont's Windsor County, using local rough-hewn stone; the Edson House (1833) in Chester Depot is one of their finest.

Forts

Sébastien Le Prestre de Vauban, Marshal of France under Louis XIV, shaped fort design. George Washington put French engineers under General de Malmedy in charge of Rhode Island "works of defense" in 1776, constructing Fort Chastellux after the British evacuation in 1779, repairing Goat Island (1784) as Fort Washington. Congress created a Corps of Artillerists and Engineers and funded the First System of Defense (1794–1800). Major Etienne de Rochefontaine, engineer for New England, designed three Narragansett forts. He used earthworks, masonry, and timber for the batteries and barracks at Fort Sewall (1794) in Marblehead. U.S. Major Louis Tousard took over (1798–1800), enlarging the Conanicut Island Fort with the nation's first stone Martello tower with roof-mounted guns.

The Second System began in 1804 as Jefferson ordered West Point to train engineers. New Hampshire ceded old Fort Constitution and its Light to the United States in 1791. Renovations began in 1808 with a stone wall around a barbette battery, a bastion, barracks, power magazines, shot furnace, and captain's brick house. A brick Martello tower was added in 1814. Gen. Henry A.S. Dearborn supervised Portland fortifications as the British blockaded New England during the War of 1812.

The Third System of forts had masonry on earthen ramparts. Lt. Col. Joseph Totten, a West Point engineer, designed one near Newport on Old Brenton's Point. It was the nation's third largest fort and was considered a showcase in the art of fortification. Stonemason Alexander McGregor built Newport's Artillery Armory with shale, brick, and granite. Totten designed Providence's Fort Adams (1824–1845) to include the most complex Vaubanian defenses and a six-acre parade area. Army Corps Capt. George Washington Cullum (1809–1892) designed the five-sided Egyptian Fort Trumbull (1839–1852) at New London with four granite bastions on a site leveled in 1812. Boston's Castle Island remains the oldest (1634). Paul Revere repaired it as Fort Independence (1777); then Col. Sylvanus Thayer constructed the five-pointed star of granite (1834–1851).

STYLES IN STONE: THE GREEK REVIVAL AND BOSTON GRANITE STYLES

A new, growing class of professional architects introduced the Greek Revival in the early 1800s, a style associated with nationalism, more "rational" than the Federal, and drawing on technological breakthroughs for processing hard granite, although the style often used wood. Parris designed two Beacon Street houses (1816–1819). The finer of them, the bowfront granite house of Col. David Sears (now the Somerset Club), had the left half added in 1832. Parris collaborated with Solomon Willard, owner of the Quincy granite quarries, on Boston's colonnaded St. Paul's Cathedral (1820). Their Stone Temple or First Church (1828) in Quincy has a portico of fluted Doric columns, its tower topped by a colonnaded cupola. Benjamin wrote in 1830, "The Roman school of architecture has been entirely changed for the Grecian."

The building of Charlestown's Bunker Hill Monument (1825–1843) signaled a new commemorative sensibility through a visionary project which expanded technologies. The Monument Association hired Willard to design an unprecedented 221-foot obelisk with internal stairs to an observation platform. Gridley J. Fox Bryant, the Quincy quarries developer, supervised construction, devising ways to transport the heavy stone by boat and the nation's first railway, oxen-drawn, thus launching an era of the "Boston Granite Style."

After Boston was incorporated as a city in 1823, mayor Josiah Quincy created Quincy Market (1826) on 167,000 square feet of new filled land with 142,000 square feet of docks and wharfs just east of Faneuil Hall. Parris designed a two-story market block of Quincy granite (555' × 50') with colonnaded façades at both ends and a central rotunda featuring a copper-covered dome. The complex, flanked by two equally massive warehouses, covered 27,000 square feet. Beyond granite and glass with post-and-beam construction, it had cast-iron columns and tension rods. Rough-hewn granite gave monumentality to the quarter-mile-long Ropewalk (1836) which Parris gave to the Charlestown Navy Yard and to Lewis Wharf (1840).

Providence investors launched the commercial Arcade (1828), a covered street-like passage between three levels of shops designed by Russell Warren and James C. Bucklin. Cast-iron balustrades lined balcony sidewalks in front of glazed storefronts. Granite Ionic colonnades on end pavilions enclosed stairways. Full of light and air with skylights, gas-lit at night, the structure had only a few precedents in Paris, New York, and Philadelphia.

The architect Ithiel Town (1784–1844) began practice in New Haven in 1813, designing a hotel there and meetinghouses in nearby Plainfield and Thompson. Town also designed the Connecticut State Capitol (1831, destroyed) and New Haven's Third Congregational Church (1829). His Trinity Church (1816) on New Haven's Green is Gothic with crenellated parapets and tower. He worked with Isaac Damon to build wooden bridges (1816–1825), obtaining patents for his lattice truss (1820, 1835). Other covered bridges used "kingpost" or "queenpost" trusses of barn construction or the Burr truss patented in 1817. The roof on the 150-foot bridge (1852) in Stark, New Hampshire, was so great that its sides needed no enclosure. Caleb Lamson built the longest covered bridge, in West Dummerston, Vermont (1872), using Town's truss. Of those covered bridges surviving in 1954, Vermont had 121; New Hampshire, 54; Massachusetts, 12; and Connecticut, 3.

Trained by Willard, Isaiah Rogers (1800–1869) specialized in granite Greek Revival. His Tremont House (1829, demolished in 1894) in Boston, the first modern hotel, innovated with public facilities and privacy in 170 "patent-locked" rooms.

A gas plant provided lighting; a steam engine provided hot water for first-floor "bathing rooms." Having passed through its Doric portico, Charles Dickens marveled at "more galleries, colonnades, piazzas, and passages" than he had ever seen. The sole survivor of Rogers' famed hotels is the Bangor House (1832). Rogers designed the Merchants' Exchange (1841, destroyed) and the Custom House Block (1847) on Boston's Long Wharf, granite in front and brick in the rear. Willard's Suffolk County Court House (1836, destroyed) had a portico of fluted Ionic columns.

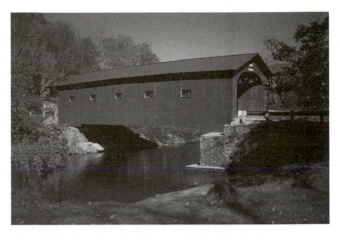

Covered bridges remain a fixture of New England's countryside. This bridge is located in Vermont.

Ammi B. Young, once apprenticed to Parris, designed the U.S. Custom House (1837–1847), a granite temple with Doric columns and a skylit dome over a rotunda, then at the water's edge, replacing an 1810 structure by Uriah Cotting. Young also designed the Vermont State Capitol (1836–1843) in Montpelier with Ionic colonnaded portico and a majestic dome. After an 1857 fire, Joseph R. Richards and T. W. Silloway oversaw its reconstruction.

The Greek style spread through Benjamin's and other pattern books and was still popular in the 1850s. Doric façades on churches, banks, and markets added a sense of permanency even on small wooden buildings like the Nantucket Athenaeum (1847). Edward Clarke Cabot designed the Boston Athenaeum (1849) using a Palladian idiom from books in that proprietary library. Its gray sandstone facade has Corinthian pilasters and pedimented windows in arches. Neoclassical simplicity inspired churches in Madison, Connecticut (1838), Slatersville, Rhode Island (1840), and Wellfleet, Cape Cod (1850).

Bryant and Louis Dwight used granite for Boston's Charles Street Jail (1851). The massive cruciform building with hipped roofs and wings off a central octagonal pavilion was a model for prison design, like Bulfinch's Charlestown State Prison. It has corner quoins and keystones above windows. Additions in 1901 and 1920 followed Bryant's plans. Bryant provided Boston's massive Mercantile Wharf Building and Commercial Block in 1856, State Street Block (1857), City Hospital (1864) in the South End, the ornate Beaux Arts Horticultural Hall (1865, destroyed), and the Italian Renaissance Revival Ballou Hall, the first Tufts College building.

THE INDUSTRIAL REVOLUTION

British law tried to keep colonists from developing industry. Once details of the Arkwright System of textile manufacture, patented in 1769, were smuggled out of England, "water frame" mills could be built by millwrights to harness waterpower through landworks, targeting the power from canals through sluiceways to run machinery. Available technology and waterpower determined a mill's size and shape, narrow on stone foundations to minimize vibration and having many windows to maximize light. Structures were of wood and masonry until 1810, when use of iron began.

Mills and Mill Towns

Samuel Slater (1768–1835) apprenticed with Arkwright before evading English customs in 1789. Moses Brown (1738–1836), a Rhode Island Quaker merchant, and his son-in-law founded Almy & Brown and had Slater "perfect" the first watermill at Pawtucket (1793) on the Blackstone River, a 29' × 43' wooden structure resembling a meetinghouse but enlarged in the 1820s into a "T" with cupola and "eyebrow" or "trapdoor monitor" roof windows for lighting. Brown built housing for poor families recruited to work for him. David Humphreys (1752–1818) copied Slater's plan in his woolens manufactory (1803) on Rimmon Falls near Derby, Connecticut. Orphans lived in boardinghouses and worked in semirural Humphreysville. Humphreys added a school, gardens, and housing for sixty families of "operatives." John Barber described it in 1836 as a "romantic and beautiful village" of white buildings.

Slater and his brother John joined Almy & Brown to buy 150 acres on the Branch River Falls near Pawtucket. Slatersville (1806) had a mill, two tenements, a company store, and a resident-owner's house. The first U.S. manufacturing census in 1810 counted twenty-six Slater-style mills in Rhode Island, fourteen in Connecticut, and fifty-four in Massachusetts. Providence had 169 mills in a thirty-six-mile radius by 1815, dislodging grist- and sawmills. Slater incorporated Webster, Massachusetts, in 1832. Brother-in-law Smith Wilkinson developed "Pomfret Factory" on Quinebaug Falls, later Putnam, Connecticut. Slater's friend Roger Rogerson became resident-owner of the Crown and Eagle mills (1825, 1829) on the Mumford River. Granite mills had clerestory roofs in North Uxbridge, Massachusetts. Canals from Worcester to Pawtucket made the Blackstone the nation's "best harnessed river" in 1828 with ninety-four cotton mills in new villages by 1844. Mills sprang up in Globe Village and North Adams in Massachusetts and as far north as Harrisville, New Hampshire. Richard Borden and friends tapped Quequechan Falls for eight Fall River mills and an ironworks by 1845.

Larger mills gave rise to cities to the north. Francis Cabot Lowell (1775–1817) studied English power looms from 1810 to 1812, returning to form the joint-stock Boston Manufacturing Company with Nathan Appleton (1779–1861). They chose ten-foot falls on the Charles in rural Waltham for two six-story brick mills and a machine shop (1814–1819). Workers were women and children living in boardinghouses. The company built houses for resident "agent" Patrick Tracy Jackson (1780–1847) and superintendents along with a school, store, and church around a common. Waltham had the first fully integrated mill with raw cotton processed to a finished product.

Jackson and Appleton located a better site in rural Chelmsford on the Merrimack Falls at the Concord River's confluence, waters draining four thousand square miles through rapids thirty-two feet high. The Patucket (1792) and the Middlesex (1804) canals bisected it. Merrimack Manufacturing (1821) bought land for Lowell, a city of twenty thousand chartered in 1836. Kirk Boott (1790–1837) constructed mills with boardinghouses, a school, and a stone church for "mill girls." John Greenleaf Whittier described Lowell in 1845 as "a city springing up of brick masonry and painted shingles." The company leased water "privileges" upriver. Nashua Manufacturing (1825) began twelve miles north of Lowell with a mill and boardinghouses. The Boston Associates sold privileges, giving rise to Dover and Great Falls. Manchester had potential for a hundred mills after canalization of the Amoskeag Falls' fifty-foot drop. Amoskeag Manufacturing's expandable plan took form in 1838.

Picturesque Landscapes

James Hillhouse, sponsor of New Haven improvements, broke from traditional common graveyards in founding the New Burial Ground (1796), its grid laid out by Josiah Meigs of Yale and planted with yews and poplars. The origins of landscape design, however, date from the first "rural" cemetery in the United States, Mount Auburn (1831), which was established by the Massachusetts Horticultural Society. With seventy-two acres four miles west of Boston, Mount Auburn became a nonprofit corporation in 1835. Gen. Henry A. S. Dearborn (1783–1851) designed the landscape based on eighteenth-century English naturalistic gardens.

Boston merchants Amos (1786–1852) and Abbott (1792–1855) Lawrence incorporated in 1830, giving rise to a mill city with their name on falls twelve miles below Lowell, a virgin location. Their Essex Company built New England's largest dam—1,629 feet long and 26 feet high. Engineers Charles Bigelow and Charles Storrow also laid out city blocks. Iron columns supported three massive Bay State Mills (1846–1855). The Pacific (1852) and the Pemberton (1854) added to the brick wall of riverside mills. The huge Machine Shop had its own mechanics' housing. The company laid out a common, built municipal buildings, founded churches and schools, and created a library while auctioning lots for a business district.

Large mill towns sprang up beyond the Merrimack. The forty-two-foot falls at Saco, Maine, gave rise to a 47' × 210' mill seven stories tall (1825), but fire ravaged it. The Boston Associates intervened, forming York Manufacturing (1831). Three companies developed Cabotville on the Connecticut and Chicopee Rivers with fourteen mills and two thousand workers by 1838. Speculators bought land on the Connecticut where the Hadley Falls drain an 8,000-square-mile watershed. Edmund Dwight persuaded the Boston Associates to fund his Hadley Falls Company and construct a dam two thousand feet long and thirty-five feet high with a two-level canal system. The first two turbine-powered Lyman Mills were completed in 1850 as Holyoke incorporated as a city.

The 1860 Pemberton Mill fire spelled the demise of the Boston Associates with bankruptcy there and at Holyoke even before the Civil War curtailed cotton supplies. Over ten thousand in Lowell were unemployed. Amoskeag machine shops retooled to make fire engines, guns, and sewing machines. Three Lewiston mills had stockpiled cotton, and the city grew by 80 percent in the 1860s while other mills languished.

Paper mills thrived in Maine. Eli Whitney's Arms Company (1798) used water-powered machines to produce muskets in Hamden, Connecticut. Samuel Colt (1814–1862) opened his firearms works in Hartford's "Coltsville" section in 1855, his Turkish domed mansion "Armsmear" overlooking the world's largest armory with model workers' housing and parks. Paternalism produced comfortable workers' housing and amenities around the Fairbanks Scale plant (1830) in St. Johnsbury, the Waltham Watch Factory (1854), and the Crane Paper Mills near Pittsfield.

ECLECTICISM: GOTHIC, ROMANESQUE, AND OTHER STYLES

New Englanders experimented with styles to replicate Romantic sensibilities. Master builder John Holden Greene (1777–1850) added "Gothick" elements to his Gibbsian Federal St. John's Cathedral (1811) in Providence. In nearby Bristol, Russell Warren did likewise in an octagonal wing of the "Linden Place" House (1810) and in the County Courthouse (1816). Daniel Wadsworth used the Gothic Revival in wood in 1818 for his "Montevideo" estate in Avon, Connecticut.

Willard used granite for English Gothic churches—the Bowdoin Street (1831) with a heavy square crenellated tower with quatrefoil window, Temple Street First Methodist (1833), and St. Peter's (1833) in Boston as well as Salem's First Unitarian (1836). Bryant designed Saints Peter and Paul (1845–1853) in South Boston. Isaiah Rogers used wood and the Carpenter Gothic for Cambridge's First Church (1833), as did Waldron, a Boston builder, for Nantucket's First Congregational Church (1834).

Richard Bond's Gore Hall, Harvard's library (1841, destroyed in 1913), had a "Pointed" style in granite, as did Yale's Dwight Hall (1846) by Henry Austin, who opened his New Haven office in 1839. Hartford's Wadsworth Athenaeum (1842), based on Austin's plans, has a Gothic stone facade credited to Davis. George M. Dexter used the Gothic for Boston's Fitchburg Railway Station (1847, destroyed), as did Rogers for the Howard Theater (1847) and Merrill G. Wheelock for the Masonic Temple (1867).

Richard Upjohn (1802–1878) adapted the Gothic for Edward King's summer villa (1835) in Newport and his stone Gardiner House (1836), "Oaklands," on the Kennebec in Gardiner, Maine. In Newport, Upjohn designed the "rustick Gothick" mansion of "Kingscote" (1841) for George N. Jones, its interior by Louis Comfort Tiffany, and the King House (1847), both of asymmetrical "picturesque-eclectic" style. The Carpenter Gothic spread through Andrew Jackson Downing's *Cottages Residences* (1842), *Architecture of Country Houses* (1850), and *Rural Essays* (1853), cultivating "domestic rusticity." The Bowens' "Roseland Cottage" (1846) by Joseph C. Wells in Woodstock, Connecticut, has vertical board-and-batten siding, as does the Morrill House (1848) in Vermont, both painted rose. Davis designed the Harrals' "Walnut Wood" (1846, demolished) in Bridgeport and used rough-hewn stone for Newport's Prescott Hall (1848), both with crenellated towers. Davis and William R. Emerson made "a Cottage-Villa in the Rural Gothic Style" for New Bedford mill owner William Rotch (1846).

Taste for Gothic cottages arrived with balloon-frame construction, the use of a skeletal structure of standardized, milled boards described in Gervase Wheeler's *Homes for the People* (1855). The new scrollsaw or jigsaw made Gothic decoration possible. Artist Thomas Waterman Wood designed his own "Athenwood" (1850) in Montpelier with leaf-like "gingerbread." Carpenters built the Soper House (1850) in South Royalton, Vermont, its dark exterior decorated by white "gingerbread." George W. Bourne clad his Federal brick structure (1810) in Kennebunk with "gingerbread" in 1855—the "Wedding Cake House" with matching stables. The faithful surrounded Wesleyan Grove at Oak Bluffs on Martha's Vineyard with tiny, ornate cottages in the 1860s to replace tents for Methodist camp meetings.

Lewis F. Allen urged simplicity in *Rural Architecture* (1852), while Cleaveland

The rose-painted "Roseland Cottage" (Woodstock, Connecticut, 1846), by Joseph C. Wells, has vertical board-and-batten siding. Photograph by David Bohl, courtesy of Historic New England/SPNEA.

and Backus in *Village and Farm Cottages* (1856) hoped that the Grecian "folly" had "had its day." The "Stick style," vertical sheathing that had lattice-like diagonal and horizontal detailing expressing the skeleton, has been judged the most American in inventiveness and flexibility. Porches abound in the Griswold House (1863) in Newport by Richard Morris Hunt; the Sturtevant House (1872) in Middletown, Rhode Island, by Dudley Newton; and "Villa Vista" (1878) by Henry Austin in Stony Creek, Connecticut. Newport's King House (1872) blends Stick–style decor with a mansard roof. William T. Comstock's *Modern Architectural Designs and Details* (1881) featured a seashore house with rambling veranda with diagonal braces.

Striving for historical accuracy advocated by ecclesiologists, Upjohn used Early English Gothic or Decorated style for St. John's Church (1839) in Bangor; St. James' Church (1850) in New London; St. Paul's Church (1851) in Brookline; the Bowdoin College Chapel (1853) in Brunswick; and Boston's Central Congregational Church (1867), setting a style emulated by Ware & Van Brunt, Alexander R. Estey, Abel C. Martin, Edward T. Potter, and others. Arthur Gilman did likewise in Dedham's St. Paul's (1857) and Brookline's Christ Church (1862). S. S. Woodcock used the Gothic for the First Baptist Church (1866), Cambridge's "most ambitious" brick church, with one tall steeple on the side of the facade, rebuilt by Hartwell & Richardson after an 1881 fire.

Patrick C. Keeley (1816–1896) designed Catholic churches as immigrants swelled the population. He blended Romanesque, Gothic, and Celtic elements in St. Francis de Sales (1859) in Charlestown. Immaculate Conception Church (1861) in Boston's South End melded Georgian, Classical, and Renaissance themes, its interior by Gilman. Keeley turned to the Gothic for Chelsea's St. Rose of Lima Church (1866) and his Cathedral of the Holy Cross (1867–1875) of Roxbury puddingstone with asymmetrical steeples. Then the nation's largest Catholic church, the Cathedral of the Holy Cross seated 3,500 with room for 7,000 standing, its nave 364 feet long and 120 feet high. Keeley designed Portland's Cathedral of the Immaculate Conception (1869) with a two-hundred-foot steeple.

Town & Davis expanded "modern" designs with the Italianate in the 1850s— low projecting roofs, bracketed eaves, ornate cornices, round-headed windows, and square towers inspired by villas in Lombardy, Tuscany, and Umbria. Joseph and Hammatt Joseph Billings used the style for the Boston Museum (1846, demolished), an opera house with a 164-foot-long facade with three levels of iron balconies and gas lights, as did C. F. Kirby for the first Boston Public Library (1858, demolished). Ammi B. Young designed Italianate post offices and customhouses, and used brownstone for R. S. Morse's "Victoria Mansion" (1859–1863) in Portland, one of the finest villas, with its interior done by Giovanni Guidirini.

Henry Hobson Richardson (1838–1886) pioneered in the Romanesque revival. Educated at Harvard and in Paris, he began to practice in New York in 1866 and received his first commissions from Springfield—the Gothic Church of the Unity (1869), the North Congregational Church (1870), the Western Rail Road offices (1869), and the Hampden County Courthouse (1871). He used Romanesque details in Springfield's Agawam National Bank (1870, destroyed). Hartford commissions included the Phoenix Insurance Building (1872) and the arcaded sandstone Cheney Building (1876), five stories filling a block.

The Richardsonian Romanesque redefined public buildings with railroad stations in Auburndale, Palmer, and North Easton (1881); in Chestnut Hill, South Framingham, and Holyoke (1883); in Brighton, Waban, Woodland, and Eliot (1884); and in Wellesley Hills (1885). New London's Union Passenger Station (1885) replaced one (1849) by Austin. Richardson's public libraries in Woburn (1878), Quincy (1883), Malden (1884), and Eliot (1885) influenced others like Van Brunt & Howe's Cambridge Public Library (1888) and City Hall (1888) by Longfellow, Alden & Harlow. Richardson worked in 1879 in North Easton with Olmsted on the hilly site of the Ames Memorial Town Hall next to his library, near his Ames shovel factory and F. L. Ames' grand "cottage" (1884). George F. Meacham's Eliot Congregational Church (1889) in Newton Corner emulated his style.

Richardson's houses include those for Stimpson in Dedham (1868), Crowninshield and Higginson in Boston (1870 and 1881), Bowles in Springfield (1873), Andrews and Sherman in Newport (1874), Bryant in Cohasset (1880), Browne in Marion (1882), Stoughton in Cambridge (1882), Channing in Brookline (1883), Paine and Gurney in Beverly Farms (1884), Bigelow in Newton (1886), and Paine in Waltham (1886). After he died, partners George F. Shepley (1860–1903), Charles Rutan (1851–1915), and George A. Coolidge (1858–1936) completed the six-story Ames Building (1889), then the second tallest masonry bearing-wall structure, and produced the Nickerson Mansion (1886) in Dedham and a porch on Trinity Church (1897).

Many copied Richardson's "Shingle style." William Ralph Emerson used asymmetrical forms and porches for grand seaside houses—"Redwood" (1879) for C. J. Morrill on Mount Desert Island; Loring and Cochrane Houses (1881) in Pride's Crossing, Massachusetts; "Thiristane" (1881) for Mrs. R. B. Scott in Bar Harbor; and his own in Milton (1886). Arthur Little designed "Shingleside" (1882) in Swampscott. In Newport, McKim, Mead & White created the Skinner House (1882), Robert Goelet's "Southside" mansion (1883), and the Bell House (1883). They melded shingles with rustic stone and brick for Joseph Choate's "Naumkeag" (1885) in Stockbridge. Robert S. Peabody and John G. Stearns used shingles for irregular gables, gambrels, and porches of "Kragsyde" (1884) in Manchester-by-the-Sea. Clarence S. Luce shingled part of Springfield's Wesson House (1884). *The Builder* published Luce's design for Newport's Van Alen House in 1886. In Maine, John Calvin Stevens used lateral extension of rooms in the Brown House (1886) at Delano Park and the Smith House (1886) in Falmouth, as did McKim in the W. G. Low House (1887, destroyed) in Bristol, Rhode Island. New Haven's Ciampolini House (1892) by Babb, Cook & Willard is similar. Rudyard Kipling hired Henry Rutger Marshall for his "Naulahka" (1893) in Dummerston, Vermont.

The Queen Anne, synonymous with the Victorian, had so many incongruities it defies description. Asymmetrical houses had verandas, bay windows, steep gables, high chimneys, and turrets mixing polychromatic materials—wood, brick, coarse stone, slate, terra cotta, shingles like fish scales, "gingerbread," and ornate iron. Windows of varied shapes and sizes mixed stained with clear glass. Catalogs of components permitted vernacular versions. Richardson's Sherman House (1874) in Newport has been called the first true Queen Anne.

The Beaux Arts was more a design methodology than a single style, eclecticism through a process from sketches refined by design review. Connecticut's High Victorian marble State Capitol (1879) by Richard Michell Upjohn (1827–1903) was dubbed a "Gothic Taj Mahal," its gilded dome rising 257 feet above turreted, mansard roofs. Architects tinkered with medieval or Venetian Gothic principles of John Ruskin, English arbiter of taste, and ideas about what styles could shape and epitomize character.

Ralph Adams Cram (1863–1942) with Charles Francis Wentworth (1861–1897) borrowed elements widely for shingled houses in 1889—half-timbered gables and wrap-around porches in the Ide House in Williamstown; the Parker House in Cambridge; and the Whittemores' "The Ledges" at York Harbor. "Casa Loma" for Edward Gale in Williamstown and Brookline's Fellner House (both 1890) were neo-Tudor. The firm designed Grundmann Studios and Stuart Terrace apartment buildings (1891) in Boston; Bridgeport's Colonial Revival Seaside Club (1889); and the Rockingham County Courthouse in New Hampshire. Cram's *Builder and Woodworker* (1882) spread the "Gothic spirit" of arts and crafts design, preaching a return to the English Gothic as ended by Henry VIII. Cram gained fame for Gothic churches—All Saints' (1894) in Ashmont, St. Stephen's (1900) in Cohasset, First Unitarian in West Newton, and All Saints (1895) and the Church of Our Saviour in Brookline. He formed a firm in 1899 with Bertram Grosvenor Goodhue (1869–1924) and Frank Ferguson (1861–1926), continuing as Cram & Ferguson after 1914.

Cape Cod Style

The Cape Cod house style is an example of Colonial Revival architecture, but it originated in seventeenth-century New England when the first settlers of Massachusetts adapted the half-timber English house with a hall and parlor to the stormy weather and natural resources of New England. The house was usually one room, perhaps including a loft, and over several generations evolved into a modest and distinctly American architectural style. In the early nineteenth century, Yale President Timothy Dwight recognized the style of these homes and coined the term "Cape Cod." Some of the general features of this style are: (1) it is small in scale and low to the ground; (2) the roof is steep, pitched at about 8 to 12 inches, and has a small overhang to protect against severe weather; (3) there is a large central chimney usually centered over the front door; and (4) the roof and outside walls are covered with wooden shingles and clapboards, and the windows have shutters.

These homes were popular in New England until about the 1840s when European styles began to dominate American architecture. The Colonial Revival reintroduced these homes in the early twentieth century, though there were two minor alternations: chimneys were usually placed at the side rather than the center of the house, and shutters simply served as decoration. When Americans were looking for small, economical housing during the 1930s and 1940s, the Cape Cod became a favorite style among middle- and working-class Americans. Even after World War II, when many Americans were moving to the suburbs, the Cape Cod maintained its popularity and can be found in almost every town across America.

COLONIAL REVIVAL

The Colonial Revival style of architecture emerged during the early 1880s, shortly after the centennial celebrations of the nation's founding when Americans began to take a new pride in their past and grew increasingly concerned with historical preservation. The Colonial Revival style borrowed from early American architecture (Georgian, Federal, Greek, and even Dutch Colonial, though mainly Georgian), combining these various colonial elements with contemporary ones. Some architects borrowed heavily and with such historical detail that it was hard to distinguish Revival buildings from their colonial counterparts, but often they built them larger with certain details, like windows or chimneys, exaggerated or out of proportion with other parts of the house. Characteristically, its design was simpler and more symmetric and included much less "gingerbread" than Victorian architecture of the period and soon was incorporated into the Four-Square and bungalow house styles of the early twentieth century.

The Revival style became popular in New England after the partners at McKim, Mead and White made a tour of New England's historical towns in 1878 and observed the features of "important colonial houses." The New England colonial home served as the ideal of the Revival style across the country, and soon McKim, Mead and White were introducing Colonial Revival elements in their buildings, like the Newport Casino (1879–1880) and the Isaac Bell House (1881–1883) in Newport, Rhode Island. Although this style quickly became fashionable in New England, well-established architectural firms initially used it to build homes or buildings for the wealthy. By the early 1900s, however, architects had adopted the style for middle-class suburban homes. They became less eclectic in their designs, simplifying the structure to one colonial tradition or influence. This contrast with the perceived opulence of Victorian architecture signified a plainer, more honest style that remained popular among middle-class New Englanders and Americans until about 1930, though the Cape Cod style persisted as one of the most favored styles in American architecture. In their catalog of house plans (1928), Sears, Roebuck & Company marketed plans for these modest colonial-style homes using what might be described as a nostalgic yet modern idealization of the colonial past: this "type of home brings forth thought of the colonial days when love of home and woman were the most sacred emotions in the hearts of men."

"CONSPICUOUS CONSUMPTION" OR THE GILDED AGE

Thorstein Veblen criticized "conspicuous consumption" in the era Mark Twain termed the "Gilded Age." Wayne Andrews called it the "Age of Indiscretion" or "Age of Exuberance" marked by "vulgarity" rather than "good taste"; but it gained a foothold before the arrival of the "Robber Barons."

Phineas T. Barnum hired Leopold Eidlitz to design "Iranistan" (1848) on seventeen acres in Bridgeport. Like Brighton's Royal Pavilion, it blended Byzantine and Moorish elements. The 124-foot-long "palace" of reddish sandstone had wings from a three-story core. Multicolored, diamond-shaped windows pierced a ninety-foot-high dome. Four onion domes rose over conservatories. Piazzas with filigreed arches ran on all levels around the core, columns terminating in minarets. The public had access to gardens with parterres, Turkish kiosks, Chinese pavilions, and a miniature palace for the gardener. Fire razed it in 1857. Barnum's "Lindencroft" (1860) in nearby Fairfield lacked eccentricities. His third mansion, the High Victorian "Waldemere" or "Woods-by-the-Sea" (1869), was in a "compound" of family cottages and grounds open to the public.

Mark Twain hired Edward Tuckerman Potter for his eccentric "Nook Farm" (1874) in Hartford, a composite of polychrome, patterned brick, colored roof tiles, turrets, porches, porte cochere, and balconies evoking steamboats, its interior by Louis Comfort Tiffany. Twain's neighbor Harriet Beecher Stowe had a house as primly reflecting New England culture as her writing.

Newport attracted the wealthy, who built elaborate "cottages" on ocean bluffs. The first were relatively modest, like the residence built for J. N. Alsop (1861); the half-timbered Henry G. Marquand House (1872); and many of the Shingle style. McKim, Mead & White used the Colonial Revival for the H.A.C. Taylor residence (1886, demolished) and made the Edward D. Morgan residence (1891) meld into a craggy cliff on the sea, although its front has Ionic colonnaded wings.

The Fearings attempted the chateauesque in 1872, followed by design for "Chateau-sur-Mer" (1877) by Richard Morris Hunt (1827–1895). Millionaires rivaled European nobility with palatial "cottages" along Belleview Avenue cliffs for "summer seasons" peaking in opulence from 1890 to 1914. Hunt designed "Ochre Court" (1890) for Ogden Goelet, a limestone Gothic chateau like those on the Loire with fifty-two rooms and walled gardens. His Louis XIV-neoclassical "Marble House" (1892) for William K. Vanderbilt boasts a portico with rose fluted Corinthian columns echoed by pilasters on wings, the rear inspired by Mansart's Grand Trianon at Versailles. Oliver Belmont hired Hunt in 1896 for the fifty-room "Belcourt," modeled after Louis XII hunting lodges. Alva Belmont, the first female professional architect, supervised John Russell Pope's redesign of the Grand Hall, eliminating traffic.

Cornelius Vanderbilt II hired Hunt for "The Breakers" (1898), an Italian Renaissance palace like those in Genoa and Turin, 250' × 150', with seventy rooms and thirty baths, set in eleven acres of gardens and lawns. Fireproof steel supports vaulted arches and high-coffered ceilings. Two-story stables are 150 feet wide. French architect Richard Bowens Van der Boyen imported pieces from chateaux, alabasters and marbles from Africa and Italy, French Caen stone, and rare woods and mosaics from five continents. The fifty-eight-foot-long dining room has red alabaster columns topped with gilded Corinthian capitals. Gas and electricity lit chandeliers. Decorative iron screens made it "kidnapper-proof."

E. J. Berwind had Horace Trumbauer design "The Elms" (1901), modeled after a Parisian chateau with fifty-six rooms and terraced gardens and stables. Hunt reinterpreted the Grand Trianon at "Rosecliff" for Mrs. Hermann Oelrichs (1902). Trumbauer used a Louis XV design for the twenty-eight-bedroom "Miramar" (1914) for Mrs. Alexander Hamilton Rice. Guan Hutton built "Shamrock Cliff" on the Bay, an Italian Revival villa with red granite walls, red roof, and thirty-five rooms.

In Boston, Willard T. Sears designed a "Palazzo turned inside-out" for Isabella Stewart Gardner's Fenway Court (1902) for her famed art collection. Its simple exterior belies the Venetian villa inside, a four-story, glass-roofed courtyard lined with pink and white Moorish arcades. Income tax, introduced in 1913, curtailed building such opulence. Still, actor William Gillette built his castle at Hadlyme (1914–1919) on the Connecticut River, a twenty-four-room, four-story mansion rising into a tower, its granite cobbled by builders.

Henry "Harry" Davis Sleeper sited "Beauport" over the rocky Gloucester harbor, expanding his three-room shingled cottage (1903) into a mansion over three decades to fifty-six rooms by his death, each showcasing the past from Plymouth to the early Republic with elements from Old England. An early professional interior decorator who lectured about antiques, Sleeper built his "House of Mystery," a collage of gabled roofs, dormers, dovecotes, and towers above wings and terraces blending wood and stone. Colonel Leslie Buswell drew from him in making "Stillington Hall," another residential museum on 110 acres across the harbor, expanded after 1922 with fourteen private suites and a vaulted hall with space for

Cornelius Vanderbilt II hired Richard Morris Hunt to design "The Breakers" (1895), an Italian Renaissance palace like those in Genoa and Turin. Courtesy Rhode Island Convention and Visitors Bureau.

250. Neighbor John Hays Hammond, Jr., copied from medieval castles for his stone mansion atop rocks, its interior pillaged from European castles and churches; it, too, was a museum.

John Russell Pope designed his own house, "The Waves" (1927), a rambling Tudor Revival structure on a rocky Newport promontory, blending into its site with gray slate roofs, half-timbering, and leaded windows. Taste for the Tudor spread in the 1920s combining stucco with half-timbering for modest and grand houses.

SUBURBS

The first suburbs appeared as the middle class commuted by train to Boston from country towns like Lexington and Concord. Architects designed depots, libraries, and churches in such suburbs from the 1870s. Underwritten by philanthropists, the German Homestead Association, a building-and-loan, hired Ware & Van Brunt with Edmund Quincy, Jr., to design "model" houses for Wollaston in the 1870s. Developers mass-produced affordable housing, moving beyond row houses.

"Triple-deckers," three stacked units, a regional style in "streetcar suburbs," spread from the 1890s into the 1930s. The form spread as trolley lines expanded from cities and towns melded into the metropolitan fabric. Gardner Bartlett, John Hasty, C. A. Russell, William H. Smith, and Charles E. Wood designed better examples, but most were formulaic, free-standing with clapboards, on half lots from 2,400 to 2,700 square feet. Interior stairways and stairs on rear porches permitted access. From 1872 to 1901, over five thousand dwellings went up in Dorchester, annexed to Boston in 1870. Better houses lined parkways from the 1880s into the 1920s, as did apartment buildings with "French flats" (luxury-style apartments).

Many towns banned multiunit structures. Single-family houses occupied 20 to 30 percent of lots from 4,500 to 6,000 square feet; double-deckers or duplexes, a third of lots from 4,000 to 4,500 square feet. Many used new concrete block covered with stucco, modest half-timbering, and slate roofs. After World War II, developers of suburban tracts accessible only by car mass-produced single-family houses.

LEISURE PLACES

In the second half of the nineteenth century, sprawling resort hotels arose: New Hampshire's Crawford (Notch) Hotel (1859), Montpelier's Pavilion Hotel (1876), and the Mount Washington Hotel (1902) in Bretton Woods, New Hampshire. Nantucket's Sea Cliff Inn (1886) was typical of the Shingle style but had Colonial Re-

The Second Industrial Revolution

Industry expanded from the 1870s on with turbines and steam engines. "Factories" could be anywhere, no longer dependent on site-specific hydrology. Smokestacks punctuated the new skyline, reviving mill cities. Immigrants replaced the "mill girl" system. Tenements sprang up like barracks in dense slums, crowding six hundred per acre in Lawrence, Lowell, and Holyoke.

Industry matured on rivers between Rhode Island and Connecticut in new villages with large turbine factories tapping maximum waterpower. William Grosvenor took over older companies and renamed two Rhode Island towns Grosvenordale in 1868. F. D. Sheldon designed a grand Romanesque brick factory with two huge towers and a tall smokestack. He similarly designed the Ponemah Mills (1867) in Taftville on Connecticut's Shetucket River—75' × 750', extended in 1871 to a third-mile long, the nation's largest cotton mill. In 1860 George Maxwell united thirteen woolen mills in Rockville on Connecticut's Hockanum River as it falls 283 feet over a mile and a half. In the next seventy-five years, the Maxwells urbanized the town with operatives' "neat and substantial cottages."

Eclectic Campuses

Expanding colleges experimented with eclectic styles. The Victorian Gothic from Ruskin and Viollet-le-Duc shaped Harvard's Memorial Hall (1866–1878) by William Ware and Henry Van Brunt, an imposing brick mass scaled like a cathedral (132' × 310') with stained glass and mansarded towers. Charles Eliot Norton believed that America had "painfully displayed disregard of the ennobling influences of fine architecture upon national character." Russell Sturgis designed Yale's Farnum Hall (1870) in Ruskinian High Victorian. Harvard hired Richardson for Sever Hall (1880) and the Law School's Austin Hall (1883). Richardson's University of Vermont Billings Library (1885) is an asymmetrical, reddish sandstone structure with two turrets and a "Syrian arch" entry.

vival elements. Maine's Poland Springs House (1876) had three hundred rooms, expanded to six hundred (1881) with turreted Queen Anne bays in wings. Harry Wilkerson added Beaux-Arts details in 1903. Portsmouth's Wentworth-by-the-Sea (1879) had mansard roofs and Stick-style piazzas. McKim, Mead & White used the Shingle style for Newport's Casino (1881), a clubhouse with theater and lawn tennis courts. "The Balsams," in fifteen thousand acres of forests in New Hampshire's Dixwell Notch, is a Victorian survivor, winterized as a ski resort.

Eclecticism shaped Boston's coalescing theater district. Clarence H. Blackall's Colonial Theatre (1900) has a sumptuous interior by H. B. Pennell. John Galen Howard tapped the Beaux Arts for the Majestic (1903). Blackall designed the Georgian Revival Wilbur (1914) with advice from Harvard's Wallace Clement Sabine, a pioneer in acoustics, who also applied his research at Symphony Hall. Blackall gave the Modern Theater (1914, now the Mayflower) a Beaux Arts facade. J. Williams Beal's Sons used the Georgian for the Repertory Theater (1925).

Movie "palace" designer Thomas W. Lamb converted the two-thousand-seat Orpheum (1852) for movie magnate Marcus Loew in 1916. Dubbed Mediterranean Baroque, the Orpheum features a grand marble staircase which leads to a theater with vaulted ceilings painted in the manner of Wedgwood. Blackall, Clapp & Whittemore made the Metropolitan (1925, now Music Hall) of "mountainous splendor" one of the largest "cathedrals of the motion picture" with 4,407 seats. The Met's Grand Lobby soars five stories, circled by marble promenades with gilding, chandeliers, and crimson velvet. Lamb produced the B. F. Keith Memorial Theater (1928), more lavish than Keith's first (1894), which was built behind the Bijou in Boston and dubbed the "mother house of American vaudeville." The Opera recycled it as the Savoy in the 1970s, preserving the flamboyant Spanish facade and soaring lobby with galleries and marble columns.

The Young Men's Christian Association (1851) and its Springfield Training School (1885) promoted gymnasiums and new sports. Sturgis & Brigham designed Boston's Richardsonian brick YMCA (1883). As football mania grew with Ivy League origins, Harvard built the nation's first stadium (1903) to keep "cheap wooden seats" off campus. Engineering professor Ira Nelson Hollis worked with McKim, Mead & White on the reinforced concrete arena, sixty feet high and seating twenty-two thousand. Modeled after Greek stadia, an Ionic colonnade (1910) topped steel bleachers expanded for forty thousand. The Yale Bowl (1914) held sixty-seven thousand fans. Both served for track, ice hockey, and theater.

Red Sox owner John Taylor hired Osborn Engineering for Fenway Park (1912) to seat thirty-five thousand in bleachers on ferroconcrete enclosed by a red brick facade with the famed thirty-seven-foot outfield wall, the "Green Monster." Less distinguished was the Boston Braves Field (1915) for owner Daniel Marr. After Dr.

James Naismith of the YMCA Training School invented basketball in 1891, Tex Richards developed the Boston Garden (1928) arena for Celtics basketball, which served also for Bruins hockey, concerts, circuses, and speakers until replaced by the Fleet Center (1995), seating 19,600.

THE COMING OF THE MODERN

Tall Buildings

The Beaux Arts defined "skylines" rising with new technologies, steel, and elevators. Peabody, Stearns & Furber produced Worcester's nine-story Commerce Building (1897), then a "skyscraper" with a marble Renaissance Revival exterior on a steel frame. Richard Howland Hunt of that firm added the City Hall's 205-foot Renaissance Campanile Tower (1898). Frost, Briggs, & Chamberlain adapted neoclassicism for the ten-story Slater Building (1907), its steel skeleton dressed in limestone. Esenwein & Johnson designed the Bancroft Hotel (1913), ten stories with a Renaissance facade. Cross & Cross with Daniel H. Burnham produced Worcester's ten-story neoclassical Park Building (1914).

Springfield built the Campanile (1913), a three-hundred-foot carillon tower by Pell & Corbett. Hartford arose with Benjamin Wistar Morris' State Armory (1909), Donn Barber's State Library (1909), the G. Fox department store (1917), and the neo-Georgian Aetna Life Building (1929). Harvey Wiley Corbett melded the Georgian with French classicism for Bushnell Memorial Hall (1930), a red brick theater with pedimented portico, tower, and cupola. New Haven's twelve-story Taft Apartments (1911) and the thirteen-story Center Court Apartments (1916) were both Beaux Arts. Howells & Stokes used neoclassical detail in granite for Providence's flatiron-shaped Turk's Head Building (1913). G. Henri Desmond created Portland's first "skyscraper," the Fidelity Trust (1910), a ten-story steel frame dressed in limestone, surpassed by the fourteen-story complex at 477 Congress Street (1924) and the thirteen-story Eastland Park Hotel (1928).

Boston resisted "skyscrapers," limiting height to 150 feet, although builders pushed to the limit in sixty-five acres razed by the Great Fire of 1872. Peabody & Stearns designed the Exchange Building (1887–1891) on State Street with 1,100 offices. Arthur Bowditch's Old South Building (1902) and C. H. Blackall's Little Building (1916) began to define a business district. Densmore, Le Clear & Robbins created the Parks Square Building (1923). The 495-foot Custom House tower (1915) by Peabody & Stearns was exempt from the height limit because it was a federal project, and it was the city's tallest building until 1947.

Boston revised its skyscraper ban in 1928. Harold F. Kellogg built the Public Services Building (1928). Parker, Thomas & Rice designed the 298-foot-tall United Shoe Machinery Building (1929). Cram & Ferguson, with James

---

The Auto Landscape

Auto tourists roamed in the 1920s. Cottage motels sprang up in groves along Route 1, an artery that followed the Atlantic coast and offered attractions like miniature golf and restaurants. Structures doubled as signs. The Sankey-Hood Milk Bottle (1934, now in Boston) sold ice cream in Taunton. Rustic clam shacks arose in Ipswich and tidal places. With the recently patented projectors (1933), Thomas Domara built the Weymouth Drive-In (1936). Among the first "open-air" or "auto" theaters were those in Lynn and Providence (1937), Shrewsbury and Methuen (1938), and Portland (1939).

Finnish architect Eliel Saarinen designed "The Music Shed" (1938) for the Boston Symphony at Tanglewood in Lenox. Photographer, Walter H. Scott.

A. Wetmore, made the Post Office and Federal Building (1931) rise 345 feet. The John Hancock Building (1947) by Cram & Ferguson dominated the skyline with its Art Deco top until the Prudential Building (1959–1965) introduced unprecedented scale in a huge multiuse complex over railroad yards and garages. Charles Luckman with Hoyle, Doran & Berry designed the 750-foot, 52-story skyscraper.

Modernism

Modernism appeared in the massive "Music Shed" (1938) which Finnish architect Eliel Saarinen designed for the Boston Symphony at Tanglewood in Lenox; but modernism gained a foothold at Harvard's Graduate School of Design. Walter Gropius (1883–1969) from the Bauhaus became the architecture department's chair (1938–1952), preaching team-design. Gropius brought Bauhaus colleague Marcel Breuer to Harvard in 1937, and they collaborated until 1943. Sightseers thronged to the first "Modern" houses, one that Carl Koch and Edward Durrell Stone designed in Cambridge and Gropius' own (1938) in rural Lincoln— efficient buildings with flat roofs, cubistic collages of windows, and concrete. Breuer designed his own (1938) and another for James Ford in Lincoln, as did Walter Bogner (1940). Breuer left Harvard in 1940, building two houses for himself in New Canaan, Connecticut, and another for neighbor Ogden Kniffin (1948).

George Howe of Yale designed the Thomas summer house (1939) on Mount Desert Island with its rough-hewn stone chimney above a shingled roof. Working for Amelia Peabody of Dover, Massachusetts, Eleanor Raymond adapted new technologies and materials in her white Plywood (1940) and Masonite (1944) houses. She worked with Dr. Maria Telkes on Peabody's innovative Solar House (1948) with wall of windows under a flat, diagonal roof. Natural wood and rough stone blended in the Loeb House (1949) by Harwell H. Harris in Redding, Connecticut, and the Klotz House (1969) by Charles W. Moore in Westerly, Rhode Island. Richard Meier designed the cubistic Smith House (1967) in Darien, Connecticut. William Reinecke melded geometric forms and angles of the Sibley House (1965–1969), a wooden ski lodge in Warren, Vermont.

Calling for "radiant and naked" design without "lying facades," Gropius recruited designers to The Architects' Collaborative (TAC, 1946), each an equal partner, including principals Sarah Pillsbury Harkness and Jean Bodman Fletcher. TAC designed the Graduate Center (1950), concrete dormitories of light brick with a central commons. TAC designed the Thomas M. Evans Science Building (1963) at the Philips Andover Academy, continuing after Gropius died.

Massachusetts Institute of Technology (MIT) professors Lawrence Anderson and Herbert Beckwith drew on a Swedish precedent for their Alumni Swimming Pool (1940). Becoming MIT dean in 1944, William Wurster promoted modernism. Alvar Aalto from Finland made the serpentine brick Baker House dormitory (1948). Eero Saarinen (1910–1961), son of Eliel, produced MIT's Kresge Auditorium (1954) and enlisted Theodore Roszak for an abstract bell tower and Harry Bertoia for the altar of his circular chapel (1955). I. M. Pei designed the Green Building (1964). Apartments at 100 Memorial Drive drew upon MIT faculty—William Brown, Vernon DeMars, Robert Kennedy, Carl Koch, and Ralph Rapson. Gordon Bunshaft and Hugh Stubbins added more modernism to MIT.

Boston University (1839) began plans in the 1920s to move from scattered sites to the banks of the Charles, but only the Hayden Memorial (1938) was completed before the war. When building continued, modernism defined the campus around an eighteen-story Law School Tower (1966) with growth along Commonwealth Avenue. Students moved into old brownstones. Brandeis (1945) chose modernism for its Waltham campus built by the Macomber Company. Max Abramovitz designed three chapels in 1955. TAC and Hugh Stubbins supplied other buildings, functional but flawed; flat roofs leak.

The Memorial Unit of the Yale-New Haven Hospital (1952, 1972) is a highrise "healing factory" by Douglas, Orr, DeCossy, Winder & Associates. Saarinen made Yale's D. S. Ingalls Ice Hockey Rink (1959) like an inverted ship's hull and designed Yale's Morse and Stiles colleges (1960–1962), textured concrete monoliths. Paul Rudolph designed the Art and Architecture Building (1962). Skidmore, Owings & Merrill (SOM) provided a gridded, shadow-boxed skin of translucent marble for the Beinecke Rare Books Library (1963). Louis I. Kahn designed the Art Gallery, and Rudolph and Bunshaft made additions to it.

After studying with Gropius, Philip C. Johnson (1906–2001) championed the "International Style," epitomized by his own glass house in New Canaan, Connecticut (1948), followed by those for neighbors Hodgson (1951), Ball (1953), Wiley (1953), and Boissonnas (1956). Johnson provided Yale's 250-foot Kline Science Tower (1966). Johnson and John Burgee designed the Boston Public Library addition (1971).

Jose Lluis Sert (1902–1983) came from Spain in 1939 to become a Yale professor in 1944. He succeeded Gropius at Harvard in 1953 and served as its planner until 1969. Working through Sert, Jackson & Gourley (1955) until 1977, Sert designed campus additions like the mixed-use Holyoke Center. Peabody Terrace Housing (1965) is a massive complex with three twenty-two-story towers amid lower buildings interspersed with green spaces. Balconies and louvered windows on concrete resemble Mondrian's geometry. Sert's Undergraduate Science Center (1973) is a similar collage.

Sert brought Le Corbusier to design Harvard's Carpenter Center for the Visual Arts (1961–1963), the only U.S. building by the famed Swiss Modernist, a cubistic and curved concrete mass pierced by glass and glass block. John Andrews, Anderson & Baldwin made a dramatic statement in Gund Hall (1972), the Graduate School of Design bastion of Modernism. It is built concrete and has open, tiered student work areas that step down under greenhouse-like glass on the east. Sert also encouraged buildings by William Caudill and Minoru Yamasaki.

Modernism appeared in Mount Holyoke's Bukland Hall. Wellesley College employed Paul Rudolph of Yale's Architecture School (1958–1965) for a building, and he teamed with Anderson, Beckwith & Haible for the Jewett Art Center (1957). Rudolph with Desmond & Lord set the sculptural character in poured concrete of the South Eastern Massachusetts Technical Institute (1965–1972) campus in North Dartmouth. Rosaria Piomelli was project designer for Warner, Burns, Toan & Lunde for Brown's Science Library (1971), its slip-formed tower walls above a high glass lobby. Louis I. Kahn produced the Phillips Exeter Academy Library (1971), its balconies framed by massive circular openings in a six-story-high central court punctuated by X-shaped concrete bracing lit from a skylight.

Modernism made a radical break in New England church building. In Stamford, Connecticut's First Presbyterian Church (1958), Wallace K. Harrison & Max Abramovitz created a soaring, triangular, tent-like nave of precast concrete, like girders inset with multicolored faceted glass segments, by French architect Gabriel Loire. Victor A. Lundy's Unitarian Meetinghouse (1964) in Hartford is tent-like but different in shape and materials. Sharp angles of soaring concrete outside belie the dramatic circular sanctuary, its ceiling of wooden strips resembling draped fabric, letting light infiltrate.

Mary Otis Stevens and Thomas McNulty of the Cambridge Institute's New City Project built their own abstract Lincoln house (1965), which stretches behind a nearly windowless facade of poured concrete members, its interior designed for "human movement" as along a street for "fluid and unconvential [sic] relationships between family members." Valerie Batorewicz erected "Environment A" (1972) in New Haven, a prototype for an energy-saving housing "system" patented and manufactured with modular pieces of fiberglass sprayed with foam.

Corporate Campuses

Multiuse renovations grew from the 1950s on, resisting "urban renewal" razing of buildings. The old structures were gutted and recycled. Old mill towns launched campaigns to bring businesses into abandoned structures. Corporations fled to tax-free New Hampshire. The Nashua Foundation lured electronics and plastics firms into 2.5 million square feet of vacant space. Sanders Associates spun off from Raytheon in Waltham in 1951, finding space for missile development in a vast, empty Nashua textile mill. Defense Department contracts permitted Sanders Associates to build a seven-story corporate headquarters between Nashua, Concord, and Manchester to become the state's second largest employer.

Raytheon moved into North Andover's old Shawsheen Mill; Digital, into the Maynard Woolen Mill; Owens-Corning, into one in Ashton, Rhode Island. Honeywell took over Lawrence's Wood Mill as the Economic Development Corporation underwrote new industry. After the Atlantic Mills in Olneyville, Rhode Island, closed in 1954, its twenty-one acres of floor space became a department store. The Hope Mill in nearby Lonsdale became a supermarket. Fall River and Lewiston mills became garment and shoe factories. Elsewhere management companies leased space.

Massachusetts Governor Paul Dever withstood criticism for championing Route 128, which ringed the inner suburbs. Bypassing the city and easing commuting, Route 128 became the "Technology Highway" as over thirty industrial parks and seven hundred firms settled after the 1960s—Digital, GE, Polaroid, Raytheon, RCA, Sylvania, and others. Corporate "campuses" had state-of-the-art glass shells surrounded by parking lots.

Near Manhattan, Stamford on Connecticut's "Gold Coast" attracted corporate headquarters—Pitney Bowes, Schweppes, Xerox, and others—and began a 130-acre downtown renewal in 1965 with a $200 million budget. The twenty-one-story obelisk centerpiece on Landmark Square boasts offices over a skating rink and a rooftop restaurant, the tallest building between New York and New Haven. A hundred headquarters moved to Greenwich in 1971 alone, where an office and store complex towers above the train station with easy access to New York city. As Fairfield County became the target of growth, towns zoned to fend off the megalopolis. Kevin Roche, John Dinkeloo & Associates designed the self-contained, aluminum-clad complex of Union Carbide's World Headquarters (1984) a quarter-mile long amid seven hundred forested acres near Danbury.

Modern headquarters arose along the I-91 corridor north of New Haven. Skidmore, Owings & Merrill (1936) created campuses for Connecticut General Life (1957) and Emhart Manufacturing (1963) in Bloomfield, north of Hartford. A single-story, horizontal structure of the latter sits atop concrete stilts, sheltering parking on a knoll amid rambling lawns. Natalie de Blois and Gordon Bunshaft were responsible for designing it.

URBAN DESIGN

Elected New Haven mayor in 1953, Richard Charles Lee made renovation of the decaying downtown his cause for sixteen years. No new buildings had gone in for three decades; vacant lots abounded. Lee used Yale professor Maurice Rotival's master plan for renewal, hiring attorney Edward Logue to manage it. Lee won $110 million in federal urban renewal funds by 1963, with twice that amount from private sources by 1970. Modernism was the credo, epitomized by the textured concrete monolithic walls of the Central Fire Station (1962) by Earl P. Carlin with Paul E. Pozzi and Peter Millard Associates. "Brutalism," a harsh architectural style characterized by massive or monolithic forms, was the word many used to describe it. The state built the six-lane Oak Street Connector to I-95 with slum clearance for the ninety-six-acre Church Street Project—offices, stores, hotel, high-rise apartments, and low-cost housing. Paul Rudolph's reinforced concrete Crawford Manor (1966) has elderly housing in a spartan tower with cantilevered balconies, mocking the term "manor" but "heroic and original." Kevin Roche, John Kinkeloo & Associates made the Knights of Columbus Headquarters (1970) and Veterans Memorial Coliseum (1972) of concrete and self-rusting steel, but New Haven's population plummeted.

Hartford lagged behind New Haven's "renewal." The neoclassical Travelers Insurance Tower (1919) of pink granite by Donn Barber was New England's tallest building until 1965, its pyramidal roof with gold cupola and beacon rising 527 feet. In 1960 Ellerbe Becket's 360-foot Fleet Bank Building appeared. Travelers hoped to revive the downtown with the $40 million International-style Constitution Plaza (1964) by Sasaki, Dawson & DeMay, enclosed by a new hotel and four high-rise buildings. The eighteen-floor, 246-foot tower by Charles DuBose with Emery Roth and Sons has a skin of glare-free tinted glass. Phoenix Mutual Life (1965) built a 160-foot biconvex glass skyscraper by Harrison & Abramovitz, dubbed "The Boat." The 420-foot Hartford Plaza (1967) added to the skyline. I. M. Pei contributed the 262-foot Bushnell Plaza Apartments (1969). The Financial Plaza Tower (1975), sheathed in golden mirrored glass, soars 335 feet. Despite Hartford's new Civic Center's convention facilities and sports arena, "white flight" grew and many judged urban renewal "a continuing disaster."

Providence began renovations in the 1970s with a capitol-area plan to create an "acropolis." As the downtown languished, a misguided solution was making the main street a pedestrian mall. Two department stores vacated in 1973, although "renewal" cleared eyesores. The Rhode Island Hospital Trust and Old Stone Bank built two high-rises as the Regency apartment complex and Civic Center, sports and performance venue, brought transitory life back, but efforts could not stem businesses and population from escaping "creeping blight" to the suburbs. New Bedford remained dilapidated until Howard Baptista started rebuilding the downtown, waterfront, and West End in 1974 with new docks, shopping malls, and housing. Worcester had a renaissance under City Manager Francis McGrath, who built the Centrum arena.

The Boston Redevelopment Authority (BRA) (1957), sought to "Manhattanize." The "New Boston" followed "urban renewal," wiping away forty-eight acres of the West End in the name of "revitalization." Developer Jerome Rappaport won BRA approval for the Charles River Park complex (1961), an enclave of high-rise apartments with amenities designed by Victor Gruen. Outcry prompted Mayor John F. Collins to bring Edward J. Logue from Hartford in 1960 to head the BRA to use federal funds in a more sensitive manner.

Famed modernist I. M. Pei (1917–) conceived the 1960 Government Center Master Plan for the BRA, a fifty-six-acre site replacing the run-down Scollay Square area with city, state, and federal complexes interspersed with retail and private office space around an immense, sterile brick "piazza." Gerhard M. Kallmann (1915–), Noel M. McKinnell, & Edward F. Knowles (1929–) won the competition for Boston's City Hall (1961–1969), a massing of concrete under three top-heavy cantilevered floors with windows divided by sun screens. Two 26-story towers of the John F. Kennedy Federal Buildings (1966) by TAC and Samuel Glaser Associates, the 22-story State Office Building (1966) by Emery Roth & Sons with Hoyle, Doran & Berry, along with lower office buildings, are equally spartan and out of scale and style. Nearby, Paul Rudolph coordinated a team for the State Service Center (1971), its textured concrete columns and ramps over a pedestrian plaza and parking, and Skidmore, Owings & Merrill inserted a stark office tower (1972) on Beacon Street.

The BRA and developers tried to bolster the Financial District, first with the State Street Bank Building (1966) by Hugh Stubbins with F. A. Stahl and Le Messurier, a thirty-four-story cruciform tower of precast concrete window frames atop lower wings. As high-rises filled the district, Stubbins' Federal Reserve Bank (1977) arose nearby, an aluminum-skinned tower with flanking pylons. The BRA hired Victor Gruen Associates in 1967 to bolster the Central Business District department-store area. Henry Cobb of the I. M. Pei & Partners designed the Hancock Tower (1975) across town. Then New England's tallest building, the 790-foot slender slab had a steel skeleton with mirrored-glass curtain walls.

Pei's firm did the Christian Science World Headquarters complex (1968–1973), dwarfing the Romanesque chapel by Franklin J. Welch (1894) and Classical Revival basilica (1906) by Charles E. Brigham and Solon S. Beman. A piazza with a seven-hundred-foot-long reflecting pool and an eighty-foot circular fountain by Sasaki, Dawson & DeMay form the core flanked by a twenty-six-story Administration Building, 525-foot-long Colonnade Building, and curved Sunday School facade. Pei also designed the John F. Kennedy Library (1979), a collage of white forms with a nine-story library and 110-foot-high gray glass pavilion. Pei's stark granite West Wing exterior (1981) of Boston's Museum of Fine Arts belies the 200' x 53' galleria lit by a glass barrel vault.

Attention also turned to the dilapidated waterfront. Peter Chermayeff (1936–) founded the Cambridge Seven (1962) and completed the New England Aquarium (1969) on Central Wharf, architectonic forms of concrete and a model for modern aquaria. Internal ramps lead visitors past four levels of exhibits around a huge central tank. Benjamin Thompson, founder of Design Research in Cambridge, undertook renovation of Quincy Market (1976–1978). Faneuil Hall Marketplace became a tourist magnet after Thompson and developer James W. Rouse persuaded the BRA of its viability. The "festival marketplace" is now emulated nationally.

A movement grew to reject modernism as monotonous and minimalistic. Postmodernism is deliberately vague, a collage of fragments borrowed in a cartoonish way. Graham Gund's Cambridge firm (1971) designed the Harvard Square Hyatt Regency Hotel (1978), condos in 1983 in the ruined shell of the Romanesque Christ Church (1891), the Boston Ballet School (1991), the University of New Hampshire Library Expansion (1998), and the Lois Foster Wing (2001) of the Rose Art Museum at Brandeis. Henry Cobb of I. M. Pei & Partners created Portland's Mu-

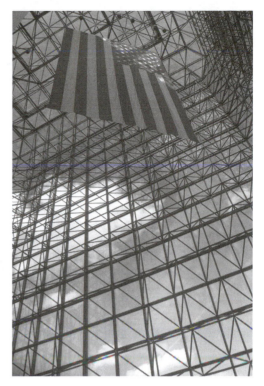

I. M. Pei designed the John F. Kennedy Library (1979), a collage of white forms with a nine-story library and a 110-foot-high gray glass pavilion. FayFoto/Greater Boston Convention & Visitors Bureau/BostonUSA.com.

seum of Art's brick Payson Building (1983) with clerestories, intended "to respect and render eloquent the living presence of history on and around the site"—the Federal McLellan House (1801) and the Sweat Memorial Galleries (1911) restored in 2002.

Boston harbor languished before the revival of Long Wharf following the Aquarium's lead. Adrian Smith of Skidmore, Owings & Merrill won the BRA competition for Rowe's Wharf (1988), a sixteen-floor complex. With huge archways under a rotunda, it is a grand entrance from the harbor but squeezed by the Central Artery (1959), which also slashes past One and Two International Place (1987, 1992) by Philip Johnson & John Burgee, the tallest building rising six hundred feet. White windows pierce the brick skin Johnson calls "eclectic traditionalism."

The "Big Dig," the largest public works project ever undertaken in the United States, began as part of an idea put forward in 1972 under Governor Michael Dukakis and Transportation Secretary Fred Salvucci to improve traffic flow by burying Boston's elevated Southeast Expressway (sometimes called, like Fenway Park's famed left field wall, the "Green Monster"). Thomas "Tip" O'Neill won approval in Congress. Two of the world's largest engineering firms, Bechtel with Parsons, Brinckerhodd, Quade & Douglas, began to replace eight miles of interstate and 161 lane miles of tunnels, bridges, viaducts, and surface roads. Ted Williams Tunnel (1995) runs under the harbor, augmenting the Sumner (1934) and Callahan (1961) tunnels. Vent Number 7 at Logan Airport won industrial design awards. After fifteen hundred years of Native Americans leaving shell middens on Spectacle Island, archaeologists have excavated the native campsites—the 1966 National Historic Preservation Act requires the recovery of artifacts before obliterating a site. Century/Weston & Sampson, Joint Venture Engineers, and Brown & Rowe are now moving soil from the Big Dig to the island and making it into a public park.

The Leonard P. Zakim Bridge (1997–2002) towers 330 feet, the world's widest (745') carrying ten lanes over a 1,457-foot span. Swiss engineer Christian Menn designed the nation's first cable-stayed bridge with obelisk towers mimicking the Bunker Hill Monument. When tunnels sink the interstate, a corridor will become the Rose Kennedy Greenway, a million square feet lined with "cultural and commercial activities" and "tree-lined promenades" reuniting city and waterfront. Landscape architect Carol R. Johnson coordinated design review in 2003 for two dozen parcels plus an acre-large, nine-story "Garden Under Glass."

Postmodernism has transformed New England. In 2002, Kyu Sung Woo created "a virtual Italian hill town" at Northeastern University atop a garage, and Stephen Holl provided a new MIT dormitory. Childs, Bertman & Tseckares (CBT, 1967) designed Trinity Place (2000) with eighteen floors of residences and worked with Gary E. Handel on the forty-story twin towers of Millennium Place (2001). CBT's 111 Huntington Avenue (2002) is a round thirty-six-floor glass tower with a crown, and Belvedere Residences (2002) have an eleven-floor curved brick facade. CBT designed Hartford's thirty-four-floor Town Square Residences (2003) and planned to begin the 395-foot Russia Wharf Tower in Boston in 2004. Chermayeff, Sollogub & Poole (1998) pursue projects such as the Connecticut River Discovery Center (2003) in Hartford, the National Marine Life Center (2004) in Bourne, and the New Bedford Oceanarium (2005), which is to be the world's largest aquarium, in an old waterfront power plant.

REVIVALISM AND PRESERVATION

Northern populations waned after 1870. Abandoned hill farms listed for $10 an acre in 1910 versus $500 for bottomlands. Dairying supported half of farms in Vermont, a third in New Hampshire, and a quarter in Maine, relying on trains and then new roads to take milk out and bring auto tourists in to discover old towns and rural beauty in the mountains. Charles Eliot created the Massachusetts Trustees of Public Reservations (1891), advocating in *Garden and Forest* saving places of scenic and historic value with private associations "to hold small and well-distributed parcels of land free of taxes, just as the Public Library holds books and the Art Museum holds pictures." The nation's first Metropolitan Park Commission (1893) amassed open space in eastern Massachusetts.

Restorations began under diverse auspices. The Ipswich Historical Society bought the Whipple House (1639) in 1898. Faneuil Hall's renovations in 1899 made it fireproof, replacing wood with iron, steel, and stone. Saving Paul Revere's house, Boston's sole surviving wooden building, began when the patriot's great-grandson blocked demolition in 1902. Joseph Chandler restored it, eliminating traces of use as a tenement, cigar factory, stores, and bank. It opened as a museum in 1908. R. Clipston Sturgis and Henry C. Ross restored the Old North Church in 1912.

Preservation was in its infancy until William Sumner Appleton's Society for the Preservation of New England Antiquities (1910) became active, publishing *Old-Time New England*. Renovations by George Francis Dow with SPNEA's advice saved Salem's House of the Seven Gables in 1910 and Topsfield's Capen House in 1914. Dow installed "period" rooms at Salem's Essex Institute in 1907; the Boston Museum of Fine Arts, three rooms from McIntire's "Oak Hill" (1800) in its American Wing. Cummings E. Davis donated fifteen "period rooms" (1685 to 1860) to the Concord Antiquarian Museum.

Litchfield began the first town-wide renovation in 1913, "colonialization" in the name of "civilization," resolving not to leave "the slightest vestige of modern design." The town had architects remodel buildings in "purely" colonial style, sanitized. The common was not a "green" with trees until the 1780s, but it had market stalls, woodpiles, and animal "pounds," unlike the Olmsted Brothers' design. The meetinghouse was not "old-fashioned white" as "restored" until 1829. Richard Henry Dana, Jr., demolished a Gothic church (1873) and salvaged a meetinghouse which had become a warehouse, barn, gym, and cinema, moving it to the green in 1929. Homeowners hired Aymar Embury II for "old-fashioned" details out of Benjamin's pattern books which Embury republished in 1917. Alain C. White set up a privately funded public trust (1913) to hold six thousand acres of scenic land as Parris T. Farwell misinterpreted Puritan reverence for "the value of natural beauty" in *Village Improvement* (1913).

The Society for the Preservation of New England Antiquities (SPNEA) restored Bulfinch's first Otis house in 1916, dilapidated from being a Turkish bath, shop, and boardinghouse, saving it from demolition to widen a street in 1926 by moving it back forty feet. Robert D. Andrews and H. Hilliard Smith renovated Bulfinch's Connecticut State House in 1921. The Providence Preservation Society saved College Hill buildings, aiding private restoration of 200 of those structures. Henry Ford restored Sudbury's Wayside Inn (1926) as autos brought people into the countryside to see the quaint. The Friends of Hartford bought Mark Twain's "Nook Farm" in 1929. Appleton and Dow advised William Cordingley on the 1930 restoration of Hingham's Old Ship Meetinghouse (1681). Work on Colonial Deerfield began in 1930. A coalition of SPNEA, Trustees of Reservations, Colonial Dames, and the Massachusetts Society of Architects created the Gore Place Society (1935), saving Waltham's Federal estate from developers. The Trustees saved Concord's Old Manse, appealing to children to fund purchase in 1939. Helena Woolworth McCann bought Harry Sleeper's "Beauport" mansion in Glouces-

Paul Revere's House, from which, on April 18, 1775, he began his famous ride, was originally built in 1680, and was opened as a museum in 1908. It is one of the few structures remaining from that time period. Courtesy of Massachusetts Office of Travel and Tourism.

Snow covers the House of the Seven Gables in Salem, Massachusetts © Getty Images/PhotoDisc.

ter when Sleeper died in 1934, transferring it to SPNEA in 1942 with a grant ensuring that it remain open to the public.

Pioneers' Village on three acres in Salem's Forest River Park in 1930 reproduced life in 1630 from dugouts to the Governor's "Fayre House." Antiquarian Albert Wells of Southbridge made his home a museum (1935), then founded Old Sturbridge Village to celebrate "arts and industry of early rural New England" (1938), hiring Perry, Shaw, & Hepburn and Arthur Shurcliff to recreate a town circa 1830, moving buildings and constructing others from prototypes. Old Sturbridge Village opened in 1946 with craftsmen and actors as "living history."

The 1935 Historic Sites and Buildings Act extended National Park Service (NPS) authority, naming Salem's waterfront the first National Historic Site (NHS) in 1937. The WPA's Federal Writers' Project's *American Guide Series* fed interest in historic places with *Massachusetts* (1937), its first volume. The American Iron and Steel Institute funded reconstruction of Saugus Ironworks (c. 1646) in the 1940s by Perry, Shaw & Hepburn based on archaeological research, and then the NPS took over the "first company town." The Marine Historical Association launched Old Mystic Seaport, moving whaling-era structures to a thirty-seven-acre village. Old Mystic Seaport and Electra Havemeyer Webb's Shelburne Museum in Vermont remained in planning in 1949 as Harry Hornblower II (1917–1985) founded Plimoth Plantation. Architect Charles Strickland reconstructed Pilgrim life in 1627 inside a palisade with the homesite of Wampanoag emissary Hobbamock outside. Inaccuracies existed until archaeologist James Deetz applied research in the 1960s and Henry Glassie joined in 1973, making it a "living history" museum.

The Newport Preservation Society began acquiring mansions in the 1940s— "The Breakers," "Chateau-sur-Mer," "Kingscote," and "Rosecliff." It saved "The Elms" in 1962 from a syndicate's plans to raze it. "Operation Clapboard" began buying old houses there in 1963, selling them to those promising rehabilitation. Doris Duke's Newport Restoration Foundation (1968) renovated dilapidated houses for rental. The Town of Sandwich bought the Cape's oldest dwelling in 1959, restoring the Hoxie House (1637) as it was in the 1680s.

The 1955 Beacon Hill Bill designated the district immune from alteration and led to state declaration of ninety-five other historic districts. The Interior Department recognized Beacon Hill as a National Historic Landmark in 1963. Richard Cardinal Cushing hired Isaac Blair and Chester Wright to restore Bulfinch's St. Stephen's Church in 1964. The Nantucket Historic Trust resold old houses for restoration. Senator Edward Kennedy helped set up the Nantucket Sound Islands Trust. Creation of the Cape Cod National Seashore preserved a thirty-mile stretch from developers.

The General Court created the Massachusetts Historical Commission (1963,

MHC) in response to the wide "urban renewal" destruction. The MHC State Reconnaissance Survey documents properties and districts, working with 332 municipal agencies and the private sector to keep preservation central to any planning. The Cambridge Historical Commission began to survey buildings in 1963. The 1966 National Historic Preservation Act and National Register program bolstered such efforts. Massachusetts launched a planning authority in 1974 with zoning over Martha's Vineyard's six towns to preserve "island culture." The MHC began giving matching grants from the state Preservation Projects Fund in 1984 and technical assistance to seventy-five projects by 1990. Investment tax credits helped while federal funds shrank in the 1980s.

Historic Boston Inc. (1960) restored the Old Corner Bookstore. Anderson, Notter Associates with Roger S. Webb recycled Boston's Old City Hall (1970) for offices and a restaurant. Carl Koch & Associates rehabilitated Lewis Wharf (1972) for shops, offices, and condos. John Sharratt renovated the Charles Street Meeting House in 1982 for commercial uses. Restoration of Bulfinch's Middlesex County Courthouse (1816) in 1983 returned to the 1848 appearance as altered by Ammi B. Young with a cast-iron portico of Corinthian columns painted to resemble stone.

Newburyport revived after the 1964 threat of bulldozers, renovating old brick buildings with "the flavor and nostalgia of the past but the con-

The Interior Department recognized Beacon Hill as a National Historic Landmark in 1963. Fay-Foto/Greater Boston Convention & Visitors Bureau/BostonUSA.com.

veniences of today." Greater Portland Landmarks remade the Old Port Exchange and waterfront with shops, restaurants, and craft studios. Local groups formed the Lowell Development and Finance Corporation as Senator Paul Tsongas won designation of the first urban-industrial National Historical Park in 1978. The Boott and Suffolk Mills became museums with canals restored. New industrial archaeology contributed to the Manchester Historic Museum and naming of Pawtucket's Slater Mill as a National Historic Landmark. Waltham mills became housing and the Charles River Museum of Industry. Watertown developers recycled the old Arsenal in the 1980s as a shopping mall with more offices, residences, and restaurants as the federal government vacated in the 1990s. Thus New England has embraced its past as antidote to unbridled change.

RESOURCE GUIDE

Printed Sources

Andrews, Wayne. *Architecture in New England: A Photographic History*. Brattleboro, VT: Stephen Green Press, 1973.

Bunting, Bainbridge. *Houses of Boston's Back Bay: An Architectural History, 1840–1917*. Cambridge: Harvard University Press, 1967.

Butler, William. "Another City upon a Hill: Litchfield, Connecticut, and the Colonial Revival." In Alan Axelrod, ed., *The Colonial Revival in America*. New York: W. W. Norton, 1985.

Curt, Bruce, and Jill Grossman. *Revelations of New England Architecture: People and Their Buildings*. New York: Grossman Publishers, 1975.

Downing, Antoinette F., and Vincent J. Scully, Jr. *The Architectural Heritage of Newport, Rhode Island*. 2nd rev. ed. New York: Clarkson N. Potter, 1967.

Garvan, Anthony N.B. *Architecture and Town Planning in Colonial Connecticut*. New Haven: Yale University Press, 1951.

Hitchcock, Henry Russell, Jr. *Rhode Island Architecture*. Providence: Rhode Island Museum Press, 1939. Reprint, DaCapo, 1969.

Kaufmann, Edgar, Jr., ed. *The Rise of an American Architecture*. New York: Praeger, 1970.

Pierson, William H., Jr. *American Buildings and Their Architects: The Colonial and Neo-Classical Styles*. New York: Doubleday, 1970.

Scully, Vincent J., Jr. *The Shingle Style: Architectural Theory and Design from Richardson to the Origins of Wright*. New Haven: Yale University Press, 1955.

Shand-Tucci, Douglass. *Built in Boston: City and Suburb, 1800–1950*. Boston: Graphic Society, 1978.

Walker, Lester. *American Homes: The Illustrated Encyclopedia of Domestic Architecture*. New York: Black Dog & Leventhal Publishers, 2002.

Web Sites

Architecture in Salem. March 8, 2004.
The City Guide to Salem, Massachusetts.
http://www.salemweb.com/guide/arch/

The site has detailed descriptions of a dozen major houses from the seventeenth through the nineteenth centuries and four historic districts, as well as detailed descriptions of architectural elements characteristic of eight period styles for understanding New England architecture.

Exploring New England Architecture. 2004.
Memorial Hall Museum.
http://www.memorialhall.mass.edu/activities/architecture/

Early colonial to Federal style.

New England Lighthouses: A Virtual Guide. 2003.
Jeremy D'Entremont.
http://www.lighthouse.cc/

Roots and Routes. 2003.
Lois Cunniff Productions, Inc.
http://www.rootsandroutes.net/body.htm?http&&&www.rootsandroutes.net/travelnow.htm

Links for New England architecture.

Skyscrapers. 2004.
Emporis Corporation.
http://www.emporis.com/en/bu/sk/

High-rise buildings twelve stories and taller, skyscrapers, and their architects.

Videos/Films

America by Design. Five-part series. Public Broadcasting Service (PBS) Video, 1987.
The American House: A Guide to Architectural Styles. Learning Seed, 1992.
Buildings, Villages, Towns: Traditions in Vermont Architecture. Dir. Susannah C. Zirblis. Perceptions, 1991.

Collections

The Plymouth Colony Archive Project
University of Virginia, 1998–2004
email: cfennell@alumni.virginia.edu
http://etext.lib.virginia.edu/users/deetz/Plymouth

A detailed compendium of the pioneering seventeenth-century architectural, archaeological, and material cultural studies of James Deetz is assembled in Patricia Scott Deetz, Christopher Fennel, and J. Eric Deetz.

Organizations

Historic Boston Incorporated (HBI)
3 School Street
Boston, MA 02108
email: hbi@historicboston.org
http://www.historicboston.org/

Organization for the preservation of historic sites in the city of Boston.

The National Historic Landmarks Program (NHL)
http://www.cr.nps.gov/nhl/INDEX.htm

Under the auspices of the U.S. National Parks System, the National Historic Landmarks Program. They are places where significant historical events occurred, where prominent Americans worked or lived, that represent those ideas that shaped the nation, that provide important information about our past, or that are outstanding examples of design or construction. This site is searchable by state and by name of landmark, providing basic information about the landmark.

National Register of Historic Places (NRHP)
http://www.cr.nps.gov/nr/

Like the NHL, the NRHP is also under the auspices of the U.S. National Parks System, and is the nation's official list of cultural resources worthy of preservation. This site includes information about 77,000 such places, including National Historic Landmarks (see the preceding text) and provides access to its database of information, travel itinerary information, and a reference service to the public.

The Preservation Society of Newport County
424 Bellevue Avenue
Newport, RI 02849
email: Info@newportmansions.org.
http://www.newportmansions.org

Newport mansions. Contains detailed information on five Gilded Age properties and other historic houses.

Society for the Preservation of New England Antiquities (SPNEA)
141 Cambridge Street
Boston, MA 02114
http://www.spnea.org

Founded in 1910 to protect New England's cultural and architectural heritage, SPNEA is an internationally known museum and national leader in preservation, research, and innovative programming. The archives hold over 1.5 million images, and a century of pioneering research is in the SPNEA journal *Old-Time New England* (1910–1999) and its quarterly magazine *Historic New England* (2000–) It is headquartered in Boston, with museums located throughout Connecticut, Maine, Massachusetts, New Hampshire, and Rhode Island. The Web site provides information on historical sites preserved by SPNEA as well as its museums and collections.

The Trustees of Reservations
http://www.thetrustees.org

The Trustees of Reservations preserves for public use properties of exceptional scenic, historic, and ecological value in Massachusetts. It owns 914 reservations, 214 properties, and more than 52,000 acres of land in the state. The Web site shows its Conservation Centers, describes its properties, and provides information on how to support the organization.

ART

*Herbert R. Hartel, Jr.,
with Michael Sletcher*

NATIVE AMERICAN ART IN NEW ENGLAND

The visual arts in New England began among the Native Americans who inhabited the region for centuries before the first European colonists arrived early in the seventeenth century. Compared to the artistic production of Native Americans in much of the rest of North America, little is known about the art produced by Northeastern tribes, because few works by Northeastern natives have survived four hundred years of intense settlement, relocation, and urbanization.

Besides wampum beads made of sea shells and quills, New England natives were probably best known for basket weaving. As historian Laurel Thatcher Ulrich has noted in her book *The Age of Homespun* (2001), in 1842 the Historical Society of Rhode Island received as a donation a basket about four and a half inches high and four inches in diameter. The basket had been "given by a squaw, a native of the forest, to Dinah Fenner, the wife of Thomas Fenner, who fought in Churche's War," in exchange for Mrs. Fenner's hospitality. Based on the "Churche's War" reference, it has been dated to the year 1676, when Captain Benjamin Church of Little Compton, Rhode Island, led New England troops in victory over the Wampanoag sachem Metacomet, also known as King Philip. As one of the few remaining artifacts of native New England art, it tells us about the complexity of basket weaving in seventeenth-century New England and earlier, or as Ulrich has explained it in relation to the lacuna of native embroidery or textiles in early New England, "Nothing survives that can fully convey the complexity of seventeenth-century Algonkian textiles, but Dinah Fenner's basket, read alongside archaeological fragments, helps us to understand some of the techniques used. The warp is of bark, the wefts of wool and a flatter material that may have been cornhusk. The construction is complex. . . . The technical details are important because they locate the basket in an ancient textile tradition. Shreds of twining very similar to that in Dinah's basket have been found in northern Vermont in archaeological sites dating from the Early

Woodland Period (1000–100 B.C.). . . . Except for the wool in its weft, Dinah's basket could have been made a thousand years before the first European excursion to North America." With the mass migrations of Europeans to New England in the seventeenth and eighteenth centuries, the quality of basket weaving appears to have declined. By the middle of the eighteenth century, natives had adapted themselves to the European market and supplied demand for that market. Indeed, by mid-century, as Ulrich has explained it, New England "twined basketry declined as Algonkian families began to manufacture and sell woodsplint baskets, brooms, axe handles and other forest products adapted to English tastes."[1]

For early New England natives, art involved the entire community and was not viewed as a profession or individual pursuit. The artist, as an individual entity, simply did not exist. Rather, the artist was someone who devoted his or her talents to the communal and subsistence living and used art to express a collective understanding of the community and everyday life. As a shared experience, the native artist was, in many respects, a craftsperson or folk artist, making canoes, bowls, pots, pipes, baskets, and a variety of utilitarian objects. Often the artist decorated these objects for hunting, trading, and eating and, as practiced in southern New England, to be buried with the dead.

Gender roles also determined the production of art in early New England. Native men typically made wooden bowls, spoons, dishes, and canoes, stone pots and pipes, and fishing nets, while women were responsible for embroidery, woven mats, baskets, and containers like birch bark pails for collecting sap from maple trees. In *New England's Prospect* (1634), William Wood described native women in New England as catering to their husbands during the winter, sewing their shoes, weaving coats of turkey feathers, and doing the ordinary tasks of the household. They also worked with pottery, though there are some seventeenth-century references to men making clay pipes, indicating that they too might have had a role in this task. The production of wampum beads from sea shells and quills, which the Northeast tribes often wove into decorative belts and sashes, was the responsibility of men, but recent evidence suggests that women also had a role in this task. Age also determined the production of native art in early New England. Older men typically made fishing nets, wooden bowls, and ladles. Younger men usually did not participate in such undertakings. Older men also might have been involved in embroidery, making clothes for their own family.

COLONIAL PORTRAITURE

The earliest painting in New England produced by white, European New Englanders originated within a few decades after the first settlers arrived in the Plymouth and Massachusetts Bay colonies and evolved gradually during the decades that followed. New England painters and sculptors were often the most capable and innovative in the United States from early colonial times to the twentieth century. They established trends and patterns that reveal both a regional character and outlook and a broader sense of national identity. Their work often epitomized what is American about American art and what is distinct about the culture and philosophy of New Englanders. Indeed, they revealed that there was much about New England that was the basis for American ideals and values regardless of region or period.

The earliest painting in New England was portraiture. Portraits were functional and practical; they recorded the likenesses of clergymen, magistrates, merchants, and farmers before the age of photography. In a society that valued spiritual purity and hard work, portraits were personal property that reinforced social status and pious morality. Since there were no art schools and no museums or private collections of paintings and few opportunities for apprenticeships, portrait painters were mostly self-taught, and their work was meager in quality compared to what was painted at the same time in Europe.

Of the few paintings from the seventeenth century that have survived, *Elizabeth and Mary Freake* from the 1670s, done by an unknown artist referred to as the Freake Limner, is a prime example of colonial New England portraiture. Elizabeth sits in a large oak chair and holds her young daughter as she stands on her mother's lap. Their garments are simple yet elegant. The limited abilities of the artist are revealed by the obvious, blunt modeling of light and shadow to create three-dimensional forms and the rigid poses and facial expressions of the two women. The girl looks like a doll in her mother's arms. The careful delineation of the garments reveals the developing materialist concerns of this new colonial society. This trait would appear in much of later American painting; even as the illusion of reality was achieved far more successfully in the years to come, this attention to the tactile reality of things would become a major characteristic of American painting. However, this austerity and rigidity in depicting the figures may be related to the sitters' discomfort with such luxury items as portraits of themselves; such property was not in keeping with the strict Puritan beliefs held by the earliest colonists.

By the early eighteenth century, painting in New England had grown in quantity and quality, and there were many more painters at work. Although painters could be found in many cities and towns, Boston quickly came to be the leading center for art in New England, and so it has remained. Throughout the era of colonial settlement and the early years of independence from England, portraiture continued to dominate. *The Bermuda Group* of 1729 by John Smibert (1688–1751) is a key example of how painting in the colonies had evolved in the fifty years after the Freake Limner was active. Smibert was an English painter who accompanied the minister Dean George Berkeley, his family, and his entourage on their voyage to English-controlled Bermuda to establish a college. On their way to Bermuda they stopped in Newport, Rhode Island, and remained there as they awaited funds from England to fund the college. The money was never provided and the college never came to be. Smibert sensed that there was a need for portrait painters in the colonies and that he would have far less competition in the New World, so he settled in Boston. *The Bermuda Group* was executed while most of the group was in Providence. It depicts Berkeley in his clerical garments. His wife and her friend, a Miss Hancock, sit to his right. Behind the women are Smibert and two friends of Berkeley, John James and Richard Dalton. Sitting on the left writing in his book is John Wainwright, who commissioned the painting before the group left England but who did not go on the voyage. His portrait was painted in absentia. The skillful brushwork in describing three-dimensional form and textures, as seen in the folds and wrinkles of the garments worn, the hair of the figures, and the landscape background, indicate how advanced Smibert's painting was compared to earlier colonial painters. The individualized gestures, poses, and facial expressions are

With little formal training and few early examples to follow, John Singleton Copley (1738–1815) achieved a bold style of vivid, highly realistic light, space, and textures in his paintings. Shown here is a portrait of Mrs. Eunice Brown Fitch (c. 1765). Courtesy Library of Congress.

also noteworthy. *The Bermuda Group* is pictorial testimony to the rapid growth of the colonies due to economic opportunity and gradual emergence of religious toleration after the Glorious Revolution (1688). Before he retired in 1746, Smibert produced about 250 paintings, held the first solo exhibition of an artist's work in the colonies, and allowed many aspiring artists to study the copies of Old Master paintings he had made during his youthful travels in Europe. He was essentially America's first professional artist. Although his talent was nothing spectacular compared to his European contemporaries, he was one of several portrait painters in the New World who contributed to the artistic maturation of what would become the United States.

A profound development in American painting occurred in Boston around 1760, when native-born John Singleton Copley (1738–1815) emerged as the city's leading portrait painter. Although Copley wanted to paint large narrative paintings of historical, mythological, and biblical subjects (what are called *history paintings*), and he left Boston for London in 1773 to do so, he painted portraits in New England for about fifteen years because they were in great demand as the colonies prospered. With little formal training and few early examples to follow, Copley achieved a bold style of vivid, highly realistic light, space, and textures. His paintings *Mary and Elizabeth Royall*, *Mrs. Thomas Boyleston*, *Henry Pelham*, and *Paul Revere*, all done from 1758 to 1769, are without precedent in the colonies.

Paul Revere of 1769 shows the silversmith, who later played a famously important role in the American Revolution, sitting at his work table, admiring a teapot of his own making. Revere sits thoughtfully in a finely pressed shirt and vest, better than one would wear in the heat of the workshop, and rubs his chin while admiring his own craftsmanship. The brushwork is so smooth and careful that a stray or loose paint stroke will never be found. The ruffled wrinkles of Revere's sleeves, the fine smoothness of his combed-back hair, the pristine shine of the silver, and the reflections on the polished wood surface of the table are remarkable for any painter, let alone one so young and lacking in formal training. The emphatic tactility of Copley's paintings is indicative of the materialistic values of his newly affluent patrons and a continuation of a trend seen in the work of the Freake Limner a century earlier. Revere's admiration for his own craftsmanship, an object of beauty and a material indication of wealth and social status, reveals a distinctly American, and particularly Yankee, sense of pride and satisfaction with one's own hard work and achievement. In essence, this painting visualizes the Puritan or Protestant work ethic, as the concept came to be known.

NARRATIVE, HISTORICAL, AND PORTRAIT PAINTING IN NEW ENGLAND DURING THE FEDERALIST ERA

Copley left the United States in 1773 for England to pursue his goal of becoming a history painter, and he never returned to the New World because he was very successful in Europe. He produced numerous large, impressive history paintings. Perhaps the finest and best-known of these is *Watson and the Shark* of 1778. It depicts a momentous and horrific event in the life of Brook Watson, the successful businessman and political figure in England who commissioned the work. As a young man working on boats in the harbor of Havana, Cuba, Watson fell overboard and was attacked by a shark. The shark tore off his leg before he could be pulled to safety. This is the story depicted in the painting. A mostly nude Watson is seen struggling to break free from the shark's ferocious hold on him, as his shipmates try to fight off the shark and throw Watson a rope to pull him out of the water. True to the facts of the event, a black man on the boat is holding the rope that was thrown to Watson. This black man figures prominently, even conspicuously, in the composition. *Watson and the Shark* is one of numerous paintings from the late 1700s that embody a major change in historical, narrative painting. This change is one toward the depiction of recent, newsworthy, actual events in large paintings. Traditionally, the scope of history painting was limited to high-minded ideals and detailed compositions about important events in ancient history, classical myth, or the Bible.

Another important history painter of the late eighteenth century who came from New England was John Trumbull (1756–1843). Trumbull came from a wealthy, prominent Connecticut family. He was born in Lebanon, Connecticut, in 1756 and his father was the governor of the state. He studied at Harvard University, from which he graduated in 1773. While at Harvard he decided to pursue a career as an artist, and after graduation he went to England to study with Copley. When the American Revolution erupted in 1776, Trumbull returned to the rebellious colonies and drew maps for the Revolutionary Army. Like his contemporary history painters, including Copley, Benjamin West, and Jacques-Louis David, Trumbull chose events that occurred recently, were highly newsworthy at the time, and would retain historical significance. Although he painted portraits and history paintings of various subjects, Trumbull is now best remembered for his paintings of the American Revolution. Trumbull was commissioned by Congress in 1817 to create a series of large canvases to decorate the walls of the rotunda in the U.S. Capitol, and seven years later he completed all four of them: *The Declaration of Independence, The Surrender of General Burgoyne at Saratoga, The Surrender of Lord Cornwallis at Yorktown*, and *The Resignation of General Washington at Annapolis*. His depiction of the signing of the Declaration of Independence is undoubtedly his most famous painting, and has firmly established our visual comprehension of this momentous event. Trumbull was elected the president of the American Academy of Fine Arts in 1817. Although this organization did not survive for long, it was an important precursor to the influential and respected National Academy of Design, which was founded in New York City in 1825 and exists to this very day.

The greatest example of Romanticism in American painting is Washington All-ston (1779–1843). Romanticism is the movement that dominated early nineteenth-century art. It is more a group of attitudes and ideas than a radical stylistic change. Romanticism, regardless of media, was about an interest in the strange, bizarre, weird, frightening, gory, morbid, deviant, and things ancient and exotic. Neoclassicism, the dominant movement in art in the late eighteenth century, was a precursor or first phase of Romanticism. Neoclassicism was more focused in that it was a rekindled awareness and deep fascination with the Greek and Roman tradition in art, architecture, drama, poetry, and philosophy. Allston was born and raised in South Carolina. His education was completed at Harvard and he spent much of his adult life, when he was not in Europe, in Boston. He started his career as an artist while studying at Harvard. In 1801 he left the United States for Europe. He spent three years in England, where he studied at the Royal Academy of Arts with Benjamin West and became further engaged in the practice of creating large historical and mythic narratives, building on his interest in historical, religious, and literary subjects, which had surfaced in his earliest paintings. In 1804 Allston went to Paris and Rome to further his artistic education by studying more works by Renaissance and Baroque painters. In Rome, Allston became a close friend of the English Romantic poet Samuel Taylor Coleridge. This personal connection strongly influenced Allston's interest in depicting literary subjects. In 1808, Allston returned to the United States, and he lived in Boston for three years before returning to England. His 1818 painting *Elijah in the Desert* is one of his quintessential Romantic paintings. The subject is from the Bible but the landscape is sublime. In the history of art, the sublime landscape is a special category of depicting nature as vast, wild, powerful, and even violent and threatening. Elijah is the small white-haired old man crawling over the rocks in the center of the composition. The canvas is dominated by the hard, craggy rocks and darkened, heavy clouds of the desert setting. Paintings such as this one seem to be more about the landscape than about the story and figures depicted. Allston's earlier painting, *The Dead Man Restored to Life by Touching the Bones of the Prophet Elisha* of 1811, is a more traditional Romantic narrative painting. Scared and confused onlookers witness the biblical miracle that is the subject of the painting. They are massive figures arranged in a semipyramidal structure with the dead man coming back to life seen at the bottom of the canvas. In its grandeur and monumentality, the composition is indebted to High Renaissance painting, particularly the work of Raphael.

Several New England painters of considerable talent succeeded Copley in portrait painting during the first few decades of the United States' independence. The most influential and capable of these portraitists was Gilbert Stuart (1755–1828), who was born and raised in Rhode Island and always lived a wild, carefree life of excessive spending, drinking alcohol, and carousing. Hence, Stuart was always in need of money and avoiding his creditors, which led him to move frequently from one city or country to another and take on as many commissioned paintings as he could. As a young man he studied painting in Europe, mostly in England with expatriate American painters such as Copley, West, and Trumbull, but also with English artists such as George Rommey. Stuart left Rhode Island for Scotland in 1772 with Cosmo Alexander, a Scottish-born painter who had been in the British colonies and had encouraged Stuart to pursue a career as an artist. Alexander died soon after the two arrived in Scotland, and Stuart spent several years in the British

Isles before he was able to scrounge up the money to return to Newport. Stuart worked in New England in a highly local, unskilled style during the 1770s. He went to London in 1777, where he perfected his craft among the American expatriates. He took to the lively brushwork of eighteenth-century English painters Thomas Gainsborough and Joshua Reynolds. He was active as a painter in England and Ireland for several years, and then returned to the United States in 1793. Upon his return to the United States, he painted portraits for wealthy and politically influential clients along the Northeast coast. He became the leading portrait painter in the United States of the Federalist era. Today Stuart is best known for his portraits of George Washington. He produced three basic types of portraits of Washington in the late 1790s, and over the next thirty years he churned out countless copies of them. These three types are now known as the Vaughan, the Atheneum, and the Lansdowne. The Atheneum type shows Washington from the chest up and looking to our left. There is an equivalent version depicting Martha Washington. The Lansdowne type is a full-length view of Washington. Stuart's portraits of Washington have been frequently criticized; the complaints started with Martha Washington's dissatisfaction with them. However, his portraits are most responsible for our current perception of what the first president of the United States looked like. They are the basis for the countless posters of Washington and his likeness on the one dollar bill. Stuart's portraits of the first six presidents of the United States are among the best-known likenesses of them that we have. All lived before the invention of photography in the 1830s, and so at that time painting, drawing, and various means of making prints were the only ways of recording the likenesses of famous people. Stuart's portraits feature a capable, lively, and loose handling of the paint brush. Although this stylistic tendency may have had much to do with his need to produce many paintings quickly for the money he needed to sustain his extravagant lifestyle, it breathed new vitality into American painting, regardless of subject or region of the new nation. Stuart's skill at recording light and shadow, textures, and the subtleties of individual likenesses are quickly apparent. In addition to his depictions of Washington and other presidents, his portraits of *The Skater (William Grant)* of 1782 and *Mrs. Richard Yates* of 1793 are fine examples of his style. The former established his reputation in England when it was exhibited at the Royal Academy in London in 1782.

Another notable New England painter of portraits and historical subjects from the early nineteenth century is Samuel F.B. Morse (1791–1872). Today, Morse is best known as the inventor of the telegraph and Morse Code. However, in his youth, Morse aspired to be a painter. He wanted to paint historical narratives and did so, but he did numerous portraits as well in order to earn a living. Morse was a great innovator in that he wanted to create historical paintings of contemporary subjects and themes which were relevant and important to the American people. He wanted to democratize history painting. Morse was born in Charlestown, Massachusetts, to a father who was a minister. He studied at Yale University and spent much of his life in Connecticut, New York City, and Europe. His historical paintings include *The Old House of Representatives* of 1822 and *Gallery of the Louvre* of 1831. The first painting depicts America's elected representatives to Congress (at the time, senators were not elected directly by the public) at work on various matters in the small room in the Capitol building that was the first home of the House of Representatives. Jedidiah Morse, the artist's father, and a Native American from the Pawnee tribe are sitting in the balcony looking down at the debate. This is a reference to then-current legislation pertaining to Native Americans as the United States was rapidly settling more land and displacing the people who had occupied it for centuries. Morse's father had been asked by Congress to study the effects of geographic dislocation on Native Americans. It is possible to identify nearly all the members of the House of Representatives who served in the Sixteenth and Seventeenth sessions of Congress, for most of them are included in the painting. As the nation grew and the number of members of the House grew with it, the House moved its meeting space to a larger room in the Capitol. Hence, the reference in the title of the painting to the "Old House." *Gallery at the Louvre* is an example of a didactic painting, one that would consist of copies of many great paintings all seen at once for study by artists. This was necessary before the invention of photography and modern methods of reproducing artworks.

Morse's portraits include *Marquis de Lafayette* of 1826 and *Susan Walker Morse as a Muse* of 1835–1837, as well as many smaller bust-length portraits of merchants, professionals, political figures, and the like. The portrait of Lafayette was made to commemorate the return visit of the aging French military leader who had helped the colonies fight Britain for their freedom nearly fifty years earlier. It is a large, full-length portrait of Lafayette standing on a Greco-Roman porch. Next to him are portrait busts of George Washington and Benjamin Franklin, two of Lafayette's closest American friends during the Revolutionary War who had been dead for many years. Next to these two busts is the base for a third one that is not yet put in place. This refers to Lafayette's appropriate place in the company of America's greatest heroes upon his own death. In the distance behind Lafayette is a blazing battlefield, a reminder of the sitter's military glory. Finally, there is a sunflower in an urn on the far right. This most likely functions as a symbol of devotion and loyalty. Frustrated with the inability to make history painting a popular and accepted category of art and bored with portraiture, Morse gave up painting in the 1830s to pursue his scientific and technological interests, for which he is far more famous today.

LANDSCAPE PAINTING IN NINETEENTH-CENTURY NEW ENGLAND

The Hudson River School

In the 1820s, landscape painting became very popular in the United States. The new movement eventually became known as the Hudson River School, but it was far from such a regionally confined development, nor was it formally a school in that sense of the word. The new style quickly spread throughout the Eastern states, and when it faded into history by the end of the nineteenth century, it involved artists who lived and worked throughout the rest of the nation. Paintings of the Hudson River School depict mountains, forests, and meadows across the United States in ways that exalt the spiritual, nationalistic, and geological beauty of the vast, unspoiled terrain of the new nation. These themes merged with and reinforced the prevailing ideology of Manifest Destiny, of the expansion of the United States across the West to the Pacific Ocean. Some painters even traveled extensively in foreign lands and brought this American-born movement and its attitudes toward nature as grandly beautiful and filled with the presence of the Divine to their depictions of foreign locales. Regardless of the particular locations depicted, Hudson River School paintings offer panoramic views from fairly high elevations and are extremely detailed in rendering trees, leaves, plants, rock formations, and the meandering shores and gleaming surfaces of rivers and lakes. Contours and textures are depicted very carefully and with extreme fidelity to optical fact. Colors are rich and diverse. The movement flourished through the 1870s and later.

The first great painter of the Hudson River School was Thomas Cole (1801–1848), and although he lived in Ohio, Philadelphia, and New York City after arriving in the United States from his native England at the age of eighteen, one of his greatest paintings was inspired by a geologically distinct New England locale. *View from Mount Holyoke, Northampton, Massachusetts, After a Thunderstorm (The Oxbow)* of 1836 depicts a loop in the Connecticut River, seen from a steep hill right after a storm has passed. The drama and beauty of the American landscape, as expressed by juxtaposing the storm clouds with the clearing sky and prominently featuring a lightning-blasted tree (Cole's signature motif) in the foreground, conveys the presence of the Divine in nature, and its associated violent, awe-inspiring powers. Such meanings are fundamental to Hudson River School paintings. On the hill in the foreground, a painter, presumably Cole, can be seen if one looks closely. It has been suggested that the trees scattered about on the hill in the distance spell "Noah" or, if viewed upside down, the Hebrew letters for "Shaddai," which means God. Thus, this optical trick would literally invoke the presence of the Divine in the vast, unspoiled American landscape.

Some of the most important Hudson River School painters came from New England. Among them were Connecticut natives Frederic Church (1826–1900) and John F. Kensett (1816–1872). Church, who came from Hartford, traveled around often and great distances, and applied the Hudson River School aesthetic to scenes of the Eastern United States, the jungles and mountains of South America, the frozen tundra of the Arctic, and the deserts of the Middle East and North Africa. *Twilight in the Wilderness* of 1857 is among his best-known paintings, and one that almost certainly depicts an American, probably Northeastern, locale. The vast spaces and radiant light of the setting sun breaking through the long, swirling clouds overhead glorify and celebrate the unspoiled beauty of the terrain. Such dramatic effects of sunlight at critical times of day are common in Church's paintings. His *Heart of the Andes* of 1859 and *Cotapaxi* of 1861 depict breathtaking vistas of the mountainous regions of South America and were highly praised when they were first exhibited in the United States. When it was shown in New York, *Heart of the Andes* was surrounded by actual tropical trees and plants, and viewers had to pay admission to see it. They were even encouraged to bring magnifying lenses and opera glasses with them to look more carefully at the minute details of the painting. Upon carefully examining the canvas, the viewer can locate voyagers on a rocky hill who stand before a tall, makeshift cross. This symbolic inclusion is a direct reference to the presence of the Divine in nature, albeit from a European Christian perspective. They can also locate Church's signature in the painting, which has been included as his handwriting scratched onto the bark of a tree in the midst of the enormous, verdant areas of plants, flowers, trees, and foliage of the equatorial tropics. The vastness of the space and the sublime wonders of nature are further implied by the snow-capped mountains in the distance. The extreme height of the distant mountains is in striking contrast to the tropical warmth of the lower-lying jungles closer to the viewer.

Numerous locations in New England were popular with Hudson River School painters, who would usually travel during the spring and summer to various places and produce sketches which they then would use to produce finished, large oils on canvas during the colder months of the year. Some of the most popular locations were North Conway in New Hampshire, Monhegan Island on the coast of Maine, and Bash Bish Falls in Massachusetts. John F. Kensett (1816–1872), who came from Cheshire, Connecticut, painted *The White Mountains from North Conway* in 1851 and *Bash Bish Falls* in 1855. Both works are stylistically indebted to the examples established by the older, New Jersey–born painter Asher B. Durand (1796–1886), whose carefully composed, tranquil scenes of mountains and meadows, rendered with meticulous detail and virtually no trace of the application of paint with the brush, were extremely popular in the middle of the nineteenth century. Cole may have pioneered the style and ideology of the Hudson River School, but the long-lived Durand popularized it and shared it with a generation of younger painters.

Luminism

Luminism is another landscape aesthetic—one related to yet very different from that of the Hudson River School—that had deep roots in New England art, culture, and philosophy. Kensett and Gloucester native Fitz Hugh Lane are important examples of painters who were closely involved with this movement, which spanned the third quarter of the nineteenth century. Luminist paintings are usually seascapes, particularly coastal views, that feature broad areas of glowing light that often fill cloudless cerulean skies, rendering details of the nearby landscape immaculately clear, no matter how large or small, obvious or inconspicuous. It is the denial or elimination of atmospheric perspective, of the possibility that the accumulation of atmosphere will diminish the clarity of any natural forms. Luminist paintings also exude an overwhelming tranquility; they make silence visible. Whereas Hudson River School paintings glorify the mountains, meadows, and forests of America with thunderous applause, luminist paintings reveal the lakes, ponds, coasts, and marines of the nation with an introspective reverence. Decades ago, scholars of American art associated luminism with certain aspects of American philosophy and spirituality, particularly Emersonian Transcendentalism. In most cases, the links between luminist paintings and Transcendentalist writings have connected individual paintings with prose passages, assuming that the written descriptions of America's terrain conjure the painted scenes with which they have been associated. However, it is also possible that Transcendentalism provided a new and different mode of vision in depicting landscape views, a mode that encouraged the suppression of individual artistic style and the avoidance of personal commentary in favor of more passively recording the scene before the artist with the utmost fidelity to optical experience. This mode of vision is implied by some of Emerson's most famous statements, such as his concept of the "all-seeing transparent eyeball" in his essay "Nature." Emerson described this comprehension of nature as follows:

> Few adult persons can see nature. Most persons do not see the sun. At least they have a very superficial seeing. The sun illuminates only the eye of the man, but shines into the eye and the heart of the child. The lover of nature is he whose inward and outward senses are still truly adjusted to each other;

who has retained the spirit of infancy even into the era of manhood. His intercourse with heaven and earth, becomes part of his daily food. In the presence of nature, a wild delight runs through the man, in spite of real sorrows. . . . Standing on the bare ground,—my head bathed by the blithe air, and uplifted into infinite space,—all mean egotism vanishes. I become a transparent eye-ball. I am nothing. I see all. The currents of the Universal Being circulate through me; I am part or particle of God.[2]

Fitz Hugh Lane's paintings of Boston Harbor and other coastal, marine views of Massachusetts' eastern shores from the 1850s and early 1860s are excellent examples of luminism. Lane came from Gloucester, Massachusetts. His Anglo-Saxon, Protestant family had very old roots in New England; they had settled on the coast of Massachusetts in the mid-1600s. As a painter, Lane was mostly self-taught. His formal training in the visual arts was in lithography. The skills of printmaking were practical and marketable; pure painting was not. Hence, numerous American painters of the nineteenth century, including Durand, Lane, and Kensett, had been engravers and lithographers at the start of their careers. Lane's *Boston Harbor* of 1850–1855 is a particularly important example of luminism in its brilliant glowing light that permeates the sky which covers most of the canvas. The light reflecting off the atmosphere is subsequently reflected off the almost motionless surface of the water in the harbor. The numerous ships in the harbor, placed evenly across the canvas, seem permanently fixed in their places, destined to remain exactly where they are forever. Other paintings by Lane explore the luminist qualities of other coastal regions, conveying a poetic, contemplative stillness that is fundamental to luminism and the essential character of the New Englanders who lived and earned their living in the northern Atlantic Ocean.

Kensett's paintings varied considerably in style and in the kinds of landscapes he chose to depict. Many of the forest and mountain scenes from throughout his career of twenty-five years fall squarely in the scope of the style of the Hudson River School, while his coastal and marine views are usually quite luminist. This dichotomy of style is difficult to explain at first, but makes much more sense if the landscape painter is understood as an Emersonian "transparent eyeball." Then the changing depictions of nature can be understood as the artist serving as a conduit for his perceptions of nature. Kensett's series of paintings of Beacon Rock in Newport Harbor in Rhode Island and of the mouth of the Shrewsbury River on the coast of New Jersey are thoroughly luminist, while his views of the White Mountains in New Hampshire and Bish Bash Falls in western Massachusetts are closer to the Hudson River School. Kensett's luminism features forms differentiated with crisp, intricately defined contours, believable and individualized textures, and sharp contrasts of tones and hues. This is evident in *Newport Harbor* of 1857, one of four known paintings of this rock formation off the coast of Rhode Island that Kensett made at this time.

PHOTOGRAPHY IN NEW ENGLAND

Photography originated around 1839 in France with the creation of the first daguerreotype, but it took only a few years for the technology to spread across national borders and oceans and for various photographers to modify and gradually improve the technology. Photography quickly appeared in the United States, and there were active and enthusiastic photographers across the nation early in the 1840s. For the first few decades of photography, most of what was produced was portraiture and the rest was documentation of diverse landscapes across the world. Albert Sands Southworth and Josiah Hews pioneered portrait photography in New England when they established a studio in Boston that they maintained from 1843 to 1862 and which produced about three thousand photographs. Other New England photographers such as Samuel Bemis (1789–1881), Anson Clark (?–1847), and James Wallace Black (1825–1896) were active documenting the terrain of rural New England from the 1840s to after the Civil War. This use of photography would become commonplace in the twentieth century, as Ansel Adams and Edward Weston documented and celebrated the Rocky Mountains, the deserts of the Southwest, and the forests of California. The earlier impulse to document the forests and mountains of the Northeast was revolutionary but has often been overlooked. It is certainly related to parallel developments in landscape painting.

NINETEENTH-CENTURY REALIST PAINTING

One of the greatest painters of genre scenes and portraits in mid-nineteenth-century New England was Eastman Johnson (1824–1906). Johnson came from Maine; he was born in Lowell and grew up there and in Augusta. He went to Boston around 1840 and trained to become a lithographer. During the 1840s he traveled around the Northeastern United States. He studied in Europe from 1849 to 1855, and traveled to Germany, the Netherlands, and Paris. In Europe, he studied with Emmanuel Leutze and Thomas Couture. He settled in New York in 1859 after traveling around the country for a few years upon his return from Europe. His first great success in the United States was with *Old Kentucky Home (Life in the South)* of 1859, which he exhibited that year at the National Academy of Design in New York. The painting was based on the daily life of African Americans in the South before the Civil War. The painting shows numerous poor southern blacks around the shanty houses that they inhabited on Antebellum estates. This scene is supposedly based on the slave house on the property owned by Johnson's father when he relocated from Maine to Washington, DC. In the painting we see a young man making sexual advances to a slightly coy young woman by an old fence, an old man strumming his banjo, a mother tending to her two children, a young girl quietly slipping out of a chicken coop after an apparent sexual interlude with a faintly seen man, and a mother who is holding her child as he stands on the shingled porch roof of the dilapidated house. By the 1870s, Johnson's palette became darker and less colorful and his paint surfaces somewhat rougher and looser. He began to depict various aspects of rural New England life. He favored scenes of Nantucket, which he visited often, and usually depicted the farmers, laborers, and craftsmen who worked on the island (it is not presented as the expensive, elite vacation spot that it is today). *The New Bonnet* and *Husking Bee, Island of Nantucket* of 1876 and *The Cranberry Harvest, Island of Nantucket* of 1880 are among the finest of Johnson's paintings of life on Nantucket in the late nineteenth century and are typical of his gloomier, neutral palette, which is reminiscent of Gustave Courbet's Realist paintings of only a few decades earlier.

Another important genre painter of the era was Thomas Waterman Wood

(1823–1903). Wood was born and raised in Montpelier, Vermont, and he spent much of his life in the capital city and other towns in his home state as well as in New York, Kentucky, and elsewhere. Many of his paintings are anecdotal, sentimental, matter-of-fact depictions of everyday life in rural New England of the nineteenth century that evoke the ultimate Yankee character and the simple rustic life that he was surrounded by when he was growing up. One such painting is the *Yankee Peddler*, done around 1872, which shows an old New England traveling salesman displaying his goods to local country people. This was how much commerce was conducted in rural America. The work also depicts the Puritan work ethic that is so closely associated with New England pragmatism and entrepreneurship.

Winslow Homer

Winslow Homer (1836–1910) is widely considered the greatest American painter to have come from New England. His intentions and sensibilities as an artist, as both a painter and an illustrator, are rooted in what might be thought of as a fundamental New England character and view of life. In his matter-of-fact depictions of rural and coastal Northeastern life and his explorations of more unusual subjects such as scenes of the Caribbean, which were made during a prolific career that lasted for more than forty years, from the Civil War until the beginning of the twentieth century, he combined keen observation with gripping storytelling, giving the viewer a lasting pictorial record of everyday life as he experienced and understood it. His paintings are particularly revealing of an America that would soon fade into history as industrialization, urbanization, and immigration transformed the United States in the fifty or so years after the Civil War. Homer excelled not only at fairly large oil paintings but also at fully developed watercolors. He was also a prolific illustrator for many of the most popular magazines in mid-nineteenth-century America.

Homer was born in Boston in 1836 to a middle-class merchant family of longtime New Englanders. His father was a hardware merchant, and Homer grew up in Boston, where as an adolescent he was apprenticed to a lithographer. In 1859 he moved to New York City, where he lived until the early 1880s. In New York, Homer embarked on a highly successful career as an illustrator for popular magazines of his time. His illustrations were often genre scenes (scenes of everyday life) depicting mid-nineteenth-century America and occasionally more specific topics related to important news events of the time, in particular the Civil War. From around 1860 until the late 1870s, he contributed illustrations to *Harper's Weekly*, *Appleton's Journal*, and other popular magazines of the era. He gave up his career as an illustrator only when he found he was able to earn a living from his paintings.

Homer's career took a profound turn during the Civil War, when he was sent to the front by *Harper's Weekly* to be an eyewitness observer and sketch artist. He made two visits to Virginia, in 1861 and 1862. Homer's visits to the front transformed his artistic vision, making him steadfastly a realist in style and temperament. Realism as an artistic movement originated in France in the 1830s, and by the 1860s it had spread rapidly throughout Europe and the Americas. The Civil War not only yielded subjects for many illustrations but also gave Homer a wealth of material for his first paintings.

Homer's paintings of the Civil War, which often parallel his illustrations of it, usually focus on ordinary, incidental moments and details of war; they depict the frustration, boredom, anxiety, and the routine activities in camp that filled up most of the time between battles. They are radical and daring in that they do not dramatize military combat or glamorize the valor of war.

His two most intellectually profound depictions of the Civil War include *Prisoners from the Front* and *A Veteran in a New Field*. The first of these is a summation of the lingering hostilities and divisions between the North and the South. The star of the painting is the Union Army general Francis Channing Barlow, a distant cousin of Homer and a native of New York who had a respectable political career in the Empire State after the Civil War was over. Barlow stands to the right, looking at four recently captured Confederate soldiers. One is young and the other considerably older, but both seem equally perplexed and uneasy in their captivity. Barlow's gaze becomes fixed on the more confident and defiant Confederate officer who stands closer to him and returns his gaze. Their linked gazes indicate conflict and mistrust between equally determined and dedicated forces on opposite sides of a fiercely divisive, highly complex political situation. The lasting, seemingly irreconcilable (at least at that time) differences that led to the Civil War are embodied by these two figures. The second painting is a cleverly obfuscated call for normalcy and peace after the war's conclusion. In it, the farmer who throws his scythe back and forth has just abandoned his military garb, which is seen on the ground to the right. This veteran has come to a new field, his farm land, and has given up the battlefields he has seen so much of in recent years. Now he swings his scythe back and forth as he cuts down wheat on his farm. Not long ago he was "cutting down" soldiers on another field, the battlefield. The image of a man swinging a scythe brings to mind the Grim Reaper and the death that this soldier saw and may have caused in combat. The fact that we do not see the man's face implies he could be any one of thousands of soldiers who recently left military service. The issue of how or if the huge armies of the North and the South could or would disband after the Civil War ended was a serious concern in 1865.

After the Civil War, Homer turned to other subjects. In the late 1860s and 1870s, he often painted the labors, simple pleasures, and pastimes of ordinary people, usually in the mountains and meadows of the Northeast, capturing the subtle nuances of their attire, behavior, lifestyles, and daily activities. Homer's paintings take mundane facts and make quietly dramatic epics of them; this is his genius, his greatest gift as a painter equipped with all the skills of an illustrator. His observations are authentic, convincing, and astute. Some of these paintings are strictly matter-of-fact; others tell stories with remarkable subtlety. Moralizing is never seen. *Snap the Whip* of 1872, of which there are two similar versions (now in the Butler Institute of American Art and the Metropolitan Museum of Art), depicts several adolescent boys playing a game of tug-of-war of sorts on a grassy field in front of a little red schoolhouse. They differ in that the Butler's version has mountains in the distance and the Metropolitan's does not. The homespun innocence of America is celebrated here; what could be more archetypically American than a red schoolhouse in the countryside? This way of life would soon fade into history as America changed, rapidly becoming urbanized and industrialized after the Civil War. There are several young girls in the background, standing in the field by the schoolhouse. Homer seems to imply that there are natural, logical divisions between the social lives, pastimes, and work of men and women.

Breezing Up (A Fair Wind) of 1876 shows three boys and a young man riding in a small sailboat off the coast of Gloucester on a partly cloudy, windy day. When first exhibited, the painting was praised for its attention to light, atmosphere, and the choppy waves of the New England coastal waters. Although some portions of the canvas are rather loosely rendered, at least compared to Homer's other works and earlier American paintings, *Breezing Up* never approaches the rapid, sketchy paint handling of French Impressionism. It succeeds in conveying the momentary qualities of light and atmosphere for which Impressionism is known, but it does so with tighter and more controlled handling of paint. Once again, a long-standing American tradition in painting is evident. The painting is believed to contain subtle symbolic meanings. The year 1876 was itself significant, since it was America's Centennial. The original title "A Fair Wind" may refer to the Centennial Fair held in Philadelphia that year. Although he rarely made specific, lengthy comments about the meanings of his paintings, Homer did seem to favor clever and telling plays on words. His titles are more than descriptive; they are sometimes indicative of deeper meanings. The sense of youthful vigor and enthusiasm conveyed in this scene of young boys sailing a small boat on the choppy seas near Gloucester may allude to America's youthfulness, optimism, and future promise, and it may indicate hopes for a new beginning with prosperity and, in the aftermath of the Civil War, peace. Although Homer said and wrote very little about the meanings of his works, he is known to have been dismayed at the harsh brutality of devious military tactics used during the Civil War.

Homer traveled much during his life. In the 1870s and again in the 1890s, he often went to the mountains of the Catskills. In 1881 he went to England and spent time in a coastal fishing village. He apparently did not travel to continental Europe. In the late 1870s and early 1880s, he often visited rural northern New England. He even made trips to the Caribbean and Florida in the 1890s. In 1884, he left New York and settled permanently in the isolated coastal town of Prout's Neck, Maine. His reasons for doing this remain unknown and open to debate. In the early 1880s, around the same time that he embraced the seclusion of Maine, his vision of life as suggested by his work became rather grim, introspective, and somewhat philosophical. He left Prout's Neck periodically to travel to other areas, but more often than not he sent his work to major cities for exhibitions and to be sold. During these years he created some of his most philosophically profound paintings. Coastal scenes, marine views, the lives of the fishermen who worked the coastal waters of Maine or farther out in the Atlantic Ocean, and themes of human beings or other living creatures in confrontation with the awesome power and danger inherent in nature are common subjects in these late works. In *The Herring Net* of 1884, two New England fishermen hoist a net full of herring onto their small boat on a dark, stormy day in the midst of the choppy waves of the Atlantic Ocean. Homer gives these honest, hardworking men a nobility and dignity through the subliminal triangular composition that is formed by the two men and their boat. It has been suggested that the crossed oars symbolically allude to the cross on which St. Anthony, the patron saint of fishermen, was crucified, although such a specific symbolic reading may be excessive. Nevertheless, honest labor, proper conduct, good morality, and other ideas associated with the Puritan and Protes-

Honest labor, proper conduct, good morality, and other ideas associated with the Puritan and Protestant work ethic are exalted in Winslow Homer's 1885 painting, *The Herring Net* (oil on canvas, 30⅛ x 48⅜ in.). Courtesy Mr. and Mrs. Martin A. Ryerson Collection, The Art Institute of Chicago.

tant work ethic are exalted in this painting. *Nor'easter* of 1895 is a pure seascape, perhaps the greatest ever painted by an American. In this large canvas, we are given a head-on, almost confrontational view of huge ocean waves crashing onto the rugged, rocky Maine shore. One is amazed when trying to imagine the time and skill that it took to depict with such conviction the movement and mass of this tiny yet incredibly powerful portion of water. The dark, overcast sky filled with stormy clouds reinforces the bleak mood of the painting. This painting is perhaps Homer's most direct, intense statement of the awesome powers of nature and its ability to conquer humanity and all it can achieve.

Artistic Training in New England

As the United States grew in population and geographic area and matured socially and culturally, the means by which artists studied their craft changed accordingly. The earliest artists in the colonies and the newly independent nation were self-taught or apprenticed as youngsters to older painters, engravers, lithographers, and commercial illustrators. Printmaking, advertising design, and illustration offered immediate and reliable means of earning a living, and so many artists in America up to the late nineteenth century began their careers in such professions and then branched out into drawing and painting. This was true of such New Englanders as Kensett, Lane, Homer, and others. Many other artists felt the need to go to Europe to further their artistic training and their ability to study first-hand the work of the Old Masters and current innovators. This was true of aspiring history painters of the late eighteenth century such as Copley, West, and Trumbull and artists whose careers began after the Civil War, including many of the American Impressionists and some of the pioneering modernists of the early twentieth century. During the nineteenth century, the creation of colleges, art academies, and artists' colonies changed how artists were taught. The school of the Museum of Fine Arts in Boston became an important center for the study of art in New England. William Morris Hunt (1824–1879), a native of Brattleboro, Vermont, was a painter who became even more important as an influential teacher in Boston in the 1860s and 1870s. Various artists' colonies appeared across New England after the Civil War; among the largest and most popular were those in Provincetown, Massachusetts, Cos Cob and Old Lyme, Connecticut, and Cornish, New Hampshire and the MacDowell Art Colony in Peterborough, New Hampshire. Although not schools in the traditional sense, they fostered artistic development and encouraged various styles, such as Impressionism, to flourish in New England. Eventually, virtually all of New England's colleges and universities created departments of visual arts. Of these, Yale University would come to be the most widely influential by the middle of the twentieth century, as it recruited numerous instructors of great talent and influence, the greatest of which is the color and design theorist Josef Albers.

IMPRESSIONISM

When Impressionism came to America in the 1880s, it first gained popularity with collectors and viewers in Boston.[3] Of the numerous American Impressionists of importance, John Singer Sargent (1856–1925) and Childe Hassam (1859–1935) have the strongest connections to New England. Sargent was born in Italy to an affluent American family that traveled extensively. He toured Europe throughout his childhood, never staying in one town, city, or country for very long, and he did not visit the United States until he was in his early twenties. He first established himself as a painter in Paris in the 1870s, when Impressionism was the latest, most radical style. Although he did some landscapes and genre scenes, most of his works, especially his largest and best, were portraits. They feature vigorous brushwork reminiscent of such Old Masters as Diego Velázquez and Franz Hals, but which had more immediate connections to French Impressionism. As with the Impressionists, Sargent was interested in convincing effects of natural light and capturing fleeting moments in time. He applied the Impressionists' attitude toward capturing personalities, social decorum, and economic class to his wealthy, Victorian-era patrons. Some of his finest portraits were large group portraits. These include *The Daughters of Edward Darley Boit* of 1882 and *The Wyndham Sisters* of 1899. In the earlier painting, Boit's four daughters are scattered about in the parlor of their large, darkened house. The two older daughters, in their early teens, stand in the space between the two rooms. The other two are in the room in the foreground. Each is a distinct personality. The oldest looks away from the viewer and leans against a large vase while the youngest sits on the floor holding her doll as she looks upward. In the later painting, the three sisters sit casually but gracefully around a couch in a large living room. In 1884, Sargent created a scandal when his recently finished *Madame X (Portrait of Mme. Victorine Gautreau)* was exhibited at the Salon in Paris. In this painting, he depicted a well-known Parisian socialite as heavily adorned with cosmetics and sexually provocative with one of the shoulder straps on her dress dangling off her shoulder. As a result of the harsh criticism the work received and the displeasure of the sitter and her family, Sargent removed the painting from the Salon and repainted the shoulder so that the strap was properly over it. Sargent then relocated to London, where his career also thrived. As with any great portraitist, Sargent had an innate sensitivity for character, temperament, and behavior and the ability to convey these observations through choice of color, light and shadow, point of view, and facial expressions, gestures, and poses. Starting around 1890, Sargent traveled often to and from the United States, the nation that had been home to his family. These trips were initiated by two major commissions in Boston, one for the Boston Public Library on the theme of the historical development of religion and another for the Museum of Fine Arts in Boston on various subjects drawn from Greek myth. For the next twenty-five years of his life, Sargent spent much of his time in America, particularly in Boston, and produced many portraits for wealthy American patrons.

Childe Hassam was born Frederick Childe Hassam in Gloucester to a family with supposedly long-standing roots in New England.[4] He was raised there and moved to Boston when he was a young man. He received his earliest training as a lithographer in Boston. He traveled to Europe to study the Old Masters and more recent painting in 1883 and remained abroad for three years. While in France, he came to know Monet and spent time at his estate in Giverny. Hassam might be most succinctly summarized as the American Monet because of his vigorous paint handling and his keen attention to subtle, nuanced, fleeting moments of perception. Like Monet, his painting reveals a keen awareness of light, atmosphere, and weather and the extraordinary talent to capture such effects with oils on canvas. Although he spent much of his career in New York, he visited Boston regularly over the years. His favorite subjects were panoramic scenes of the modern city and close-up, more detailed genre scenes of urban and rural themes. Later in his career, Hassam painted many scenes of flags hanging from city skyscrapers after the victory of the United States and its allies in World War I.

Willard Metcalf (1858–1925) was another American Impressionist who lived and worked in New England for most of his career. He was born and raised in Boston and studied painting there before he went to Paris to further his training. He was one of the first American painters to go to Giverny to study with Claude Monet. Impressionism did not take hold in his work until around 1903, when he made a sketching trip to Maine. At this time, his handling of paint became looser and his choice of colors brighter. He is now best known for his sparkling, light-suffused depictions of the countryside of New Hampshire and Vermont, which often provide sensitive observations of the subtleties of weather and seasons; his winter scenes are particularly striking. Late in his career he was active in the art colony at Old Lyme, Connecticut. John Twachtman (1853–1902) was another Impressionist who produced some of his greatest paintings in New England. He was born and raised in Cincinnati. In 1874 he went to Europe for the first time, and for the next fifteen years he traveled back and forth between America and Paris, Florence, Venice, and Munich. In 1889 he bought a farm in Greenwich, Connecticut, which became his own American Giverny. In these last years spent in Connecticut, Twachtman produced some of his finest, most original paintings. They feature diaphanous, broadly applied layers of white and grays to create thick atmospheric effects, particularly of winter weather.

Two of the most intriguing painters of the female figure in late nineteenth-century America, Thomas Wilmer Dewing (1851–1938) and Abbott Henderson Thayer (1849–1921), spent much of their careers in New Hampshire, including the years in which they created some of their most important works. Dewing is best known today for his hazy, atmospheric depictions of willowy young women in meadows or domestic interiors, where they are usually walking and standing alone or in groups of two or three. *The Hermit Thrush* of 1893 is perhaps Dewing's most famous painting of such subjects. Stylistically, these works are part of Tonalism, a late nineteenth-century development in American painting in which landscapes, figures, and genre scenes are depicted as diaphanous objects immersed in thick, hazy atmospheric spaces, with heavy reliance on shifts of tones (variations from white to grays to black) rather than distinct hues to define forms and spaces only vaguely. The thick, hazy environments are not responses to natural conditions of light and atmosphere, and so this movement is quite distinct from Impressionism. Dewing lived in Cornish, New Hampshire, from 1886 until 1905. He began his Tonalist paintings of women shortly after he settled in Cornish. Thayer lived in Dublin, New Hampshire, beginning in 1888. He is best known for his paintings of young women or girls who simultaneously seem very real and contemporary and yet are somewhat ethereal and otherworldly. Many of his females are considered modernized variations of the Virgin Mary, saints, or angels, even though they are never clearly identified with traditional symbols and attributes of Christian figures such as haloes and wings. Thayer's paintings are associated with the Symbolist tendency in late nineteenth-century painting that began in Europe around 1880.

NORMAN ROCKWELL

Although born in New York City and establishing himself as successful illustrator before moving to Arlington, Vermont, in 1839, Norman Rockwell (1894–1978) became a New England artist, exploring the theme of small-town America. In Arlington, Rockwell began work on his Vermont rural life series, which the *Saturday Evening Post* published under the title "Norman Rockwell Visits." Depicting "the clean, simple life" of rural New England, the paintings, which include *Family Doctor* (1947), are some of his best work during the 1940s. Rockwell's move to New England coincided with events in Europe and once the United States was at war with Germany and Japan, he joined the war effort by creating the "Willie Gillis" series, depicting a quiet and carefree private in the U.S. army. Gillis, as Rockwell described him, was "an inoffensive, ordinary little guy thrown into the chaos of war." Rockwell also painted *The Four Freedoms* series for the *Evening Post* after President Franklin D. Roosevelt's gave his Four Freedoms speech in 1943. The paintings, which raised nearly $133 million in war bonds, were simple illustrations of American life: In *Freedom of Speech* (1943), a man in working clothes stands determined amongst men wearing suits; in *Freedom of Worship* (1943), multiethnic profiles look reflective under the text "Each According to the Dictates of His Own Conscience"; in *Freedom from Want* (1943), a family gathers for Thanksgiving dinner; and in *Freedom from Fear* (1943), a mother and father tuck their children into bed while the father holds a newspaper with war-time headlines. The same year as Rockwell completed his *Four Freedom* series, a fire destroyed his studio in Arlington, and so he moved with his family to West Arlington, Vermont, where he built another studio. The family moved again in 1953, this time to Stockbridge, Massachusetts, so Rockwell's second wife, Mary Barstow, could receive treatment for depression. It was around this time that Rockwell produced his paintings of warm and humorous family life for which he is so well known today. He continued to publish his work in the *Evening Post* and some of his best known illustrations, including *Girl at Mirror* (1954), *The Marriage License* (1955), and *The Runaway* (1958), appeared on the cover of the *Post* during the 1950s. The Massachusetts Mutual Life Insurance Company also commissioned him for eighty-one advertisements, as part of the company's American Family series campaign, which Rockwell completed by the early 1960s.

The death of Rockwell's second wife in 1959 had a profound effect on the artist. He married Mary "Molly" Punderson, a retired school teacher from Milton Academy, Massachusetts, two years later. In 1963 he ended his forty-seven-year association with the *Saturday Evening Post* and began to travel with Molly in Europe, the Soviet Union, and the United States. While traveling, he established a working relationship with *Look* magazine and collaborated with his wife on a children's book, *Willie Was Different* (1967), illustrating fourteen oils and a number of black-and-white sketches.

Rockwell's travels and new association with *Look* magazine gave his work a seriousness that had not been there before. International politics, involving the Middle East and Soviet Union, and social issues, involving poverty and civil rights, became typical themes in his paintings for *Look* magazine. In 1964, for example, he produced *The Problem We All Live*, in which a young black girl is being escorted to school by U.S. marshals. In *Southern Justice* (1965), which also appeared in *Look*, he depicted the murders of Andrew Goodman, Michael Schwerner, and James Chaney, the civil rights activists who had been killed in a small Mississippi town. This was a dramatic change from his 1946 image of a white boy being served by a black waiter on a train. Rockwell later claimed that he had done this, because the editor of the *Evening Post* had "told me never to show coloured people except as servants."

Although Rockwell had done portraiture of world leaders for the *Evening Post* during the 1950s and early 1960s, his work now took on a new social and political gravity, and politicians and celebrities alike offered him commissions. He was sought after by Frank Sinatra, John Wayne, and Arnold Palmer and painted the likenesses of five U.S. presidents—Dwight D. Eisenhower, John F. Kennedy, Lyndon B. Johnson, Richard M. Nixon, and Ronald Reagan. His 1966 portrait of Kennedy, painted alongside young Peace Corp volunteers, is an exemplary model of his new social and political outlook on the world and the role of the artist in portraying it.

By the 1970s, Rockwell, who had received little recognition from the art community for his work, was now acceptable in certain art circles. Thomas S. Beuchner, director of the Brooklyn Museum, wrote a critical review of his work to accompany a national exhibition tour in 1970. Two years later, his work appeared in the Bernard Danenberg Galleries of New York City and Madison Avenue art galleries, and New York auction houses began to show his work as well. In 1976, the town of Stockbridge honored him with a parade, and the following year President Gerald Ford honored him with the Presidential Medal of Freedom for his "vivid and affectionate portraits of our country." After he died, Stockbridge honored him again by building the Norman Rockwell Museum on the site of his last studio. It houses the largest public collection of the artist's original works and is one of the few museums in the United States devoted to a single artist.

SCULPTURE IN NEW ENGLAND

Several of the most prominent sculptors of nineteenth-century America were New Englanders. Some were born there, while others moved there to study and practice their craft. Their styles and subjects varied, from grand historical monuments to small genre pieces. Horatio Greenough (1805–1852), who came from Boston, may be one of America's most famous sculptors because of his notorious sculpture of George Washington. Greenough studied at Harvard before he traveled to Europe. He settled in Italy in 1827 and spent most of the rest of his life there. During his career he produced many busts of American political and military leaders as well as fairly small sculptures of narrative, literary subjects. His famous, larger-than-life sculpture of Washington depicts the first president of the United States in the tradition of Greek sculpture. This was done near the end of the era of Neoclassicism, when an interest in Greek art and architecture pervaded artistic developments throughout Europe and the Americas. Washington is shown seated, bare-chested and clad in a Roman toga. He is addressing the people as he raises his right arm above his head and points upward. Greenough was commissioned by Congress in 1832 to do this idealized, heroic image of a monumental, muscular Washington for display in the rotunda of the U.S. Capitol. Such commissions were almost unheard of in America up to this time, and the few that had been arranged were given to foreign artists. Greenough's commission was an indication of America's gradual, uneven artistic maturation. The sculpture was so poorly received that it was eventually placed outside the Capitol building, on the grounds nearby, where it remained for decades until it was given to the Smithsonian American Art Museum and placed indoors. The dress, attire, and demeanor of Washington in this work, so regally classical, were foreign to the republican artistic tastes of the American people, who scoffed at it mercilessly. Today most viewers would conclude that it is false, silly, campy, and heavy handed in conveying its meaning. Artistic tastes have changed greatly over the past 150 years; most contemporary viewers would not think that this sculpture flatters Washington.

Daniel Chester French (1850–1931) was born in Exeter, New Hampshire, and raised there and in Concord, Massachusetts. One of his earliest and best-known sculptures is *The Minuteman*, which was commissioned in 1874 for the town square of Concord, Massachusetts, where it remains. *The Minuteman* depicts a young, rural farm-worker holding a rifle and dressed for laboring on his land, not fighting on the battlefield. He stands tall, square-shouldered, and alert; he is ready to fight. Although the pose is based on the ancient Greek sculpture the *Apollo Belvedere*, the figure's garments and the equipment he holds are historically accurate for this time and place. This reflects the shifting tastes of the nineteenth century from the timeless idealism of Neoclassicism to the factuality of Realism. Late in his career, French produced his most famous work, the figure of a sitting, brooding Abraham Lincoln, for the Lincoln Memorial in Washington, D.C. French's figure is massive, far greater than life-size. Lincoln sits in a large chair, his shoulders square, his knees raised up and angled straight and parallel to one another,

Daniel Chester French's *The Minuteman* reflects the shifting tastes of the nineteenth century from the timeless idealism of Neoclassicism to the factuality of Realism. Fay-Foto/Greater Boston Convention & Visitors Bureau/BostonUSA.com.

and his arms resting on the sides of his chair which he grasps with his large, powerful hands. Lincoln looks down slightly. This gaze serves to connect the viewer to the subject, since any visitor to the memorial must look up to see Lincoln's face. However, this tilted head gives a resigned melancholy to the president whose election divided a nation and whose presidency was dominated by a war to reunite it. The melancholy may also be very self-directed; Lincoln was also the first president to be assassinated. The spacious memorial in which this sculpture is centrally placed has walls on which have been engraved excerpts from Lincoln's most famous speeches, including the Gettysburg Address, the Emancipation Proclamation, and his Second Inaugural Address.

One of the most notorious cases of a publicly controversial sculpture in American history occurred in Boston in 1894. The work was *The Bacchante and Faun*, a nearly life-size bronze sculpture, and the sculptor was Brooklyn-born Frederic MacMonnies (1863–1937). This sculpture was commissioned for the front of the newly built Boston Public Library. It depicts an exuberant, voluptuous nude woman holding the infant Dionysus, the Greek god of wine and, by extension, parties, celebrations, and physical pleasures. The laughing woman taunts the child with a bunch of grapes in her right hand, which is raised far above the child. The grapes are used to make wine, and Dionysus yearns for them out of instinct. This sculpture generated a lot of criticism for its wanton nudity, and it shocked many people who considered it amoral and unsuitable for its public location. The work was removed and sent to the Metropolitan Museum of Art in New York City, in whose collection it remains.

Another well-known sculpture in New England was done for a public location but not by a native New Englander. Augustus Saint-Gaudens (1848–1907), who came to the United States from Ireland as a young child and who lived most of his life in New York, traveled far and wide to fulfill his many illustrious commissions. One of his finest works is the *Shaw Memorial*, which is still found in Boston, at the very site for which it was commissioned. It commemorates the Civil War military hero Robert Gould Shaw and the brave regiment he led into battle. This regiment consisted entirely of African Americans who joined the Union Army to fight the Confederacy. Although slavery did not exist in the North during the Civil War, segregation existed in both the North and South. This was particularly true of institutions like the military that would have normally spanned the divisions of North and South (the U.S. military was finally integrated by President Harry S Truman in 1948, more than eighty years after the Civil War ended). The elaborate, deep relief sculpture is considered remarkable for the sensitive, realistic, and individualized depictions of the many African Americans in this corps.

Shaw rides high and proud on his horse, surrounded by his regiment. Depth and space are suggested by the many raised rifles. This is a device for creating space in relief sculpture that can be found as early as the relief of Titus riding into battle on the inside of the Arch of Titus constructed in Rome around 81 C.E. In the mid-1880s, Saint-Gaudens helped to establish an art colony in Cornish, New Hampshire.

Harriet Hosmer and Edmonia Lewis were two of the leading women sculptors in nineteenth-century America, and both had ties to Boston. Hosmer (1830–1908) came from Watertown, Massachusetts. Her father was quite liberal in his thinking for early nineteenth-century America, and he encouraged his daughter's artistic pursuits. She began her career studying in Boston with the artist Paul Stevenson. The difficulties associated with allowing a woman artist to study human anatomy from observing nude male models led Hosmer to travel to St. Louis, Missouri, to study anatomy at a medical school there whose student population had been entirely male. In 1852, Hosmer went to Rome, where she could study the works of ancient and more recent European masters and could practice her craft in a social environment that was more tolerant of women artists. She spent much of the rest of her life in Europe, but when she returned to the United States, she stayed for extensive periods of time in Boston. One of her best works is her 1858 marble *Zenobia*, which depicts this ancient queen held captive while retaining a beauty, dignity, and grace throughout her ordeal. Another well-known work by her is *Puck*, a marble sculpture which she also made in the mid-1850s. It became so popular that she produced many copies of it. It depicts the angelic elf from Shakespeare's play *A Midsummer Night's Dream*. Hosmer gave up sculpture around 1875 to pursue her interest in mechanical inventions. She was truly ahead of her time—a Renaissance woman of Victorian America.

Edmonia Lewis (1845–?) is a fascinating yet mysterious figure in the history of American art. She was born in Ohio to an African American father and a mother who was a Native American of the Chippewa tribe. She studied at Oberlin College and then went to Boston in 1865, where she lived for several years. In Boston, she studied sculpture with Harriet Hosmer. Lewis produced two works that were reproduced and sold in large numbers in New England shortly after the Civil War. These were busts of the abolitionist John Brown and Union Army officer General Shaw. Lewis eventually went to Rome to study ancient sculpture and further her career in a social environment that was considered less racially biased. For a while, she received much attention in Europe; then she abruptly faded into obscurity. Records of her life end mysteriously around 1880; it is not known when and where she died. The fact that a woman who was also an African American could succeed as an artist in nineteenth-century America or Europe is itself remarkable. Few of her works have survived. Today, her most famous sculpture is probably *Forever Free*. This marble sculpture depicts two African Americans, a man who is standing and a woman who is kneeling by his legs. The muscular, bare-chested man is proudly breaking free of chains which symbolize slavery. The woman, dressed in a long robe, is less commanding and threatening, but nonetheless has been liberated from slavery as well.

Another intriguing New England sculptor is William Rimmer (1816–1879), who was based in Boston. Rimmer was a trained and practicing physician who took a serious interest in sculpture early in life and returned to it periodically over the years. His sculptures *The Fallen Gladiator* and *The Dying Centaur* are small, richly modeled sculptures which are fascinating in their poetic explorations of themes of suffering, despair, and death and their reliance on mythic creatures depicted with great attention to anatomical truth. Rimmer's study of human anatomy as a physician and his awareness of Greek sculptors of the Classical era as well as Renaissance masters such as Michelangelo are quickly apparent in these works. Furthermore, Rimmer's tendency to emphasize the musculature of his heroic figures with rather bold, vigorous modeling of the clay from which the bronzes were cast anticipates the revolutionary sculpture of Rodin by decades.

MODERNISM IN NEW ENGLAND

Of the pioneers of modernist art in the United States, James Abbot McNeill Whistler (1830–1903), Maurice Prendergast (1859–1924), and Marsden Hartley (1877–1944) are among the most prominent to have come from New England. Whistler, the oldest and probably most radically innovative of the three, was born and raised in Lowell, Massachusetts, but spent most of his adult life in England. His father was an engineer who designed railroads, and as a teenager Whistler traveled to wherever his father was working. Whistler returned to the United States as a young man to study at the U.S. Military Academy at West Point, New York. Although he became a military draftsman and mapmaker during this time, his stay at the Military Academy was short; he was expelled for poor grades. Whistler returned to Europe, this time settling first in Paris for a while before moving to London, where he spent the rest of his life. Known for his sardonic wit, Whistler became an integral part of Victorian London high society and was a close friend of the English playwright Oscar Wilde, also legendary for his wit. By the early 1860s, Whistler became part of the nascent Aesthetic movement, also known by its fundamental credo, "Art for art's sake." Whistler began to execute simplified, tonal paintings of landscapes, city views, figures, and portraits, which he often named using generic terms such as "composition," "nocturne," and "symphony," and adding numbers to differentiate them. By doing this, Whistler was emphasizing that these works were about compositional and visual issues and effects, and not about the subjects they depicted. Without ever realizing it, he pioneered many of the basic concepts of early twentieth-century abstract art, with its emphasis on the expressive and visual power of pure formal elements and its belief that the visual arts could be expressive in the same way that music without lyrics could be expressive (a concept known as synaesthesia).

The two most famous examples of Whistler's ideas put to full use are his paintings *Composition in Black and Grey: The Artist's Mother* of 1871 (commonly known as "Whistler's Mother") and *Nocturne in Black and Gold: The Falling Rocket* of 1876. The first painting shows the artist's elderly mother wearing a black dress and white bonnet as she sits in a chair by a black curtain. She is seen in strict profile, unemotional and seemingly oblivious to the presence of the viewer. The careful relationships of different forms to one another and the use of only black, grays, tans, and browns is unusual and very protomodern for its time. It is very different from Impressionism, which was spreading rapidly in France at the same time, and yet both Whistler's unique painting and the more abundant practice of Impressionism across the English Channel were pointing the way toward full-fledged modernism.

The second painting by Whistler led to heated controversy and debate when it was exhibited in 1877, shortly after it was painted. The English art critic John Ruskin hated it and criticized it in a published review by writing that Whistler "has thrown a pot of paint in the face of the public." The comment infuriated Whistler, who sued Ruskin for libel. A lengthy and lively trial ensued, in which the merits of the beginnings of modern art were inadvertently debated. Although Whistler won, he had so outraged the judge that he was awarded a settlement that amounted to less than $1.00; the trial ruined him financially more than it ever really vindicated him artistically.

Maurice Prendergast was associated with the Eight, a loose-knit group of artists who were based in New York and who often painted the rough living conditions of the urban poor and newly arrived immigrants in America's rapidly growing cities. Of the Eight, Prendergast was the only one to have come from Boston. Most of the group had come from Philadelphia and relocated to New York in the first few years of the twentieth century. Prendergast was also the most stylistically radical of the group. His connection to them was social in that they interacted at the same parties but artistic only in that they exhibited their works together. Prendergast's depiction of urban themes was more modernist than that of the other members of the Eight. He favored vivid, exaggerated colors, loose brushwork that often did nothing to re-create believable textures and shapes, and the balance of personal optical sensations and compositional structure pursued by Cezanne.

Marsden Hartley was born in Lewiston, Maine, and was raised there and in nearby towns for most of his childhood. His parents were English Episcopalians who came to the United States before Hartley was born. After his mother died when he was a teenager, Hartley lived with his older sister and her husband in Cleveland. Hartley's given first name was Edmund, but he abandoned it as a young man for "Marsden" as a gesture to endear himself to his stepmother, whose maiden name was Marsden. As a young man in Cleveland he worked various menial jobs, including one at a shoe factory, but he found such work very dissatisfying. Art caught his interest, and as a young man he started drawing and painting. Hartley received his earliest formal training at the Cleveland School of Art (now the Cleveland Art Institute). He moved to New York in 1898, where he soon came to know many other up-and-coming artists of his era. He studied first at the Chase School (the art academy founded by William Merritt Chase) and then at the National Academy of Design, but was not particularly happy at either institution. Hartley's painting is inextricably woven into his New England character and view of life but also into his personal needs and compulsions. Hartley was an insecure, lonely, withdrawn, and unhappy child. He was also a homosexual, and spent his adult life in search of meaningful love and affection, be it purely emotional or sexual. His art was a means of self-expression and also self-validation and spiritual fulfillment. He was also a restless soul and traveled often to places near and far. In the years before World War I, he traveled in Europe and studied much of the painting he found there. He spent nearly three years, from 1912 to 1915, in France and Germany. Unlike most of his contemporaries, he preferred Germany for both its art and its social environment. Once he returned to the United States he lived mostly in New York, which was beneficial to his career because he was surrounded by other artists and was near his supporter and benefactor, the art dealer and collector and photographer Alfred Stieglitz. Stieglitz promoted Hartley and several other leading modernists, including John Marin, Arthur Dove, and Georgia O'Keeffe, in his galleries, the first of which was formally called the Little Galleries of the Photo-Secession but which was informally known by its address on Madison Avenue, "291." Hartley often went to rural, isolated places in northern New England, especially in the summers of the last fifteen years of his life. The isolation was, oddly enough, a source of comfort, tranquility, and artistic inspiration for this lonely and unhappy man.

Hartley's earliest paintings, done before the Armory Show, are mostly landscapes that reflect various Post-Impressionist styles, in particular the exaggerated colors and loose paint application of Van Gogh, Gauguin, and Matisse. Hartley's breakthrough came during his visits to Europe in 1912 to 1915. In several paintings, mostly done while he was in Germany, Hartley combined Fauve and Expressionist color, Cubist handling of space, and the spiritual longing of abstractionists from across Europe to achieve his own artistic voice. *Portrait of a German Officer* of 1914 is probably the best-known of these paintings. This is an abstract "portrait" of Karl von Freyburg, a young German soldier whom Hartley met while in Germany and who became the object of his affections. Von Freyburg died in combat early in World War I, and the deeply saddened Hartley made this painting as a commemoration of the subject's heroism and his own feelings about him. In this tightly clustered composition of roughly painted forms, references to von Freyburg are everywhere and include his regiment tags, his initials, and the German flag and iron cross. Other paintings from around 1914 are similar in their dense packing of forms, rough paint texture, and use of disparate, virtually clashing colors ranging from vibrant hues in small areas to larger areas of grays and black. Some are about Native American culture, which also interested Hartley at this time. Along with his fellow artists of the Stieglitz circle, Hartley was one of the most innovative and daring artists from America in the early years of the twentieth century. He fully explored and assimilated current modernist styles that originated in France and Germany and made them into something very much his own and highly expressive. In the late 1910s and early 1920s, Hartley's paintings became more subdued in color and strictly linear; he ventured further into Cubism and abstraction than ever before. At this time, he seemed to have disavowed personal expression in art, but such inclinations were foreign to Hartley and did not last long. In the mid-1920s, his painting became overtly expressionistic in color, paint handling, and subjects. His dark, moody colors and raw paint handling are almost disturbing in their fierce emotive power.

Some of Hartley's greatest late works were done in Dogtown, Massachusetts, in the late 1930s. The sublime, unspoiled, wild grandeur of the New England landscape and the hardy, sincere, straightforward character of the rural, Puritan-like New Englanders he knew are seen in many of these late paintings. *Fisherman's Last Supper* of 1940–1941 commemorates a young Maine fisherman who died at sea. Hartley and the family were friendly and the young man was yet another object of Hartley's sexual interests. Hartley's painting takes the traditional Christian theme and applies it in a matter-of-fact, secular way to the New Englanders he knew. He shows several members of the family sitting at their dining table. They are dressed in old work clothes and their home is sparsely furnished. A glowing yellow star floats above the head of the dead young man. Hartley has virtually canonized him in paint.

REGIONALISM AND SOCIAL REALISM BETWEEN THE WORLD WARS IN NEW ENGLAND

During the Great Depression and World War II, more realistic styles and subjects taken from contemporary life and its problems became common among American artists. These styles are referred to as Regionalism, American Scene Painting, and Social Realism, and they carry with them complex distinctions of regional and cultural identity (Midwest versus Northeast, rural versus urban, Anglo-Saxon and Northern European versus Southern and Eastern European, etc.). Whereas Regionalism is usually associated with the rural Midwest and Social Realism with the large cities of the Northeast, there were artists practicing these more realistic styles across the United States. Perhaps the most impressive realist of this era to have close ties to New England is the painter Andrew Wyeth (1917–). Wyeth comes from a large family of painters; most of his siblings and his son Jamie are painters and his father, N. C. Wyeth, was a famous book illustrator in the early twentieth century. Although Wyeth was born in Chadds Ford, Pennsylvania, as were generations of his family before him, and he continues to live there, he spent much of his time in Maine, where his family has a farm and a house near the coast. *Christina's World* of 1948 is perhaps his most famous painting, and is strikingly different from the emergent Abstract Expressionism of the late 1940s. The painting is about Christina Olson, a woman handicapped by polio (infantile paralysis) who lived near Wyeth's family's farm in Maine. She was unable to walk and got around by crawling, using her arms to drag herself. Yet she was able to take care of the home that she shared with her brother. Hence, her "world" was severely limited. As indicated in this painting, it was geographically limited to her house and its surrounding farmland. The painting features Wyeth's characteristic meticulous, dry painting style. This unpainterly style can be attributed to Wyeth's use of tempera (traditionally, *tempera* is paint in which pigments, the materials that give paint their colors, are mixed into a binder that holds the pigment and allows it to be used). Christina Olson's frail yet determined physique looms large in the foreground, while her house seems impossibly far away at the top of the hill that fills the canvas.

Numerous photographers took great interest in the architecture of New England at this time. Among them were Charles Currier, Paul Strand, and Edward Weston. Currier worked in Boston in the 1930s and 1940s as he created many photographs of domestic interiors of New England which reflect his interest in precise, geometric order and stability in the decoration and furnishings of homes. The more famous Edward Weston (1886–1958) took a similar interest in New England architecture at around the same time. In 1965, he joined the faculty of Yale University. The equally famous Paul Strand (1890–1976) visited many places during his career, and around 1925 he went to Maine to photograph local scenery and people.

CONTEMPORARY ART IN NEW ENGLAND

In the aftermath of World War I and World War II, the Great Depression, and the Cold War and the rapid spread of mass communication, no single region of the United States is as socially and culturally distinct as it once was. Hence, identifying particular trends, styles, or attitudes in art that identify one region and distinguish it from another is much more difficult. Nevertheless, it is worth noting that certain artistic trends were developing in New England after World War II. Although few of the better-known Abstract Expressionists had ties to New England, several of the Color-Field Painters and Minimalists of the 1960s did. Frank Stella (1936–) was born and raised in Malden, Massachusetts. Stella started painting while he was a student at Princeton University. He was one of several young painters who, around 1960, embraced hard-edged, smooth-surfaced abstract painting and the use of canvases that were irregularly shaped (such supports are often called *shaped canvases*; they are not rectangles, squares, or circles). *Agbatana III* of 1968 exemplifies this new attitude toward the shape of the picture plane and the use of lines, shapes, colors, and textures. This large painting consists of several large arc-shapes arranged in a curving pattern. Within this multishaped canvas are numerous firmly defined shapes, many of them slightly triangular areas of various colors, some of them rich and vibrant, others dark and muted. Stella's titles are often mysterious and suggestive. One cannot help but wonder what cryptic levels of meaning they impart to sparse, seemingly unemotional, geometric abstraction.

Yale University

Yale University in New Haven, Connecticut, became one of the leading institutions for the study of art when the German abstract artist, art theorist, and teacher Josef Albers (1888–1976) joined the faculty. Albers became an influential art theorist and teacher in Germany in the 1920s. He studied at the Bauhaus from 1920 to 1923. The Bauhaus was founded in 1919 in Weimar, Germany, by the architects Walter Gropius and Mies van der Rohe, with the intention of training new generations of artists in styles considered appropriate to the modern era and demolishing traditional boundaries of media, style, and function and regional, ethnic, or cultural identity.[5] The Bauhaus revolutionized the ways that design and color were taught, and Albers was essential to its success. Albers taught at the Bauhaus from 1923 to 1933; he usually taught the introductory course required of all students. Albers came to America in 1933 after the Nazis closed the Bauhaus that year. He started teaching at Black Mountain College in North Carolina shortly after he arrived in America. He subsequently taught at Yale from 1950 to 1960. Teaching at the Bauhaus had made Albers acutely aware of issues of perception and the optical experience of color, shape, space, and depth. Around 1930 he began to develop series in various media to explore what and how we see. In 1942 he worked on the Graphic Tectonics and from 1947 to 1957 he worked on the Graphic Constellations. In these series, he explored optical illusions through the manipulation of shape and line. Around 1950 he began the series of color experiments for which he remains best known: *Homage to the Square*. Albers produced hundreds of paintings in this series, which he continued until his death in 1976. In *Homage to the Square*, Albers explored how changes in hue, brightness, tone, and purity, be they subtle or extreme, affect neighboring colors and how we perceive them. Albers' writings, theories, and artwork provided enormously useful insights into the ways that humans comprehend and respond to visual experience. His ideas and teaching methods spread far and wide, and their legacy is alive and well today in art academies and universities all over the world. Countless artists studied with Albers or with artists who adhered to and promoted his color theories and adopted his teaching methods; his influence has been enormous.

Louise Nevelson

One of America's greatest women sculptors of the post–World War II era has close ties to New England. Louise Nevelson (1899–) was born Louisa Berliowsky in Kiev, Russia, to a Russian-Jewish family. Her family relocated to Portland, Maine, in 1905, when she was six years old. She remained there until 1920, when at the age of twenty-one she went to New York City. In the 1920s and 1930s she studied with various artists in cities across the United States, including Kenneth Hayes Miller, Hans Hofmann, and Diego Rivera. Her artistic maturation was gradual and irregular; although she was older than most Minimalists, she came of age artistically at nearly the same time as they did. In the mid-1950s, she began to produce the tall, wide, semirelief sculptures placed against walls for which she is now famous. They are reliefs in that they are usually not intended to be viewed by walking completely around them. They often feature deeply and intricately carved recessions. Sometimes they are constructed by compiling box-like forms, such as wine and produce crates, with their open sides facing the viewer. In these spaces many different found objects or carved forms are placed. These sculptures are usually made of wood, and regardless of the materials used to make them, all the items and objects are usually painted one color, with black being quite popular. Nevelson's signature sculptures show the merging of Surrealist and abstract influences and thought processes. *Sky Cathedral* of 1958 is a particularly good example of Nevelson's distinct approach to sculptural form and space.

FOLK ART

Although the term originated in the twentieth century, folk art has a long history, and folk artists, though hard to define in a singular way, might be described as painters, sculptors, and craft artisans who have little or no formal training as artists. Folk artists are usually ordinary people who create art for themselves and others but mostly for those people living within their community. Similar to Native American artists, folk artists reflect the attitudes and ideals of their folk community and participate in the traditions of that community. In following tradition, folk artists tend to be conservative rather than innovative, concrete rather than abstract, and ignore the latest trends of the art world. They follow their own traditions, creating an object or scene that is familiar to them and the rest of the community. Although folk art has become more acceptable in the established art world since the founding of the American Folk Art Museum in New York (1961), it is still sometimes referred to—namely by academic artists—as "primitive," "naive," "self taught," "outsider art," "provincial," or "country." Nonetheless, the genre maintains its popularity in many small and large American communities, including those of New England.

Art had a practical function for the first Puritan settlers of North America. Like Native Americans, the Puritan settlers often decorated utilitarian objects for daily use. One of the first forms of New England folk art, therefore, was wood carving or "treening"—that is, the art of making something from a tree. In the seventeenth century, wood carving usually involved small objects used in domestic and farm life as well as in the trades and professions. Kitchenware, for example, was usually carved from wood using simple or plain designs. More intricate designs were sometimes found on wooden knitting sheaths or on wooden stay busks (love tokens) carved for young women by their admirers. During the eighteenth century, pewter, copper, and earthenware replaced wooden kitchenware, but the fascination with wood carving continued into the nineteenth and twentieth centuries as cabinetmakers increasingly incorporated designs and patterns into their furniture, and other craftsmen or artists simply made small wooden figures and pieces for the sake of ornament. One of the four garden ornaments carved by John and Simeon Skillins at the end of the eighteenth century for Elias Hasket Derby of Boston, and now located at the Peabody Museum in Salem, Massachusetts, is a perfect example of this growing attention to detail. The Figure of Plenty (now called Pomona) depicts a woman wearing a long, billowing dress and holding a cornucopia. She represents the prosperity of the new republic but also demonstrates the evolution of folk art in early New England.

Other folk art that originated in the colonial period included pottery, metalwork, needlework, sewing, embroidery, and lacemaking, but perhaps the best-known New England tradition often associated with folk art was quilt making. Although it is a popular belief that many New England women were holding quilting parties or quilting next to the fire during the colonial period, there is no evidence to suggest that New England women were quilting in the seventeenth century. Cloth was simply too expensive, and wealthy families were known to import whole cloth quilts from Europe. By the middle of the eighteenth century, however, New England women were beginning to make their own quilts. These quilts, consisting of three layers (a top, a filler or batting, and a backing), were made of "whole cloth," usually expensive silk or glazed worsted (long-fiber wool). New England women created patterns by stitching the layers together and creating elaborate motifs like the popular "Tree of Life." Stars were another important motif until about 1825 when New England women also began to quilt comforters or "comfortables."

The earliest examples of quilting, which included petticoats, skirts, cloaks, coats, bonnets, and other garments as well as bed quilts, displayed wealth, showing the household's ability to purchase expensive hand-block-printed cloth. With the advent of the Industrial Revolution, however, the price of fabric dropped considerably and larger numbers of middle- and working-class women were able to afford cloth for quilt making. It was around this time that quilting became associated with frugality and women increasingly began to make quilts out of bits of worn-out clothing and left-over sewing scraps. Some of these scrap quilts, which later became known as "crazy quilts," were elaborate, like the one made by a member of the Haskins family of Granville, Vermont, in the third quarter of the nineteenth century (now in the collection of the Shelburne Museum). It was also around this time that the myth of women quilting in early New England emerged, reinforced by the 1920s and 1930s revival in everything colonial, which included the romantic vision of colonial quilting bees. Today the folk art of quilting does not have the appeal that it once did in New England, but there are still quilting bees and dedicated quilters in rural parts of the region. In 1976, for example, a group of women founded the New England Quilter's Guild, and it now has sixty chapters across

New England. In 1980, the guild founded the New England Quilt Museum in Lowell, Massachusetts, Lowell also hosts the annual Lowell Quilt Festival, while Northfield, Vermont, hosts another quilt festival during the summer.

Another early form of New England folk art to emerge during the colonial period was primitive painting. Colonial primitive painting first emerged in New England in the early eighteenth century when untrained painters traveled the countryside looking for commissions. These itinerant painters were often called "limners," in reference to "limning," or simple unrefined sketching, which is indicative of their undistinguished place in early American society and its economy. These primitive painters typically painted flat portraits and landscapes and sought their commissions from middle-class families who could not afford the cost of professional paintings. Although many of these limners are unknown to us today, a few made a name for themselves as portrait and landscape painters. John Greenwood (1727–1792) of Boston, for example, was one of New England's earliest primitive painters. As a young man, Greenwood was apprenticed to a Boston artisan involved in engraving, japanning, cutting gravestones, and painting houses and ships. Having received no formal training, Greenwood set his mind on becoming a portrait painter and was soon well known around Boston. An obscure engraving of one of his paintings depicting an old lady, entitled *Jersey Nanny*, is in the Boston Museum of Fine Arts with the following verse beneath it:

Nature her various skill displays
In thousand shapes, a thousand ways;
Tho' one form differs from another,
She's still of all the common mother;
Then, Ladies, let not pride resist her,
But own that Nanny is your Sister.

Greenwood's work parted from the norm and was often satirical, peopled with small, energetic figures reminiscent of William Hogarth's work. As a self-taught artist, Greenwood developed a new genre of American painting before leaving Boston at the young age of twenty-five for Surinam, South America, and later for England, where he established himself as a successful art dealer.

Winthrop Chandler (1747–1790) of Woodstock, Connecticut, Ralph Earl (1751–1801) of New Haven, Connecticut, Rufus Hathaway (1770–1822) of Freetown, Massachusetts, Ruth Henshaw Bascom (1772–1848) of Leicester, Massachusetts, Chester Harding (1792–1866) of Conway, Massachusetts, Erastus Salisbury Field (1805–1900) of Leverett, Massachusetts, Horace Bundy (1814–1883) of Hardwick, Vermont, and Joseph Whiting (1815–1855) of Springfield, Massachusetts, were all part of this limner tradition. Perhaps the most successful of the limner painters, however, was William Matthew Prior (1806–1873) of Bath, Maine. He was born the son of a shipbuilder from Duxbury, Massachusetts, and claimed to be a descendant of the Pilgrims. Without any professional training, Prior became an itinerant painter, traveling to Portland, Maine, and later to Boston, where he set up the "Painting Garret" studio. Unlike a lot of other primitive painters, Prior was able to make a good living at his trade and painted in both the flat and academic traditions. He simply advertised that less expensive portraits would be "flat likeness without shade and shadow" and that those persons paying more would have more realistic depictions. Prior, however, was best known for his primitive flat work, namely full-length child portraits like *Baby with Whip* (in the Abby Aldrich Rockefeller Folk Art Collection), and typically painted them with vibrant colors and little attention to details on the hands and feet. Unlike his contemporaries, Prior also tended to paint his subjects against a soft atmospheric background instead of one with bright colors. Throughout his career, he painted and sold hundreds of paintings and departed from the norm by painting the likeness of Andrew Jackson on bed ticking and the likeness of George and Martha Washington on glass. Prior also painted the portrait of such notable figures as Charles Dickens, Abraham Lincoln, and Theodore Parker.

Another unschooled painter to receive recognition in her day was Grandma Moses. Born Anna Mary Robertson in 1860 in upstate New York, she became a farmer's wife, marrying Robert Moses and living first in the Shenandoah Valley and then at Eagle Bridge, New York. As a farmer's wife, she raised five children and did chores around the farm; in her spare time, she painted traditional New England farm scenes from memory. At the age of seventy, when she had grown too old for farm work, she began to paint full time, creating idealized images of New England farm life. Her paintings typically depict a simple and nostalgic way of life, including images of quiltmaking, haying, and milking, and were full of bright colors. Such examples can be found in her paintings *Haying Time* (1945), *Apple Butter Making* (1947), and *The Quilting Bee* (1950), among many others.

By the 1940s, shortly after she had been noticed by a New York art dealer and her work had been exhibited at the Museum of Modern Art in New York City, she began to paint more rolling hills in the landscape and showed small figures engaged in activity, as in *The Old Checkered House* (1944) in the Yasuda Kasai Museum in Tokyo, Japan, in which small figures are riding horses or carriages outside the farmhouse. Grandma Moses' name quickly spread throughout America, becoming a household name. Her paintings with their idealized nostalgia for a happier past appealed to the American public, and she was invited to the White House and was commissioned by Hallmark. She painted her last painting, *The Rainbow* (1961), at the age of 101. She died that same year. Today, a large collection of her paintings can be found in the Bennington Museum in Vermont, where two galleries are devoted to her work.

CONCLUSION

The visual arts in New England have a long, vibrant, and rich history. With culturally thriving cities like Boston, Providence, and New Haven and many artists' colonies in rural parts of Vermont, New Hampshire, and Maine, that artistic legacy survives and continues to prosper to this day, and no doubt will prosper in the future.

RESOURCE GUIDE

Printed Sources

Berlo, Janet Catherine, and Ruth Phillips. *Native North American Art*. New York: Oxford University Press, 1999.

Bjelejac, David. *American Art: A Cultural History*. New York: Harry N. Abrams/Prentice-Hall, 2001.

Cikovsky, Nicolai, Jr., et al. *Winslow Homer*. Washington, DC: National Gallery of Art, 1995.

Gerdts, William H. *American Impressionism*. New York: Abbeville Press, 2002.

Hartel, Herbert R., Jr. "Luminism, Abstraction and Transcendentalism in the Landscape Paintings of John F. Kensett." *Source: Notes in the History of Art* 21, no. 4 (Summer 2002): 23–30.

Howat, John K., et al. *The American Paradise: The World of the Hudson River School*. New York: Metropolitan Museum of Art, 1986.

Rebora, Carrie, et al. *John Singleton Copley in America*. New York: Metropolitan Museum of Art, 1996.

Robertson, Bruce. *Marsden Hartley*. New York: Harry N. Abrams, 1995.

Truettner, William H., et al. *Picturing Old New England: Image and Memory*. New Haven: Yale University Press, 1999.

Wilmerding, John. *American Marine Painting*. 2nd ed. New York: Harry N. Abrams, 1987.

Wilmerding, John, et al. *American Light: The Luminist Movement, 1850–1875*. Washington, DC: National Gallery of Art, 1980.

Web Sites

Native Tech. 2004.
Nativetech.org. March 28, 2004.
http://www.nativetech.org/

Internet resource guide for indigenous ethno-technology focusing on the arts of the Eastern Woodland Indian peoples.

Smithsonian Archives of American Art. March 24, 2004.
Smithsonian Institution. March 28, 2004.
http://www.aaa.si.edu/

The Archives of American Art is a division of the Smithsonian Institution with branches in Washington, D.C., New York, Boston, and California.

Museums and Organizations

Abby Aldrich Rockefeller Folk Art Museum
Colonial Williamsbury Foundation
P.O. Box 1776
Williamsburg, VA 23187-1776
http://www.history.org/history/museums/abby_art.cfm

Part of the Colonial Williamsburg collection, this folk art museum exhibits many examples of New England Folk Art, such as tavern signs, quilts, toys, and illustrations.

American Folk Art Museum
45 W. 53rd Street
New York, NY 10019
http://www.folkartmuseum.org

Collection features many New England artists from the eighteenth century to the present.

Bowdoin College Museum of Art
Bowdoin College
9400 College Station
Brunswick, ME 04011
http://academic.bowdoin.edu/artmuseum/

Fogg Art Museum
Harvard University
32 Quincy Street
Cambridge, MA 02138
http://www.artmuseums.harvard.edu/fogg/index.html

Fuller Museum of Art
455 Oak Street
Brockton, MA 02301
http://www.fullermuseum.org/

Metropolitan Museum of Art
1000 Fifth Avenue at 82nd Street
New York, NY 10028
http://www.metmuseum.org/

The museum houses collections of New England drawings, paintings, sculptures, and crafts, including works by John Singleton Copley, Gilbert Stuart, John Townsend, and Paul Revere, Jr.

Museum of Fine Arts, Boston
Avenue of the Arts
465 Huntington Avenue
Boston, MA 02115
http://www.mfa.org/

National Gallery of Art, Washington, DC
National Mall between Third and Ninth Streets
Constitution Avenue, N.W.
Washington, DC
http://www.nga.gov/

The museum houses a small collection of New England art, including the works of John Marin and Winslow Homer.

New England Carousel Museum
95 Riverside Avenue, Route 72
Bristol, CT 06010
http://www.thecarouselmuseum.com

The Museum is proud to house one of the largest collections of antique carousel pieces in the country. It sponsors programs for children and teachers and provides art exhibits of local artists.

New England Quilt Museum
18 Shattuck Street
Lowell, MA 01852
http://www.nequiltmuseum.org/index.shtml

The New England Quilt Museum was founded in 1987 to preserve and exhibit antique and contemporary quilts. It sponsors an annual juried quilt show and provides a library and Web site with links to other New England quilt sites.

Shelburne Museum
U.S. Route 7
P.O. Box 10
Shelburne, VT 05482
http://www.shelburnemuseum.org/

Eclectic American art, architecture, and artifacts.

Wadsworth Atheneum Museum of Art
600 Main Street
Hartford, CT 06103
http://www.wadsworthatheneum.org/

Whitney Museum of American Art
945 Madison Avenue at 75th Street
New York, NY 10021
http://www.whitney.org/

Winterthur Museum, Garden, and Library
Route 52
Winterthur, DE 19735
http://www.winterthur.org

Worcester Art Museum
55 Salisbury Street
Worcester, MA 01609
http://www.worcesterart.org/

Yale University Art Gallery
1111 Chapel Street
New Haven, CT 06520
http://www.yale.edu/artgallery/

State Arts Councils and Regional Foundations

Connecticut Commission on Arts, Tourism, Culture, History & Film
One Financial Plaza, 755 Main Street
Hartford, CT 06103
http://www.ctarts.org

Maine Arts Commission
193 State Street
25 State House Station
Augusta, ME 04333-0025
http://www.mainearts.com

Massachusetts Cultural Council
10 St. James Ave.
3rd Floor
Boston, MA 02116
http://www.massculturalcouncil.org

New England Foundation for the Arts
266 Summer Street
2nd Floor
Boston, MA 02210
http://www.nefa.org/

New Hampshire Council on the Arts
New Hampshire State Council of the Arts
21½ Beacon St., 2nd floor
Concord, NH 03301-4974
http://www.state.nh.us/nharts/

Features New England Cultural Database, an extensive listing of arts organizations and groups throughout New England.

Rhode Island State Council on the Arts
One Capitol Hill
3rd Floor
Providence, RI 02908
http://www.arts.ri.gov/

Vermont Arts Council
136 State Street—Drawer 33
Montpelier, VT 05633-6001
http://www.vermontartscouncil.org/

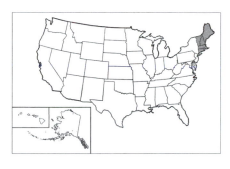

ECOLOGY AND ENVIRONMENT

Lisa Krissoff Boehm

PHYSICAL ENVIRONMENT

As a region, New England shares some features with the mid-Atlantic states, yet it has a much more rock-covered landscape and is marked by many swamps and bogs. New England's location on the Atlantic Ocean made it among the first regions settled by the European colonizers of the New World. The access to the sea allowed for the growth of the region's cities as centers of international trade. New England's gritty mixture of clay, sand, and rock soil, a substance called "till," translates into very difficult conditions for farming, much of the impetus that brought industrialization to the region. Industrialization established itself early in New England—the region led the nation in turning to manufacturing—and although the region gained from the practice economically, industrialization and dense settlement left New England with severe environmental consequences.

New England has a variety of impressive mountain ranges. While not as high as the ranges of the American West, the mountains offer an abundance of hiking and skiing options to visitors and memorable vistas. The Green Mountains of Vermont and Massachusetts resemble the Blue Ridge Mountains of Virginia, in that both are the much eroded remains of very old mountain ranges. Several of the Green Mountains—Mt. Killington, Mt. Ellen, the Camel's Hump, and Mt. Mansfield—are over four thousand feet above sea level. The Berkshire Hills of western Massachusetts are related in origin to the Green Mountains. Both are components of a general upfolding of land that stretches from central Pennsylvania to southern New York state and westward into New England. The Taconic Mountains are a narrow range that sits on the border of New York State and New England, working its way from northern Connecticut to central Vermont. The White Mountains of New Hampshire and its Presidential Range are the highest mountains in New England. Mt. Washington is the single highest peak in the region at over six thousand feet. The mountain receives over seventy inches of precipitation yearly. Its

Primarily Pine Forests

CANADA

St. Lawrence Seaway

St. John

Churchill Lake

Chamberlain Lake

Chesuncook Lake

Mt. Katahdin

Moosehead Lake

Kennebec

MAINE

Penobscot

Bangor

Augusta

VERMONT

Lake Champlain

Charlotte
Montpelier

Connecticut

Berlin

Androscoggin

Mt. Washington

Presidential Range

WHITE MOUNTAINS

Bar Harbor

Acadia Nat'l Park

Prehistoric Lake Hitchcock Area

GREEN MOUNTAINS

Mt. Whiteface

Nancy Brook Virgin Forest

Lake Winnipesaukee

Portland

Lebanon

Claremont

Merrimack

Rochester

Somersworth

Concord

Dover

NEW HAMPSHIRE

Portsmouth

NEW YORK

TACONIC MOUNTAINS

Manchester

Nashua

MASSACHUSETTS

Lowell

Lawrence

Cape Ann

Middlesex Canal

Worcester

Lake Cochituate

Boston

Charles

Berkshire Hills

Springfield

Quabbin Reservoir

Blackstone Canal River

CONNECTICUT

Hartford

Providence

Pawtucket

Cape Cod

ATLANTIC OCEAN

Waterbury

Cranston

Fall River

Meriden

New London

RHODE ISLAND

Newport

New Bedford

Danbury

New Haven

Bridgeport

Stamford

Block Island

Martha's Vineyard

Nantucket

winter snow blankets the slopes, keeping underlying plant life at a relatively warm thirty-two degrees Fahrenheit underneath. Few of New England's ranges are high enough to claim a truly alpine zone, with its requisite low-lying plant life and lack of trees. Just below New England's alpine zone one encounters shrubs and trees prostrate from the fierce winds, known as *krummholz*, the German word for "twisted wood." The alpine plant community also includes wildflowers, lichens, and other low-lying plants. A single alpine plant may be over one hundred years old. The treeline lies at 5,200 feet on south-facing sides of the mountain, and at 4,800 feet on north-facing sides. Part of the difference in vegetation lies in the fact that rising up four hundred feet is equivalent to traveling northward for one hundred miles, in terms of climate change. The Presidential Range has eight square miles above the alpine zone, and Mt. Katahdin claims a small zone as well. The Presidential Range offers one of the best places in the world to observe vegetation changes at different altitude levels.[1]

Less striking than New England's many mountain ranges, yet still part of the region's captivating uneven landscape, are the rounded drumlins. Drumlins are long ridges or oval shaped hills produced by glaciers, although the exact nature of their formation is still debated. The longest of the drumlins are less than one mile in length, and 250 feet tall. Boston's Bunker Hill is perhaps the most famous regional drumlin. Formed by glaciers, most of the drumlins point generally in the same direction, or approximately east-west. In the modern day, many of the drumlins have been altered by development and no longer remain such an obvious feature of the region.

Glaciations caused a variety of lakes to be scattered across New England, although many have become dried out over time and have left only their tell-tale shapes and soils behind. For example, a lake later named Lake Hitchcock was once located in the Connecticut Valley. Thousands of these ancient bodies of water remain. Vermont's Lake Champlain, for example, is the remaining component of the former Champlain Sea, and much of coastal Maine and New Hampshire was formerly underwater. Findings like the 1848 unearthing of a whale skeleton well inland at Charlotte, Vermont, point to this watery past.

New England remains the U.S. region with the least resources of commercially viable minerals. The region can boast of no oil and relatively little in terms of coal. The mining in the region primarily focuses on slate, marble, and granite as well as a now disbanded industry, pegmatite mining. Pegmatite is a rock formation with masses of sought-after minerals like feldspar and mica within it. Pegmatite mining began in New England during the 1800s and reached its height in the 1940s. The mining of the colorful tourmaline crystals has also been pursued in the region.[2]

New England contains a number of significant rivers, some of which provided the waterpower that made the Industrial Revolution possible in the region. The Merrimack River, the heart of much of the region's early manufacturing efforts, flows southward from New Hampshire into northeastern Massachusetts. The Blackstone River originates near the city of Worcester, Massachusetts, and works its way southward through Rhode Island and connects with the Atlantic Ocean at Narragansett Bay. The Blackstone Canal, which enabled central Massachusetts to blossom, was opened 1828. The Blackstone Canal paralleled the Blackstone River in many places, and with forty-nine locks enabled the connection of Worcester,

New England's island vacation retreats, including Nantucket and Martha's Vineyard in Massachusetts (shown here) and Block Island in Rhode Island, contributed greatly to the region's early economic health and encouraged settlement. Courtesy of Massachusetts Office of Travel and Tourism.

Massachusetts, with Providence, Rhode Island, despite the 438-foot difference in elevation between the two cities. The Connecticut River, the longest river in New England at 407 miles, begins in northern New Hampshire and makes up the border between that state and Vermont, running southward through Massachusetts and Connecticut.[3]

New England contains several moderately sized freshwater lakes. In Maine, one can enjoy Eagle Lake, Moosehead Lake, and West Grand Lake. Maine's largest lake, Moosehead, covers about 120 square miles of area and serves as the source of the Kennebec River. The Moosehead offers coved areas that are ideal for fishing. Lake Winnipesaukee, the largest lake entirely within New England, is located in central New Hampshire at the foothills of the White Mountains. Winnipesaukee is twenty miles long with a width of up to twelve miles. Vermont's Lake Champlain serves as the boundary between New York State and Vermont. The largest of all lakes mentioned (although not entirely within New England's borders), Lake Champlain is part of the link between the Atlantic Ocean and the St. Lawrence Seaway and thus has significant commercial traffic.

In addition to New England's important rivers and lakes, the region includes an extensive ocean coastline, stretching from Maine to Connecticut. New England's ocean harbors, like those at Boston, Massachusetts, and Newport, Rhode Island, contributed greatly to the region's early economic health and encouraged settlement. In modern times, New England's Atlantic coastline provides a draw to numerous tourists. Of special interest to many are New England's island vacation retreats, including Nantucket and Martha's Vineyard in Massachusetts and Block Island in Rhode Island.

The New England region was greatly shaped by the immense continental ice sheet, which finally receded about twelve thousand years ago, leaving the rocky debris and rocky soil behind with which New Englanders today are so familiar. In some areas, the glaciers dislodged solid bedrock, forming huge boulders, like those that adorn the landscape in Massachusetts' northern coastal region, Cape Ann. During the Ice Age, animals like woolly mammoths, American mastodons, and sabre-toothed cats inhabited the region. The region played host to an arctic type of vegetation for the two thousand years following the melting of the ice sheet. Large mammals like caribou and musk-oxen roamed the landscape, and hardy plants such as sedges and dwarf shrubs constituted the region's vegetation. As the region warmed, both the flora and fauna diversified. Spruces constituted the earliest conifers, followed by fir trees. Trees with broad leaves began to take root in the lower areas of the region. For the following four to six thousand years, New England was a warmer region than it is today.

New England is a region of trees. Just two thousand years ago, New England developed the diversity of trees considered the primary representatives of the northern hardwood forest, including the American beech, the sugar maple, and the yellow birch tree. The forests of northern New England resemble closely the boreal forests of southern Canada (typified by white spruce, balsam fir, and moose) except for the presence of the red spruce in New England, but the similarities gradually lessen as one moves into southern New England. Northern Maine does sit five hundred miles closer to the North Pole than Connecticut, so the types of trees found in different parts of New England vary. New England's forests are a composite, with boreal forests in northern Maine, northern hardwood forests (including such trees as orange-red sugar maples and yellow birch) in Maine, New Hampshire, Vermont, and Massachusetts, oak-hickory forests in Connecticut, Rhode Island, and Massachusetts, and maple-basswood forests in Connecticut, Rhode Island, and Massachusetts. Today's largely wooded landscape evokes thoughts of virgin woodlands, but the region has been heavily logged. In the 1850s, southern New England was for all intents and purposes deforested. Most of New England has been logged at least once, and in many areas two to three times. Just a few virgin spruce-fir forests remain—including what is known as "The Bowl" on Mt. Whiteface near Waterville, New Hampshire, the Nancy Brook Virgin Forest in Livermore Township, New Hampshire, and some of the upper slopes of the White Mountains. New England is known for its evergreen wilderness, yet this type of forestation covers less than one-third of the northern states of New Hampshire, Vermont, and Maine. The tallest trees in New England in modern times are the red spruces, some of which acquire trunks as wide as three feet in diameter.

Weather

New England has a temperamental weather system, known for sudden changes. The region's growing season spans approximately 150 days, with the last killing frost taking place between mid-March and some time in May. New England has famed vibrant colors in its trees during luxuriant fall seasons, yet it also hosts the infamous damaging storms, the nor'easters, caused by the influx of weather systems on this relatively narrow band of land near the cold Atlantic Ocean. Weather systems from the South Atlantic, the Gulf region, and the Pacific Northwest all meet in New England. Low-pressure systems hit the region on a continual basis, sweeping in air in a counterclockwise fashion. The counterclockwise winds of a low-pressure system draw in the cool temperatures of Canada, making New England perhaps the coldest place on earth at the same latitude. The only areas occupying similar latitudes that can claim weather as cold as that in New England are northeastern China and Hokkaido, Japan. New England also faces an unusually high frequency of cloudy days. Mt. Washington, the region's tallest peak, is considered by many to have the worst weather in the world. Plagued by hurricane winds, the mountain receives seventy inches of precipitation yearly, much of it in the form of snow. Snow falls there even in the summer months. It was once thought that the ocean brought Europe a climate much warmer than that of the areas of eastern North America at the same latitudes because of the flow of the Gulf Stream. New studies show that the colder climates of the East Coast come from the flow of cold winds from the Rocky Mountains. In the winter, when the

Mt. Washington, New England's tallest peak, is considered by many to have the worst weather in the world, including hurricane winds and seventy inches of yearly precipitation. Courtesy National Park Service.

strongest winds blow, it is this inland mountain range that is responsible for the bitter northwest winds hitting New England. Only in the winter, scientists argue, does the ocean significantly affect the temperature of New England, warming the region by approximately five degrees.

NATIVE AMERICAN AND EUROPEAN LAND USAGE

The European colonists built their cities and towns on land that had previously been settled by Native Americans, or had at least been seen as part of the native people's domain. New England was home to the Nipmuc, the Pokanoket, and Narragansett peoples before the arrival of the colonists. Since the first European settlers arrived in North America, clashes between European groups and peoples native to the land had erupted. Many of the troubles stemmed from the two parties' opposing ideas regarding land usage. European immigrants believed for their part that land should be privately held. Plots were purchased with money or credit and then utilized by one owner or family until sold or passed down to heirs in the next generation. In New England, some Europeans shared grazing pastures, and sometimes this land was located conveniently in the center of cities, such as in the case of the Boston Common and the Worcester Common.

Native Americans tended not to own land individually, and in fact their belief system stipulated that most land was shared by the group. Native Americans who were involved with agriculture typically moved seasonally between summer plant-ing grounds and woodland winter camps. Native agriculturalists also relocated their farming plots occasionally so as not to exhaust the soil—a technique usually impossible for European farmers who owned only a certain piece of land. Also in contrast to Europeans was the native technique of group farming. Native Ameri-cans worked together to feed their families, farming all of the land as a group proj-ect rather than dividing the land into family holdings. Native women tended to work the land, day in and day out, and women assumed the authority for issues of land use, such as what share of the harvest each family could claim. Groups of women planted corn, beans, and other staples in their fields, often utilizing the same field for a combination of crops—a practice that later research proved highly effective and beneficial to the soil.

European colonists viewed the Native American land use practices with disdain. The colonists eschewed the native people's failure to own land in the European sense, and balked at the native women's hard labor in the fields. To Europeans, no land was properly used if not tended continually. The Europeans believed the Na-tive Americans were wasting the apparent bounty of their lands. These new ar-rivals failed to understand how careful practices employed by the Native Americans had kept the vegetation lush and the wildlife plentiful. The Native American prac-tice of "swidden," or clearing the land by burning the underbrush, ultimately re-sulted in the wide-open and dark green pastures filled with game animals, yet Europeans failed to credit the natives for this work. What the Europeans labeled the "natural" bounty of their new home actually was brought about by a careful agricultural process that stood outside their paradigms regarding land usage. The Europeans, cognizant of the richness of the land, believed the Native Americans ought to have traded more of their goods for wealth in the European sense of the word, expressing incredulity that the natives were so "poor" when the land offered so many opportunities for wealth building.

Early European colonists believed they could take what they needed to survive, and even what they needed to build trade routes, from the land without extensive labor. In their assessment, the land offered so many goods that the living would be easy. Historian William Cronon, author of *Changes in the Land: Indians, Colonists, and the Ecology of New England*, explains, "In New England, most colonists antici-pated that they would be able to live much as they had done in England, in an ar-tisanal and farming community with work rhythms, class relations, and a social order similar to the one they had left behind—the only difference being their own improved stature in society." This erroneous judgment led many colonial peoples in the New World to starvation and near-starvation, and often the colonists sought out the indigenous people's assistance in tough times. Native Americans died of hunger to a significant degree less than the early colonists. Part of the reason for this stems from the native practice of living in lower density populations on the land. Native peoples tended to live in densities of approximately forty-one people per 100 square miles, while farming colonists lived at densities of approximately 287 people per 100 square miles—a population that at times the land could not support.

Another historical issue that paved the way for European colonial settlement that we should not overlook is the fact that the majority of the Native Americans died soon after contact with colonial peoples because of coming into contact with

European diseases. Scholars estimate that the land that is now the United States and Canada had anywhere between 5 million and 12.5 million Native American peoples at the time of contact. Most historians cautiously estimate the number at somewhere in the 6 to 7 million range. At the time of colonization, an estimated 120,000 Native Americans lived in New England. Eighty to ninety percent of the natives died after contact, falling victim to diseases that they had never built up any immunity to as a population. Additional numbers also fell victim to battles with Europeans and to the hardships that came from attempting to share space with European populations—such as dwindling food sources. Although this aspect of the settlement saga is grim, we must acknowledge that the rapid pace of European town building in New England would not have been possible without this turn of events. Thus William Cronon points out that the European colonists did not encounter "virgin land" (land that had never been utilized by humans) at the time of settlement, but rather "widowed land" that had lost its human partners. The colonists often took advantage of the actual building sites once home to Native Americans—this step saved clearing the land and streamlined access to clean water sources.

European contact quickly altered the landscape. Ecological change would not come over an extended time, but rather followed almost immediately upon the heels of European arrival. European settlers had gained motivation to relocate to New England in part because of the lack of resources such as timber back in Europe. New England families took advantage of the bounty of their new home, typically using one acre of timber a year as fuel. The increase of cleared land altered the region's climate; the region grew hotter and windier, snow melted faster, and flooding increased. Soils were exhausted. European peoples also brought new pests with them from the Old World, such as the ubiquitous cockroach, and pesky weeds such as the stinging nettle. Cronon explains, "the colonists themselves understood what they were doing almost wholly in positive terms, not as 'deforestation'; but as 'the progress of cultivation.'" The European brands of wealth acquisition, mercantilism, and capitalism came as one piece with extensive environmental change.[4] This early reality would become a legacy of European settlement, an inheritance that New England communities still struggle mightily with today.

European colonists, coming from a continent short on wood, probably had never before personally viewed trees as tall as those found in New England. In the colonial period, white pine and hemlock trees could be as large as three feet in diameter and as much as 150 feet high. The shortage of trees had spurred the emigration from Europe; the needed resource—which was available in the New World in such quantities—constituted a significant draw. In addition to supplying the fuel and raw materials for settlement, tall trees provided much-needed masts for the British Royal Navy. New ships needed masts of about forty inches across at the bottom and 120 feet tall. The tall trees of the colonies could provide this commodity, and more. This bounty of wood was soon depleted, however. Colonists had begun settlement in the region in earnest by the early 1700s, clearing many of the forested areas. According to ecologist Peter Marchand, author of *North Woods: An Inside Look at the Nature of Forests in the Northeast*, by the 1830s, central New England was perhaps 80 percent cleared. Wood for the process of settlement—the erection of buildings and fences, necessary fuel, the production of tools and furniture—had to be brought in from Maine and the western United

States. Logging and the growing railroad system were closely linked. Some railroad systems relied on wood for fuel; all counted on wood for the railroad ties that supported the weight of the iron rails. The presence of train service also proved valuable in getting access to additional forests for logging, and for shipping the product to its desired point of sale. By 1850, the railroad had helped bring the lumber business into the Adirondack High Peaks region; many areas were clear-cut. By 1890, almost all softwood viable for the commercial market had been taken from the White Mountains of New England. Although New England's railroads increasingly used coal for fuel after the 1870s, area forests remained troubled. New Hampshire's woods, for example, declined until the 1870s, Massachusetts jumped down from above 60 to below 50 percent forest cover between 1820 and 1860, and Vermont's forests only stabilized in the 1880s, when only 35 percent of the state remained forested.

NEW ENGLAND WILDLIFE

Dramatically altering the vegetation of the region had clear effects on the wildlife of New England. Some forms of wildlife that inhabit New England today had been all but extinct in earlier periods, and have only come back with better environmental tactics and organized species reintroduction in the late twentieth century. An 1854 document declared that the last known beaver in Vermont had been sighted twelve years earlier. Surprisingly, both the white-tailed deer and the wild turkey had previously been extinct, their populations later reintroduced to the region. New England's mature hardwood forests provided the tree seeds needed for the wild turkey's diet; as forested landscape returns today, wild turkeys return as well. In these related changes we see that greater diversity in vegetation enables greater diversity of animal life, an environmental maxim at the cornerstone of restoring any region to full environmental health. In addition to the clearing of forests, the colonial (and later American) penchant for placing bounties on large animals of prey led to their extinction in certain areas. Perceptions regarding the safety of livestock and human residents informed these decisions, rather than any analysis of the mechanics of the food chain. Colonists placed bounties on wolves, mountain lions, and black bears. In the 1600s, the Massachusetts Bay Colony determined the bounty for killing a wolf in proportion to the number of livestock in town that would be protected by the action. By the 1800s, spotting a wolf or a mountain lion in New England was a rare event, except in remote areas.

Despite significant environmental concerns in modern New England (covered at the end of this chapter), New England has made strides toward recovering forested land. Peter Marchand notes, "With the decline of agriculture in the Northeast after the middle of the nineteenth century and the dramatic reversal of land use throughout the region, many areas have reverted in less than one hundred years from as little as twenty percent to more than eighty percent forest cover." With the return of forested land, New Englanders have begun to witness the return of large mammals and can foresee the possibility of wolves and mountain lions resettling the area. The presence of the eastern coyote, a new species of coyote, leads to speculation on the settlement of these other large animals. First seen in Vermont and New Hampshire in the 1940s, the eastern coyote has now established itself in a wide swath of New England. The eastern coyote represents

With increased logging in Canada, Maine, Vermont, and New Hampshire since the mid-1980s, moose have become much more prevalent in central New England. Courtesy Maine Office of Tourism.

its own unique species and is not, as some have supposed, a simple mix between domesticated dogs and western coyotes. The eastern coyote subsists on a diet of both vegetation and animal foods, and has been known to kill sheep or deer. An opportunist, the eastern coyote primarily looks for injured or otherwise compromised prey. Thousands of eastern coyote now live in the northern Appalachian mountains.

The region is known for its aquatic wildlife, such as cod, herring, lobsters, crabs, oysters, and mussels. New England is home to fascinating tideland creatures, such as snails, barnacles, and starfish.

Black bears have expanded their habitat in the New England area, much to the chagrin of urban dwellers who must now confront the wild and dangerous animals. Black bears are mostly carnivorous, but will also consume a wide range of vegetable matter. Other New England regional wildlife includes the big brown bat, the skunk, and the sometimes overly populous white-tailed deer. Beavers and raccoons are nearly ubiquitous, increasingly becoming unwelcome neighbors for those living on the edge of Nww England's suburban sprawl. The region contains two species of tree-frogs. A wide spectrum of birds can be found in New England, including hawks, crows, herons, great horned owls, the ruffed grouse, and the great crested flycatcher. New England also offers a home to red fox, eastern cottontails, New England cottontails, and moose. Massachusetts alone contained five hundred moose in 2003. Moose moved into central New England in response to increased logging in Canada, Maine, Vermont, and New Hampshire during the mid-1980s. Between 2000 and 2003, the increased moose population led to fifty accidents on Massachusetts roadways, including the death of teacher Amber Ronzoni on the Massachusetts Turnpike on July 23, 2003.[5]

COLONIAL SETTLEMENT AND THE ESTABLISHMENT OF CITIES

Native American peoples in North America, contrary to common belief, did build some permanent urban settlements. The prime examples remain the city of Cahokia, located outside present-day St. Louis, and towns in the Southwest. In New England, Native Americans tended to live in seasonal settlements. Some of the earliest permanent Native American towns came at the prompting of proselytizing Puritans, who created fourteen "praying towns" for Christianized Native Americans between 1651 and 1676. New England's colonial peoples established towns as their bases of command for commercial networks because this was the system they had become accustomed to in Europe. And although the Spanish, the French, and the Dutch had footholds in other areas of what would become the

United States, the English colonists established the pattern of settlement building that would most influence town-founding in the new nation.

In 1800, 6.8 percent of the residents of Massachusetts lived in towns of more than ten thousand. By 1840, 22 percent did, and by 1870, almost one-half of the state lived in towns of over ten thousand. As the United States considered a location to be urban if it contained 2,500 people or more, and because by this standard the United States would not become an urban nation (more than one-half of the population living in places of 2,500 or more until 1920), we can see that the urbanization of New England precedes that of the United States as a whole.[6]

Historian Kenneth Lockridge, author of *A New England Town: The First Hundred Years*, offers readers a detailed case-study of New England town formation. He explains how the first New England settlements gave birth to new towns, a process which other scholars have termed sequential town formation. Lockridge takes the reader through the initial establishment and subsequent growth of Dedham, Massachusetts. The town held its first town meeting in 1636. By 1656, seventy men constituted the official membership of the town, owning the public lands of Dedham and able to choose by themselves any new additions to the community. Being an active part of the Dedham church, or at the very least an involved town participant, was a critical requirement for male town members (although women joined the church as well). In 1648, 70 percent of the town's adult men had joined the church; between 1644 and 1653, 80 percent of the children born in Dedham underwent baptism. Greater swathes of land were rewarded to men with higher social standings in the town.

Dedham, like many small New England towns, was a rather insular community, with few new additions after its founding. In the seventeenth century, Dedham maintained a constant population of just about five hundred people. The number of family names represented in the city actually grew smaller over time, with sixty-three surnames showing up in town records from 1648, but just fifty-seven surnames in 1688. Overall, the town was healthier than similar European villages, with higher birth rates and lower death rates than its Old World equivalents. A better diet and/or improved housing partially accounted for the additional births and longevity of the Dedham residents. Additionally, New England avoided some of the disastrous events like famine and plague which Europe faced in this period.

In just one generation, the commitment to church membership had dwindled. Many of those making the crossing to colonial New England from England had been at least in part fueled by the drive for religious freedom—their children were not so devoted to the church. By 1662 almost half of the men in Dedham had not joined the church. The compromise of becoming a "half-way" member of the church, under the "Half-Way" Covenant, failed to catch on initially in Dedham. The practice of the Half-Way Covenant enabled residents in other cities to take part in church and town life and have their children baptized by pledging to uphold the moral standards of the church despite their own failure to feel called by God to enter into the church as "saints." As New England towns were built around church membership, this compromise allowed the communities to continue to grow despite lagging religious enthusiasm and commitment.

Eventually, religious disagreement and cultural rifts caused by spatial differentiation spearheaded the formation of new towns out of the original Dedham grant. By 1720, four new towns had been created within the original Dedham. The first two towns had the support of Dedham itself, most likely created to provide a wall of safety between Dedham and Native American groups. A group from Dedham founded the town of Medfield in 1649, and the town gained incorporation in 1651. Similarly, Wrentham was begun in 1652 and incorporated in 1673. A northeast portion of the grant area became Needham, incorporated in 1711. Buildings clustered around the town sawmill, twelve miles south of central Dedham, evolved into the town of Walpole, incorporated in 1724. The Dedham Grant of 1637 eventually came to hold the towns of Natick, Wellesley, Needham, Dedham, Dover, Westwood, Norwood, Medfield, Walpole, Norfolk, Bellingham, Franklin, and Wrentham.[7]

Leading Colonial Cities—Boston and Newport

Boston, Massachusetts, and Newport, Rhode Island, ranked as the most populous cities in colonial New England. Both cities, like the other leading colonial cities—New Amsterdam/New York City, Philadelphia, and Charleston—owed their existence to the importance of sea trade. Boston was officially founded in 1630 when English settlers in Charlestown crossed the Charles River seeking access to a better harbor and clean drinking water. Despite Massachusetts Bay Governor John Winthrop's claim that the region would be a "Citty upon a Hill," and a moral beacon for all peoples, Boston's initial years clearly established it as a center for commerce. Boston claimed only three hundred inhabitants during the 1630s, but grew to house seven thousand inhabitants in 1690 and over sixteen thousand in 1742, despite weathering wars with Native Americans. In 1742, Boston ranked as the largest colonial city, the second largest being Philadelphia at thirteen thousand inhabitants. Yet in 1775, Boston ranked only third with a population of sixteen thousand, outpaced by Philadelphia at twenty-four thousand and New York at twenty-five thousand people. The city's primary source of growth was its ship building industry and its role as a trading center and harbor; New England's rocky soil made the hinterland a difficult place to farm productively, and Boston never pulled in the kind of rich harvests that New York City could claim from the rich soils of its region.

Newport's founders fled the religious discrimination of Massachusetts and formally established the port city in 1639. Newport could claim the best harbor in southern New England, so its location proved a solid choice for growth—although the pace was slow and steady rather than the rapid rise of Boston. In 1739, one hundred years after its founding, Newport had 6,200 residents.[8]

INDUSTRIALIZATION AND THE ENVIRONMENT

At the forefront of commerce, and later industrialization, New England faced urban problems earlier on than some regions, but also took a leadership role at posing solutions to these problems. Boston championed road grading as early as 1713, engineering streets that rose in the middle so that runoff could spill off into side gutters and keep the city cleaner. Of all colonial cities, Boston and Newport, whose relatively independent governments had the authority to tax residents, had the most well-maintained streets.[9] Those living with the lack of planning in these early English towns, however, might long for the grid-system employed by the Spanish. Boston especially is known for the confusion of its street layout.

What once had been largely an agriculturally based economy changed dramatically in the middle of the nineteenth century. In the early 1800s, farming in New England had become increasingly linked to the commercial world. In order to procure the products they needed, farmers grew market-oriented crops, like flax, favored by the storeowners with which they did trade. Consistently farming the market product could be detrimental to the soil. The manure fertilizer, utilized to increase yields for market-driven farming, left nitrates and salts in the soil. The switch from raising crops to livestock farming—at first sheep for wool and increasingly dairy farming—could also damage the soil. Even New England's virgin forests offered little in the way of topsoil—just two to four inches of rich soil. Raising animals meant clearing additional land; the loss of forest cover led to exposed river banks, rising water temperatures, and the failure of precipitation to be absorbed into the water table. Floods ensued. The slope of the land alone caused significant loss of valuable topsoil. By the 1850s, many families found it difficult to make a living in New England's rocky and uneven earth. As the nation grew, the bounty of the richer soils of the Midwest competed, and increasingly won out over eastern agricultural products, even with the additional transportation cost of shipping goods from farms in the Midwest to consumers in the East.

The rural areas of New England grew more sparsely populated despite the rising population in the rest of the region. For example, Hampshire County, Massachusetts, lost 33 percent of its population in the second half of the 1850s, while the state as a whole gained residents. Dairy and "truck farming"—farming food products for sale in local markets—took hold while other types of farming in the region declined. The city's need for fresh milk and milk products pushed merchants ever northward in search of suppliers. Specialized crops like tobacco and onions secured livelihoods for farmers in Connecticut and Massachusetts who were willing to adhere to market demands. Increasingly, New England's rural areas catered to tourism more than farming; the rural linked in the imagination as a healthy escape from the city rather than a region of agricultural labor. Rural resorts began to open in the late 1800s to cater to urban tourists.

Families began to abandon their farms in the 1860s, and the land, where not utilized immediately for housing or urban growth, filled in again with forest. Much of this succession of vegetation filled in with white pine. Yet in approximately fifty years' time, these white pines proved a tempting crop to a new generation of eastern loggers, and the land was clear-cut again. Between 1895 and 1925, those working in the New England uplands obtained approximately fifteen billion feet of lumber, worth about four hundred million dollars. This white pine cutting occupied residents for just thirty years. After this

A Vermont dairy farm.

second clearing, the hardwood forests now typical of the landscape took hold, dominating by the 1930s. While today's New England forests may evoke thoughts of the earliest colonial settlers or even of Native American villages, they most likely represent reforestation following turn-of-the-century logging. The agricultural origins of today's forested areas are quickly attested to by the nearly ubiquitous New England rock wall; the walls run through what is now heavily forested land, but they once set a farmer's fields apart.

Early Mills and Factories

John T. Cumbler's book, *Reasonable Use: The People, the Environment, and the State, New England, 1790–1930*, captures the story of the way in which industry significantly changed the environment of the Connecticut River Valley in the 1800s. Cumbler contends that the Connecticut River, which stretches the four hundred miles from northern New Hampshire to Long Island Sound at Saybrook, Connecticut, constitutes the longest and most important inland waterway in New England. In 1790, the region was environmentally strong. By the 1830s, however, industrialists had taken to damming the Connecticut's falls to provide the energy necessary to power their factories and releasing the wastes into the river. The burgeoning cities—filled with the excess population of New England's rural areas, now displaced by the failure of their farms and looking for a new livelihood—dirtied regional waters with the trash and the sewage of their populations. Combined, the communities of Holyoke, Chicopee, Springfield, Hartford, and New Britain dumped about 42.25 tons of fecal matter and 45,900 gallons of urine into the Connecticut River a day in the 1800s. Keene, New Hampshire, located on the Connecticut River tributary, the Ashuelot River, released its raw sewage into a formerly clear brook that ran through town. The brook came to be known as the "Town Brook Sewer" by the latter half of the 1800s, and the city eventually covered over the brook and transformed this natural waterway into what was essentially a drain, handling rain runoff and sewage for Keene.

Cumbler points out, like many historians, that New England's rocky soils made industrialization necessary for the area's long-term economic survival, yet the consequences of this necessity were grim. Cumbler summarizes, "These capitalists created an environment in which rivers and streams were polluted by wastes dumped from the mills and tenements, fish were excluded from spawning grounds, and mill towns filled with smoke and foul odors."

New England's conception of how water ought to be considered in legal terms evolved as industry evolved. The New England rulings known as the Mill Acts of 1795 and 1797, as well as earlier colonial laws, helped to promote the establishment of mills, which were necessary users of the region's waters yet uncomfortable neighbors for many. The first mills appeared in New England in the 1630s. Gristmills ground the grains necessary for a neighborhood's flour; sawmills used waterpower to cut the boards needed for the rapid building in the area. Yet mills commandeered water to provide energy at times not necessarily convenient for their neighbors, disturbing the flow of New England's vital and inexpensive food source, fish. Mills also periodically flooded into land owned by others, disturbing crops, animals, and human life. Was it right that the mills and the nuisances caused by them were exempt from the usual conceptions of private property due to a greater good they provided their communities? Or were laws protecting mills and their owners a form of protecting business at the expense of others?

The New England residents' vision of mills as a vital, yet localized, part of the economy changed drastically with President Thomas Jefferson's embargo on goods manufactured outside of the United States, which led to the War of 1812. Although the peace of 1815 again brought English manufactured goods to American shores, New England industrialists had joined a wider marketplace beyond their own region. Business owners now called on local resources to serve a national and even at times an international market. The question remained, could New England's environmental resources withstand the stresses placed by this challenge?[10]

In the late 1700s, the First Industrial Revolution began in Great Britain. At its heart, this revolution consisted of the replacement of human and animal energy by machine-powered production, including steam-powered and coal-powered mechanisms. By the 1790s, the First Industrial Revolution had begun in New England, and then spread into the Atlantic states and into the Midwest. The Southern region of the United States was largely unaffected by the revolution until after the Civil War. As in England, this adoption of an industrial way of life brought significant changes to New England. People began leaving the rural areas to resettle in urban settings near their new places of work. In 1790, the entire country had only twenty-four towns with populations over 2,500; by the dawn of the Civil War era, the United States could claim nearly four hundred towns and cities. And over one-third of all northeasterners lived in cities or towns.

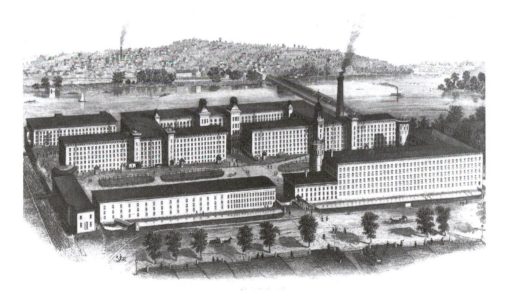

BOOTT COTTON MILLS.
LOWELL, MASS

Mills helped create an environment in which the rivers and streams were polluted, the towns were filled with smoke, and the air was rife with foul smells. Courtesy Lowell National Historical Park.

In the United States, labor recruiters supplied the demand for a new kind of worker by urging the native-born daughters of New England farmers to enter the factories. As agricultural pursuits became increasingly affected by the market economy and New England farms faced competition from the rich soils of the Midwest, the young women relied on income generated before marriage to secure dowries and enable the establishment of their future homes. These young women, New England born and bred, constituted the majority of the workers in New England factories in the 1820s and 1830s. By the 1840s, however, the new immigrant populations entering the United States, willing to work for lower wages than the New England farm women would work for, increasingly took on factory work. The labor pool remained highly female, however; by the 1860s, the textile workers remained 58 percent female.

The mill established by Samuel Slater in Pawtucket, Rhode Island, in 1790 is considered the first modern factory in the United States. Samuel Slater, formerly an overseer in an English cotton factory, opened the factory utilizing investments from the Brown family of Rhode Island, who had made a family fortune on the rum and slave trade. This early factory spun cotton yarn by a mechanical process. By 1793, the corporation of Brown, Slater and Almy had founded a factory producing completed textiles. This example led to more small operations opening in the region of Rhode Island and southeastern Massachusetts.

By 1814, manufacturing in New England had metamorphosed into a larger-scale production with the opening of the Boston Manufacturing Company plant in Waltham, Massachusetts. Situated at a dam on the Charles River, the new facility took cotton through the processes of carding, spinning, and weaving and transformed it into finished cloth. Francis Cabot Lowell had taken plans for a modern power loom from Great Britain during his travels and used what he learned abroad to great effect in the United States. Soon the Charles River proved unequal to the power needs of the Boston Manufacturing Company. By 1822, the company built the industrial town of Lowell, named after the then-deceased entrepreneur, on the Merrimack River in Massachusetts. Use of waterpower for industry spread to Lawrence, Massachusetts, and Nashua and Manchester, New Hampshire. While substantial investments were needed—the Boston Manufacturing Company had put four hundred thousand dollars into the Waltham plant initially—waterpower was in many respects a virtually free source of power for the industrialists. The absence of a suitable environment for large-scale agriculture fueled the rush to industrialize in New England, yet other factors contributed as well. The high education levels of the region certainly encouraged industrialization, as did the Puritan belief in hard work. At a very basic level, too, New England's willingness to invest in building an infrastructure of transportation enabled manufacturing to blossom. Connecticut proved an early road builder, opening the Monhegan turnpike, running the twelve miles between Norwich and New London, in 1792. Canals, however, revolutionized shipping because they provided an inexpensive way of hauling freight. The South Hadley Canal was established to enable a route around the falls of the Connecticut River in 1794. The Middlesex Canal, consisting of twenty locks and twenty-eight miles of water linking the Merrimack Valley of New Hampshire to Boston, opened in 1803. The region's most influential canal, the Blackstone Canal, joined hilly and relatively isolated Worcester County with Providence, Rhode Island, and opened in 1828. Despite their importance, the region's canals were quickly displaced by railroads, as they were throughout the United States. New England's first railroad, the Boston and Worcester, opened in 1834. Track stretched from Boston to Worcester by 1835 and connected with Albany by 1841.[11]

Many industries dumped their waste materials directly into rivers. The moving waters of New England rivers had been considered safe sewer systems by many early New England residents. Rivers could break down a limited amount of organic pollution with few residual substances left behind. Mills such as those that processed textiles utilized organic substances in their manufacturing that found their way (intentionally and otherwise) into the water. Organic dyes like madder, logwood, and peachwood were joined by the more dangerous, inorganic substances of sulfuric acid, muriatic acid, lime, and arsenate of soda. The tanning industry, which had long been a necessary component of New England settlement, flourished as the region industrialized. The machinery of the new plants drew its power from generators by means of great leather belting. The region's shoe industry also necessitated vast resources of finished leather. By 1849, Maine, New Hampshire, and Massachusetts produced over one-half of the nation's shoes. Tanning dumped materials like tannin, oil, and grease and, with later processes, chromium and metallics into New England water, killing organisms.[12] While these types of processing severely affected New England's waterways, papermaking had an even greater impact on the environment. The early process of making paper out of rag material left waste products of dirt, grease, and oils from the rags and the chemicals from the processing. Froth visibly showed up on the surface of nearby rivers and streams. (Later use of wood pulp also left dangerous chemical by-products and also stripped the region of its forests.)

New England's industrialization, particularly the use of waterpower to fuel manufacturing and the pollution that made its way into regional watersources as industrial by-products, disturbed the fish supply throughout the region. As farming in New England grew less profitable, fish—an inexpensive food source—grew perhaps even more important as a food source in the region. States began to form commissions to study the effects of industrialization on fishing, and passed laws designed to keep the waterways stocked with fish. Massachusetts launched the nation's first fish hatchery, located on the Connecticut River, to produce shad. Run by Seth Green of New York state, the hatchery soon evolved into the source of millions of fish for the Connecticut. The effect of this effort was short-lived, however, because the Connecticut ran through state boundaries and the states' efforts did not all coincide. Connecticut overturned restrictions on fishing in the lower Connecticut in the late 1800s, a counteractive step in the process of restoring the wildlife of the river. Vermont and New Hampshire gave up their endeavors to hatch shad, seeing little effect for their work. Unfortunately, too, the fishways that activists had so long planned as a way around manufacturing facilities for migrating fish turned out not to function efficiently.

In 1867, the New England Commission of River Fisheries was formed, with Judge Henry Adams Bellows of New Hampshire as chair and Theodore Lyman III of Massachusetts as secretary. As the nation matured, a second argument for conservation was added to that of the poor and hungry farmer in need of an inexpensive food supply. Fishing had evolved into a popular sport, pursued in large part by the wealthier urban elite who wielded considerable political power. These fishermen fought to retain or restore fishing for its sport value. Would-be conservationists could openly make the argument that this outdoor sport restored the human soul dulled by the increasing pressures of urban life by acquainting people with the balance of nature.[13]

An 1896 article by N. S. Shaler illustrates the relationship between New Englanders and their environment at the turn of the century. The article proves especially interesting for its commentary on the evolution of a specific New England character, forged in part by the landscape of the region:

> In considering the matter, we should in the first place note that New England is much more like Old England than is any other part of America; this likeness is shown in many ways. To begin with, the surface of the country, unlike that of the continent in general, is extremely diversified; it has indeed the localized character of surface soil and in a measure of climate which we find in Great Britain. When as a young man I came from the tableland of Kentucky to study in New England, I remarked to the elder Agassiz that impression of relatively great variety which this seaboard country made upon me. He said that the area seemed to him essentially like that of the old world in that it had an exceedingly diversified character.
>
> Between the mountains of New Hampshire and Vermont and the lowlands of Southeastern Massachusetts there are as great differences in conditions as are found in Great Britain, in passing from the Highlands of Scotland to the plains of Norfolk. In the area of almost any county of the six New England States we discover a range of soil-conditions extending from the arid pastures of the thinly covered rocky uplands to the swamps of the valleys, or it may be the marine marshes of the seashore. Everywhere there is lacking the consolidated character of the inner part, the centre, of this continent. . . .
>
> Turning now to the conditions which from their nature are likely to have a shaping influence upon the population of New England, we find at once a number of physical features which not directly but in a secondary way have had a great effect upon the character of the population. Taking these in their natural order, we may begin with the subterranean stores of mineral wealth of the district. In this subterranean field we find extremely limited resources. From the first settlement to the present day the result of explorations has been to turn the minds of the people away from the occupations of the mine, from that generally delusive and usually disastrous expectation that fortune was to be won by finding precious metals. In later days stone quarries and occasional veins of pyrite and other ores have opened the way to profit, but these are matters of modern times. . . .
>
> The soil of New England is, on the whole, not unlike that of Wales and Scotland. It yields the same crops, in rather scantier measure; as in those more rugged parts of the mother country, not more than one-half the area is or can be made in any way fit for the plow. Like as are the conditions of the earth in the old land and the new, there were certain circumstances of contact which were peculiar, and which were very effective in determining the history of the people. The whole of New England has been in a remarkable way affected by the action of the ice and water of the last glacial

period. Although the same calamitous period affected the British Isles as well, the diversity of actions there was much less than on the western side of the Atlantic. In the old world region the effect of the visitation, so far as the soil is concerned, was, in the main, to leave a tolerably deep covering of what is commonly termed till or boulder clay upon the surface, which, though rather bouldery, is generally brought under tillage without much difficulty. In New England the division of the surface was usually into very stony fields, where it required from fifty to two hundred days of labor to bring about a good tilth, and into sandy areas, where the soil was ready for the plow as soon as the forest had been cleared away, and decay had removed the roots of the trees. . . .

. . . .

The effect of these soil conditions in New England was quickly to turn the attention of the enterprising colonists away from any expectation of winning wealth from the earth; the general understructure had denied them mineral resources, the state of the surface made it evident that they would not, like the colonists further south, look to agricultural resources as the basis of commercial success. In fact, though there was from time to time some small outgoings of field products, New England never succeeded in doing much more than supply its own demands, in the way of food such as the fields of the land afford. Baffled in the effort to found success on the subterranean or the soil resources of the country, the New Englanders quickly turned their attention to the fisheries. In this realm of the seas, the same geological events which had deprived the land of its fertility gave an excellent opportunity for profit. The irregular, usually bouldery, waste formed by the glacial actions extends far beyond the limits of the shore; it creates at many points extensive shallows, such as Georges Bank, which affords the best natural feeding grounds for the food fishes, which have been in such large measure the basis of the commercial prosperity of the country. A bouldery field above the plane of the ocean is poor ground for the nurture of anything that man can turn to profit; from that level downward to a depth of one hundred fathoms, a surface of this nature is admirably suited for the development of a marine life; it is especially fitted to support and attract the cod fish, the creature which was the pilot of the New Englanders to their first commercial prosperity. Fortunately, these fishing grounds, the product of glaciation, abound along the seashores of New England, are very extensive, and lie near a great number of harbors, which, though shallow for modern ships, afforded ample room for fishing vessels. The forests, moreover, abounded in excellent timber for building ships. Thus, though the colonists were not to any considerable extent from the seafaring folk of the old country, they shortly were led, we may say driven, by their necessities, to seek gain beyond the shore.

The industry of fishing was naturally the first step toward the larger enterprises of the sea. This industry was from the start successful. The blessed cod, perhaps the best good fish of all the known tenants of the ocean, was found in great numbers; it was readily taken; its flesh was savory and so easily cured that it will keep for years. There was an almost unlimited market for the product of the fisheries in the more southern plantations of the continent, where a soil more easily won was yielding a great though temporary profit to the colonists. From the cod to the whale fishery was an easy transition, and the two combined made the best possible foundations for the marine commerce which grew up among the people after they had been trained in seafaring in the most natural way through the art of fishing. In this largest part of the sailor's work the development was again in the same way as with the fisheries, but in even greater measure, favored by the very many good harbors that exist along the shore, and which are due also to glacial action. For the ships of the last century the New England coast afforded the greatest number of good havens that exist in any part of the American coast where the other conditions permitted settlement. These natural ports are very accessible, they usually carry deep waters to their shores. They are not much encumbered with ice, the back country abounds in construction woods such as the ship carpenter demands, and also afforded a fair supply of the food stores required for voyages. Thus the environment led the shore line folk of this district straight forth to the sea and stamped a large part of its people with the admirable and enduring mark of that peculiar culture. Although there are no accurate data for determination, it appears likely that, in the two centuries from 1650 to 1850, somewhere near one-fourth of the population of this district were distinctly influenced by the maritime life which had become the basis of its prosperity.

The same conditions of soil which in a way compelled the New Englanders to essay fortune upon the sea led them in another direction of endeavor which has proved in its effects more lasting. The glacial event, as we have already noticed, covered the surface of the earth with a prevailingly deep deposit of very porous material; this of itself gives the streams an uncommon steadfastness of flow. Moreover, the drift is laid on in a very irregular manner so that it forms a multitude of depressions all of which were originally lakes, though the greater number of them have now been converted into bogs or swamps; these basins still further retard the flow of the water to the sea, delivering the rain fall in a gradual and tolerably constant manner. Furthermore, the country is tolerably elevated, so that the aggregate of available power that may be won from the streams is very great. The value of these sources of energy for mill use was easily appreciated: very soon after the settlement, many of the lesser streams were the seats of corn mills, to which wool carding appliances were soon added. The records show that the authorities were early awake to the value of these sources of wealth: thus among the many regulations we may note an order that the curious division of the Charles River near Boston known as Mother Brook, which leaves the main stream in Dedham and by flowing into the Neponset River makes that city an island, has a right to carry one third of the water of the Charles. This law which was established in the later part of the seventeenth century attests the value of the mill privileges at that early day.

In its valuable water powers which owe their advantages to the glacial history of the country, the New Englanders found a feature which was destined in a remarkable manner to influence their future, even to the time beyond our day. At first these opportunities were sought for domestic needs alone, but as the expansion of the marine adventures came about, the little mills grew to be great factories and their varied products found a market the world over. In a way this industry, particularly that in woollen cloths, helped the needy agriculture. The sheep, a thrifty feeder, could pick up a sufficient living in fields where cattle would fare ill. To prepare the way for them it was not necessary to clear the land as for tillage, the timber could be felled and burned and the animals turned into the partly cleared ground where they would find subsistence among the boulders. In time they would extirpate the brushwood and so give room for grass. A large portion of the vast area of stony fields in this part of the country thus came to be deforested. Much of these old sheep ranges has been recovered by the woods since the cheaper wool of Australia and the Mississippi Valley has made it unprofitable to keep the creatures where they have to be fed through the long winter. The forests of New England afford excellent varieties of wood for the manufacture of tools and furniture; the bog iron ores, accumulations which often form beneath swamps, served for a time for the manufacture of iron. These advantages led to a very great diversity in the manufacturing work which depended on the water powers for the needed energy.

As the value of the water powers was enhanced by the development of the agricultural interest, the people found that the swamps which had, by a natural process, the growth of peat, to a great extent taken the place of the glacial lakes, were no longer worthless lands but had a peculiar value, in that by slight dams at their outlets they could be converted into reservoirs for storing water to be used at the mills. . . .

The combined effects of a varied relation to the sea, and the yet more diversified influences of a manufacturing industry which concerned a wider range of work than had ever been undertaken in any other country of like area, in time gave to the characteristic New Englander some peculiar qualities or habits of mind. He became, as he is now, of all the world, the aptest man to discover in any situation some measure of advantage which might be turned to profitable account. He learned the precious lesson that in every place there is something which if well done will pay for the doing. The impress of this way of looking at the world may to the observant traveller be seen in every part of the area which has been subject to New England influences. Within this part of the country we find the most complete subdivision of industries which exists in any part of the world. In most cases these employments have taken root because of some local advantage in the way of access to peculiar natural stores or to certain lines of transportation. In other instances they have been founded by some discerning person who, looking over the fields of employment, has seen that his place was fit for some pursuit which had not been essayed in his neighborhood, or was perhaps altogether novel. Thus, to note but a few of these specialized occupations, we find that the Attleboros are given to making jewelry, Leicester to the manufacture of "Card clothing," i.e., the hook covered leather which is used for carding wool; the region about Gardiner to the making of chairs. At least fifty towns could be cited as the seats of such special callings, the peculiar conditions being due to the development of an active-minded people compelled to look beyond the soil or the resources which lay beneath it for the basis of their fortunes, indeed—we may say, of their existence. Such eager and efficient application of wit and work to the possibilities of a situation has no parallel in the old world, and is unequalled in this country of expedients: it is a peculiarity of the New England conditions; it can be accounted for by the circumstances in which the people were placed. It is, in a word, the effect of environment. . . .

The same eminent inventiveness which has brought about the institution of industries has made it possible for the New Englanders, when the need arose, quickly to change their occupation to fit the altered requirements. In the formative period the same people often followed several callings at once: farming, fishing and shoemaking were often combined. Though the greater part of this elasticity has been lost through the more elaborate organizations of labor, it is easy to see the marks of it to this day. The quality is in the folk, it is ready to meet such changes as are by some apprehended through the Southern competition in the manufacture of cotton cloth. Should this industry betake itself to the neighborhood of the fields where the fibre is produced, it will probably change rather than lessen the industrial life of this region. We often find in New England manufacturing districts which have preserved their activities, though the nature of their labor has greatly and sometimes frequently altered. . . .

There is no reason to believe that the settlers of New England, if they had found a home in an easily tilled land such as lies beside the James River or Chesapeake Bay, would have had a history greatly different from that which awaited the colonists of those more southern countries. Notwithstanding certain differences of faith, these peoples were essentially alike in all those features which serve to direct the course of populations. But the northern colonists, because they fell upon lands which bore the peculiar stamp which has been given them by the singular processes of the glacial epoch, were forced to peculiar and, to them, unnatural ways of progress. They could look to the earth for no mote than a bare and hardly earned subsistence. This incidentally spared them the evils of slavery, for the African slave was profitable only in agricultural districts, and then only in the production of important exportable crops of which New England could produce—none. Although they were not by inheritance seafarers or manufacturers, the New Englanders were forced to look to the deep for all their first gains and to the water powers for all their more permanent and larger profits. And in these occupations, through the impress giving effect of labor in peculiar fields, they came by their remarkable qualities.[14]

Early Steps to Confront Environmental Problems

Because New England came to industrialization earlier than the rest of the United States, the region was one of the first to experience the environmental consequences of manufacturing. Luckily, the region also led the nation in trying to solve the damage of pollution in its air, water, and soils. Of course, the optimum balance between the economic need for industry and the desire for a healthful environment has never been found. New England continues to struggle with environmental issues even in the twenty-first century.

New England's citizens showed an early understanding of the need for a clean environment. Massachusetts, for instance, in 1869 became the first state in the nation to establish a board of health. The Massachusetts Board of Health argued in a progressive manner, "All citizens have an inherent right to the enjoyment of pure and uncontaminated air, and water, and soil, that this right should be regarded as belonging to the whole community, and that no one should be allowed to trespass upon it by his carelessness or his avarice." New Hampshire's Board of Health similarly stated in its first report, "every person has a legitimate right to nature's gifts—pure water, air, and soil—a right belonging to every individual, and every community, upon which no one should be allowed to trespass through carelessness, ignorance, or other cause." The Connecticut State Board of Health posited, "as condensation of population in cities goes increasingly on, the supply of necessities of life become more and more matters of public concern and less and less within the direction and knowledge of individuals." While such claims might appear mundane today, these statements actually represented a revolutionary understanding toward the use and responsibility of natural resources. Here, state agencies proclaimed the right to a healthy environment and the government's responsibility to help procure it for its citizens. Following Massachusetts' lead, Connecticut established a board of health in 1877, New Hampshire in 1881, and Vermont in 1886.[15]

In the 1830s and 1840s, Boston built sewer lines that drained the fouled waters into the ocean. Other New England cities followed this example. By the 1870s and 1880s, European scientists had completed research linking germs to disease. Americans were relatively slow in embracing this scientific concept. Once understood, sewage became a greater cause of concern for New Englanders. In 1887, Ellen Swallow Richards launched a project to determine the best method for dealing with regional sewage. She also developed the first water purity tables in the world, so as to better judge the cleanliness of the water supply. Swallow Richards set standards for water cleanliness in Massachusetts.

In 1893, the city of Lawrence began filtering its sewage through sand, leaching out 90 percent of the bacteria from the waters, and disease rates fell. Brockton, Massachusetts, followed with an even more advanced system. By the mid-1890s, Connecticut's state government urged its towns to adopt the practices of either Brockton or Lawrence to clean water.[16]

EVOLUTION OF URBAN LAND USE

New England, as one of the first areas in the nation to be settled by the colonists, has had a considerable tenure during which to develop its towns and cities. The region's early industrialization, too, meant that it urbanized earlier than other parts of the United States. Today, New England's population constitutes one of the nation's most densely settled landscapes. Yet, because of the high numbers of people settled in the region, New England also suffers from urban sprawl, or the expansion of once discrete urban areas across an extended area. Perhaps as the region develops solutions to the problems that accompany sprawl—like rising commute times to work and air pollution from growing automobile use—New England can serve as a pioneer in finding solutions to environmental concerns that will soon plague the rest of the nation, if they have not already.

The U.S. census recognized the existence of "metropolitan districts," or urban areas that extend past the traditional political boundaries of the city, in 1910. Today's metropolitan regions are so complex that new terms must be employed; urbanists and government officials now use the term Metropolitan Statistical Area (MSA) to refer to a county or group of counties that have a central city or cities with a population over fifty thousand but function together as a socially and economically integrated unit. The largest MSAs are known as Primary Metropolitan Statistical Areas (PMSAs), and the very largest of these, consistituting a number of PMSAs that function together, constitute a Consolidated Metropolitan Statistical Area (CMSA). The density of New England towns actually translates into a slightly different definition of an MSA for the New England region than elsewhere in the United States; in New England, an MSA is built around a collection of towns or villages (rather than counties) with a central city of over fifty thousand in population. New England contains a number of important Metropolitan Statistical Areas; in fact, New England contains two Consolidated Metropolitan Statistical Areas, the Worcester-Lawrence-Manchester area and the New York–Northern New Jersey–Long Island, New York, area, which includes a sizable area of southeastern Connecticut.

The geographic spread of urban areas has matured to the point that the central business districts or traditional downtowns of cities no longer provide the center of urban activity in many cases. To serve suburban residents, new outlying areas have evolved that offer job opportunities, entertainment, and other community resources. These locations came into general understanding with the publication of Joel Garreau's influential work, *Edge City: Life on the New Frontier* (1991). Although Garreau was not the only one to discuss the phenomenon, Garreau's term *edge city* became the one commonly used to describe the new centers that had come to supplant traditional downtowns. In order to qualify as an edge city, the area must comply with Garreau's five-part definition. The area should have at least five million square feet of office space and it should have at least six hundred thousand square feet of retail space (equivalent to a good-sized regional shopping center). An edge city should offer more jobs than bedrooms; thus it is not the traditional bedroom suburb. The entity should be considered to be a single place by local residents, although it might span several town boundaries on the map. Very importantly, too, it ought to be a new arrival to the region, evolving, perhaps from countryside, in the past thirty years.

New England offers such prime examples of edge cities that Garreau features the Boston metropolitan area in one of his nine chapters based around a single edge city. As Boston is the most mature large city in the United States, Boston's case of sprawl proves informative and perhaps predictive of the problems of other American cities in the future. Boston's edge city in large part followed its highway development, a typical edge city phenomenon. Route 128 spawned development along its corridor, particularly rich in settlement at the highway exits. Along Route 128, the so-called Massachusetts Miracle was born, with information companies like Digital, Lotus, and Wang making possible the economic boom of the 1980s. In later years, Boston's Route 495, a highway even farther out from the city's downtown, spurred the growth of another edge city. The economic blossoming affected much of New England, and in 1988, New Hampshire found itself with the lowest state unemployment rate of all time for the nation—a slim 2.0 percent. In that same year, Vermont ranked second with a 2.5 percent unemployment rate, Connecticut tied for third at 3.0 percent, Rhode Island tied for fourth with 3.1 percent, and Massachusetts ranked sixth with 3.4 percent.

In the 1990s, however, the economy took a tumble, and the "miracle" earned the sobriquet the "Massachusetts Massacre" instead. Urban sprawl had spread so fast and so furiously in New England that the housing prices rose to untenable levels. Housing in reasonable (and increasingly unreasonable) driving distances from the city were priced out of the range of many workers. Housing costs hurt recruitment of the labor force and ultimately damaged the economy. Garreau explains, "Here is where the Edge Cities of Boston had the distinction of being the first but by no means the last to hit the wall. No matter how far out you go, the dollars-per-hour of the jobs available within a reasonable commute go down quickly. But the dollars-per-quarter acre do not."[17]

In New England, the economy, the environment, and urban sprawl remain complexly interrelated. In this relatively compact and long-settled region, fewer parcels of undeveloped land remain than in other parts of the United States. Because of the history of long-standing environmental concerns due to industrialization, New England residents stand more firmly against growth in their communities than residents of other areas. Thus, even to the detriment of the economy, New Englanders will avoid the building of new homes. Adopting an antigrowth policy does not insulate the landscape against all environmental concerns, however. Strapped for housing resources, regional workers must select homes farther and farther from their place of business. Longer commute times lead to increased automobile pollution, the effects of which will be explored later in this chapter.

Concern for commute times in and out of Boston and increasing respect for the harbor front environment of that city have led to the largest single public works project in American history, the Central Artery/Tunnel project, or "Big Dig," to move the city's main highway underground. The amount of soil being removed from the Big Dig site has led to environmental concerns—where will the excavated material be relocated? Some of the material, along with material from other regional sites, may find its way to a previously closed Greenwood Street landfill in Worcester, Massachusetts, abutting the newly created and environmentally sensitive Blackstone River Valley National Heritage Corridor.[18]

Modern Ecological Issues

New England, once so tempting to the European colonists because of its lush, wildly healthy natural landscape, now faces the daily onslaught of man-made environmental poisons. Acid rain and pollution that is borne over the land by snow, fog, and even the region's very air attack the region. Acid rain, or precipitation carrying sulfur dioxide and nitrogen oxide from industrial emissions, attacks both the foliage and the animal life of the region. Most of the problems stem from our use of fossil fuels to propel today's nonstop industrialized lifestyle. Fuels used in our homes, our cars, and our factories simultaneously propel our world forward yet pollute the regions in which we live, and even go on to destroy the homes of others. Acid rain, among other effects, leaves behind a level of aluminum toxic to many organisms.[19]

New England has made some small yet significant steps in addressing its envi-

Quabbin Reservoir

Access to fresh drinking water is of great concern to New Englanders, especially with growing population density. Large cities like Boston face considerable challenges in maintaining adequate drinking water resources. In the early twentieth century, Boston created the Quabbin Reservoir in central Massachusetts to meet its growing needs.

The Quabbin Reservoir gets its name from the Nipmuc chief, NaniQuaben or NineQuabin, who once ruled the area. This hearkening back to the historic roots of the region is ironic, for not only were the native populations displaced from the site, but the white residents, most of Scottish descent, were also relocated by Boston's drive for water.

The farming communities of the Swift River Valley grew out of one another as populations increased, in the sequential town formation style so common throughout New England. The towns centered around the Congregational churches established there. The first white settlers arrived in the areas during the 1730s. Just before the Civil War, the valley reached its peak population. As railroad lines grew, many of the early lines bypassed the region and populations thinned. The farmers faced competition from farms farther west, and agricultural opportunities lessened. Those who persisted in farming often moved into diary farming, as did other farmers around New England. Between 1850 and 1890, the towns of the valley lost over one-third of their population. The four main towns that would eventually be cleared out for the formation of the reservoir, Dana, Enfield, Greenwich, and Prescott, were in a state of obvious decline. In 1924, Prescott lost its Congregational church, once a mainstay of the community, because of population decline. The town had no fire department, either. Ironically, the return of the area to wilderness sparked growing interest from hunters and fishermen and led to the founding of several summer camps in the area catering to urban children. Yet this interest in the valley came too late to save it from Boston's great thirst.

Boston had sought access to better water supplies as early as 1652. In fact the original founders of the city had settled in Boston in 1630 over Charlestown because of Boston's fresh water springs. Boston's very existence was linked with the essential quest for water. By 1822, Boston had formally incorporated as a city and had fifty thousand inhabitants. The once island city juxtaposed to the vast body of salt water needed reliable sources of fresh water. The city commissioned several studies regarding regional water sources. One of the early measures to provide water to the city involved transforming Long Pond of Natick, Massachusetts, into Lake Cochituate and building an aqueduct to carry the man-made lake's water to a reservoir in Brookline, Massachusetts, for Boston's use. This system became fully operational in 1848. Lake Cochituate served the city adequately for almost twenty years. But Boston was growing at a rapid pace. Between 1820 and 1890 the land mass of the city had increased by four times, due to landfill and the annexation of surrounding cities.

Boston officials considered Sebago Lake in Maine and Lake Winnipesaukee in New Hampshire, but rejected the sources because of their remoteness and the complexity of working out a legal deal with another state. The Merrimack River and the Charles River were deemed too polluted, although the water could have been filtered. Boston officials directed their energies to a plan that would form a reservoir out of the South Branch of the Nashua River. This became the Wachusett Reservoir, serving Boston and Worcester by the early 1900s.

The Swift River Act of 1927 set the actions in motion that would lead to the formation of the Quabbin Reservoir. The legislation would provide more than adequate water resources to the Boston metropolitan area, but it would disrupt life in the valley and would entail an enormous undertaking. A tunnel would be built between the Swift

Valley and the Ware River to the Wachusett Reservoir, a distance of twenty-four miles, cutting through dense rock. The state had to negotiate buy-outs with all real estate owners in the valley who would be displaced. Massachusetts paid an average of $103.64 per acre (including the purchase of buildings) to remove the valley population. Additionally, entire cemeteries needed to be relocated. A total of 6,551 bodies were reinterred in the Quabbin Park, just off Route 9, while more than one thousand other bodies were moved to other cemeteries. Two dams were built to hold back the Swift River; four others were built to form the reservoir itself. In 1936, the valley towns still functioned, but in the fall of 1937 farmers were informed not to plant more crops. The towns legally existed until March 28, 1938. In April 1938, the Enfield firemen hosted a final party for nearly one thousand area guests; partygoers were moved to tears by the end of the festivities.

By June 1938, area elementary schools closed. (The towns had never been populous enough to run their own high schools.) The last buildings were sold off, including the Dana town hall, which fetched just $90. The very last residents left the site in 1939. All told, about 2,500 residents had left the Swift River Valley, most of them choosing to settle in a twenty-five-mile radius from their former homes. Even area fish were relocated where they could be utilized by sport fishermen.

The area began to be flooded in August of 1939, and was not fully filled until 1946. The Quabbin Reservoir claimed one hundred thousand acres of land. Just 10 percent of the area of the reservoir had been utilized for agriculture—what was lost was not agricultural land as much as towns to which many families were attached. The Quabbin Reservoir safely yields three hundred million gallons of water a day, providing water for the metropolitan areas of Massachusetts. The reservoir and adjacent land are controlled by two government agencies. The Metropolitan Water Resources Authority owns the reservoir itself, while the Metropolitan District Commission Watershed Management Division manages the land surrounding the reservoir. Activities in the region are limited so as to assure the public of a safe water supply.[20]

ronmental problems, yet troublesome issues remain. The changes in regional air quality, for one, illustrate the tiny, yet positive, steps that have been made. In the summer of 2002, New England registered thirty-one smog alert days in which the air quality was deemed unsafe, demonstrating better air quality today than in the mid-1980s, but also showing that room for improvement remains. New England faces challenges from the level of nitrogen oxides, volatile organic compounds, and other airborne toxic substances.

The majority of New England's air problems stem from the production of energy and regional transportation. Facilities like incinerators and power plants lead to high mercury levels in regional air and water and contaminated fish supplies. The majority of New England's medical waste incinerators have recently closed, but toxins also move into New England from other regions of the United States. Dioxin, a by-product of incinerators and paper mills, also pollutes New England and so far has not been sufficiently addressed. Twenty-six new power plants that adhere to tighter standards on emissions have been granted permits to operate in the region since the late 1990s. Yet automobiles and trucks in the region are responsible for approximately one-third of the volatile organic compounds and about one-half of the nitrogen oxides and other airborne toxins. The Environmental Protection Agency estimates that in the past thirty years, the number of miles driven in New England has doubled.

The U.S. Global Change Research Program found in 2001 that New England had warmed significantly in the past one hundred years, with temperatures up by 0.7 degrees for the yearly cycle. Most of the upward trend occurs during the winter months, the region's net temperature for the winter season up 1.8 degrees. This warming trend may be the result of greater greenhouse gases regionally. The warmer temperatures may encourage the spread of insects and a decrease in the healthiness of trees and aquatic life.

New England's unique tidal wetlands, an ecosystem among the most diverse in the world, have encountered severe threats from urban development. Tidal marshes have also been drained to kill off mosquito populations or to be used as garbage dumps. Today, efforts go forward to preserve and rebuild wetlands, yet not at the needed pace. Other ecological treasures, like the Atlantic Ocean's George's Bank, face destruction from overfishing. George's Bank, an offshore region whose surface comes just twenty feet from the water's surface, once netted New England fishermen fifteen thousand pounds of halibut in a single day. The area stretches 150 miles in length and 75 miles in width, making it larger than the state of Massachusetts, and lies 75 miles off the coast. In 1850, the halibut populations of the region began to decline. By the 1920s, the United States had joined Great Britain in the use of trawlers—boats dragging nets—to capture fish. In 1925, the Birdseye Corporation, located in Gloucester, produced a frozen fish stick that introduced fish to many American homes for the first time. The factory ships of the late 1900s caught as many fish in an hour (about one hundred tons) as a seventeenth-century ship would harvest in an entire season. In 1993, Canada placed restrictions on fishermen in their zone of George's Bank, and on December 7, 1994, the United States closed 3,707 square miles of George's Bank to further fishing. The United States made the ban indefinite in April 1995 and the restrictions remain. In January 1999, scientists at New England's Woods Hole noted that cod populations still were undergoing decline.

In 2003, the United States Geological Service concluded that while wastewater treatment improvements had led to a reduction of chemicals in the important New England rivers, the Blackstone, the Connecticut, and the Merrimack, the rivers have also experienced a rise in salt levels. The salt contaminant stems from the salt used to increase traction on roads during the winter months. For instance, on the Merrimack River, chloride (salt) levels have risen a startling 760 percent in one hundred years. The Connecticut River underwent a 344 percent increase in chloride in the same period and the Blackstone River has seen a 186 percent rise. The Blackstone River, of the three, had the highest levels of the pollutants sulfate, phosphorus, nitrate, chloride, and solid residues. Fertilizer and emissions from power plants account for raised levels of nitrates in all three major rivers. All three have seen a decline in phosphorus contaminant due to controls over the addition of the substance to soaps and detergents as well as improved wastewater treatment in the region. Sulfate levels have fallen over the last few decades due to increasing conversion from coal to natural gas at electric power plants. This information demonstrates the direct impact human choices have on the environment. The chief scientist of the U.S. Geological Service study, Keith Robinson, explains, "Certainly, this study shows that our lifestyles have an effect on the area's rivers. Using what we have learned from this study will help water resource managers and private citizens to understand what the future of New England's Rivers might be."

New England's industrial legacy translates to communities haunted by the highly polluted land parcels known as brownfields. Brownfields make development cumbersome, but modern techniques have enabled the government and private developers to recycle particular sites. In New England, a paper factory in Old Town, Maine, got reworked into shops and a museum; a Bridgeport, Connecticut, industrial site became a baseball park; and the economically troubled New Bedford received a new industrial park on a previously abandoned parcel.[21]

All three major New England rivers have seen a decline in phosphorus contaminants due to controls over the addition of dangerous substances to soaps and detergents as well as improved wastewater treatment in the region. © Getty Images/PhotoDisc.

CONCLUSION

In New England, as we have seen, environmental issues, industrialization, and urbanization are intricately intertwined. The rocky soils of the region, combined with the bent toward education and hard work brought to the New World by the Puritans, led New England into manufacturing much earlier than the rest of the United States. Industrialization in turn caused the growth of urban centers, for while agriculture requires a scattered population, industrialization encourages dense settlement, with all workers in easy reach of their work sites. New England's early adoption of manufacturing meant that its factories developed before the environmental consequences of the chemicals released into the landscape were fully understood. New England can be considered a leader in many kinds of environmental protection, yet it also has to grapple with complex problems, some of them of long standing. Among New England's gravest modern problems are urban sprawl, producing enough energy for its people, and the pollution caused by automobiles and trucks in the region. It remains to be seen if New England can formulate and implement environmental action plans that could substantially alleviate some of these long-standing problems, and whether it can serve as an example to other regions facing similar challenges.

RESOURCE GUIDE

Printed Sources

Axtell, James. *The Invasion Within: The Contest of Cultures in Colonial North America*. New York: Oxford University Press, 1985.

Chudacoff, Howard P., and Judith E. Smith. *The Evolution of American Urban Society*. Upper Saddle River, NJ: Prentice-Hall, 2000.

Corey, Steven H. "Waste Management." In Burt Feintuch and David H. Watters, eds., *Encyclopedia of New England Culture*. New Haven: Yale University Press, forthcoming.

Cronon, William. *Changes in the Land: Indians, Colonists, and the Ecology of New England.* New York: Hill and Wang, 1983.

Cumbler, John T. *Reasonable Use: The People, the Environment, and the State, New England, 1790–1930.* New York: Oxford University Press, 2001.

———. "Whatever Happened to Industrial Waste? Reform, Compromise, and Science in Nineteenth Century New England." *Journal of Social History* (Fall 1995): 149–172.

Davis, Mary Byrd, ed. *Eastern Old Growth Forests: Prospects for Rediscovery and Recovery.* Washington, DC: Island Press, 1996.

Garreau, Joel. *Edge City: Life on the New Frontier.* New York: Random House, 1991.

Greene, J. R. *The Creation of Quabbin Reservoir: The Death of the Swift River Valley.* N.p.: J&R Printers, 2001.

———. *The Day Four Quabbin Towns Died.* N.p.: The Transcript Press, 1985.

Jaffee, David. *People of the Wachusett: Greater New England in History and Memory, 1630–1860.* Ithaca, NY: Cornell University, 1999.

Jorgensen, Neil. *A Guide to New England's Landscape.* Barre, MA: Barre Publishers, 1971.

Kricher, John. *Eastern Forests: A Field Guide to Birds, Mammals, Trees, Flowers, and More.* New York: Houghton Mifflin, 1998.

Krieger, Alex., David Cobb, and Amy Turner. *Mapping Boston.* Boston: Muriel G. and Norman B. Leventhal Family Foundation, 1999.

Lockridge, Kenneth A. *A New England Town: The First Hundred Years.* New York: W. W. Norton, 1985.

Lucarelli, Jennifer. "Moose Crash Kills Woman." *Worcester Telegram,* July 25, 2003.

Marchand, Peter J. *North Woods: An Inside Look at the Nature of Forests in the Northeast.* Boston: Appalachian Mountain Club Books, 1987.

Monahan, John J. "Tainted Soil May Give Life to Old Dump." *Worcester Telegram,* July 27, 2003.

"More Salt, Less Phosphate Found in 3 Rivers." *Worcester Telegram,* July 25, 2003.

Muir, Diana. *Reflections in Bullough's Pond: Economy and Ecosystem in New England.* Hanover, NH: University Press of New England, 2000.

Palen, J. John. *The Urban World.* Boston: McGraw-Hill, 1997.

Revkin, Andrew. "Study Outlines Arsenic Risk in Some New England Well Water." *New York Times,* May 5, 2003.

Reynolds, Douglas, and Katheryn Viens, eds. *New England's Disharmony: The Consequences of the Industrial Revolution.* Woonsocket: Rhode Island Labor History Society and Labor Research Center at the University of Rhode Island, 1993.

Shaler, N. S. "Environment and Man in New England." *The North American Review,* no. 162 (June 1896): 725–740.

Steinberg, Theodore. *Nature Incorporated: Industrialization and the Waters of New England.* Amherst: University of Massachusetts Press, 1991.

Web Sites

EPA New England Annual Reports. April 23, 2003.
U.S. Environmental Protection Agency. February 16, 2004.
http://www.epa.gov/region01/ra/soeindex.html

Annual reports by EPA on the New England environment.

The Exchange. 2004.
NH Public Radio. February 16, 2004.
http://nhpr.org/view_content/3123/

New England environment.

Major Topics in New England. January 31, 2004.
U.S. Environmental Protection Agency. February 16, 2004.
http://www.epa.gov/region01/topics/index.html

Environmental issues regarding New England.

Protecting New England's Environment. 2004.
NewenglandWOW.com. February 12, 2004.
http://newenglandwow.com/environmental.htm

An environmental site on the New England environment by state and region.

Sprawl in New England. May 16, 2002.
Regional Review (Quarter 1, 2000) Vol. 10, No. 1.
Federal Reserve Bank of Boston. January 27, 2004.
http://www.bos.frb.org/economic/nerr/rr2000/q1/sprl_ne.htm

State of the New England Environment 1970–2000. April 23, 2003.
U.S. Environmental Protection Agency. February 16, 2004.
http://www.epa.gov/region01/ra/soe00/soe2000.html

EPA report covering the New England environment from 1970 to 2000.

Students and Teachers. January 31, 2004.
U.S. Environmental Protection Agency. February 16, 2004.
http://www.epa.gov/region01/students/index.html

A resource guide on the environment for New England teachers and students.

U.S. Environmental Protection Agency. January 31, 2004.
February 16, 2004.
http://www.epa.gov/

Includes a variety of sites addressing environmental issues, including New England and its regions.

Woonsocket. 2004.
Erik Eckilson. January 29, 2004.
http://www.woonsocket.org/

History and industrialization of Woonsocket, Rhode Island.

Videos/Films

A Civil Action. Dir. Steve Zallian. Perf. John Travolta, Robert Duvall. Touchstone/Paramount Pictures, 1998.
A Rich and Ancient Heritage, Vermont's Archaeological Sites. VT Division for Historic Preservation, 1991.

Organizations

Environment Business Council of New England, Inc.
333 Trapelo Road
Belmont, MA 02478
http://www.ebc-ne.org/

Council for promoting the development of environmental industry.

National Park Service
1849 C Street, N.W.
Washington, DC 20240
http://www.nps.gov/

Federal Parks, including New England.

U.S. Environmental Protection Agency
Ariel Rios Building
1200 Pennsylvania Avenue, N.W.
Washington, DC 20460
http://www.epa.gov/

Government organization for the environment.

Museums

American Museum of Natural History
Central Park West at 79th Street
New York, NY 10024
http://www.sciencebulletins.amnh.org/

American natural history. Includes "The Sorry Story of George's Bank."

The Davistown Museum
Prescott Block
58 Main Street # 4
P.O. Box 346
Liberty, ME 04949
http://www.davistownmuseum.org/

Promotes community awareness of environmental history.

Ecotarium
222 Harrington Way
Worcester, MA
http://www.ecotarium.org/

Museum and center for the study of the New England environment.

Fisher Museum Harvard Forest
324 North Main Street
Petersham, MA 01366
http://harvardforest.fas.harvard.edu/museum.html

Museum of New England forest ecology and the history of land use.

Museum of Science
Science Park
Boston, MA 02114
http://www.mos.org/

Permanent exhibit of New England habitats.

New England Aquarium
Central Wharf
Boston, MA 02110
http://www.neaq.org/index.flash4.html

Aquarium of marine life and aquatic environments.

ETHNICITY

*Enrique Morales-Díaz
and Gabriel Aquino,
with Michael Sletcher*

The history of ethnicity in New England has been shaped by group conflict. The persistence of ethnic identity in the region is a process that is shaped equally by common internal group identification, through the belief in a common culture, a process that is shaped by a belief in the differences in the customs of others. These stories, therefore, are fashioned by the common memories shared by ethnic groups and how these ethnic identities are further strengthened through their relationship and notion of what and who constitutes "otherness." For a clearer perspective on ethnicity in New England, it is important to understand what is meant by *ethnicity* and how society has shaped the way people look at themselves as individuals, as a society, and as a result how they view and treat others based on how they have been socialized. It is important, however, to explore the views that those who believe themselves to be superior to others have of those they identify as inferior, since "Each man calls barbarism whatever is not his own practice. . . . Barbarians are no more marvelous to us than we are to them, nor for better cause."[1]

Ethnicity is a concept that is seldom defined by scholars and is usually interpreted as referring to a "people."[2] Of course, what constitutes a people does require some serious consideration, especially when attempting to understand how New England society and culture have developed. According to Max Weber,[3] ethnicity is a social construct in which people hold a belief in their shared language, culture, and history. Furthermore, ethnicity is intensified when groups come in contact with each other and differences in customs, language, and memories are sharpened by economic and political conflict. In other words, a group's belief in their common ancestral link grows out of the differences that they see in other groups' customs. These differences become stronger as the contact between groups increases economic and political competition and by the increase of skills that promoted group survival. Geographic differentiation or social distance has meant the development of distinct forms of survival skills that were imitated by individuals from within the family and others in close proximity.[4] These distinct skills that promoted survival for these groups became the customs that allowed for the differentiation of others. How is one defined as a member of an ethnic group in the United States? How can we apply this understanding to the case of New England? In this society the meaning of ethnicity, as well as race, has been shaped politically.[5] The construction of ethnic "definitions" changes over time as the country's historical arena continues to change.

Who were the Native Americans present in the area when the Europeans, specifically the Puritans, arrived? How did their arrival affect native life, customs, and traditions? How did the natives react to the changes imposed on them? The appearance of the Puritans in New England signaled the beginning of ethnic relations in what would become the United States. Contact with the Native Americans and the introduction of the African slave established the bases for ethnic diversity in New England. How did the arrival of the Puritans affect the lives of those already there, and consequently, shape ethnic relations? Who were the Puritans? Why did they settle in New England? What motivated them to treat the native population as they did?

The forced introduction and involuntary presence of the African slave in the New World accelerated interracial relationships at all levels, necessitating the creation of cultural and personal bonds with others in similar situations that helped in their struggle to survive in a world and a culture that were alien to them. Why were they brought to New England? Was there a need for slavery in the area? How were they treated in comparison to slaves in other colonies?

The Puritans' presence also established a formula for future European immigration, particularly the Irish, French, and Portuguese, although other European groups, specifically from Eastern Europe, would follow. Understanding the importance of European settlement enables us to construct a cohesive and inclusive New England ethnic tapestry of the region as it has been "constructed." New immigrant groups, such as Asians, Eastern Europeans, and Hispanics/Latinos, have made lasting and important contributions as did their predecessors.

NATIVE AMERICANS

There were approximately two million natives in the Northeast region including the New England states (Connecticut, Maine, Massachusetts, New Hampshire, Rhode Island, and Vermont).[6] By the time the Europeans arrived to the region they encountered populated areas with various established civilizations, each with their own customs, traditions, and religious practices, which supports the idea that the area was already populated by a variety of indigenous groups.[7] Some historians, whose research was based primarily on accounts by early explorers, established that the native populations "encountered" in the New World did not posses anything resembling a "civilization." Nevertheless, contemporary research has contradicted earlier findings and has established that the Native Americans whom the Puritans encountered in 1630 were in fact part of organized and civilized societies. This can be seen in how the natives adapted the newly arrived culture into their own. Their eventual conversion to Puritanism, however, was based on a need for survival. Thus, the Native Americans found themselves forced to accept English law, customs, and traditions, and as a result they needed to redefine who they were and what their culture meant to them. It meant altering their existing societies and assimilating themselves into new ones, emphasizing their ability to adapt to their changing environment, even when forced to do so.

According to James Axtell, the millions of Native Americans in the Western Hemisphere spoke "221 unintelligible languages, each fractured into myriad dialects that were themselves confounding even to native ears."[8] The fact that even one family of languages differed among tribes and villages within close proximity to each other attests to the notion that the Native Americans were people who adapted their way of life to their environment as a form of survival. For example, Roger Williams (1603–1683), founder of the Rhode Island colony, observed that among the Algonquian-speakers of New England "the varietie of their Dialects and proper speech within thirtie or fortie miles each of the other is very great."[9] At the dawn of the twenty-first century the U.S. government recognized approximately 550 Indian communities.[10] This figure attests to the survival instincts that continue as part of Native American life in the United States.

Within the Northeast cultural area, five subgroups of tribes were present at the time of the encounter. This chapter focuses on part of the first, which includes Nova Scotia, New England, Long Island, Hudson Valley, and Delaware Valley Algonquian-speaking tribes such as Abenaki, Massachusetts, Narragansett, Wampanoag, Pennacook, Pequot, Mahican, and Wappinger, as well as Maliseet, Nipmuc, Passamaquoddy, Paugassett, Penobscot, Podunk, and Schaghticoke.[11] Each native group varied in size depending on where they had settled.[12] To be more precise, Sharon Malinowski and Anna Sheets list fourteen specific groups not only connected to the region but also descending from the Algonquian family of tribes, which is reflected in their shared language.[13] Even though many of the groups were divided, they could all "trace" their heritage to the Algonquians.[14]

Native American Tribes of New England

Tribe	Location
Abenaki	Maine to Lake Champlain, south to the Merrimack River, north to Quebec
Maliseet	St. John's River in northern Maine
Massachusetts	Valleys of the Charles and Neponset rivers in eastern Massachusetts
Mattabesic	Western Connecticut
Mohawk	Western and northern frontier of Massachusetts, Vermont, and New Hampshire
Mohegan	Upper Hudson River to western parts of Connecticut, Massachusetts, and Vermont
Narragansett	Narragansett Bay, western Rhode Island, southern Massachusetts, and eastern Connecticut to the Pawcatuck River
Nauset	Cape Cod
Niantic	Southern coast of New England
Nipmuc	Central and western Massachusetts from the Seekonk River to the Connecticut River
Passamaquoddy	Northeastern United States, primarily Maine
Paugassett	Southwestern Connecticut, along the Merrimack River
Pawtucket	Cape Ann
Pennacook	Merrimack River valley of southern and central New Hampshire, northeastern Massachusetts, and southeastern Maine
Penobscot	Old Town, Maine
Pequot	Southeastern Connecticut between the Pawcatuck and Connecticut rivers
Pocumtuck	Connecticut River valley in Massachusetts
Podunk	East of Hartford, Connecticut, in the South Windsor vicinity
Schaghticoke	West-central Connecticut, Litchfield County, near Kent
Siciaoggs	Connecticut River valley
Wampanoag	Southeastern Massachusetts, northern Rhode Island, Martha's Vineyard, and Nantucket
Wongunk	Connecticut River Valley

Just as there have been debates regarding the exact number of Native Americans present at the time of European arrival, there have also been debates with regard to the groups themselves: Who were they? Where were they located? As Margo Burns stated, the region was populated by various native groups, all sharing some similarities and connections with each other, without making them a homogenous group.[15] Burns provides us with a list of native groups present throughout the region, but differing in terms of groups and locations with that previously listed.

Alden T. Vaughan, on the other hand, states that by the time the Europeans arrived there were ten prominent groups, some more important than others, but all had an impact on the developing relationships between the natives and newcomers. One of the important points derived from these lists is the fact that there were a variety of tribal groups throughout the New England region. While not equally divided, at one point there was at least one group in each of the states. Also important is the fact that although many of these tribes belonged to the same family of language they differed in terms of their customs, beliefs, traditions, and locations. Regardless of the differences, the Europeans would use uniformity in order to classify them, which also extended to the attitudes that existed toward the natives. For example, the Puritans saw the natives as merciless, and this belief affected their relationship with them. Many Europeans believed that the Native Americans enjoyed mutilating their victims—among the most popular Western myths of natives is the fact that "scalping" became their calling card.

What was New England like before the encounter between the Puritans and the native tribes? How were the first settlers of the region affected by contact with the Europeans? What attitudes about the natives did the European newcomers develop? Because census information was not available until the end of the eighteenth century, to establish an exact number of Native Americans in the region, even today, is almost impossible. It is perhaps necessary to state that the number of natives in the New England region at the time of contact is unknown.[16] Dinnerstein, Nichols, and Reimers speculate that the most common accepted figure is that of 3–5 million indigenous peoples.[17] However, Claudia Durst Johnson estimates that there were seventy-five thousand Native Americans in the region by 1620,[18] while Kathleen Bragdon has estimated that there were approximately seventy-two thousand distributed throughout southern New England.[19] Thus, a substantial portion of the two million Native Americans could be connected to New England before disease ravaged their numbers.

Penobscot woman in original Gala-Day costume. Courtesy Library of Congress.

Johnson's analysis affirms that the most prominent indigenous groups in the region between 1620 and 1630 were the Pawtucket, Wampanoag, Massachusetts, Pequot, Paugassett, Mohegan, Narragansett, Pocumtuck, Mohawk, Penobscot, and Abenaki. Based on Klein's compilation of reservations and tribal councils, the tribes that continue to have recognized representation and are present in Johnson's list are the Pequonock, Pequot, Mohegan, Schaghticoke, Maliseet, Passamaquoddy, Penobscot, Wampanoag, and Narragansett. Johnson's list corresponds to Bragdon's distribution of the seventy-two thousand natives in the southern New England region. She lists among them the Pawtucket, Massachusett, Pokanoket, Narragansett, and Pequot or Mohegan.[21]

Native Americans in New England Today

According to Barry T. Klein in the *Reference Encyclopedia of the American Indian* (2000), there are many reservations and tribal councils in the United States today, some of which are in the New England region. In Connecticut there are four: Golden Hill Indian Reservation, Mashantucket Pequot Tribal Nation, Mohegan Tribe, and Schaghticoke Tribal Nation of Kent, Inc. In Maine there are five: Aroostook Band of Micmac Indians, Houlton Band of Maliseet Indians, Indian Township Reservation (Indian Township Passamaquoddy Tribal Council), Penobscot Nation Reservation, and Pleasant Point Reservation (Pleasant Point Passamaquoddy Tribal Council). In Massachusetts there is one: Wampanoag Reservation. And in Rhode Island there is also one: Narragansett Indian Reservation.[20]

The European View of the New World and Its Native People

How did the Europeans envision the region? New England, as coined by Captain John Smith in 1616 (although other sources claim that it was in 1614 when he mapped out the New England coast),[22] had been described as "a blur of contradictory images, of barren rock and beckoning pasture, crippling cold and balmy sunshine," as communication between the New and Old World promoted the idea of migration.[23] While a first attempt at establishing a settlement had been made in 1607 "at present day Popham," this enterprise was abandoned.[24] The failure at the first attempt to establish a colony in the New England region affected those individuals who would eventually arrive and attempt to settle once more in the area.[25] The failure of this initial venture affected the beginning of a migratory process, although by 1630 a substantial number of Puritans would find their way to New England in the hopes of establishing roots without the fear of religious persecution.

Those already in the New World maintained constant communication with England in the hopes that more settlers would travel and establish colonies in what at the time was known as "northern Virginia." For Captain John Smith, the region would allow newcomers to establish new homes, considering the problems taking place in the Jamestown outpost.[26] According to Smith, New England was "'a most excellent place, both for health and fertility,' and blessed with 'an excellent climate.'"[27] However, when there was communication between these two parts of the world, references regarding the "original" settlers were rarely made, and when information about them was included, much of it was based on observations made by fur traders or temporary visitors. Nevertheless, according to Vaughan, the year 1605 was significant because of two specific events: the beginning of Puritan migration to the New World, and first contact with the natives.[28] It can also be said that the Puritans' encounter with the natives echoes the continuous conflict that exists between the "Other"/"other," those who see themselves as superior and others as inferior, reflected in their own relationship with the English crown and the Church of England. As a result, they would impose upon the natives (and later on the Africans brought over and treated as "perpetual servants," as the natives were) a series of beliefs, ideas, and attitudes that would undermine the development of cordial ethnic relations. Louis Martin Sears remarks that "The relations between the Puritans and the Indians constitute an important phase of early American society. Conquest of the barbarians was part of the taming of the wilderness, with the added variable of a human element, the influence of the Indian upon the Puritan being second only to that of the Puritan upon the Indian."[29] The classification of the Native American as "barbarian" would determine the relationship between the "first" inhabitants of the area and the new European arrivals. Also, the idea that Puritan influence was more important goes far into establishing the hierarchical power structure that was not present in the various native civilizations. Martin Sears states that, "Lacking the hypotheses of civilized man, [the native] nevertheless possessed the experience of centuries of forest roaming," establishing a clear differentiation between the two groups under discussion.[30] However, Sears also states that while the Puritan influence on the Native American was more "important," it would be the Native Americans' influence on the Puritans that would last: "Each introduced many arts, both of war and peace, into the fashioning of New England civilization. But since ultimate survival constituted the Puritan as final legatee, the Indians' contributions to the Puritans, however minor, have survived, while the Puritans' contributions to the Indians, however great, have perished."[31]

By the time the Puritans arrived in the region they already had preconceived notions of what the Indian was and why. William Simmons writes that many of the attitudes the English Puritans held stemmed from "mythological" stories about the region's "barbarians."[32] Hence, the Europeans had already imposed on the Native Americans old beliefs brought from the Old World; they "tended to conceive of the new in terms of the old, to classify novelties according to conventional wisdom."[33] The old classifications of new individuals, then, are not a new phenomenon. Dinnerstein, Nichols, and Reimers support this notion by adding, "The English regarded those who differed from them as inferior. Toward the Native American Indians they held two contradictory views. On the one hand Englishmen hoped to meet friendly tribesmen who would help, guide and trade with them. At the same time they feared these 'savage and backward' people."[34] Also, the English had developed similar attitudes toward Africans, specifically based on skin color, values, and traditions, as well as toward other Europeans, such as the Irish.[35]

At the same time that the Europeans were developing notions about the first inhabitants of the region, the natives themselves had developed their own attitudes and notions about the Europeans since contact between them predated the Puritans' arrival. Some of the initial contacts with early European visitors can be traced back to the beginning of the sixteenth century.[36] Only the new arrivals in the mid-seventeenth century believed that it was the first time natives had come in contact with people like them. As such, the Europeans' reaction to the treatment they initially received was based on their own beliefs. However, the natives' reaction to the new European arrivals was based on "a well founded sense of revenge for injuries inflicted by earlier European visitors."[37]

Kathleen Bragdon asserts that with the increased contact between the natives and Europeans, the natives' behavior changed as they became familiar with the needs and desires of the newcomers, and how that would affect their own lives. She writes that "As the number of those encounters increased, however, explorers noted an increasing cynicism and suspicion, and a tendency to respond with violence in uncertain situations."[38] As the experiences acquired by the Europeans in the region increased, so did the natives' own perspective on the newcomers. The Europeans' own exploratory exploits "familiarized the New England natives with the white man as trader, kidnapper, deceiver, murderer, and friend."[39] Accounts as early as that of Giovanni da Verrazzano (1485–1528) describe encounters with the native populations.

Verrazano's account, however, is an interpretation through the eyes of a literate European with a written language, and it is "this version" of history, from the colonizer's perspective, that we are familiar with. According to Bragdon, Verrazano's account "depicts a joyful paradise, an encounter between strangers unmarred by fear or violence. As participants in a literate tradition . . . Europeans have been awarded ascendancy in historical accounts partly because of the permanency of their written impressions, the most enduring artifacts of such early encounters."[44] Thus, while this encounter was a description of the natives that Giovanni da Verrazzano encountered in Newport Bay, it is still a version of history that does not include the other side, because colonialism can be seen as "a denial of all culture, history and value outside the colonizer's frame; in short, 'a systematic negation of the other person.' "[45]

The Europeans' early accounts of encounters with native inhabitants of North America reflect a universalistic approach to history that reflects a Euro/ethnocentric view of the "universe." Many of the Puritans encountered the Native Americans in New England with a universal and homogenous notion of who the natives were.[46] Their lack of knowledge of the "first" inhabitants also reflected the conflicting reports about the region itself. For instance, Captain John Smith hailed the area as a great opportunity for new settlements, but Cressy writes that by the middle of the seventeenth century a series of other views on the area affected the Puritans' attitude and relationship with the natives and the land. These attitudes ranged from viewing the region as a wonderful place to settle to viewing it as a worthless area that needed to be avoided.[47]

Conquest and Prejudice

Some of the prejudices and stereotypes that exist in our society and in our time are a legacy of our past, even before the initial contact between Europeans and natives. Jan Nederveen Pieterse believes that current attitudes toward differences are a consistent practice since "virtually all the images and stereotypes projected outside Europe in the age of empire had been used first within Europe."[40] Stereotypes and prejudice are often restructured to fit the group on which those notions are placed upon, often labeling one group with the name formerly used for another. The process of labeling, of naming one group and placing upon it the characteristics initially used to describe an earlier group of people stems from the fear of losing power; thus, it is a process of discrimination, and as Pieterse states, of humiliation.[41] "The top-dog position," which plays an important role in ethnic and power relations, refers to "white, western, civilized, male, adult, urban, middle-class, heterosexual. . . . It is this profile that has monopolized the definition of humanity in mainstream western imagery. It is a programme of fear for the rest of the world population."[42] Hence, "it was this process of 'conquest, colonization, and destruction' of the native in the New World which created binary patterns of identification that separated not only the colonized from her/his roots, but distanced any understanding between the colonizer and the colonized subject."[43]

First Impressions

The following excerpt portrays da Verrazzano's first impressions of an initial contact with a group in what is known today as "Newport Bay." Also of importance in this account is the Native Americans' reaction to the encounter with the Europeans.

[June (?), 1524] We . . . proceeded to another place, fifteen leagues distant from the island [Block Island], where we found a very excellent harbor. Before entering it, we saw about twenty small boats full of people, who came about our ship, uttering many cries of astonishment, but they would not approach nearer than within fifty paces; stopping, they looked at the structure of our ship, our persons and dress, afterwards they all raised a loud shout together, signifying that they were pleased. By imitating their signs, we inspired them in some measure with confidence, so that they came near enough for us to toss to them some little bells and glasses, and many toys, which they took and looked at, laughing, and then came on board without fear. Among them were two kings more beautiful in form and stature than can possibly be described; one was about forty years old, the other about twenty-four, and they were dressed in the following manner: The oldest had a deer's skin around his body, artificially wrought in damask figures, his head was without covering, his hair was tied back in various knots; around his neck he wore a large chain ornamented with many stones of different colors. The young man was similar in his general appearance. This is the finest looking tribe, the handsomest in their costumes that we have found in our voyage. They exceeded us in size, and they are of a very fair complexion; some of them incline more to a white, and others to a tawny color; their faces are sharp, and their hair long and black, upon the adorning of which they bestow great pains; their eyes are black and sharp, their expression mild and pleasant, greatly resembling the antique.[48]

While the initial contact between the natives and the Europeans was not one based on a power hierarchy, the dynamics of their relationship changed at the arrival of more Europeans. According to Norman Yetman, one of the main conflicts between the European arrivals and the Native Americans was the increased demand for land by the newcomers.[49] For instance, the Abenakis, Etchemins, and Souriquois of Maine, according to Bourque, were dying in large numbers as a result of exposure to foreign diseases introduced by Europeans, such as smallpox and measles, which acted like "shock troops," decimating the population.[50] Thus, the arrival of large numbers of Europeans, together with the surviving indigenous population and the introduction of the African slave, would serve to create the basis for the establishment of ethnic New England. As Mandell articulates, "New England was shaped by the cultures and desires of native and newcomers."[51]

Frederick Wiseman, in his narrative account of the introduction of new diseases to the region as it relates to the Abenaki Nation (in what is known today as Vermont), states, "Disease from the East is the other singularity of the period. Beginning in the 1530s a series of afflictions washed over Wôbanakik, carrying away the knowledge of our elders, the potential of our young, and the strength of our adults."[52] The period he is referring to is the "Christian years 1600 to 1820," or "The Years of the Beaver."[53] Wiseman's statement supports a series of notions: first, the native inhabitants of the region were aware of the changes taking place, specifically the introduction of certain metals and other items which were causing changes affecting their people, directly related to the Europeans' presence; second, the period in question, the 1530s, refers to the period of first contact between Europeans and Native Americans; third, "The Years of the Beaver" is directly connected to fur and skin trading agreements between warring tribes and their alliances with the newcomers, the Europeans, or "Agemenokak."

While the beaver did not play a major role in the Abenaki annual hunting cycle, it nonetheless interested the Agemenokak. This interest caused a rift in the relationships that existed among the region's tribes. Wiseman says of this situation, "Our respect for conservation and game animals was challenged for the first time in scores of generations. To survive in a changing world, we could not refuse the new technology, no matter what the environmental consequences."[54] In "The Departure of Koluscap," Wiseman relates how the killing of the beaver in the territory changed the well being not only of the people, but also of the land, introducing the native population to the changes that were to escalate with the arrival of the Puritans.

Wiseman's account reflects the concerns of the spirits over the influences introduced by the "newcomers," or the Europeans, over the Abenaki. The treatment of the beaver by the once respectful and caring tribe reflects the dangers that the spirits felt the European presence posed in the region. The specific reference to the Black Robes was a direct parallel to the French Jesuits' attempt to convert the Huron natives north of New England. Like the Huron, many New England natives who converted to Protestantism after the arrival of the Puritans did so as a way to survive the changes taking place in their environment. Daniel Mandell writes, "Many of those most directly affected by the arrival of the newcomers may have converted because the aboriginal cosmos could not adequately explain or affect the technology, writing, sense of superiority, power, or disease brought by the Anglo-Americans."[55]

Not all natives converted, however. According to Donna Keith Baron, J. Edward Hood, and Holly V. Izard, those natives who did not convert relocated. They assert that what was once a populated region, particularly in reference to central New England, turned into a deserted area, depopulated by King Philip's War (1675–1676), and by the mid-nineteenth century "there remained in New England's inland towns perhaps a sole survivor of the first inhabitants or, in most cases, only a memory of their presence."[56] They add that the supposed disappearance of the natives from the lower central New England region added to the existing idea that they were inferior to the Europeans, and their "conversion" only proved Anglo-American "superiority" over them. What the Europeans did not take into account were cultural traditions and practices that included "seasonal mobility" which could explain why many natives moved into Anglo-American "settlements."[57]

Other aspects of the encounter explain the "disappearance" of the first New England inhabitants and the relationship between the survivors and the newly arrived Europeans: how indigenous societies were structured and how their social systems dealt with European influences. "Native society operated on three levels: clan, village, and tribe. The clan, an extended family that claimed a common ancestor, dominated an individual's life. Clans worked and held fields and hunting territories. The village, containing up to several hundred people from one or more clans, set field boundaries and organized the political and economic life. The tribe, the largest and least powerful grouping, connected the villages and clans with a common dialect and culture, but lacked stable hierarchies and could be reshaped by outside influences or internal conflicts."[58] Most tribes had stationary settlements, which changed according to the seasons but existed within the confines of a recognized tribal territory.[59] Land was shared by everyone in the tribe, with the exception of the house the family lived in and the bit of land cultivated for vegetables. Native Americans' concept of ownership explains the relationship between all par-

King Philip's War

In 1675, New England colonists and native groups came into conflict when King Philip (Metacomet) of the Wampanoag nation and other native nations attacked some houses on the outskirts of Swansea, Massachusetts. The war, which had resulted from cultural differences, a changing economy, and competition for limited land resources, quickly spread northward to New Hampshire and southward to Connecticut and ended in 1676 with the killing King Philip by a Wampanoag Indian fighting on the side of the colonists. The war was bloody and costly, resulting in more fatalities per capita than any other war in American history.

The following Native Americans played significant roles in King Philip's War:

Massasoit (1580–1661)	Sachem of the Wampanoag Indians
Wamsutta (d. 1676)	(Alexander)—son of Massasoit
Metacomet (1639?–1676)	(Philip)—Grand Sachem of the Wampanoag
John Sassamon (d. 1674)	The "praying Indian"
Canonchet (d. 1676)	Sachem of the Narragansetts

ties involved.[60] Conflicts erupted between the Native Americans and Puritans because the Puritans failed to understand traditional tribal land practices.

SETTLERS TO THE AREA

Who were the Puritans, and why did they settle in New England? The answers to those questions will give us a clearer picture of how ethnicity developed in New England. While the Puritans were not the only English settlers in the area, they do put in motion the ethnic mosaic that develops in the New England region.

The Puritans left England in search of a place that would allow them the freedom of religion they sought; they wanted the opportunity to worship without the constant fear of persecution and reprisal for not conforming to the norms of the English church. Because of fear of the Anglican reach, rather than settling in Ireland, the doors opened for those who wanted to seek adventure and opportunity and settle in the North American colonies.[61] The Puritans there had specific reasons to immigrate. Cressy writes that "Arminianism, Laudianism, and Charles I's drive for Anglican conformity are identified as the goals that drove the Puritans to despair, and thence to America."[62] New England seemed like the perfect place for the Puritans to start anew.

A series of characteristics distinguished the Puritans from their forefathers, for example, the brief duration of the migratory process known as the "Great Migration." The circumstances that forced the Puritans to leave England would change within a few years, however, so that some decided to remain at home. As Anderson writes, "Why travel 3,000 miles to create a new society when one could now remake the world at home?"[63] Another characteristic that distinguishes this group was their destination. Rather than heading for Virginia, those who migrated between 1630 and 1640 (approximately thirteen thousand men, women, and children) decided to go to New England, and once there settled in areas that were less populated by Native Americans.[64] Nevertheless, when the Puritans did encounter natives they pursued the appropriation of land. Mandell writes that "The English not only wrought demographic, political, and social changes among the Indians of southern New England, but altered the very environment on which the natives depended. The growing number of colonists cut deeply into the forests; trees were felled for fuel, shelter, and export, and an increasing amount of land was taken for farms."[65] Hence, the Puritans' attitudes with regard to land ownership and displacement portrayed them as "inflexible and authoritarian," eventually leading to conflicts such as King Philip's War.[66]

The Puritans who migrated to New England "resembled the English population as a whole."[67] The fact that the Great Migration was, for the most part, "a transplantation of families" was important because those settling in New England were already bringing with them close-knit ties that would differentiate them from those who established the first colonies. Also, the immediate establishment of familiar institutions facilitated the creation of their New England society, particularly since those individuals not of the same religious inclinations were required to convert before settling in the area.[68]

Once the settlement of New England began, the treatment toward the Native Americans changed. While the colonization of North America differed from that of the rest of the hemisphere, some of the same practices were implemented in New England, such as the enslavement of the native population. For example, according to Juan González, one characteristic that differentiated the colonization process between the English and the Spaniards were their attitudes toward land and "first" inhabitants. He writes that "While all European settlers justified the Indian conquest and genocide as God's will, the Spanish and English differed substantially in their methods of subjugation, and this eventually led to radically different colonial societies. English kings, for instance, ordered their agents to 'conquer, occupy and possess' the lands of the 'heathens and infidels,' but said nothing of the people inhabiting them."[69] Their enslavement and the subsequent introduction of the African to the region established the basis for ethnic conflict, which would reach its climax in the mid-twentieth century. The forced labor of natives, however, did not last as long as that of the Africans because many of the earlier inhabitants had been killed off by the newly introduced diseases, and because attitudes toward Native Americans changed. Consequently, the colonists needed to import more laborers, as indentured servants or slaves.

Restrictions Under the Law

Although African slaves in the North had certain rights, they were considered property that could be sold or inherited and their daily lives were restricted in many ways:

They were not allowed to leave their villages without a pass.
They were not allowed to ride ferries.
They were not allowed to be on the streets after 9 p.m.
They were not allowed to buy merchandise for themselves, only through white men.
They were not allowed to be on the streets during church.
They could not hold social gatherings out of doors.
They were forbidden from carrying sticks or canes unless they were physically disabled.
They could not keep domestic livestock.

Free blacks in the North were also subject to many restrictions:

Free blacks were not allowed to entertain black or mulatto slaves or natives in their houses.
They could not own certain kinds of property.
They could not own swine.
They could not serve on juries.
They were not considered full citizens.
They were taxed but could not vote.
They were excluded from the peacetime militia yet subject to the draft in time of war.
They were socially ostracized and segregated in harborside ghettos.
In New London, Connecticut, free blacks were forbidden to own any property at all and forbidden to reside in the community.
Their children were forbidden from attending public schools.[70]

AFRICANS IN NEW ENGLAND

While the number of African slaves in New England during the colonial era was lower in comparison to those found in the southern states throughout the same period, the institution of slavery did exist in the North. There were perhaps less than one thousand Africans found in the region during the eighteenth century.[71] While scholars such as Johnson and Lorenzo Johnston Greene assert that the exact date in which the first African slave was identified in the region is not known, they do nonetheless confirm that at around the mid-1600s slavery was a thriving commercial enterprise. Scholars also identify Massachusetts as one of the first states to have partaken in the aforementioned institution, making it the leader in terms of the number of Africans with "one hundred Negroes in 1680,"[72] followed closely by Rhode Island. Credit for having introduced the first "Negroes" to New England has been given to Captain William Pierce of the ship *Desire*, who in 1638 brought Africans with him from the West Indies. Winthrop D. Jordan states that the trade relationship that existed between the New England and English Caribbean colonies (specifically Barbados) fomented the attitude toward slavery that developed in the northern region. The fact that many white settlers from the Caribbean migrated to New England also added to the belief that the region was in need of African slaves, as Jordan states that they "undoubtedly [brought] with them their opinions about the suitable status of black persons."[73]

Governmental documents had recorded the presence of Africans throughout New England. Reference had been made as well in the *News Letter*, the first North American established newspaper (Boston, c. 1704). Most of the allusions to the Africans were often in the form of advertisements for the sale of slaves. Johnston Greene states that by 1639, Hartford, Connecticut, had slaves, as well as the New Haven colony in 1644 and New Hampshire in 1645. In the case of Rhode Island, reference to the presence of slaves dates back as far as 1652.[74] Africans, while not the only slaves in the region, were the only "perpetual servants." Johnston Greene writes that the "Negroes were the only persons held in bondage in New England. . . . Combined . . . were the several kinds of unfree labor current in that day; white, Negro and Indian indentured servitude, Indian slavery and, in occasional instances, the slavery of white people."[75] The fact that Africans were the only "permanent" slaves reflects the power relationship that the institution entailed, which according to Louis Ruchames is also a reflection of ethnocentrism, which "provided the rationale and apology for slavery and the slave trade."[76]

Dinnerstein, Nichols, and Reimers add that one of the reasons Africans were enslaved by the Europeans had to do with the differences that the latter identified in them. They believed that "Africans were not Christians," and whites "gradually began to consider blacks, as they considered Indians, savage and uncivilized."[77] Ruchames also adds that "Christianity, as the only true religion, and Christians as the new 'chosen People,' could do with the earth and its non-Christian populations as they saw fit."[78] Hence, the treatment of the African by the Puritans, according to Jordan, was based on a religious belief that the African, and any other group identified as inferior or uncivilized, was meant to serve those more advanced and superior.[79] This practice provided credence to the notion that God had created certain groups superior to others, a belief used to justify the treatment of whole ethnic groups throughout the twentieth century. Many of the religious beliefs in the superiority of one group over another were based on biblical texts in Leviticus 25, 45, and 46: "Of the children of the strangers that do sojourn among you, of them shall ye buy, and of their families . . . and they shall be your possession. And ye shall take them as an inheritance for your children . . . they shall be your bondmen for ever: but over your brethren the children of Israel, ye shall not rule one over another with rigor."[80]

Another reason why Africans were enslaved in New England had to do with the belief that natives were more of a threat to the established Puritan society. Since Native Americans were native to the territory, their escape and possible union with other tribal members was a likely prospect due to their familiarity with the terrain. This is one reason why in exchange for tobacco, and African slaves, New Englanders heading toward the West Indies brought "Indian" warriors with them. For the New Englander the threat of a Native American uprising made Native Americans unsuitable as a labor force; thus Native Americans were deterritorialized and in their place black slaves were brought to the region. The Africans, unlike the Native Americans, did not have that same possibility for escape and "unionization," because by the time they were brought over to New England, most of them had already been separated from their families, had been mixed with members of other African tribes, and had been slaves in the West Indies. As a consequence, the African slaves have been described as "defenseless and powerless."[81]

The attitudes practiced toward any group viewed and believed inferior to those possessing power were often based on the fear of differences and the unknown. The relationship between the New Englanders, natives, and Africans reflected a hierarchical structure that would allow some to dominate through the belief that certain individuals were meant to be dominated. Much of the prejudice directed toward Africans was based on physical differences identified by Europeans through years of contact with the African continent.[82] Ruchames adds that Aristotle's philosophy toward power hierarchy influenced the Europeans' belief in their own superiority. He writes that "Aristotle propounded the view that some men are destined by nature to be masters and others to be slaves, with each given those qualities appropriate to his position in society."[83]

While the institution of slavery was not a New World phenomenon, the needs that the North American colonists had for "perpetual servants" differed from the needs that other cultures and civilizations had for instituting the same practice. Also, the treatment that the Africans received reflected the conflicts in Europe and the way certain groups, such as the Irish, were treated. The Europeans, particularly the Anglo-Americans, saw the Africans in a very distinct way that stemmed from the ethnocentrism that continued to develop as they succeeded in their colonization. Yetman writes that "From the beginning, these contacts were marked by extreme ethnocentrism on the part of the English. Because Africans had vastly different customs, languages, religious practices, and skin color, they were viewed negatively by the English."[84]

New England has been credited with having "introduced and expanded" the slave trade during the colonial period. While the number of slaves in New England did not come close to those found in the South, New Englanders profited from the venture, even taking over the trading of slaves after competitors such as the Dutch withdrew.[85] By 1776 "slave trading was a cornerstone of the New England economy."[86] The institution of slavery did end much sooner in New England than it had in the South; however, the treatment that the Africans received in the North did not differ much from the treatment that they received in the South, with the exception that slaves had access to New England courts.

THE IRISH COME TO NEW ENGLAND

As the Puritans saw differences in the Native American and African other, so did they see a great difference in the Irish other. The history of the Irish in America has been shaped by the historical relationship between Britain and Ireland. The political and military conquest of Ireland by Britain helped to create the conditions for the dichotomy between Catholic and Protestant, Irish and Scotch-Irish, Ireland and Northern Ireland, and eventually Irish and others.

The earliest immigrants to the New England region from Ireland were those identified as Scotch-Irish. Who exactly the Scotch-Irish were has been difficult to discern and may itself have been affected by the conflicting relationship between Irish Catholics and Irish Protestants.[87] Historically in the United States, Scotch-Irish immigration to the New England region dates back to the 1600s. Additionally, many scholars have described these early immigrants as Presbyterian Irish from Ulster County's Scottish borderlands. Yet, the earliest records of the use of Scotch-Irish identity appeared in Ulster County and referred to "Catholics," "Gaelic-Speaking MacDonnells" and other Highlanders who were not Ulster Presbyterians, but who were referred as "Ulster Scots" or "Scottish Nation." Additionally, the term Scotch-Irish had negative connotations when used by officials in the colonies and, as in its use in Ulster County, referred to Catholics and Gaelic-speaking Highlanders.[88]

By the end of the eighteenth century the term "Scotch-Irish" had all but disappeared from use in the colonies. Instead, "Protestant Irish" or "North Irish" were used to refer to immigrants from Ulster County, and the term "Irish" came into general use as a panethnic identity favoring an American patriotism and shunning a Scottish identity because of Scotland's siding with King George III during the American Revolution. However, the resurgence of the term Scotch-Irish and its new meaning defining Protestant Irish or more specifically the Presbyterian Irish came into use with the vast Irish Catholic immigration that began in the 1840s.[89]

Although immigration by Irish Catholics had occurred before the famine of 1846, the famine in Ireland began a unique process of immigration to the United States.[90] Hasia Diner separated the process into four periods and types of immigration. The first was the prefamine experience before 1846, which was almost evenly divided between Protestant and Catholic Irish immigrants. Much of this immigration was also dispersed equally among many of the states outside the New England area. The second period of Irish immigration began with the start of the Irish potato famine. In the fall of 1846, the first potato crop failure occurred.[91] The potato was a staple of the Irish middle and lower classes. The failure of the crop was the catalyst for a profound demographic and social transition in Ireland. The population of Ireland went from eight million to four million during this period of crisis. Half of the missing population in Ireland died because of starvation and diseases exacerbated by malnutrition, while the other half emigrated.[92] By 1851 over four hundred thousand had emigrated from Ireland to the United States. The new Irish immigrants to the United States were distinctively poorer and disproportionately more Catholic.

According to census figures for 1790, the Irish made up less than 1 percent of the entire population in the region. By 1870, Irish-born were 11 percent of the population in New England and 55 percent of all foreign-born in New England.[93] The mass migration to the area has helped transform the image of the New England ethnic landscape from that of Yankee Puritanism to one of Irish Catholicism. With the Irish came many of the religious institutions that would assist other Catholic immigrants who were to come to New England. By 1980, those of Irish ancestry were 14 percent of the region, second to those who claimed English ancestry with 16.43 percent. However, in 1990, those who claimed Irish ancestry were claiming the principal ancestry in the area with 15.18 percent; the second group was English with 11.55 percent. In the year 2000, those who did not report an ancestry were number one with 14.25 percent, although the Irish were second with 13.25 percent.[94]

Other Roman Catholic Immigrant Groups

As Catholics, the Irish presence in the New England region opened the doors for other (im)migrant groups who shared their faith. Peoples from Latin America have always been a presence in the United States, even in the New England region. One group in particular that has made its presence felt due primarily to its close political and economic relationship to the United States has been the Puerto Ricans. Because Puerto Ricans were granted American citizenship through the Jones Act in 1917, many have formed enclaves throughout the United States. Puerto Ricans began to migrate to New England in large numbers during the 1940s and 1950s as agricultural laborers,[95] primarily to the Connecticut River Valley to work on the tobacco farms. Recruiters on the island brought many Puerto Ricans to the valley during this early stage of migration. Because of the decline in immigration during World War II and a general decline on agricultural laborers, New England farmers were forced to find a new source of labor.[96] Economic conditions in Puerto Rico made Puerto Ricans a willing labor force for the New England agricultural industry.

Puerto Rico had a surplus labor force created by an industrialization initiative that was exacerbating the island's unemployment problem.[97] Migration to the United States became part of the island's government policy in dealing with the high unemployment.[98] Additionally, the United States had initiated a labor migration program earlier in the century, when the sugar conglomerates dislocated agricultural workers out of the rural areas.[99]

Opportunities in New England's cities attracted Puerto Rican workers from the surrounding farmlands.[100] Cities like Hartford, Lowell, Worcester, Springfield, Lawrence, and Holyoke became destinations for Puerto Ricans from the surrounding farms, from New York, and from the island. Many of the cities in New England have some of the highest proportions of Puerto Ricans.[101]

The transformation of the New England region's urban economy became a further obstacle for Puerto Ricans. It was the manufacturing sectors in these cities that attracted Puerto Ricans in the first place. With the industrial transformation, many Puerto Ricans eventually found themselves in lower-end jobs. According to the 2000 Census, Puerto Ricans in New England are overrepresented in less-skilled occupations in sectors like precision production, and as operators and laborers.

During the 1990s Latin American and Caribbean migration to New England was lower than the percentage of immigrants from Europe or Asia.[102] Dominicans were the largest immigrant group from Latin America and the Caribbean, followed by Colombians, Jamaicans, and Haitians. Mexicans were the eighth largest immigrant groups from Latin America and the Caribbean.[103] However, in 2000, Dominicans and Mexicans each represented less than half of 1 percent of the total New England population. Like Puerto Ricans, Dominicans are concentrated in the lower occupations, but have a greater percent in labor occupations. Mexicans, on the other hand, have a much larger proportion as farm laborers than all of the other ethnic groups in New England.

CENSUS STATISTICS ON ETHNIC GROUPS IN NEW ENGLAND

The United States must enumerate the population in order to properly allocate representatives of Congress' House of Representatives. The U.S. Census counts the population of the United States every ten years in order to apportion representation. The first count of the U.S. population took place in 1790. English and Welsh nationality made up the majority of the population in New England with 95 percent of the population. Those of Scottish nationality comprised 3.5 percent, and the rest were less than 1 percent.

In 1980, English ancestry made up the largest of all chosen ancestry groups in the New England region with 16.43 percent, followed by Irish with 14.33 percent. By 1990, English ancestry had moved to second place after those reporting Irish ancestry. By 2000, English ancestry placed fourth with 8.46 percent, following "Not Reported," Irish, and Italians, with 14.25 percent, 13.25 percent, and 10.85 percent, respectively.

Between 1980 and 1990, the English had the largest change with a 4.87 percent decrease from one census to the next. The largest increase during the same period occurred for those who chose French Canadian ancestry, a 3.18 percent change. The most dramatic change for any of the choices occurred for the "Not Reported" category between 1990 and 2000, a 7.38 percent increase. It is difficult to truly understand why there was such an increase in the "Not Reported" category; however, many may have found the White racial category sufficient.

European Americans were the largest of all of the ethnic and racial groups in New England. African Americans followed with 3.4 percent and Puerto Ricans were second with 2.36 percent. Aside from the combinations of smaller ethnic groups in the "Other Latino" and "Other Race" category, all groups were less than 1 percent of the New England population.

THE FRENCH IN NEW ENGLAND

According to the 2000 Census, over 10 percent of New Englanders identified their ancestry as French or French Canadian. The history of French Canadians in

New England, although recently "rediscovered," helped shape much of the character of the region. Most of the immigrants from French Canada arrived between 1840 and 1930. However, immigration by North American French to the British colonies that became the United States began with the expulsion of the French-speaking population from Nova Scotia in 1755 on the onset of the Seven Years War between England and France.[104] This first period of migration was spread throughout most of the thirteen colonies.

The contentious relationship be-

The French

Franco-Americans comprise a large part of New England's non-English population. In Maine, nearly a quarter of the population is of French origin, and the other northern New England states have significant populations as well. One group, the Acadians, are descendants of French colonists who were expelled from Canada in the mid-1700s when they refused to take a loyalty oath to the British crown. Other Acadians migrated to Louisiana, where "Acadian" became *Cajun*; today there are cultural links between the French community of northern New England and that of Louisiana, who have joined together to try to preserve Acadian culture.

tween the Anglos and Francos in North America began in the antagonism created in the historical global positioning of their respective countries. In 1604, a French colony was established on the island of St. Croix, in the Bay of Fundy, which was moved to what is now Annapolis Basin. By 1613, the British captured the settlement, and in 1763 through the Treaty of Paris, eastern North America became a British territory. In 1791, Canada was divided into Upper Canada and Lower Canada, reflecting the Anglo and French origins of the majority of the populations.[105] In 1840, the British government presented an act to unify Lower and Upper Canada. This act, although intending to give Upper Canada greater equity with Lower Canada, formed the first elements that led to the development of a French-Quebecois national identity. By 1849, the provinces were unified but the distinct national character of French Canadians in Quebec had already been formed. Additionally, border disputes between Lower Canada and the United States intensified for several decades after the American Revolution. With the Webster-Ashburton Treaty of 1842, the French agricultural lands on either side of the St. John River (between present-day Maine and New Brunswick, Canada) were divided, ending a boundary dispute between Canada and the United States. Those on the right bank became Americans, while those on the left bank became Canadians.[106]

The mass migration between 1840 and 1930 comprised nine hundred thousand French Canadian immigrants arriving into the United States, the bulk of them moving to New England. According to Claude Bélanger, the lower quality of Quebec's agricultural lands added to a large economic disparity between Quebec and New England. New England had an industrializing economy with a great need for laborers. The push from Quebec and the pull of New England influenced much of this immigration. Consequently, most French Canadians settled in textile mill towns and villages, concentrating the population in certain New England towns. For example, by 1900, Fall River, Massachusetts, had a population of 33,000 and Lowell, Massachusetts, had 24,800.[107]

French identity during this period of great immigration to New England prospered in some areas and was lost in many others. French Canadian identity was particularly maintained in towns with large French Canadian populations; conversely, French Canadians were assimilated into Anglo-American culture where they were fewer in numbers. Since the acquisition of most of North America by the British, North American French have been under pressure to assimilate into Anglo culture both in Canada and in the United States. This pressure has helped to sustain their cultural identity. Much of this identity has been maintained under the auspices of a belief in the "three pillars" (church, language, and institutions).[108]

In New England, particularly in areas where French Canadians made up a large proportion of the town's population, control of the church helped with the maintenance of their cultural ethnic identity. Many Catholic churches were formed in New England towns with French names. Between 1861 and 1900, eighty-four national French Canadian parishes were created throughout New England. Nevertheless, control over the Catholic church in New England was problematic due to the Irish control and influence. Most churches created by the French had Irish priests appointed as their clergy.[109]

In 1884 in Fall River, Massachusetts, the Flint affair, an incident named after the textile factory, sparked a challenge to the traditional Irish control of the church. The presiding priest of French origins in Fall River died. Beloved by his parishioners, he had established a cooperative relationship with the parishioners in Quebec. This had angered the controlling archdiocese of Providence. The monsignor of the Providence archdiocese appointed an Irish pastor who was trained in Quebec and spoke excellent French,[110] yet the parishioners rejected him and eventually won the appointment of a French Canadian pastor. This, of course, was not the case in other towns where French Canadians found themselves assimilating into Anglo-American culture rapidly.

Many French Canadians, during this period, lived in urban centers. According to Bélanger, French Canadians lived in ghetto-like conditions. French Canadian ascension out of their ghetto state did not occur until after World War II when the changing economy allowed for the suburbanization and further assimilation of French Canadians in New England.

JEWS IN NEW ENGLAND

Until the close of the nineteenth century, the number of Jews in New England was relatively small in comparison with other regions of the United States, namely, the metropolitan areas of New York City, Philadelphia, and Baltimore. The intolerance of Puritanism during the colonial period, and later that of the Protestant establishment, had made Jews unwelcome in the region. The one exception was Rhode Island, where Roger Williams had ensured religious freedom. Consequently, in 1658, Sephardic Jews established a congregation in Newport, and in 1763, Touro Synagogue became the first synagogue to be erected in America. In other parts of New England, Jews were less welcome. Despite a few references to Jewish names or traders during the seventeenth century, it was not until the eighteenth century that a Jew settled in the Boston area. His name was Judah Monis, and he filled the chair of Hebrew at Harvard College (1722–1764), but only after he converted to Christianity. In New Haven, Connecticut, Ezra Stiles, President of Yale College, reported the arrival of a Jewish family from Venice, Italy, whom he said, in 1772, were worshipping according to the Jewish faith. This marked the first settlers of the Jewish faith in New Haven, but no congregation emerged until about 1840 with the immigration of Bavarian Jews to the Hill district of the city.

German and Russian Jews, fleeing political upheavals in Europe during the nineteenth and early twentieth centuries, established a much larger Jewish community in different parts of New England. In Boston, for example, the immigration and settlement of German Jews in Boston's South End resulted in the establishment of the first congregation in 1843, and the first synagogue in 1852. The Russian Jews arrived in the latter part of the nineteenth century, fleeing czarist pogroms (and later the Bolshevik uprisings), and, like the Germans, settled in more urban areas like Boston and New Haven. The population grew, and many more settled in Massachusetts. By the early twentieth century, about 60,000 of an estimated 80,000 to 90,000 New England Jews lived in Massachusetts, and today, according to U.S. Census figures published in 2001, there are 275,000 Jewish residents. The second largest Jewish population in early twentieth-century New England was in Connecticut, where an estimated 5,500 were living in New Haven, and about 2,000 in Hartford. In other parts of the state, namely, Bridgeport, Ansonia, Derby, Waterbury, and New London, there were another estimated 1,000. Today, approximately 111,000 Jews live in Connecticut.[111] Their population was not so large in the northern states of Maine, Vermont, and New Hampshire, where they barely exceeded 2,000 souls at the beginning of the last century. According to U.S. Census figures published in 2001, however, 9,300 Jews live in Maine; 10,000 live in New Hampshire; 16,000 are in Rhode Island; and 5,500 reside in Vermont. In particular, there are now thriving Jewish communities in Portland and Lewiston-Auburn, Maine, as well as in Burlington and Stowe, Vermont; and in Portsmouth, Manchester, and Nashua, New Hampshire.

THE PORTUGUESE IN NEW ENGLAND

Another important non-English ethnic group that has emerged in the region in the last two hundred years is the Portuguese. Their communities are particularly prominent in southern New England, namely in New Bedford, Massachusetts, nearby Fall River, and the island of Martha's Vineyard. The first Portuguese were whalers who came to the region because it was a center of the industry. Today the community still thrives in these areas, as is evident from the continued use of the Portuguese language and cultural activities, often centered around the church. It should be remembered, however, that when one speaks of the "Portuguese community," often one is speaking about people from Madeira or the Cape Verde islands; thus, the community may be Portuguese speaking, but the culture also contains important African elements.

A recent study of the Portuguese community, the first in twenty-five years, found that Portuguese Americans continue to be concentrated in the working class. After the decline of whaling, the Portuguese went into fishing and factory work, such as textiles and the New England shoe industry. With fishing and the shoe industry both in serious trouble, the community recognizes the need to develop a larger middle-class base and raise its college education rates, but gains have been slow. As happens in any immigrant population, the desire to maintain community cohesiveness and traditions has come into conflict with the desire to advance economically and socially, which pushes immigrants toward assimilation.

Today, those of Portuguese descent account for nearly 3 percent of New England's total population, comprising the largest concentration of Portuguese im-

A group of Portuguese in the hold of a Menhaden Fishery steamer fill the hoisting tubs. Courtesy NOAA National Marine Fisheries Service.

migrants in the United States. Massachusetts ranks seventh in the nation in terms of the size of its immigrant population; in the last thirty years of the twentieth century, about 14 percent of new immigrants to the state were from Portugal, the Azores, Cape Verde, and Brazil. The strength of the Massachusetts economy, combined with its already long-established Portuguese communities, make it a magnet for new immigration. Massachusetts and Rhode Island, respectively, have the region's largest Portuguese population. Developments in the Brazilian community are particularly interesting. There are as many as two hundred thousand Brazilians, many if not most undocumented, living in Massachusetts. A mini-migration is now taking place within the state, with more and more Brazilians moving from the Boston area to more affordable Fall River and the south coast, where many of them work in the manufacturing and service sectors. Economic upheaval in Brazil has also meant that many professionals have immigrated to New England, adding to the social-economic makeup of the Portuguese community.

ASIAN IMMIGRANTS TO NEW ENGLAND

More recently, there have been migrations from Asia. The entire United States has seen a huge growth in Asian population—three times the rate of that of the U.S. population as a whole. But because 96 percent of Asian and Pacific Islanders live in metropolitan areas, New England has not been a major destination as New

Table 1. U.S. Census ancestry classification in New
England, 1980–2000 (by percent)

Reported Ancestry	1980	1990	2000
Not reported	7.76	6.87	14.25
Irish	14.33	15.18	13.25
Italian	10.40	10.96	10.85
English	16.43	11.55	8.46
French	10.98	8.48	6.02
French Canadian	1.81	4.99	4.58
American	3.95	2.95	4.44
German	4.71	6.72	4.17
Polish	4.35	4.23	3.74
Portuguese	2.20	2.72	2.63
African	n/a	n/a	2.33
Puerto Rican	0.97	1.51	2.21
Scottish	2.83	2.14	1.77
Scotch Irish	n/a	1.34	1.21
Swedish	1.57	1.38	1.12
Russian	1.46	1.36	1.11
Greek	0.78	0.93	0.81
Chinese	0.24	0.51	0.66
Other	0.48	0.63	0.66
Dominican	0.03	0.30	0.61
Canadian	0.66	0.59	0.50
European	0.05	0.12	0.47
Indian	n/a	0.21	0.46
Lithuanian	0.70	0.61	0.46
Dutch	0.55	0.56	0.43
Cape Verde	0.15	0.27	0.41
Haitian	0.05	0.27	0.41
Norwegian	0.31	0.32	0.40
British	0.07	0.40	0.38
Jamaican	0.16	0.22	0.38
Spanish	0.47	0.41	0.37
White	0.21	0.43	0.35
Uncodeable	n/a	0.47	0.35
Hungarian	0.46	0.40	0.34
Hispanic	0.07	0.18	0.34
Vietnamese	0.05	0.15	0.31
American Indian	0.53	0.70	0.31
Brazilian	n/a	0.08	0.30
Lebanese	0.22	0.28	0.29
Ukrainian	0.31	0.27	0.28
Finnish	0.29	0.30	0.27
Mixture	0.07	0.19	0.27
Black	n/a	n/a	0.26
Mexican	0.05	0.15	0.26
Colombian	0.07	0.14	0.26
Armenian	0.27	0.28	0.25
Cambodian	n/a	0.13	0.24
Korean	0.09	0.17	0.23

Table 1. (continued)

Reported Ancestry	1980	1990	2000
Welsh	0.22	0.29	0.22
Eastern	0.06	0.07	0.21
African	0.07	n/a	0.20
Danish	0.26	0.24	0.18
Filipino	0.06	0.12	0.17
Japanese	0.07	0.11	0.17
Native American	n/a	n/a	0.17
Guatemalan	n/a	0.07	0.17
Indian	n/a	n/a	0.16
Slovak	0.23	0.37	0.16
Salvadoran	n/a	0.07	0.16
Austrian	0.26	0.23	0.15
Czech	n/a	0.11	0.13
Ecuadorian	n/a	0.04	0.12
Swiss	0.14	0.16	0.11
Albanian	0.07	0.09	0.10
Cuban	0.07	0.08	0.10
Anglo	n/a	n/a	0.10
Peruvian	n/a	0.06	0.09
United States	0.09	0.19	0.08
Afro American	2.96	2.92	0.08
Romanian	0.07	0.09	0.08
West Indian	0.10	0.09	0.08
Syrian	0.07	0.08	0.08
Laotian	n/a	0.07	0.08
Scandinavian	0.06	0.09	0.07
Czech	0.26	0.08	0.07
Northern	n/a	n/a	0.07
Nigerian	n/a	n/a	0.07
Central	n/a	0.07	n/a
Belgian	0.06	0.06	n/a
Spaniard	n/a	0.06	n/a
Latvian	0.06	0.05	n/a
Taiwanese	n/a	0.04	n/a
Croatian	n/a	0.04	n/a
Israeli	0.03	0.03	n/a
Iranian	0.04	0.03	n/a
Spanish American	0.05	n/a	n/a
Yugoslavian	0.04	n/a	n/a
Slavic	0.03	n/a	n/a

Source: U.S. Census, 1980, 1990, 2000.

York and California have been. This ethnic community is solidly middle class. It has the highest median income of any racial group according to the 2000 Census, as well as the highest proportion of college graduates. Urban centers like Boston, New Haven, and Hartford not surprisingly have significant Asian populations. The Chinatown neighborhood of Boston, however, the largest city in New

England, does not rank in the top ten in statistics for Chinatowns across the nation.

Asian immigration into New England increased after 1975 and at the end of the Vietnam War. Boston has a significant Vietnamese population, in addition to Chinese, Filipino, and Indian communities. The city's large number of universities attracts thousands of Asian students, some of whom stay in the area, particularly because it is a financial and high technology center. Because the Boston suburban area has spread to southern New Hampshire and Maine, Asians have begun to move into those states as well. The number of Asians in New Hampshire, for example, nearly doubled between 1990 and 2000.

Asian success has, unfortunately, not always found acceptance. The Asian population is the fastest growing in Massachusetts, and has sometimes encountered hostility; a study financed by the Ford Foundation found that Asians had a 41 percent chance of being subject to job discrimination. In a 2003 incident, an Indian student at the University of Massachusetts–Dartmouth was the victim of a hate crime. The student was reported to have been mistaken for an Iraqi and brutalized and stabbed. Thus Asians face multiple challenges, from jealousy of their economic success to ignorance and violence.

CONCLUSION

This chapter provides a simple overview of the ethnic make-up of the New England states. Many groups have not been included due to the space allotted to this endeavor. Nevertheless, while traveling or living in the region, it is impossible to deny the contributions that all ethnic groups have made in various New England cities, towns, and villages. Considering names of cities, towns, rivers, and parks, as well as listening to the radio and looking for places to eat, we recognize that ethnic influence has been an important part of the diversity that New England has to offer, which could explain why so many ethnic and racial groups have found it appealing to move and settle in the region. Whether it is for economic or educational opportunities, or just simply for a change of scenery, New England continues to become, although slowly, one of the most diverse regions in the United States.

RESOURCE GUIDE

Printed Sources

Axtell, James. *Native and Newcomers: The Cultural Origins of North America*. New York: Oxford University Press, 2001.

Chartier, Armand. *The Franco-Americans of New England: A History*. Trans. Robert J. Lemieux and Claire Quintal. Worcester, MA: ACA Assurance; Institut Français of Assumption College, 2000.

Cressy, David. *Coming Over: Migration and Communication Between England and New England in the Seventeenth Century*. New York: Cambridge University Press, 1987.

DeJohn Anderson, Virginia. *New England's Generation: The Great Migration and the Formation of Society and Culture in the Seventeenth Century*. New York: Cambridge University Press, 1991.

Duany, Jorge. *The Puerto Rican Nation on the Move: Identities on the Island and in the United States*. Chapel Hill: University of North Carolina Press, 2002.

Glasser, Ruth. *Aquí me quedo: Puerto Ricans in Connecticut.* Hartford: Connecticut Humanities Council, 1997.

Johnston Greene, Lorenzo. *The Negro in Colonial New England.* New York: Atheneum, 1968.

Jordan, Winthrop D. *White over Black: American Attitudes Toward the Negro, 1550–1812.* New York: W.W. Norton, 1977.

Mandell, Daniel R. *Behind the Frontier: Indians in Eighteenth-Century Eastern Massachusetts.* Lincoln: University of Nebraska Press, 1996.

Pedraza, Susan, and Ruben G. Rumbaut, eds. *Origins and Destinies: Immigration, Race, and Ethnicity in America.* Albany: Wadsworth Publishing Group, 1996.

Pritzker, Barry M. *Native Americans: An Encyclopedia of History, Culture, and Peoples.* Volume 2. Santa Barbara, CA: ABC-CLIO, 1998.

Vaughan, Alden T. *New England Frontier: Puritans and Indians 1620–1675.* Norman: University of Oklahoma Press, 1995.

Web Sites

Black Americans in New England Reunion Online. 2003.
Reunion Publishing Group. February 12, 2004.
http://www.blacknewengland.net/

African American history and culture around New England.

Boston Irish Online. 2003.
Boston Irish Online. January 16, 2004.
http://www.bostonirishonline.com/

Boston Irish businesses and culture.

Integrated Public Use Microdata Series: Version 3.0. 2003.
S. Ruggles, M. Sobek, et al. Minneapolis: Historical Census Projects, University of Minnesota. February 12, 2004.
http://www.ipums.org

National census database spanning from 1850 to 2000.

The Irish Heritage Trail. 2004.
Boston Irish Tourism Association. January 16, 2004.
http://www.irishheritagetrail.com/

Three-mile walking trail through Boston and its Irish past.

Maine's French Communities. 2004.
Franco-American Center at the University of Maine and
Department of Geography of Laval University. January 25, 2004.
http://www.francomaine.org/index.htm

French culture and history in Maine.

Rhodeirish.net. 2004.
John Harvey. January 16, 2004.
http://www.rhodeirish.net/

Rhode Island's Irish community.

17th Century New England. February 28, 2004.
Margo Burns. March 1, 2004.
http://www.17thc.us/

Resource for seventeenth-century New England, including Native Americans.

University of Virginia Geospatial and Statistical Data Center. 2003.

United States Historical Census Data Browser, University of Virginia. January 16, 2004.
http://fisher.lib.virginia.edu/census/

National population and economy database spanning from 1790 to 1960.

Videos/Films

Captains Courageous. Dir. Victor Fleming. Perf. Freddie Bartholomew, Spencer Tracy, Lionel Barrymore, Melvyn Douglas, Charley Grapewin, Mickey Rooney. MGM, 1937.

The Inkwell. Dir. Matty Rich. Perf. Larenz Tate, Joe Morton, Suzzanne Douglas, Glynn Turman, Vanessa Bell-Calloway, Adrienne-Joi Johnson. Touchstone, 1994.

The Last Hurrah. Dir. John Ford. Perf. Spencer Tracy, Jeffrey Hunter, Dianne Foster, Pat O'Brien, Basil Rathbone, Donald Crisp. Columbia, 1958.

Little Women. Dir. Gillian Armstrong. Perf. Winona Ryder, Susan Sarandon, Gabriel Byrne, Eric Stoltz, Samantha Mathis, Trini Alvarado. Columbia, 1994; remake of the 1933 and 1949 productions.

Mermaids. Dir. Richard Benjamin. Perf. Cher, Bob Hoskins, Winona Ryder, Michael Schoeffling, Christina Ricci, Caroline McWilliams. Nicita-Lloyd-Palmer, 1990.

The Scarlet Letter. Dir. Roland Joffe. Perf. Demi Moore, Gary Oldman, Robert Duvall, Lisa Jolliff-Andoh, Edward Hardwicke, Robert Prosky. Hollywood Pictures, 1995; remake of the 1926 and 1934 productions.

Where the Rivers Flow North. Dir. Jay Craven. Perf. Rip Torn, Tantoo Cardinal, Bill Raymond, Michael J. Fox, Treat Williams, Amy Wright. Caledonia Pictures, 1992.

Museums

The Amistad Foundation
600 Main Street
Hartford, CT 06103
http://www.theamistadfoundation.org/

Housed at the Wadsworth Atheneum Museum of Art, the Amistad Foundation holds a large collection of art, photographs, and artifacts depicting the African American experience in the region.

The Mashantucket and Pequot Museum and Research Center
110 Pequot Trail
P.O. Box 3180
Mashantucket, CT 06338
http://www.pequotmuseum.org/

This museum holds one of the world's largest collections of Native American artifacts and information, not just from the region, but from the United States and Canada as well.

Plimoth Plantation
137 Warren Avenue
Plymouth, MA 02360
http://www.plimoth.org

This museum, located in Plymouth, Massachusetts, allows its visitors to experience a day in the life of 1627. Included in the museum is a historical account of Thanksgiving from its first celebration to our present day.

Organizations and Festivals

American Jewish Historical Society
160 Herrick Road
Newton Centre, MA 02459
http://www.ajhs.org/

Belgian American Society of New England
P.O. Box 382
Lexington, MA 02420
http://www.bas-ne.org/welcome/main/welcome.asp

Federation of Hellenic-American Societies of New England
P.O. Box 525
Accord, MA 02018
http://www.fhasne.com/

Franco-American Centre
52 Concord Street
Manchester NH 03101
http://www.francoamericancentrenh.com/

Hispanic American Chamber of Commerce of Massachusetts
67 Broad Street
Boston, MA 02109
http://www.hacc.com/

Hispanic American Chamber of Commerce of Rhode Island
45 Royal Little Drive
Providence, RI 02904
http://www.haccri.org/

Hungarian American Chamber of Commerce of New England
111 Huntington Avenue
26th Floor
Boston, MA 02199
http://www.hungarianamericanchamber.com/

Latino Professional Network
P.O. Box 6019
Boston, MA 02209
http://www.lpn.org/content/sponsors/sponsors.cfm

Rhode Island Scottish Highland Festival and Scottish Heritage Society
Washington County Fair Ground, RI
http://www.riscot.org/

Sri Lanka Association of New England
P.O. Box 442
North Chelmsford, MA 01863
http://www.slaneusa.com/

Turkish-American Cultural Society of New England, Inc.
P.O. Box 230162
Boston, MA 02123-0162
http://www.tacsne.org/

FASHION

Linda Welters

Fashion is defined as the prevailing style accepted by large numbers of people at any given time. When applied to regional culture, fashion gains an added dimension—it becomes associated with a place. The way in which clothing and personal appearance reflect regional culture is an especially challenging notion to investigate in today's global society.

Five principles help determine how certain styles or looks come to represent a place. Such principles have generated regional styles in the past and, to a limited extent, the present. One or more of the principles may operate at any given time. First, locally available materials may be used in making articles of clothing. This is particularly true of communities with limited access to raw materials from outside the region, such as New England's Native Americans prior to contact with Europeans. Second, specific styles may emerge from the collective physical and social needs of a region's inhabitants. For example, the substantial snowfalls in northern New England demand functional outerwear that would be out of place in warmer sections of the country. Third, a unique regional or local word may be used to name an item of dress. Subcultures are especially prone to naming items of apparel or certain looks. Fourth, an individual may choose to dress in a particular manner that expresses identity with a community. Sports fans who wear caps, sweatshirts, or T-shirts bearing the logos of their regional teams provide a common example. Last, through memory and representation, regional dress may symbolize a place both in and out of the region. For example, imagined versions of New England's Pilgrims appear every November in commemoration of the first Thanksgiving at Plymouth, Massachusetts. Throughout this chapter, these principles will be exemplified.

This chapter examines dress and appearance in New England culture from both a topical and a historical perspective. The context is somewhat broader than "fashion," which by definition is temporal. In the past, some styles worn in New England were more akin to traditional dress, for instance, the dress of Native

Americans or the garb of utopian religious communities such as the Shakers. Such styles changed slowly, more often responding to changes in materials than new styles. In today's world, fashion changes rapidly. Some industry observers, such as *Wall Street Journal* reporter Teri Agins, have speculated that fashion no longer exists in a market where trends come and go within a single season among selected demographic groups.[1] Yet new styles continue to be accepted. Many Americans recognize that fashion varies regionally. Seasoned travelers see that styles acceptable in Boston differ from those worn in New York, Chicago, or Los Angeles. Let us examine the geographic and climatic factors that have influenced fashion in New England.

GEOGRAPHY

Geography has been, and continues to be, a critical influence on fashion in New England. Historically, the lay of the land determined settlement patterns, which in turn affected both the availability and popularity of fashionable goods in each community. The geography of New England varies considerably. Five of its six states—Maine, New Hampshire, Massachusetts, Rhode Island, and Connecticut—have at least some coastal access. The sixth state, Vermont, is accessible via inland waterways, specifically the Connecticut River and Lake Champlain. Historically, proximity to oceans, rivers, and lakes allowed ships to bring the latest fashionable goods from abroad to port cities.

Boston has been the center of the entire region since the seventeenth century. The city even goes by the nickname "the hub." From Boston's docks, newly arrived goods made their way to the hinterlands through a network of tradesmen and shopkeepers. Other port towns on the coast that developed into important commercial centers in the colonial period include Portland, Maine; Portsmouth and Dover, New Hampshire; Salem, Massachusetts; Newport and Providence, Rhode Island; and New Haven, Connecticut. The Connecticut River, New England's longest river, offered a navigable waterway to the interior. Beginning in Canada, the river flows between the Green Mountains and White Mountains, forming the boundary between Vermont and New Hampshire. It winds through Massachusetts into Connecticut, emptying into Long Island Sound near Old Saybrook. Many of the region's early settlements began along the "Great River" in the colonial period including Hartford, Windsor, Springfield, Northampton, Hadley, Deerfield, and Fort Dummer (Brattleboro). It was via the river that fashionable goods made their way from Dutch, French, and English ships to these "frontier" communities.

"Frontier" is a concept that Americans typically associate with prairies and mountains in the Midwestern and Rocky Mountain states. But at one time much of New England was sparsely settled. The dense forests and thick undergrowth of the southern New England colonies made for challenging travel in the early years before land was cleared. By the mid-eighteenth century, the Post Road, which runs along the coastline, became the major turnpike from Boston to New York. The northern New England states remained frontier areas well into the nineteenth century because of their rough topography. Vermont and the inland areas of New Hampshire and Maine were settled much later than Massachusetts, Connecticut, and Rhode Island. Geographical isolation encourages regionalism in dress.

Geography also influences fashion through the establishment and diffusion of regional trends. A fashion cycle operates in a predictable manner. A few style leaders begin to wear a new style; other fashion-forward people in contact with the leaders soon adopt the look. As more people see the fashion on others, they start wearing it too. Eventually, when the majority appears in a particular style, the leaders abandon it and move on to something new. By the end of a style's life cycle, no one buys it anymore, although a few fashion laggards may continue to wear it. A critical mass of people must exist for a trend to start in a particular place. Thus, it is not surprising that styles start in major cities. People who live in smaller outlying towns look to city dwellers as arbiters of style. In colonial New England, Boston set the trends because the city's merchants offered the latest goods from London. Often the new styles were seen first in church, where the young rapidly adapted them. Older people retained their more conservative styles. In more recent years, resort areas for the rich and famous served as birthplaces of certain looks. Rural areas are acknowledged to be less fashion forward, both in the past and in the present.

CLIMATE

Climate is another critical influence on regional styles. New England's first settlers, who mostly came from the midlands of England, encountered hotter summers and colder winters than they were accustomed to in the Old World. New England's reputation for long, cold winters is well deserved, especially in areas away from the coast, which is more temperate than inland zones. The northern states receive snowfalls averaging more than sixty inches per year. Near-zero temperatures occur nearly every winter. How did people survive in drafty post-and-beam buildings heated by fireplaces or wood stoves before the days of down-filled jackets and Polartec fleece?

Diaries and letters offer some clues. Anne Jean Lyman of Milton, Massachusetts, recalled that "we wore our great coats in the house half the time."[3] Diarists noted the day in spring when the warmer weather allowed them to switch to lightweight

Town and Country

In 1752, fifteen-year-old Joseph Gilman moved from Exeter, New Hampshire, to Boston to begin an apprenticeship with a merchant. He soon found that his country clothes did not meet city standards. Owning enough clean clothes in good condition was just one issue that concerned him; the other was the quality of the materials and the workmanship. Over the next few years, Gilman wrote to his widowed mother on numerous occasions asking for additional stockings, shirts, and outerwear. Stockings featured repeatedly in his requests. He complained that he was "forced to go with holes In my Stockings very often" and that his "feet Sweat so that when I have Wore a Pair of Stockings three or four days they are Stiff that I can Scarce Weare them." Clean shirts were also important: "one of my shirts I have worn for a week and tried to Keep clean as far as it Lay in my power." Additionally, he specified the materials to be used for his shirts. Instead of country-style checked fabric, he requested that his mother send seven white shirts made with "bag Holland sleeves." "Holland" was a fine linen cloth originally imported from the Netherlands. Such fine linen sleeves would have been visible from under his waistcoat while the rest of the shirt remained covered. Joseph's requests extended to breeches, coats, and shoes, revealing a marked difference between clothes made in town by professionals and those made in the country by amateurs. He asked for a "handsome" pair of black breeches and a broadcloth jacket made by a professional tailor. Sounding like any teenager, he warned his mother not to send his "homespun Cloth coulerd jacket if you do I shall not wear it." He also griped about the Exeter-made shoes his mother sent him: "I scarce Ever saw a Worse pair...than the Last you sent me." In eighteenth-century New England, people walked a fine line between dressing well and being considered vain. Joseph Gilman's requests were tempered with claims that he was not being prideful; he just wanted to "dress neat and Clean but not fine."[2]

stockings or to take off the flannel underwear. From these comments we learn that before the advent of central heating, people wore multiple layers of clothing for warmth from October to April. Wool was the fiber of choice. Women kept warm with wool petticoats, some of which were quilted. Men wore woolen coats or jackets over waistcoats. Both genders donned hooded cloaks or great coats of heavy, thick wool to journey out of doors or to keep warm inside the house on especially frigid days. Stockings, mittens, and caps, also of wool, covered the extremities.

Museum collections of historic costumes provide other clues. Numerous full-length cloaks with deep collars or hoods survive in the region's historical societies and museums. A seventeenth-century version in wool camlet that belonged to Richard Smith (1630–1690) exists at the Rhode Island Historical Society. Cloaks were sometimes called "cardinals" or "riding hoods." Often these cloaks were scarlet colored. The best ones were made from English broadcloth that had been heavily fulled, giving it a felt-like texture. If one could not afford English broadcloth, homespun could substitute. These long-wearing, water-resistant cloaks found favor with both men and women well into the nineteenth century. Sarah Bryant of Cummington, Massachusetts, made a scarlet cloak in 1797 that she used until 1825. Reverend Edward Holyoke, president of Harvard University from 1737 to 1769, had a crimson cloak that also was worn by Judge Blaney and Dr. Edward Augustus Holyoke of Salem before finding its way into the Essex Institute in Salem, Massachusetts, where it is preserved today.

Drenching rains also posed a problem for New Englanders. Early waterproofing methods included a variety of unappealing techniques to render cloth impervious to water, namely brushing tar, paraffin, or liquefied rubber on shoes, jackets, coats and hats. In the nineteenth century, commercially produced rubber products became available.

The real weather-related challenge was keeping feet dry in rainy or snowy weather. Museum collections throughout New England preserve many pairs of eighteenth-century shoes in brocade or satin, often imported from London. These shoes generally were saved because of their association with a sentimental or historic event—a wedding, a ball, or a visit from a revered statesman—rather than for everyday wear. The vast majority of men, women, and children wore plain brown leather or cloth shoes with buckled straps. Occasionally such shoes are found in walls or chimneys of antique houses, placed there by builders for good luck. Made in a simple, little-changing style with leather soles and leather or cloth uppers, these shoes quickly became wet in snow or rain. Leather shoes stiffened while drying in front of a fire, rendering them uncomfortable to wear.

New Englanders wore protective pattens or clogs over their shoes in inclement weather. Pattens had thick leather or wooden soles with leather straps; the soles were attached to iron rings that raised the foot above the ground. Pattens were noisy on paved streets, and in wet weather, the rings sank into the mud. Clogs were wooden-soled overshoes secured to the foot by a leather strap over the instep. A hinged sole made it easier to walk. They were used in rain, in snow, and on board ship.

New Englanders used other strategies to protect their footwear in bad weather and to prevent slipping and falling. One young woman attending a winter "assembly" in Portland, Maine, in 1802 pulled woolen stockings over her dancing shoes to protect them and to keep her feet warm in the carriage. Gentlemen friends carried her into and out of the assembly hall. Martha Ballard, a midwife in Hallowell, Maine, who crossed the Kennebec River and cut through snowdrifts to deliver babies, upon occasion walked in her stocking feet to prevent soaking her shoes.[4] Men also carried Martha over snowdrifts when her horse had difficulty negotiating the path. How the men's footwear fared in both these situations is not known.

The nineteenth century brought welcome changes to protective footwear. Rubber shoes were imported to Boston from Brazil as early as 1823. Within a decade, Boston companies began working with natural rubber, manufacturing rubberized fabrics as well as footwear. However, New England's extreme weather conditions caused the rubber to get sticky and smelly in the summer and brittle and cracked in the winter. In 1839, Charles Goodyear discovered that treating rubber with sulfur cured its defects, thus ushering in the vulcanization process that gave rise to the lucrative rubber industry. Shoes dominated the industry until the invention of the automobile. Rubber also was a component in elastic webbing used as inserts in boots.

> ### Shag Mittens
>
> Keeping hands warm posed challenges during the winter. Fur muffs provided a fashionable alternative for those with ample financial resources. Knitted mittens and gloves kept many a person from having cold fingers. In northern New England, a distinctive style of hand wear developed known as "shag" mittens and gloves. In the seventeenth and eighteenth centuries, the term *shag* referred to wool or silk cloth with a long nap. Shag mittens and gloves were hand knitted with pile loops on the outer surface. The loops could be cut or left uncut. Sometimes patterns were created by using different colored yarns.
>
> Surviving examples from the nineteenth century display colorful patterns. The Maine State Museum owns a pair of red, gold, brown, and black shag mittens that resemble gauntlets. Eliza Hunnewell Dean (1826–1855) made and wore them. The Farrar-Mansur House in Weston, Vermont, has a pair of shag gloves in white with red flowers made by Lois (Walker) Mansur (1809–1886) for her son Frank Mansur as a twenty-first birthday present. Today some older northern New Englanders can remember wearing shag mittens as children.
>
> Shag mittens are an example of a regional style that developed out of a physical need. The care with which women designed and made them produced a functional accessory that bordered on folk art.

A REPUTATION FOR CONSERVATIVE DRESS

New England has long held a reputation for conservative dress. To many Americans, the phrase "New England fashion" is an oxymoron. This reputation is well deserved, going back to the seventeenth century when the first English settlers put their stamp on New England style.

The somber colors and pared-down clothes of the Puritans had their roots in religious doctrine. The Puritans were members of a reform movement within the Church of England. Their aim was to "purify" religious practices, removing what they believed to be excesses. This austere view of religious expression extended to everyday life, including dress. The Puritans preferred plain fabrics and simple styles devoid of ornamentation. The church elders railed against excessive display, to the point where they attempted to regulate dress through legislation. Although the Puritans splintered off into a number of religious groups by the middle of the eighteenth century, their belief in simplicity in dress lived on in the region.

Even during the excesses of the second half of the nineteenth century, Boston's cultural elite practiced sartorial conservatism. The city's wealthy families, the so-called Brahmins, shopped in Paris at the leading couture houses. However, they were rumored to have sometimes left their French dresses in the boxes for a year before wearing them lest they appear too ostentatious. Boston women scoffed at the outrageous styles worn on Broadway in New York City, describing fashion-conscious New York women as "vulgar." On July 25, 1868, Bostonian Mary Putnam, who had moved to New York after her marriage, wrote to her sister Sarah: "I have never seen the dressing in Broadway so bad as it is this fall. You see girls with light hair all frizzed up like wool, with long fuzzy curls hanging down behind, eyes painted, complexions painted, and chalked, and tremendous bustles, hundred flying ends, high pinching boots, Grecian bend and nothing to do. Men turn and look at them and laugh and make comments that the woman herself may hear."[5]

In the twentieth century, New Englanders solidified their reputation for practical, functional clothes. Simple, classic styles held sway. The only fashions that have an association with New England are the Ivy League looks of the 1950s and the Preppy looks of the 1980s. To this day, New Englanders avoid extremes in fashion. In the national eye, New England is better known as the home of L.L.Bean than a hotbed of fashion-forward trendsetters. To see how this conservatism evolved over time, we will look at the historical development of New England fashion.

NATIVE AMERICANS

For several thousand years prior to the arrival of the Pilgrims in 1620, Native Americans inhabited the region that became New England. By the late Woodland period, New England's tribal groups had organized themselves into numerous cultural and political entities. These included the Pokanoket, Massachusett, Narragansett, Niantic, Pawtucket, and Pequot-Mohegans in southern New England; the Abenaki in Vermont, New Hampshire, and Maine; and the Mahican in western Massachusetts and Vermont. Dress varied among tribes to signal affinity with a particular tribe.

Before English settlement of the colonies, tribes along the eastern seaboard exchanged furs with European traders for a wide range of goods including cloth and ready-made clothing. In 1602, near the Elizabeth Islands off Cape Cod, a Native American came out to Bartholomew Gosnold's ship dressed in a black waistcoat and breeches cut like those of English sailors, complete with hose and shoes. Establishment of the Plymouth and Massachusetts Bay colonies accelerated the pace of such encounters. Native Americans acquired English-style clothes through trade, which they wore when negotiating with European explorers, traders, and settlers. They found tailored coats rather restrictive and reportedly took them off as soon as they were out of sight of the English. When in their own company, they wore garments made from deerskins and furs. They dressed their black hair in ways that Europeans found fascinating, sometimes donning crowns of bird feathers. Natives abhorred facial hair, pulling out any hairs as soon as they appeared. They also painted their faces in various colors, tattooed their skin, and decorated themselves with ornaments.

One of the most valuable forms of native ornamentation was "wampum," cylindrical beads made from seashells found along the coast of southern New England. White beads came from the shells of whelks, while blue-purple beads came from hard-shelled clams known as quahogs. Wampum was produced in areas with abundant whelk and quahog shells, specifically along the coast of Connecticut and Rhode Island. Bead blanks were roughed out, drilled, then ground into their final tubular shape. Beads were threaded onto strings of Indian hemp to be worn as necklaces, or made into multistrand assemblages for use as belts, headbands, and bandoliers. Men drilled the beads, while women worked them into wide bands using rigid looms. In precontact times, wampum was used as currency as far north as Nova Scotia. When Europeans introduced metal drills, wampum production increased, as did its importance as a medium of exchange. High-ranking tribal members—the chiefs and important young men and women—began wearing wampum belts, headbands, necklaces, and links to hang on their ears. The archaeological record reveals that the tribes of southern New England buried their dead, particularly young children, with wampum jewelry.

As the supply of furs and skins declined, the New England Indians began incorporating European cloth into their traditional attire. Coarse wool cloth imported from England replaced skins for breechcloths and mantles. From 1620 to 1676, the time of King Philip's War, documentary sources mention that Indians acquired coats (especially red ones), shirts, gold and silver laces, and woolen mantles through gift or exchange. Native Americans adapted these European goods as they saw fit. The sagamore Quanopin, for example, wore a Holland shirt with "laces" (trim) trailing off the hem.

Dress varied among tribes to signal affinity with a particular tribe. Pictured here is a woman in traditional Pequot dress. Photo by Nancy Walker.

European Americans found native attire to be "uncivilized." Their reasons varied. First, native garments were not tailored, as were English clothes. Second, the shoulder mantles and breech cloths revealed too much of the body, thus making the wearer "indecent." Third, although the English attired themselves in beaver hats and fur-trimmed coats, unfinished skins and furs were judged to be the robes of "savages." Most importantly, native dress signified to the English that the natives were not Christians. Attempts to convert natives to Christianity included coercing them to wear European-style clothing and cutting their long hair. The natives in the so-called praying towns of Massachusetts abandoned their native attire relatively early and wore "suits of clothes," although a few ethnic markers remained in the manner in which they dressed their hair. Eventually, the small number of natives who lived on reservations and in towns succumbed to European-style clothing. Eventually in the twentieth century, pride in Native American heritage brought

John Josselyn, Colonial Traveler

John Josselyn visited the province of Maine on two occasions, once from 1638 to 1639, and again from 1663 to 1671. He reported on the attire of Native Americans that he encountered, most probably the Abenaki.

Their Apparel before the *English* came amongst them, was the skins of wild Beasts with the hair on, Buskins of *Deers*-skin or *Moose* drest and drawn with lines into several works, the lines being coloured with yellow, blew or red. Pumps [footwear] too they have, made of tough skins without soles. In the winter when the snow will bear them, they fasten to their feet their snow shooes which are made like a large Racket we play at *Tennis* with, lacing them with *Deers*-guts and the like, under their belly they wear a square piece of leather and the like upon their posteriors, both fastened to a string tyed about them to hide their secrets; on their heads they ware nothing: But since they have had to do with the English, they purchase of them a sort of Cloth called trading cloth of which they make Mantles, Coats with short sleeves, and caps for their heads which the women use, but the men continue their old fashion going bare-headed, excepting some old men amongst them. They are very proud as appeareth by their setting themselves out with white and blew Beads of their own making, and painting of their faces with the above mentioned colours, they weave sometimes curious Coats with *Turkie* feathers for their Children.[6]

back the wearing of indigenous styles for ceremonial purposes. More often than not, the ceremonial outfits worn by New England tribes were based on Plains Indians' styles because so little was known about their own dress prior to the arrival of European settlers.

Despite their appraisal of Indian dress as "savage" and "uncivilized," New Englanders admired the utility of Indian footwear. Leather moccasins and leggings made from carefully tanned and oiled skins functioned well in rain and snow. Roger Williams, founder of the Rhode Island colony, observed that Indian leggings could be wrung out and dried in front of a fire with ease. Colonists also adopted the snowshoes worn by Native Americans to travel over deep snow. In the nineteenth century moccasins were much admired as indoor footwear for invalids and children.

Turkey-feather coats, wampum headbands, and deerskin garments exemplify the principle of using locally available raw materials to make clothing. The word *wampum*, a term understood by Europeans and natives alike, demonstrates the utilization of a unique regional or local word to name an item of dress.

PURITAN NEW ENGLAND

The first Europeans to settle in New England emigrated from the midlands and the southeastern part of England to escape religious persecution. Known as Puritans, their doctrines professed a firm belief in a strict social order. Every man and woman knew his or her place in society and acted accordingly. Puritan clothing reflected styles worn among the middling classes in England. Seventeenth-century attire consisted of several basic garments cut in the same general style for everyone. Fabric and ornamentation determined the difference between a lady and her servant.

In 1620 men's clothing consisted of breeches, doublets, short or long cloaks, stockings, and buckled shoes or boots. The doublet—also called a coat, jacket, or waistcoat—fastened in the front with buttons or ties. Under the doublet men wore shirts of linen or cotton. On their heads they wore high-crowned, brimmed hats or knitted stocking caps known as Monmouth caps.

Women's wardrobes began with a cotton or linen shift. No other underwear was worn. Over the shift a woman wore one or more "coats," "cotes," or "[petti]coats" similar to a modern skirt gathered to a waistband. The uppermost skirt was sometimes lifted and tucked into the waistband. Aprons were common. On the upper body a woman wore a jacket or wescoat (waist-cote), cap, or hood. Like men, women wore cloaks, stockings, and buckled shoes.

During the first half of the seventeenth century, plain white collars known as falling bands accented the jackets of both men and women. At this time sleeves were not sewn into the armscye (the armhole opening in a garment); instead they were hooked, or tied in place with "points." The practice of making repeated decorative slits in fabric—known as "slashing"—was very fashionable among the wealthy in Europe.

A Catalogue of Useful Apparel

In 1630, Francis Higginson penned a guide for his fellow countrymen considering emigration entitled *New England's Plantation, A Catalogue of such needful things as every planter doth or ought to provide to go to New-England*. He included a list of supplies to bring from England because "here are neither markets nor faires to buy what you want." For apparel, he listed:

1 Monmouth cap
3 falling bands
3 shirts
1 waistcoat
1 suit of canvass
1 suit of frieze
1 suit of cloth
3 pair of stockings
4 pair of shoes[7]

During the second half of the century, fashions changed. From the Near East came the three-piece man's suit. Adopted quickly in England, it consisted of breeches, a long waistcoat, and an outer coat with large buttons down the front and on the cuffs and pockets. Cravats that tied around the neck replaced the old square collars. Women's fashionable dress also changed to the mantua, a full-length gown that opened in the front to reveal a petticoat of the same or contrasting fabric. A triangular piece known as a stomacher covered the gap at the front of the bodice. First seen in the courts of France, this new silhouette had an elongated bodice that required stiff stays called a "pair of bodies."

In England, the highest level of society had their best suits of clothes made from silks, fine linens, and woolens. They trimmed their clothes with costly braids of precious metals and added lace to collars, cuffs, and caps. Clothing from the seventeenth century is extremely rare, but extant examples show how luxurious fashionable clothes could be. Museum collections contain suits, cloaks, and gowns of slashed silks and fine wools embroidered in silver and gold and trimmed in ribbons and lace.

New Englanders of "gentle" status followed English fashions, eagerly awaiting news of the latest styles seen in London. Surviving artifacts show that the well to do followed English fashion closely. When Penelope Pelham Winslow married in London in 1651, she wore silk mules trimmed with gold braid that she brought back with her to Plymouth Colony. A stomacher of the 1690s worn in Massachusetts by Margaret Halcie Armstrong, niece of Sir William Phippsall, is embroidered with gold and silver thread in a manner typical of English work.

Only high-ranking members of New England society could afford such fancy goods. More common among the yeoman, husbandmen, merchants, innkeepers, goodmen, and goodwives were undecorated wools and linens. Puritan beliefs discouraged excess interest in fashion. Nevertheless, those in lower ranks, particularly servants, aspired to look their best, sometimes too closely approximating the appearance of their masters.

Pilgrims and Witches

Two of the most recognizable costumed images in America had their genesis in seventeenth-century New England history. The first is the Pilgrim, whose familiar figure appears every Thanksgiving season along with the turkey. Thanksgiving is a New England tradition that commemorates the first harvest at Plymouth, Massachusetts, in 1621. Celebrated only intermittently at first, it became an annual event by 1676. Each of New England's governors proclaimed a Thursday in late November or early December as a day of thanksgiving. This was not always the same day in each colony. Originally the main event had been a sermon at the meetinghouse, but gradually it became a traditional holiday when families assembled over a harvest meal. The menu included chicken or turkey and a variety of pies. Preparations often included making new clothes. In 1834 the editor of the New Hampshire *Patriot* observed that "the increased demand for laces, ribbons and dancing pumps—the hurrying of tailors, milliners and mantua makers" signaled the approaching holiday.[8]

The image of the somber Thanksgiving pilgrim derives from seventeenth-century Massachusetts dress practices. The stereotypical male pilgrim typically wears a black doublet with a large, square-edged white collar over black breeches. Frequently he wears a tall black hat with a metal buckle on the hatband. His leather shoes also are fastened with a buckle. His female counterpart wears a doublet, also collared, over a dark skirt and apron. On her head she wears a white cap. The costume historian Elisabeth McClellan included a drawing of a Puritan couple in her 1904 *Historic Dress in America*, one of the earliest books devoted to American costume history. This drawing is a likely source of the contemporary stereotype.

A second persistent New England image is the witch. Witches are depicted as old crones wearing black cloaks and tall pointed hats with flat brims. A witch's clothes are often tattered, and her hair is wild and unkempt. She carries a broom and is frequently accompanied by a black cat or a raven. Every American school child learns of this image when choosing a Halloween costume.

In the seventeenth century, the practice of witchcraft was punishable by death. The best-known incident of persecution of so-called witches occurred in Salem, Massachusetts, in 1692 when nineteen accused witches were executed from the hundreds charged and arrested. Accusations of witchcraft typically grew out of conflict between two parties. Although both men and women could be accused of superstitious behavior, most of the accused were women. Proceedings of the Salem trials and other witchcraft trials reveal that the accused women did not wear any clothing that set them apart from other women. The accused witches were almost always older women of lower social status living on the margins of society. The clothing mentioned in the legal accounts is the same as that worn by others of similar social standing. They wore "coats" or "cotes" (skirts) and jackets, often of red wool with black caps or hats. The witches of our imagination are the only ones wearing black cloaks or loose robes with black steeple-crown hats.

Pilgrims and witches are examples of dress associated with a region that are still alive in the American imagination. Both of these costumed images had their roots in seventeenth-century New England dress practices; as time wore on, the imagined representation superseded anything based on historical fact. Today, every American recognizes the pilgrim and the witch.

To encourage conformity to the perceived social order, several of the colonies enacted sumptuary laws. These were attempts to regulate personal expenditures. The Massachusetts Bay, Plymouth, and Connecticut colonies enacted a series of laws restricting excessive spending on clothing, prohibiting the wearing of "strange and new" fashions, and restricting "lascivious" or "immodest" fashions. The first law enacted by the Massachusetts Bay Colony in 1634 prohibited the wearing of long wigs, slashed apparel, knots of ribbons, and gold and silver laces. (It is ironic that some of these same gold and silver laces were being traded to Native Americans in exchange for land.) By the mid-seventeenth century, the laws were updated to accommodate variations in social standing. The Massachusetts Bay Colony's 1651 law divided people into two categories: those with estates worth over £200 and those worth under £200. Men belonging to the higher rank were permitted to wear great boots, silver or gold lace, silver or gold buttons, and "points" (ribbons) at the knee. Women were allowed to wear bone lace as well as hoods made from silk or a gauze fabric called "tiffany." Many offenders were servant girls aspiring to a more fashionable life at a higher rank. The laws were hard to prosecute. The last law was enacted in 1676 in Connecticut.

The New England colonies depended on England for their clothing. Ships carrying new settlers also brought fabrics, ready-made clothes, and shoes from London merchants who thrived on the developing new market. Emigrants to the colonies were advised to bring clothing with them. Only after emigration rates declined in the 1640s did colonial governors worry about "manufactures." Various government bounties encouraged farm families to grow flax, raise sheep, spin yarn, and weave cloth. However, the New England colonies never became self-sufficient. The most they could do was to supplement their clothing needs by spinning yarn to knit stockings, weaving linen for shirts, or weaving rough woolens for outerwear.

Contrary to historical legend, the Puritans were not restricted to black or gray colors for their clothes. The "sadd" colors mentioned in the records of the time were so called because of a dye process that dulled or "saddened" the intensity of the color. Colors with names like "tawney," "russet," and "Kendall green" appear in inventories, revealing that the Puritans were more colorful than we thought. The preferred colors for men's suits included gray, blue, and green as well as black; colors for women's clothes were brown, green, blue ("sky-colored"), purple, and various shades of red.

COLONIAL SOCIETY IN THE EIGHTEENTH CENTURY

The availability of consumer goods on the eastern coast of North America began to increase at the end of the seventeenth century. By the early 1700s, people of modest means could afford a wide range of consumer goods. With the abandonment of sumptuary laws, people were limited only by what they could afford. Still, one was expected to dress to one's station in life. For families of means, this meant dressing as "gentlemen" and "gentlewomen." In New England, society was divided into three ranks: gentry, middling folk, and the poor. The region did not have a parallel to the English aristocracy with their grand country houses and London town houses. Yet the taste of the English aristocracy set the wheels of fashion in motion for New England. Letters surviving from the period indicate that gentlemen and gentlewomen often sent to London for the latest in stylish goods, both lengths of fabric and finished garments and accessories. A visitor to Boston in 1740 reported: "Both the ladies and gentlemen dress and appear as gay in common as courtiers in England on a coronation or birthday."[9]

Gentlemen wore suits of clothes—coats, waistcoats, and breeches—made by professional tailors from good English cloth, preferably superfine broadcloth. The women of the family had the needle skills to sew men's linen shirts. The quality of accessories such as hats, gloves, and cravats sent out silent messages about a man's position in society. Proper deportment, meaning posture and pose, signified a well-bred person. New Englanders abhorred the upper-class pretensions that were associated with British officers. They infrequently wore wigs, which were commonly worn by the wealthy in Europe. Those of a scholarly or philosophical persuasion wore eastern-inspired robes known as banyans for at-home wear along with caps.

Gentlewomen wore fashionable gowns made from patterned silks, cotton chintz, wool worsteds, and embroidered linen for best dress. The gowns had three-quarter-length sleeves, cone-shaped bodices to fit over stays, and full skirts split in front to reveal the petticoats. Finely quilted petticoats made from silk or worsted wool calamanco were fashionable, judging by the number that survive in regional collections. Talented needlewomen sometimes quilted their own petticoats; others purchased ready-made ones imported from London where they were produced in factories. Women kept small items in separate pockets that they attached at the waist under their skirts. Pockets belonging to gentlewomen display colorful embroidery on linen. Some stylish women wore hoops and powdered their hair. Paradoxically, to appear too interested in the latest fashions risked accusations of "prideful" behavior.

Yeoman farmers and husbandmen, a step below the gentility on the social scale, dressed in the manner expected for the "middling sort." Sometimes they spun the yarn and wove the cloth for their own fabrics; often they purchased imported cloth. Men wore the same coats, waistcoats, and breeches as did the gentry, albeit in plainer cloth. Leather breeches attained popularity for their longwearing, durable qualities. When engaging in hard physical labor, men often wore oversized shirts called "frocks." Women in this social rank often owned a gown of silk, worsted wool, or printed cotton to be worn with an imported chip hat for best dress. Their everyday attire consisted of skirts, or "petticoats," worn with abbreviated gowns called short gowns or bed gowns. Work aprons protected their clothes. Their everyday pockets were plain.

The clothes of the poor—servants, farm hands, African slaves, and indentured Native Americans—revealed their lowly station in society. Men who worked in the fields or on board ship wore long "trowsers" that ended at the top of the shoes. The poor had few clothes. Although servants might wear cast-offs from their masters or mistresses, they did not have the financial resources to buy the cloth or finished clothing afforded by their social superiors. For indentured servants and slaves, their masters provided their clothing. Cloth was an expensive commodity before the Industrial Revolution. This fact manifested itself in two ways in the dress of the poor. First, the makers of working men's coats and jackets economized on cloth, making them appear skimpy-looking. Women wore short gowns that stopped just below the waist instead of being full-length. Most of the poor's attire was made from homespun fabrics such as blue-and-white checked or striped linen and coarse woolen flannels. The few surviving garments of these humble fabrics reveal multiple patches and darned areas, thus speaking to the paucity of servant or slave wardrobes. Shoes and stockings were a constant worry. Stockings developed holes and shoe leather wore out. To extend the life of their shoes and stockings, poor people often went barefoot.

Local tailors and seamstresses provided cutting and sewing services for the gentry and middling folk. They cut and sewed the more complicated, fitted garments. Some specialists traveled to rural homesteads, residing with families while completing the garments. All women knew how to sew straight seams, but they did not all know how to cut and sew the more complicated, fitted garments. Often they took apart old garments to use as patterns for shirts, aprons, and caps.

> ## Runaway Ads
>
> Clothing worn by the poor rarely survives. Thus, costume scholars look to documentary sources for information about the attire of the lower rungs of the social ladder. Ads for slaves or indentured servants who ran away from their masters provide detailed descriptions of what the runaway was wearing when last seen. An ad in the *Newport Mercury* (1759) lists what was most likely the entire wardrobe of a runaway male: "dark colour'd Cloth coat with flat metal buttons, a new kersey dark colour'd jacket, with flat metal button, an old brown jacket, a flannel jacket and flannel shirts, a check linen shirt and a pair of white wide trowsers, red broadcloth breeches, a pair of blue breeches and clocked stockings." A runaway slave in 1773 wore an "oznabrig shirt, jacket, & trousers new beaver hat, great coat half worn." A Native American woman named Vice Hill, twenty-five years of age, ran away from James Hardy, Innholder, in 1760, wearing a light striped short gown and a black quilted petticoat.
>
> Kersey, check linen, and oznaberg fabrics—short gowns, wide trousers, and half-worn garments—together these components told of low socioeconomic status.

What distinguished New England dress in the colonial period? As scholar Linda Baumgarten has noted, very little. She states that "the widespread use of export textiles in all the British colonies mean that regional preferences were somewhat blurred."[10] Fabrics from all over the world were imported into Boston—cottons painted and dyed in India, silks woven and sometimes painted in China, and from England block prints, silks, and an infinite variety of wool fabrics. The reliance on London for style news by all the colonies also muddled regional preferences during this period. As Lord Cornbury, Governor of New York, noted in 1705, all of the colonies were but "twigs belonging to the main tree."[11]

The War for Independence

American dependency on British textiles became a political issue in the 1760s. When colonists grew increasingly hostile toward the British crown, the politically minded Daughters of Liberty began hosting spinning bees. Interestingly, some of these women did not know how to make cloth themselves, having been accustomed to purchasing fabric or hiring girls to spin and weave. As their skills improved, the wearing of homespun became a common sight in the cities and towns of New England. In fact, Harvard's class of 1768 took their degrees dressed in the "manufacture of this country."

New England played a critical part in the Revolutionary War. In December 1773, sixty members of the Sons of Liberty disguised themselves as Native Americans, boarded British ships in Boston Harbor, and dumped chests of tea overboard to protest the Tea Act. The Native American disguise allowed them to dress in clothing different from their own breeches, coats, and waistcoats and to paint their faces, making them unrecognizable. The Boston Tea Party led to the battle of Lexington in 1775.

British soldiers were easily recognizable in battle, for they wore three-piece regimental uniforms with red wool coats, giving them the moniker "redcoats." The colonial militia units wore ordinary clothing as well as styles based on Native American hunting shirts and leggings. The shirts, modeled after fringed leather shirts, were made from tow cloth, an inexpensive linen fabric. In 1775, George Washington wrote to Connecticut's governor Jonathan Trumbull requesting "from the colonies of Rhode Island and Connecticut, a Quantity of Tow Cloth, for the Purpose of making of Indian or Hunting Shirts for the Men, many of whom are destitute of Cloathing."[12] Native American leggings—a type of woolen gaitor that fastened around the calves and ankles—protected a soldier's legs from sharp rocks and underbrush. In 1779, the Continental Congress ordered blue uniforms with distinctive trims for every state. However, not everyone conformed because the necessary wool fabric to outfit a regiment was both expensive and scarce.

Civilian clothing during the war changed out of necessity. The hostilities disrupted the flow of textiles from Britain, so the colonists had to make do with what they had. When General Washington attended a ball in his honor in Newport in 1781, the local belles dressed in whatever finery they had available. Women all over New England established mini-factories in their homes to spin and weave cloth to be made into suits for their families and to provision the soldiers.

A Revolutionary War reenactment at Minuteman National Historic Park. Courtesy National Park Service.

The Republic

After the war ceased, New Englanders, like their fellow Americans, were of two minds when it came to dress. While many continued to be "cloathed in their own manufactures," others rushed to buy the latest imported goods from England, France, and the Far East.

Fashion, inspired by the radical changes in French politics and culture, changed for both men and women. The luxurious ensembles made from silk brocades, embroideries, and laces disappeared after the French Revolution; in their place came democratic fashions modeled after classical Greek and Roman art. From 1790 to 1820 fashionable women wore simple high-waisted, one-piece gowns of plain lightweight silks or cottons. Country women continued to wear short gowns and petticoats for a brief period but soon switched to high-waisted one-piece dresses, albeit in homespun or calico. Men cut their hair short "à la Brutus" and wore tailcoats, short waistcoats, fine linens, and tight-fitting breeches in subdued colors. By about 1815, pantaloons replaced breeches, and top hats appeared on fashionable heads. Fine fabrics, good fit, and exquisite details distinguished the gentleman from the rustic. Youthful enthusiasm for the new fashions offended the sensibilities of some New Englanders, including the Reverend Timothy Dwight of New Haven, who stated that a young lady dressing *à la grecque* "in a New-England winter violates alike good sense, correct taste, sound morals and the duty of self-preservation."[13]

Those who participated in fashionable social events such as dancing assemblies, balls, and cotillions wanted to keep up with fashion and needed imports to do so. New England merchants resumed trade with England right after the war ended. Entrepreneurial merchant families in several New England port towns, particularly Salem, Providence, and New London, commenced trade with China and India in the 1790s. Soon Chinese and Indian goods—including fabrics, ready-to-wear silk and muslin dresses, nankeen breeches, shawls, and shoes—became readily available. The War of 1812 frustrated American efforts to acquire the latest fabrics and fashions from Europe, but it offered fledgling American manufacturing concerns an eager market for their goods, at least for a short time.

In the early days of the Republic, the wearing of homespun signified Republican virtue. In Hartford, one hundred elegant women formed a Patriotic and Economical Association devoted to dressing plainly and simply, avoiding silks and decorations in favor of domestic manufactures. George Washington himself wore a suit of wool made at the Hartford Woolen Manufactory for his inauguration as President in 1789. Alexander Hamilton, in his *Report on Manufactures*, found that in Connecticut in 1791, "a great proportion of our most substantial Farmers and mechanicks appear dressed on Sundays and holydays in the manufactures of their Wives and daughters; & this is becoming every day more reputable."[14]

Abigail Adams (1744–1818), wife of John Adams of Braintree, Massachusetts, second president of the United States, spent four years in London and France in the 1780s when her husband served as envoy. Her views on fashion reflect the New England belief in the moral superiority of simple living over European sophistication. Abigail Adams was "neat and trim in dress."[15] She kept up with fashion, yet she was critical of its excesses. When she was First Lady, she found the popular neoclassical chemise to be transparent and flimsy and cut shockingly low in the

Quaker Attitudes Toward Dress

The diaries of Hannah Fisher of Newport, Rhode Island, reveal Quaker attitudes toward dress. Hannah stated her admiration for "humility of appearance and the simplicity of . . . clothing." Inspired by the testimony she heard at the North Meeting House while visiting Nantucket in 1793, she wrote: "Recommending the example of our blessed Lord and Saviour, that we might obey, and follow *Him* in meekness, in regard to apparel, Furniture, & conduct—particularly advising against *silk gowns* & *spotted* Calico's."

Hannah herself had succumbed to a calico in her youth, as this diary entry dated December 30, 1787, shows:

I think I was my 16th year, when reading Jane Hoskins life, I observ'd her Saviour's gracious promise upon condition of her obedience, "I will be with thee to the end of time, I make thee an heir of my kingdom."—Such an assurance I though[t] a wonderful favour, and wish'd it for myself—but when I was requir'd to take up the Cross, upon the same conditions if I continued faithful—the sinful part prevail'd—the Cross then presented to my view was this. I had some Calico to make a gown, which my pride thought I stood in need of—but I think the evidence was clear, that I should refuse it for Christ's sake and something plainer would be provided for me—but I did not obey—tho I had great inward encouragement so to do—the Holy Cross I shyn'd—I had the gown made-& thereby was in measure depriv'd of that sweet consolation which before frequently accompanied my spirit.[17]

front. She attempted to set more conservative standards by introducing medium-weight silks in place of sheer cottons.

As the young country grew, Americans gave up homespun for the new factory-made goods. This first occurred in cities and towns, then spread to rural areas. By 1840, anyone wearing homespun garments in New England was seen as an old-fashioned country person. Yet the striving for simplicity and practicality in dress persevered in New England through the twentieth century.

Religious Doctrine and Dress: Quakers and Shakers

Communities centered on religious beliefs wore simple yet atypical clothing that was easily recognizable by others. Although not unique to New England, two religious groups—the Quakers and the Shakers—left their mark on the region's dress history in the nineteenth century.

The Society of Friends, better known as the Quakers, was prominent in Massachusetts, Rhode Island, Connecticut, New York, and Pennsylvania. Quaker doctrines advised against excess in dress. As antiquarian author Alice Morse Earle said, "the dress of the Quaker was simply the dress of everybody, with all the extravagances left off."[16] Quakers believed in plain, undecorated fabrics. They avoided printed fabrics, hooped petticoats, ribbons, and laces. They did, however, dress in good wools and silks in colors of soft "dove" gray and brown.

By the early nineteenth century, a codified dress developed for Quaker men and women that distinguished them from the rest of New Englanders. Men wore old-fashioned knee breeches and coats with flat-crowned beaver hats. Women wore simple unadorned dresses with white neck cloths and shawls. A distinctive Quaker bonnet developed, many of which survive in the region's historical society collections.

The Shakers, or United Society of Believers in Christ's Second Appearing, is a communal society. They began in England in the 1750s as a breakaway group of Quakers. Because they danced and moved their bodies during worship, they were called "Shaking Quakers," or Shakers. Shakers led by Ann Lee emigrated to America in 1774 in pursuit of religious freedom. They first established a settlement in Albany, New York, gradually spreading to Connecticut, Massachusetts, New Hampshire, and Maine, where converts gathered into communities bound by shared beliefs in common property, celibacy, equality of men and women, pacifism, and separation from the world. Shakerism peaked in the mid-1800s. Today one Shaker community with four members remains at Sabbathday Lake, Maine.

Shaker attire, like that of the Quakers, consisted of pared-down versions of styles popular when the communities were formed. Men wore simple suits and broad-brimmed hats. The women, in plain dresses, wore white kerchiefs over their necks and bosoms and covered their heads with white caps. The Shakers were known for simple, functional, exquisitely designed furniture and other items that they offered for sale to the outside world. One such item was the Shaker cloak, a long hooded garment made of russet-colored or dull-blue homespun.

FACTORY TOWNS

The economic ambitions of the new republic gave birth to numerous industries connected to fashion in New England. Textile manufacturing led the way. Every state in New England was involved in textiles, thanks to the region's many rivers, which provided waterpower.

Cotton yarn was first spun by waterpower in the United States at Slater Mill in Pawtucket, Rhode Island, in 1790. In 1814, a factory in Waltham, Massachusetts, wove the first machine-made American cloth on power looms. Soon mill villages arose on major rivers all over New England. One of the largest was created by the Boston Associates at a small town on the Merrimack River that they named Lowell after the company's founder. Labor shortages sent agents to northern New England to recruit workers, who succeeded in attracting young girls to work in the

The so-called Lowell Mill girls. Courtesy Lowell National Historical Park.

mills. The so-called Lowell Mill girls spent some of their wages at shops that catered to their desires for the latest in fashion. In 1845, fifteen-year-old Mary Paul of Barnard, Vermont, left a job as a domestic servant to work in the Lowell factories, explaining that "It would be much better for me [in Lowell] than to stay about here. . . . I am in need of clothes which I cannot get about here and for that reason I want to go to Lowell or some other place."[18]

The industry continued to expand with the building of woolen mills, dye houses, and print works. Investors built large mill complexes on the region's most powerful rivers. Fall River's vast mills were developed when water wheels changed to turbines. Amoskeag in Manchester, New Hampshire, was the largest cotton mill in the world in the late 1800s. Rhode Island and Massachusetts dominated textile manufacturing in North America until the 1920s.

The result of the rapid development of the textile industry was the widespread availability of inexpensive cloth. The price of printed cotton, for example, dropped from $1.00 per yard in 1800 to $0.16 in the 1830s. Even the working class could afford to dress in reasonably fashionable clothes at those prices. The making and wearing of homespun cloth disappeared in the areas around the mill villages, continuing a decade or two longer in the more remote regions.

Footwear has been a major industry for New England, particularly Massachusetts, since the seventeenth century. Boston had at least twenty-six active shoemakers before 1650. Four shoes excavated from the Nanny Privy site (1660–1670), in a settlement near the harbor, display a unique square-gap toe design that may have been exclusive to shoemakers in the Boston area.[19] The craft of shoemaking spread to outlying towns on the north shore like Lynn, Haverhill, and Lawrence. Traveling peddlers sold ready-made shoes throughout the region. The invention of the sewing machine in 1846 by Elias Howe of Massachusetts allowed soles to be machine-sewn to uppers. The need for soldiers' boots during Civil War provided a boost to the industry. Shoe manufacturing continued in the late nineteenth and early twentieth centuries, with the development of such nationally famous brands as Bass, Converse, and Timberland.

Bass Shoe of Portland, Maine, began in 1876 when George Henry Bass entered the shoe trade. The company introduced the camp moccasin in 1910 and the "Weejun" in 1936. Both of these styles are associated with the Ivy League and preppy looks discussed later. Marquis William Converse started in 1908 with production of winterized footwear for men, women, and children. Soon the company, based in Andover, Massachusetts, moved into canvas sneakers. Basketball star Chuck Taylor offered suggestions for improvements, resulting in the now famous All Star basketball sneaker in 1917. The company's long association with basketball peaked in the 1970s with endorsements by Celtics star Julius Irving ("Dr. J."). Timberland started in 1918 when Nathan Swartz began making boots in Boston. In the 1950s he purchased an existing company for the production of waterproof boots. The company acquired its present name in 1973 and added casual and boat shoes to the line. Currently, the company, which is located in Stratham, New Hampshire, also manufactures sports apparel that embodies the New England philosophy of well-made, functional clothing.

Hat making was another industry that thrived in New England. When costly straw bonnets from England and Italy appeared on the New England fashion scene in the 1790s, enterprising young women learned how to replicate them in rye straw. Betsy Metcalf of Providence is credited with introducing the art of straw braiding and bonnet making to New England. After her marriage, she moved to Dedham, Massachusetts, where she taught many women how to split and braid straw. Soon bonnet making became a widespread cottage industry with whole families involved in production. By the 1840s, small factories bleached, blocked, and finished the bonnets.

Connecticut led the nation in manufacturing men's hats in the nineteenth and twentieth centuries. Since the early years of the republic, the towns of Danbury and Derby, located in the southwestern part of the state, dominated. Danbury had eighty hat manufacturers in 1900. The official city seal includes a derby hat. As men abandoned the wearing of hats in the 1960s, the industry faded.

The costume jewelry industry has long been concentrated in Providence, Rhode Island. One well-known brand, Monet, has been headquartered there since 1929. Costume jewelry came into its own as an accessory in the 1920s at the hands of Paris designers Coco Chanel and Elsa Schiaparelli, who produced fashionable pieces.

OCCUPATIONAL DRESS

New England's extensive coastline made it possible for its residents to make a living from the sea. Fishing was and still is a major industry in Connecticut, Rhode Island, Massachusetts, New Hampshire, and Maine. Gloucester and New Bedford, Massachusetts, are just two of the many ports with thriving fishing businesses. Some fishermen head out to the abundant fishing grounds, known as "the banks," while others stay close to shore to harvest shellfish. The waters of coastal Maine are rich with lobster. During the colonial period, salted fish, especially cod, were shipped as far away as the West Indies. The image of the New England fisherman or lobsterman in his rubberized coat and broad-brimmed Sou'wester hat is a familiar one in American culture.

Fishermen began harpooning whales off the coast of Cape Cod around 1700. Thus commenced New England's long association with these large mammals, whose oil provided both lighting and lubrication. In the first part of the nineteenth century, Nantucket led the nation in whaling. When the island's harbor filled in, the center of the industry shifted to New Bedford. The discovery of mineral oils in 1859 caused a long, slow decline in the industry. The last whaling ships went out of New England ports in the 1920s.

Whaling ships went out to sea for up to two years, stopping in distant ports for supplies. Sailors wore shirts, wide sailors' trousers, and a variety of short wool jackets that allowed them free movement when climbing up masts and hauling sails. These jackets, the forerunners of today's pea coats, are listed in journals, outfitting books, and ship's logs as pea jackets, monkey jackets, or reefer jackets. Shops in port sold sailors' "slops," which are recognized as the earliest ready-made clothing in the history of dress. Captains also sold replacement clothing from their chests during a voyage.

New Englanders' first attempts at creating foul-weather gear involved tarring or waxing shoes, hats, and jackets. The importation of natural rubber from Central and South America did much to improve the lot of fishermen and sailors in the nineteenth century. At first, chunks of rubber were dissolved in turpentine and brushed onto cloth and leather. Later, two fabrics coated with dissolved rubber were sandwiched together, making a waterproof fabric. However, New England's hot summers and cold winters caused stickiness, cracking, and offensive odors. With the advent of vulcanization in 1839, the disadvantages of rubber were eliminated. Comfortable shoes, hats, coats, and overalls could be made from "India rubber."

PRIVATE FAMILY AND PUBLIC DISPLAY IN THE NINETEENTH CENTURY

The industrialization of New England contributed to a separation of work and home. With the decline in agriculture, the family lost importance as an economic unit, and gender roles for men and women shifted. Men went off to work while women stayed home to raise the children and take care of the house. Through their appearance, and that of their children and homes, women defined their husbands' status. Among the rising middle class, being in fashion became a concern.

At the same time, women's styles changed from the simple neoclassical styles to narrow-waisted dresses with wide skirts, requiring corsets and multiple petticoats. Trims and accessories changed with every season. To keep up to date, women read magazines like the popular *Godey's Lady's Book*, which offered advice on etiquette and showed fashion plates. These publications informed female readers about how to behave and what to wear for every social occasion—visiting, dinners, parties, balls—resulting in a rigid social code for both men and women. Mourning a loved one became a complicated practice involving full mourning attire for a year and a day, then half mourning for another six months. Not following the rules guaranteed gossip, rumors, or worse—social ostracism. The amount of clothing in people's wardrobes proliferated.

This growing concern with appearance filtered down to all social levels. William Apes, a Native American of Pequot heritage, left his home on the Connecticut reservation to find gainful employment. When he returned for visits, he tried to "look decent"; he thought looking decent was important because he had worn rags as a child. Once he was only one hundred miles from home but avoided making a visit because he did not have "clothes suitable for the season."[20]

New England's penchant for intellectualism led to concerns about society's obsession with fashion. Leading thinkers preached moderation and sobriety since Boston, the region's center, considered itself the Athens of America. One of these intellectuals was Henry David Thoreau, who decried society's increasing interest in fashion in "Economy":

> As for Clothing, to come at once to the practical part of the question, perhaps we are led oftener by the love of novelty and a regard for the opinions of men, in procuring it, than by a true utility. . . . No man ever stood lower in my estimation for having a patch in his clothes; yet I am sure that there is greater anxiety, commonly, to have fashionable, or at least clean and unpatched clothes, than to have a sound conscience. . . . Who could wear a patch, or two extra seams, over the knee? Most behave as if they believed that their prospects for life would be ruined if they should do it. It would be easier for them to hobble to town with a broken leg than with a broken pantaloon.[21]

Thoreau himself wore clothes made of homespun when he resided at Walden Pond in 1854: "The pantaloons which I now wear were woven in a farmer's family—thank Heaven there is so much virtue still in man; for I think the fall from the farmer to the operative as great and memorable as that from the man to the farmer."[22]

New England women responded to fashion's foibles by becoming active participants in the dress reform movement. Dress reformers objected to fashion's extremes: restrictive corsets, voluminous heavy skirts, and the expense of keeping up with rapid changes in styles. Alternative styles of dress were

Fall clothing display, Windsor Locks, Connecticut, 1939. Courtesy Library of Congress.

variously called rational, reform, aesthetic, or artistic dress. The New England Women's Club formed a dress reform committee, and members began lecturing on dress reform in 1874. They recommended reforming underwear and aesthetic dress. Boston women devised a Rational Dress, a divided skirt (trousers) and short jacket based on Syrian national dress. Annie Jenness-Miller and Mabel Jenness, two nationally known dress reformers in the 1880s and 1890s, were born in New England and educated in Boston. The sisters promoted freeing women from constricting clothing and promoting exercise.

Shops and Shopping

Every city, town, and village in New England had a dry goods store or general store where customers could obtain fabrics, trims, and accessories. In the early national period, Yankee peddlers sold goods to rural dwellers while traveling on foot or horseback. Specialists—dressmakers and tailors—made clothing or helped people cut out fabric. Most women learned to sew at home or in finishing schools and academies and were capable of putting together a garment. They often took apart worn-out dresses and modified them to achieve the latest silhouettes and details, resulting in unique regional characteristics. For example, many women's dresses in New England from the 1830s and 1840s had matching shoulder capes that helped keep them warm.

As more manufactured goods became available, the department store evolved. Department stores grew from dry goods stores into large, centrally located buildings that offered a wide variety of products to the growing middle class, including fashion products. Several factors coincided in the mid-nineteenth century to bring about this change in the way people shopped. Elias Howe invented the sewing machine in 1846, paving the way for mass manufacture of clothing. All types of fabrics, including lace and velvets, were made industrially by the 1850s. Chemical dyes gradually replaced natural and mineral dyes after William Perkin discovered aniline dye in 1856. During the Civil War, the Union Army developed standardized sizing for soldiers' uniforms. This resulted in the widespread availability of man-

Department Stores

New England had three major department stores: Filene's, Jordan Marsh, and G. Fox. William Filene (1830–1901) founded Filene's in Boston in 1851, turning operations over to his sons Edward and Lincoln in 1890. Edward (1860–1937) was noted for numerous innovations in retail distribution, notably the bargain basement. Filene's Basement still exists at the flagship Washington Street store and has branches in twenty other locations around the country.

Eben Jordan (1822–1895) of Danville, Maine, and Benjamin Marsh (1825–1865) of Chesterfield, New Hampshire, joined forces in 1851 to found Jordan Marsh in Boston. The store's mail order business thrived in the late 1800s. The store's policy that "the customer was always right" earned a loyal following.

Gerson Fox (1811–1880), a German Jewish immigrant, established a dry goods store in Hartford in 1845, which eventually grew into G. Fox. When Gerson died, his son Moses Fox became president. Moses' daughter Beatrice Fox Auerbach eventually took over presidency of the store in 1938. She expanded the business tenfold, then sold her shares to the May Company in 1965.

All three stores were synonymous with New England taste. When Americans moved to the suburbs in the 1950s and 1960s, these three department stores followed them by expanding to the new malls. Only Filene's and Filene's Basement survived the retail shakeouts of the late twentieth century.

Shopping Abroad

When Eliza Park of North Bennington, Vermont (1848–1938), married John McCullough (1835–1915) in 1871, both of their families decided to join them on their honeymoon trip to Europe. John McCullough, originally of Bennington, was a laywer who had made his money filing claims in the California Gold Rush. Eliza's diary reveals that the family shopped daily in both London and Paris. The women spent a fortune on suits, dresses, shawls, furs, cloaks, bonnets, gloves, fans, jewelry, and handkerchiefs. The men did not shrink back, buying suits, shirts, boots, pins, and watches for themselves. Eliza visited C. F. Worth and another top couturier, Emile Pingat, on January 8, 1871, but did not buy anything. She purchased at less celebrated houses such as Mme. Marquerite, Louis Hillé, and Caroline Reboux. When she returned to the United States, she noted in her diary that people looked at her when she wore her French dresses.

ufactured clothing, particularly for men, making it possible not only to dress in neat clothing, but also to follow changes in fashion.

High Fashion

Those with money, such as the Boston Brahmins, sought to distinguish themselves from the fashionable middle class by patronizing the developing couture system. Haute couture, literally "fine sewing," began in Paris in 1856 when the Englishman Charles Frederick Worth started showing his gowns on live models at his salon located at 7, Rue de la Paix. Soon other dressmakers joined the couture system, and the designer label was born. New Englanders participated in the Paris shopping experience almost from the beginning. French dresses from the 1860s, particularly those by Madame Roger, are preserved in New England museums. Worth may have been a little too avant-garde for New England taste at this time, as few of his clothes exist in area collections. Isabella Stewart Gardner reportedly wore Worth gowns. The New Yorker married Jack Gardner in 1860, and moved to Boston. The couple visited Paris in 1867, where she was introduced to the pleasures of owning Worth gowns. One young Boston society woman disapproved, noting that "Mrs. Jack Gardner has a queer way of dressing."[23] At the time, Worth was moving away from hoop skirts by designing dresses with bare shoulders and draped skirts.

For those women who could not afford the time or money to sail to Paris for their wardrobes, local dressmakers adapted the latest styles. Boston in particular had several dressmakers whose work rivaled the French in the skillful selection and use of fabric, such as John J. Stevens of Washington Street. The "little dressmaker" was replicated in every city in New England. In 1911, the Providence City Directory listed over five pages of custom dressmakers. Many women on a budget made clothes at home. With the widespread availability of sewing machines and the invention of paper patterns, the home sewer could easily obtain a fashionable cut from the 1860s on.

Centennial and Colonial Revival in the Nineteenth Century

The nation's celebration of its one hundredth birthday gave New Englanders the opportunity to look back with pride on their Yankee heritage. They

Rhode Island women at the turn of the twentieth century. Courtesy Library of Congress.

participated in parades, fairs, pageants, balls, Martha Washington teas, and other social events that focused on the colonial past. The culmination was the Centennial Celebration in Philadelphia and its popular "New England Kitchen."

Colonial costume became an important component of the centennial celebration. Fancy dress balls allowed the elite Yankees the chance to wear the family "relics," thus reaffirming their exalted social rank. For those who did not have ancestors' clothing to wear, dressmakers and tailors made updated versions of colonial gowns and breeches suits for them to wear. Fabric manufacturers printed calicos with Centennial motifs such as "1776" and George Washington's portrait. The public's fascination with the past continued into the twentieth century in the guise of the colonial revival.

THE TWENTIETH CENTURY BEGINS

At the beginning of the twentieth century, New England enjoyed a booming economy. New immigrants arriving from southern Europe found work in the region's manufacturing facilities or in the fishing industry. Thanks to affordable mass-manufactured clothing and widespread distribution, the styles available to men, women, and children in New England were similar to other areas of the country.

If the same fashions were available throughout the United States, what characterizes New England dress in the twentieth century? The answer encompasses two generalities. First, specific styles became associated with places in New England, mostly locations where the affluent spent their leisure time. Second, manufacturers or retailers located in New England developed specific styles or looks that project the region's tradition of well-bred conservatism.

Resort Wear

New England's mountains, coastline, and quaint port cities offered numerous locations for the well to do to spend their leisure time. Some enjoyed the sea at

Newport, Kennebunkport, Cape Cod, and the Islands during the summer. Others cooled off in the Berkshires or camps in Maine. In winter, they headed to northern New England to ski country.

During the Gilded Age, Newport, Rhode Island, became one of the nation's premier summer resorts where old money families mixed with newly wealthy industrialists in their "cottages." Newport, home to the America's Cup 12-meter sailing races until 1983, became associated with yachting. The classic navy blazer and white wool flannel trousers originally worn for yachting are still popular today for social engagements in sailing communities throughout the region, although the white flannels have been replaced by chinos.

With improved transportation, Cape Cod and the islands of Martha's Vineyard and Nantucket became popular vacation destinations. Philip C. Murray of Murray's Toggery Shop on Nantucket began selling brick-red sailcloth slacks in the 1940s based on pants made in Brittany, France. They became so popular that Murray trademarked them as "Nantucket Reds." Today Murray's shop, still family owned, features shirts, shorts, baseball caps, bib overalls, trousers, and other casual clothing in the famous red fabric. The line spread to Martha's Vineyard where Brickman's sells them in its shops in Edgartown and Vineyard Haven. Nantucket Reds enjoy a devoted local, national, and international clientele who communicate to those "in the know" that they have been to the islands. In the past few years, men in some wedding parties on the islands wear Nantucket Red shorts or trousers with navy blazers.

The Outdoorsman

Maine's Leon Leonwood Bean (1872–1967) developed a waterproof duck hunting boot with rubber bottoms and leather uppers in 1911. In 1912, he launched a mail-order business geared to the outdoorsman featuring the boots. He expanded with an apparel line in the 1920s, including the still popular Bean field coat (now known as the barn coat) and chamois shirt. Today the company sells a full line of sports and casual clothing for men, women, and children in stores in the United States and Japan, through its catalog, and over the Internet. The flagship store in Freeport, Maine, is a destination for many Bean devotees. In the early 1980s, a couple wed in front of the in-store trout pond.

The practical, comfortable, long-wearing styles developed by L.L.Bean suit the New England lifestyle. Residents of rural New England swear by L.L.Bean, finding its mail order business to be fast and convenient. The rugged outdoor boots, jackets, and casual wear work for New England's snowy winters, particularly in mountainous Vermont, New Hampshire, and Maine. Bean's conservative sporting styles enjoyed great popularity among the preppies during the late 1970s and early 1980s.

L.L.Bean is known for high-quality fabrics and functional designs. Their outdoor gear is designed for any weather situation faced by hunters and sports enthusiasts. The company retains customers' old favorites while developing new products. In 1979, the company offered its first Gore-Tex jacket, which has since gained "classic" status. Gore-Tex is a waterproof breathable fabric, ideal for sporting gear.

Skiing

The sport of skiing came to America from Europe in the 1930s. The mountains of Vermont and New Hampshire were among the first locations in the United States where one could learn to ski. Enthusiasts of the new sport stayed at inns in mountain villages, climbing up hills to ski down them. During the early years of the Depression, the Civilian Conservation Corps cut ski trails in northern New England's mountains, creating the foundation for the region's future ski industry.

In the mid-1930s, a number of factors contributed to the growth of the sport in New England. Ski schools established at inns and hotels began offering lessons with ski instructors from Austria. The limiting of the workweek to forty hours established "the weekend" as a time period when city dwellers could take short trips. Ski trains brought skiers from New York, Boston, and Montreal to the mountains. The passenger cars served as combination clubs, shops, and dorms. Soon entrepreneurs built resorts, installing rope tows, J-bars, and T-bars. Skiing became the winter sport of the upper middle class.

The locations of the first ski resorts were at Cannon Mountain near Franconia Notch, New Hampshire; Wildcat at Jackson and Mt. Cranmore at North Conway, New Hampshire; and Suicide Six at Woodstock and Mt. Mansfield near Stowe, Vermont.

Initially, ski ensembles consisted of anything that passed as winter clothes. By the second half of the 1930s, entrepreneurs produced specialized ski attire. Mostly of wool, a typical ski outfit consisted of baggy wool pants gathered at the ankle, a wool jacket, and sweater. Designs for sweaters drew upon Norwegian and Swiss folk motifs. With advances in fiber technology after World War II, innovative new styles became available. In 1949, ski instructor Klaus Obermeyer designed a quilted nylon parka filled with down feathers. The German Maria Bogner introduced stretch pants in 1953 made from Helanca, a fabric blend of stretch nylon and wool.

Several well-known skiwear companies got their start in New England. B. F. Moore of Newport, Vermont, began manufacturing skiwear in the late 1920s. The company grew over the years, expanding into the highly successful Slalom Skiwear Incorporated. Harold S. Hirsch, a member of the Dartmouth ski team, created a one-piece jumping suit for the team in 1929. He continued to develop clothing exclusively for skiers; his company eventually became White Stag.

Carroll Reed of North Conway was at the forefront of bringing skiing to New England. After a bad skiing accident in 1934, he established a ski school there in 1936 and took over management of the Saks Ski Shop. When Saks did not renew the lease, he and his wife Kay opened the Carroll Reed shop in the same space. In 1938, he sold the ski school and concentrated on building his retail business, which he finally sold in 1969. Initially, Reed hired local women to knit ski sweaters. Later he bought innovative merchandise from international sources for his stores. He was the first to import Bogner stretch pants into the United States, to buy the Italian designer Emilio Pucci's ski clothing, and to buy Icelandic sweaters. He is credited with inventing the cotton turtleneck, which is ubiquitous in New England today.

Priscilla of Boston

New England was known for more than just functional sportswear in the twentieth century. One of the nation's most prestigious bridal wear manufacturers was Priscilla of Boston. Priscilla Kidder (1918–), born in Quincy, Massachusetts, opened her bridal salon on Boston's Newbury Street in 1945. The limited selection of bridal gowns available to women right after World War II made her shop an instant success. She expanded and began selling dresses to bridal salons throughout the country. Journalists referred to her as the "Dior" of bridal design.

Priscilla and her sister Natalie designed the first gowns but soon turned over the design function to a team of talented designers. John Burbidge was senior designer for decades. The company prided itself on innovation by blending fashion trends with classic looks. For example, in the 1940s Priscilla incorporated large amounts of lace into her gowns when other houses showed undecorated styles. Priscilla gowns featured elaborate designs, yet they had elegant lines in keeping with New England's conservatism.

Gowns by Priscilla were especially desirable in the 1950s and 1960s. When movie star Grace Kelly married Rainer III of Monaco in 1956, her bridesmaids wore Priscilla of Boston gowns. The company's fame continued to grow when Priscilla bridal gowns were worn by three presidential daughters: Luci Baines Johnson in 1966, Julie Nixon in 1968, and Tricia Nixon in 1971.

IVY LEAGUE AND PREPPY LOOK

New England is home to four of the colleges that comprise the Ivy League athletic conference: Harvard, Yale, Brown, and Dartmouth. The other colleges—Princeton, Cornell, University of Pennsylvania, and Columbia—are also in the Northeast. The feminine counterparts are the seven sisters schools, four of which are in New England (Mt. Holyoke, Radcliffe, Smith, and Wellesley). In the conformist 1950s, students at these colleges popularized the Ivy League look, which had its roots in the conservative styles of New England.

For men, the Ivy League look consisted of a suit with a narrow-shouldered unfitted jacket, worn with a button-down shirt, skinny tie, and penny loafers (preferably Bass Weejuns). Charcoal gray and olive were the preferred colors. Chinos and tweed blazers offered a casual alternative. The look spread beyond campuses to young men in all parts of suburban America where details such as buckle straps from Ivy trousers were transplanted to caps, shirts, and shoes. High school students wore a more extreme four-button jacket bearing the name "Jivey Ivy."

By 1960, most men sported modified Ivy models that incorporated unpadded shoulders, narrow lapels, and tapered trousers. Brooks Brothers, a citadel of conservatism, came to the forefront as the Ivy League style became popular. When the young John Fitzgerald Kennedy, a senator from Massachusetts, became the president of the United States, the Ivy League look reached the White House.

Ivy League women wore cashmere twin sets, Shetland sweaters, or blazers with kilts or tweed skirts. In the summer, blouses with peter pan collars were worn with Bermuda shorts. A pearl necklace set off any outfit.

The Ivy look is well bred, understated, but not fussy. Many New England men and women held to the conservative, classic styles that comprised the Ivy League look during the sartorial upheavals of the 1960s and 1970s. In the late 1970s, conservative styles once again seemed right for the times, and the Ivy League look resurfaced as the preppy look.

The essential ingredients for the male preppy wardrobe included a conservative gray flannel suit, preferably made by Brooks Brothers, a long-time favorite label of New Englanders. For less formal wear, button-down oxford shirts or Lacoste polo shirts worn with khakis or corduroys sufficed. Other favorites included Harris Tweed jackets, navy blazers, heavy sweaters, down vests, Burberry trench coats, L.L.Bean field coats, and camel hair Polo coats.

Preppy women wore female versions of masculine styles: khaki, flannel, or corduroy slacks; a kilt or plaid skirt; a blazer or tweed jacket; and a Shetland or Fair-Isle sweater over a ruffle-necked white blouse or cotton turtleneck.

THE PREPPY LOOK

New England's propensity for conservative dressing spread to the nation once again in the late 1970s as the economy entered a recession. The so-called preppy look was named after the styles worn by students at the region's numerous private preparatory schools, some of which are listed here.

Massachusetts

Phillips Academy	Dana Hall School
Deerfield Academy	Groton School
Winsor School	Middlesex School

New Hampshire

Phillips Exeter Academy	St. Paul's School

Rhode Island

Portsmouth Abbey	St. George's

Connecticut

Miss Porter's School	Hotchkiss School
Choate Rosemary Hall	Kent School

Preppy styles for women were rather androgynous: female versions of the men's styles produced by the same companies. Both genders wore clothes made of Indian madras, a cotton plaid fabric that had first become popular in the early 1960s. Shoes common to both men and women were loafers or Sperry Top-Siders (boat shoes). Socks were optional. Men donned wing tips for dressy affairs while women wore simple pumps.

Like the Ivy League look before it, the preppy look emphasized the wearing of classics evolved from British men's wear. The clothes were conservatively styled in classic fabrics from natural fibers. The only departure from conservative dressing was the bright pink and green color combinations seen in preppy ensembles. Preppy clothes were well made, with attention to detail. Brand names were important. The American designer Ralph Lauren has built a financial empire on fashions inspired by this old money New England look.

Jack and Jackie Kennedy

John F. Kennedy (1917–1963), son of Boston businessman and ambassador to Great Britain Joseph P. Kennedy (1888–1969), became president of the United States in 1961. A graduate of Harvard University and a World War II veteran, he entered political life as a congressman in 1946, becoming a senator in 1952. On September 12, 1953, Senator Kennedy married Jacqueline Bouvier at St. Mary's in Newport, Rhode Island. The reception was held at Hammersmith Farm overlooking Narragansett Bay where Jackie had summered since 1942, when her mother married Hugh D. Auchincloss, Sr., an investment banker.

Becoming president and first lady in 1961 placed Jack and Jackie in a position

As president and first lady, Jack and Jackie Kennedy influenced American fashion, and the couple soon became symbols of youth and vitality—Jackie's oversized pillbox hat, simple suits with boxy jackets, and shift dresses became a national sensation. Courtesy Library of Congress.

to influence fashion. The couple became symbols of youth and vitality. JFK's tanned good looks and Ivy League style inspired men to adopt his sartorial habits. Kennedy preferred two-button suits that had broader shoulders, longer lapels, and more chest room than the three-button styles of the late fifties. He also disliked wearing hats, which sounded the death knell for the men's hat industry.

Jackie was an even greater fashion influence than her husband. Glamorous and elegant, she had a highly developed sense of style. She was named "Debutante of the Year" in 1947, the year she graduated from Miss Porter's in Farmington, Connecticut. That fall, she entered Vassar College. She met Congressman Kennedy in 1951 and again in 1952, at which time their courtship commenced. For her wedding, Jackie wore a dress created by Ann Lowe, an African American dressmaker whose clientele included New York society women. It was made of more than fifty yards of ivory silk taffeta. She wore an antique family wedding veil and a single-strand pearl necklace. Three-strand pearl necklaces later became a signature look for Jackie.

During the campaign for the presidency, Jackie showed that she had the potential to become an international fashion icon. The Kennedy family wealth allowed her to acquire a wardrobe from the best European and American fashion houses. Jackie worked with a number of designers and fashion experts to create a look of understated elegance for the campaign and, later, in her role as First Lady. Fashion doyenne Diana Vreeland, then an editor at *Harper's Bazaar*, was an influential advisor. As the president's wife, Jackie was encouraged to wear American fashions. California designer Oleg Cassini became her official dressmaker. Her clothes had simple lines and flattering colors. She rarely wore printed or patterned fabrics, understanding that these would have less of an impact in a crowd.

Jackie was highly photogenic. Her image at White House events, while traveling on presidential business, and with her two children at the Kennedy compound at Hyannisport, Massachusetts, appeared everywhere. Her clothing choices were an unqualified success, unleashing a national mania for the "Jackie" look. Women adopted her bouffant hairdo, an oversized pillbox hat set back on the head, simple suits with boxy jackets, and shift dresses. After JFK's assassination in 1963, Jackie returned to life as a private citizen but continued to be a fashion inspiration to many American women.

MULTICULTURALISM

New England is home to many ethnic and racial populations. Industrialization brought immigrants to the region in search of employment. The sartorial preferences of each of the following groups contributed to regionalism in dress.

New England was predominantly English until the nineteenth century when immigrants of European extraction came to the region. The Irish, fleeing the potato blight, came first. They sailed to New York or Boston, either settling in those port cities or traveling overland to mill villages in search of work. Despite discrimination, they assimilated into the dominant culture. They became factory workers, domestics, and unskilled laborers. Some of the women worked as seamstresses; a few eventually became mistresses of their own dressmaking establishments, such as Mary Ruby of Boston. Mary, the daughter of Irish immigrant Anne Kenar, owned a highly successful salon on fashionable Newbury Street from 1912 to 1949. Irish Americans who rose to prominence, such as the Kennedy's, wore the conservative styles espoused by the well-to-do Yankees. Irish style is currently represented in the region by craft shops that sell handcrafted Irish fisherman's sweaters, Kinsale smocks, and outerwear made of wool tweeds handwoven in Ireland.

French Canadians, who came from rural Quebec to work in the textile mills, dominated the second wave of immigrants. They preserved their Quebecois customs, particularly the French language, in tight-knit communities, isolating from the dominant Yankee culture longer than other immigrant groups. In dress, however, they assimilated quickly. In Quebec, farmers wore old-fashioned *habitant* clothes of homespun materials along with distinctive hooded coats called *capotes* tied with colorful sashes (*ceinture fléchée*). Immediately upon settling in the United States, they shed their rural clothes and donned fashionable styles. A Jesuit priest who served in French Canadian parishes in New England wrote the following about French Canadians in 1890: "The boys, wearing clean and well cared for clothes, now look like little gentlemen. The girls are elegantly dressed and, to be sure, there are plenty of ribbons. Even the grandparents have been won over; the oldtimer and his wife are very nearly converted to American fashions."[24]

French Canadians have a flair for fashion. Many of the women knew how to sew and made fashionable clothes for themselves and their children. In Maine, Arthur Benoit began a clothing business that developed into a well-known chain of retail stores. Benoit came to Maine from St. Dominique, Quebec, as a factory hand in the 1870s. He moved into the men's clothing business, eventually establishing Benoit's. His son and grandson continued the family business, expanding it into the largest chain of men's clothing stores in Maine. In business for over one hundred years, Benoit's closed in 1990.

Italian Americans form another important component of New England's diverse ethnic landscape. In the late nineteenth and early twentieth centuries, ships brought emigrants from Italy directly to New England ports. They settled in specific neighborhoods, some of which still retain a strong Italian flavor, such as Boston's North End and Providence's Federal Hill. In the old neighborhoods, elderly men wore cardigan sweaters and hats in keeping with the customs in the old country they left behind. Older women often wore village black to signify mourning. As the twentieth century progressed, many Italian American families moved to the suburbs and diversified their clothing practices. Some Italian Americans developed a flamboyant "Guido" or "Vinnie" look complete with gold chains, a visual symbol of wealth and achievement. Young females preferred flashy styles and chunky jewelry. They patronized beauty salons to maintain their nails and voluminous hairstyles. This manner of dressing contrasted sharply with the region's long-established conservative White Anglo Saxon Protestant (WASP) attire.

Current Italian Americans are fashion innovators who are sophisticated in their dress. Men wear Italian cut suits, which fit more closely to the body than English suits. The fabrics differ from the gray flannel and navy blue worsted preferred by New England Yankees. The more successful Italian American may patronize a tailor, perhaps one trained in Italy. Fine leather products from Gucci or Prada, for which Italy is well known, also feature in these men's wardrobes. Throughout southern New England, one can find men's clothing stores that cater to this Italian American trade.

As elsewhere in the United States, Native Americans in New England stopped trying to blend into the dominant culture after the social upheaval of the 1960s. They began to wear markers of their ethnicity on an everyday basis—long hair for men, braid hairstyles for women, clothes decorated with Indian motifs. For the pow-wow tribal celebrations that take place annually, many wear full native costume termed "regalia." Because little is known about the original appearance of the various tribes in the region, regalia often is based on historical examples of the Iroquois. The "big four" powwows in New England are sponsored by the Shinnecock (on Long Island, once part of New England), the Narragansett, the Mohegan, and the Mashantucket-Pequot. Although other powwows occur, the "big four" offer the most prize money for dance competitions. One of the region's largest is Schemitzun, sponsored by Mashantucket-Pequots for all North American Indians. Authenticity is not required for the regalia worn to the dance competitions; however, a dancer must understand the origins of his or her costume and be able to defend it.

Compared to other regions of the country, New England has a low percentage of African Americans and Hispanics. Neither of these two groups has a distinctive look that is tied to the New England region.

PROFESSIONAL SPORTS TEAMS

New England is home to four national sports teams: the Boston Red Sox, the Boston Bruins, the Boston Celtics, and the New England Patriots. Like sports fans across the country, New England fans wear T-shirts, jerseys, sweatshirts, casual jackets, and baseball caps emblazoned with team logos. As elsewhere, colors of team uniforms become symbols. Wearing team logos and colors expresses an individual's affiliation with a sports team that extends to a community of people and a region of the country. Together, fans watch games, follow the team's progress during a season, and share the lore of previous seasons.

The Boston Red Sox is the oldest professional sports team in New England. Founded in 1901, it became part of the American League. The team's home, Fenway Park, built in 1912, is one of baseball's few remaining old-time stadiums. The uniform with the red socks developed from customary sports attire of the early twentieth century: a shirt and knickers buttoned below the knee worn with knitted stockings and athletic shoes. The red socks gave the team its name. The history of the Red Sox is part of New England legend. Some of the great names of baseball played for Boston including Babe Ruth, Ted Williams, and Cy Young. After Babe Ruth was traded to the New York Yankees before the 1920 season, an intense rivalry developed between the two teams. Since 1918, the Red Sox have not won a World Series, resulting in the continuance of belief in the "curse of the Bambino." The Red Sox inspire strong feelings throughout the entire region. Fans wear Red Sox paraphernalia year round.

The Boston Bruins played their first National Hockey League game in 1924. The team's uniform has not changed much since then. Ice hockey inspires winter attire. Boys throughout the region who play hockey wear Bruins jackets and caps during the colder months. Today, fans may choose from a wide array of jackets, sweatshirts, jerseys, fleece vests, and knitted stocking caps to display their interest in and support for the team. The clothes are in team colors of black, yellow, and white accompanied by the trademark "B" logo.

The Boston Celtics were founded in 1946. The basketball team's color is green, a hue associated with Ireland. The team's first heyday began with the arrival of Bill Russell, winning eight consecutive championships from the 1957–1958 season to the 1965–1966 season. The second heyday occurred in the late 1970s and early 1980s with Hall-of-Famers Larry Bird, Robert Parrish, and Kevin McHale. During recent years, the hip-hop generation has taken to wearing the team jerseys of their favorite professional basketball player-heroes. Even the girls of the hip-hop generation wear basketball gear these days: the NBA is selling snug team jersey minidresses in the colors and logos of the Celtics, 76ers, Knicks, and Lakers.

In 1959 the Boston Patriots became the eighth franchise in the American Football League. After years of playing in other teams' parks (including Fenway Park), the Patriots played their first season in their own stadium at Foxboro, Massachusetts, in 1971. That same year the name was changed to the New England Patriots. When Bill Parcells became coach under a new owner, the team adopted a new logo and changed the primary color of the uniform from red to blue. For many years, fans suffered through mediocre seasons, but in 2002, the Patriots won their first Super Bowl. During the frenzy of a playoff season, the fans went all out to support their team. "Extreme" fans painted their skin in red, white, and blue and braved the elements at Foxboro Stadium.

FASHION REGIONALISM TODAY

Despite today's global society, New England fashion still differs from that of other regions of the country. Climate continues to play a part in how New Englanders dress, if simply to protect them during cold winters and cool, rainy weather in spring and fall. The ways in which New Englanders spend their leisure time, particularly the outdoor sports they engage in, influence their casual attitudes toward dress.

The Puritan belief in simplicity and avoidance of excess has cast a long shadow on New England's sartorial habits. We have seen how the Puritan preference for plain simple styles devoid of decoration persisted into the early years of the new Republic and beyond, establishing a reputation for conservative dress. Some New Englanders—the ex-hippies who have settled in Vermont, or the intellectuals around Harvard Square—feign a seeming lack of interest in fashion.

All five of the principles that affect fashion's development in a particular region still operate in New England to some extent. Locally made materials, such as Polartec fleece made by Malden Mills of Lawrence, Massachusetts, can become favorites. Styles that emerge from collective physical needs—L.L.Bean's duck boots and field coats—have longevity throughout the region. Unique naming of styles, as in Nantucket Reds, signifies regional affiliation, if only as a seasonal visitor. Expression of community identity through clothing thrives, particularly with the caps, T-shirts, jerseys, and jackets of the region's professional sports teams. Lastly, the memory and celebration of historical events in New England are represented through reenactment, or through familiar imagery such as the Thanksgiving Pilgrims.

RESOURCE GUIDE

Printed Sources

Baumgarten, Linda. *What Clothes Reveal: The Language of Clothing in Colonial and Federal America*. Williamsburg, VA: Colonial Williamsburg Foundation, 2002.

Birnbach, Lisa. *The Official Preppy Handbook*. New York: Workman Publishing, 1980.

Craughwell-Varda, Kathleen. *Looking for Jackie: American Fashion Icons*. New York: Hearst Books, 1999.

Cunningham, Patricia A. *Reforming Women's Fashion, 1850–1920*. Kent, OH: Kent State University Press, 2003.

Earle, Alice Morse. *Two Centuries of Costume in America, 1620–1820*. 2 vols. 1903. Reprint, New York: Dover, 1970.

Fischer, Hackett David. *Albion's Seed: Four British Folkways in America*. New York and Oxford: Oxford University Press, 1989.

Gordon, Beverly. "Dressing the Colonial Past: Nineteenth Century New Englanders Look Back." In Patricia C. Cunningham and Susan Voso Lab, eds., *Dress in American Culture*. Bowling Green, OH: Bowling Green State University Popular Press, 1993.

McClellan, Elisabeth. *Historic Dress in America, 1607–1870*. 1904–1910. Reprint, New York and London: Benjamin Blom, 1969.

Nylander, Jane C. *Our Own Snug Fireside: Images of the New England Home, 1760–1860*. New York: Alfred A. Knopf, 1993.

Rexford, Nancy. *Women's Shoes in America, 1795–1930*. Kent, OH: Kent State University Press, 2000.

Trautman, Pat. "Witches' Weeds." In Patricia C. Cunningham and Susan Voso Lab, eds., *Dress and Popular Culture*. Bowling Green, OH: Bowling Green State University Popular Press, 1991.

Trautman, Patricia. "When Gentlemen Wore Lace: Sumptuary Legislation and Dress in 17th-Century New England." *Journal of Regional Cultures* 3, no. 2 (1983): 9–21.

Ulrich, Laurel Thatcher. *Good Wives: Image and Reality in the Lives of Women in Northern New England, 1650–1750*. New York: Vintage Books, 1980.

Welters, Linda. "From Moccasins to Frock Coats and Back Again: Ethic Identity and Native American Dress in Southern New England." In Patricia C. Cunningham and Susan Voso Lab, eds., *Dress in American Culture*. Bowling Green, OH: Bowling Green State University Popular Press, 1993.

Winner, Viola Hopkins. "Abigail Adams and 'The Rage of Fashion.'" *Dress* 28 (2001): 64–76.

Wright, Merideth. *Put On Thy Beautiful Garments: Rural New England Clothing, 1783–1800*. East Montpelier, VT: The Clothes Press, 1990.

Web Sites

Costume Society of America. 2004. Studying and Shaping World Dress. January 15, 2004.
http://www.costumesocietyamerica.com/

Society for the promotion and study of world dress and fashion. The site also includes a link for New England and the eastern provinces of Canada.

Organizations

American Textile History Museum
491 Dutton Street
Lowell, MA 01854
http://www.athm.org/home2.htm

This museum, housed in an old factory building, is devoted to the art, science, and history of textiles in America. The permanent exhibition details the history of cloth. Temporary exhibitions sometimes focus on costume history.

Darien Historical Society
45 Old Kings Highway North
Darien, CT 06820
http://historical.darien.org/

The society has a costume collection for the nineteenth and twentieth centuries.

Historic Deerfield, Inc.
Box 321
Deerfield, MA 01342-0321
http://www.historic-deerfield.org/

Historic Deerfield is a museum of New England history and art within the carefully preserved 330-year-old western Massachusetts village of Deerfield. It also houses a collection of eighteenth-century garments worn by ladies, gentlemen, and children.

Mashantucket-Pequot Museum and Research Center
110 Pequot Trail
P.O. Box 3180
Mashantucket, CT 06338-3180
http://www.pequotmuseum.org/

This state-of-the-art museum has eighty-five thousand square feet of exhibition space including examples of Native American clothing. The adjoining research center contains a library and archives.

Shelburne Museum
U.S. Route 7, P.O. Box 10
Shelburne, VT 05482
http://www.shelburnemuseum.org/

Shelburne Museum is one of the nation's most eclectic museums of art, Americana, architecture, and artifacts. Thirty-nine galleries and exhibition structures display over 150,000 objects spanning four centuries, including historical garments.

Living History Museums

Mystic Seaport
P.O. Box 6000
75 Greenmanville Ave.
Mystic, CT 06355-0990
http://www.mysticseaport.com/

Mystic Seaport is the largest and most comprehensive maritime museum in North America. Exhibits include historic clothing, and role-players wear nineteenth-century costumes.

Old Sturbridge Village
1 Old Sturbridge Village Road
Sturbridge, MA 01566
http://www.osv.org

This two-hundred-acre village shows everyday life as it was during the period 1790 to 1840. Guides wear historical costumes.

Plimoth Plantation
137 Warren Avenue
Plymouth, MA 02360
http://www.plimoth.org/

Plimoth Plantation is a reconstructed village set in 1627, seven years after the Pilgrims landed. Role-players are in historic costume, and there is also a Native American (Wampanoag) site.

FILM AND THEATER

Bruce F. Murphy

New England was the first great intellectual center of the United States, and maintained its primacy in American intellectual life at least through the Civil War. It was the site of the nation's first university (Harvard, founded in 1636), and later gave birth to America's first philosophical movement, Transcendentalism, whose central figure was Boston-born Ralph Waldo Emerson (1803–1882). It was also the source of that tremendous flowering of American literature and culture in the first half of the nineteenth century known as the "American Renaissance" (sometimes referred to as the New England Renaissance). New England was also arguably the birthplace of American political consciousness, as well as being the actual battleground of the initial phase of the War of Independence. Now only a minuscule part of the United States in a geographical sense—all of New England would fit comfortably into Wyoming—the region has had a giant effect on who we are, how we live, and what we think. How strange, then, that one of the arts—the one that virtually defined Elizabethan England, for example—lagged behind all the others: theater.

EARLY AMERICAN VIEWS OF THEATER

The first theaters in colonial America were built not in New England but in Williamsburg, Virginia (1716), and Charleston, South Carolina (1730). Two points should be kept in mind with regard to this omission. First, although a late starter, New England would abundantly make up for its shortcomings in the area of drama (both staged and filmed). Second and more important, the reasons for early New England's lack of a theatrical culture tell us much about the character of the region and what Perry Miller called "the New England mind," which was to leave an indelible stamp on the national character as a whole. More particularly (and ironically), the very culture that retarded the development of the theater in New England would later be strongly represented in it; even down to the present day, a signature "New England style" in theater and film betrays the influence of the region's original founders, their values, and, for better or for worse, their legacy.

Those founders were, of course, the Pilgrims of Plymouth Colony and the Puritans of the Massachusetts Bay Colony. The settlers who landed at Plymouth, Massachusetts, in 1620 were an offshoot from the Puritans, a nonconformist English sect that had existed for decades. The English Puritans notoriously disapproved of plays, and with their party in ascendance the English parliament closed all the theaters in 1642. Around the same time, Shakespeare's theater, the Globe, was torn down. The attitude of the New England Puritans—who, of course, thought of themselves as English—mirrored that of their counterparts in the home country. The dour theology expressed in Connecticut divine Jonathan Edwards' famous sermon, "Sinners in the Hands of an Angry God," found all the drama it needed in the struggle for redemption. This was far more than a metaphor; in *From Puritanism to Postmodernism*, Richard Ruland and Malcolm Bradbury write that

> for each pious settler, personal life was a theatre for an inner drama comparable to the history of the community as a whole. Each day's experiences could be scrutinized for indications of God's will and evidence of predestination, and so the story of individual lives grew in the pages of diaries and journals in much the way historians shaped their accounts of historical crises and public events.[1]

Thus, though it lacked a theater, Puritan New England did not lack theatricality. It was in these devotional forms, not in stage drama, that the concerns of the age were enacted. The Puritans, however, were not without aesthetic sensibilities; in fact, one of their objections to the English church was its stale, pro forma readings and sermons, against which they asserted "the right to choose a minister who would preach and not merely read the officially prepared homilies, and some right for the congregation to hear the preachers they preferred."[2] This was a free speech issue, but it was also an aesthetic and even artistic one—a demand, so to speak, for a literally inspired performance.

It remains true that in Puritan thought, God's plan for salvation did not leave much room for entertainment. Amusements such as hunting, games, and nondevotional music—not to mention gambling and drinking—were hardly thought to be "innocent pastimes." But the familiar image of the fun-hating and self-loathing Puritan who repressed every sensory and sensual pleasure has been shown to be a caricature. Margot Heinemann points out that in England, many Puritans did not disapprove of the theater; many of those who did disapprove were not Puritans; and many of the reasons were practical or political rather than doctrinal. Although some thought "disguise is sinful and imitation a form of lying,"[3] concerns that the theaters fomented dissent and drew people away from church and work were probably much greater worries. But whatever the reasons for the disapproval, it should be recognized that Puritan New England must have been stony soil indeed for the development of theater, since virtually nothing grew there for 150 years after the Pilgrims landed.

Puritanical opposition to the theater was eventually breached, but other aspects of Puritan thought, many of them positive, lived on. "Puritanism may have set limits on the American imagination; it was also one of its essential roots," remark Ruland and Bradbury.[4] To be sure, there are other strands in New England culture, but the Puritan "commitment to self-scrutiny and conscience"[5] can still be traced, even in the dramatic art of which they disapproved—as well as in the film art they could not have imagined.

ENTER THE YANKEE

The first theatrical performance in New England is said to have been the dramatization of Thomas Otway's *The Orphan* in a Boston coffee shop in 1750. A scuffle of some kind erupted, which led the government to ban any more plays. Disapproval of the theater was still prevalent in New England (and, to be fair, in other colonies as well), and it would be more than a decade before the next attempt was made. The theater company of David Douglass played in Newport, Rhode Island, in 1761–1762, including a benefit performance for the poor. Apparently this generosity did

> ## An Act to Prevent State Plays and other Theatrical Entertainments within this Colony. Rhode Island, 1762
>
> For preventing and avoiding the many mischiefs which arise from public stage-plays, interludes and other theatrical entertainments which not only occasion great and unnecessary expenses and discourage industry and frugality but likewise tend generally to increase immorality, impiety and contempt of religion.
>
> Be it therefore enacted by this General Assembly and by the authority thereof it is enacted that immediately from and after the publication of this Act, no person or persons whatsoever shall or may for his or her gain or any price or valuable consideration, by or under any pretence whatsoever, let or suffer to be used or improved, any house room or place whatsoever in this colony, acting or carrying on any stage plays, interludes or other theatrical entertainments, on pain of forfeiting and paying for each and every day or time such house room or place shall be let, used or improved, contrary to the true intent and meaning of this Act £50 lawful money.

little to thaw the antitheatrical mood, because when Douglass went to build a theater in Providence, he had to disguise it as a schoolhouse. No one was fooled; the colonial government responded with "An Act to Prevent Stage Plays and other Theatrical Entertainments within this Colony," following the example of the Massachusetts legislature.

It should be clear that here we are speaking of early theatrical performances by European immigrants; performance among Native American peoples had probably been going on for centuries before the settlers arrived. The entire American "mission," as it were, was predicated on the displacement, disenfranchisement, and destruction of the Native Americans. This harsh reality, however, would remain invisible in American theater for a long time to come. The long tradition of Native American ritual performance is not recorded because these were not literate societies, but also because those who could have recorded it—the colonists—saw no value in it. One New England colonist who observed an Indian "harvest dance" in 1674 found it "impious."[6] No doubt other performances, if they were noticed at all, were met by the same incomprehension; if the Puritans disapproved of other *Christian* denominations, how likely was it that the practices of Native Americans—dismissed as "savages"—would be considered worthy of transmittal?

The growing rebelliousness of the colonies in the years leading up to the American Revolution seems to have stimulated theater in New England. One of its practitioners was Mercy Otis Warren (1928–1814), who wrote several plays satirizing the English governor of the Massachusetts Bay Colony, Thomas Hutchinson. War-

167

ren was born in Barnstable, Massachusetts. Her first play was *The Adulateur* (1772), written in the wake of the Boston Massacre. New England history was already supplying material for the theater, as it would continue to do for the next two centuries. The stage was beginning to show its political power. Hugh Henry Brackenridge (1748–1816) wrote *The Battle of Bunker's-Hill* (1776) the year after the battle occurred; Addison's *Cato* (1709), which celebrated Roman civic virtue rising up against tyranny, was popular for obvious reasons. For the opposition, British general John Burgoyne wrote a farce about the blockade of Boston and had it performed in Faneuil Hall practically as the event was happening. Theater boomed during the Revolution as both sides used it to advance their cause—and the Continental Congress followed the by-now established tradition and took measures to suppress it.

Royall Tyler (1757–1826), born in Boston, is often but incorrectly credited with the first play by an American playwright to be performed in North America. However, his comedy *The Contrast* (1787) was certainly the first homegrown play to achieve enduring theatrical influence. One of the reasons was that he established the Yankee character as a stock stage figure. He had ample experience of the type: Tyler was educated at Harvard College, served in the American Revolution, and would live much of his later life in Vermont, where he was a justice of the state supreme court. The plot of *The Contrast* is a familiar comedy of manners about true love triumphing over rogues and social conventions. But the figure of the servant Jonathan was a new contribution, the plain-spoken Yankee of dry wit and hard sense, often comical but also wise. Another theme, "the contrast" between the corrupt manners and morals of old Europe and the virtuous new republic, was also destined to be repeated over and over on stage and in film. Thus New England values were entwined with the shaping of an ideal of the national character and destiny. Yet another theme, the contrast between city sophistication and rural simplicity, provided opportunities for humor at the Yankee's expense, while also mirroring the European/American dichotomy.

Interestingly, Jonathan echoes Puritan disapproval of drama from within the play when he calls the theater "the devil's drawing room."[7] At the same time, Tyler shared the view of many writers of his age who believed that it was imperative to create a national literature that would be distinctly American, and that included drama. For the most part, the plays that had been performed in the colonies were English classics such as Shakespeare or more recent imports. Now it was time to produce theater out of the conditions of the New World and the new country itself. Drawing "the contrast" of corrupt old Europe with young republican America was part of the nationalist strategy—and it dovetailed nicely with earlier defenses of the theater as morally uplifting. For Puritanism held the moral high ground, and aspiring thespians had been forced to justify theater on those terms. Thus, the productions of Douglass' company in the 1760s had begun with a prologue exculpating theater:

> Much has been said at this unlucky time,
> To prove the treading of the stage a crime.
> Mistaken zeal, in terms oft not so civil,
> Consigns both play and players to the devil.
> Yet wise men own, a play well chose may teach

Such useful moral truths as the parsons preach,
May teach the heart another's grief to know,
And melt the soul in tears of generous woe.[8]

The most successful plays of the following century—Shakespeare and the classics apart—would indeed be those that advanced moral causes. As theater expanded, a division would emerge between "high" and "low" theater, with edifying melodramas being played before high-class audiences and republican celebrations of the American victory in the war appealing to tradesmen, immigrants, and the working class. But at both levels, plays adopted the requisite tone of celebrating virtue.

THE NINETEENTH CENTURY

In the first half of the nineteenth century, theaters began to spring up in New England; lit by the open flame, they also frequently burned down. Sometimes they were actually torn down or burnt by mobs, because theaters became a locus for confrontations between political factions. New England was making up for its theatrical backwardness, and "probably the finest theater of the early republic years was built in Boston, the fortress of Puritanism."[9] An assortment of what we would call "alternative spaces" also existed. One popular practice was the mounting of theatrical productions in museums. W. H. Smith was a stage manager and actor at the Boston Museum for more than fifteen years. In 1844, he wrote *The Drunkard*, which had over a hundred performances in its first year—in fact, it became one of the great theatrical hits of the nineteenth century and a nationwide phenomenon. The play chronicles the deterioration of the hero's life under the influence of drink, and his later social rehabilitation through abstinence and sobriety. So popular was Smith's play that it was still being performed decades later. Obviously, this melodrama of personal salvation appealed to the century-long temperance movement that would eventually result in Prohibition. It affirmed traditional values and the Puritan metaphysical drama of salvation. We can only speculate whether the concomitant scenes of drunkenness, vice, and dissolution were thrilling—in the way that, for example, the moral framework of the contemporary cop show licenses depictions of violence, murder, rape, and brutality. The temperance drama became so widespread that it inevitably led to parody; Charles H. Hoyt, born in Concord, New Hampshire, wrote *A Temperance Town* (1893), a send-up of the temperance movement in which the leading citizens of a Vermont town are immoral and it is the drunks who display Yankee virtue.

Burlesque and sensational theatrics were growing side by side with the theater of moral uplift, and often catered to immigrants. Leaders of the Transcendental movement like Henry Ward Beecher (Harriet Beecher Stowe's brother) and Ralph Waldo Emerson opposed the surviving puritanical bias against theater, but "low" theater is not what they had in mind. At Brook Farm, the commune founded in West Roxbury, Massachusetts, by the movement, theater was an integral part of the utopian experiment, facilitating group cohesion. To be sure, it provided amusement, but of a restrained and philosophical kind.

Two developments, immigration and industrialization, were radically transforming New England, and with it the theater. Together they provided new themes, new audiences, and new problems. For the ethnically English and religiously orthodox class that had dominated the region for almost two centuries, it was tremendously challenging (and with hindsight, we might say invigorating), particularly as many of the new immigrants were from Catholic nations. Then as now, new immigrants provoked the hostility of the older immigrants, even as they performed jobs that the established immigrants were no longer willing to do. First the Irish and the Germans, and later the Italians and Eastern Europeans, were satirized and caricatured in theatrical works. The beer-swilling German, loquacious and lazy Irishman, and knife-wielding Italian villain became common stereotypes. Representations of African Americans were the most appalling, with more than a hundred theatrical pieces in the postrevolutionary period featuring "foolish and degrading images of black characters."[10] In melodramas that showed virtue rewarded and vice punished, and the damsel rescued from the villain's clutches, an immigrant was unlikely to be cast as hero.

It could be argued that the rise of moralistic melodrama was general and not specific to this region. However, as has already been discussed, the growing national culture was already suffused with New England values, which the melodramas reflected. Once the legal suppression of theater was removed, the theater grew explosively and variously, including "military parades, gothic thrillers, circus horsemanship, and domestic melodramas."[11] Another theatrical genre was "tableaux" depicting historical events and idealized scenes from American life. One of its best-known practitioners was William Chauncy Langdon, who staged pageants around New England. Yet it was theatrical melodrama that best fitted the pious metaphysical "drama" of carving out a new world in the wilderness, now being secularized from a Puritan vision to a national-republican one:

> And if that drama was frequently presented as a melodrama, in which freedom challenged tyranny, the virtuously new rejected the villainously old, and humans struggled against nature to achieve their destiny, then why should we wonder that melodrama eventually proved the natural mode of the American theatre in its formative years? The posturing actor, compelling attention, was a paradigm, a prototype, an ideal for a society that genuinely believed that the curtain had risen on a new epic in which human possibility would stand as an animating faith and Proteus be elevated to a central position.[12]

But idealism entails disillusionment, and the theater of this period was plagued by a divergence of the ideal and the real. No aberration was more heinous to New Englanders than slavery. America may have been a protean land of possibilities, growing and changing minute by minute, but it was its inability to transform itself with respect to its most shameful institution that brought on the horror of civil war. Harriet Beecher Stowe (1811–1896), born in Litchfield, Connecticut, gave America not only the most popular novel of the century in *Uncle Tom's Cabin* (1852), but the most popular play as well. Like the temperance play, the abolition play was hugely successful—in fact, the play adaptation of Stowe's novel by George Aiken continued to be successful long after the Civil War was over. In 1879, there were forty-nine touring companies performing the play, and in 1899, as many as five hundred. Stowe herself maintained a dubious Yankee attitude toward theater and suspicion of its corrupting influence. Melodrama satisfied the New England bluestocking demand for *moral* theater; unfortunately, this meant that theater more and more showed the world not as it was, but as one wished it to be. Playwright Thornton Wilder would later identify the unreality of melodrama with the fact that it "deals with tragic possibilities in such a way that you know from the beginning that all will end happily." The ascendance of melodrama and sentimentality in nineteenth-century theater led Wilder to make the astonishing claim that "between the plays that Sheridan wrote in his twenties and the first works of Wilde and Shaw there was no play of even moderate interest in the English language."[13]

> ## Harriet Beecher Stowe's Criticism of Theater
>
> It is thought with the present state of theatrical performances in this country, that any attempt on the part of Christians to identify themselves with them will be productive of danger to the individual character, and to the general cause. If the barrier which now keeps young people of Christian families from theatrical entertainments is once broken down by the introduction of respectable and moral plays, they will then be open to all the temptations of those who are not such, as there will be, as the world now is, five bad plays to one good.[14]

But the theater continued to grow, even if it did not improve. The increasing population and cultural diversity of New England produced some interesting results. As the "star system" came into play, it was the idea of Boston theatrical impresario John Stetson to bring European stars to the United States and pair them with American troupes. Thus, he presented Italian stars Tomasso Salvini and Ernesto Rossi in productions in which they spoke Italian and everyone else on stage spoke English. Rossi opened in Boston in October 1881 in *King Lear* and received rave reviews for this unlikely form of bilingual theater[15] (one can hardly imagine a similar reaction today).

Although New York was well established as the theatrical center of the country, it did not enjoy the virtual monopoly on talent and taste that it has now. Thanks to the growth of towns and audiences, touring companies mushroomed; major stars crisscrossed the continent and appeared in small towns throughout New England in tours that are unimaginable today. It had become "a matter of pride for any community, large or small, that fancied its position in its region, to have its own 'op'ry house.'"[16] Many of these opera houses—which were not exclusively for opera, but for all sorts of theatrical and musical performances—can still be found throughout the region, from fishing towns like Camden, Maine, to Claremont, New Hampshire, in the White Mountains. They are often the most imposing and majestic building in town, attesting to the cultural importance of theater in the period before film, television, and radio. Like the republican dramas of the postrevolutionary period, they also served a unifying function. Critic David Krasner writes that "Shakespeare, minstrel shows, touring shows, tragedies, comedies, vaudeville, etc., all had to appear in the same place. This led to a kind of egalitarian spirit in the theatres."[17] In some ways, remote parts of New England were less "provincial" than they are today, and certainly with respect to live performance.

In the latter part of the nineteenth century, the pace of immigration into the United States accelerated rapidly (ending only with the passage of xenophobic restrictions on immigration after World War I). American theater probably reached its maximum dispersion at this time, including in New England. It also achieved a variety not seen since. Ethnic or foreign language drama was common; several

Italian theaters existed in Boston, New Haven, and Vermont. Polish, Greek, and Latvian theaters existed as well. The rise of the labor movement led to worker's productions, sometimes as benefit performances for imprisoned activists, that dramatized the conditions in factories and disparities of wealth. At the same time, European realism was finally having its effect on American theater, sounding the death knell of the melodramatic style (which, however, would live on for decades, particularly in film).

MODERN THEATER IN NEW ENGLAND

As early as the last decades of the nineteenth century, William Dean Howells (1837–1920), who was the leading realist of his day and one of the country's main arbiters of taste (he also wrote dozens of plays), had called for theater that reflected American reality. What modernists like Wilder wanted to do was to restore drama's connection to reality as well as its sincerity. While striking workers were being shot down, Jim Crow laws extended, and women jailed for demanding civil rights (starting with the right to vote), the gross inequalities of the Gilded Age maintained a nation of haves and have-nots. In this environment, it was absurd for melodramas like *Way Down East* (written in 1897, and later filmed by W. D. Griffith) to insist that women were destined to achieve happiness solely in an idealized domestic realm and in marriage. It was farcical to continue to present nationalistic plays that asserted that America had left backward Europe behind and realized human freedom. Somehow, the sincere if flawed spiritual vision of the first colonists had devolved into the fatuous projection of a myth. The "city on a hill" that John Winthrop had exhorted the faithful to build in the Massachusetts Bay Colony had turned out otherwise. Melodrama had failed to keep pace with reality, and probably did not want to; Henry James (1843–1916) felt that the theater of his day offered empty entertainment without social or aesthetic value, a mere parade of types—"an Irish image, a French image, an English image."[18] One has only to make the effort to think of a major American dramatist to see his and Wilder's point; whatever name springs to mind, it almost certainly belongs to the twentieth rather than the nineteenth century.

The foremost name is probably that of Eugene O'Neill (1888–1953). The man who changed American theater more than any other, O'Neill came from an acting family and was brought up in the rootless atmosphere of a touring company. The family's only home was in New London, Connecticut. O'Neill was instrumental in the "little theater" movement, which sought to introduce modernist drama along the lines of the naturalistic theater of Ibsen, Strindberg, and Shaw, and also to discover new American playwrights. At the same time, he was deeply influenced by melodrama. The elder O'Neill toured for years in the role of the Count of Monte Cristo, and the son sometimes took part in the acting company as well. O'Neill's first plays were written in New London; the first performances of his works were by the Provincetown Players in the mid-teens of the new century. The genesis of the players began when George Cram Cook (1873–1924) and his wife Susan Glaspell (1876?–1948) staged a performance at the Lewis Wharf Theatre in an old fish house in Provincetown, Massachusetts, in 1915. O'Neill also lived in Provincetown in 1916–1917; in the summer of 1916, the Players put on his *Bound East for Cardiff*, the first-ever performance of an O'Neill play. Although the Provincetown Players soon moved to New York City's Greenwich Village, the literary community continued to frequent Provincetown in the summers and to put on theatricals.

O'Neill was not the only New England connection to the burgeoning "little theater" movement. In fact, a whole network of forces were converging to revitalize American drama. The poet Edna St. Vincent Millay (1892–1950) was born in Rockland, Maine, and after graduation from college moved to New York, where she became involved with the Provincetown Players as an actress. The Players later produced her one-act verse play *Aria da Capo*, which became a staple of the little theaters. Another Provincetown contributor was Harvard-educated John Reed, author of *Ten Days that Shook the World*, about his first-hand observation of the Russian Revolution. In 1916, the same summer they presented O'Neill's first plays, the Provincetown Players performed Reed's *Freedom* and *Eternal Triangle*. Reed's participation points to another aspect of the Players: their espousal of radical politics. The radical movement and the horrors of World War I deepened the group's commitment to presenting socially relevant and realistic theater. Indeed, many of O'Neill's early plays, such as *Abortion*, could not be performed at all, and in some cases were not staged until decades after his death. Still, O'Neill's produced plays did present workers, prostitutes, criminals, drug addicts, and others who had been left out of the dominant narrative of America as presented in the nineteenth-century tradition, and treated them sympathetically. Perhaps most startlingly, in such works as *The Emperor Jones* (1920), he presented African Americans as major dramatic protagonists, not the racist "comic relief" figures of the previous century.

New England also contributed to the theatrical revival through its schools. College theater groups like Harvard's Hasty Pudding—known as the oldest undergraduate theatrical organization in the country—had been performing on campus since the eighteenth century. Universities also played a role in the development of professional theater. Especially important in the early twentieth century was the famous Workshop 47 at Harvard taught by George Pierce Baker. O'Neill studied playwriting with Baker in 1914; other students who went on to make a mark on the theater were Philip Barry (1896–1949), Sidney Howard (1891–1939), and S. N. Behrman (1893–1973). Baker later moved to Yale, whose school of drama continues to be prominent not only locally but nationally.

S. N. Behrman was born in Worcester, Massachusetts, and although like Barry he was known for sophisticated comedy, he invested it with deeper psychological elements. Like O'Neill, he brought previously stereotyped or ignored people onto the stage, in his case the New England Jewish community he had grown up in—portrayed in *The Cold Wind and the Warm* (1958), which was based on his memoir *The Worcester Account* (1958). It would not be too much to say that the idea of "New England Jews" was nonexistent in nineteenth-century theater (except, perhaps, in Shylockian caricature). Now excluded faces and ignored realities were finding their way into drama. The old cliché-ridden melodrama was breaking up, though as we shall see it found a new home in the burgeoning film industry; likewise, the hackneyed opposition of Yankee rural virtue and the corruption of the city (now not only culturally Eurocentric, but filled with "foreigners") that went back at least as far as Tyler's *The Contrast* was being challenged. Behrman's play *Meteor* (1929) opened in Boston starring the famous acting couple Alfred Lunt and Lynn Fontanne; it concerned a maniacal capitalist who moves to a small New

England college town, and was an incisive exploration of the rapaciousness that would lead to the crash of '29. The character was based on notorious Boston "businessman" Charles Ponzi, whose very name has become synonymous with swindling.

The revisioning of New England was perhaps most evident in O'Neill's *Desire Under the Elms* (1924). Set in rural New England in the 1850s, it was a more mature exploration of the playwright's recurrent theme of twisted relationships warped by a repressive society—and perhaps by the land itself, symbolized by the trees of the title. O'Neill, known for his almost essayistic stage directions, wrote: "They appear to protect and at the same time subdue. There is a sinister maternity in their aspect, a crushing, jealous absorption. They have developed from their intimate contact with the life of man in the house an appalling humaneness. They brood oppressively over the house." For Eben Cabot, one of the sons of the house, "each day is a cage in which he finds himself trapped."[19] The play develops into a story of greed, adultery, and infanticide. Interestingly, it was banned in Boston. It was not the last of his plays to receive such treatment in the "fortress of Puritanism." (Thus, New England was in the odd position of providing writers and subjects for the revolutionary theater while also harboring a reactionary party that stood for the very things that the new movement was criticizing.)

O'Neill wrote other plays set in New England and exploring its darker side. In *Mourning Becomes Electra* (1931), set in 1865, O'Neill again presents a dwelling—the Mannon mansion—that is a kind of pressure cooker of perverse relationships that end (as so many of his plays do) in murder and suicide. He does, however, also give his own take on the Yankee character in Seth Beckwith, a gardener and workman ("Seth" is the giveaway, a name associated with the Yankee). His crowning achievement, the highly autobiographical *Long Day's Journey into Night*, was written in the early forties, but he did not want it published until after his death. Set in New London, it dramatizes O'Neill's own early life. James Tyrone is an actor terrified of poverty, his wife a drug-addict; they have two sons, one tubercular and the other an alcoholic. They are a perfect example of what psychology terms an enmeshed family, its members slowly tearing each other apart, yearning for escape but paralyzed by the relations that torture them. Like Sartre's *No Exit*, but for very different reasons, the play probes the hellishness that is possible in human relationships.

In a way analogous to how Jonathan had criticized theater from within *The Contrast*, O'Neill criticized New England's puritanical aspects while demonstrating the Puritans' "commitment to self-scrutiny and conscience," which in turn was subversive of their other legacy, the myth of the "city on a hill"—still very much alive in melodrama and the culture as a whole. In fact, it was about to be given a whole new interpretation and fresh impetus in the idea of the "American century." The Puritans had envisioned their experiment in North America as a unique break in history and a new beginning; now time itself was to be Americanized in this new century that, in some sense, America "owned." O'Neill's view of New England was especially negative; he was also especially influential, being far and away the most important dramatist of his time. Later commentators (the Smithsonian exhibition "Picturing Old New England," for example) would feel that the dark image of Puritanism was exaggerated during this period.

Theater Venues in New England

Despite the excitement it created, the little theater movement was short lived. It is generally felt to have failed for economic reasons. The little theaters revolted against the star system by placing art over commerce, emphasizing new writers and amateur talent. But although their commitment to amateurism in acting may have been noble, in relation to finances it was disastrous. Eventually, they were absorbed into Broadway, which badly needed their energy and seriousness and offered them profitability in return. The Provincetown Players are a case in point; after the move to New York, founders George Cram Cook and Susan Glaspell became disillusioned with the project and left to live as expatriates in Greece. The Provincetown Players survived for a few years, but collapsed in the same year as the stock market crash, 1929. The advent of the Depression seemed to spell a quick end to the theatrical resurgence.

Oddly enough, however, the Depression years also offered opportunities. The Federal Theatre Project, part of the New Deal, provided employment for thousands of out-of-work theater professionals, and has been called the most democratic experiment in theater in American history. Although putatively national, it was focused on New York, though it did pursue some activities in Massachusetts. The Federal Theatre Project was eventually killed off by conservative lawmakers who feared its radical leanings, and this reminds us of the serious political unrest of the period, to which theater was not immune. On the other hand, theater was also able to creatively embody leftist causes, most notably in Clifford Odets' *Waiting for Lefty* (1935). But the greatest cause célèbre for liberal activists in the interwar years was undoubtedly the Sacco and Vanzetti case, which stemmed from a robbery-homicide in South Braintree, Massachusetts, in 1920. The movement to free the two Italian immigrants became an international protest, and continued until their execution in 1927. Maxwell Anderson (1888–1959) based his play *Winterset* (1935) on the case. Set in a slum, its characters include a judge who justifies the sacrifice of a few innocent men in the interest of public order, the son of a man unjustly executed, and a coward who knows the truth but lets others die to save his own skin. Such plays tried to close what one critic has called the gap between "stage and age,"[20] the legacy of nineteenth-century melodrama. Like the Federal Theatre Project, these plays antagonized those who sought to maintain the so-called exceptionalist view of American history and the status quo.

While some little theaters went out of business, others flourished. The Peterborough Players, founded in 1933 in Peterborough, New Hampshire, is still in existence. From the beginning, they pursued a little theater agenda. In 1940, they presented Thornton Wilder's *Our Town* in the town where he had written the play (at the nearby MacDowell Colony), Peterborough being his fictionalized "Grover's Corners." *Our Town* has been called sentimental and Wilder himself said Grover's Corners was meant to be a universal setting rather than a portrait of a New Hampshire town at the turn of the century, and yet the play's austerity, lack of a set, and efforts toward dialect still seem to bear the stamp of its New England roots. Another New England theatrical institution dating from the same period (1928) and still thriving is the Berkshire Theatre Festival in western Massachusetts, one of the oldest in the country. The nearby Williamstown Theatre Festival received the Regional Theatre Tony Award in 2002 for its contribution to the growth of theater nationally, the only summer theater to have received such an award to date.

As the little theater movement was failing, the regional theater movement was being born, and really gained momentum after 1945. The movement for little theaters was principally aesthetic; it was opposed to the values of Broadway, not the existence of Broadway itself. At the turn of the century, when there were two thousand theater companies throughout the country and the opera houses flourished, theater was regional. Radio, film, the Depression, and, starting in the 1940s, television all helped to shrink regional theater to a shadow of itself, a development quickly answered with calls for a revival. For the moment, New England summer stock theaters still attracted New Yorkers anxious to escape the heat of the city and the low point of the theatrical season. The "tryout" system still existed, by which plays opened in New England—Boston, New Haven, and Hartford—before moving to New York. But these institutions were slipping. By 1958, when Archibald MacLeish's version of the book of Job, *J.B.*, opened at the University Theatre at Yale in its world premiere, it was cause for comment. Following decades were to see a resurgence of theater in the region despite difficult circumstances.

A distinction is generally made between community theater and regional theater, the former being amateur and the latter professional. Community theater is alive in all parts of New England; creating viable regional theaters with the resources not only to perform classics but to foster new talent and mount world premieres has been more challenging. New England theater was plagued in the postwar period by economic factors and increasing centralization. The plays that appear on the Boston stage and in other cities in the region tend to be proven New York products, which in turn may be imports—in contrast to O'Neill's time, a hit play today is more likely to have its origin in London than New London. Costs and the difficulty of competing with New York have meant that few if any regional theaters have been able to survive without institutional or government support. The Trinity Repertory theater in Providence, Rhode Island, founded in 1964, received an early boost from grants from the federal government to present plays in high schools. It later started a conservatory linked to degree programs at local colleges, and receives local, state, and federal funding.

New England theater has been able to hold its own, particularly in New Haven, which benefits by its proximity to New York. One of the most important developments in American theater in the past two decades has been the meteoric rise of the African American playwright August Wilson (1945–). Several of his plays have had their premieres at the Yale Repertory Theatre, including Pulitzer Prize winners *Fences* (1985) and *The Piano Lesson* (1987). The Yale Repertory was founded by Robert Brustein, a dean of the Yale School of Drama, in 1966. Unlike the University Theatre where *J.B.* premiered, the Yale Repertory is a professional theater, and has sent ten plays on to Broadway. The Yale School of Drama was founded in 1924, and its first chairman was George Pierce Baker, who was previously at Harvard (Brustein has been a figure similar to Baker, having also cofounded the American Repertory Theatre at Harvard in 1980). Brustein has been at the forefront of innovative American theater. Only a year after its founding, the Yale Repertory premiered *We Bombed in New Haven* (1967), Joseph Heller's stage adaptation of his antiwar and highly experimental novel *Catch-22* (1961). Just as the novel had satirized McCarthyism and militaristic thinking, the play criticized the U.S. war in Vietnam.

New Haven has another repertory theater, the Long Wharf Theatre, founded in 1965 by graduates of Yale. It also has a share of premieres that have transferred to Broadway, as well as at least two Pulitzers. Other important theaters in the region include the Huntington Theatre Company (at Boston University), the Merrimack Repertory Theatre (Lowell, Massachusetts), and the Hartford Stage Company (founded in 1964 in Hartford, Connecticut, in an old grocery warehouse). In northern New England, low population density has made it difficult to maintain vibrant regional theaters. Vermont has only six hundred thousand residents; Maine has twice that many, but is geographically almost as large as all the other New England states combined. The largest regional theater in northern New England is the Portland Stage Company, founded in 1974 in Portland, Maine.

A revival of a different kind is taking place in the French-speaking community of Maine (20 percent of the population of the state). It is important to remember that a large portion of this state was under French control until the end of the seventeenth century, and was known as Acadia. French colonists, unlike their English counterparts, were often landless aristocrats, and they did everything they could to imitate the fashions of the home country. French theatrical performances took place in Nova Scotia in the early 1600s; it is at least possible that the first play performed in New England was actually in French and put on by Acadians. Marc Lescarbot (c. 1570–1642), for example, was a poet and playwright who emigrated to Acadia in 1606. Today, the theater troupe Les gens d'à côté and playwright Grégoire Chabot are reviving Franco-American theater; Susan Poulin is another figure in the movement.

There are signs that professional theater is moving back into the space left empty with the decline of regional theater (perhaps we should say rural theater) in the early twentieth century. In 1997 the Penobscot Theatre Company, an outgrowth of a small summer theater founded in the seventies, acquired the Bangor Opera House. The industries that made small cities in rural New England rich during the nineteenth century have either aged or died; it remains to be seen whether these smaller localities can sustain a local theatrical culture in the twenty-first century.

NEW ENGLAND FILM

The history of film is obviously intimately tied to the history of theater, in New England as elsewhere. Some of the earliest films shot in New England have been preserved at the Library of Congress and the Northeast Historic Film archive in Bucksport, Maine. Many others have been lost. In the first days of film, the medium exploited what film historian Gerald Mast called "visual amazement"—the fact that anything could be represented at all was seen as a marvel. Thus, *Yale Football Team at Practice* (1896) was probably as enthralling as a Super Bowl to the viewers who first saw it. Films of people at work like *Drawing a Lobster Pot* (1901) have a long history, and have provided invaluable documentation of New England industries, such as factory work, logging, farming, and fishing. The first films lasted only a few minutes at most, and were often shown before or after theatrical entertainment of some other kind.

The narrative element had come into film by the turn of the twentieth century and revolutionized it. From this point on, the history of New England film in many ways recapitulates the history of New England theater. The region had two deep resources, history and literature, that provided narrative material for early filmmakers, just as they had for theater in previous centuries. In addition, film also went through a melodramatic phase, ironically beginning at about the same time when the theatrical stage was abandoning it. Harriet Beecher Stowe's *Uncle Tom's Cabin* again proved its enduring popularity, the first of many film versions appearing as early as 1903 (the most famous version was made in 1927 by Carl Laemmle at a cost of $2 million). A film based on Henry Wadsworth Longfellow's poem *Evangeline*, a romance set against the tragic deportation of the Acadians (French-speaking Nova Scotians) to Maine by the British, was made with Dolores Del Rio in 1929. Nathaniel Hawthorne's *The Scarlet Letter*—the touchstone for any treatment of Puritanism—was filmed in 1908, 1911, 1913, 1917, 1926, and 1934. *The House of the Seven Gables* was first filmed in 1910, and Hawthorne's short story "Feathertop" was very popular, having its third version in 1923 as *Puritan Passions*. Herman Melville's *Moby Dick* was filmed in 1930 with John Barrymore, whose brother Lionel would make a somewhat larger mark in New England films in a series of sea captain roles. Mark Twain's *A Connecticut Yankee in King Arthur's Court* was filmed in 1921 and again in 1949, with Bing Crosby. Several of popular novelist Kenneth Roberts' works were made into films, including *Captain Caution* (1940) starring Victor Mature, in which a Maine vessel is attacked during the War of 1812. *As the Earth Turns* (1934) was based on a nineteenth-century novel by Gladys Hasty Carroll.

History was a bread-and-butter subject for the industry from the beginning. *The Battle of Bunker Hill* (1911) featured Boston-born Ralph Ince (1887–1937), one of three Ince brothers who would be important in the early days of film. Another early picture, *The Midnight Ride of Paul Revere* (1914), had silent star Augustus Phillips in the title role. *Paul Revere* followed in 1924. *Benedict Arnold* was made in 1909. It would be interesting to know how this lost film portrayed Arnold, who on the one hand was the hero who made an unimaginably daring and indescribably painful winter trek through New England to attack Quebec, but whose name has become synonymous with *traitor*. New England history films have continued down to the present day. Some of the milestones along the way have been *Johnny Tremain* (1957), a fictional Disney story about a young silversmith who becomes involved in the American Revolution, and *Glory* (1989), a Civil War film about the first black regiment commanded by Bostonian Robert Gould Shaw, in which Denzel Washington and Morgan Freeman made significant appearances. Freeman also starred in Steven Spielberg's *Amistad* (1997), portions of which were filmed in Connecticut, Massachusetts, and Rhode Island. The story is based on a slave revolt aboard a Spanish ship in 1839.

History of course includes criminal history, and New England has had some celebrated cases. *The Brinks Job* (1979) was based on what was the biggest robbery of all time, which became a relatively lighthearted vehicle for Peter Falk and Peter Boyle. *Reversal of Fortune* (1990), with Jeremy Irons and Glenn Close, explored the bizarre case surrounding the death of Newport socialite Sunny von Bulow and her husband's trial. *A Civil Action* (1998) concerns a different kind of case, involving a suit against polluters whose dumping of toxic chemicals is suspected to have led to the death of several children from leukemia. Sherwood Anderson's play based on the Sacco and Vanzetti case, *Winterset*, was filmed in 1936 with Burgess Meredith reprising his stage performance. Most famous of all is the strange story of Albert DeSalvo; despite his conviction, doubt continues as to whether he was really the Boston Strangler. *The Boston Strangler* (1968), a film with Tony Curtis, Henry Fonda, and George Kennedy, was especially dark for its time and prefigured the later style of intense crime dramas.

The use of literary works about New England (but not always by New Englanders) as a basis for films has continued down to the present day—Richard Russo's novel of life in a depressed Maine mill town, *Empire Falls* (2004), being only the latest. *The Hotel New Hampshire* (1984) and *The Cider House*

Portions of Steven Spielberg's *Amistad* (1997) were filmed in Connecticut, Massachusetts, and Rhode Island. Photofest.

Rules (1999), based on John Irving novels; *Ethan Frome* (1993), from Edith Wharton's novel set in rural New England; and Carolyn Chute's *The Beans of Egypt, Maine* (1994) are other recent examples. *Mystic River* (2003), based on a crime novel by Dennis Lehane and directed by Clint Eastwood, starred Sean Penn, Tim Robbins, Kevin Bacon, and Laurence Fishburne.

No New England author has been adapted as much as Henry James. Ironically, James spent five long years in midcareer trying to become a successful playwright, and failed. But his novels have had stunning success in a theatrical medium that was still in its infancy when he died in 1916. James was the perfect vehicle for costume drama master James Ivory, who filmed *The Europeans* in 1979 with Lee Remick and a screenplay by Ruth Prawer Jhabvala. Set in the New England countryside, the story is a knowing and ironic exploration of American-European relations, benefiting from all of James' expatriate wisdom. The simple oppositions of melodrama—jaded, immoral Europe and young, idealistic America—are exploded in James' subtle and witty novel, which is fairly well transmitted. The film was made on location in New Hampshire and Massachusetts. Also deserving of mention among the flurry of James adaptations by Ivory (several are set in Europe) is *The Bostonians* (1984), in which a young suffragette meets a Mississippian who is hardly her ideal man.

Locating New England

Even this preliminary examination of New England films brings out a general feeling for the territory; what we find there is brought into even sharper relief by a reminder of what is missing. For example, New England does not have the equivalent of the French sex comedy, nor has it found its own Woody Allen. Instead, New England film has taken its cues from New England literature and the region's past, and even from its landscape. From the beginning, film began duplicating the twin images of a dark, puritanical inwardness and the pastoral New England village with its humorous, wise Yankee. New England rarely seems to be "neutral ground." Rather, the region continues to be the perfect backdrop for dramas of the soul, as it was for the Puritans. Its cold, harsh winters, blazing fall colors, brilliant but brief summers, and long-awaited (and muddy) springs were long ago turned into metaphors for moral concepts—punishment, redemption, penance, grace. For example, in *On Golden Pond* (1981), filmed largely at Squam Lake in New Hampshire, the golden summer offers Henry Fonda's character—an elderly father and harsh New Englander who cannot show his feelings—one last chance to connect emotionally with his daughter. *The Whales of August* (1987), set during the summer on the coast of Maine, brought together actresses Lillian Gish (1893–1993) and Bette Davis (1908–1989) as two elderly sisters for whom time is running out. In *The Ice Storm* (1997), director Ang Lee used weather to symbolize the emptiness of suburbia for children growing up in Connecticut during the 1970s.

Both *On Golden Pond* and *The Whales of August* were based on plays. Eugene O'Neill's plays have often been filmed, and Thornton Wilder's *Our Town* was adapted in 1940. But that is not the only way in which film and theater continue to overlap; even today, in rural New England the nearest movie theater may be the local opera house and not a multiplex cinema. The silent era is particularly interesting for New England film because the industry had not yet been centralized. Location shooting was far more of a necessity because of the lack of technologies that could replace it. In the early days, regional distributors were also prevalent in small cities, so a film could be regionally distributed and be successful and never appear on the national scene at all. In this sense, in the period 1895–1915 film and theater were more similar than they ever would be again. They appeared in the same venues; they could be successful without vast expenditures of money; and they penetrated into even remote communities.

Location raises the question of just what is a "New England film." Simply being made in the region does not always qualify a work—some films shot on location in New England have nothing to do with the region at all. For two early films, *The Spoilers* (1914) and *The Girl from Porcupine* (1921), the directors shot in New England rather than go all the way to the Yukon, where the films were set. Today, the reverse circumstance is more likely; with the growth of population and creeping sprawl, directors have gone to Canada to find the "look" of New England of yesteryear. But if New England has been built up, the situation in the New York area is far worse. When director Francis Ford Coppola wanted to find a setting for *The Great Gatsby* (1974), he went to Newport, Rhode Island, even though F. Scott Fitzgerald's novel is entirely set on Long Island and in New York City.

New England Culture in Film

From the start, films generally located New England on the same cultural map as theater (especially melodrama) had been doing for two hundred years. In *The Seventh Day* (1921), a yacht stops along the coast of Maine and finds rural peace and piety—yet another reprise of the popular country/city theme. The film was made, appropriately enough, by Inspiration Pictures. The story, by New Englander Porter Emerson Browne (1879–1934), had already been filmed four times before 1921. Dating from the next year, *Shadows*, with Lon Chaney, was also set on the Maine coast, but viewed it less idyllically. In this case, the Yankee character is the bad guy, who is foiled by a Chinese laundryman (Chaney). The film is ahead of its time in its message about racial stereotypes (though *Within Our Gates*, made in 1919, had dealt with African American professionals in Boston). Descendants of this kind of film include *The Inkwell* (1994), about African Americans on Martha's Vineyard; *Mermaids* (1990), about a Jewish couple (Bob Hoskins and Cher) living in Massachusetts; and *Mystic Pizza* (1988), which dealt in part with Portuguese living in Connecticut. *The Blue Diner* (2001) is about a Puerto Rican woman who moves to Boston and the troubles she faces; *Passionada* (2002) is a romantic story about the Portuguese community of New Bedford and the widow of a fisherman who finds love again.

The New England village, with its prim little houses and picturesque village green, is to some a vision of utopia and to others just a mask concealing a darker side. In *Housesitter* (1992), Goldie Hawn plays a con artist who moves into Steve Martin's "dream house" in a small New England town. The director, Frank Oz (1944–), seems to like using the New England village as a place where city folks go to find peace and simplicity but are pursued by the relationships they sought to leave behind. In Oz's *What About Bob?* (1991), some of which was filmed in New England, psychiatrist Richard Dreyfuss is pursued by a clinging and dependent patient (Bill Murray) who ruins his vacation.

These are comic treatments of the theme; but in *Misery* (1990), based on a novel by Stephen King (1947–), the result is sinister if not gruesome. James Caan is a writer who has an accident and is taken in by Kathy Bates. She turns out to be a fan of his work, but a deranged one. Caan is brutalized and held captive (though the film stops short of the novel's more extreme violence, such as her cutting off the writer's feet).

The comical side of small-town New England life is, as we have seen, a theme with incredible longevity. In recent film, however, the potential for contrast with the darker side has become more important. Stephen King is both an exemplar of the trend and, perhaps, its prime motivator. As the most influential New Englander to be connected with the movies, he has probably done more to shape popular culture images of New England than anyone since Eugene O'Neill. And like O'Neill, he has an obsession with looking behind the picket-fence facades of the small town. The difference, of course, is that for King, the evil often has a supernatural cause. Born in Portland, Maine, he has lived most of his adult life in Bangor. His work could be characterized as New England *noir*. In *Dolores Claiborne* (1995), an island community is unromantically presented. Murder, alcoholism, and incest are lurking just below the surface. Relationships are dominated by silence and repression. A film with a similar setting is *The Man Without a Face* (1993), in which Mel Gibson plays a former schoolmaster whose scars mark him for past transgressions just as Hester Prynne was marked by her scarlet "A." He is an outsider and the locals for the most part treat him badly. Also set on an island, *The Man Without a Face* is more problematic and unrealistic than *Dolores Claiborne*. For example, although an ex-con who makes his living as a freelance artist, Gibson lives in a waterfront mansion and keeps a horse.

King is famous for his use of not only horror, but also the supernatural. In *Needful Things* (1993), the devil in human form comes to a small New England town and brings out the worst in people, unleashing the cruel and murderous instincts that have been carefully suppressed behind a neat exterior. *Return to Salem's Lot* (1987), a poor film, is based on King's story of vampires living in Vermont. King's use of the supernatural to talk about human evil links him to Nathaniel Hawthorne, whose short stories were popular film subjects during the silent era. More recently, in *Meet Joe Black* (1998), a man bargains for his life with the personification of Death, who finds out during his terrestrial stay that life has its pleasures. In another use of the supernatural, filmmakers have returned again and again to New England to treat the haunted house theme. Some of these, like *Beetlejuice* (1988), are comical, while others, such as the recent *What Lies Beneath* (2000), most definitely are not. New England's long history of settlement seems to promote it as the setting for such films; it is harder to imagine an evil spirit haunting a split-level ranch in the Sun Belt than a ramshackle house surrounded by pine trees and snow.

In the Salem witchcraft trials, supernaturalism intersects New England history in one of its darkest chapters. *Maid of Salem* (1937) was an early Hollywood approach to the subject. The recent film version of *The Crucible* (1996) with Daniel Day-Lewis benefits not only from being based on a great play, but also from the decades of interpretation of it as a political parable. *The Witches of Eastwick* (1986) was based on a novel by John Updike and had an all-star cast of Jack Nicholson, Susan Sarandon, Cher, and Michelle Pfeiffer. It expanded the theme of witchcraft in New England, while *The Stepford Wives* (1975) took a different approach to the idea of possession (a remake of this film was released in 2004).

Perhaps the most interesting films of the region are those that bring together a combination of New England stories, New England actors, or New England settings—and sometimes all three. Interestingly enough, some of these films are among the landmark pictures in the history of the medium. Others provide continuity between the theatrical past and the modern world of film. *The Old Homestead* (1922) is one of these; *Way Down East* (1920) falls into both categories.

The Old Homestead (1922) is based on one of the most enduring plays in American theater history. Written by Denman Thompson (d. 1911) in the last quarter of the nineteenth century, it concerns a Yankee character, Josh Whitcomb, who travels to New York City to rescue his son Reuben, who has fallen into evil city ways and become a drunk. He succeeds in finding his son after many comical encounters and brings him back to the old homestead, which symbolizes rustic peace and Yankee virtue. Thompson himself starred in the role until his death, and to this day it is still performed every summer in his hometown of Swanzey, New Hampshire.

The play was first filmed in 1915, but that version seems to be lost. The fact that it existed means that this melodrama featuring themes that went back over a hundred years was playing on stage and on screen almost contemporaneously. The mass audience that flocked to the cinema after World War I had been raised on nineteenth-century melodrama, and this is what it expected in the narratives of the new medium.

No one knew this better than D. W. Griffith (1875–1948), the legendary and controversial director who established many of film's conventions and techniques. The son of a Confederate officer and notoriously conservative, he was attacked for glorifying the Ku Klux Klan in *The Birth of a Nation* (1915). In 1920 he took a sentimental drama about a "fallen" woman and turned it into his biggest (and last) box office hit. The film, *Way Down East*, was based on a play by an obscure author which had premiered in Newport, Rhode Island, in 1897. The play had be-

Filmed on the Connecticut River in Vermont, this scene from D. W. Griffith's silent melodramatic film *Way Down East* (1920) stars Lillian Gish. Photofest.

come a hit with touring companies, and Griffith had to pay the enormous sum of $175,000 for the film rights.

The story concerns a young woman, Anna Moore (played by Lillian Gish), who is seduced by wealthy Lennox Sanderson (Lowell Sherman). She becomes pregnant, loses her child, and flees to the countryside. There she is taken in by a country squire, and the interlude provides opportunities for Yankee humor. After her shame is discovered, however, she is thrown out into the storm, and in the most famous scene escapes across ice floes in a nearby river. These scenes were filmed on the Connecticut River in Vermont, and Gish was in serious danger, both of being swept over the falls and of freezing in her skimpy costume. The cinematographer who shot these legendary sequences was Billy Bitzer (1872–1944), who was born in Roxbury, Massachusetts. Bitzer had a long association with Griffith and shot all his landmark films. The reason the film was such a success, and why melodrama would receive such a boost from the new genre, is that the camera could do things that a play could never do—you could not put rushing ice floes and driving snow on stage. Although the matter of melodrama was hackneyed and it reproduced tired myths and stereotypes that modern drama was challenging, film could present them in ways that were totally new and visually breathtaking. As a film, *Way Down East* was revolutionary, even if its content was reactionary.

Way Back Home (1932) reused many of the plot devices of *Way Down East*—one of the characters even alludes to having seen the earlier film in Boston. The stars of the film are a young Bette Davis (born in Lowell, Massachusetts, her family summered on the coast of Maine) and Phillips Lord (1902–1975), an actor and radio personality. Lord was born in Vermont and became famous for his Yankee character "Seth Parker," which is the role he played in *Way Back Home*. Although comical, Seth is truly kind and plots to prevent Davis from making a similar mistake to Anna Moore's. He also upbraids his neighbors for ostracizing a local woman and her illegitimate son, saying that he does not sit in judgment on his neighbors, phrasing his criticism with a religiosity that is far removed from the caricature of puritanical moralism associated with Yankees.

The ongoing influence of melodrama remains evident in the film industry's penchant for happy endings, no matter how implausible—Hollywood actually made a version of *Moby Dick* in which Captain Ahab comes back alive and, of course, marries. It was not until 1956 that a reasonably faithful version of Melville's classic was produced, directed by John Huston and starring Gregory Peck as Ahab. It takes some of its dialogue directly from the book, including Ahab's "pasteboard masks" speech in which he says that all things (including Moby Dick) are but signs of some greater and more awful reality behind them. Ahab's Puritanism run amok is countered by the Quaker Starbuck, who says that the whale is just a whale, and to think anything else is "blasphemous." The film is also notable for a riveting sermon by Orson Welles as a minister.

The New England coast and its maritime tradition have often been made to carry a "voyage of discovery" theme. The recent *Message in a Bottle* (1999) is a romantic (and rather hokey) take on this trope. Another version is *Down to the Sea in Ships* (1949). It starred Richard Widmark as a "modern" whaling man who serves as first mate under the crusty old captain with the symbolic name of Bering Joy (played by Lionel Barrymore). Barrymore's grandson comes along on the voyage, which becomes his voyage to manhood.

Better than any of these films is *Captains Courageous* (1937), marred by Spencer Tracy's now outmoded presentation of a Portuguese fisherman (for which he won an Oscar). Harvey Cheyne (Freddie Bartholomew) is a young boy who lives in Connecticut with his father (Melvyn Douglas), a tycoon and widower. After Freddie is thrown out of his prep school for dishonesty, his father takes him to Europe—but Freddie falls overboard, and is picked up by a fishing schooner, whose captain is Lionel Barrymore. Manuel (Tracy) befriends the boy, and he is gradually transformed from a spoiled brat into an honest, hard-working member of the crew. The film contains wonderful footage of the old Grand Banks fishing schooners. Another New England connection is that the film is based on the novel by Rudyard Kipling, which he wrote while living in Vermont with his American wife. The story is not so incredible as it at first seems; Hollywood leading man Sterling Hayden (1916–1986) grew up in New England and actually lived the experience of the Harvey in *Captains Courageous*. Although poor, he attended prep school and then went away to sea to be a doryman on the Grand Banks, and commanded his first vessel at the tender age of nineteen.

Of all New England films, perhaps *Now, Voyager* (1942) manages to capture most of the strands of New England's dramatic complexity. Bette Davis plays Charlotte Vale, a spinster aunt of a prominent Boston family who is tortured by her mother's suffocating treatment, which reflects the wealthy, narrow, and repressive society they live in. Her liberation and blossoming into a full human being begins with a retreat to Cascades, a sanitarium operated by Dr. Jacquith (Claude Rains) in Vermont—a subtle version of the old country/city dichotomy. But Charlotte's journey is far more complex; in order to really be free, she has to leave New England altogether. On a cruise, she meets and falls in love with a married man (Paul Henreid), who on an impulse introduces her to other passengers as "Camille Beauchamps." Critic Stanley Cavell has compared Charlotte to Nora in Henrik Ibsen's *A Doll's House*, who in the end leaves a false and stifling situation (her marriage) in order to become a real human being. In that case, *Now, Voyager* marks a kind of successful merging of melodrama with the reality principle of naturalistic drama. Instead of a happy ending, the lovers arrive at a temporary solution and hope for the best—far more like real life than the usual Hollywood product. It is particularly interesting that Charlotte, after her transformation, is able to return and live with her mother and even appreciate her; geography is not destiny after all, and very different people can inhabit the same space. In a sense, they can even inhabit the same body, as her two names show.

Film People from New England

Bette Davis is one of those actresses who was born in New England, often returned there, and made films that had a direct connection to the region; Katharine Hepburn

Of all New England films, perhaps *Now, Voyager* (1942) manages to capture most of the strands of New England's dramatic complexity. This scene features Bette Davis and Claude Rains. Photofest.

was another. A list of people from New England who have become known in the film industry would be enormous, running from silent stars Dustin and William Farnum to Liv Tyler of the *Lord of the Rings* trilogy. Connecticut alone has produced Danny Aiello, camp filmmaker Jack Arnold (*Creature from the Black Lagoon*), Ernest Borgnine, blacklisted director Jules Dassin (*Topkapi*), Brian Dennehy, Glenn Close, Rosalind Russell, and Meg Ryan, to name a few. Jack Lemmon (born in Newton, Massachusetts) got his start at Harvard's Hasty Pudding, as did Fred Gwynne; two of Dorothy's companions in *The Wizard of Oz*, Ray Bolger and Jack Haley, were from Boston (as anyone who heard the Tin Man's accent would know); Rudy Vallee was born in Island Pond, Vermont; Robert Aldrich (who directed Bette Davis in *Whatever Happened to Baby Jane?*) was from Cranston, Rhode Island; and the playwright and screenwriter Israel Horovitz was born in Wakefield, Massachusetts.

One New Englander who made a lasting contribution to film and maintained some connection to his native region was Thomas H. Ince (1882–1924), born in Newport, Rhode Island. Now remembered mainly by historians of the silent era, Ince was the first to make a film of a Eugene O'Neill play (*Anna Christie*, in 1923). Famous for his towering ego, he virtually created the role of producer, institutionalizing many production and financial practices and giving care to every aspect of the film (even writing dialogue that, though it was never heard, helped the actors understand their characters). The films Ince shot in Rhode Island have unfortunately been lost.

No consideration of New England film would be complete without mention of the Ford brothers from Portland, Maine. Francis Ford (1881–1953) directed and acted in more than a hundred films in the silent era, then turned exclusively to acting. He was overshadowed by his younger brother John (1894–1973), who became one of the most famous directors of all time. Although John Ford's name is forever associated with the Western, he also made films set in New England. These included *The Village Blacksmith* (1922), based on a Longfellow poem; the nautical *Hearts of Oak* (1924); and *Doctor Bull* (1933), an unromanticized depiction of small-town life starring Will Rogers. In the last film, once again we find a plot examining the sexual mores of a New England village. Rogers, the doctor of the title, is having an affair, which provokes the town's "respectable" people.

The subgenres of New England film are still alive and well. *The Perfect Storm* (2000), loosely based on the loss of a Gloucester fishing boat in the infamous "Halloween Gale" of 1991, is the latest tale of New England's most dangerous industry. *Man with a Plan* (1996), directed by Vermont-born John O'Brien, updates the Yankee comedy. O'Brien cast retired dairy farmer Fred Tuttle as a retired dairy farmer who runs for office to raise money for his father's hip replacement. *Where the River Flows North* (1993), set in Vermont in 1927, played on the theme of the honest Yankee (Rip Torn, as a logger) opposed by big city interests (a dam company that wants his land), but introduced a Native American character (played by Tantoo Cardinal) as his companion. It was not so long ago that interracial relationships on screen were taboo. Though not entirely successful, the film is an example of more diverse depictions of New England as it is today, and not as it exists in myth. The industry is also becoming ever more conscious of itself: David Mamet's *State and Main* (2000) makes fun of New England film by showing the mess that occurs when a crew tries to make a film in Vermont. Besides mocking the sharp and sometimes unscrupulous individuals associated with the movie industry, Mamet shows how the local New Englanders are equally crafty and self-serving. Finally, *In the Bedroom* (2001) is an intense drama about relationships, including one between a college student and an estranged young mother, and ends in violence and tragedy (the O'Neill strain in New England drama). Thus, in its slow abandonment of romantic melodrama, Hollywood has found its way to the antiromantic melodrama, which substitutes an unhappy ending for a happy one.

In the film industry as a whole, independent film is making a comeback, as the national distribution of low-budget films like *El Mariachi* (1992) and *The Blair Witch Project* (1999) show. Dozens of small films are made in the region each year, as well as increasing numbers of large mainstream productions. There are currently more than five hundred independent film production companies based in New England. Three films by directors with New England connections made a strong impression at the Sundance Film Festival of 2004, including Brad Anderson, maker of *Next Stop Wonderland* (1998). We can expect in the future to see more, and more diverse, representations of the region in film. Filmmakers will continue to be drawn by New England's physical attractions, from the rugged Maine coast to the small village in Vermont or the Berkshires. On a deeper level, New England remains a frequent background and starting point for examinations of relationships (particularly illicit ones) and how they are treated by society, as in *The Scarlet Letter* (filmed yet again in 1995, with Demi Moore), and how conflicts lead to introspection and self-discovery. Doubtless the region will remain a source, returned to again and again, for the restless self-examination of the American mind.

RESOURCE GUIDE

Printed Sources

Bank, Rosemarie K. *Theatre Culture in America, 1825–1860*. Cambridge: Cambridge University Press, 1997.

Bercovitch, Sacvan. *The Puritan Origins of the American Self*. New Haven: Yale University Press, 1975.

Buell, Lawrence. *New England Literary Culture from Revolution through Renaissance*. Cambridge: Cambridge University Press, 1989.

Cavell, Stanley. "Ugly Duckling, Funny Butterfly: Bette Davis and *Now Voyager*." In *Contesting Tears*. Chicago: University of Chicago Press, 1996. 114–148.

Conforti, Joseph A. *Imagining New England: Explorations of Regional Identity from the Pilgrims to the Mid-Twentieth Century*. Chapel Hill: University of North Carolina Press, 2001.

Ruland, Richard, and Malcolm Bradbury. *From Puritanism to Postmodernism: A History of American Literature*. New York: Viking, 1991.

Westbrook, Perry D. *A Literary History of New England*. Bethlehem, PA: Lehigh University Press; London; Cranbury, NJ: Associated University Presses, 1988.

Wilmeth, Don B., and Christopher Bigsby, eds. *The Cambridge History of American Theatre*. 3 vols. Cambridge: Cambridge University Press, 1998.

Web Sites

Deflumeri, Richard. *ArtTix Rhode Island*.
Arts & Business Council for Rhode Island. February 16, 2004.
http://www.arttixri.com

Contains information on performances throughout Rhode Island.

Gale, Bill. *TheaterNewEngland.com*.
February 17, 2004.
http://www.theaternewengland.com

Contains, news, reviews, and interviews related to New England theater.

Meek, Michele. *Newenglandfilm.com*. August 1997.
New England Film. February 17, 2004.
http://www.newenglandfilm.com

A resource for the industry in New England, particularly local film and video professionals, including reviews; it maintains an extensive link page.

Needham, Col. *IMDb.com*. October 17, 1990.
Internet Movie Database, Inc. An amazon.com company. February 17, 2004.
http://www.imdb.com

The largest film database on the Web.

Schilling, Falko. *Summertheater.com*. 1997– .
Falko Schilling. February 17, 2004.
http://www.summertheater.com/Region/region.html

Summer theaters in America; maintains lists of summer theater by region.

Stark, Larry. *The Theater Mirror*. 1995– .
Larry Stark. February 17, 2004.
http://www.theatermirror.com

An on-line magazine covering New England with particular focus on Boston and Massachusetts. Many links provided.

Videos/Films (in Chronological Order)

Within Our Gates. Dir. Oscar Micheaux. Perf. Evelyn Preer, Flo Clements. Micheaux Book & Film Co., 1919.

Way Down East. Dir. D.W. Griffith. Perf. Richard Barthelmess, Lowell Sherman, Burr McIntosh. D.W. Griffith Productions, 1920.

The Seventh Day. Dir. Henry King. Perf. Frederick Barthelmess, Frank Losee. Inspiration Pictures, 1921.

The Old Homestead. Dir. James Cruse. Perf. Theodore Roberts, George Fawcett, Harrison Ford. Famous Players/Lasky, 1922.

Shadows. Dir. Tom Forman. Perf. Lon Chaney, Marguerite De la Motte, Harrison Ford. Preferred Pictures, 1922.

The Village Blacksmith. Poem Henry Wadsworth Longfellow. Dir. John Ford. Perf. Will Walling, Virginia True Boardman. Fox, 1922.

Anna Christie. Dir. Thomas H. Ince, John Griffith Wray. Perf. Blanche Sweet, William Russell. Associated First National/Thomas H. Ince, 1923.

Hearts of Oak. Dir. John Ford. Perf. Hobart Bosworth, Pauline Starke. Fox, 1924.

Uncle Tom's Cabin. Dir. Harry A. Pollard. Perf. James B. Lowe, Virginia Gray, George Siegmann. Universal, 1927.

Evangeline. Dir. Edwin Carewe. Perf. Dolores del Rio, Roland Drew. Edwin Carewe/Feature Productions, 1929.

Way Back Home. Dir. William A. Seiter. Perf. Bette Davis, Phillips Lord, Effie Palmer, Mrs. Phillips Lord, 1932.

Doctor Bull. Dir. John Ford. Perf. Will Rogers, Vera Allen. Fox, 1933.

As the Earth Turns. Dir. Alfred E. Green. Perf. Jean Muir, Donald Woods. Warner Bros, 1934.

Ah Wilderness. Dir. Clarence Brown. Perf. Wallace Beery, Lionel Barrymore, Aline MacMahon. Metro-Goldwyn-Mayer (MGM), 1935.

Captains Courageous. Dir. Victor Fleming. Perf. Spencer Tracy, Melvyn Douglas, Freddie Bartholomew, Lionel Barrymore, Mickey Rooney. MGM, 1937.

Maid of Salem. Dir. Frank Lloyd. Perf. Claudette Colbert, Fred MacMurray. Paramount, 1937.

Captain Caution. Dir. Richard Wallace. Perf. Victor Mature. Favorite Films/United Artists, 1940.

Our Town. Dir. Sam Wood. Perf. William Holden, Martha Scott. Principal Artists, 1940.

Now, Voyager. Dir. Irving Rapper. Perf. Bette Davis, Paul Henreid, Claude Rains. Warner Bros, 1942.

The Strange Affair of Uncle Harry. Dir. Robert Siodmak. Perf. George Sanders, Geraldine Fitzgerald. Universal Pictures, 1945.

Boomerang. Dir. Elia Kazan. Perf. Dana Andrews, Jane Wyatt. 20th Century Fox, 1947.

Mourning Becomes Electra. Dir. Dudley Nichols. Writing credits Dudley Nichols; Eugene O'Neill (play). Perf. Rosalind Russell, Michael Redgrave, Raymond Massey. RKO Radio Pictures, 1947.

Time Out of Mind. Dir. Robert Siodmak. Perf. Phyllis Calvert, Robert Hutton, Ella Raines. Universal International Pictures, 1947.

A Connecticut Yankee in King Arthur's Court. Dir. Tay Garnett. Perf. Bing Crosby, Rhonda Fleming, William Bendix, Cedric Hardwicke. Paramount, 1949.

Down to the Sea in Ships. Dir. Henry Hathaway. Perf. Richard Widmark, Lionel Barrymore, Dean Stockwell. 20th Century Fox, 1949.

The Trouble with Harry. Dir. Alfred Hitchcock. Perf. Edmund Gwenn, John Forsythe, Mildred Natwick. Paramount, 1955.

High Society. Dir. William Beaudine. Perf. Grace Kelly, Bing Crosby, Frank Sinatra, Celeste Holm. Allied Artists Pictures, 1956.

Moby Dick. Dir. John Huston. Perf. Gregory Peck, Orson Welles, Richard Basehart. MGM/United Artists, 1956.

Johnny Tremain. Dir. Robert Stevenson. Perf. Hal Stalmaster, Sebastian Cabot, Luana Patten. Disney, 1957.

Desire Under the Elms. Dir. Delbert Mann. Writing credits Eugene O'Neill (play), Irwin Shaw. Perf. Sophia Loren, Anthony Perkins. Don Hartman Productions; Paramount Pictures, 1958.

Long Day's Journey Into Night. Dir. Sidney Lumet. Perf. Katharine Hepburn, Ralph Richardson. Embassy Pictures, 1962.

Hallelujah the Hills. Dir. Ed Emshwiller and Adolfas Mekas. Perf. Peter H. Beard, Martin Greenbaum, Sheila Finn. Vermont Productions, 1963.

Those Calloways. Dir. Norman Tokar. Perf. Brian Keith, Vera Miles, Brandon De Wilde. Walt Disney Pictures, 1965.

The Group. Dir. Sidney Lumet. Perf. Candice Bergen, Joan Hackett, Elizabeth Hartman. Famartists Productions S.A., 1966.

The Boston Strangler. Dir. Richard Fleischer. Perf. Tony Curtis, Henry Fonda, George Kennedy. 20th Century Fox, 1968.

Rachel, Rachel. Dir. Paul Newman. Perf. Joanne Woodward, James Olson. Kayos, 1968.

The Catamount Killing. Dir. Krzysztof Zanussi. Perf. Horst Buchholz, Ann Wedgeworth. Hallmark Releasing Corp., 1974.

The Stepford Wives. Dir. Bryan Forbes. Perf. Katharine Ross. Fadsin Cinema Associates Palomar Pictures, 1975.

The Brinks Job. Dir. William Friedkin. Perf. Peter Falk, Peter Boyle, Gena Rowlands. Dino Di Laurentiis, 1979.

The Europeans. Dir. James Ivory. Perf. Lee Remick, Robin Ellis. Merchant-Ivory, 1979.

Ghost Story. Dir. John Irvin. Perf. Fred Astaire, Melvyn Douglas, Douglas Fairbanks Jr. Universal Pictures, 1981.

On Golden Pond. Dir. Mark Rydell. Perf. Henry Fonda, Katharine Hepburn, Jane Fonda. IPC/Universal, 1981.

I Am the Cheese. Dir. Robert Jiras. Perf. Robert MacNaughton, Hope Lange, Don Murray. Almi Pictures, 1983.

Something Wicked This Way Comes. Dir. Jack Clayton. Perf. Jason Robards, Jonathan Pryce, Diane Ladd. Walt Disney Pictures, 1983.

The Survivors. Dir. Michael Ritchie. Perf. Walter Matthau, Robin Williams. Columbia Pictures, 1983.

The Bostonians. Dir. James Ivory. Perf. Christopher Reeve, Vanessa Redgrave, Madeline Potter, Jessica Tandy, Wallace Shawn, 1984.

The Hotel New Hampshire. Dir. Tony Richardson. Perf. Rob Lowe, Jodie Foster. Filmline/Graham Jennings, 1984.

Baby Boom. Dir. Charles Shyer. Perf. Diane Keaton, Sam Shepard. MGM, 1987.

The Birthmark. Dir. Jay Woelfel. Story Nathaniel Hawthorne. Film Ideas, 1987.

A Return to Salem's Lot. Dir. Larry Cohen. Novel by Stephen King. Perf. Michael Moriarty, Ricky Addison Reed, Samuel Fuller. Larco Productions, 1987.

The Whales of August. Dir. Lindsay Anderson. Perf. Lillian Gish, Bette Davis, Vincent Price. Nelson Entertainment, 1987.

Beetlejuice. Dir. Tim Burton. Perf. Alec Baldwin, Geena Davis, Michael Keaton. Warner Bros., 1988.

Funny Farm. Dir. George Roy Hill. Perf. Chevy Chase, Madolyn Smith-Osborne. Warner Bros., 1988.

Mr. North. Dir. Danny Huston. Perf. Anthony Edwards, Anjelica Huston, Harry Dean Stanton, Lauren Bacall, Robert Mitchum. Samuel Goldwyn Company, 1988.

Mystic Pizza. Dir. Donald Petrie Amy Jones. Perf. Annabeth Gish, Julia Roberts, Lili Taylor. Samuel Goldwyn Company, 1988.

Sweet Hearts Dance. Dir. Robert Greenwald. Perf. Don Johnson, Susan Sarandon. ML Delphi Premier Productions, 1988.

The Wizard of Loneliness. Dir. H. Anne Riley. Perf. Alan Wright, Lukas Haas, Steve Hendrickson. American Playhouse, 1988.

Everybody Wins. Dir. Karel Reisz. Script. Arthur Miller. Perf. Debra Winger, Nick Nolte, Will Patton. Film Trustees Ltd.; Orion Pictures, 1989.

Glory. Dir. Edward Zwick. Perf. Matthew Broderick, Denzel Washington, Morgan Freeman. TriStar, 1989.

Mermaids. Dir. Richard Benjamin. Perf. Bob Hoskins, Cher, Winona Ryder. Fox, 1990.

Misery. Dir. Rob Reiner. Perf. James Caan, Kathy Bates. Castle Rock, 1990.

Reversal of Fortune. Dir. Barbet Shroeder. Perf. Jeremy Irons, Glenn Close. Warner Bros./Reversal Films, 1990.

What About Bob? Dir. Frank Oz. Perf. Richard Dreyfuss, Bill Murray, Julie Hagerty. Touchstone, 1991.

Housesitter. Dir. Frank Oz. Perf. Goldie Hawn, Steve Martin. Imagine/Universal, 1992.

Ethan Frome. Dir. John Madden. Perf. Liam Neeson, Gil Rood. American Playhouse, 1993.

The Man Without a Face. Dir. Mel Gibson. Perf. Mel Gibson, Nick Stahl. Icon, 1993.

Needful Things. Dir. Fraser Clark Heston. Perf. Ed Harris, Max von Sydow. Castle Rock, 1993.

Where the Rivers Flow North. Dir. Jay Craven. Perf. Rip Torn, Tantoo Cardinal, Bill Raymond. Caledonia Pictures, 1993.

The Beans of Egypt Maine. Dir. Jennifer Warren. Perf. Martha Plimpton, Kelly Lynch, Rutger Hauer, Patrick McGaw. American Playhouse, 1994.

Federal Hill. Dir. Michael Corrente. Perf. Nicholas Turturro. Trimark Pictures, 1994.

The Inkwell. Dir. Matty Rich. Perf. Larenz Tate, Joe Morton. Touchstone, 1994.

Oleanna. Dir. David Mamet. Perf. William H. Macy, Debra Eisenstadt. Samuel Goldwyn Company, 1994.

Party. Dir. Eric Swelstad. Story Nathaniel Hawthorne. Perf. Jay Woelfel, Floyd Harden, DeAnna Hawkins, Ron Litman. J & E Studio Productions, 1994.

Dolores Claiborne. Dir. Taylor Hackford. Perf. Kathy Bates, Jennifer Jason Leigh, Christopher Plummer. Castle Rock, 1995.

The Scarlet Letter. Dir. Roland Joffé. Novel Nathaniel Hawthorne. Perf. Demi Moore, Gary Oldman, Robert Duvall. Moving Pictures, 1995.

American Buffalo. Dir. Michael Corrente. Perf. Dustin Hoffman, Dennis Franz. Samuel Goldwyn Company, 1996.

The Crucible. Dir. Nicholas Hytner. Perf. Winona Ryder, Daniel Day-Lewis, Paul Scofield. 20th Century Fox, 1996.

Killer: A Journal of Murder. Dir. Tim Metcalfe. Perf. James Woods, Robert Sean Leonard. Spelling Films International, 1996.

Long Day's Journey Into Night. Dir. David Wellington. Play Eugene O'Neill. Perf. Martha Burns, Peter Donaldson. Rhombus Media (Canada), 1996.

Man with a Plan. Dir. John O'Brien. Perf. Fred Tuttle, Bill Blachly. F-Stop/J. G. Films, 1996.

Mrs. Winterbourne. Dir. Richard Benjamin. Perf. Ricki Lake, Shirley MacLaine, Brendan Fraser. Columbia/Tristar, 1996.

The Spanish Prisoner. Dir. David Mamet. Perf. Campbell Scott, Steve Martin, Rebecca Pidgeon, Ben Gazzara. Jasmine Productions, 1996.

The Spitfire Grill. Dir. Lee David Zlotoff. Perf. Alison Elliott, Ellen Burstyn. Columbia Pictures, 1996.

Amistad. Dir. Steven Spielberg. Perf. Morgan Freeman, Nigel Hawthorne, Anthony Hopkins. DreamWorks SKG, 1997.

Good Will Hunting. Dir. Gus Van Sant. Perf. Robin Williams, Matt Damon, Ben Affleck. Miramax Films/Buena Vista, 1997.

Home Before Dark. Dir. Maureen Foley. Perf. Stephanie Castellarin, Brian Delate. Hazelwood Films with Scout Productions, 1997.

The Ice Storm. Dir. Ang Lee. Perf. Kevin Kline, Joan Allen, Henry Czerny. Canal + Droits Audiovisuels; Fox Searchlight Pictures; Good Machine, 1997.

The Matchmaker. Dir. Mark Joffe. Perf. Janeane Garofalo, David O'Hara, Milo O'Shea, Denis Leary. PolyGram Filmed Entertainment, 1997.

Monument Ave. Dir. Ted Demme. Perf. Jason Barry, Billy Crudup, John Diehl, Denis Leary. Charlestown Inc./Tribeca Films, 1997.

The Myth of Fingerprints. Dir. Bart Freundlich. Perf. Randee Allen, Arija Bareikis, Justin Barreto. Good Machine Production, 1997.

Say You'll Be Mine. Dir. Brad Kane. Perf. Nicky Katt, Libby Langdon. Eagle Beach Productions, 1997.

Ties to Rachel. Dir. Jon Resnick. Perf. Joanna Adler, Arija Bareikis. Counter Productions and Ocelot Films, 1997.

Anima. Dir. Craig Richardson. Perf. George Bartenieff, Jacqueline Bertrand, Bray Poor. Tangent Films, 1998.

A Civil Action. Dir. Steven Zaillian. Perf. John Travolta, Robert Duvall, William H. Macy. Touchstone Pictures, 1998.

Meet Joe Black. Dir. Martin Brest. Perf. Anthony Hopkins, Brad Pitt. City Light/Universal, 1998.

The Proposition (a.k.a. Shakespeare's Sister). Dir. Lesli Linka Glatter. Perf. Robert Loggia, Bronia Wheeler, Sister Mary Frances, Kenneth Branagh. Interscope Communications, 1998.

Stranger in the Kingdom. Dir. Jay Craven. Perf. David Lansbury, Ernie Hudson, Martin Sheen. Kingdom Come Pictures, 1998.

Williamstowne. Dir. Richard Horian. Perf. Deni DeLory, Richard Horian, Lynn Britt. Woodleaf Productions, 1998.

Autumn Heart. Dir. Steven Maler. Perf. Tyne Daly, Ally Sheedy, Jack Davidson. The Film Cellar, 1999.

The Cider House Rules. Dir. Lasse Hallström. Novel John Irving. Perf. Tobey Maguire, Charlize Theron, Delroy Lindo, Michael Caine. Miramax Films, 1999.

In Jest. Dir. Jay Craven. Perf. Tantoo Cardinal, Sascha Craven. Kingdom County Productions, 1999.

Letters to My Mother's Early Lovers. Dir. Nora Jacobson. Perf. Sue Ball, George Woodard, Molly Hickok. Off The Grid Productions, 1999.

Message in a Bottle. Dir. Luis Mandoki. Perf. Kevin Costner, Paul Newman. BelAir/Di Novi Pictures, 1999.

Mud Season. Dir. Anthony Hall. Perf. Rusty De Wees, Linda Shing. Zia Film Distribution, 1999.

Outside Providence. Dir. Michael Corrente. Perf. Alec Baldwin, George Wendt. Eagle Beach Productions, 1999.

The Blue Diner. Dir. Jan Egleson. Perf. Miriam Colon, Lisa Vidal, Jose Yenque. The Blue Diner Film Project, 2000.

Lift. Dir. DeMane Davis and Khari Streeter. Perf. Kerry Washington, Lonette McKee, Eugene Byrd. Hart-Sharp Entertainment, 2000.

Me, Myself & Irene. Dir. Bobby Farrelly and Peter Farrelly. Perf. Jim Carrey, Renée Zellweger. 20th Century Fox, 2000.

The Perfect Storm. Dir. Wolfgang Petersen. Perf. George Clooney, Mark Wahlberg, Mary Elizabeth Mastrantonio. Baltimore Spring Creek/Radiant/Warner, 2000.

Peril. Dir. David Giancola. Perf. Michael Paré, Morgan Fairchild. Artist View Entertainment, 2000.

State and Main. Dir. David Mamet. Perf. Michael Higgins, Michael Bradshaw. Eldorado/Filmtown, 2000.

Title To Murder. Dir. Steven Furst. Perf. Maureen McCormick. Deco L.A. Productions, 2000.

What Lies Beneath. Dir. Robert Zemeckis. Perf. Harrison Ford, Michelle Pfeiffer. 20th Century Fox, 2000.

What's the Worst That Could Happen? Dir. Sam Weisman. Perf. Danny DeVito and Martin Lawrence. MGM, 2000.

In the Bedroom. Dir. Todd Field. Perf. Tom Wilkinson, Sissy Spacek, Marisa Tomei. Good Machine/Greene Street, 2001.

By the Sea. Dir. Dean Barnes. Perf. Elena Aaron, Tori Davis. Latigo Filmworks, 2002.

Mr. Deeds. Dir. Steven Brill. Perf. Adam Sandler, Winona Ryder. Columbia Pictures, 2002.

Passionada. Dir. Dan Ireland. Perf. Jason Isaacs, Sofia Milos. Sandyo Productions, 2002.

Swimming Upstream. Dir. Robert J. Emery. Perf. Michael Moriarty, Ben Savage, Kelly Rutherford. Media Entertainment, 2002.

Beacon Hill (a.k.a. The Gentleman from Boston). Dir. John Stimpson and Michael Connolly. Perf. Michael Landes, Wendy Benson-Landes, 2003.

Mona Lisa Smile. Dir. Mike Newell. Perf. Julia Roberts, Kirsten Dunst, Julia Stiles. Columbia Pictures, 2003.

Mystic River. Dir. Clint Eastwood. Perf. Sean Penn, Tim Robbins, Kevin Bacon, and Laurence Fishburne. Warner Bros., 2003.

The Stepford Wives. Dir. Frank Oz. Perf. Nicole Kidman, Bette Midler, Matthew Broderick, Christopher Walken. Paramount Pictures; Scott Rudin Productions; De Line Pictures; DreamWorks SKG, 2004.

Festivals

Boston International Comedy & Movie Festival
119 Braintree Street
Allston, MA 02134-1628
e-mail: film@bostoncomedyfestival.com
http://www.bostoncomedyfestival.com

April/May.

Boston International Latino Film Festival
P.O. Box 391794
Cambridge, MA 02139
e-mail: info@cambridgelatinofilmfestival.org
http://www.cambridgelatinofilmfestival.org

October–November; event is in process of moving to Boston for 2004.

Boston Jewish Film Festival
1001 Watertown Street, 3rd Floor
West Newton, MA 02465
e-mail: info@bjff.org
http://www.bjff.org

Annually in November.

Boston Underground Film Festival
The Boston Underground Film Festival (B.U.F.F.)
441 Washington St. Suite 2
Brookline, MA 02446
e-mail: bostonundergroundfilm@verizonmail.com
http://www.bostonundergroundfilmfestival.com

Annually in the fall.

Film Fest New Haven
P.O. Box 9644
New Haven, CT 06536
http://www.filmfest.org

Annually in September. Festival of independent feature, documentary, and short films.

Maine International Film Festival
10 Railroad Square
Waterville, ME 04901
e-mail: info@miff.org
http://www.miff.org

Major festival of international, national, and local film and video projects.

New England Film & Video Festival
Boston Film & Video Foundation
119 Braintree Street, Suite 104
Boston, MA 02134
http://bfvf.org/festival/

Founded in 1976 by the Boston Film & Video Foundation, it is an important festival for independent film and video, both by students and by established filmmakers.

Rhode Island International Film Festival
P.O. Box 162

Newport, RI 02840
http://www.film-festival.org

Showcasing international features, documentaries, and shorts, as well as promoting opportunities for distribution.

Williamstown Theatre Festival
Williamstown Theatre Foundation Inc.
P.O. Box 517
Williamstown, MA 01267
e-mail: webmaster@wtfestival.org
http://www.wtfestival.org

Held annually from mid-June to late August. One of the major theater festivals in the country; it presents over two hundred performances in each session. The festival also provides a training ground for almost two hundred aspiring new talents.

World Population Film/Video Festival
46 Fox Hill Road
Bernardston, MA 01337
e-mail: info@wpfvf.com
http://www.wtfestival.org. or http://www.wpfvf.com

Submissions in June. Competitive film/video festival for high school and college student productions on population growth, the environment, consumption, and sustainability. Offers up to $10,000 in prizes plus national exposure.

Organizations

Boston Film & Video Foundation
119 Braintree Street, Suite 104
Boston, MA 02134
e-mail: info@bfvf.org
http://www.bfvf.org

Offers financial, technical, and educational support to film and electronic media creation and organizes the New England Film & Video Festival.

Berkshire Theatre Festival
P.O. Box 797
Stockbridge, MA 01262
e-mail: info@berkshiretheatre.org
http://www.berkshiretheatre.org

An institution rather than an event, this is one of the oldest professional performance venues in the United States and comprises two theaters, the Main Stage and the Unicorn. Also has training programs, including a children's program and a performing arts students program in the summer which produces two plays every season.

Connecticut Commission on the Arts
One Financial Plaza, 755 Main Street
Hartford, CT 06103
e-mail: artsinfo@ctarts.org
http://www.ctarts.org

Fledgling Films
949 Somers Rd.

Barnet, VT 05821
http://www.fledglingfilms.com

Nonprofit media arts education organization and independent film production company. Also offers an annual intensive media writing and production program for teenagers.

League of Resident Theatres
1501 Broadway, Suite 2401
New York, NY 10036
http://www.lort.org

A national organization, whose Web site contains links to repertory theaters in New England.

Maine Arts Commission
193 State Street
25 State House Station
Augusta, ME 04333-0025
e-mail: MaineArts.info@maine.gov
http://www.mainearts.com/

New England Theatre Conference, Inc.
PMB 502
198 Tremont Street
Boston, MA 02116-4750
http://www.netconline.org

Founded in 1952, it is the region's most important organization that promotes and supports theater and theater professionals. It publishes the *New England Theatre Journal*, as well as a quarterly newsletter *NETC NEWS*, and the annual *NETC Resource Directory*. The annual convention includes lectures, performances, and workshops and competitive awards, including the John Gassner Playwriting Award Competition for new playwrights and the Moss Hart Award Competition for outstanding play productions that dignify the human condition.

New Hampshire State Council on the Arts
2½ Beacon Street—2nd Floor
Concord, NH 03301-4974
http://www.state.nh.us/nharts/

Northeast Historic Film
P.O. Box 900
Bucksport, ME 04416
http://www.oldfilm.org

A leading archive, theater, and study center, it hosts the Northeast Silent Film Festival annually in August. Karan Sheldon, "New England in Feature Films," can be read on the Web site.

Vermont Arts Council
136 State Street—Drawer 33
Montpelier, VT 05633-6001
e-mail: info@vermontartscouncil.org
http://www.vermontartscouncil.org

Women in Film & Video/New England
50 Hunt St.
Watertown, MA 02472
http://www.wifvne.org

Promotes positive images of women on screen, serves as a source of information, and works to empower all women working in film, video, and new media.

FOLKLORE

Michael Hoberman

New England's folklore is diverse in origin and dynamic in scope. Every group that has settled in New England has influenced and been influenced by the region's multifaceted vernacular culture—its oral traditions, holiday customs, and building styles. What all of these groups and traditions have in common is their relationship to a changing landscape of rural, urban, and suburban places. Folklore in New England is a vital and continually evolving marker of its inhabitants' regional identity. Hardly a relic of bygone eras or a vanishing way of life, the region's folklore has always constituted a living link between the past and present and reminds us of how geography continues to both unite and diversify its people.

The region's folklore stretches back historically to the precontact period when dozens of loosely affiliated Native American tribal groups developed and sustained their own linguistic, material, and decorative traditions, some of which persevere—in transmuted form—to the present. Since much of native cosmology identified the land as a transcendent and spiritual entity, and since tribal economies, although often enriched by extraregional trade, were based on local resources, the pre- and postcontact-era Native American folk culture in the New England area was inherently regional, or place-based, in its derivation. Even as the ranks of native peoples were thinned by the relentless forces of European colonialism and its attendant wars, diseases, famines, and policies of forced assimilation, New England native peoples maintained and built upon their original, folk cultural connection to place and the environment. From the bark-covered longhouse to the local legend that tells the origin of a given mountain or lake, New England native people's cultural traditions have evolved out of and responded to local geographical circumstances.

Successive generations of Old World settlement may not have resulted in the same degree of investment in the landscape; nonnative peoples brought with them prior allegiances to other places and preexisting worldviews. But all New Englanders, even the most urbanized among them, have had to respond and adapt to the local geography and climate, and, in doing so, they too have created a distinctly regional set of folk styles. When the Puritans built their first settlements, they worked to shape the landscape in their own worldview image; patchworks of cultivated fields stood as bulwarks, in their minds, against a surrounding forest full of demons and wild animals. To this day, the bare rocky summit of Mt. Monadnock, in southwestern New Hampshire, stands as a testament to this folk mentality. In his many visits to the mountain in the mid-nineteenth century, Henry David Thoreau recalled having been told that for generations, the entire mountain had been forested. The early English settlers had set fire to the top during the eighteenth century in order to drive away the wolves living up there. Neither the trees nor the wolves have returned as yet, but thousands of annual visitors to the mountain experience the trip to its rocky summit as a quintessentially regional pilgrimage.

Present-day New Englanders, of all cultural backgrounds, continue to shape a set of folk regional styles that derive from their multifaceted relationship to this place. Gloucester, Massachusetts' annual blessing of the fleet, which began as a predominantly Italian festival devoted to St. Peter, has clear Old World roots. But in its celebration of the local North Atlantic fishing fleet and of the continuing legacy of Gloucester's centuries-old nautical tradition, this festival speaks as well to a complex region-specific history of both devotion to and fear of the local waters—appreciation for the gifts they bear and mourning over the mortal toll they have so long exacted. Even sports fans in New England carry on various folk traditions that derive from particular places. Red Sox fans continue to speculate about the mystical properties of a pond in Sudbury that is reputed to contain a legacy of the famous "curse of the Bambino," a grand piano that Babe Ruth was said to have sunk while attending a party there in 1918. According to the legend, as soon as someone finds the piano and manages to play it again, the Red Sox will win the World Series again.

NATIVE AMERICAN FOLKLORE

Native New Englanders' settlement in the region dates back approximately ten thousand years. Members of the New England tribes are the bearers of an ancient tradition whose origins predate European colonization, but whose perseverance through the settlement and later periods is marked by the dynamism of cross-cultural encounter. Native oral, decorative, ceremonial, and building traditions offer consistent evidence of folklore's inherent regional, or geography-specific, nature. Like other ancient peoples, the Wampanoags, whose home is southeastern Massachusetts and includes Cape Cod ("the Narrow Land"), tell all sorts of creation stories that explain post-glacial topography. "Years ago," one such tale begins,

> in the days before the first white people came across the sea, a young giant named Maushop lived in the Narrow Land. He was so large that no wigwam or council house could hold him, so he slept under the stars. Sometimes he lay on one part of the Cape, sometimes on another. The high snowdrifts were like handfuls of beach sand. If he awakened on an icy night and found that the chill had crept under his robe, he warmed himself by jumping back and forth across-Cape.[1]

The tale goes on to narrate how on one particularly muggy summer night, when "the stars hung heavy with unshed lightning," Maushop slept so fitfully that his moccasins became full of sand. Upon waking in the morning, he rose and tossed the sand out of them, forming, in the process, both Nantucket and Martha's Vineyard. Folk memory, in other words, was as old as the land itself. Oral tradition derived, at least in a story like this one, from the depth of that perceived connection.

Native American creation myths persist into the present day. Contemporary storyteller Marge Bruchac, who is of Abenaki origin, tells a tale that explains the origin of a major landscape feature in the western Massachusetts town of Deerfield:

> A giant beaver took up residence in the lower Connecticut Valley, damming up the river and constructing a lodge. When the creature refused to move, the humans appeared to Hobbamock, the shaper, who did battle with the stubborn beaver and broke its neck. Hobbamock allowed the River to flow free once more, and turned the body of the beaver to stone. Those who visit this site today will notice to the east the shape of the head of the creature in the form of Mount Sugarloaf.[2]

Tales like this one remain in circulation because they continue to be relevant. As contemporary New Englanders, native and nonnative alike, face the daily prospect of encroaching development, perhaps Hobbamock's determination to keep the river flowing serves as an appropriate example of spirited resistance to the impositions of economically motivated human endeavors.

In time, as indigenous storytellers came into contact with European colonizers starting in the 1600s, Native American tales changed and, in some cases, began to incorporate Old World motifs. In mid-nineteenth-century Nova Scotia, the Mi'kmaq and Passamaquoddy narrators with whom Baptist missionary Silas T. Rand came into contact had adapted the north European Cinderella to their own traditional cycle of stories about the Invisible One. Desired by all the young women in his village, the Invisible One is pursued by the daughters of one old widower:

> The youngest of those was very small, weak, and often ill, which did not prevent her sisters, especially the eldest, treating her with great cruelty. The second daughter was kinder and sometimes took the part of the abused little girl, but the other one would burn her hands and face with hot coals. Yes, her whole body was scarred with the marks made by torture, so that people called her *Oochigeaska* (rough-skin or burnt-skin girl).[3]

At the end of the tale, when Oochigeaska wins the hand of the Invisible One, she does so by seeing what all the other village girls, including her sisters, have failed to see: that the Invisible One's shoulder strap or sled harness is not a strip of rawhide but the rainbow itself. (She also sees that his bow-string is *Ketak' soo wowcht*—the Milky Way.) The story of Oochigeaska conveys a much different meaning, clearly, than Cinderella; its completion is contingent not on a properly fitted glass slipper but on the rough-skin girl's courageous refusal not to pretend, as her sisters have, to see a piece of rawhide—or an actual man—where none existed. Rand theorized that this story had its origins in native exposure to French Acadian tales, among which Cinderella would most certainly have been found. The influence of such encounters seems undeniable, but it hardly implies that Oochigeaska wouldn't exist without Cinderella.

FOLKLORE OF THE COLONIAL ERA

Among the English, folklore in the earliest days of New England's settlement comprised an entire worldview. Although the Puritans were a famously literate people (few religious sects in history have been so thoroughly devoted to the reading and interpretation of Scripture as they were), they also cultivated and were influenced by an active and pervasive oral tradition, which they had transplanted to the New World. As believers in an all-powerful God, whose whim and direct involvement in all human endeavors knew no bounds, the early English settlers of the region habitually interpreted all natural phenomena as messages to them from an either merciful or vengeful deity. The dominating geographical reality in the colonial period, of course, was the "howling wilderness" itself, which they believed to be the preserve of demonic animals, savage Indians, and sundry other malevolent climactic and topographical forces. What did this all mean? Although influenced by a literate theology, the reading of what was known among the Puritans as "divine providence" relied heavily upon oral traditions and superstitions whose provenance, clearly, was ancient and preliterate.

Increase Mather, the famous chronicler of New England's early history, had, as folklorist Richard Dorson has pointed out, a particular interest in the mystical meanings associated with thunderstorms:

> On the 18th of may (being the Lord's day), A.D. 1673, the people at Wenham [Massachusetts] (their worldly pastor, Mr. Antipas Newman, being lately dead) prevailed with the Reverend Mr. Higginson of Salem to spend that Sabbath among them.
>
> The afternoon sermon being ended, he, with several of the town, went to Mr. Newman his house. While they were in discourse there about the Word and Works of God, a thunderstorm arose. After a while, a smart clap of thunder broke upon the house and especially into the room where they were sitting and discoursing together; it did for the present deafen them all, filling the room with smoke, and a strong smell as brimstone. With the thunderclap came in a ball of fire as big as the bullet of a great gun, which suddenly went up the chimney, as also the smoke did. This ball of fire was seen at the feet of Richard Goldsmith, who sat on a leather chair next to the chimney, at which instant he fell off the chair on the ground.[4]

Although Goldsmith had seemed, to his neighbors, to be a good and Godly man, he had, as Mather put it, "blemished his Christian profession by frequent breaking of his promise."[5] God's way of punishing him was hardly subtle, and his neighbors, who certainly would have heard of the incident, as evidenced by the fact that Mather's testimony was drawn from local accounts of the event, could not fail to see the connection between God's wrath and the lightning itself. Through the lightning strike and by other means as well, Mather writes, "God gave him a deep sense of his evils."[6]

Author Edgar Rowe Snow recounts the tale of the *Fellowship*, a ship bound from

New Haven to England, whose disappearance in 1646 was marked by a ghostly reappearance in the sky. Having left New Haven in January, the ship was expected to return, laden with English goods, by spring. The Connecticut colonists had all but given up on the ship by June, when a strange sight was seen over the harbor. In the wake of an enormous thunderstorm, "a miracle was said to occur":

> An hour before sunset the clouds unmistakably gave way to a strange image high in the firmament. It was the lost ship of New Haven, floating in toward them, sailing on a cloud through the sky. The news was relayed from house to house, and soon the people were all out in the streets, staring in astonishment at the miracle taking place before their eyes. . . .
>
> There was the *Fellowship*, just as she had left New Haven—her keel, masts, sails and rigging—all exactly as they had last seen her two winters before. . . .
>
> Then, suddenly, without warning, the topmasts blew away, to hang tangled in the rigging. The masts soon went by the board, and within a few minutes the proud vessel was reduced to a battered hulk.[7]

Interpreting the chilling event, the Reverend John Davenport, leader of the New Haven flock, interpreted the event: "God has condescended to send this account of His Sovereign disposal of those for whom so many prayers have been made."[8]

Divine providence could also be used to explain larger-scale climatological events, and even geopolitical ones. King Philip's War, which raged throughout southern New England from 1675 to 1676 and pitted the English against an alliance of Pequots, Narragansetts, Nipmucks, and Wampanoags, was, to our view of it today, an early example of a racializing, colonial war. The Puritans, however, saw it differently; much of their discourse reflects on the war's divine origins and implications—their conviction, in other words, that God was out to punish someone. In 1676, Englishman Philip Walker wrote these words regarding the war and the cruelties of the Indians:

> The Righteous God hath heightened our calamity and given commission to the Barbarous Heathen to rise up against us, and, to become a smart Rod, and severe scourge to us, in Burning and Depopulating several hopeful Plantations, Murdering many of our people of all sorts and seeming as like to cast us off.[9]

Fervent belief in biblical prophecy, in combination with a superstitious belief in signs and portents, explained the worldly phenomena of war and English suffering. As historian Jill Lepore has pointed out, Puritan churches throughout the New England colonies declared dozens of fast days as means of atonement in the face of so many perceived sins.[10]

The conclusion of King Philip's War brought about a brief hiatus in the armed hostilities between colonists and Native Americans in the region. Peace can hardly be said to have settled upon the New England colonies, however. As mercantile opportunities burgeoned, as an ever-widening economic margin separated English settlers of high station from those below them, and as more external enemies were vanquished, social and cultural tensions grew. Ever a barometer of regional tumult, the cultural life of New England was profoundly affected at the close of the sev-

enteenth century by what has gone down in history as one of the most fascinating eruptions of folk phenomena ever. The Salem witch trials of 1692 merely marked the culmination of a lengthy obsession on the part of New Englanders with a myriad of demonic forces. As Richard Dorson has described it, "in 1692, the Massachusetts Bay Colony was nervous; they had lost their charter, they feared the pagan Indian enemy without, the Satanic enemy within, and their critics in England overseas."[11] Whether the trials were the result of mass hysteria, the machinations of the power-hungry or any other sort of worldly or supernatural phenomena, they came about at a time of great uncertainty, tension, and fear. Articulated through a complex weave of contemporary Puritan theology and an ancient, paganistic superstitious fear of invisible evil forces, the various accounts of witchcraft in late seventeenth-century New England illustrate just how responsive oral traditions and folk beliefs can be to real world concerns.

Whether the Salem witch trials were the result of mass hysteria, the machinations of the power-hungry, or any other sort of worldly or supernatural phenomena, they were held at a time of great uncertainty, tension, and fear. Courtesy Library of Congress.

Witches and Ghosts

The witch trials were unique in the manner in which they brought about a shared discourse among the most highly placed intellectuals and the lowliest of lay parishioners. For all of the learned theology of the Mathers, whose devoted study of such things put them on exact notice as to what to look out for in a witch, the account of farmer John Allen, of Salisbury, Massachusetts, as Dorson has pointed out, shows how broadly based and deeply rooted in folk tradition the fear of witches could be. Allen's testimony, like that of many of his neighbors, was really no different from the sort of story one might hear today of an encounter with the supernatural. Susanna Martin had asked him to employ his oxen in transporting some staves for him. He turned her down, insisting that the oxen were too weak for such work. At this point

> She threatened him, saying his oxen would never do him much more service. Allen replied, "dost thou threaten me, thou old witch?" . . .
> "I'll throw thee into the brook" [Martin replied]. Off she "flew" over the bridge. Allen led his oxen to Salisbury Beach, a customary resting place, but they all ran off into the Merrimack River and swam out to sea, and only one swam back.[12]

Allen's account seems to constitute flimsy evidence for a claim in court, even by 1692 standards, but as it is corroborated by dozens of other claims of witchcraft, it certainly stands as a useful illustration of how such testimonials clearly emerged from everyday circumstances—from one neighbor's interaction with another. Indeed, rather than arising from extraordinary occurrences, most folk accounts mirror this one in the practically prosaic nature of their original context.

The accounts of Salemites and other New Englanders of their encounters with witches are no different from the sorts of stories we might tell today about ghostly hitch-hikers and demonic babysitters. They gave voice, on a mass level, to societal fears and petty differences and every sort of tension that existed in between. Although these sorts of tales emerge in all cultures, they were thoroughly regionalized in late seventeenth- and early eighteenth-century New England—adapted both to local geography and local social and economic circumstances. Cape Cod storytellers, for example, recount the tale of Captain Sylvanus Rich and the witch of Truro, which features both local landscape features and, more importantly, a set of region-specific circumstances that spoke to the facts of life in a seafaring community. Rich was the captain of a coastal vessel that was returning to Massachusetts with "a load of North Carolina corn to the Boston trade." Waiting for improved weather so that he could round Race Point (the promontory off Provincetown, Massachusetts, that marks the outermost tip of the Cape), and having tired, as the account in Elizabeth Reynard's *The Narrow Land* puts it, of the North Atlantic seaman's "eternal cod muddle," Rich went ashore in Truro to buy himself a bucket of milk from a shabby old woman who had on a pair of "scarlet heels."

> As soon as the shipmaster boarded his vessel the bad weather abated and he put out to sea. No sooner had he reached open water than a great gale began to blow. The ship wallowed; the sails tore. . . . The milk, he maintained, was bewitched. For every night at moon rise an old woman with scarlet heels on her slippers came into his cabin. She put a bit in the captain's teeth. She saddled him and bridled him and all night long she rode him over the Truro hills. Along the Coombs and through the woods, up the dunes and down the dunes, across the inlets, through the town, even around Bound Brook.[13]

The story does not end there either; now under the influence of the night's enchantment, the captain lost his wits and his ship was headed for the Grand Banks before his son was able to talk enough sense into his father and get him to gain control of the situation. What the tale suggests in the way of insight into a regional mindset is noteworthy: Seafarers have no business, it seems, going ashore for such mammalian, domestic comforts as milk. Even if the captain is lord over the sea, his authority gives way on land, where a woman rides him roughshod. Indeed, the tale's inclusion of such an exhaustive survey of the local topography seems calculated to emphasize such a conclusion. In the end, only the determined male partnership of father and son proves powerful enough to overcome the witch's curse.

Witchcraft rumors and ghostly occurrences were clearly hallmarks of the colonial period, when a supernaturalism and concomitant fear of the wilderness and other forces beyond human control dominated so much of the New England mentality. But even as their once dominant influence waned, they hardly disappeared. Nineteenth- and twentieth-century New Englanders continued to take their haunts seriously. Richard Dorson, who conducted an extensive field study of Downeast Maine folklore during the 1940s and 1950s, found that belief in witches was rampant in many coastal communities. The following account, which Dorson recorded in an interview with his informant James Alley, suggests just how persistent belief in witches could be, and offers us an illustration of how tales of first-hand encounters with them remain in dynamic circulation. The story's theme and circumstances resonate with the seventeenth- and eighteenth-century tales of Susanna Martin and the witch of Truro:

> Mother Hicks was a witch. I heard father tell about her. She was a witch. If she wanted anything and you didn't give it, she'd bewitch it, see. And it wouldn't be no good. And they had a cow on Beals Island, and she wanted that cow. And she bewitched the cow. And that cow'd swing around, take jumps, bite herself. Well, they said only thing to do was to kill that cow. That's all there is to it.
>
> So a fellow comes along and say, "Look, do you want to get rid of Mother Hicks?" And they say yes. "You take that cow and kill her and build you up a roaring fire, and fire her innards into that fire, and you'll get rid of Mother Hicks." And they done it. "And it wasn't no time," he says, "they'll be somebody here after something. If they get anything out of your house, she'll get well.... And it wasn't no time before there was two boys come, and they said they had all they could do to keep that innards into that fire, bounds to get it out. And he said, "Mother Hicks is burning up, she wants something out of the house." And they wouldn't gin it to her and that's the end of her.[14]

Alley indicates immediately after telling his story that his father was only one source of the tale; he had grown up hearing it from others in the community as well.

As various non-Anglo immigrant groups began to occupy the region, they brought with them their own witch- and ghost-related traditions. From the Irish, whose ancient All Hallows Eve customs lay behind the eventual creation of Halloween, to the French Canadians, whose harrowing werewolf tales of the *Loup Garou* entered the regional tradition in the border areas and other Franco enclaves in the mid- to late nineteenth century, New Englanders of all backgrounds have long inscribed their landscape with the memory of one legendarily fearsome occurrence after the next. Folklorist Julien Olivier, who studies Franco-American traditions in New England, heard the tale of Aunt Anna from a member of the Levesque family of Taunton, Massachusetts, sometime in the 1970s:

> During the fall, there was something that began to make noise in the house. You know, in those times, they used coal for heat. They began to hear shoveling of coal at night, in the basement. So Charles went down; he thought that someone was in the house. Nothing. He looks at all the windows. It was all double-windows, and they were all locked. The door was barred. He climbs back up. As soon as he gets back up, it began to shovel again. Shovel and shovel.
>
> Not a long time afterwards, they go to spend the weekend at a brother's house, Joe's, in Fall River [Massachusetts]. They tell him the story. "Oh, okay," Joe says to them, "You're easily scared! I'll go there myself and then," he says, "if there's something in the basement, we'll find it."

So, the following week, big Joe goes there. At night, after supper, he goes down into the basement; he looks at all the doors and windows, outside and inside. He says to Charles, "You won't hear noise tonight." During the watch they don't hear anything. But once they're in bed it begins to shovel coal again. . . . It was shoveling and it was walking in the basement. It takes the stairs and climbs up.

[In the morning, Joe] gives his advice: "You would do well to move away from here." . . . Charles goes to the parish priest, to tell him about it. The priest says, "There is something which you have promised to some people. They are in need. You promised a couple of masses to some people.

So, Charles sang a couple of masses—and the thing left. They didn't hear it ever again.[15]

As Olivier suggests in his introduction to the tale, "Aunt Anna" offers insight into the role of faith and religious practice within the Franco-American community. In this regard, the tale is not so very different from the sorts of accounts we associate with the earlier English settlers of New England. Folklore offers a consistent reminder of how frequently our various religious traditions tend to be reinforced by ancestral fears and beliefs in the supernatural.

"THE YANKEE BROKE IN": FOLKLORE BETWEEN THE REVOLUTION AND THE CIVIL WAR

The Revolution and its aftermath brought a new more thoroughly prideful and regionalized folklife to the New England states. If the colonial New Englander was in the habit of judging his or her relationship to the new land through the lens of an Old World mentality, denizens of the early Republic demonstrated an interest in establishing a cultural connection to their own pastures. The overwhelming emphasis in New England oral traditions of the period was on establishing an indigenous character-type, the Yankee. The derivation of the Yankee—his immediate precursor was a rural figure known to many as Brother Jonathan—was in large part theatrical as well as folkloric. As cultural historian Constance Rourke has written in her classic *American Humor* (1931), "Yankee plays," in which this symbolically American and vernacular-steeped New England character was featured, were popular throughout the country. The Yankee, Rourke suggests, "was a looming figure. He might be a peddler, a sailor, a Vermont wool-dealer, or merely a Green Mountain boy who traded and drawled and upset calculations."[16] Sometimes the stage Yankee was the world's greenest of greenhorns, just rolled out from a sheepfold in Vermont and experiencing his first taste of town life. As often as not, however, he knew just exactly what he was doing and where he was. If the Yankee, on stage and in real life, was known for anything it was his understated quick-wittedness, his ability to out-talk and out-trade anyone while seeming all the while, in his ill-fitting clothes and stranger colloquialisms, to have been born yesterday.

The Yankee Character

Stage presence notwithstanding—and these Yankee character-types held forth well into the nineteenth century not only in the United States but in England as well—we might as well ask whether such a type was true-to-life or wholly manu-factured. A more pertinent question from a folklorist's point of view might be, did the oral traditions of actual New Englanders, as opposed to the stereotyping over-lays of traveling theater troupes, feature the Yankee as a central character? To the extent that folklore among rural New Englanders today continues to feature the dry-witted, outwardly humble, and, often enough, crotchety Yankee as a central character, the tradition itself would appear to bear evidence of the dialect Yankee as an important figure. Moreover, published collections of nineteenth-century New England folklore, like Richard Dorson's *Jonathan Draws the Long Bow* (1946) and B. A. Botkin's *Treasury of New England Folklore* (1947), which are largely based on popular accounts circulated in local newspapers of the age in question, would suggest that the theater Yankee, even if he drove some of the indigenous folk tra-ditions himself, was not an imagined type, but a figure whose speech and manner were based on regional actualities.

Given the changed circumstances of life in early to mid-nineteenth-century New England, factors such as the recent independence of the United States from Britain, the expansion of trade, both domestic and foreign, the rising sectional con-flict between New England and the South, and the prospect of westward expan-sion, it is no wonder that a new kind of cultural hero was born and widely cultivated during this period. As New Englanders' relationship to their own environment and to the world beyond their borders became increasingly fraught with both native pride and provincial testiness, it could hardly be an accident or a mere playwright's whim that gave them sketches like this one, which was recorded in the *Saturday Rambler* magazine in 1848:

> A Yankee sat one day in a barroom in western New York, listening to some farmers bragging of their rich wheat lands. At length, one of them taking oc-casion to sneer at New England soil, the Yankee broke in:
> "Wal, now, gentlemen, you're greatly mistaken about the soil in the Old Bay State. Fact, they wouldn't *have* such land as your'n in Massachusetts. Why, there is a piece of land so poor that nobody won't own it, and they call it No-town, because nobody don't live there, and yet even there the land is so rich that taller [i.e., tallow] grows on the bushes. It *is* a fact, gentlemen, though I won't say as some do, that the old women of the neighboring towns go over there after a rain to dip candles in the puddles, but it is a fact that taller grows on the bushes and I've sot by the light of candles made of it." The New Yorkers owned beat.[17]

The beaten New Yorkers, of course, still possessed, and knew that they possessed, the more fertile soil. They were, after all, receiving hundreds of migrant New En-gland farm families year after year, people in flight from soil that could hardly sup-port the large-scale cultivation of anything. They had been beaten, on the contrary, by the now famous Yankee wit, which could turn general misfortune and agricul-tural paucity into a source of quick-witted verbal triumph. Generations of simi-larly resourceful dialect Yankees, on stage, to be sure, but also in actual bar-rooms, general stores, and, more recently, filling stations, have come to be associated with a New England folk mentality. An exaggerated understatement seems to be the common thread running through such sketches, and the multifaceted ambivalence that so many New Englanders bore toward their home region was a never-ending source of inspiration.

Given the disappointments of their agricultural endeavors and the inherent dangers of going to sea, Yankees of the nineteenth century couldn't afford any overt displays of pride. Indeed, on the occasions when the heroes of their oral traditions commit the sin of hubris, they invariably pay the price. Among Maine's Downeasters, as folklorist Richard Dorson has discovered, all manner of tales existed to chasten those who would act too imperiously in the face of misfortune. The cycle of tales that Dorson entitles "Buying the Wind" offer a case in point. Dorson was interviewing Maurice Alley, of Jonesport:

Paris Kaler was the captain of a vessel, and he got out one day and got becalmed. He was going to the west'ard and wasn't no wind. And he wanted some wind, so he throwed quarter overboard. He wanted to buy a quarter's worth. He said he wished it would blow so hard she wouldn't lug a nail in a paulpost. He said, "I'll stand by with a pin maul to drive it in."

So he said it commenced to blow, it blowed till it blowed the sails off her, and he was three or four days off his course; he was three or four days getting back again. He said if he knew it was as cheap as that he wouldn't have bought half as much.[18]

Good fortune could not be purchased in a world that, despite the passing of the Puritan era, was still ruled over by a predestinarian God, whose whim could never be predicted, much less won over by obviously blasphemous behavior. Success could hardly be anticipated or sought after.

It could, however, be encountered accidentally. Tales that folklorists label with the "Wonderful Hunt" motif offer further evidence of this principle. Many regional groups in the United States, not to mention rural people the world over, tell stories like the following, which has a New Hampshire provenance:

One morning, Old Man Moses went out his kitchen door and found twelve turkeys on his fence. He figured one of them would make a good dinner, but he was afeared that if he went to get his gun, the turkeys would be gone when he returned.

So Old Man Moses tossed his ax at them turkeys, hoping to get at least one. But his ax caught the tree branch above the turkeys on the fence. The branch fell into the pond, taking the turkeys with it and trapping their legs right good. Old Man Moses went right into the pond after them turkeys, his great coat floating around him like a fishing net. By the time he came ashore, Old Man Moses had snagged himself twelve turkeys and a passel of fish.[19]

Since the tellers of such tales hardly expect to be believed, their use would appear to suggest an actual absence of resources. Like the story about the tallow-bearing bushes, the anecdote about Old Man Moses appears to use hyperbole as a humorous commentary on such inspiring results.

Another salient Yankee rhetorical characteristic—the famous New England reserve—looks as well to derive from the land's evident reluctance to be bountiful on demand. One of the most ubiquitous features of New England's agricultural history and attendant folklore, even to this day, is the stoniness of the region's soil, at least in upland areas removed from the more fertile river valleys. The oral traditions that follow from this circumstance speak with what we might mark as a characteristically wry humor about the Sisyphean work involved in removing newly frost-heaved stones from upland fields. Although we might expect all farmers to have used such impediments to agricultural progress as excuses to complain, at least one farmer of the era spoke, in an anecdote that the late Robert Ripley of Montague, Massachusetts, grew up hearing, with a defiant spirit of resistance. Farmers who stayed in the uplands while their neighbors ran downhill might have appreciated Mr. Ware's attitude. "He had a little farm," Ripley says, "and it was awful stony. But he never picked up one. Somebody asked him one time, says, 'Why don't you pick up these stones? [Don't] they bother you?'

" 'Well,' he [Mr. Ware] says, 'I knowed those stones was made for something,' and he left them right there."[20] Mr. Ware might just as well have been talking about the farmers themselves who, though they might have been expected to know better than to stay put, elected not to move away, come what may. The Yankee wit, in other words, was laconic in its clear recognition and acceptance of hardship, and its use suggested the opposite of insularity.

If New Englanders of this period were united by any one factor it would have to have been their universal grudging acceptance of less than ideal geographical and economic circumstances. Seafaring Yankees, as the tale of Captain Sylvanus Rich illustrates, were wedded, in a sense, to a hazardous but somehow compelling way of life. Similarly, along the Maine coast, generations of sailors found themselves reflecting on their limited prospects; they were, as early twentieth-century folksong collector Joanna Colcord has described it:

> cautious New Englanders doing a hard job which some of them even disliked, because by its means, they could make a better livelihood for their families than in any other way open to them. But here was where they loved to be; and at home most of them now lie, in the cemetery facing south across Penobscot Bay.[21]

Surely it was this mentality that led to the shipboard culture of sailors, whose song lyrics continue to haunt us. Colcord would most likely have been led to see things as she did based on the content of the songs she collected, which included the famous Nantucket whaling song, "Blow, Ye Winds," a version of which we find excerpted in B. A. Botkin's *Treasury of American Folklore* (1944). On the return trip home, sailors who sang about their voyage being nearly concluded must have known, as Bulkington in Melville's *Moby-Dick* knew, that the touch of solid ground would only be a fleeting one:

> now that our ship is full and we don't give a damn
> We'll bend all our stu'n'sails and sail for Yankee land.
>
> When we get home, our ship made fast, and we get through our sailing
> A winding glass around we'll pass and damn this blubber whaling![22]

The call of the sea would prove too powerful for many of them, and the songs of nineteenth-century sailors, while they certainly curse the dangers and drudgeries of seaboard life, convey an equal portion of stoic acceptance and even romance.

Yankee farmers, too, as evidenced perhaps by the story about the paucity of the Massachusetts soil, betrayed a similar ambivalence, a tireless devotion to their rocky and unforgiving soil, mingled with a realistic acceptance of just how impoverished it rendered them. Nonetheless, the early to mid-nineteenth century was the age of New England's agricultural ascendancy. Despite the steady flow of New England emigrants to the thicker topsoils of upstate New York and the Ohio Valley, "those who stayed behind," as the title of one social history of the phenomenon calls them, knew a limited prosperity in the years preceding the Civil War. In part, this circumstance was owing to rural New Englanders' embrace of a seasonally determined, mixed-resource economy. Even beyond the confines of fertile areas such as the Connecticut River valley bottomlands of central Connecticut and western Massachusetts, New England farmers of the nineteenth century mastered the art of mixed production and collective enterprise. A salient feature of the period, though even the gradual decline of New England agriculture didn't entirely phase it out until the twentieth century, was a set of rural folkways that combined economic necessity with communal cultural endeavor. Corn-huskings, apple pairings, and barn-raisings, events that brought together extended family members but also neighbors and friends from throughout the community, made for lighter work. Loyce Dunbar, who grew up in the western Massachusetts farm community of North Leverett in the early twentieth century, grew up hearing about one such event:

> [Washburn] Ripley was a deacon. And he had a pair of oxen. He used to have a husking here every fall. Out in the big barn, and a big bushel basket. If you could get a red ear you could hold it up and jump up and kiss any woman you wanted to. My father always took a red ear from home with him. And then after the husking bee, you'd go in your house, you had doughnuts, cider, coffee, cheese and [then] you'd go out [to] the barn. They'd sweep away all the corn husks and you'd have a little dance.[23]

Farmers drawing a sustenance from reluctant soil developed a folklife fully in keeping with the physically harsh but occasionally revivifying cultural circumstances of their community.

For all of the visibility of the rural Yankee, both in the public eye and on the farmsteads of the region, we can't help but notice how exclusively male his type is. However, where some women might otherwise have hesitated to step into the male-dominated world of hunting, Mary Turner took naturally to that role. She spent her entire life in West Peru, Maine, and when a crew of young folklorists came to visit her there in the 1970s, she regaled them with this personal narrative.

> I shot a moose. That mornin' I had on my red pajamas[,] eatin' breakfast. It started raining. . . .
>
> It was a moose. I come downstairs. I grabbed the gun and the shells, my .30-30, and back up there I went. Well, he come down the hill a bit, so I got a standin' broadside shot.

Well, I didn't have the least idea I'd got him. I leaned up against the side of the building, so I could let him run. He started to run, then he slowed up, and went across to the field. I paunched him. I knowed I hit him.

So he slowed up. I thought I'd get him again, so I shot him in the rear end. Well, he ran over and he run around the tree. Well, I was still here at half past six in the morning.[24]

Mary Turner was not only unfazed by the moose in her farmyard. She must certainly have dazzled the high school students who had come to document her story as she continued her account:

The old cow kicked Gus [a local pensioner whom Mary had taken in] off the stool. He said, "That's nobody but the goddamn game warden that would do a trick like that in the morning!" So I went in these old red trousers . . . wobbling up the road with a gun.

I heard a car coming. I figgered it was the friggin' game warden. I'd bet you a dollar I shot twice. Well, I come running down the road just as fast as I could. And some fellas [friends of Mary's] drove up in the yard.

"What in hell are you running for?" one of them yelled.

"I just shot a moose!" I said.

"Well, don't you know that's pretty serious?"

"Well, yes, I guess it is, kinda," I said. "I sure don't need my name in the newspaper."

"Well, just you shut your mouth or you will."[25]

Turner concludes her account by explaining how she just barely managed to avoid getting caught red-handed by the game wardens, six of whom did in fact show up a few days later. For all of its high adventure, hunting moose was just her way of adhering to the code of female domestic economy and hospitality. One of the first things she had told her interviewers was that "there's not too many people come here and not go away feeded."[26]

FACTORIES, IMMIGRANTS, AND A CHANGING LANDSCAPE: FOLKLORE IN THE INDUSTRIAL ERA

Despite our tendency to imagine ante- and postbellum New England as a quaint and self-absorbed pastoral world unto itself, the facts of history tell us quite another story. As historian Stephen Nissenbaum has observed, "By 1860," right around the time when Americans began to manufacture this image of regional tranquility, "New England as a whole had become the single most urban part of the nation, the most industrial, the most Catholic, the most heavily immigrant in population."[27] The folklore of this era, understandably, reflects this duality of myth and actuality. In a myriad of ways, New Englanders, both of the "old timer" and "newcomer" variety, fashioned vernacular styles that spoke both to their devotion to cherished images of the past and to engagement with the conditions of the present. The single constant, as always, was a shared, though rapidly diversifying, cultural geography, a mutual commitment to a landscape that, in itself, could never be fashioned into any one group's single preserve.

The several salient factors outlined by Nissenbaum and other historians of nineteenth- and early twentieth-century New England—urbanization, immigration, and the resulting ethnic diversification—are outgrowths, clearly, of the region's status as the birthplace of the Industrial Revolution in America. Long-settled cities such as Boston and Hartford, though obviously transformed by the industrial experience, evolved during the period beginning in 1850 into ever more important commercial and trading centers, where capital resources and workforces could be centralized. The urban folklife of this period, however, might more properly be understood as being concentrated in the newer cities, where vast brick factories increasingly came to dominate local landscapes. Places which not long before had been the sites of small water-powered mills evolved into gigantic industrial complexes. Even the mere juxtaposition of the attendant place-names suggests an odd duality. The Amoskeag mills, which produced textiles well into the twentieth century in Manchester, New Hampshire, occupied several square miles along the western bank of the Merrimack River, where, as local lore (as corroborated by considerable archaeological evidence) has it, various native tribes had gathered for thousands of years to fish peacefully on what they believed to be sacred ground. Indeed, as historians of Native American life in New England indicate, "*Amoskeag*, in the language of the Penacook Indians, meant 'to take small fish.' This is what the Indians did when they lived along the banks of this river near the falls [of] . . . the river Merrimack, which means 'place of strong current.' "[28]

The industrial age in New England saw the development of dozens of similarly burgeoning urban manufacturing enclaves, among them, Lewiston, Maine; Holyoke, Massachusetts; Pawtucket, Rhode Island; Waterbury, Connecticut; and South Burlington, Vermont. Cities such as these, though they could certainly constitute oppressive environments in which to work and live, also generated a new and dynamic sort of folk regionalism in which the immigrant culture of the factory and the neighborhood came to dominate. Exile and poverty bred alienation, but they also constituted fertile ground from which new folk forms emerged, as we see in these lyrics from a French Canadian song of the late nineteenth century:

> C'est dans un' maison de pension
> La ou l'on trouv le temps bien long
> La ou l'on pleure et l'on s'ennuie
> D'etre eloigne de ses parents.
> De son amie. De son pays
> Et ceux qu'on aim' bien tendrement
>
> [It's in the boarding house
> That one is bored to tears
> That is where we cry and suffer
> At being separated from our parents
> Our girlfriend, our country
> And those we love so tenderly][29]

The predominantly young and female workers of the Lowell textile mills, as is well known, came eventually to publish their own newspaper, the *Lowell Offering*. What is less known, however, is that the same city, as an eventual magnet for French Canadian immigrants, saw a Saint Jean the Baptist day celebration in 1881 that included two thousand parade participants, and as many as 180 carriages.[30] Similar ethnic-based festivals occurred on a grand scale throughout the late nineteenth and early twentieth centuries in all of New England's midsized cities.

The remnants of these once so clearly demarcated neighborhoods can still be seen in some cities, as old billboards are visible on brick walls and different sorts of church steeples and church names continue to loom high above the postindustrial skyline. Ruth Brown of North Adams, Massachusetts, has described the neighborhood geography of her turn-of-the-century childhood:

> They [ethnics] kept to themselves, over what's State Street. . . . Well, we still have State Street, I guess. It was called Little Italy. And that's where the Italians [lived]. And the French people lived up East Main. They built that big church, Notre Dame. And, yes, that was where they lived. The Jewish people in those days, why, on Sabbath you had to live close enough so you could walk—you didn't drive on the Sabbath. So they had to live nearby and the synagogue was here in the center of North Adams. . . . We didn't have too many black people, although some of them I know lived down the end of River Street, down near where the Salvation Army citadel is now.[31]

The burgeoning of such ethnic neighborhoods spoke to the dynamism of regional folklore during the post–Civil War era. On the one hand, the mere existence of cities suggested that New England as a whole was undergoing a profoundly modernizing transformation. Even the predominantly rural states of Maine, New Hampshire, and Vermont, by the 1870s, were now home to at least a few significantly industrial enclaves. But as ethnic neighborhoods developed, so too did New Englanders' ties to an Old World and to traditional, or at least *reinvented* traditional, cultures increase.

The French spoken in the Little Canadas, deriving as it did from Quebec, was older than the French spoken on the streets of Paris. Holiday customs, foodways, and oral traditions, many of which originated in premodern Europe, connected life in the liveliest of New England cities to a distant past on a daily basis, in homes, churches, and community halls. Often enough, their songs used traditional forms to convey a sad longing for the homes they had left behind. The lyrics of one Franco-American *complainte*, or lament, tell the story of a family whose members actually returned northward in the face of New England's cold disappointments:

> Apres ce temps de quelques mois
> Que je demeurs dans les Etats
> J'ai ravoisee peu de richesee
> Pour temps j'epuis pour travailler
> Jusque s'u'abord claire de la lune
> Et reveiller avant soleil leve
>
> [After a few months
> Of living in the States
> I changed my mind about the pittance
> That I had labored so hard to earn
> Working until the moon rose
> And waking before the sun came up][32]

The *complainte* and other similarly conceived first-hand accounts gave musical voice to ethnic suffering, and in so doing, offered one form of redemption within the urban industrial folk milieu. Irish immigrants too sang of their distress but—more often than not—their balladry was a means of sustenance and supplied the necessary inspiration for perseverance. "No life was too hard," writes Doris Kirkpatrick about the men who—at the expense of nearly two hundred lives—built the Hoosac Tunnel, "but what an Irishman could season his troubles with a song such as

> And drill ye tarriers drill,
> It's work all day without sugar in your tay,
> And drill, ye tarriers drill."[33]

If nothing else, songs such as these could assist in the passage of time. They were an improvement, to be sure, over silence.

Of equal stature to songs of complaint in many immigrant communities were spoken accounts, first person and otherwise, which could give voice to a life devoted to back-breaking but nonetheless dignifying labor. Jim Carron, who was interviewed in 1977 by Julien Olivier, tells of his family's and his own laboring odyssey. Carron had begun his working life helping his father in the woods, at age 9: "At age 11 I moved to Waterville, Maine. There, they put me into the cotton . . . mill. I worked there for five years . . . six [o'clock] to six. Sunday and all. No . . . days off . . . 25 cents a day. To work like little devils."[34] Even as the majority of residents in ethnic neighborhoods were often steeped in traditional lore, certain individuals seemed destined to become the primary bearers of such things, and it is to the existence of these individuals that we owe our contemporary awareness of the traditions in the first place. Sophia Bielli was born in Medford, Massachusetts, in 1893, but grew up in the "purely Italian" North End of Barre, Vermont. In June of 1979, folklorist Dick Sweterlitsch made his first acquaintance with her; in the course of several subsequent interviews, he recorded dozens of Italian stories, tongue-twisters, rhymes, and songs. The origins of these traditions lay in Italy and in the traditional village culture that Italian immigrants had brought with them to America.

> Di mi con shi vai, che ti diro chi tisei
> [Tell me who you go with; I'll tell you who you are]
> Chi non ha testa, gamba
> [Who has no head, walks]
> Snobbishness is the mother of ignorance
> The first chicken that cackles is the one who laid the egg[35]

"When you are a child," Bielli's husband pointed out in one of Sweterlisch's interviews, "You didn't get slapped. You got a proverb thrown at you."

For all the Old World origins of Bielli's stories and proverbs, their provenance was modern and American. Folklore lives in its daily usage, not in its distant past. Bielli was known in her community not just as someone who remembered ancient tales and proverbs, but as a person whose life and lore reflected the very contemporary, and often troubling, history of Italian immigrants in an American context. As often as she told the old stories, she could present her listeners with harrowing portrayals of the ordeals of acculturation that her parents—first-generation im-migrants—had suffered through. The Italians who came to Barre in the early 1900s were employed, for the most part, in granite quarries:

> The poor men, they would get up at six o'clock and go to work at seven. Seven to four. Seven to twelve and then one to four. And they'd go in the morning and be near the stove and you'd burn in the back and freeze in the front. They'd get great big—I remember—even my husband had a big cal-lous—on their fingers, where they held tools. And they would come home exhausted and they'd catch cold and die.[36]

Granite quarries, textile mills, dangerous fishing grounds, and the like tested the fortitude of immigrants to the region and, in so doing, helped to make them na-tives in the process.

The folklore of industrial New England is the dynamic record of this collective ordeal, and the spiritual survival of those who lived through such times seems, in large part, to have derived from the sense of dignity that folk traditions passed on. We made this place, the stories tell us; it is our home because our bodies and souls gave it its current shape. Anna May Sevigny, a Vermonter of Irish ancestry, told her interviewer in 1979 what she had grown up hearing about her predecessors' stake in New England:

> The Irish came and they stayed because they didn't branch out, didn't travel. Although some of them came from Ireland and built the railroads. . . . As I've heard my grandparents tell about, the Americans didn't relish an Irishman or appreciate him when he came to this country. They were looked down upon. They were laborers.[37]

If "new-comers" did, eventually, evolve into "old-timers," what enabled them to do so, ultimately, was their reputation for being hard workers. Indeed, what urban and rural New Englanders had in common was their adherence to a regional code of sorts, devotion to place, as demonstrated through hard and often enough self-destructive work.

Mary Doyle Curran grew up hearing stories like this one, which adapted a tra-ditional motif to modern-day, New England circumstances, and seems to sum up centuries' worth of Irish history in the process:

> In the old days of Ireland when the O'Sullivans were among its kings and there was wealth and glory for them . . . they had seven golden castles and seven silver, and there was some said it was fairy gold. There has ever been a story that they had more to do with the Sidhe than they would say. There was even one O'Sullivan who was gone for fifteen years, and there was no age upon her when she came back.
> Well, it's that one gave birth to a child two months after her return, and it was no natural birth, for the swans were circling the house the whole day. It was a boy, and they say he heard the Sidhe, and since that time there is no one of the O'Sullivans who has not had to shut his door tight on a windy night for fear of them. Some say they took to the hills of Kerry with the

coming of the English and lost their wealth doing it . . . some say that the old ones that went to the hills buried their treasure and the young ones have been seeking it ever since. One of the girls looked for it in dreams and was told to seek it in a fairy forth. She did, and lifted the rock it was supposed to be under and found nothing but a heap of dung. Some say the Sidhe moved to America and there will be O'Sullivans looking for it yet.[38]

The woman from whom Curran heard the tale while sitting in the hushed kitchen of her family's Holyoke tenement added, at the end, that men like Mary's father John were bound to fail in their quest, for they could only succeed by relinquishing their Irishness. "He'll find no pot of gold here unless it be the one buried at the foot of Money Hole Hill and he's more than welcome to Yankee gold, for I'd want none of it," she says.

Occupations and Folkways

Rural folkways during this period, though they certainly existed at a significant remove from the rapidly diversifying cultures of the urban areas, were hardly unaffected by the large-scale shifts occurring throughout New England. If nothing else, even the most insulated upland dwellers knew what was happening all around them. In 1899, sometime rural-dweller Rollin Lynde Hartt could hardly have been the only person to notice that hill-town communities were being decimated by the combined forces of increasing industrialization, not to mention the draw of cheaper, more fertile western lands and the social and economic attractions of city life. "Steadily the river valleys, rich in water power, are robbing the uplands of their population," Hartt wrote. "The people of New England are running down hill, [sic] Massachusetts has built the factory and mortgaged the farm . . . says Noah, 'All the spunkiest ones have up and got out.' "[39] The devotion to place that lay at the heart of so much rural New England folklore during this era speaks not just to the "stick-to-itiveness" of "those who stayed behind" but to their adaptability as well; that is, their conscious choice *not* to run downhill was an aspect of their knowing engagement of modernity, and hardly a flight from it. Rob Ripley of Montague, Massachusetts, recalled hearing his father tell about the opportunity the family had once had to move out of the hills and to buy a farm along the Connecticut River floodplain, where growing crops would have been much easier. "Nice, level, flat land, no stones, he said, but his grandfather couldn't leave Chestnut Hill. Every time he'd go that way he'd say, 'Oh, plowing up there amongst all those rocks, and look at this nice level land, no stones.' "[40] The Ripleys stayed where they were in an attempt to retain their identity as hillfolk, not because they were unaware of the alternatives.

The major changes in the agricultural folklife of the turn-of-the-century period were clearly matched by similar shifts occurring in the other outdoor industries. Backcountry dwellers had long known a mixed resource-based economy, and lived in accordance with a seasonal work cycle. Wood-cutting, typically a winter activity, generated its own customs and traditions. In some areas of rural New England—notably in the "northwoods" areas of northern Vermont, New Hampshire, and interior Maine, logging was the dominant economic activity, and loggers, though they might be employed in other sectors during the warmer months, constituted a specialized economic and folk-cultural group. Folklorist Edward "Sandy" Ives has, over the course of his career, documented the folklife of these men—their music, oral narratives, material traditions, and so forth. His study of logging culture grew out of his deep admiration for the complexity of the work woodcutters did. "I could find practically nothing in the written records," Ives told his interviewer in 2000, "that told how that work was done."[41] Another folklorist, Richard Dorson, explains the cultural heroism of these woodsmen by comparing their feats and, significantly, their own folk representation of these feats to those of their western contemporaries, the cowboys. "In his spring role as river driver, balancing on logs, careening down swollen streams and prying loose with his peavey the giant logs piled up into jams, the woodsman played a role as dangerous as the cowpuncher attempting to stem a stampede."[42] Various versions of the famous "The Jam on Gerry's Rock" capture this swaggering but mournful heroism. The following lines, which former Maine lumberman John Porter sang to Dorson in 1956, speak both to the dangers and to the spirit of the men who faced them. The verse presents to us the words of the foreman and the misfortune that follows immediately from his instructions to the six Canadian volunteers who fearlessly did his bidding:

> They had not rolled off many a log
> When they heard his clear voice say,
> "I'd have you on your guard, boys
> The jam will soon give way."
> These words were scarcely spoken
> When an ash did break and go.
> It carried off those six brave youths
> And the foreman Jack Monroe.[43]

Stoic heroism in the face of dangers such as these is the hallmark of the era's logging folklore. Woodsmen everywhere, whether of the Maine logging camp variety or of the type seen more typically in less wild tracts, generated a folk tradition which, like that of the farmers of the day, spoke to their sense of themselves as a dying breed of sorts.

In some woodsmen's tales, the dangers are overcome, of course, but an ever-present factor seems to be the looming pressure exerted by a voracious market economy. Vernon Aiken of Leverett, Massachusetts, recounts the following story, which he had heard from his father. In some regards a typical woodsman's "strong man story," the anecdote Aiken provides is marked as well by the spirit of an industrial age, during which even rural people, at least in New England, prided themselves on their ability not just to survive but to exceed expectations and work faster and harder than the machines that threatened to eclipse their power could. Aiken describes the work of a portable mill, and the heroic exploits of Walter Carey, a local hero, also of Leverett, whose strength, apparently, knew few bounds:

> They [the woodsmen] would find a place on the timber lot that they were cutting where [they] could be near the water. And then . . . they'd burn the slabs from the logs they were cutting and they'd make steam and run the mill on steam power. And . . . they had a whistle. And if the mill could saw all the logs before they got the next load in there, they'd blow the whistle.

And if the mill could saw all the logs before they got the next load in there, they'd blow the whistle. And that was quite a . . . feat with them to do that. And Mr. Carey was doing the logging, Walter Carey. And . . . some of the boys were driving the horses and they had a pretty big load on. Just before they got to the mill, it was kind of muddy, and they got stuck. And he [Carey] heard the commotion down there, and he run down there and said, "What's the matter?"

"Oh," he [one of the boys] say, "they're going to blow the whistle on us, they're going to blow the whistle on us." So he [Carey] took a huge log right off the top of the load on his shoulder and he walked over and dropped it on the skids so they couldn't blow the whistle. And then he went back and he grabbed the wheel . . . and spoke to the horses at the same time. And he lifted up on that wheel and brought the load of logs up to the skidway, so they weren't able to blow the whistle.[44]

If this tale reminds us of any story from the vast compendium of widely known stories in the American tradition it might be that of John Henry, another turn-of-the-century folk hero well-known to Americans from all regions who have heard about the man who was, in the exact words of the famous ballad, either from Texas or Maine and who died "with his hammer in his hand" when pitted against another sort of voracious machine—in this case, his boss's steam-drill. The prevalence of such tales among New England storytellers of the age speaks to an overall awareness that they carried of their own impending obsolescence, and their pride in resisting—but not denying—the strength of the forces, both natural and human-made, arrayed against them.

CONTEMPORARY REINVENTIONS: FOLKLORE IN THE PRESENT DAY

Clearly, the industrializing and urbanizing changes of the twentieth century, while they exerted a considerable *reshaping* effect on the vernacular culture of New England, can hardly be said to have eliminated the enormous importance of folklore from the region. Various transformations of local landscapes, like the reforestation of open pasturelands, for instance, the gradual abandonment of industrial centers after World War II, and the expansion of suburban development into rural areas, demanded all manner of reinventions from New Englanders. Where farmlands became forests, locals were suddenly surrounded by ghostly reminders of how quickly their agricultural self-sufficiency had given way to a sort of bleak dormancy; oral tradition reflected this sense of decline. "Nobody cuts the trees down no more," remarked one Massachusetts informant when asked about reforestation. "There used to be farms and now they're all grown in," offered another old Yankee.[45] Eclipsed industrial centers evolved into centers of ethnic revival, even as economic decline wore away at local morale. Where tract housing and strip malls took over, a new folk culture of urban legend, white collar occupational lore and, often enough, a reconstituted New England heritage came to dominate. New Englanders are currently learning to adapt to these sorts of changes, both economically and culturally. If any element of the region's collective vernacular past has been retained, it would be the tradition of dynamic versatility—the famous "Yankee ingenuity"—some version of which has enabled the region's residents to thrive in an environment of constant economic change by dint of continual experimentation combined with an adherence to core values of hard work and devotion to place.

In rural sections of New England, old folkways associated with an agricultural or resource-based economy have, in certain respects, been rendered obsolete. The tractor has long since replaced the ox-driven plow, and mechanized harvesters have long eliminated the need either for scythe-wielding fieldworkers or for the once popular corn-huskings and the like. But New England farmers still raise oxen, and whether or not they employ them for plowing or wood-hauling, ox-pulls—contests in which various teams of oxen are yoked to two- and three-ton sledges and challenged to draw their loads over increasing distances—provide frequent and well-attended fare at town and county fairs region-wide. The equipment and verbal commands used in these contests derive directly from the days when oxen were not merely shown at fairs but employed as the literal engines of landscape transformation throughout rural districts of New England. The same is true for any number of other rural folkways that have persevered despite technological advances. Although many maple sugar producers have switched from hanging metal sap buckets on their trees to using plastic tubing for reverse osmosis collection, hundreds of large-scale producers continue with buckets, and with good reason—they cost much less than miles and miles of plastic tubing.

New Englanders continue as well to manage a uniquely diverse rural economy, a circumstance which in turn lends itself to all manner of cultural reinventions. Where crop cultivation is concerned, changing times, in combination with the region's inherited hilly topography, encouraged farmers and rural communities in general to emphasize variety in production and efficiency in scale. For this reason, the most visible and influential of folk artifacts—the landscape itself—bears a remarkable resemblance in many rural areas to its former incarnations. As many recent historians have pointed out, the "classic" New England village, complete with white church and a handsome town green, was a mid-nineteenth-century invention, as opposed to a holdover from the communitarian days of Puritan settlement. But whatever the era of its invention was, the ideal of clustered development, in which open space and forested land still defines the space between towns and villages throughout sections of Maine, New Hampshire, Vermont, western Massachusetts, and Connecticut, still prevails.

The traditions of rural life in New England—storytelling, musical, artifactual, and otherwise—have likewise been transformed but not eliminated by the changes wrought by the late twentieth century. In many cases, indeed, preexisting pastimes that had nearly died out have been entirely revived, though in new configurations. A notable case in point, familiar beyond the confines of New England but of a distinctly New England provenance, would be contra dancing. Community dancing in which opposing lines of participants face each other and enact various do-si-do's, swing-your-partner's, and *alle-mains* right and left as instructed by a caller, contra dancing had all but disappeared from rural New England life in the early twentieth century. But a handful of players and callers, having themselves been taught the dance and music by elders, passed the tradition on to enthusiastic back-to-the-landers in the early 1970s and the dance style caught on. Small-town New England currently abounds in weekly contra dances, and the players get both younger and more numerous by the year.

Back-to-the-landers and other countercultural types, though hardly comprising majorities in any but a few rural New England communities, have nonetheless done a great deal both to revive and to maintain other folk pastimes. Yankee ingenuity, reborn in the late twentieth century, has often manifested itself in the form of various arts, crafts, and small-scale building operations in which old styles, which in their inception were outgrowths of a regional cultural geography, shape the production of cabinetry and other fine woodworking, house and barn building and refurbishing, quilt-making, and a host of other livelihoods inspired by or derived from New England's vernacular heritage. Regional foodways are also maintained in rural districts in accordance with long-standing agricultural and culinary traditions. Maple syrup continues in many instances to be produced and used in accordance with the old ways, and is a ubiquitous element of cultural life during the period between late February and early April. St. Albans, Vermont, plays host to an annual maple syrup festival at the season's end. The community pancake breakfasts that are served in church basements and in enterprising sugarhouses throughout the region during this season are only one element in a year-long cycle of food-based community celebrations. Typical fare in many communities might mark the growing year with a "sugar supper" in March, a ham and bean supper supplemented by the spring's "first mess of peas" to mark the Memorial Day weekend, and a dinner at which strawberry shortcake features as the main attraction in June. Midsummer festivals feature barbequed chicken and corn, and blueberries figure prominently in August. Several communities in the region have now begun featuring garlic festivals in September; tastes have certainly evolved in this regard. Fall, the primary harvest season throughout the northern temperate zones, is marked by events featuring apple cider- and pie-making and, of course, the native pumpkin.

Halloween and Thanksgiving

The pumpkin offers a case in point for the convergence of foodways, decorative traditions, and holiday celebrations. Keene, New Hampshire, has been nationally renowned for its annual jack-o-lantern festival, in which tens of thousands of individually carved pumpkins and assorted gourds are placed on sidewalks and in windows throughout the downtown area, and visitors from throughout the region and beyond attend a Halloween gathering on an enormous scale. Indeed, between the Fourth of July, Halloween, and Thanksgiving, New Englanders can be said to have created the template by which other people's observations of the "indigenous" American holidays have been perhaps unwarrantedly judged. Community and family observances of these holidays are of course derivations of all sorts of transregional and even transnational traditions. Halloween, whose origins lie in premodern European pagan rituals and Christianized Europe's All Saints' Day, has been thoroughly regionalized in New England, and is also a cross-cultural construct. The jack-o-lantern, a figure which was originally carved out of the potato in Ireland, made its way across the Atlantic as Irish men and women arrived in New England in the nineteenth century, but was reinvented in the image of the locally ubiquitous and supple pumpkin, originally a fruit raised by New England's native tribes. Still more recently, Salem, Massachusetts, as the renowned site of the 1692 witch trials, has hosted enormous Halloween festivities for several years

Keene, New Hampshire, has been nationally renowned for its annual jack-o-lantern festival. Courtesy Center Stage, Keene, New Hampshire, Pumpkin Festival.

now and even adapted the word "wicked," a choice regional slang term, in its advertising for the event.

Halloween, though it has certainly been *regionalized* in many ways to "fit" in a New England context (how else do we explain the Salem connection?), can justifiably be said to have originated elsewhere. Thanksgiving, on the other hand, though it has been made to fit in all kinds of *other* places, strikes us as a quintessentially New England holiday. Indeed, though we may never really know exactly what foods the Pilgrims and Wampanoags shared with each other back in 1621, the tradition of holding a welcome-home dinner during the harvest season does derive from a New England–specific origin. It is important to note, however, that the contemporary Thanksgiving—turkey dinner and so forth—is a modern invention. Like every other folk pastime, its derivation lies somewhere in the past, but its application speaks to the circumstances of the present. First celebrated as a civic holiday in 1863, as Northerners gave thanks for the Union victories at Gettysburg and Vicksburg, Thanksgiving manifests itself as a regional holiday because of its symbolic associations rather than its "actual" history. Hence, when a regional connection can be found, its origin will likely prove to be not so much in any sort of New England–wide practice, but rather in the discrete traditions of specific families. Folklorist Barre Toelken offers a fascinating case in point. His own family's recent history lies in central Massachusetts. When family members get together for Thanksgiving—wherever they happen to be in the United States—they sing an old New England sea song, "Rolling Home," while seated around the table. The song itself, as Toelken explains, memorializes "family members who did not come home from the sea."[46]

> Rolling home, rolling home
> rolling home across the sea
> rolling home to old New England,
> rolling home, dear land, to thee.[47]

Given such clear references, the song's (coastal) New England pedigree would seem intact. But as the family, whose members have long since been removed from the nautical life, continues to sing it, they have come to adapt its meaning to changed circumstances. Like the holiday itself, the singing of the song reminds family members of one regional past but is applied to the regional (and extraregional) circumstances of the present.

Folk celebrations punctuate the lives of urban New Englanders as well as those of their rural compatriots. The same large and mid-sized cities that evolved in the nineteenth century into immigrant enclaves still play host to dozens of ethnic festivals, all celebrated in a modern milieu. Lowell, Massachusetts, hosts a national folk festival every July, in which contemporary music, dance, and storytelling traditions from throughout the region are showcased. New England's Franco communities throughout the region continue to mark St. Jean le Baptiste Day (in June), and French Canadian folk music continues to be played over the airwaves and in dancehalls. This is especially true in some sections of New Hampshire and Maine, where Franco Americans constitute the largest ethnic group. But southern New England, too, boasts large Franco populations. The annual Franco American heritage festival, held every August in West Warwick, Rhode Island, is one of many such regional gatherings. Celtic music, which has seen a large-scale revival throughout the Atlantic world and beyond, continues to be enormously popular, and several clubs in the region offer a weeklong fare of Irish fiddling, step-dancing, and the like. Boston in particular, as home to hundreds of thousands of Irish Americans, boasts many venues for such music. In addition, Irish festivals are held annually in New Haven and Hartford, Connecticut; Billerica, Marlboro, and Lawrence, Massachusetts; and Lincoln, Rhode Island. Holyoke, Massachusetts' annual St. Patrick's Day parade, which is one of many in the area, hosts—in addition to the usual procession of floats and bands—one of New England's largest running races. Newer immigrants, too, have made their mark on the folklife of New England. Chinese New Year celebrations, southeast Asian dance styles, and, in some

Reproduction of the painting *The First Thanksgiving 1621*. Courtesy of Library of Congress.

sections, Tibetan stone masonry manifest the presence of the many Asian immigrants who have made their homes in New England since the beginning of the twentieth century and have long exceeded the confines of Boston's Chinatown. Lowell, Massachusetts, which is the second largest population center for Cambodians in the United States, as well as home to thousands of Laotian immigrants, has hosted an annual Southeast Asian arts festival for nearly a decade now. Operating on the premise that adaptation to a new home would be easiest if the new immigrants could bond with the local landscape, the event has transplanted the practices associated with the ancient water festivals indigenous to the Mekong River delta to the highly industrialized banks of the Merrimack. As Linda Silka writes, "Each new year has brought additional groups on board to celebrate water and its life-giving properties."[48] As in the rest of the country, Latino immigrants of various origins have played a considerable role in the reinhabitation of many industrial and postindustrial cities in New England. Spanish-speaking residents of many New England cities, namely, Bridgeport, Connecticut; Holyoke, Massachusetts; and Manchester, New Hampshire, have revived urban centers with neighborhood *bodegas*, ethnic eateries, and, from time to time, outdoor festivals of Puerto Rican and other Latino cultures, such as the ones held annually on Boston's South End and in West Springfield, Massachusetts.

Lest we make the mistake of assuming that folk music is everywhere rendered by guitar-strumming or fiddle-scraping "folkies," the revival—going back to the 1960s and 1970s—of traditional Hispanic folk music in urban New England should serve as a reminder of just how diverse regional traditions have become. In 1991, folklorist Michael Kline and luthier and community scholar William Cumpiano recorded several interview and music sessions with the Cabrera family of Holyoke, Massachusetts. The father, Alejandro, had taught his sons, Alex and Axel, the songs and musical styles he had inherited from his father in rural Puerto Rico. Cumpiano later recounted his experience of meeting the Cabreras:

> At that moment, I felt as if I were witnessing the rarest of spectacles; two youngsters, clearly uncoerced, intently absorbed in the playing of turn-of-the-century Puerto Rican ballads, torch songs and ancient melodies; singing alongside their father in that small Holyoke tenement. And they played so unhesitatingly, so unselfconsciously—as if there was nothing at all remarkable about it, as if it was the most natural thing in the world to do.[49]

Musical traditions such as these suggest an incontrovertible tie, on the part of the singers, to a home and a culture left behind—to a world beyond the region. But they also suggest and enforce connection to this place. In Puerto Rico, for all we know, the Cabreras—at least in the younger generation—might very likely have discarded their musical heritage and opted for a less traditional style, feeling less pressure to maintain cultural integrity. In Holyoke, removed from their original context, the music and the tradition mean all the more; as Cumpiano writes, "it now keeps their family together through the adversities of life in a strange, forbidding, far off land."[50] The barrios of Holyoke—once home to the likes of Mary Curran Doyle—now host thousands of Puerto Rican families, many of whom still listen and dance to the traditional forms of the *plena*, *bomba*, and *jíbaro* but in new urban settings.

The barrios of Holyoke, Massachusetts, host thousands of Puerto Rican families, many of whom, like the Cabreras, remain attached to traditional forms of Puerto Rican music despite—or perhaps precisely because of—their new urban settings. Photograph courtesy of Michael Hoberman.

The regional context, especially in an urban setting, also shrinks once unbridgeable gulfs between rival ethnic subcultures and, in the process, creates a new set of amalgamated cultural entities. Through the process of what cultural historians call *syncretism*, in which uprooted cultures re-create themselves in the image of an Old World past and in the actuality of a modern-day, dynamic present, ethnic styles dovetail. Early twentieth-century immigrants to North Adams, Massachusetts, a formerly small industrial city in the Berkshires of western Massachusetts, included people from both the northern, or Tyrolean, region of Alpine Italy and from the extreme southern area of Calabria. As John Lipa put it in a 1998 interview,

The Italians, the old-timers, are pretty much divided along either the northern or the southern Italians. It's about equally the same number of people, and there are families from both the south and the north part of Italy. Their traditions are a little different. The southern Italians eat more sardines and pasta and tomatoes, and the northern Italians are more into chickens and the polenta and the wild birds—pheasants, fowls and quail and stuff like that. . . . [But] over at St. Anthony's church, which is the Italian parish . . . it is becoming more and more homogenous as the older people pass away—when they do spaghetti suppers, we also do a polenta and chicken dinner to keep both aspects of the culture alive.[51]

In the eyes of their non-Italian neighbors, in any case, northern or southern origin was clearly irrelevant. And hence, in North Adams and beyond, we see the creation of the "Italian American" branch of New England regional folk culture. Such hybrids are, in this way, not imports to the region but direct products of its cross-fertilizations.

Nautical Lore

Even in rural places where folkways and ethnic revival has been less of a factor in daily life, a region-specific folklore continues to play a role in people's lives. Coastal sections of New England—even the ones that have been turned into vacationlands and resort communities—maintain an allegiance of sorts to a traditional nautical past—reconfigured, of course, in accordance with contemporary touristic trends. But the occupational lore of fishing communities remains, if not unchanged in the face of economic constraints and environmental concerns, in keeping with old ways. In his best-selling book *A Perfect Storm* (1997), Sebastian Junger writes about one captain who fishes on what people in the trade refer to as "the frontside" of the moon—"the quarters leading to the full." "Boats that fish the frontside," Junger writes, "tend to get small males on the line; boats that fish on the backside get large females. . . . On the day of the full moon the catch abruptly switches over to huge females and stays that way for a couple of weeks."[52] The lobstermen of coastal Maine still ply their trade using traps whose design has remained basically unchanged since the practice was begun, and still follow a tightly maintained, traditional code of ethics and protocols when it comes to respecting one another's trapping "turf." Storytelling remains a primary means for passing and maintaining traditional knowledge, practice, superstition, and work ethic. Jeff Fogman, a New Hampshire boat-builder, recounts the following story that was told to him by his mentor. Boat-builders, a species of leprechaun, used to live in caves. "The devil came to the boat builders in the cave, and he said: 'Listen, you guys living in caves. You have an absolutely abysmal existence.' . . . And the devil said: 'I'll give you anything on a material level you need. All you have to do is to make every seventh boat not so good.' And they said, 'Sorry, we really like this stuff. We can't do that.'"[53]

Moreover, even in the cultivation of a tourist trade, many residents of coastal areas continue, in a dynamic way, to follow the cultural practices pioneered by their forebears. The clambake offers a particularly illustrative case in point. In 1992, folklorist Kathy Neustadt published a carefully researched study of the pastime, devoting attention to its obscure, precolonial native origins, its uses among early settlers, its late nineteenth-century reinvention, and its contemporary role in the tourist trade around Allen's Neck, along the south shore of Massachusetts. "From the prehistoric clambaking of native Americans to clambake pavilions filled with hungry voters, from pictures in old family albums of church bakes to glossy ad photos of robust Yuppies in 100 percent cotton sweatshirts steaming shellfish on the beach," writes Neustadt, "the images of the clambake have communicated a wide range of messages about time and place and the role of community therein."[54]

Despite all manner of changes in the context for and practice of clambaking, certain aspects of the tradition remain intact. Clams are still baked in large hand-dug pits lined with salt-water soaked seaweed; clambakes have always celebrated coastal New England's summer bounty on both land and sea, its local flora and fauna. Corn continues to be husked by many people seated around a large table; the meal continues to be a markedly communal affair.

Even suburban sections of New England have inherited and engendered their own folk pastimes. New England suburbs are somewhat unique in the fact that they occupy formerly inhabited areas. Consequently, even as new buildings and streetscapes come to dominate, a few old houses and other sorts of landmarks almost invariably remain to remind residents of a departed, often ghostly past. "Spidergates" Cemetery, in Worcester, Massachusetts, comes to mind as a favorite haunt and preserve for thrill-seeking teenagers. Urban legends, which in many instances might properly be labeled as *suburban* legends given their ubiquity in bedroom communities, take root quickly in such environments, where old and new structures, landscapes, and worldviews coincide and residents work to balance their modern lives with divergent forms of cultural and often folk engagement. Even the seemingly nontraditional milieus such as office parks and college campuses can often become points of origin for all manner of folk pastimes. The company Halloween or Christmas party, though clearly a product of a postrural, commercializing culture, is choreographed in the image of regional and extraregional traditions and myths, and the foods and beverages served at such functions, store-bought or homemade, represent a collective effort, in any case, to adhere to a preexisting cultural template. College campuses, on the other hand (and New England is home to great plurality of them), have long generated their own traditions and, in true folk form, perpetuated them through the informal, "intergenerational" passing down from class to class. Students in the so-called Five College region, home to Amherst, Smith, Mt. Holyoke, Hampshire College, and the University of Massachusetts flagship campus, have generated several oral traditions over the years. On the University of Massachusetts campus, so the story goes, the statue behind the Student Union building of the native chief Metawampe will be sure to drop his tomohawk as soon as the first virgin walks past him. And as one joke has it, on the first day of class at each of the colleges, the professor's "Good morning, class" greeting is met by a gamut of responses. At competitive Amherst College, the students direct the professor to "Prove it." At Hampshire, which is by reputation one of the nation's premier "hippie" schools, "Good morning" evokes a chorus of "Wows." Students at the University of Massachusetts, who are held by their counterparts at the other colleges to be grade-obsessed but lacking in intellectual curiosity, respond by asking, "Will that be on the final exam?"

The folklore of a region, it is useful for us to remember, is rarely an elderly-specific culture. Rather, as in the case of Alejandro Cabrera's sons, it is the very youth of its practitioners that ensures and refreshes its continued practice. Indeed, since an active imagination and willingness to believe so often constitute the central factor in one or another folk practice's tenure, young people can be said to be the guarantors of vernacular culture. We can reach back as far as 1692 or earlier for tales of witches in New England, but a far more compelling case for the region's integral belief in witchcraft can be made as we look to a more contemporary account. An interview recorded in 1992 with a fifteen-year-old high schooler suggests the continued prevalence of such tales. The center of her town of Wendell, Massachusetts, is known for one landmark in particular, the "Eyeball House" (the tall picket fence that surrounds the place is covered by a large mural that depicts a multicolored eye), which has been home to members of a local reggae band since the 1970s. "In sixth grade," the girl says,

> They said that witches lived there and they'd steal kids. And everybody was really freaked out. And whenever we'd ride our bikes or something . . . we'd always go the long way around. . . . We'd never ride by the "hippie" house. We thought that witches were there and they were going to take us and use us in their potions.[55]

An oral tradition like this one bears so many of the earmarks of a contemporary lore—the social, cultural, and racial tension arising within an increasingly diversifying population, the primordial fear known throughout the ages to the children who naturally in such an unstable world fear for their well-being and safety and are all too susceptible to adult paranoias. Perhaps its most salient feature, however, is its simultaneously ancient and modern provenance, the way in which it collapses the departed world with the world of the present and delineates a landscape of meaning, a cultural practice in which specific places and the traditions that arise around them define the terms of people's collective existence. The New England landscape—a folk entity in itself—will continue to inspire regional folkways for as long as there are New Englanders to inhabit and shape it.

RESOURCE GUIDE

Printed Sources

Dorson, Richard. *Buying the Wind.* Chicago: University of Chicago, 1964.

————. *Jonathan Draws the Long Bow.* Cambridge, MA: Harvard University Press, 1946.

Hoberman, Michael. *Yankee Moderns: Folk Regional Identity in the Sawmill Valley of Western Massachusetts, 1890–1920.* Knoxville: University of Tennessee Press, 2000.

Ives, Edward "Sandy." In *Joe Scott: The Woodsman Songmaker.* Urbana: University of Illinois Press, 1978.

Neustadt, Kathy. *Clambake.* Amherst: University of Massachusetts Press, 1992.

Snow, Edward Rowe. *Ghosts, Gales and Gold.* Cornwall, NY: Cornwall Press, 1972.

Vermont Folklife Center. *Many Cultures, One People: A Multicultural Handbook about Vermont for Teachers.* Middlebury, VT: VFC, 1992.

Web Sites

The American Folklore Society. 2004.
February 23, 2004.
http://www.afsnet.org

Primary academic and public folklore site. Includes announcements, publications, book reviews, and links.

Maine Folklife Center. 2004.
University of Maine, Orono (also the home of the Northeast Archives of Folklore and Folklife).
February 23, 2004.
http://www.umaine.edu/folklife/

Includes newsletter, guide to public programs, archives, and links.

*The Vermont Folklife Cent*er. 2004.
February 23, 2004.
www.vermontfolklifecenter.org

Features publications, educational resources, exhibit guide, and links.

Native American Lore Index Page. 1996.
February 24, 2004.
http://www.ilhawaii.net/~stony/loreindx.html

Features narratives and index.

Videos/Films

Carousel. Dir. Henry King. Perf. Gordon MacRae, Shirley Jones. 20th Century Fox, 1956.
From Stump to Ship: A 1930 Logging Film. Dir. Alfred Ames. Narrated by Tim Sample. Stone
      E. Productions, 1930.
Together in Time (documentary about New England contra dancing). Dir. Steve Alwes. Nar-
      rated by Peter Coyote. 2001.

Recordings

Choose Your Partner: Contra Dancing and Square Dancing Music of New Hampshire. Smithson-
      ian Folkways, 1999.
Mademoiselle, Voulez-Vous Danser? Franco-American Music from the New England Borderlands.
      Smithsonian Folkways, 1999.

Festivals/Events

Haunted Salem
Salem, MA
www.hauntedhappenings.org

Spans three weeks in October.

Lowell Folk Festival
Lowell, MA
www.lowellfolkfestival.org

Held on the fourth weekend in July.

Pumpkin Festival
Keene, NH
www.pumpkinfestival.com

Held on the weekend in October closest to Halloween.

St. Peter's Fiesta (Blessing of the Fleet)
Stacy Boulevard and St. Peter's Square

Gloucester, MA
www.stpetersfiesta.org

Held on the weekend closest to the Feast Day of St Peter (June 29).

Southern New Hampshire Scottish and Celtic Festival
Greenfield, NH
www.snhscotcelt.org

Held in June.

FOOD

Robert F. Moss

FOOD AND GEOGRAPHY

As in all regions, the food of New England directly reflects the local geography and climate. The soil is mostly rocky and poor, but it is interspersed with fertile pockets, particularly in the lowland valleys of rivers such as the Connecticut and the Merrimack. New England has never been suited to large-scale grain production of the type seen in the Midwest, but it does support dairy farming and the raising of a few staple crops such as potatoes, apples, and sweet corn. The relative poverty of its soil is more than made up for by the richness of its seacoast, which not only provides an abundance of fish and seafood for the local diet but also offers excellent harbors that have made New England an important shipping center. From the early colonial days, Puritans maintained a brisk import and export trade, which brought into the region foreign foodstuffs such as spices, fruits, and sugars that added variety to the local produce.

The climate of New England has also had an important influence on its foodways. The region has late springs, short summers, and harsh winters, resulting in a short growing season—as little as one hundred days in the northernmost areas. For this reason, the harvest plays a crucial role in New England's food culture. Food was not only gathered during this time but also cooked, preserved, and stockpiled against the coming of winter. Autumn is a time of abundance and feasting, as typified by the Thanksgiving celebrations that began in the Northeast and evolved into a nationwide holiday. Historically, the long, cold winters dictated a style of cooking that was plain, hearty, and filling. For much of the year, the diet was composed largely of preserved foods such as salt pork, dried cod, and corned beef, all of which still play important roles in New England cookery. The area is not without its seasonal delicacies, however, and its residents relish the brief availability of foods such as alewives, blueberries, and fiddlehead ferns.

CLASSIC NEW ENGLAND FOODS & RECIPES

Seafood

Because of the importance of the sea to the New England food supply, many of the region's classic dishes are based upon seafood. Perhaps most iconic of New England cuisine is the lobster. The American lobster can be found in Atlantic waters as far south as North Carolina, but, because it thrives in colder water, it is most commonly found off the coast of Maine and Newfoundland. Larger than related varieties from Europe, Maine lobsters commonly weigh between one and five pounds, though specimens as large as forty pounds have been caught. Protected by a hard, thick shell, a mature lobster is nearly invulnerable to sea predators. It has a thick, powerful tail and two strong claws, the larger of which is used for crushing shells and the smaller to catch small fish and other fast-moving prey.

The shellfish are caught using "lobster pots," large traps made of wooden laths and nylon netting. A typical pot has two compartments, the inner one holding bait such as fish carcasses, and the large one serving as the actual trap. Two funnels at either end of the pot allow lobsters, attracted by the bait, to enter into the trap but, since the narrow end of the funnel is on the inside, prevent them from escaping. Lobster fishermen place their pots among rocks at depths of ten to fifty feet, and they use small boats to tend them. Often working alone, the fisherman moves from pot to pot, which are marked by brightly painted buoys, hauling up each one and removing the captured lobsters. Lobster fishing is a major industry in New England, bringing in revenues of more than $200 million a year. Although the shellfish are expensive outside the region, live lobsters can be purchased for as little as two dollars a pound in Maine.

The rich, sweet meat of the lobster is found mostly in its large tail and claws. The most common way to prepare the shellfish is to boil it in salted water or steam it in a pot with only a half-inch of water. Lobster is frequently served whole, and diners use mallets, nutcrackers, or special shears to break open the claws and remove the meat. Generally it is accompanied by melted butter for dipping. Lobster meat is also commonly used in cold salads or cream-based stews. Then there is the lobster roll. In most recipes, cooked lobster meat is combined with enough mayonnaise to bind it, and it is served on a buttered and toasted hot dog or hamburger bun. New Englanders fiercely debate the details of the preparation, such as the type of bun that should be used and whether spices, onion, celery, or lemon juice should be mixed in with the meat. A ubiquitous feature of Maine cuisine, lobster rolls can be found in restaurants and roadside stands up and down the coast, and they are popular with local residents and tourists alike.

Of equal importance to New England cooking are clams, which come in two main varieties: soft-shelled and hard-shelled. The first, often called "steamers," live beneath the ocean sand, using long neck-like siphons to reach up and draw in seawater, filter its nutrients, and discharge it. Because of this "neck," the clams are often given colorful nicknames such as "gapers" or "squirts." To harvest steamers, New Englanders go out onto sand flats at low tide and scoop up the clams with their hands or with a hoe-like tool called a clam differ, which has long, flat tines instead of a solid blade.

The other main variety of clam, the hard-shell, is also known as a "quahog" (pronounced "co-hog"), and it has a thick, round shell with a bright purple spot inside. Because of this color, Native American tribes would trim and polish the shells and use them as a form of money. Hard-shell clams are usually found in mud, not sand. To find them, fishermen wade out into three- or four-foot water, feel for the shells with their bare feet, and dig them out of the mud with long-handled rakes. Hard-shelled clams are categorized by size, the smallest being called "littlenecks," the medium ones "cherrystones," and the largest simply "quahogs."

The way clams are cooked depends upon the variety. Littlenecks and cherrystones are often served raw on the half shell, while the largest quahogs are generally chopped and used in soups and stews. In New England restaurants, the large clams are also cut into strips, breaded, and deep fried. Soft-shelled clams are usually steamed and served in the shell with melted butter for dipping. Perhaps the region's most famous dish is clam chowder. In most incarnations it is a cream-based soup that contains clams, onions, and potatoes, but recipes vary greatly from state to state. On Cape Cod in Massachusetts, chopped quahogs form the clam base, while in Maine whole steamers are used, along with roughly chopped celery. The Vermont variety contains no milk or cream, consisting of a clear broth with clams, onions, and potatoes.

Lobster pots line a commercial pier near the Portland Fish Exchange, Portland, Maine. Photograph by William B. Folsom/Courtesy NOAA.

One of the oldest ways to cook clams dates back to the Native American inhabitants: the clambake. A large pit is dug in the sand and its inside lined with stones. A wood fire is built in the pit and allowed to burn down to coals, which are then raked out and removed. The white-hot rocks are covered with wet seaweed, which creates steam for cooking, then clams, lobsters, and corn are placed into the pit. A variety of other ingredients are sometimes added to the clambake, including crabs, mussels, fish, chicken, sausage, potatoes, and other vegetables. Then, the pit is covered with a heavy tarp, and the food steamed. More than just a cooking method, the clambake is a popular form of social gathering in New England. Clambakes are regularly held as celebrations and fundraisers by churches, clubs, volunteer fire departments, and other organizations, the largest drawing thousands of diners to the shore.

In addition to lobster and clams, the New England seas produce an array of fish that form an integral part of the region's cookery. Most common are white-fleshed, bottom-feeding fish such as cod, pollack, haddock, sole, flounder, whiting, and halibut. These are typically baked whole, often draped with bacon or salt pork, and served with mild butter- and egg-based sauces. Smaller fish and fish fillets are fried

Recipes for clam chowder vary greatly from state to state: on Cape Cod in Massachusetts, chopped quahogs form the clam base, while in Maine whole steamers are used, along with roughly chopped celery.

and broiled; the fried haddock sandwich, served with tartar sauce and French fries, is a classic Maine treat. Fish chowder is popular throughout the region as well, although—like clam varieties—recipes differ greatly from place to place. The typical fish chowder includes onions and potatoes fried with salt pork or bacon, to which are added large chunks of white fish along with milk or cream. Each spring alewives—small, bony herring—make runs up smaller streams to spawning ponds, and their roe is considered a local delicacy. Another seasonal treat is salmon. Though not nearly as abundant as it once was, due to the damming of New England's rivers, salmon can still be caught in midsummer in Maine. Whole poached salmon with new potatoes and green peas remains the traditional dish served at Fourth of July celebrations in New England.

Other seafood staples of the region are scallops, oysters, and mussels. Scallops can be found both in the bays of Massachusetts and in the deeper ocean off the New England coast. Bay scallops are in season between November and April and are harvested by dredgers who pull trawling nets behind their boats. Small and tender, the bay scallop meat is about the size of a thimble and has a sweet, delicate flavor. They are often sautéed, marinated for salads, breaded and fried, and even eaten raw. Sea scallops are much larger—from one to four inches in diameter—and can be harvested year round in the North Atlantic. They are generally broiled, grilled, or sautéed—quick methods of cooking that keep their interior creamy, for overcooked scallops are tough and rubbery. Oysters are found along Cape Cod and in scattered spots along the northern coast, and they are generally served raw, though sometimes they are baked into casseroles and pies or deep fried. Though long avoided by New Englanders, who considered them poisonous, mussels are plentiful in the region. Like clams, they can be steamed in a wine and garlic sauce or made into soups and chowders. The popularity of mussels has grown rapidly over the past twenty years, and they can now be considered a regular part of New England cuisine.

Baked Beans

The natural produce of the oceans, of course, is only one aspect of New England foodways. Many of the most common dishes in the region have English roots, being introduced by British colonists in the seventeenth and eighteenth centuries. Baked beans are one such example. The bean varieties themselves are natives of the New World, and Native Americans had their own version of baked beans, which were cooked in the ground in an ember-filled "beanhole." British colonists adopted this recipe readily, for it was very similar to pease porridge, a staple of English cooking. Today, the dish is best known outside the region as "Boston baked beans," but it is prepared throughout New England, with the ingredients varying from state to state. In Massachusetts, navy or white pea beans are most commonly used. Jacob's Cattle and soldier beans are favored in Maine, while yellow-eyed beans are popular in Vermont. Despite the variety of bean used, the basic preparation is the same. The dried beans are soaked overnight, and in the morning they are simmered until tender but not overcooked. The classic test of a bean's doneness is to blow on it; if the skin cracks, it is ready. The parboiled beans are then placed in a bean pot, which is an earthenware vessel with high sides, a narrow neck, and a tightly fitting top. Scored salt pork is added to the beans along with sweetener, which can be molasses, maple syrup, brown or white sugar, or a combination. In some areas, an onion or mustard is added for additional flavor. The covered bean pot is placed in a slow (300 degree) oven and the beans allowed to cook anywhere from a few hours to all day long. The pork fat melts during cooking, permeating the beans with its rich flavor and mixing with the sweetness of the molasses or sugar. The resulting dish, though inexpensive to prepare, is hearty and filling, and it is a traditional Saturday evening meal throughout New England.

The classic accompaniment for baked beans is brown bread, which is also an adaptation of old English dishes to the food available in the New World. Unlike most breads, New England brown bread is not baked in an oven but is instead steamed inside a metal mold, a mode of cooking borrowed from the English pudding. Brown bread is made with a mixture of cornmeal, rye, and whole wheat flours, along with molasses or maple syrup for sweetening, buttermilk or sour milk, and baking soda for leavening. The batter is put into a greased mold (or, if a mold is not available, a one-pound coffee can), which is in turn placed in a large kettle or pot with enough boiling water to halfway cover the mold and is steamed for two to three hours.

Berries and Fruit

The New England soil is not well-suited to the large-scale production of grains such as wheat and corn, but it does produce a rich variety of berries and fruit. Because of its role in the traditional Thanksgiving dinner, the cranberry is perhaps the most well-known of New England berries. Cranberries are a native wetland fruit that, much like strawberries, grow low to the ground on trailing vines. They are most

Cranberries are a native wetland fruit that, much like strawberries, grow low to the ground on trailing vines. They are most commonly found in Massachusetts, where they grow in unique formations called cranberry bogs. Courtesy of Massachusetts Office of Travel and Tourism.

Strawberries, blackberries, and blueberries are found throughout New England. Courtesy USDA. Photo by Scott Bauer.

commonly found in Massachusetts, where they grow in unique formations called "cranberry bogs." The natural bogs were created when retreating glaciers left behind clay-lined "kettle holes" in the earth, which were then filled with water and organic matter, making an ideal environment for cranberry vines. Domestic cultivation techniques were perfected in the early nineteenth century, and since then growers have created their own bogs with impermeable beds layered with sand, peat, gravel, and clay. The mature berries produced from these bogs have a dark red color, firm texture, and very sour taste. Because of their tartness and acidity, cranberries are a good complement to the sweet flavor of sugar and other fruits. One of the most common preparations is to cook the berries with sugar and water to produce cranberry sauce, an essential accompaniment to turkey in the classic New England Thanksgiving dinner. There are two main varieties of cranberry sauce: whole berry, in which the full fruit adds texture, and jellied, from which the berry seeds and skins have been strained. Another popular preparation is cranberry relish, in which the berries are ground along with other fruits such as apple and oranges. Cranberries can be added to breads, muffins, and cakes, and their tartness is used to add zip to salads. Nationwide marketing of cranberry juice began in the 1960s, and the juice can now be found throughout the country, much of it made from berries raised in New England.

The blueberry is another important New England fruit, and Maine is widely acknowledged to produce the highest-quality blueberries in the country. These grow wild in "barrens," treeless tracts of land with acidic soil in which the low blueberry bush—and little else—flourishes. Maine is the only state that produces wild blueberries commercially, and its small, compact berries are ideal for industrial food products such as packaged muffin and pancake mixes. Locally, the berries are baked into pies, cakes, cobblers, and breads and made into jams and jellies. Other berry varieties can be found both wild and domesticated in New England, including strawberries, raspberries, and blackberries. These fruits ripen in the late summer and are an important seasonal addition to the cookery of the region.

Maple Syrup

Maple syrup is another distinctive New England food that is drawn from the local landscape. It is made from the sap of the hard or sugar maple tree, which, like cranberries and blueberries, is well-adapted to the harsh environment. Maple trees are hardy enough to stand up to New England's bitter winters, and they flourish on the steep, rocky slopes that are typical of the region. At the start of spring—generally in early to mid-March—the trees begin to produce large quantities of sugar-rich sap. To collect it, farmers drill holes two to three inches deep into the tree trunks and hammer in iron spouts. The clear sap begins to flow as the temperature warms above 40 degrees Fahrenheit, dripping slowly into buckets hung from the spouts. The flow lasts for several weeks, and during that time the farmer periodically collects the buckets and

To collect maple sap, farmers drill holes 2 to 3 inches deep into the tree trunks and hammer in iron spouts. Courtesy Library of Congress.

transfers their contents to a sugarhouse, where it will be transformed into maple syrup. This is done by slowly boiling the sap in large pans to remove the water, reducing it until it is thick, dark, and has a strong, rich flavor. It takes between thirty and forty gallons of sap to produce a single gallon of pure maple syrup; a farm of one thousand trees can produce from two hundred to three hundred gallons of syrup in a single season. The finished syrup is categorized by quality into a range of grades. The best (Grade A Light Amber) is the lightest and most delicately flavored, while the two middle grades (Grade A Medium Amber and Grade A Dark Amber) grow progressively darker and are more strongly flavored. The lowest grade (Grade B) is often called "cooking syrup" because its intense maple taste is better suited to flavoring dishes than being served by itself.

Maple syrup is the only sweetener that is native to New England (honeybees being introduced by English settlers in the eighteenth century), and it figures prominently in the cooking of the region. In colonial days, the syrup was widely used as a substitute for cane sugar and molasses, which had to be imported and were very expensive. Today, maple syrup is more expensive than conventional sugars, but it is still used because of its unique flavor. Pure maple syrup is poured on pancakes and waffles, and it is used to sweeten a variety of desserts such as pies, cookies, and doughnuts. The rich flavor makes a welcome addition to other dishes as well, including baked apples, candied sweet potatoes, and baked beans. By further heating, which removes all moisture, the syrup can be crystallized into maple sugar, which is then poured into molds or granulated. Maple candy is made through a similar process, boiling the syrup to remove excess water, though it is allowed to cool until soft and plastic. Now exported throughout the United States and the world, maple syrup is one of the best known natural products of New England.

Fiddleheads

In late April or early May, a different sort of seasonal treat becomes available in northern New England: the fiddlehead. Little known outside the region, fiddleheads are the young fronds of the ostrich fern, picked as they are just beginning to unfurl in the spring. Only the top few inches are snapped off the plants, and the curled shoots are dark green in color and have a flavor similar to asparagus. The most common way to prepare fiddleheads is the simplest: boiled or steamed and topped with melted butter and sometimes lemon juice or vinegar. A wide variety of more complicated recipes have been devised for this Maine delicacy, including fiddlehead soups, salads, stir-fries, ragouts, and pies.

NATIVE AMERICAN COOKERY

The foodways of the Native Americans laid the foundation for modern New England cookery. The principal Northeastern tribes—the Wampanoag, the Massachusetts, the Narrangansett, the Pequot, and the Pennacook—share a common diet and mode of cooking. Three domesticated crops formed the base of this diet: corn, beans, and squash. Their basic farming technique was to clear a patch of forest land by girdling the trees or by piling brush around their trunks and burning it. Once the land was cleared, the Native Americans used clamshell hoes to turn the soil and build a series of low mounds, two or three feet apart. Into each mound they planted corn and, once the first shoots were showing, beans as well. As the corn stalks grew, the bean vines would wrap around them and climb upward, producing a two-staple crop. The local corn varieties produced small (four- to five-inch) ears and had weak root systems, which was the reason native farmers planted them in mounds. One common technique was to place a small fish, such as the herring-like alewife, into each hill. The fish would rot into the soil, providing fertilizer for the growing corn and beans.

After they had harvested the corn, Native Americans generally made it into meal. To do so, they boiled the corn so that the kernels would swell and the hulls would loosen. They then rinsed the kernels, rubbed them to remove the hulls, and dried them in the sun. Then, using mortars and pestles, they ground the dried corn flesh and sifted the resulting meal, dividing it into several grades of coarseness. The finer meal was baked into bread, while the coarser meal was boiled into mush or cooked like hulled corn, creating a hominy-like dish. The beans grown by the New England tribes were generally of the kidney variety, and they were cooked by boiling and made into soups and stews. The squash included yellow summer, crook-neck, acorn, butternut, and pumpkin and were most often baked whole in the ashes of a fire.

The three main staples of corn, beans, and squash were supplemented by gathering wild plants. The edible greens available in New England included milkweed shoots, poke, and skunk cabbage, and there were a variety of native tubers such as arrowhead, cattail, and bulrush root knobs. A particularly important tuber in the Native American diet was the groundnut, a variety of wild bean whose walnut-sized roots are similar to sweet potatoes. The local tribes, of course, took full advantage of wild berries, which included strawberries, blueberries, raspberries, blackberries, and cranberries. They preserved the wild fruits by drying them and including them in pemmican cakes. Preserved berries were an important source of vitamins, preventing diseases during the long winter when fresh produce was not available.

For meat, the New England natives hunted deer, bear, and game birds such as turkeys, geese, and ducks. They cooked the meat primarily by roasting it over a fire or grilling it over hot coals. This was supplemented by the rich variety of fish and seafood from the ocean and inland rivers. Coastal tribes fished for cod, sole, flounder, herring, halibut, and sturgeon, and they gathered shellfish such as shrimp, lobsters, clams, and oysters. The indigenous method of cooking clams in a large pit was adopted by the first settlers and remains largely unchanged to this day.

Many other Native American recipes were adopted by European settlers and became a lasting part of the cookery of New England. The "beanhole," for example, was a pit dug in the ground, filled with hot coals, and used to cook a mixture of beans, maple syrup, and bear fat. The recipe—when Puritans replaced the pit with an oven, the maple syrup with molasses, and the bear fat with salt pork—evolved into Boston baked beans. More recently, John Mariani has claimed in *The Dictionary of American Food and Drink* (1994) that baked beans originated in North Africa and came to America with New England sea captains, but the Native American origin of baked beans still remains the popular view of Boston baked beans.

Northeastern tribes incorporated fish and clams into a variety of hearty soups and chowders, and they used maple sugar as their primary sweetener. They made whole-kernel corn into soups as well, to which beans and meat were often added. The Narrangansett word for this soup, "Msickquatash," is the origin of the English word "succotash," a dish of mixed corn and beans that became a staple of English colonial cooking. In this way—through ingredients, cooking techniques, and indigenous recipes—Native Americans laid the foundation on which the rest of New England cooking would be created.

EARLY COLONIAL COOKING

When English settlers first arrived in Massachusetts in the 1620s, they did not adopt Native American cookery completely. The Puritans were intent on maintaining the foodways of their native England—particularly the East Anglia region from where they primarily came—but they were forced by necessity to use the foodstuffs they found in the New World. As a result, the diet of the early colonists can be characterized as indigenous ingredients prepared by traditional English cooking methods. Baking was the primary mode of cooking in East Anglia, and brick ovens were among the first structures built in the Massachusetts colonies. The Puritans considered the outward senses to be a source of spiritual danger, so they preferred plain, mildly seasoned dishes—a style of cooking that cultural historian David Hackett Fisher has called "one of the more austere food ways of the Western World." A typical Puritan dish is the New England boiled dinner, which consists of beef and vegetables boiled for hours in plain, unseasoned water. Similarly plain was the popular "pease porridge": field peas boiled or baked to a mush-like consistency, which would be eaten, hot or cold, for breakfast, lunch, and dinner. When the field peas the settlers brought with them from Europe failed to grow in the harsh New England climate, they adapted the recipe to use local bean varieties.

The Puritans also brought wheat to the new world, but, like their peas, it did not grow well in the new climate. In its place the colonists substituted corn, which they learned to grow from the Native Americans, and corn meal became the main ingredient in their breads and puddings. Within a decade, the colony had a small number of cattle, goats, pigs, and chickens—all European imports—but they were still dependent upon local fish and eels for protein. Lobsters were abundant and easy to catch, but they were loathed by the early New Englanders, who would eat them only when nothing else could be had. They considered the region's plentiful mussels to be fit only for feeding pigs. The English settlers did relish many of the local wild plants, though, and edible mushrooms, nuts, cherries, and berries were an important supplement to their diet. They also hunted the local game, which included duck, rabbits, turkey, quail, and grouse and added some variety to their otherwise austere tables.

In the autumn of 1621, less than a year after their arrival in the New World and following a harsh winter and difficult summer that killed almost half of the colony, the surviving Plymouth residents celebrated their first harvest of corn and barley. Governor William Bradford proclaimed a day of thanksgiving and invited representatives from the neighboring Native American tribes to share in the feast that is now remembered as the first Thanksgiving dinner. The exact menu for the feast is not recorded, but we do know that for the occasion the Puritans killed many different fowl—probably partridges, ducks, geese, and turkey—and the visiting Wampanoag natives contributed five deer. Other likely dishes included pumpkins, squash, berries, and nuts, along with puddings or rustic bread made from the newly harvested corn. These items would form the basic New England diet for many decades to come.

The foodways of the early colonists were firmly controlled by the changing seasons. During the spring (from the first of April until mid-May) they engaged themselves in planting fields and gardens while subsisting largely on food preserved from the previous year. The early summer months of May and June, when these food stores were almost depleted, were times of privation, and the colonists depended on fish and dairy products for survival. By July, the gardens would begin to produce vegetables, and the full harvest (which lasted from late August to early October) would finally bring abundance. During these months, farmers would take in their grain and corn, and vegetables, wild fruits, berries, and nuts would be plentiful. As the weather turned cold in late October, the colonists would begin to put away food for the long winter. They slaughtered, smoked, and salted beef and pork; ground wheat into flour and corn into meal; and stored away bushels of tubers and root vegetables. They also brewed beer from newly harvested barley, and this drink would be an important source of carbohydrates during the long months ahead. The deepest part of winter lasted from December until the end of March, when the growing cycle would begin once more. Over the centuries, trade and technology have freed New Englanders from the harsh dictates of the climate, but the cyclical patterns of seasonal treats and harvest celebration remain an important part of the cooking of New England.

MATURE COLONIAL COOKING

By the eighteenth century, New England had grown from a few struggling settlements to a fully populated region, and new settlers were pushing westward into the mountainous frontier. The cookery of the region had also matured and was no longer a matter of bare subsistence, but the images of harvest feasts have led to a somewhat distorted popular perception of eighteenth-century eating. For most of the year, the colonial New England diet was plain and unvaried. The primary source of protein was salt-preserved meats and fish, and boiled tubers and roots were the predominant vegetables. In the countryside, the standard meals were an early breakfast, a large dinner at midday, and a lighter supper or tea around dark. Meat, grains, and dairy were the mainstays of the diet. The midday meal usually included boiled pork or beef with vegetables such as potatoes, beets, carrots, and cabbage, served together from a large platter placed in the center of the table for all to share. Supper was a much smaller meal and might consist solely of bread and milk; toast, cheese, and cider; or perhaps just a slice of pie. Breakfasts were usually austere as well, sometimes amounting to nothing more than reheated peas or beans accompanied by rustic bread.

The First Thanksgiving

Our harvest being gotten in, our governor sent four men on fowling, that so we might after have a special manner rejoice together after we had gathered the fruit of our labors; they four in one day killed as much fowl, as with a little help beside, served the company almost a week, at which time amongst other recreations, we exercised our arms, many of the Indians coming amongst us, and among the rest their greatest King Massasoit, with some ninety men, whom for three days we entertained and feasted, and they went out and killed five deer, which they brought to the plantation and bestowed on our governor, and upon the captain, and others. And although it be not always so plentiful as it was at this time with us, yet by the goodness of God, we are so far from want that we often wish you partakers of our plenty.[1]

Colonial Cooking Methods

In the days before stoves (and long before electricity or gas), almost all cooking was performed over an open fire and required a tremendous amount of labor. The typical kitchen had a large brick fireplace with a broad hearth, and a fire was kindled in it in the early morning and kept burning for much of the day. Most colonial fireplaces had some sort of suspension system that was used to hold the large pots and kettles used for cooking. The simplest of these was the "lug pole," a green log mounted high in the chimney from which pots could be hung. An important innovation during the colonial period was the iron crane, which was mounted on a hinge and could be swung out into the room to give the cook access to the pots. It also allowed her to raise and lower the pots and kettles more easily to control the cooking temperature. These were supplemented by footed pots and "spiders"—iron skillets with short legs on the bottom—that were placed directly on a bed of hot coals. Although a middle- or upper-class family might have a large array of pots and utensils, most families made do with a single iron kettle, a long-handled spoon, and perhaps a spider. Some of the most common meals were therefore one-pot recipes such as stews, soups, and chowders.

Baking was one of the most important forms of cooking in colonial New England, and the region's cooks produced a wide variety of breads, pies, and puddings. Because wheat was rare and expensive, New Englanders made a dense, hard-crusted bread from rye and corn meal (which was popularly called "rye 'n' injun") and a coarse brown bread from a mixture of whole wheat flour and corn meal. Typical pies included egg, mince, chicken, apple, pumpkin, and squash, and sweets such as gingerbread and pound cake were popular as well. All of these would be baked either in a so-called Dutch oven or in a brick oven that was specially constructed as part of the fireplace. The latter was the more labor-intensive way to bake, but it allowed for a much greater volume of production. To prepare for baking, the cook would light a fire directly inside the oven and allow it to burn for up to two hours. Once the coals had burned down sufficiently, they were emptied out and the food placed inside, where it would be cooked by the radiant heat stored in the oven's bricks.

Cooking in such an oven required considerable skill to judge the temperature of the oven and to know when to put in and remove the various breads and pies. Because of the work and time required to light and heat the oven, colonial housewives did their baking in large batches, cooking a series of items in an order determined by the level of heat required by each. Breads were cooked first, followed by puddings, then pastries, and finally cakes and gingerbread. Oven baking was generally done only once a week, and sometimes a single oven would be shared by two or more neighbors so that the hard-won heat would not be wasted. The second method of baking was the Dutch oven, a heavy, shallow iron kettle with three legs that allowed it to be set directly over hot coals. The kettle had a heavy lid on which more coals could be shoveled, allowing the contents to be cooked from both top and bottom. Dutch ovens were widely used by colonists who lacked a fireplace oven, and also between baking days by those with larger ovens. They would continue to be used throughout New England until well into the nineteenth century, when iron cook stoves became widely available.

Dairy Products and Meat

Like bread, dairy products were available year round and thus were an indispensable part of the New England diet. Most of the region's farms produced their own butter and cheese, and the work, which was generally performed by women, was not easy. They first had to milk the cows, strain the milk, and skim the cream from it. Most farmhouses had a room called a "buttery" that was located on the north side of the house (to keep it as cool as possible) and near to a water supply. In this room the women would churn the cream into butter and make cheese by allowing the milk to curdle and ripen. Dairy products were both an important part of any farm family's diet and a source of revenue. They sold their excess butter and cheese to town and city merchants (often exchanging them for other goods), and Boston exporters regularly purchased cheese from rural Massachusetts farmers to be sold throughout the colonies.

Though dairying went on throughout the year, butchering occurred only in the late fall. Sheep and cattle could not be fattened at pasture during the cold winter months, and they had to be slaughtered when the weather was cold enough for the meat not to spoil during the multiday process. Late November and early December, after the first frost but before hard freezes had set in, were the prime weeks for the task. Butchering required huge amounts of labor, and the work would take upward of a week to complete. A farmer began the process by killing the selected animals, draining them of blood, and removing their internal organs. The entire family was involved in the work, cleaning tripe, trying out tallow or lard, making sausages, and salting hams. The most important step was the preservation of the meat, which had to last through the long winter and well into spring. If the weather was cold enough, the meat could be frozen and stored in the farmhouse attic or an outbuilding. This method was not very reliable, however, because even in the northernmost parts of New England a midwinter warm spell could raise the temperature enough to spoil the entire stock. The most common way to preserve beef and pork was to pack it in salt and store it in large barrels in the cellar. Other popular methods included drying, smoking, and pickling. Preserved meats were an indispensable part of the region's cuisine, and to this day many of New England's signature recipes are based on salt pork, dried fish, or corned beef.

The Character of New England Food

It was in the eighteenth century, in fact, that the predominant character of New England food was established. Though later immigration, imported products, and new technology would add new flavors and variants, most of the ingredients and techniques of today's New England cuisine became available during the colonial period. Apples, for example, are not native to the region (with the exception of crabapples). The Puritans brought apple seeds with them from Europe, and orchards were flourishing in the colonies by 1650. In the 1740s, Boston merchants began exporting apples to the West Indies. New England's growers experimented with cross-pollination to create new strains, and by 1800 over a hundred different varieties of apples were being grown. Ready for harvest in the early fall, apples were eaten raw and baked into pies, tarts, and other pastries. Properly preserved, the fruit would last for months, and dried apples and barrels of applesauce were an important part of wintertime food stores.

The potato, though a native of the New World, was also an import to New England, being introduced there in a rather roundabout fashion. Spanish explorers found potatoes among the Incas of South America and brought them back to Europe in the sixteenth century. Within a century they had become a staple food item in Ireland, though they remained almost unknown in England and were not part of the diet of the original English colonists in Massachusetts. Potatoes were introduced in New England by Scotch-Irish settlers, who came to the area around Colrain and Pelham, Massachusetts, in the 1710s. These immigrants had good success growing potatoes in New England's rocky soil, and the vegetable was soon adopted by their English neighbors. Like carrots, turnips, and beets, potatoes were hardy and could be stored through the long winters in families' root cellars, a feature that helped them become an indispensable part of the region's cuisine. This was one of the first of many instances in which non-English immigrants introduced new foods and techniques to New England cookery.

Most desserts require some sort of sweetener, and there were several options available to colonial bakers. Cane sugar had to be imported from the West Indies, and as a result was quite expensive. The highest quality sugars, known as Jamaica or loaf sugar, were used sparingly and reserved for the better-quality desserts such as cakes and pies. Molasses, the dark sap-like by-product of the sugar refining process, was imported in large quantities as well. Though it was frequently used as a less-expensive alternative to white sugar, much of the molasses brought into the colonies was distilled into rum. Two types of sweeteners were produced locally: maple syrup, a native New England product, and honey, which was made by bees that had been brought to the New World by the Puritans. While maple syrup (and maple sugar) served as general-purpose sweeteners for a variety of recipes, honey was used principally to brew a thick, mead-like drink called metheglin, which was very popular in the eighteenth century.

Alcoholic beverages were an important part of the food culture of colonial New England, even among the most devout Puritans. The records of the Reverend Jonathan Ashley of Deerfield, Massachusetts, for example, show him budgeting 8 percent of his salary to purchase various types of alcoholic products for his household—a sum approved by his church and apparently quite typical. Rum was by far the most popular liquor during this period, and it was purchased in large quantities by all social classes. Much of the supply was brewed locally from imported molasses, and it was both strong and inexpensive. "Punch"—a mixture of rum, sugar, boiling water, and lemon or lime, was the preferred drink at parties and weddings. Until the nineteenth century, farm workers commonly received a quantity of rum as part of their wages, and soldiers were rationed a half cup a day. At mealtime, the standard New England table drinks were beer and hard apple cider. Most families brewed their own beer from barley, malt, and hops, and making apple cider was a regular harvest-time task. Other beverages such as wine, brandy, and gin had to be imported from Europe, so they were expensive, but they were available throughout New England, particularly for the upper classes.

The economy of New England during the colonial period was dominated by fishing, and the principal fish was cod. New England fleets would range from Massachusetts to the coast of Labrador in search of the fish, and their catch was taken ashore to be dried and salted. The best-quality salt cod was exported to southern Europe, where it was traded for wine, cloth, and manufactured goods, while the middle quality was sold domestically, particularly to the backcountry regions of New England. The lowest-quality fish was sent to the West Indies, where it was used to feed slaves and was exchanged for rum and molasses. The cod trade was a lucrative business, and it helped make many Massachusetts merchants extremely rich. These men, who included George Cabot, used their wealth to gain social and political prominence, earning themselves the nickname "the Codfish Aristocracy." As a percentage of the region's economy, cod fishing peaked around 1760. During the Revolutionary War, many fishing vessels were converted into privateers. After the war, the fleet was only one-quarter of its original size, but fishing would continue to be an important part of New England's economy and its food culture, although on a much smaller scale.

Variations in New England Food Culture

Although all of colonial New England shared a common food culture, there were some important variations. Vermont and northern New Hampshire were frontier regions much longer than the rest of New England, and its terrain was more mountainous and difficult to access, all of which contributed to its distinctive cooking. Because of their isolation and distance from the coast, hill-country residents had very little seafood in their diet, salted cod brought over the mountains from Boston being the only fish readily available. Vermont was cattle country, so beef took the place of seafood in the local cuisine. Because of the cold mountain winters, meat was often preserved by freezing instead of salting or drying, and fresh meat was available for much of the year. Highland beef was relatively tough and stringy, so typical early recipes are for dishes such as stews and pot roasts, which made the meat tender through long, slow cooking. Because of the many local dairy cows, milk and cream play a more prominent role in hill country cooking than elsewhere in New England, and to this day Vermont is known for the quality of its cheeses.

In colonial times only a small minority of New Englanders lived in towns and cities, and their foodways differed significantly from those in rural areas. Apart from the occasional vegetable garden, townspeople did not raise their own food, relying on meat and produce brought in from the surrounding countryside. Throughout much of the eighteenth century food was regularly sold by hucksters who carried their goods from house to house on foot or in small carts, offering vegetables, meats, eggs, butter, and fish for sale. Just before the Revolution, many of the cities and larger towns established produce markets where residents could go to select their vegetables and fruits rather than waiting for the sellers to come to them, and going to market soon became a regular part of the housekeeper's day. Most townspeople did not have large ovens for baking bread and pastries, buying them instead from commercial bakers. Because of the shipping trade, a wide assortment of imported foodstuffs were available, such as raisins, citrus fruit, salted meats, and spices. As a result, the typical town dweller in the eighteenth century had a much more varied and balanced diet than those living on farms, who were dependent upon the seasons and what they could produce, preserve, and prepare themselves.

FOOD AND THE EARLY REPUBLIC

Imported Food and Goods

In the years immediately following the American Revolution, the foodways of New England began to be altered by trade. The war had devastated the region's fishing industry, reducing its fleet to only a quarter of its prewar size. These vessels were replaced not by fishing boats but by merchant ships, for independence from Britain had freed New England from restrictions on foreign trade and helped spark a boom in shipping and shipbuilding. The Northeast produced few raw materials of its own for export: there was little large-scale farming of grains or cotton, and no iron or coal. Instead, New Englanders became merchants and shipping middlemen, importing products from around the globe and reexporting them to different places. In the early nineteenth century, merchants from Salem, Massachusetts, cornered the lucrative pepper trade, a spice that was popular throughout the Western world for food preservation (largely because it helped disguise the flavor of spoiled meat). Salem's middlemen imported pepper from Sumatra in massive quantities—7.5 million tons in 1805—and exported it everywhere, in the process creating fortunes for the new shipping aristocracy.

The traders' ships returned from overseas filled with an array of foods and beverages. From the West Indies came molasses, limes, oranges, and rum; from the Mediterranean, wines, brandy, raisins, figs, and olive oil. Ale, pork, and butter were common imports from Britain, and Brazil contributed coffee and tapioca. By the end of the eighteenth century, New England cooking was enlivened by imported spices, including mace, cloves, nutmeg, pepper, ginger, cinnamon, aniseed, and allspice—all of which have since become traditional flavors in the region's recipes.

The coastal trade with other American states brought in additional foodstuffs, such as onions, pork, and flour from the mid-Atlantic, rice and corn from the South, and wheat and oats from the farmlands of the newly opened frontier. All of these imports supplemented local produce and helped make New England's food supply less dependent upon the seasons.

Two imported beverages, coffee and tea, formed an important part of New England foodways during this period. Both drinks had been popular in the region since the early colonial days: Boston's first coffeehouse had been licensed in 1670, and its first tea room in 1690. Tea remained cheaper (and therefore more popular) until the Revolution, when high import duties led to American boycotts and protests, including the famous Boston Tea Party in 1773, when a band of colonists boarded British ships and dumped more than three hundred crates of tea into Boston Harbor. Tea sales recovered after the Revolution, but the War of 1812 once again cut off the supply, resulting in higher prices and lower-quality tea. Americans turned instead to coffee, which was by then widely available from Brazil, and it became the standard hot beverage in New England.

Most of the Northeast remained rural during the early years of the Republic, and the country store played an important role in rural life. Such stores were usually small but sold a wide variety of general merchandise, from cloth and buttons to jams, preserves, and candies. Though most New England farms were largely self-sufficient, families turned to the country store to augment what they raised for themselves. Common food items included eggs, vinegar, rum, coffee, tea, sugar, molasses, salt, and spices. Milled flour and corn meal were available by the barrel, and large wheels of cheddar cheese—often called simply "store cheese"—were kept under glass and sliced into one- or two-pound wedges for customers. This cheese was often eaten along with "common crackers," a round, nugget-like New England staple, which were kept in large barrels in almost every country store. Barter was often the medium of exchange, and farm families regularly swapped their excess butter, eggs, and cheese for store credits.

Holiday Feasts

By the early nineteenth century, the character of traditional New England cookery was solidly established. Although the cuisine would continue to evolve and expand over the next two hundred years, the ingredients and recipes that most people think of as classically New England were already set. To a large extent, the popular image of New England food is rooted in the institution of Thanksgiving, which grew from a strictly regional holiday into a national celebration during the Antebellum years. Throughout the colonial period, following the tradition established by the Puritans of Plymouth Plantation, the governor of each New England colony would declare a day of Thanksgiving in late November or early December. The morning would be spent in religious services, where ministers preached special sermons on the topic of civic affairs, reviewing current events and addressing the political duties of Christians. But the centerpiece of the day—then as now—was the Thanksgiving dinner.

The dishes served at the traditional Thanksgiving feast during the early nineteenth century were very similar to those served today, though the dinners were usually longer (two hours or more) and more ritualized. The feast began with a

"The National Thanksgiving"

Editorial by Sara Josepha Hale (1865)

"Then he said unto them, Go your way, eat the fat, and drink the sweet, and send portions unto them for whom nothing is prepared; for this day is holy unto our Lord: neither be ye sorry; for the joy of the Lord is your strength."—Nehemiah viii.10.

Such was the order given to the people of Israel for the celebration of their *National and Religious Festival*, the "Feast of Weeks." We learn from this that a day of yearly rejoicing and giving of gifts was not only sanctioned but enjoined, by Divine authority, on God's chosen people. Such yearly festival is not positively enjoined on Christians; but that it is both expedient and beneficial may be safely urged, when we find that the practice was approved by our God and Father in heaven. We have, for many past years, urged the advantages of having a day set apart by the civil authorities of each State, which every heart in our wide land may welcome as the time of joy and thankfulness for the American people.

Our Day of Thanksgiving represents, in many striking coincidences, the Jewish Feast of Weeks; only make our day national, and we should then represent the union of joy that was the grand proof of the Divine blessing.

Such social rejoicings tend greatly to expand the generous feelings of our nature, and strengthen the bond of union that binds us brothers and sisters in that true sympathy of American patriotism which makes the Atlantic and Pacific Oceans mingle in our minds as waters that wash the shores of kindred homes, and mark, from east to west, the boundaries of our dominion.

The Creator has so constituted the race of mankind that their minds need a moderate portion of amusement as imperatively as the body at times wants stimulating food. The recreative joyousness, the return, if you please, to the gayeties of childhood, is good for the soul. It sweetens the temper, it brightens hope; it increases our love for each other, and our faith in the goodness of God. There are individuals and nations who, from an unhappy state of things, vice in themselves or in other persons, from poverty, or political oppression, never "drink the sweet, nor eat the fat," but drag on a starved and miserable existence. These are not, physically, true specimens of the human being; want is written on the sunken cheek, and wasting despondency cripples the feeble limbs.

Even thus the mental starvation from all the sweet joys of social intercourse and innocent merry-making, has a wasting and deforming effect upon human character, similar to bad or insufficient diet on the bodily constitution. God intended that all our faculties should, in the right way, be exercised; and neglect of such exercise changes us to incomplete creatures. One has but a lame existence who has lost or neglected to cultivate "the store that nature to her votary yields." Our busy, wealth seeking people require to have days of national festivity, when the fashion and the custom will call them to the feast of love and thanksgiving.

So we agree with the large majority of the governors of different States, that THE LAST THURSDAY IN NOVEMBER should be the DAY OF NATIONAL THANKSGIVING for the American people. Let this day, from this time forth, as long as our Banner of Stars floats on the breeze, be the grand THANKSGIVING HOLIDAY of our nation, when the noise and tumult of worldliness may be exchanged for the laugh of happy children, the glad greetings of family reunion, and the humble gratitude of the Christian heart.

> Consecrate the day to benevolence of action, by sending good gifts to the poor, and doing those deeds of charity that will, for one day, make every American home the place of plenty and rejoicing. These seasons of refreshing are of inestimable advantage to the popular heart; and, if rightly managed, will greatly aid and strengthen public harmony of feeling. Let the people of all the States and Territories set down together to the "feast of fat things" and drink, in the sweet draught of joy and gratitude to the Divine giver of all our blessings, the pledge of renewed love to the Union, and to each other; and of peace and good-will to all the world. *Then the last Thursday in November will soon become the day of* AMERICAN THANKSGIVING throughout the world.[2]

meat course that featured roast turkey and chicken pie, and ham, beef, goose, and duck might also be served. The meat was accompanied by vegetables, pickles, bread, butter, and cheese. Next came a parade of pies—often dozens of them. The most popular varieties were apple, mince, and Marlborough (a blend of apple and lemon custard), but pumpkin, cranberry, blueberry, cherry, peach, and plum pies were common as well. The pies were usually followed by a fruit course that included exotic imports such as dates, prunes, oranges, raisins, and figs. Finally, the dinner was completed with the service of coffee and tea. Such a feast, of course, required days of preparation, and it was generally considered to be the culmination of the entire harvest season.

Similar holidays were celebrated outside of New England in the early nineteenth century, but they tended to be general days of Thanksgiving and did not necessarily involve a formal dinner. As New Englanders migrated westward into the new frontier states of Ohio, Michigan, Illinois, and Wisconsin, they took their holiday traditions with them and began spreading their customs into new areas. The nationwide adoption of Thanksgiving, however, was largely the result of a two-decade campaign by Sara Josepha Hale, a New Hampshire author who became the editor of *Godey's Lady's Book*, the most widely read and influential periodical in the United States. In 1846, Hale published the first of a series of editorials praising Thanksgiving and advocating its declaration as a national holiday. Each November, the *Lady's Book* devoted an entire issue to Thanksgiving, featuring poems and stories about idealized family gatherings and columns full of recipes and tips for stuffing turkeys and baking pies. Hale also wrote letters to the governors of every state, encouraging them to declare a day of Thanksgiving on the last Thursday of November. Her efforts were rewarded in 1863, which Abraham Lincoln declared the first national Thanksgiving Day. By promoting the Thanksgiving traditions and recipes from her native New England, Hale helped determine the symbols and rituals of the holiday for the entire country. As a result, the national dinner of the United States was, in effect, a Yankee dinner, one of the first of several factors that would help establish New England cookery as the quintessentially American cuisine.

EARLY NEW ENGLAND RESTAURANTS

Up to this point, the history of New England cookery has been limited to home cooking, for there truly was little else. There were no restaurants as we think of them today, and eating out simply for entertainment was virtually unheard of. During the eighteenth century, those who dined outside their homes were usually travelers stopping at taverns or inns, and most New England villages had a tavern located on the main through-road. These were generally rude establishments, and the food they served was notoriously poor. Meals were served at set times during the day, and guests had little if any choice of what they would eat. As factory towns and industrial cities grew, more and more single men and women lived in boardinghouses, and their rent included breakfast, dinner, and tea served in a common dining room. As in taverns, the quality of the food was widely reviled, as were the manners of the average boarder, who had to race to wolf down enough food to make a meal before his or her fellow diners ate it all.

A Nineteenth-Century Tavern

Next to the store was the tavern,—with a tall sign-post which used to creak and flap in the summer winds, with a leisurely, rich, easy sort of note of invitation,—a broad veranda in front, with benches,—an open tap-room, where great barrels of beer were kept on draft, and a bar where the various articles proscribed by the temperance society were in those days allowed an open and respectable standing. This tavern veranda and taproom was another general exchange, not in those days held in the ill repute of such resorts now. The minister himself, in all the magnificence of his cocked hat and ample clerical wig, with his gold-headed cane in his hand, would sometimes step into the tap-room of a cold winter morning, and order a mug of flip from obsequious Amaziah the host, and, while he sipped it, would lecture with a severe gravity a few idle, ragged fellows who were spending too much time in those seductive precincts.[3]

Restaurants that specialized solely in the serving of food first appeared in larger cities in the late eighteenth century. The name for these places varied from region to region, with "eating house" being common in New York City while "dining room" and "dining hall" were used in the Southern states. In New England (particularly Boston), the term *restorator* was widespread, a variation of the French word *restaurant*, which would enter general usage in the 1840s. The first real restaurants in New England were coffeehouses and oyster houses, which proliferated in Boston and other cities in the early nineteenth century. Coffeehouses, which were modeled after the popular institutions in Britain, were fashionable urban gathering places where men socialized, talked about politics, and conducted business over mugs of hot coffee. The popularity of these establishment saw two surges, the first during the Revolution and the second during the War of 1812, when Americans were either boycotting British tea or found the commodity hard to come by. Although some coffeehouses served food, the beverage itself was the primary draw, and coffeehouses functioned much in the manner of taverns.

In the 1820s and 1830s the United States was swept by an oyster craze, and oyster houses opened across New England. Also called oyster cellars, oyster bars, oyster lunchrooms, oyster parlors, and oyster saloons, these establishments served cheap oysters and plentiful alcoholic beverages. They were not elegant restaurants but rather plain eating dens, with large, heavy tables and floors covered with sawdust to absorb dropped shells and other detritus. The menu was simple, consisting of oysters served raw or roasted on the half-shell, oyster stew, and perhaps clams, along with a few accompaniments such as toast and pie. One of the most famous of these early restaurants is the Union Oyster House at 41 Union Street in Boston. Originally named "Atwood & Bacon," it was established in 1826 in an old dry goods store and had a famous semicircular oyster bar that served many fa-

Originally named "Atwood & Bacon," the Union Oyster House was established in 1826 in an old dry goods store. It is still open today, serving as many as 3,000 oysters daily, and lays claim to being Boston's oldest continually running restaurant. Courtesy of Massachusetts Office of Travel and Tourism.

mous diners, including Daniel Webster, who regularly washed down several dozen oysters with tumblers of brandy and water. The Union Oyster House is still open today, serving as many as three thousand oysters daily, and lays claim to being Boston's oldest continually running restaurant.

Dining in Boston was not limited to the rough pleasures of the oyster house. As the city grew in population and wealth, it soon became home to some of the country's best restaurants. Unlike New York and Philadelphia, whose chefs were heavily influenced by French recipes and techniques, Boston's restaurants remained dedicated to traditional New England dishes, particularly those featuring fresh local seafood. The Parker House Hotel, whose dining room was among the city's best and most expensive, was founded by Henry D. Parker in 1855, and its many contributions to Boston's (and America's) cuisine include the Parker House roll, the Boston Cream pie, and "scrod"—Parker's term for the fresh white catch of the day, which usually was a tender baby cod. Parker also introduced the "European plan" to American hotels, wherein meals could be ordered by guests at any time during the day rather than being served at fixed times. Two competitors to the Parker House soon opened: the Ritz-Carlton Hotel, which was loosely associated with the Ritz Hotel of Paris, and the Winter Place Hotel, which is now known as the Locke-Ober. All three are still in operation today, and they helped Boston establish a reputation in the nineteenth century as one of America's leading restaurant cities.

THE TRANSFORMATION OF NEW ENGLAND COOKING

The rise of industrial America in the nineteenth century caused dramatic changes in every aspect of life in New England, including what people ate and the way they prepared it. The era brought new techniques for growing, preserving, transporting, and cooking food as well as new ideas about diet and nutrition. These changes were accompanied by a surge of immigration, which brought an influx of new cultures and foodways into the region. By 1900, New England's cooking had been radically altered.

One of industrialism's first changes was the invention of improved cookstoves for the home kitchen. Between 1820 and 1850, more than 550 patents were issued for stoves. The main purpose of these devices was to relieve the backbreaking labor required to cook over a fire. The earliest stoves were made of iron and had a central firebox, in which a cook would tinder a wood fire, and a large stove pipe that vented the smoke through the kitchen ceiling. The stove had a baking oven in its side and two large "boiling holes" in the top into which custom-fitted cookware such as pans, griddles, and steamers could be placed to be heated by the fire below. These stoves provided raised cooking surfaces, reducing the amount of bending and heavy lifting required to cook a meal, and they let the cook use smaller pieces of wood to build the fire. Over the next few decades, inventors added a succession of minor improvements and enhancements, and by the 1850s completely enclosed ranges were widely available throughout New England.

In addition to making cooks' work easier, the new stoves also changed cooking and eating habits. Because their fires were easier to build and their ovens quicker to heat, cookstoves allowed baking to be performed more frequently and in smaller batches than it could with a fireplace oven. The stove tops allowed a cook to use multiple pots and pans simultaneously, which reduced the dependence on one-pot recipes such as soups and stews and allowed cooks to prepare a wider variety of dishes for a single meal. Also, because it was no longer heated by a continuous fire, the kitchen became less of the home's gathering point, and meals and social activities shifted more to dining rooms and parlors.

Not just the tools for cooking changed during this period but the ingredients as well. In the early nineteenth century, the only leavening agents available to bakers were yeast and egg whites beaten to a froth. Yeast was not purchased in packages but rather kept as "starter," a portion of dough saved from previous batches of baking. There were no "quick breads": muffins and biscuits were raised with yeast, and cakes resembled sweetened bread dough made with eggs, spices, and candied fruit. By the 1820s, new leavening agents began to be introduced. The first of these, pearl-ash (potassium bicarbonate) and saleratus (an impure form of sodium bicarbonate) could be substituted for beaten eggs or yeast and speeded baking because they did not require hours to rise. But, they left cakes with a coarser texture, a darker color, and an unpleasant flavor. In the 1850s, cooks began using baking soda mixed with cream of tartar, and in the 1870s the two were mixed and sold commercially as baking powder. The result was an increased popularity of quick breads and a new texture and flavor for New England cakes, muffins, and biscuits. Traditional cooks deplored the new chemical leavening agents, which resulted in cakes that lacked the richness of yeast-risen varieties and often had a metallic aftertaste, but most housewives liked the speed and convenience of the new products. By the turn of the twentieth century, what had once been known as "economy cakes" had become the norm.

Perhaps the biggest change in what New Englanders ate was caused by the developments of new ways to preserve food for commercial sale. The canning industry began in the Northeast in the 1840s as a way to preserve fish and seafood, and among the first foods to be canned were lobster, salmon, and oyster. These were soon followed by canned vegetables such as corn, tomatoes, and peas. The earliest cans were made by tinsmiths and soldered by hand, though by the 1850s new machines had been invented to mass produce the can bodies. By the 1870s, fully automated canning factories were in production, in which cans were filled, sealed, and packed mechanically on an assembly line.

These packing methods were accompanied by two revolutionary developments in transportation: the transcontinental railroad and refrigerated freight cars. The transcontinental railroad made it possible to ship goods from one part of the country to the other, and refrigerated freight cars allowed perishables to survive the trip from coast to coast. In 1868, the first shipment of refrigerated meat from Chicago arrived in Boston. By the 1880s, fresh fruit and vegetables from California could be purchased in New England. Around the same time, Lorenzo Baker, a Cape Cod fishing captain, and Andrew Preston, a Boston produce agent, began importing bananas from Central America and selling them in the Boston market. In the space of only a few decades, a wide array of inexpensive imported foods became available throughout New England.

These changes had both a traumatic and a revolutionary effect on the region's foodways. New England farming was decimated, for its smaller scale of production could not compete against the cheaper prices of wheat, barley, and rye from the Midwest and fruit and vegetables from California. Yankee farmers increasingly turned from grains to dairy farming. At the same time, cooks became much less dependent on indigenous foods and the local growing seasons. Wheat—once so prohibitively expensive that it was reserved for special desserts and pastries—became much cheaper, and it quickly replaced corn and rye as the staple ingredient in New England breads and rolls. Exotic foods could now be afforded by middle-class families, and imported fruits and vegetables became fashionable. Oranges were commonplace in the Northeast by the 1870s, and bananas by the 1880s. Canned goods, because of their novelty and their image as sanitary and modern, enjoyed something of a vogue during the late nineteenth century, and products such as canned salmon and sardines were high-status foods for middle-class dining tables.

These advances in food production and transportation proved to be something of a double-edged sword. On the one hand, cooks gained access to new sources of meats and produce, food prices on the whole dropped, and the New Englander diet was no longer constrained by the harsh cycle of the seasons. On the other hand, the general quality and freshness of foods declined. Produce was now available year round instead of just at harvest time, but it had to be picked days or weeks before it was fully ripe in order to survive the trip across the country. Innovations such as canned goods and chemical leavening agents reduced the hours cooks had to spend in the kitchen, but convenience came at a price: the general quality of traditional dishes declined. It would be almost a century before these trends would be reversed and New England's cooks would once again seek out fresh, locally grown produce.

IMMIGRATION AND NEW ENGLAND COOKING

Irish Influence

An additional force that contributed to the transformation of New England's cookery was the wave of European immigrants who came to the region during the nineteenth century. Before this period, newcomers to New England had been almost exclusively Protestant English; immigrants from other European countries such as Scotland, Ireland, and Germany had tended to settle in the middle and southern colonies. This changed in the 1820s when Boston, its port a major gateway to the United States, began to attract Irish Catholic immigrants. In the 1840s the Great Potato Famine forced more and more Irish to leave their homes to escape starvation, and by 1847 more than thirty-seven thousand Irish-born persons were living in Boston, making them the city's largest immigrant group. Over the succeeding decades, these immigrants and their descendants came to dominate Boston's political life, and the city today remains strongly influenced by Irish American culture. Irish immigration was not limited to Boston; the newcomers settled throughout much of New England. By 1860, for example, some fifty-five thousand Irish-born persons were living in Connecticut, most of whom worked in new industrial cities such as Hartford and New Haven.

The effect of Irish immigration on New England cookery was less dramatic than on other aspects of the region's culture, because Irish foodways were similar to those of earlier English immigrants. To be sure, traditional Irish dishes such as beef and lamb stews, shepherd's pie, and potato and leek soup have now become classic New England recipes, but these were variations of the many one-pot dishes already widespread throughout the Northeast. A more radical difference was introduced by the wave of immigrants from Southern Europe—notably from Italy and Portugal—who began arriving in New England after the Civil War.

Italian Influence

Italian immigration, which had been almost nonexistent before 1870, swelled in the 1880s, as tens of thousands of Italians departed for the United States, seeking to escape low wages and high taxes. Most of the immigrants were from rural communities and had little education, and they intended to find work in America, save money, and eventually return to their families in Italy. Though some Italian immigrants did indeed return to their homes, most ended up staying in America, bringing their families over to live with them. These immigrants settled primarily in urban industrial areas, where they found work as unskilled laborers in New England's many booming factories. For this reason, the largest concentration of Italian American communities in New England are in the cities of Connecticut, Rhode Island, and Massachusetts.

Italian immigrants brought with them a rich cooking tradition, and they kept these foodways alive in their new country. Italian cooking was diverse, with recipes and ingredients that varied dramatically from one region to the next. In general, though, it was much bolder and more heavily spiced than traditional New England fare, characterized by strong flavors such as olive oil, garlic, and anchovies. Initially, Italian cooking had little influence on the foodways of New England. Labeled "ethnic" food, for more than half a century it could be found only in the Italian American neighborhoods in large cities. One such neighborhood was Boston's North End, the city's oldest residential neighborhood. Once populated by a succession of British, Irish, German, and Russian immigrants, in the late nineteenth century the North End became the city's largest Italian American community and supported a wide array of shops selling traditional Italian produce, breads, pasta, and meats. By World War I, the area was home to three large pasta manufacturing factories, including the Prince Macaroni Company, which was founded by three Sicilian immigrants in 1912. For forty years, Prince sold its products almost exclusively to Italian Americans, marketing them through advertisements in Italian-language newspapers. In the 1950s, however, Prince began marketing ag-

In the late nineteenth century the North End became Boston's largest Italian American community and supported a wide array of shops selling traditional Italian produce, breads, pasta, and meats. Courtesy of Massachusetts Office of Travel and Tourism.

gressively to non-Italian customers in an effort to introduce them to pasta products such as macaroni and spaghetti. They built a series of successful advertising campaigns around the slogan "Wednesday is Prince Spaghetti Day," which was broadcast to consumers throughout New England. Efforts such as these helped Italian food move into the mainstream culture. Pasta, long ignored as an ethnic oddity, is now a staple of New England cooking, as are other once-exotic ingredients such as garlic, basil, and parmesan cheese.

Portuguese Influence

There are strong Italian American communities in many cities outside New England, and their cookery has had a strong influence on dining habits throughout the United States. An immigrant culture unique to the region is that of the Portuguese, who with the exception of a small enclave in San Francisco settled almost exclusively in Rhode Island and Massachusetts. The first Portuguese immigrants came to this country from the Azores, Madeira, and the Cape Verde Islands to seek employment in New England's whaling business. A large Portuguese American community developed first in New Bedford—then the home of the American whaling industry—and then in other coastal cities, including Newport, Nantucket, and Provincetown. In the 1870s the whaling industry collapsed as Americans switched to petroleum-based kerosene rather than whale oil to fuel their lanterns. Portuguese immigration increased, however, as new arrivals began seeking work in the textile centers of southern New England. This second wave of immigrants settled mostly in New Bedford, Fall River, and Boston in Massachusetts and Providence in Rhode Island. By 1905, 16 percent of the New Bedford population were first- or second-generation Portuguese Americans.

These immigrants, most of whom came from Portuguese islands or coastal areas, brought with them a distinctive style of cooking based around seafood and sausages, which they quickly adapted to local ingredients. There are three primary varieties of sausage. *Linguica* is a sweet and spicy pork sausage and forms the basis of a range of classic Portuguese dishes. *Chourico*, similar to the Spanish *chorizo*, is larger and hotter than linguica and is commonly used in soups. *Morcella* is a dark, almost black sausage similar to blood pudding, and it is often fried with onions and served with baked beans and beer. Another classic Portuguese dish is kale soup. Like most classic recipes, its exact ingredients vary from cook to cook, but most versions include kale, linguica sausage or salt pork, potatoes, onions, and beans. Portuguese cooking is now a specialty of the restaurant trade in the Cape Cod region, particularly in tourist destinations such as Provincetown, with fresh fish, kale soup, clam chowder, and rich Portuguese pastries characterizing the menus.

THE DOMESTIC SCIENCE MOVEMENT
AND NEW ENGLAND COOKING

At the same time that immigrants were bringing new styles and ingredients to New England, a countervailing force arose that led native cooks to resist the immigrant influences and radically altered cooking not only in the Northeast but throughout the United States. Known as the Domestic Science movement, it sought to reform cooking and eating habits through the rigorous application of scientific principles. The movement had strong New England roots. The first institution promoting it was the Women's Laboratory, which was founded by Ellen Richards in 1876 at the Massachusetts Institute of Technology. Richards' specialty was household chemistry, which applied scientific techniques to analyze cooking processes, identify adulterated foods, and improve housekeeping methods. Richards trained many of the early Domestic Science leaders, who began teaching and lecturing first in Boston, then throughout New England, and finally throughout the country.

A second influential institution in the Domestic Science movement was the Boston Cooking School, which was founded in 1879 by the philanthropic Women's Education Association as a force for social betterment. The school taught a range of cooking courses in tracks such as plain cooking, richer cooking, and fancy cooking, along with general domestic science courses such as bacteriology, laundry work, and physiology and hygiene. Mary J. Lincoln, the school's principal, was raised on plain New England dishes such as baked beans, brown bread, and fish balls, and these types of recipes dominated the school's curriculum. Fannie Merritt Farmer, a Massachusetts native and graduate of the Boston Cooking School, took over as the school's principal in 1893. Farmer became the best-known cooking teacher of her day, and her *Boston Cooking School Cook Book* was a huge success. Later renamed *The Fannie Farmer Cook Book* and periodically revised and updated, the volume is one of the best-selling cookbooks of all time and is still in print today. Although it was initially founded with the goal of giving lower-class women the skills they needed to find employment as domestic workers, the Boston Cooking School's mission soon changed—largely for financial reasons—to teaching middle-class housewives to cook for their families and guests. The school also had a respected "normal class," which trained women to be cooking teachers. The graduates of the program readily found work in public schools and cooking schools throughout the country, helping spread the principles of Domestic Science nationwide.

Improving Cooking and Housekeeping in the Late Nineteenth Century

The guiding tenet for the movement—which was also known as "scientific housekeeping," "home science," and "progressing housekeeping"—was that the empirical methods of science could and should be applied to the domestic sphere of cooking and housekeeping. In many ways, the movement was a reaction against the problems and uncertainties faced by women in the new industrial age. Despite recent innovations such as improved cookstoves, cooking still required a lot of guesswork and intuition. It was difficult to accurately gauge the temperature of wood-fired ovens and stoves, and the quality of the nineteenth-century food supply was notoriously variable, particularly with products such as flour, eggs, butter, sugar, and milk, which were now produced on a mass scale but with few health controls. Most recipes of the period were simply guidelines, using vague measurements such as "a teacup full" and "a lump the size of an egg." To be a good cook required years of tutelage under a more experienced cook—typically a daughter learning in her mother's kitchen—and as industrialism disrupted more and more families, this informal apprentice system had begun to break down. The goal of domestic science was to remove guesswork and uncertainty from the kitchen. It did so by instituting rules, formulas, and procedures to be rigidly followed, transforming cooking from an art to a science.

The movement's practitioners emphasized cleanliness, including the identification of adulterated food and the prevention of spoilage and bacterial contamination. Drawing on the latest research into the nutritional properties of food, they stressed the importance of properly balancing protein, carbohydrates, and fats as a means of achieving good health. But nutrition was more than a matter of physical well-being. Domestic scientists considered bad cooking to be a source of bad morals, leading to other ills such as alcoholism and crime. Scientific cookery would not only ease the lot of the housekeeper but also reform society and alleviate the problems of urban poverty. Many of its dictates were directly aimed at allaying the anxieties of the middle class as they were increasingly surrounded by unfamiliar immigrants. The ideal "domestic scientist" was portrayed as dainty and spotless in an immaculate kitchen and contrasted with rough, clumsy immigrant servants (usually German or Irish). As newer waves of immigrants from Southern and Eastern Europe brought even more unfamiliar flavors and ingredients to New England, middle-class cooks increasingly took refuge in the reassuring formulas of scientific cookery.

Flavorless Food

Unfortunately for New England cuisine, the aspect of cooking that concerned the domestic scientists least was the flavor of food. In fact, many of the movement's leaders actively distrusted taste as a dangerous sensual force. Speaking at the Chicago World's Fair in 1893, Mary J. Lincoln declared that "eating is something more than an animal indulgence, and that cooking has a nobler purpose than the gratification of appetite and the sense of taste. Cooking has been defined as 'the art of preparing food for the nourishment of the human body.'" This stance led to the minute analysis of the chemical properties of foods, a tireless concern with the effects of foods on digestion and heavy emphasis on garnishing and presentation. Whether a dish was actually pleasing to eat was not considered very important. As a result, New England cooking—which was traditionally characterized by plainness and simplicity—became frequently bland. Because of their concern for easing digestion, domestic scientists recommended that vegetables be boiled for long periods of time: celery for half an hour, asparagus for forty-five minutes, and string beans for upwards of three hours. "White sauce"—milk thickened with butter and flour—became a staple of cooking-school recipes, which used it to cover everything from fish to chicken to vegetables. Also popular were an array of gelatin-based salads, which consisted of chopped meats, vegetables, or fruit suspended in molded gelatin. "Perfection Salad"—which food historian Laura Shapiro has identified as a defining recipe of the Domestic Science movement—is a particularly stark example: finely chopped cabbage, celery, and red peppers bound in plain or tomato aspic. These recipes were circulated widely through best-selling cookbooks and women's magazines, and they steadily began replacing more traditional dishes on New England's tables.

As is suggested by the popularity of salads based on new commercial gelatin products (Knox introduced the first granulated gelatin in 1894), the tenets of scientific cookery helped make New England's cooks more accepting of mass-produced foods. Many of the movement's leading proponents had close ties with national food processors, conducting lectures and demonstrations at industry-sponsored "Pure Food Fairs" and contributing testimonials for new food products. These ties were not necessarily based on crass commercialism, for the notable characteristics of canned and other processed foods—uniformity, sterility, and predictability—were consonant with the values of Domestic Science. Mary J. Lincoln, writing in *American Kitchen Magazine* in 1902, concisely expressed these values in respect to cheese: "Those who can remember the great diversity in taste, structure, and composition which was so noticeable in the old farmhouse cheeses can appreciate the greater uniformity in the factory product." A similar attitude underlay the widespread adoption of manufactured shortenings such as Crisco, which was introduced in 1912, as replacements for butter and lard. Locally churned butter could melt and spoil and differed in flavor from season to season and farm to farm, but the new shortenings were pure, white, and always the same. They were also virtually flavorless.

The long-term effect of the Domestic Science movement on New England cooking was the fading of its regional distinctiveness. Where Yankee cooks once used local ingredients almost exclusively and prepared them with the recipes and techniques learned from their parents, they were now depending more and more on commercial food products and recipes from nationally circulated magazines. By World War II, a typical middle-class family dinner looked almost the same in New England as it did in California or Nebraska.

EARLY TWENTIETH-CENTURY RESTAURANTS

Beginning in the late nineteenth century, dining outside the home became a more common part of everyday life in America, and in New England a distinctive new type of restaurant emerged: the diner. The diner was a direct outgrowth of the new food needs of industrial workers. The earliest form of diners developed in Providence, Rhode Island, a major New England industrial center which specialized in textile and jewelry manufacturing. Night-shift factory workers needed to eat, but the city's boardinghouses and taverns served meals only during the day. So, thousands of workers bought their meals from vendors who peddled home-cooked foods from hand-carried baskets on the streets in front of the factories. In 1872 one such vendor, Walter Scott, decided to trade his basket for a horse-drawn wagon, which allowed him to serve many more customers without returning home to restock. His customers stood in the street and ordered through a window in the side of the wagon, choosing from a menu that included chicken salad sandwiches, frankfurters, and boiled eggs with buttered bread. Scott's "lunch wagon" was an immediate success and was quickly imitated by other vendors in Providence and then throughout southern New England.

As lunch wagons became popular, their operators began ordering custom-made wagons designed specifically for the selling of food. In 1887, Samuel Messer Jones of Worcester, Massachusetts, ordered a wagon that allowed his customers to sit inside and eat. Charles H. Palmer, another Worcester vendor, patented a similar design in 1891 and created a factory for manufacturing his models, launching the lunch wagon industry in New England. Many competitors soon followed, and their factories produced wagons that were complete turnkey operations, including tables, plates, and silverware. Fancier models boasted tiled interiors, marble counters, and brass cash registers. By the turn of the century, lunch wagons, which would remain almost exclusively a New England phenomenon, were in operation in almost three hundred communities throughout the Northeast.

Around World War I, New England's lunch wagons evolved into diners. In 1912, the city of Providence, whose streets were becoming clogged with dozens of lunch wagons, passed a law mandating that all food vending wagons must be off the streets by 10 a.m. Many operators responded by finding off-street parking and setting up shop semipermanently in vacant lots. Soon they added skirts to hide the wagon wheels and began hooking up water and electricity. And thus the diner was born. The lunch wagon manufacturers began producing stationary versions of their products that could be delivered fully built to the installation site. Newer models began to look more like railroad dining cars than wagons, with longer counters, more tables and booths, and indoor bathrooms. (Many were actually made out of refitted trolley or railroad cars.) The menu at these restaurants remained simple and quick to prepare: ham, bacon, eggs, hamburgers, and sandwiches. During the 1920s, diners and diner manufacturing expanded beyond New England, with some of the largest manufacturers operating out of New York and New Jersey, but the diner remained primarily a feature of the Northeast. Diners maintained their popularity through the 1950s, when they began losing market share to newer fast food restaurants. Most of New England's diners are now gone, but in the past two decades they have begun to be recognized as a classic part of the region's culture, and increasing numbers of old diners are being refurbished and once again serve their distinctive short-order cooking.

Diners were the first restaurants to cater to a working-class clientele. In the years between World War I and World War II, other types of restaurants developed to serve more affluent customers, particularly tourists and middle-class families. These dinner houses or

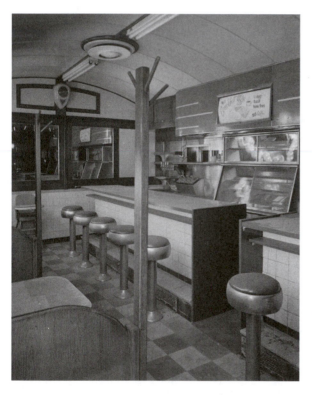

In 1872, food-vendor Walter Scott decided to trade his basket for a horse-drawn wagon, which allowed him to serve many more customers without returning home to restock. Because of this innovation, Providence is often credited as being the birthplace of the modern diner. Courtesy Library of Congress.

"destination restaurants" were usually located alongside major highways, and they specialized in prime (or "status") dishes. The "shore dinner"—a popular menu item at destination restaurants—was an indoor version of a traditional New England clambake, including steamed clams, lobster, corn, and potatoes. Other standard offerings were steaks, chops, chicken, fried clams, and ice cream. Many of these establishments were the first examples of American "theme restaurants," which were decorated according to a guiding motif such as sailing, with an interior contrived to look like the deck of a ship, wall murals showing sea scenes, and sails and rigging draped from the ceilings.

The "shore dinner," derived from the traditional New England clambake, often includes steamed clams, lobster, corn, and potatoes. Courtesy Maine Office of Tourism.

As automobile tourism increased, some destination restaurants expanded into chains. One of the first of these was Dutchland Farm Stores, which was founded in the 1920s by D. W. Field. Field owned a large dairy in Brockton, Massachusetts, and he sold his ice cream and other dairy products in a store with orange roofs, white walls, and blue-green trim. The concept proved popular, and by 1940 Dutchland Farm Stores had outlets in Massachusetts, Rhode Island, Connecticut, and New Hampshire. The chain's success was noticed by Howard Johnson, a soda fountain owner from Quincy, Massachusetts, who applied many of Field's marketing techniques—including the orange, white, and blue-green color scheme—when he opened a series of new highway-oriented restaurants. Johnson's restaurants catered specifically to tourists, with a menu based on ice cream, chicken, clams, and hot dogs. A unique feature of Howard Johnson's restaurants was that their food was cooked, frozen, and distributed from a central commissary in Wollaston, Massachusetts, then reheated and served at the individual restaurants, most of which were owned by franchisees. Johnson maintained tight control of every aspect of his franchisees' operations, particularly the store and employee appearance and the menu. The reliable format was a hit with automobile travelers after World War II, and Howard Johnson's expanded from 39 units in 1936 to 255 in 1951, most of which were located in the Boston, New York, and Philadelphia metropolitan areas.

Howard Johnson's was not the only restaurant chain with New England roots. The first Friendly's opened in Springfield, Massachusetts, in 1938 and soon developed into a chain of highway soda fountains notable for their Georgian Revival–styled buildings. Dunkin Donuts, founded in Quincy, Massachusetts, in 1950, now has over three thousand shops worldwide. Other prominent New England–based chains include Subway sandwich shops (Milford, Connecticut), Au Bon Pain (Boston), and Ben and Jerry's (South Burlington, Vermont). Their New England roots aside, these chains were part of a larger postwar movement in which dining out in America was increasingly dominated by national chains, starting with fast food outlets such as McDonald's and Burger King and expanding into almost every category of restaurant. By the 1960s, many local New England restaurants could no longer compete against the efficiencies and scale of the national chains. New England's diners were gradually replaced by fast food burger joints, and local destination restaurants lost ground to a succession of highway-oriented chains. Just as the rise of industrial food production and the Domestic Science movement helped make New England home cooking very much the same as cooking everywhere else in the United States, so did chain restaurants help make dining out in New England more similar to dining out everywhere else.

CONTEMPORARY NEW ENGLAND COOKING

Although the distinctive features of New England cooking were greatly diminished during the twentieth century, they were never lost completely. Recent years have seen a strong revival of traditional ways of cooking and eating. One of the first areas in which this revival occurred was in the dining rooms of inns and bed-and-breakfasts. Country inns had flourished in the early part of the twentieth century, catering to the ever-growing number of tourists who came to New England by automobile. After World War II, they began to lose their lodging customers to chain motels and their dining customers to chain restaurants, and many inns went out of business. A revival began in the 1970s, however, as travelers began to tire of the predictable sameness of national chain establishments and began seeking out more distinctive places to stay. Many of the region's older inns, once shuttered or converted to other uses, were restored and reopened, and by the early 1980s over five hundred inns and bed-and-breakfasts were in operation in New England, attracting visitors from all over America and the world. In keeping with their historic roots, most New England inns today have dining rooms that specialize in traditional regional dishes made with fresh, locally grown ingredients. At the same time, many of their chefs are European immigrants or Americans who have studied classic French and Italian techniques. The result is a blend of traditional and international cooking. It is quite common to see menus that mix New England favorites such as clam chowder, lobster, and halibut along with European- and Asian-inspired dishes such as Country Pate in Terrine, Beef Carpaccio, or Thai Spring Rolls.

This revival of traditional cooking is aided by a growing agricultural movement in New England that places renewed emphasis on fresh, locally grown produce, dairy, and meat. The movement has its roots in the counterculture of the 1960s, which rejected modern industrial society and sought to live more simply and more in tune with the natural world. New England—particularly the rural areas of Vermont and New Hampshire—was a natural magnet for these "dropouts," many of whom took up farming to raise their own food. In recent years, the counterculture ethic has matured into a philosophy that values small-scale farming, traditional methods, and "heirloom" plant and livestock varieties—those that were available for New Englanders before industrialization. Although much of the new ideology is rooted in ecological and moral concerns, an equal portion is based on a concern for food quality, particularly for fresh ingredients with distinctively local flavors. As a result, a new abundance of fresh, high-quality produce is now available both for serving in restaurants and for preparing at home. Orchards grow countless varieties of heirloom apples, farmers sell grass-fed beef and free-range chickens, and dozens of dairy farms—particularly in Vermont—produce handcrafted cheese with milk from their own cows and goats. These small-scale enterprises continue to attract outsiders to New England, many of whom trade high-powered urban careers for a new, more rustic farming life. In doing so, they help preserve the ingredients and recipes that define classic New England cooking.

This food is also celebrated at hundreds of local festivals in communities across New England. Generally held in autumn—the time of traditional harvest celebrations—these gatherings can draw anywhere from a few hundred to tens of thousands of attendees. Many festivals are dedicated to a particular local food, such as the Wild Blueberry Festival in Machias, Maine, which features a blueberry pancake breakfast, blueberry cooking contest, and a blueberry pie-eating contest, or the Harwich Cranberry Festival in Harwich Port, Massachusetts, on Cape Cod. Many of the festivals celebrate the abundance of local seafood, such as the Yarmouth Clam Festival in Yarmouth, Maine, where attendees can sample steamed clams, fried clams, clam chowder, and clam cakes; the Bourne Scallop Festival in Bourne, Massachusetts, which serves scallop dinners under outdoor tents; and the Maine Lobster Festival in Rockland, Maine, which in 2002 prepared over ten tons of lobster in the world's largest lobster cooker. All of these festivals feature live music, parades, craft fairs, and other outdoor entertainment, and they are a time for people to come together and celebrate their communities and the distinctive aspects of local culture. In doing so, they are helping to keep alive traditional New England foodways for the generations to come.

RESOURCE GUIDE

Printed Sources

Appelbaum, Diana Karter. *Thanksgiving: An American Holiday, an American History*. New York: Facts on File, 1984.

Chase, Sarah Leah, and Jonathan Chase. *Saltwater Seasonings: Good Food from Coastal Maine*. Boston: Little, Brown, 1992.

Coe, Michael D., and Sophie D. Coe. "Mid-Eighteenth Century Food and Drink on the Massachusetts Frontier." In Peter Benes, ed., *Foodways in the Northeast*. Boston: Boston University Press, 1984. 39–46.

Derven, Daphne L. "Wholesome, Toothsome, and Diverse: Eighteenth-Century Foodways in Deerfield, Massachusetts." In Peter Benes, ed., *Foodways in the Northeast*. Boston: Boston University Press, 1984. 48–56.

Fisher, David Hackett. *Albion's Seed: Four British Folkways in America*. New York: Oxford University Press, 1989.

Hornblower, Malabar. *The Plimoth Plantation New England Cookery Book*. Boston: Harvard Common Press, 1990.

Jackle, John A., and Keirh A. Sculle. *Fast Food: Roadside Restaurants in the Automobile Age*. Baltimore: Johns Hopkins University Press, 1999.

Leonard, Justin. *American Cooking: New England*. New York: Time-Life, 1970.

Mariani, John F. *The Dictionary of American Food and Drink*. New York: Hearst Books, 1994.

Nylander, Jane. *Our Snug Fireside: Images of the New England Home, 1760–1860*. New York: Knopf, 1994.

Pillsbury, Richard. *From Boarding House to Bistro: The American Restaurant Then and Now*. Boston: Unwin Hyman, 1990.

Root, Waverley, and Richard de Rochemont. *Eating in America: A History*. New York: Morrow, 1976.

Whitehill, Jane. *Food, Drink, and Recipes of Early New England*. Sturbridge, MA: Old Sturbridge Village, 1963.

Web Sites

Avellar, Mary Jo. *Provincetown Portuguese Cookbook*. 2002.
Blessing of the Fleet, Inc.
Cape Cod Access at Shank Painter Co. Inc. February 27, 2003.
http://www.capecodaccess.com/cookbook/index.html

Recipes from Provincetown's finest cooks and restaurants, and many Portuguese recipes from the Portuguese community.

Epicurious. 2004.
CondéNet Inc. January 26, 2004.
http://eat.epicurious.com/

World recipes, including New England regions, and food resource guide.

New England Cooks. 2003.
New England Cooks, Inc. January 25, 2004.
http://www.newenglandcooks.com/

New England food and travel information.

Union Oyster House. 2003.
Union Oyster House, Boston. May 5, 2002.
http://www.unionoysterhouse.com

History of America's oldest restaurant and oysters.

Museums

American Diner Museum, Inc.
350 Eddy Street
Providence, RI
http://www.dinermuseum.org

Affiliated with the Heritage Harbor Museum in Rhode Island and opening soon on the old site of the Narragansett Electric Company.

Old Sturbridge Village
1 Old Sturbridge Village Road
Sturbridge, MA
http://www.osv.org/

A two-hundred-acre village that offers a picture of New England life between 1790 and 1840, including farming, cooking, flour and apple cider milling, and dining at a reconstructed rural tavern.

Plimoth Plantation
137 Warren Avenue
Plymouth, MA
http://www.plimoth.org/

A re-creation of seventeenth-century Pilgrim and Native American villages that features historically accurate displays of early cooking habits, including original harvest dinners.

Festivals/Events

Bourne Scallop Fest
Buzzards Bay Park
Bourne, MA
http://www.capecodcanalchamber.org/aboutsf.html

The largest scallop festival on the East Coast, held three days each September by the Cape Cod Canal Region Chamber of Commerce.

The Green Mountain CHEW CHEW
Burlington's Waterfront Park
Burlington, VT
http://www.vtliving.com/events/chewchew/index.shtml

Annual summer food and music festival in Burlington, Vermont.

Harwich Cranberry Festival
Harwich Port, MA
http://www.harwichcranberryfestival.com

An annual Cape Cod celebration of cranberries and other regional foods, along with fireworks, arts and crafts, and entertainment.

Machias Blueberry Festival
Machias, ME
http://www.machiasblueberry.com/

An annual celebration of the harvest in Washington County, Maine, which produces 85 percent of the world's blueberries.

Maine Lobster Festival
Harbour Park
Rockland, ME
http://www.mainelobsterfestival.com/

An August celebration of Maine's signature seafood.

Pumpkin Festival
Keene, NH
http://www.pumpkinfestival.com

Annual festival held on the weekend in October closest to Halloween.

Yarmouth Clam Festival
Yarmouth, ME
http://www.clamfestival.com

Held each July, features fried clams, clam cakes, shore dinners, and clam-shucking contests.

LANGUAGE

Bruce F. Murphy

Writing about the local color novelist George Savary Wasson (1855–1932) in the early part of the twentieth century, critic Thomas Wentworth Higgins noted with some regret the loss of the "quaint dialect, now passing away, of the old New England coast."[1] He was neither the first nor the last to bemoan the disappearance of distinctive regional forms of speech. But his sentiment underscores how linguistic habits take root in a region because of local conditions, and how the users of the dialect and idiom become attached to it—as a practical tool, a badge of identity, or even a defense against outsiders. The other observation that is immediately invited by Higgins' comment, written nearly a hundred years ago, is that the Yankee dialect has not died, though it has been transmuted.

Although there are "dead" languages, when a dialect of a living language wanes it is hard to imagine how it could be replaced simply by nothing; rather, a new dialect is probably emerging, or an adjacent one taking over. As in evolution, physical isolation plays a large role in the development of local dialect. In the period since the end of World War II, vastly increased mobility, electronic communication, economic trends, and new immigration patterns have all changed American communities, and with them their dialects, leaving the popular impression that the colorful old dialects are "disappearing" into a single, national, watered-down speech. On the other hand, as linguists Walt Wolfram and Natalie Schilling-Estes remark, recent studies of American dialects actually show that some of them are becoming less like each other rather than more. New England, however, may be an exception; the authors state that "New England speech appears to be becoming less distinctive from that of surrounding areas."[2]

New England has undergone a long dialectal evolution. It was one of the first areas of the continent of North America to be visited by Europeans, and one of the earliest to be settled. It retains to this day distinctive speech forms, which vast social changes and successive waves of immigration have altered but never eradicated; some of its most notable phonological features today go all the way back to the seventeenth century. In an age when television is perceived to have dampened regional linguistic patterns, simultaneously offering a homogenized English to the entire nation, there is still no *r* in that famous phrase, "Pahk yuh cah in Hahvahd yahd." Though perhaps less recognizable than the Southern drawl or "New Yorkese," the dialect of New England is a distinctive blend of influences from the region's past.

Of course, there is no single "Yankee" dialect. Speech forms vary from seacoast to mountains and between major cities such as Boston and Providence. While the pronunciation "cah" can be heard in most of New England (except the northwestern part that has been drawn into the dialect zone of New York State), many words and pronunciations are more localized. The affirmative "Ayuh" associated with northern New England is not heard in Boston or Connecticut; the negative "Na-ah" (used when other Americans might say "Uh-uh") is distinctively Bostonian. At a narrower level of focus, even city neighborhoods in Boston may have their own vocabulary. In Charlestown, "woof" means *cocaine*; a "moosh" is a *friend* in Nonantum. Nor are such localisms restricted to cities. In Down East Maine, when someone is "a plaster," it means he or she is an idiot. Distinctions can be made even finer. Linguistics recognizes not only dialect, a form of language spoken by a group of people, but also idiolect, a form spoken by one person. There is obviously an enormous amount of overlap in dialect and idiolect. Although dialect "maps" have been constructed, language variation is less like geography than it is like weather; the lines called "isoglosses" on dialect maps which show where one dialect borders another look strangely like the frontal boundaries drawn by meteorologists using "isobars." Language change may move slower than storm fronts, but it can occur anyplace where two speakers come into contact, and dialect zones overlap and sometimes simply bypass isolated areas. Any "standard" form of a language is a construct, while the language (and its dialects) continues to change organically in a never-ending process. In New England, this process has been going on for at least four hundred years—and, if we include the presettlement period, about which we know very little, for thousands of years before that. To understand how New Englanders talk, obviously one has to know something of who New Englanders are. The complex human geography that has led to the current spectrum of language in the region began with the original "immigrants" into the area more than ten millennia ago.

PRE-EUROPEAN NEW ENGLAND AND ITS ABORIGINAL INHABITANTS

The first settlers to arrive in North America are believed to have traveled from Asia across a land bridge to Alaska sometime during the last Ice Age. By about eleven thousand years ago, they had reached New England and the Atlantic coast. Little is known of these people, and nothing of their language, since they were a preliterate society. It is not even clear how they are related to the Native American people that the first European settlers encountered. A broad outline, however, can be traced.

The Clovis people (the name comes from a particular style of spear head) were hunter-gatherers who spread across North America between twelve thousand and ten thousand years ago. This remarkably uniform culture—evidenced by very similar finds in widely separated areas, from New Mexico to Maine—later gave way to more distinct regional groups. In New England, for example, a group known as the "red paint" people flourished in the late archaic period, about five thousand years ago. Although there are still no concrete data about their language, it has been inferred from similarities in artifacts that these people were the ancestors of the Algonquian Native American tribes, and so it is likely that their language was an ancestor of the Algonquian languages that were prevalent in New England at the time of European settlement. Thus, English is a relative latecomer to the region, where the Algonquian language group had been in place for thousands of years. It is a commonplace of history that the language of the conqueror is often imposed on the conquered and suppresses the native tongue. That English submerged and virtually annihilated the Algonquian languages is a result of the decimation and dispossession of the Algonquian people themselves.

As early as the fifteenth century, Portuguese, Basque, Irish, and English sailors had discovered the rich fishing grounds off the New England coast. Explorers from several nations, including John Cabot, Giovanni da Verazzano, and Samuel de Champlain, literally followed in their wake. The fishermen and explorers stopped along the coast but did not erect permanent settlements; islands like Monhegan and Damariscove provided a refuge and a place to dry cod. Because of the fishing industry, activity was oriented toward northeastern New England. The first English colonists sent to New England were the Popham colonists, who were settled in Maine in 1607. The colony failed, as had a French attempt a few years earlier. But with the arrival of the Pilgrims and the Puritans farther south beginning in 1620, the Europeans began to gain a permanent foothold in New England. The image of the landing of the Pilgrims as a new beginning is in some ways erroneous. When the Pilgrims met Samoset, he spoke to them in English—probably a pidgin form learned from sailors in his native Maine. Pidgins are trading languages with a root stock but often incorporating terms taken from several different tongues. Sailors, as a multinational group, were early developers of pidgins and brought them to the New England coast, where they used them to trade with the native peoples. As J. L. Dillard writes, "early contact with the Basque pidgin seems to have been extensive," going back perhaps to the sixteenth century.[3]

Native American Languages

The Algonquian Native Americans who inhabited the region were not a homogeneous group. In northern New England, they were divided between the Eastern Abenaki who lived on the coast and the Western Abenaki (or Sokoki) who lived in the mountains and as far west as Lake Champlain. These groups were further subdivided into many individual tribes. The Algonquian tribes in southern New England included the Narragansett, Pennacook, Nipmuc, Mattabesic, and Pequot. The fate of these tribes depended on many factors: their own culture, the vicissitudes of European politics, and even geography. The Abenaki of northeastern New England inhabited a far more forbidding land than, for example, Cape Cod, and were repeatedly able to melt away into the wilderness during times of trouble and later return to their lands. The Abenaki also tried to remain neutral in the struggles between England and France over possession of the "New World." It is not by accident that the largest concentration of Native Americans and tribal reservations in the region today is in northern and eastern Maine.

The tragic story of the Pequot is emblematic. The Pequot were far more war-like than many other Algonquian tribes, and had evolved a more organized political structure and actually built fortified villages. But social cohesion and centralized authority proved a liability rather than a strength. The European colonizers exploited both the Pequot's power and the resentment of other tribes toward them—and were themselves the target of Pequot wrath from time to time. This all ended in 1637 with the Pequot War, during which an English expedition attacked and burned a Pequot fort at what is now Mystic, Connecticut, killing hundreds of women and children (the warriors were off on a raid of Hartford). The tribe was effectively crushed and went into centuries-long decline. By 1910, there were only sixty-six Pequot left. Although the remaining Pequot recently obtained redress for the confiscation of their lands and now run a profitable casino, their language is considered to be extinct.

Other tribes have fared little better, and possibly even worse. Most of southern New England had been conquered by the early eighteenth century. As a result, the Abenaki and Sokoki absorbed refugees from all the southern tribes. The Sokoki, however, soon became embroiled in other conflicts, with Europeans but especially with the Iroquois and Mohawk, either acting alone or as the Europeans' surrogates. During this period of upheaval and migration, the southern tribes who were joined to the Abenaki effectively ceased to exist, and their languages were lost. There are still groups of Sokoki in Vermont, but their numerous attempts to gain recognition of their status and reclaim some of their land have been rejected by the state. Of the eastern Abenaki, the Penobscot, Passamaquoddy, and Maliseet tribes were able to obtain small reservations in northeastern Maine in 1798, which they continue to occupy today. Federal recognition of the tribes only came in 1980.

Contact with Europeans was disastrous for New England's Native Americans. Precontact, the eastern Abenaki and Sokoki probably numbered about forty thousand. A succession of epidemics had already reduced the eastern Abenaki population by three-quarters, to about five thousand, by the time the Pilgrims arrived. Algonqian culture and language left little mark on colonial America partly because the native population had been so devastated. In addition, Europeans viewed the natives as "savages" who were racially inferior and, as non-Christians, heathen at best and diabolical at worst. The main object was to expropriate their land; although the Algonquian peoples of New England built villages and farmed, because they spent part of the year on hunting trips the self-serving myth was created among settlers that they were nomads, justifying the view that the land was not really their property in a European sense. The only other uses that the Europeans had for the Native Americans were as mercenaries in their own internecine wars, as a resource for the valuable fur trade, and as a prize in the religious competition of French Jesuit missionaries from Canada and their Puritan counterparts in New England.

A handful of Algonquian words did enter the English vocabulary, mainly because they designated North American flora and fauna for which no English equivalents existed. Words like "raccoon," "skunk," "menhaden," "moose," "hominy," and "squash" come from Algonquian roots, as do terms such as "wigwam" and "sachem," which refer to native culture and society. Some explorers, such as Captain John Smith, did take notes on the native languages, probably from the necessity of communicating with the Native Americans and indicating unfamiliar objects and things. It is not clear that

Europeans took any interest in Native American language as such until much later, and by then, many languages were already extinct. The number of Algonquian loan words in English also shrank steadily; at the end of the nineteenth century there were well over a hundred, but by the middle of the next century the number in common usage had decreased to a couple of dozen, owing to what H. L. Mencken called—apparently without irony—"the recession of the Red Man from the popular consciousness."[4]

In an oral culture, once the last speaker of a language dies, the language itself dies as well. Some Algonquian languages were preserved in translations of the Bible (for example, the Wampanoag Bible of 1663), even though the language died out as a spoken tongue. One exception to the neglect of Native American language was the work of Jonathan Fisher (1768–1847), a Congregational minister born in central Massachusetts and educated at Harvard College. After taking up his duties in Blue Hill, Maine, Fisher invented a phonetic alphabet for representing English and foreign languages. One of the languages he applied it to was the Penobscot dialect of Algonquian; he visited local villages and recorded lists of words and phrases in his new notation. Fisher hoped that his phonetic alphabet might provide a way

THE
HOLY BIBLE:
CONTAINING THE
OLD TESTAMENT
AND THE *NEW.*

Tranſlated into the
INDIAN LANGUAGE,
AND
Ordered to be Printed by the *Commiſſioners of the United Colonies* in *NEW-ENGLAND,*

At the Charge, and with the Conſent of the
CORPORATION IN ENGLAND
For the *Propagation of the Goſpel amongſt the* Indians in New-Eng land.

CAMBRIDGE:
Printed by *Samuel Green* and *Marmaduke Johnſon.*
MDCLXIII.

The first Indian Bible printed in America was translated into the Algonquian language by John Eliot. Photo by Eliot Elisofan/Getty Images.

for "savage nations" to become literate—that is, to develop an accurate written form of their language.[5] We may object to Fisher's terminology, but his impulse was an enlightened one. The language Penobscot is now considered almost extinct.

Today, attempts are being made to save the dialects of Algonquian, and Native American speech does retain a small foothold in New England. The Maliseet dialect, also spoken by the Passamaquoddy in Maine, had nearly nine hundred speakers according to the 1990 U.S. census, but many of them were elderly. The Micmac have a large community in Canada and about two hundred people in Maine, with another one thousand living in the Boston area. As in the other tribes, native speakers are usually older people, and economic pressures to assimilate to the mainstream do not bode well for the survival of the language.

While hundreds of Native American names still dot the New England map, from the Quinnipiac River to Lake Mooslookmeguntic, one word that ironically has not come over into English is Abenaki *Ndakinna*—"our land." The Algonquian people may have "receded" from mainstream consciousness, but the linguistic traces of their presence are everywhere. Theirs was the language of the region for hundreds and possibly thousands of years. They were generally peaceful farmer-hunters, whose *sachems* (chiefs) held qualified power, and whose tribal decisions were made by a consensus of adults—admirably "American" values. Indeed, perhaps most ironic of all is the theory that the Algonquian term *caucauasu*, meaning to advise or encourage, gives us the word "caucus," a part of the vaunted American political process from which the Native Americans were long excluded, and from which they have seldom benefited.

ENGLISH IN NEW ENGLAND

Whether linguists focus on lexical elements or phonology, vocabulary or pronunciation, the breakdown of dialects within New England looks generally the same. Perhaps surprisingly, the linguistic map of New England still shows the pattern of immigration from the British Isles four hundred years ago, and the dialects of the region continue to reflect the dialects that were extant in Britain in Shakespeare's time. Immigrants from London and southeastern England brought to the Massachusetts Bay Colony and coastal New England the *r*-less pronunciation ("cah" for *car*, "fahthah" for *father*) that is still typical of the region, and in fact is also dominant in standard British English. The "postvocalic" *r* is also dropped when it occurs within words, so that *forty* becomes "fotty," *short* sounds like "shot," *marsh* like "mahsh," and so on. Meanwhile, dialects of English in which the *r* was sounded were prevalent in other parts of England; this pronunciation became the standard in the Connecticut River valley and spread into western New England and upper New York State. (Today western Vermont is grouped by linguists with the dialect of New York State and areas farther west.) The barrier of the Appalachian Mountains reinforced the east-west split, as did the continued contact of coastal New Englanders involved in trade with the mother country, where the *r*-less pronunciation was dominant. (It is interesting to note in passing that these American English speakers were responding to the land in the same way as the eastern Abenaki and the Sokoki, who also separated into coastal and inland dwellers and developed different dialects.)

Class and Dialect in New England

This regional-geographic distinction was coupled with one of class. Thousands of colonial settlers were of Scotch-Irish origin (Scots who had emigrated to Northern Ireland), and their speech was marked by a strong *r*. The "*r*-ful" pronunciation won out in the United States, and eastern New England has been called an *r*-less island in the middle of an ocean of *r*-pronouncers. That the heavy concentration of Irish immigrants in Boston failed to overcome the *r*-less pronunciation attests to the often noticed tendency for upper-class speech to define what is "standard" in a given region. In addition to the classism that relegated Scotch-Irish to a subordinate role, there was also the religious divide, the Irish being Roman Catholic. The Puritan horror of "popery" was even more intense than their own doctrinal arguments among themselves (which led, for example, to Roger Williams' removal to Rhode Island to start his own colony). Resistance to French existed for the same reason; the struggles in which northern New England changed hands many times in the seventeenth and eighteenth centuries were not only territorial, but also reflective of the ideological struggle between Catholic France and Protestant England.

Another feature of New England speech that has been around since at least the American Revolution and still persists is the famous "broad *a*." Thus, the word *path* sounds like "pahth," and *bath* becomes "bahth" (note that these two distinctly New England traits, broad-*a* and loss of *r*, are combined in "pahk the cah," though the *a* in "car" is closer to *cat* than the British pronunciation of *car*). It has been said that the broad-*a* originated in London and southeastern England as an upper-class fad; thus, the typical American short-*a* that now dominates contemporary American English usage actually predates the broad-*a*. Noah Webster, au-

> ### Noah Webster
>
> Perhaps no one person has had as much of an effect on American English as New England's Noah Webster (1758–1843). Born in the western division of Hartford, Connecticut, Webster attended Yale University and then became a schoolteacher. This led him to produce several publications aimed at standardizing spelling and creating a specifically *American* English. It is Webster who standardized American spellings such as "color" and "plow," distinguishing them from British usage (some of his phonetic spellings, like "tung," "and "wimmen," have not survived). His spelling book for children taught many generations of Americans to spell and sold 68 million copies in its hundred years of dominance. His dictionary, first published in 1806, was even more influential.
>
> It is interesting that Webster's western Connecticut home lay on the fault line of the eastern and western New England dialect, and perhaps that explains his flip-flopping on such burning issues as the broad-*a*. His move to New Haven later in life may have tipped the scale toward eastern New England pronunciation, which he did much to preserve.

thor of the first dictionary of American English, disliked the broad-*a* and campaigned against it, promoting the use of the short-*a* (*plant, ant*) even for words like *calm*. Broad-*a* was once used in *matter, hammer, apple,* and *stamp.* There are signs that the broad-*a* is in decline. Today, few New Englanders would pronounce *dance* in the English fashion (with a broad-*a*, as "dahnce"). To some extent, especially in northeastern New England, one can still hear *can't* pronounced like the name of the German philosopher Kant. Boston vowel pronunciations in general have more nasality than those of northern New England. *Vase* and *aunt* are contested territory, pronounced differently by different people, but with the "ahnt" pronunciation still predominant to the north and east. "Bahth" for *bath* is still heard; but a speaker like the late writer George Plimpton who used broad-*a* almost across the board now sounds affected, upper class, Anglophile, or all three.

As has been shown, the English settlers' contribution to New England dialect was great. David Hackett Fischer notes in his book on English folkways in America that the nasal aspect of Yankee speech, or the "Yankee twang," is related to the "Norfolk twang" of East Anglia. Although Fischer tends to oversimplify the derivation of New England speech, he does account for some of its more peculiar vowel sounds. He describes the Yankee accent as "exceptionally harsh and high-pitched."[6] Certainly, some vowels were raised, such that *yolk* was pronounced "yelk," and *yesterday* was "yistidy"; these dialectal pronunciations can still be heard, but more and more rarely. By contrast, other vowels were shortened and lowered, as in the well-known New England "checked-*o*" (for example, "hoss" for "horse"). In the term *nor'easter*, the "*o*" is not the sound in *oar*, but more similar to the sound in *moth*. The Fourth of July might be pronounced "Fawth," and *road* almost like "rawd."

Another old Yankee pronunciation is that the vowel in *first* can be shortened and lowered to sound like "fust," but this is likely to be heard now only in rural northern New England. *Broom* sometimes has the vowel of *full*; even more striking but still rarer is for *roof* to be shortened so that it rhymes with *woof*, and *root* to rhyme with *soot*. Still important in New England dialect (particularly in the east) is the lack of a distinction between the vowels in *mourning* and *morning* and the lack of an *h* sound after *w*, for example in *while* and *whale*. Another distinctly New England speech habit which still can be observed is the addition of *r* to words that end with an *a*-sound, such that *diploma* comes out "diplomer" and *thaw* "thawr." Less commonly, other extra consonants are sometimes added, for example, in the pronunciation "wharft" for *wharf*. One language habit that New Englanders share with most of the rest of the country is so-called "*g*-dropping," represented as "writin'," "readin'," and so on. Linguists point out that this is not *g*-dropping but the substitution of one nasal sound for another. There are some differences in this sound within the region, however. For example, *goin'* in Boston sounds like "gowen," while in some places in northeastern New England you will hear the word pronounced as two distinct syllables and a strong *i*-sound ("go-in").

The lexical method of plotting dialect boundaries results in lists of local words and pronunciations, but does not necessarily give an idea of how a local accent sounds. Today there are recordings, but of course this was not the case in nineteenth-century New England. Fortunately, a number of writers have taken enough of an interest in dialect to preserve it. The quality varies, of course, but the best local color authors produced representations that are actually of use to linguists. One of the most admired was Sarah Orne Jewett (1849–1909), best known for *The Country of the Pointed Firs* (1896). Jewett lived in southern Maine (South Berwick) near the New Hampshire border for most of her life. She records many once common but now rare or lost forms, such as "wa'n't" for *wasn't*, "kag" for *keg*, and "bot" for *boat*. Almost every bit of dialogue shows an attentive ear for dialect:

> She opened the glass door of a little cupboard beside the chimney. "These I call my best things, dear," she said. "You'd laugh to see how we enjoy 'em Sunday nights in winter: we have a real company tea 'stead o' livin' right along just the same, an' I made somethin' good for a s'prise an' put on some o' my preserves, an' we get a-talkin' together an' have real pleasant times."[7]

Even this small selection shows several interesting features. The use of *dear* as a general form of address (akin to New Yorkese "hon" or "hun"), continues to be common today in Maine and is pronounced as two syllables, "de-ah." The dropping of syllables, known as syncope ("s'prise"), and what linguists call neutralization ("somethin'," "livin'") were long ago noticed as part of New England speech. Further, it has been proposed that verb forms like "a-talkin'" found their way into Yankee dialect from Irish speech patterns.

Another New Englander, Harriet Beecher Stowe (1811–1896), is famous for *Uncle Tom's Cabin*, which in her day became the second-best-selling book in America after the Bible. However, she also wrote novels about New England, including *Oldtown Folks*, in which she paid careful attention to dialect.

You know, Mis' Badger, that 'ere cold night we hed last winter. Wal, I was off with Jake Marshall that night; ye see, Jake, he hed to take old General Dearborn's corpse into Boston, to the family vault, and Jake he kind o' hated to go alone; 't was a drefful cold time, and he ses to me, 'Sam, you jes' go 'long with me'; so I was sort o' sorry for him, and I kind o' thought I'd go 'long. Wal, come 'long to Josh Bissel's tahvern, there at the Halfway House, you know, 't was so swinging cold we stopped to take a little suthin' warmin', an' we sort of sot an' sot an' sot over the fire, till, fust we knew, we kind o' got asleep; an' when we woke up we found we'd left the old General hitched up t' th' post pretty much all night. Wal, didn't hurt him none, poor man; 'was allers a favorite spot o' his'n.[8]

This passage illustrates many of the aspects of New England dialect already discussed, particularly the sounding of vowels ("tahvern," "fust"). The use of *ye* was authentic, and possessive forms like "his'n" were recorded in Vermont among old timers until the 1970s. The dropping of syllables—"'long" for *along*—is still common in some rural areas, including in the middle of words (for example, "gin'ly" for *generally*). Stowe also records turns of phrase (*swinging cold*) that may or may not survive. In a larger sense, as a story it is a good example of Yankee humor, which to this day continues to rely on dialect. Traces of old New England speech can still be found, illustrating the durability of dialect patterns. However, whole communities speaking the Yankee dialect no longer exist—the "old town" having changed, and its folks with it.

Yankee Humorists

There is a rich tradition of Yankee humorists, who have often made use of and sometimes exaggerated the regional accent. One of the earliest was Charles Farrar Browne (1834–1867), who was born in Waterford, Maine, and created the humorous character Artemus Ward. Browne was a favorite of Abraham Lincoln and also mentor to Mark Twain. The character Ward is a circus entrepreneur who wrote letters lampooning customs, current events, and hypocrisy in pre–Civil War America. Browne first published Ward's letters in the Cleveland *Plain Dealer*, where he was an editor. Although he built on an earlier tradition of Yankee comic writing and performance, "in his hands the dialect of Down East humor emerges as a supple literary idiom, fraught with expressive possibility," and laid the groundwork for later Yankee humorists.[9] It is unfortunate that his work is out of print.

Vermont-born Phillips Lord (1902–1975), an actor and radio personality, has had his performance of Yankee "Seth Parker" recorded on film. After a successful career in radio, he played the role of Seth in *Way Back Home* (1932)—a conventional melodrama in which he stands head and shoulders above all the rest. Marshall Dodge (killed in 1982 in a hit-and-run accident) also invented a famous Yankee character, who was featured in the "Bert and I" series of books and recordings. More recently, retired Vermont dairy farmer Fred Tuttle played himself in the comedy film *Man with a Plan* (1996), and humorist Tim Sample has re-recorded some of the "Bert and I" material (including "How to Talk Yankee") with Dodge's partner, Robert Bryan.

POLITICS, TECHNOLOGY, AND INDUSTRY AND LANGUAGE

The movement of people, their coming together and drifting apart, is obviously motivated to a large degree by economic and political factors, and thus economics and politics play a significant role in language change. For example, political realities in England—such as religious intolerance—brought the first English settlers to New England. In turn, Roger Williams and Anne Hutchinson left the Massachusetts Bay Colony to found Rhode Island in order to escape Puritan intolerance (yet another group split off from Providence and moved down to Newport). Later, the expulsion of the French in eastern Canada (Acadians) by the English brought another linguistic influence to the area (primarily Maine, where it continues today). Politics is also closely related to class. West Africans were brought to New England against their will as slaves; many early Irish immigrants came as indentured servants. Their dialects of English were quite different from the dominant one and were stigmatized. However, it is impossible for people speaking the same language and living in close proximity to avoid the inexorable processes of language change, and eventually the speech of lower-class and disenfranchised groups influences the "standard" language.

The presence of particular industries in the region also invited migration from particular groups. Quarrying in northern New England attracted Italian stone masons; fishing and whaling attracted the Portuguese to Narragansett Bay as early as the colonial period. With the coming of the Industrial Revolution, new groups with new languages (such as the Italians and Eastern Europeans) were motivated by economic and political conditions in their home countries to emigrate to the United States. At the same time, the early growth of factories in New England made it a magnet for unskilled laborers, who congregated in booming mill towns such as Lowell, Massachusetts, where the first mills were built in 1822. Thus, three interrelated socioeconomic phenomena—immigration, industrialization, and urbanization—changed the face of New England in a process that began with the first settlers but accelerated enormously in the nineteenth century.

Rapid industrialization in New England also had a secondary effect—it began to overtake the traditional agrarian economy. With the opening of the West and the rich agricultural lands of the Great Plains, farming in New England became less and less economical. This caused out-migration of the original immigrants to other parts of the United States, even as the new immigrants were moving in to take up the new industrial jobs. It is therefore not surprising that already at the close of the nineteenth century, writers were eulogizing the disappearance of the dialect of "old New England"; this linguistic phenomenon merely reflected the breakup of the old social-economic structure. The dialect of coastal New England probably remained more stable because the maritime industries of fishing and trading continued to thrive long after farming had become uneconomical.

The out-migration, in turn, had a significant effect: it spread Yankee forms of speech across the country. Settlers moved primarily along the same longitude, so that New Englanders wound up in northern areas of the West while Southerners migrated through the southern half of the continent. Large numbers of whalers jumped ship and joined the California Gold Rush of 1849, and New England woodsmen moved west to play a role in the start of the Pacific lumber industry—so much so that, according to John Gould, "with the exception of two words, lumberjack and timberjack, almost all of the lumbering terms of the western forests originated in the pine and spruce history of Down East."[10]

Nautical Words

Just as Europeans needed new names for the unfamiliar plants and animals of New England, every industry generates words for the implements and activities involved in it. In one small coastal area of New England, there were until recently several dialect words just for "clam basket": *hod, bonny, roller,* and *keeler.* Every dialectologist has noted the obvious fact that nautical and marine language is abundant in New England; much of it has its origins in the dialects of western England and the early fishermen and sailors, as well as from the Celtic regions. The word *schooner,* the name for the type of fast vessel used by New Englanders on the Grand Banks and other rich fishing grounds, was apparently coined in Gloucester, Massachusetts, with the launching of the first such vessel in 1713. The word comes from a Scottish dialect verb, *to scoon,* meaning to glide across the water. Like many other words related to seafaring, such as *nor'easter,* the term has long since passed into the general American vocabulary. Others, such as *up on the hard* (referring to dry land), have not.

Naturally, many nautical words and expressions are still in use on the water. To *gunkhole* is to poke around (by boat) in out-of-the-way places. Other terms refer to the weather, such as the characteristic expression *it came on to blow,* meaning that a strong wind came up. When the breeze dies, one says that "the wind *dropped out* around sunset." The term *Down East,* now the name of a popular magazine devoted to Maine, derived from the fact that the prevailing winds of the New England coast are from the southwest, and so a sailing vessel ran downwind when sailing toward Maine. Today in Maine the term does not designate the whole state, but generally the part east of Mount Desert Island (and, further down east, Nova Scotia and the rest of Atlantic Canada). Of course, there are many words for types of boats, including *dory, punt, peapod, pram, batteau,* and *Rangley boat.*

Some nautical words have been brought ashore, so to speak, and have become dialect words with wider meanings, a process that has been going on since long before New England was settled (to be *taken aback* is probably the best-known example). A *gam* originally meant a school of whales, and later came to mean a gathering of sailors or get-together of ships (as it is used in *Moby Dick,* to describe the meeting of two New Bedford whalers on the high seas). The word is still used in some coastal areas both in its original meaning and also generally for getting together for a chat. Similarly, *mug up* means to share a mug of something or a snack, and was the term for a coffee break in New England canneries. The word *gurry,* which is used by fishermen to refer to fish guts, is also sometimes used to denote waste material, usually loose and messy. The verb *founder* has a number of uses, for example, "I ate until I was foundered."[11] Similarly, the adjective *beamy* no longer applies only to boats, and is now in general use. A more restricted dialect word is *cull,* the term in the Maine lobstering industry for a *bug* (lobster) with only one claw. This word has been known to be used in other contexts for anything of inferior quality (e.g., "he acted in some cull films").

Bulkhead has been taken by linguists to be a defining term. It still exists in its original meaning of a partition between areas of a boat or ship. In eastern New England, however, it also came to refer to sloping doors giving access to a cellar from outdoors. This usage never penetrated beyond the mountains into western New England, apparently, where the term *hatchway* would be used. *Hatchway,* of course, is also a nautical word, referring to the opening in a deck through which cargo is passed to and from the hold. Some researchers have suggested that the word *tempest* is still in general use along the New England coast, but the assertion is based on older surveys and it is more likely to encounter the terms *storm, gale,* or *blow.* Other weather terms that survive include the expression *turn off*, as in "it's supposed to turn off cold later this week." And although winters have become milder, *ice out* is still the word for the time in spring when the ice leaves the harbors.

Rural Areas

Linguistic surveys have tended to focus on rural areas, because dialect terms tend to survive longer in isolation. As a result, isoglosses have been plotted for many agricultural terms. *Webbins* refers to the reins of a horse; *rowan* is a fourteenth-century English word for a second crop of hay; and hay may be *tedded*, or spread for drying (a term almost as old as *rowan*). But agricultural dialect words in New England are rapidly dying out. E. B. White, the author of *Charlotte's Web*, collected a number of farming terms while living in Maine in the 1940s. A thin pasture is *snug*; a sheep whom other sheep follow to the barn *tolls* the others in; when a ewe's udder appears she *bags out*; a mild day is a *soft* day. These expressions have all disappeared, though the term "soft day" is in general use today in Ireland for a day of light mist or rain.

Something similar occurred in Vermont. Scott E. Hastings, Jr., who was the founder and director of the Vermont Folklife Research Project, began documenting the crafts and speech of old New Englanders in what he called the "Yankee Highlands." This area, spanning both sides of the Connecticut River in Vermont and New Hampshire, happened to coincide with the traditional dividing line between the eastern and western New England dialect areas. Some of the terms he collected, like "angle dog" for earthworm, "bonnyclabber" for sour milk, "belly bunt" for sliding on your stomach on a sled, and "intervale" for meadows along a river, are terms that linguists have considered definitive of New England dialect. Some of Hastings' words, such as "nooning" for lunch, were also on White's list years before. Thus, the anecdotal work of White and Hastings matched the boundary posited by linguists. Although it is less scientific, such work has the advantage of depicting the words as embedded within the life of the people. For comparison, consider that for the *Linguistic Atlas of New England*, four individuals were interviewed on the island of Martha's Vineyard; by contrast, George Savary Wasson filled two notebooks with folkloric and linguistic material about his community of Kittery Point over a period of ten years.

As technology changes, whole classes of words may die out. Thus, in his memoir of his career as a Yankee *drummer* (pronounced "drummah") or traveling salesman, R. E. Gould uses such terms as a *setover* rig, which allowed a single horse to pull a sleigh over a track set by two horses; a *tallyho* was a wagon drawn by a team of six; and a *turnout* was a space left, often at the tops of hills, for teams to pass each other. He uses other dialect terms that were distinctive of the rural territory he covered. But the terminology of horse-drawn locomotion, even more than that of agriculture, is destined to survive only in old books or as a specialist vocabulary.

ETHNIC AND OTHER CONTRIBUTIONS

Food Words

Although the root stock of the New England dialect consists of the dialects brought from England by the first settlers, various influences have been grafted onto it. These additions are primarily loan words rather than pronunciations. Words relating to cuisine are often cited as examples of words contributed by other languages and cultures to the New England dialect. Thus, Italian gives us *spaghetti* and *macaroni*; Portuguese *linguica* is a type of sausage commonly found on the coast from Cape Cod south; and Algonquian provided *squash*. Most of these words, however, are now in general use throughout the country. It is not only that these words are not particularly interesting anymore, because they are so assimilated; agribusiness and the nationwide distribution of food have made food terms less useful for defining regions than they once were. For example, before World War II, dialectologists could still use synonyms for *cottage cheese* to mark the boundaries of eastern and western New England. Today, any supermarket shelves various national and local brands of cottage cheese, but none of them say "sour-milk cheese" or "bonnyclabber cheese" on the label.

Food words, however, are among the most frequently encountered by travelers. "Tonic" continues to be a name in parts of New England for what other Americans call *soda* or *pop*, and the term "grinder" coexists with the more common *sub* or *submarine sandwich*. New Englanders are well-known for "frappes," the ice cream drink that other parts of the country call a *milkshake*. The expression is derived from a French verb, or possibly from Italian *frappé*, an old-fashioned term for a type of iced drink. Perhaps less known is that in Rhode Island milkshakes are called "cabinets." Among the food peculiarities of New England that dialectologists have tabulated is the use of "hamburg" instead of *hamburger*, and a similar shortening of *frankfurter* to "frankfurt." A hard-boiled egg is still sometimes called a "dropped egg" in New England. As in other regions, brand names sometimes provide regionalisms, as the old New England soft drink Moxie gave rise to the expression, "you've got a lot of moxie," in the sense of "you have a lot of nerve." An interesting New England word with a French derivation is "chowder," for the familiar fish stew of the region. The name comes from *chaudrière*, a cooking pot. French also gave Americans *portage*, *prairie*, *rapids*, and *batteau*, words not restricted to or associated with New England. Italian provided the word *piazza*, which in New England was once used to mean a covered or screened porch, or a patio (this usage is dying out, except in Boston). It has been suggested that the term came not from Italian immigrants, but from settlers from England, where it had already been introduced. Italian *toro* for "bull" was once a distinctive dialect word in central Massachusetts. In Boston, the term *spuckie* for submarine sandwich apparently comes from Italian *spucadella*, a type of roll.

Scotch-Irish and Irish Terms

The Scotch-Irish influence on New England dialect has been greater than that of any other non-English group. Many expressions had to do with the sea or seafaring and hang on, if at all, in the remoter coastal towns. A *killick* is an anchor made of stone, a term drawn from Gaelic, Manx, or Dorset dialect. *Krawm* is Scotch for "refuse" or a useless thing—for which there are many other dialect words, including *culch* or *sculch*. A *glinn* (a Scotch dialect word, also used in Newfoundland) means a faint light or glimmering; a *dite* (Scotch *doit*) of something is a small amount. *Nash* (Scotch *nesh*) once meant "dainty" or "sensitive." The Irish influence is seen in the old habit of *a-* prefixes ("a-going," "a-thinking") and phrases like *by gorry*, and the use of *dead* as an intensifier ("that board is dead flat"). These words and idioms, insofar as they survive, are still dialectal in that they have not spread out of New England into general American usage. Other words have, of course, such as *donnybrook* (an Irish term for a brawl, taken from the name of a Dublin neighborhood), *shenanigans*, and *smithereens*.

Native American Words

Lastly, Native American loan words are not restricted to the usual examples known to every American, such as *skunk* and *raccoon*. Some words retain a special New England connection and are little known outside the region. One of these is *monadnock* (Algonquian), a term for a mountain which, like Mount Monadnock in southern New Hampshire, sits alone by itself. The phrase *wickie-up* or *wickiup*, still current among old-timers and backwoodsmen, comes from an Indian word and means to make a temporary shelter in the wild.

Pronunciation by Ethnic Groups

Beyond vocabulary, another interesting aspect is how different ethnic groups react to dialect change in different ways and at different rates. One study, for example, looked at the pronunciation of *-or* in Boston among persons of Jewish, Irish, and Italian origin. The dialectal Boston pronunciation of *short*, for example, comes out like "shot," and *dog* like "dahg," and *corn* like "kahn." Jewish informants used this pronunciation the least; that is, their speech was closest to standard English. On the other hand, Italians' speech was most vernacular, with Irish somewhere in between. Sociolinguistics has become more and more interested in why these kinds of differences occur. In fact, linguist William Labov was so committed to the idea of studying language in its social context that he disliked the term "sociolinguistics" altogether, because it implied that there was some kind of nonsocial linguistics. This has had profound ramifications for the study of language change as it is occurring—something that was once thought to be impossible.

Pronunciation differences based on ethnicity have also been noticed in relation to Portuguese and French. In northern Maine communities of French speakers, vowel pronunciations have less broad values than they do in New England speech in general. Thus, *day* sounds more like "dey" than the broad Down East "dai-y." In addition, stress is often different. For example, French speakers may place the stress in *Brunswick* (as in "Nouveau Brunswick," or New Brunswick) on the second syllable, whereas English speakers place it on the first syllable. In southern coastal New England, where there is a Portuguese influence, this community often substitutes *k-* for *t*-sounds, resulting in pronunciations like "Darkmouth" (*Dartmouth*) and *throak* ("throat"). These differences remain those of Franco American or Portuguese American groups, however, and have not passed into mainstream speech. Even in an isolated situation like an island (Martha's Vineyard, Massachusetts) where descendants of English settlers and Portuguese speakers have coexisted in relative harmony for a century, the pronunciations have not crossed over into the dominant speech group—which is in line with sociolinguists' observations of how the speech patterns of socially powerful groups become "standard," while those of lower classes and immigrants are seen as "dialectal."

LANGUAGE CHANGE

The rapidity of language change in New England since the mid-twentieth century is evidenced by the landmark work of Hans Kurath. In his *Linguistic Atlas of New England* (1939–1943), or *LANE*, as it is commonly called, Kurath distinguished two major dialect regions, eastern and western New England, but a further seven subregions. Ten years later, in *A Word Geography of the Eastern United States*, his subdivisions had shrunk to three: northeastern, southeastern, and southwestern New England. Kurath's regional boundaries remained the accepted ones for decades. But starting in the mid-sixties, major changes—not only in New England but also in the discipline of dialectology itself—would vastly alter the picture of language use in New England and the country as a whole.

Craig Carver has called the changes of the mid-century "cataclysmic":

> Specifically, the mass exodus of people from the country to the cities during this period and the dramatic shift to a commercially and technologically based economy and life-style accelerated the decline of the old, rural folk terms and precipitated the spatial and semantic drift of other regionalisms.[12]

Carver suggests that the *LANE* divisions were already out of date at the time Kurath made them, even implying that some of his seven subregions may never have existed at all. For example, the use of fewer than half a dozen unique dialect terms determined *LANE*'s isogloss outlining the Merrimack Valley region of Massachusetts and southern New Hampshire, and they had all disappeared by the time of Carver's work. Kurath's model was based on the idea that large cities were the engines of dialect change, which spread outward to smaller cities and eventually to rural areas, which were most resistant and saw the greatest retention of relic terms. Carver proposed a newer model, based on the concept of "layering." The numbers that define an isogloss represent shared words used by informants. The weakness of the method is that a boundary may be pinned on just a few words, and the sampling represents only a small fraction of the population.

With his idea that "heterogeneity is an aspect of the internal order," Carver advanced a vision of dialect akin to chaos theory; by thinking of different boundaries existing in the same place but at various levels of detail, he was able to map discontinuity and dispersion in a meaningful way: "clusters of relatively low numbers appear as valleys and depressions: sudden drop-offs in the numbers define plateaus and mesa-like areas."[13] Walt Wolfram is skeptical of drawing analogies from chaos or other scientific theories, and treats all mapping with a fair amount of skepticism. Dialect maps are constructs based on limited data:

> The idealized isoglosses imposed by dialect geographers—and Labov's survey based on a couple of people in locations around the country—are at best only vague indicators as well. In fact, at times they almost seem more fictional than real. Local communities may come under such taxonomic rubrics like Southern, New England, etc., but they hardly work in terms of community. That's why locals confuse dialectologists with assertations that "every island/hollow/community" has its own dialect. On one level that's also a fabrication but on another level it's as true as the classifications imposed on them.[14]

However innovative in some ways, Carver's method, like the earlier *LANE*, depended on lexical differences. More recently, "some linguists have maintained that lexical differences are among the least reliable indicators of dialect areas"; in fact, the study of dialect has changed so much that "a traditional dialectologist, frozen in the time frame of the 1950s, would hardly recognize what takes place under the guise of dialect studies today."[15] Carver based his study on the field work that was done for the *Dictionary of American Regional English*, known as *DARE*. The massiveness of this project is evidenced by the fact that the interviews were conducted in 1965–1970, and the processing of the data has taken decades. During the five years of the *DARE* project, eighty-five workers collected 2.5 million responses from informants. As of 2004, the published volumes of the dictionary had reached the middle of the letter S. Meanwhile, the field of dialectology has swept on.

Dialectologists today take account of the rise of the suburbs as the focus of American middle-class life, as well as class- and sex-based differences in language habits. Gone are the days when field work consisted solely of asking respondents a series of questions such as "What do you call the parts of an egg?" or "What is the biggest meal of the day and when do you eat it?" Dialectologists now seek to learn how people in a region use language in ordinary conversation, which depends on far more than geography alone. Within a region, "sociolects" reflect how status and other social factors contribute to the way we use language. Thus, there can be speakers sharing the same physical space but using different manners of speech, and even individuals may use different dialects in different contexts—the most obvious example being the use of African American Vernacular English (AAVE) by individuals in their community, but "standard" English when dealing with political and economic institutions. Also of major concern to linguists today is the study of language change as it is happening; this may account for the greater focus on phonology, in contrast to the lexical mapping of Kurath's day.

New England is famously "conservative" in its language habits—one almost detects a hint of disapproval in Craig Carver's comments on "this strongly conservative parent dialect, which hangs onto old, even relic expressions and which is generally less colloquial than any other American regional dialect."[16] New England was remarkably stable both in language and culture for decades, if not centuries. It is astonishing that in the 1960s when Ruth Schell Porter did her study of the dialect of Dartmouth, Massachusetts, located on the coast south of Cape Cod, one of her "informants" was a former whaler. Born in 1906, he was taken to sea by his father before he was two years old and had gone on three whaling expeditions to the Southern Ocean before he was twelve. Kurath interviewed adult language-speakers whose linguistic habits had been formed in their youth, and thus he was taking a snapshot of the New England dialect of twenty or thirty years earlier, or about 1900–1910—and this English was essentially that of the nineteenth century. But given the continuity, conservatism, and incredible staying power of "old New England," it could hardly have been otherwise.

Similar problems attend the *DARE* project. Considering that children born even a decade after *DARE*'s closing date of 1970 are now out of college, one sees how dated the material may be. More than 66 percent of *DARE*'s informants were over sixty, a further 24 percent were between forty and fifty-nine, and almost 93 percent were white. Were a similar project undertaken today, it would have to be far less homogenous to be representative of "new" New England.

Sociolinguistics and New England

Interestingly, New England played a major role in revolutionary developments in dialectology. William Labov, a towering figure in contemporary dialect studies, conducted "the earliest community-based research in sociolinguistics" in the early sixties on the island of Martha's Vineyard, Massachusetts.[17] Labov studied two centralized diphthongs—the "ay" and "aw" sounds—which he found were increasing in strength in the dialect of Martha's Vineyard natives. He broke down the data and correlated it with various social factors, such as the informant's attitude to the island (positive, neutral, or negative), and membership in one of three groups: descendants of the original English settlers, people of Portuguese background, and the Gay Head community of Native Americans. Labov found that the phonological changes were rooted in demography and economics. Already in 1961–1963, the traditional island industries of farming and fishing were in decline and the island was inundated with wealthy vacationers in the summer. The "summer people" were not only better off than the islanders, but were actually buying up the island itself for vacation homes. Thus, a great deal of hostility had grown in some quarters, and an intensified sense of being "natives" to whom the island really "belonged."

James Russell Lowell
The Biglow Papers (1848)

James Russell Lowell (1819–1891) came from one of New England's foremost intellectual families. He was a leading poet and the best-known political satirist of his time. In *The Biglow Papers*, he created a homespun Yankee, Hosea Biglow, who protests against hypocrisy and corruption—for example, in the passage below, against the American war with Mexico. A virtuoso performance, the passage illustrates most of the aspects of the Yankee dialect discussed in this chapter.

> Ez fer war, I call it murder,—
> There you hev it plain an' flat;
> I don't want to go no furder
> Than my Testyment fer that;
> God hez sed so plump an' fairly,
> It's ez long ez it is broad,
> An' you've gut to git up airly
> If you want to take in God.
>
> 'Tain your eppyletts an' feathers
> Make the thing a grain more right;
> 'Tain afollerin' your bell-wethers
> Will excuse ye in His sight;
> Ef you take a sword an' dror it,
> An' go stick a feller thru,
> Guv'ment aint to answer for it,
> God'll send the bill to you.
>
> Wut's the use o' meetin'-goin'
> Every Sabbath, wet or dry,
> Ef it's right to go amowin'
> Feller-men like oats an' rye?
> I dunno but wut it's pooty
> Trainin' round in bobtail coats,—
> But it's curus Christian dooty
> This 'ere cuttin' folks's throats.

The dialect of the fishermen of English descent became a linguistic lightning rod for this resentment. Labov noted that the traditional dialect of Martha's Vineyard had been full of whaling terms, which had become obsolete. As vocabulary was lost, pronunciation became more important, and even exaggerated, among those who saw themselves as real "Vineyarders." The phonological trend began with the fishermen, who were the most independent and cohesive group of islanders, as well as the most hostile to the summer people. The fishermen were then emulated by those who admired their independence and who identified with them—including third- or fourth-generation Portuguese who had at times been looked askance at by the old Yankees, and even the Wampanoag Native Americans at Gay Head, who had a better right than anyone to consider it "their" island. In fact, an interesting aspect of the whole phenomenon was that the term "Yankee" ceased to have any meaning, and was replaced by the distinction between those committed to staying on the island and those who move away. Labov noticed a lack of the centralized diphthongs among those who were going away to college and mainland professions, and even a case where one of those who had left decided to return, and only then began to acquire the new pronunciations (and apparently unconsciously). The dialect became a badge and a defense for those who considered themselves true Vineyarders.

Forty years later, the social dynamics that Labov observed on Martha's Vineyard can be seen in many places in New England. It is what might be called the "vanishing breed" phenomenon: under pressure from tourism, a failing traditional economy, and new demographics, some who view themselves not just as people living in New England, but as *New Englanders*, have become attached to the dialect as a sign of membership and a token of a tradition. But whereas Labov showed that the Vineyarders were unaware of how their diphthongs were changing, some New Englanders—whether Vermont farmers in the "Yankee Highlands" or lobstermen on the coast of Maine—can play up or "turn on" the accent at will. Some, of course, speak the dialect unconsciously and simply because it is the way they grew up speaking. But trying to consciously alter dialect or direct the course of language change may be futile. From Noah Webster's efforts to get people to pronounce *deaf* like *leaf* to the campaign of the Academie Française to stamp out forms like *le hot dog* and *le weekend*, language "reform" has not met with great success. Demographic and economic trends are too powerful to resist.

THE FUTURE OF DIALECT

The tendency of the evidence from *LANE* to *DARE* and beyond is for New England to break down into two main dialect areas, eastern and western, which are clear in northern New England but then become confused south of Massachusetts. The traditional subregions defined by Kurath appear to be shrinking or disappearing altogether, while at the same time, urban sprawl means that Boston spreads out as a larger and larger subregion, while New York City steadily encroaches on nearby Connecticut. These divisions are reinforced by ones of class, geography, economics, demography, and what we might call infrastructure. The number of changes that these phenomena have wrought since *DARE*, or even since Carver's work on the *DARE* data (1987), are worth considering because they might be predictive of the future.

Linguists have noted that language change spreads along transportation routes, such as train lines and highways, and that a region isolated from these networks can become a dialect "island," unaffected by a region-wide shift, or preserving forms that have long since died out elsewhere. The major travel routes in New England radiate out from Boston, with the northern Massachusetts border marking a significant divide. Above this line, there are no major east-west routes, reinforcing the natural geographic split defined by the Appalachian Mountains. Thus, a community like Kezar Falls, Maine (the locus of the dialect reproduced in Carolyn Chute's novel *The Beans of Egypt, Maine*), may be closer in miles to Boston than towns in northern New Hampshire and Vermont that lie along the major skiing-and-foliage tourist routes, but its strong dialect suggests that linguists' idea that dialects tend to develop where groups of speakers are separated both spatially and socially also goes for dialect *retention*.

Transportation reinforces, and indeed follows the fortunes of, economics. Down East Maine had train service from Boston until about 1960. About the time it lost its train service, it began to go into economic decline. It is now an area of strong dialect survival. By contrast, southern New Hampshire experienced a boom starting around 1970 as a result of the growth of high-technology industry centered around the Route 128 belt. This area also saw an influx of "tax refugees"— many of them young professionals who worked in the tech sector—attracted by the fact that New Hampshire has no sales tax or personal income tax. These movements illustrate that a key feature of suburbs is that often their residents share economic rather than cultural interests, and may be migrants from other parts of the country with little common frame of reference. It is not hard to see why, after the suburbanization of the farm belt that once surrounded Boston, the city's linguistic influence swept through the area and even into southern New Hampshire.

Thus, New England has in a sense become "balkanized," at least dialectally. Patterns of dilution or preservation—Carver's "plateaus" and "mesas"—may depend on whether a town has a paper mill, discount malls, a shipyard, or a fishing industry. A town like Gloucester, Massachusetts, which maintains its historically large fishing fleet and in which this profession is handed down from generation to generation, can be expected to have more speakers of eastern New England dialect than Camden, Maine, located hundreds of miles to the northeast but also a major tourist attraction, as well as the headquarters of the country's second-largest credit card company. Thus, Camden attracts both college students seeking summer jobs and financial industry professionals, whose children are likely to go away to college and enter similar professions themselves. The incentive for young people to adopt local Maine dialect rather than a more neutral (and in a sense portable) form of standard English is weak or nonexistent, just as Labov had observed on Martha's Vineyard.

The older Yankee dialect seems to be receding northward as the glaciers once did, leaving a few isolated pockets or moraines as it goes. Hence Gloucester, at the eastern end of Cape Ann in Essex county, is a sort of island. Better roads, better vehicles, and high real estate prices have expanded the Boston suburbs out as far as York, Maine's southernmost county, which lies to the north of Gloucester. The population of York county is growing dramatically, but from the outside. The pattern of dialect breakup can be tracked in the fortunes of the word *orts*, meaning "garbage" and especially table scraps or refuse. Once prevalent as far south as Cape Cod, it was a relic in Massachusetts already at the time of *LANE*. Decades later, the *DARE* survey found it in two places only, Bar Harbor, Maine, and New Bedford, Massachusetts. The locations are revealing; both are large harbors frequented by fishermen. Today the word still survives among older people on the Maine coast, though not much used. Gloucester might be a good place to observe overlapping sociolects. Being close to Boston, idioms and patterns of that city can be found there.

In southern New England, the pattern is even more complex. Carver found that between *LANE* and *DARE*, all but two of the dozen distinctive isoglosses of the Narragansett Bay subregion had either disappeared or become so widespread as to be national rather than regional. Carver seems determined to save the lower Connecticut River valley as a separate subregion, though he says that all of its distinctive isoglosses from *LANE* had virtually disappeared by *DARE*. This is not surprising; one of the distinctive terms that *DARE* failed to elicit was the expression *topgallant* for the tassel of an ear of corn. Since a "top gallant" (or "t'gallant") is one of the uppermost sails on a full-rigged sailing ship, it is not hard to see why it has died out. The same is true of the four or five other isogloss terms from *LANE*: the *DARE* fieldworkers found only one informant who used the term "round clam" for *quahog*. Southern Connecticut is under constant pressure from New York City, which has undergone huge expansion since *DARE*, just as Boston has. Again, transportation helps define boundaries; commuter train lines reaching as far as New Haven make the region attractive to suburbanites who work in New York City. In the never-ending search of the middle class for affordable housing near major cities, even communities within driving distance of New Haven become "commutable." One boundary of the southernmost New England state has traditionally been very firm: the Hudson River. The dialect of the Hudson River valley has historically had a strong Dutch influence. While this remains true, some of Carver's mappings of *DARE* data seemed to show encroachment of the upper north dialect into Connecticut (including such words as "babushka" for *head scarf*), as is also happening in western Vermont.

An aspect of New England speech not commonly factored into the equation is the influence of AAVE. New Haven, Hartford, and Boston all have significant African American populations. Some of the hallmarks of AAVE that are most consistent nationally are what is known as copula absence ("he bad" for *he is bad*, "he reading a book" for *he is reading a book*) and the deletion of the *-s* ending in the third person singular. At least one common aspect of AAVE, postvocalic *r*-lessness, is held in common with the traditional eastern New England dialect. It is unclear how much influence AAVE has had on New England speech, beyond its existence as a separate sociolect within the region. However, it might be more accurate for future dialect maps to indicate the major cities and their suburban coronas as subregions in themselves, having multiple dialect layers, one of which is AAVE. This will become more evident in the discussion of languages other than English (below). What does seem clear is that the pattern of overlap in southern New England is ripe for the kind of redefinition described by Carver, in which "new innovative centers emerge" and become "future nodes for linguistic innovation, from which new dialects will develop."[18]

Another area that is geographically in New England but dialectally linked to a region outside it is the northwestern section. It has been established that the part of northern New England west of the Appalachians is now being absorbed into the northern dialect region, which spreads across New York State and beyond. Evidence for this dynamic includes the fact that central and western Vermont are participating in what is called the Northern Cities Vowel Shift, in which long low vowels move upward and short vowels move downward. Thus *coffee* starts to have the vowel of *water*, and sounds like "cahffee" (the upper New York State pronunciation of the word). In fact, a study funded by the National Science Foundation is being conducted to record the older dialect of the area before it fades away. Western Vermont was settled by Scotch-Irish immigrants, and so it was not an *r*-less region. Some of its other pronunciations that go back to these settlers include "kee-ow" for *cow*, "hay-nd" for *hand*, and "woy-il" for *while*. It shared some features, such as broad-*a*, with eastern New England.

Boston

One New England dialect that appears extremely durable and is also expanding rather than shrinking is that of the region's largest city. Boston speech has highly distinctive features, some of which have already been mentioned. Many of these have spread elsewhere in New England. The city's most noticeable lexical item is *wicked*. It is used in much the same way as *bad* in African American speech; that is, it means its opposite (i.e., good). *Wicked* is most often used in combination with an adjective, for example, *wicked good, wicked cool, wicked nice*. This idiom does not interfere with or replace the original negative meaning of the word, so phrases like "the wind was wicked" are still possible, and the hearer will not make the mistake of thinking that the wind referred to was pleasant (though "the wind was wicked *cold*" is probably more idiomatic). Although *wicked* is very much associated with Boston, it has been disseminated far and wide—even electronically. The Boston dialect is now a source of pride among some of those who use it; a Boston radio station named its remote transmission vehicle "Wicked Big Yellow Van," and in 2004, a television advertisement showed a recently acquired Red Sox pitcher listening to language tapes to learn how to say he was throwing the ball "wickid hahd." But at the same time that some Bostonians have become proud of their accents, others have gone to great lengths to shed it, and several agencies have sprung up to help professionals "de-regionalize" their speech. The Boston accent has increasingly been labeled as "low class." Much of this has to do with demographics; half of Bostonians now hail from somewhere else. One professional (an art dealer) who moved to the city said the accent was "not very polished, and it doesn't speak very well of the education of the person."[19] It is ironic that *r*-lessness and the broad-*a*, which may have originated as an affectation of upper-class Londoners in the eighteenth century, are now stigmatized as blue collar.

Another distinctive Boston expression is *So don't I*, which, though negative, actually means "So do I." Hence the rejoinder to the statement "I hate the Yankees" could be "So don't I!" Another negative that is used positively is *can't get*; for example, in the phrase "Let me see if I can't get this door open," where the speaker wants to try if he *can* get it open. There is a plethora of Boston vocabulary that is not heard elsewhere in New England, such as *nizza*, a synonym for "wicked," and to be *skeeved*, by something, meaning to be disgusted. Dialectologists have plotted *rotary* (elsewhere, a "traffic circle") as a New Englandism, but it is more colorfully referred to as a *suicide circle*. *Directional* for "turn signal" is another automotive idiom of Boston and environs. A *three decker* is a wood-frame building with three separate apartments, often with porches on the back. The term *bubbler* or *water bubbler* has been plotted as a Boston-area variant for "water fountain" or "drinking fountain." Mention must also be made of the city's greatest though little-recognized gift to the language: the term *OK* was coined in Boston in 1839, and has by now become indispensible to English speakers the world over.

There may once have been as many as ten subdialects of Boston English. Many have disappeared. Boston's subdialects rested on the city's neighborhoods, some of which retain their distinctive ethnic quality, such as the Italian North End and the

Irish-dominated South Boston, known as "Southie." Although many Bostonians lament the loss of dialect because they see it as a link with the past, some of that past was fairly ugly. South Boston and its speech were made famous by the film *Good Will Hunting* (1997); the last time the neighborhood had received so much national attention was during the school busing crisis of the mid-1970s, when it was a focus of antiblack violence. The South Boston accent is said to have a touch of the Irish brogue in it, but since the neighborhood is still a destination for Irish immigrants, this may be a confusion—many people on the street *are* Irish. Also, South Boston English is as *r*-less as the rest of Boston, which is not an Irish trait.

At the other end of the social spectrum is the so-called Brahmin dialect of blue-blood Bostonians. This upper-class accent is strongly nonrhotic (*r*-less), with broad vowels and less nasality than the typical Boston accent. The Kennedy family has been identified with Brahmin speech, but many have said the Kennedys have an accent all their own. John F. Kennedy's famous *vigor* would certainly be pronounced "viguh" (as opposed to standard American "viggr"), but no Kennedy would ever say "loo-suh" for *loser*; perhaps as a concession to public life, the Kennedys seem to have adapted some strategic *r*-fulness. Indeed, in 2004, the *Boston Globe* suggested that another Massachusetts political figure, Senator John Kerry, might need to "de-Brahminize" his speech patterns.

Comparing Boston and Yankee Dialects

Some words, obviously, are more closely related to urban living than others, and therefore less likely to spread. The same is true of course for the rural vocabulary. It is interesting to compare Boston with northeastern New England, the major remnant area of the old Yankee dialect. Some words are shared between the two subregions, such as *supper* (pronounced "suppah") for the evening meal, though it overlaps with *dinner*. The term *wicked* has reached as far as Down East. In Boston, *friggin'* serves as a synonym for the more obscene "F-word," but in Maine it also has a second and older meaning, "to mess around with" or try to mend (often unsuccessfully). *Spider* for "frying pan" is a mostly dead relic word in both areas.

Rural areas of northeastern New England maintain particular usages. People from outside the area are *from away* (in northern New Hampshire, they are often called *flatlanders*). Returning to E. B. White's corner of Maine, one finds that although many agricultural words have passed out of existence, *dressing* can still mean "manure." Heating with wood is common in the region, and so *dozy* or *punky* is used to describe wood that is rotten, and *biscuit wood* is kindling to get the fire going. To give something a tap, you *tunk* it. A person who is *spleeny* is overly sensitive to pain or discomfort, and someone who is *contrary* has a stubborn or difficult nature. A *hubbly* surface is uneven, for example, loose stones or pebbles. A *dite* is a small amount. A thick fog is a *fog mull*, and *willy-wag* is used to designate what is elsewhere called "the boonies" or "the puckerbrush." *Cussèd* as a synonym for "darned" or "damned" is definitely a northeastern word and not a Boston one. Similarly, widespread throughout Maine is the use of *dear* (pronounced "de-ah") as a term of address, and *cunnin'* as a synonym for "cute" or "clever." The sound of the Maine accent is quite different from that of Boston, even if they share features such as *r*-lessness and broad *a*. Many vowel sounds seem to be lower and shorter in Maine dialect. *Idea* is a good example: in the Boston English it sounds like a two-syllable word, "ideer," whereas in Maine it may sound like three-syllable "idee-yuh." (Here the added-*r* reinforces the distinction.) *Shore* will sound more like "shaw" in Boston, and in Maine, almost like "show-uh"; similarly "befaw" and "befo-uh" (*before*). The Maine equivalent of "Pahk ya cah in Hahvahd Yahd" is "Y'cahn't get they-uh from h'yuh."

It is impossible to predict what will happen to the Yankee dialect, but if the speech patterns of the "old timers" are disappearing, no doubt it is because the region is not creating any new old-timers. Carver states that "with the strong influence of national culture, only those subcultures with tenacious social features, such as religion, language, and ethnic background, survive."[20] To these factors can be added economics. The potato industry of Aroostook County, Maine, may be the last large-scale economically viable agriculture in New England; the lumber and fishing industries in the region, perpetually under siege, will provide another stable basis for the Yankee ideal upon which the traditional dialect of the region is based. In Vermont, the maple sugar industry now produces only 20 percent of U.S. consumption, the rest coming from Canada. As traditional jobs disappear, they are replaced by new professions with different vocabularies and orientations. In some cases, they are not replaced by anything at all: the two most northeasterly counties in Maine have become depopulated, and may actually have fewer residents than they did in the nineteenth century. Thus, when we lament the decline of dialect, we may be confusing cause and effect, for behind the passing of a manner of speaking is the loss of a way of life.

OTHER LANGUAGES IN NEW ENGLAND

It is not only dialects and sociolects that overlap, of course; different languages may also coexist within the same region (and of course within a family, or an individual). This is particularly so in cities. The Boston city government's Office of New Bostonians lists 140 different languages in use in the Boston area. The major languages other than English are Spanish, Chinese, Vietnamese, Cape Verdean Creole, Haitian Creole, Portuguese, and Russian. One indicator of the size of some of these communities is that the Commonwealth Business Network, which assists the growth of new businesses, provides services in several dialects of Chinese, French, Haitian Creole, Portuguese, Spanish, and Vietnamese. The spectrum of languages in Boston is both different and a good deal larger than it was in the nineteenth, not to mention the eighteenth, century. Nor are the immigrants all of one class. With its global reputation in education and medicine, and such institutions as Harvard, the Massachusetts Institute of Technology, and Mass General Hospital, Boston is a magnet for students and professionals from all over the world. Similarly, southern Connecticut gets a share of all those who are attracted to New York for economic, educational, and cultural reasons.

But the existence of non-English linguistic communities is not restricted to large metropolitan areas. The first Portuguese parish in the United States was established in 1871 in New Bedford, Massachusetts, though Portuguese whalers had been in the area since the late eighteenth century. With the decline in whaling the Portuguese became factory workers in the newly developed mills. With the mills now defunct, they have moved into various sectors of the economy, including the professional class. A large part of the community today is made up of Madeirans and Cape Verdeans. The Portuguese-speaking community is still linguistically and culturally intact, and indeed sponsors several religious feasts and other events each year to promote and recognize the culture.

The situation of francophone New England is in some ways more complex, because the immigration has gone on for a much longer time. During the first period, until the close of the seventeenth century, the part of New England north of Penobscot Bay was held by the French. Northeastern New England was a contested prize and changed hands many times before finally becoming British. A wave of emigration occurred starting around the mid-1700s after the fall of Quebec; French colonists who refused to take a loyalty oath to the British crown were ejected from Canada (these were the Acadians). Most settled in Maine. Emigration into northern New England from Canada continued for over 150 years. French speaking may have peaked in the United States in 1930, when the census found that more than half a million people reported French to be their mother tongue. The numbers began to decline after that. Still, when Mary R. Miller studied bilingualism in northern New England in the late sixties, she found that more than half of households in Burlington, Vermont, were French-speaking, which is certainly not the case today. She found significant French-speaking communities in the Burlington-Winooski area; Manchester, Claremont, and Berlin, New Hampshire; and in Maine. Her most startling finding was that there were still small numbers of people monolingual in French; these were either elderly people, or very young children who did not learn English until they went to school. See Table 2 for figures on the use of French at home according to the 2000 Census.

The French influence in New England has taken not so much the form of borrowing French words as speaking French instead of English. Obviously there are great pressures working against this; business and government dictate facility in English. Some of the pressures were less oblique. As Miller says, public school is "the great leveler in American society,"[21] and for much of the postwar period it was forbidden for high school students to speak French on school grounds. (Probably not coincidentally, it was in the 1920s during the period of high immigra-

Table 2. Use of French at home, 2000 Census

State	Total population	Population of French origin	French at home	French speakers compared to ancestry	French speakers as percentage of total population
MA	6,349,097	559,818	84,484	15%	1%
CT	3,405,565	217,713	42,947	20%	1%
RI	1,048,319	129,306	19,385	15%	2%
ME	1,274,923	238,423	63,640	27%	5%
NH	1,235,786	241,232	39,551	16%	3%
VT	608,827	110,274	14,624	13%	2%
NY	2,160,691	188,963	18,292	10%	1%
Total	16,083,208	1,468,629	282,923	19%	2%

Source: Cynthia A. Fox and Jane S. Smith, "La situation du français franco-américain: aspects linguistique et sociolinguistique," in *Le Français aux Etats-Unis*, ed. Albert Valdman, Julie Auger, and Deborah Piston-Hatlen (Quebec: Presses Universitaires Laval, forthcoming).

tion that French was banned as a language for classroom instruction.) The outlook forecast by Miller for francophone Americans was bleak. Her predictions have almost come to pass, but in recent years there have been grassroots efforts to save the culture and language of the Acadians, as well as increased academic interest in French-speaking communities of the United States. There is now a program in Franco-American studies at the University of Maine, and a study is underway to update the very outdated material on the French-speaking community in New England.

It is interesting to note that dialect is an issue within Franco-American studies as well, for the dialect of the St. John Valley where Maine borders New Brunswick is different from that of Quebecois French. For example, the word *fougère* refers to boiled fiddlehead ferns, a specialty of the area (most Americans would recognize "fiddleheads" as a regionalism in its own right). Acadian French also refers to stairs not as *les escaliers* as in standard French but as *les échelles*, meaning "ladders"—perhaps a reference to the cruder homes of the original Acadian colonists of the eighteenth century, in which a ladder led to a second-story loft. The pronunciation of some vowels is also different from Canadian French. The issue of dialects within the foreign languages of New England is a fascinating one but lies beyond the scope of this essay.

French has had some effect on pronunciation and even syntax among bilingual Franco-Americans in northern Maine, as has been documented in recent work by Jane S. Smith. The vowel in *day*, for example, is not diphthongized as it is in typical Down East speech (hard to represent, but something like the diphthong in *die*). Plosive consonants like *p* and *b* are less aspirated than in standard forms of English, which also reflects these sounds' French pronunciation. Finally, Smith cites the curious example of "*Our generation is weird, us*" as a kind of construction imported into English from French.[22]

It is a cliché that Americans are "bad" at foreign languages, when they bother to learn them. We are often presented with the ideology of a monolingual culture. But this is one of those clichés that turns out to be false. Dialectologists refer to Massachusetts Bay as one of the "hearths" of American dialect; the Connecticut Valley is another. And yet, dominant as the English stock was, these hearths were from the beginning multicultural in the modern sense, whether they liked it or not. New England is often wrongly depicted as monocultural. The language map sketched here should show the region as anything but unitary. In the nineteenth century, New England seamen held their *gams* from Montevideo to Kowloon Bay, and sailors from the four corners of the earth walked the streets of every New England coastal town. Today, that culture is long past. However, the cities of New England have become crucibles of even greater influences, and while intact communities carry on the language traditions of the past, new forces are no doubt forming within the sometimes ambiguous conglomerations of the present. Labov's study seemed to show that forty years ago, "Yankee" was already a sort of loose signifier, available to anyone in the region who wanted to identify with that self-conceived tradition of independence, self-reliance, and rectitude. Whatever words are used to formulate that identification, whether by Russians, African Americans, or sixth-generation Scotch-Irish, will help to shape the Yankee dialect. Of course, other strains will develop with ethnic, national, or international allegiances that are socialectal, rather than dialectal. Only for the Algonquian, perhaps, is there a seamless bond between language and *Ndakinna*. Through language, it may become apparent that *New England* is less a place than an idea; one place, many tongues.

RESOURCE GUIDE

Printed Sources

Bennett, Jacob. "George Savary Wasson's Approach to Dialect Writing." *American Speech*, Summer 1979, 90–101.

Bombardieri, Marcella. "It's Still a Mahk of Distinction: The Accent Sets Bostonians Apart." *Boston Globe*, September 23, 1999, B1–3.

Carver, Craig M. *American Regional Dialects*. Ann Arbor: University of Michigan Press, 1987.

Colcord, Joanna Carver. *Sea Language Comes Ashore*. New York: Cornell Maritime Press, 1945.

Cutler, Charles L. *O Brave New Words! Native American Loanwords in Current English*. Norman: University of Oklahoma Press, 1994.

Dillard, J. L. *A History of American English*. London: Longman, 1992.

Gould, John. *Maine Lingo*. Camden, ME: Down East Magazine, 1975.

Gould, R. E. *Yankee Drummer*. New York: McGraw-Hill, 1947.

Hall, Joan Houston, chief ed. *The Dictionary of American Regional English*. Vol. 4. Cambridge, MA: Belknap, 2002.

Hastings, Scott E. *The Last Yankees: Folkways in Eastern Vermont and the Border Country*. Hanover, NH: University Press of New England, 1990.

Holliday, Carl. *The Wit and Humor of Colonial Days*. Williamstown, MA: Corner House, 1975.

Kamensky, Jane. *Governing the Tongue: The Politics of Speech in Early New England*. New York: Oxford University Press, 1997.

Kurath, Hans. *Studies in Area Linguistics*. Bloomington: Indiana University Press, 1972.

———. *A Word Geography of the Eastern United States*. Ann Arbor: University of Michigan Press, 1949.

Labov, William. *Sociolinguistic Patterns*. Philadelphia: University of Pennsylvania Press, 1972.

MacQuarrie, Brian. "Talking 'Bah-k' in Vermont." *Boston Globe*, February 12, 2004, B-1.

Wolfram, Walt. *Dialects and American English*. Englewood Cliffs, NJ: Prentice-Hall, 1991.

Wolfram, Walt, and Natalie Schilling-Estes. *American English*. Malden, MA: Blackwell, 1998.

Web Sites

Cassidy, Frederic. *Dictionary of American Regional English*.
Dictionary of American Regional English. March 23, 2004.
http://polyglot.lss.wisc.edu/dare/dare.html

The main page of one of the *DARE* projects, which was compiled under the direction of the late Frederic Cassidy, from field work carried out in 1965–1970. Harvard University Press/Belknap has already published volumes of the dictionary, which should soon be completed.

Gaffin, Adam. *The Wicked Good Guide to Boston English*.
Boston Online.com. March 23, 2004.
http://www.boston-online.com/glossary.html

This site catalogs Boston English alphabetically, and has many posts about recent developments in the dialect. Though not "scholarly," it is far more up-to-the-minute.

Labov, William. *TELSUR.*
The Atlas of North American English. March 23, 2004.
http://www.ling.upenn.edu/phonoatlas/

The Web site through which one can access the TELSUR project, a survey of linguistic changes now under way in North America, which seeks to systematically describe the phonology of the United States and Canada. Contains a William Labov paper entitled "The Organization of Dialect Diversity in North America," as well as maps.

Varieties of English (with sound samples).
http://www.ic.arizona.edu/~lsp/main.html.

This dialect site has a good overview of general linguistics (phonology, IPA, etc.). Features information on: African American English, American Indian English, British English, Canadian English, Chicano English, Northeast United States, and the Southern English.

Videos/Films

The Beans of Egypt Maine. Dir. Jennifer Warren. Perf. Martha Plimpton, Kelly Lynch, Rutger Hauer, Patrick McGaw. American Playhouse, 1994.
Good Will Hunting. Dir. Gus Van Sant. Perf. Robin Williams, Matt Damon, Ben Affleck. Miramax Films/Buena Vista, 1997.
Man with a Plan. Dir. John O'Brien. Perf. Fred Tuttle, Bill Blachly. F-Stop/J.G. Films, 1996.
Way Back Home. Dir. William A. Seiter. Perf. Bette Davis, Phillips Lord, Effie Palmer, Mrs. Phillips Lord. 1932.

Festivals

Acadian Festival
Greater Madawaska Chamber of Commerce
Laurie A. Sirois, Executive Director
P.O. Box 144
Madawaska, ME 04756
phone: (207) 728-7000 /fax: (207) 728-4696
e-mail: valleyvisit@pwless.net or valleyvisit@nci1.net
http://www.townofmadawaska.com/cc.html/

Held annually from last Sunday in June to first Sunday in July.

Maine's largest cultural festival celebrating Acadian heritage through a special family reunion honoring one of the Acadian pioneer families (for example, the Gendreau/Jandreau/Johndro family in 2004) and a number of events including a reenactment of the first Acadian landing in northern Maine, traditional Acadian supper, a softball tournament, barge rides on Long Lake, and a variety of shows. Takes place in French-speaking Madawaska and adjoining areas.

Annual Feast of the Blessed Sacrament
Madeira Field on Belleville Ave. & Earle Street
50 Madeira Avenue
New Bedford, MA 02746
phone: (508) 992-6911
e-mail: clubesss@gis.net
http://www.portuguesefeast.com

Held annually on the weekend which ends with the first Sunday in August.

Founded in 1915 and sponsored by the Clube Madeirense S.S. Sacramento, this admission-free "festa" is the oldest and largest Portuguese Feast in North America. Entertainment is offered on three stages featuring music, folkloric dances, and shows, and Portuguese food and drinks are available. A portal to Portuguese language and culture in New England.

National Folk Festival
Penobscot Riverfront
30 Main Street, Suite 220
Bangor, ME 04401
phone: (207) 992-2630
e-mail: info@nationalfolkfestival.com
http://www.nationalfolkfestival.com

Held annually on the last weekend in August.

Founded in 1939, the festival features three days of music, dance, traditional crafts, storytelling, and food celebrating the roots, the richness, and the variety of American culture. With special emphasis on Maine and New England traditions. Some of the oral events feature "Yankee" storytellers.

Organizations

The American Dialect Society
Executive Secretary, Allan Metcalf
English Department, MacMurray College
Jacksonville, IL 62650
phone: (217) 479-7117 or (217) 243-3403
e-mail: AAllan@aol.com
http://www.americandialect.org

The primary organization dedicated to the study of regional American speech. The society publishes the journal *American Speech*.

LITERATURE

Luca Prono

Questions on the very existence of a unified and coherent "New England mind" have haunted scholars ever since the cultural historian Perry Miller devised the phrase in 1939. Andrew Delbanco has summarized such questions in the introduction to his anthology of New England writing: "Can one speak of an enduring New England mentality that has somehow persisted from the Pilgrim Fathers to the present day? Or is New England merely a collective name for six states—Vermont, New Hampshire, Maine, Massachusetts, Rhode Island, and Connecticut—a big parcel of real estate stretching from the Northeast Kingdom of Vermont to the New York suburbs of Fairfield County, bounded on the east by the Atlantic, on the north by Canada, and on the west and south by the Vermont, Massachusetts, and Connecticut state lines."[1] It would be foolish to try to impose cultural and literary homogeneity on New England, and Delbanco has pointed out that "the transience and diversity of cultural memory and the slippage of history into myth" make the discontinuities and confrontations as important as the continuities and accommodations. This chapter addresses the literature of New England from its Puritan founding to the present day, emphasizing the complex and different contributions to the region's literary culture.

NATIVE AMERICAN LITERATURE

New England literature, like American literature as a whole, started well before the arrival of explorers or religious dissenters. It started with the oral legends, myths, and songs of the Native American tribes that populated the region before the colonists. The literary production was quite diverse from tribe to tribe. Yet, central to all traditions was a sense of nature as a living entity endowed with spiritual forces, a portrayal strikingly similar to that which Ralph Waldo Emerson would give in his essays in the nineteenth century. With the arrival of the Puritans in the seventeenth century, a written literary tradition was introduced to New England.

THE COLONIAL PERIOD

Puritans were suspicious of those traditional literary products which stressed the importance of aesthetics per se and rejected artistic forms such as theater and painting. This attitude is frequently justified by referring to Max Weber's famous thesis of the roots of modern capitalism in Puritan thought and also to the often invoked Puritan suspicion of worldliness. Yet, the Pilgrims started to produce a steady flow of writings from their very arrival in New England. If the colonists were God's chosen people and the eyes of the entire humankind were upon them, as their leaders suggested, it was only obvious that they should make their experience known to the world. They were persuaded that, through propagandizing, their model of union of church and state would be eventually followed everywhere. The importance given to culture and education also led to the founding of Harvard College in 1636 and the establishment of a printing press in 1639.

New England writing of this era can be divided into two broad categories: religious texts such as sermons, polemics, and ecclesiastical and political theory; and personal memoirs like diaries, journals, correspondence, and histories. In addition to these two categories, seventeenth-century New England literature also witnessed a considerable production of poetry. Not surprisingly, the first publishing projects of the Massachusetts Bay Colony were *The Bay Psalm Book* and *The New England Primer* whose aim was to spread Puritan values and beliefs and to make accessible all the basic texts of Puritan faith. *The Bay Psalm Book* adapted the Hebrew psalms of David into English so that congregations could understand, sing, and even memorize them. *The New England Primer* was instead addressed specifically to children and gave them the opportunity to learn religious and moral precepts.

Puritan sermons, though far from contemporary sensibility, were central to the Puritan idea of literature. New England colonists derived from them not only religious edification but also artistic pleasure. In sermons, preachers developed passages from the Bible to an audience who was familiar with biblical language, metaphors, and expressions and found in them parallels that would make bearable their life in an otherwise forbidding reality. As it can be expected from the Puritan mistrust of art for art's sake, sermons were constructed in the so-called plain style, that is, not so much with attention to elegance of style, but to facilitate their memorization. Each sermon would start with the exposition of the doctrine contained in the biblical passage in question followed by a series of practical applications. Sermons were also often published, and this made ministers the literary class of the colonies.

The first person to write in and about New England, and to give the region its name, was Captain John Smith (1580–1631), a shopkeeper apprentice from Lincolnshire turned adventurer and explorer. The region was first described as an earthly, rather than a spiritual, paradise: "Here nature and liberty afford us that freely which in New England we want, or it costs us dearly." In his *Description of New England* (1616), Smith, whose name has become inextricably linked to that of Pocahontas, the Indian chief's daughter who seemed to have saved his life, reported his own journey along the coast from Monhegan Island to Cape Cod. Although he soon returned to England and never went back to the colonies again, he kept promoting the colonization of New England with his volumes *New England Trials* (1620) and *Advertisements for the Unexperienced Planters of New England* (1631).

While Puritans were fleeing to New England shores predominantly for religious reasons, it is impossible to separate religion from economics. In fact, Puritans thought that work and economic success had a moral dimension. They were means through which God could be glorified. Led by William Bradford (1590–1657), the first Pilgrims to arrive in America were per-

Bradford's *History of Plymouth Plantation*

Bradford's manuscript itself had a legendary fate. Although known to early historians, it disappeared from Boston after the American Revolution, and while a copy of the first volume was kept in the Plymouth church records, the second volume was considered lost until it was found in the residence of the bishop of London and was published in 1856.

suaded that the Church of England had departed from the simple Protestant creed to which they adhered, and thought that it could not be reformed from within. This group was not representative of the majority of the Puritans that would eventually settle in New England. Rather than a national church, they favored Calvin's model of setting up local churches, each founded on a covenant between the believers, recalling the Old Testament Covenant between God and Adam.

The literary construction of the myth of the Puritan experience in New England began with Bradford's *History of Plymouth Plantation* which he wrote during the last twenty years of his life.

In his *History*, Bradford draws explicit parallels between the Puritans' expedition to America and the Israelites' errand into the wilderness. His congregation is thus described as a "chosen people" struggling into and against the wilderness to bring into existence the City of God on earth. The struggle is directed not only toward external forces, but also within the community to defeat its corrupt worldliness. This was a danger that soon materialized when the colony was charged with doctrinal looseness. Bradford first dramatizes in his account a characteristic theme of American literature, the common man's discovery of his potential when he is faced with his own nature and the wilderness, as well as a recurrent image in American history, that of a "redeemer nation." Talking about the longevity of the Pilgrim Fathers, for example, Bradford comments: "I cannot but here take occasion not only to mention but greatly to admire the marvelous providence of God! That notwithstanding the many changes and hardships that these people went through, and the many enemies they had and difficulties they met withal, that so many of them should live to very old age." Problematically, however, Bradford used spirituality and redemption to justify violence against natives, claiming that resistance to God's chosen people was the work of the devil.

The attitude toward the Church of England by the colonists who settled in the Massachusetts Bay Colony in 1630 and were led by John Winthrop (1588–1649) was more representative of New England settlement. This colony quickly overshadowed the Plymouth settlement which was officially incorporated in 1684. The Massachusetts Bay Colony was dissenting but nonseparating, wishing to reform the church from within. While still on board the ship which was taking them to New England, Winthrop preached the famous sermon *A Model of Christian Charity*, where he theorized the guiding principles to build a balanced Christian community. Just like Bradford and many other Puritan thinkers, Winthrop described the immigrants to New England as chosen by God to preserve and show His glory to the entire world. Therefore, the Puritan experiment becomes, in one of the most quoted images of American literature, like a "city upon a hill." The new settlement would have the

Thomas Morton

Although he adopted the Puritans' parallels between themselves and the Israelites from the very title of his only published work *New English Canaan*, Thomas Morton (1579–1647) was so far from Puritan sensibility that Bradford renamed him Lord of Misrule. Establishing a settlement in 1625 which he later renamed Merry Mount, Morton was condemned by Puritan communities as licentious and was repeatedly arrested and deported back to England. His book was an effort to persuade political and religious authorities in England that New England communities had betrayed both the church and the state and that action against them was necessary.

eyes of the world scrutinizing its results. If it were not successful, it would give enemies of the Puritan creed arguments to speak against it: "We shall shame the faces of many of God's worthy servants, and cause their prayers to be turned into curses upon us 'til we be consumed out of the good land wither we are going." The type of community described by Winthrop in his sermon was to remain an abstraction more than a historical reality, and in his *Journal* he devotes several passages to the contrasts that arose within the colonies, such as those with the religious dissenters Roger Williams (1603–1683) and Anne Hutchinson (1591–1643).

Williams escaped from Massachusetts to Narragansett Bay, founding in Rhode Island his Providence Plantation, whose name was synonymous with religious freedom for many years to come. Williams' banishment from Massachusetts became the central event in his life, and his writings were influenced by his condition. While his most famous book, *The Bloudy Tenent of Persecution* (1644), never mentioned Williams' forced exile, its main theme of religious freedom was surely shaped by Williams' personal encounter with intolerance. In his works, Williams denounced the unity of church and state as violating the teachings of Christ: "When they have opened a gap in the hedge or wall of separation between the garden of the Church and the wilderness of the world, God hath ever broke down the wall itself, removed the candlestick, and made his garden a wilderness, as at this day. And that there fore if He will ever please to restore His garden and paradise again, it must of necessity be walled in peculiarly unto Himself from the world."

John Cotton (1585–1652), who reluctantly emigrated to New England in 1633 after being suspended twice by the Church of England for nonconformity, was considered by the original settlers to be one of the most inspiring preachers. In his sermons and theological works (*Treatise of the Covenant of Grace*, *The Keyes of the Kingdom of Heaven*, and *The Way of the Churches of Christ*), Cotton read images, characters, places, and events of the Testaments as the foreshadowing of secular history, confirming New England's sacred mission as the Promised Land for the chosen people. Cotton's vision of New England rested on a gathering of congregations, which included a group of noticeable human saints who would incarnate the experience of religious conversion for the whole community. Though separate, these congregations would be encouraged to gather in synods, thus striking a balance between Presbyterianism and radical separatism. As far as the structure of the state was concerned, Cotton supported the cornerstone of the Puritan polity by positing a theocratic relationship between church and state.

Born in the same year as the symbolic defeat of Catholicism in England—when Guy Fawkes was charged with the Gunpowder Plot—Thomas Shepard (1605–1649) was also considered to be one of New England's most inspiring preachers. Through a careful use of imagery, Shepard attempted to make sermons a truly emotional experience so that his audience would react to them as to pieces of poetry. His style was to influence the more psychologically oriented eighteenth-century sermons by Jonathan Edwards (1703–1758), who explicitly acknowledged his debt to Shepard. The focus on the audience is clear in the following passage where Shepard speaks emotionally in the first person:

> There is a number among us, young and old, of all sorts almost among us, that swarm up and down towns, and woods, and fields, whose care and work hitherto hath been like bees, only to get honey to their own hive, only to live here comfortably with their houses, and lots, and victuals, and fine clothes, etc., but not to live hereafter eternally. Suppose the Lord should stop thy breath, and cut thee off, what would become of thee? . . . are you ready for Christ? Yes, I hope I am; O, poor wretch! why cost hope so? if thou never hadst one hour's serious thoughts, What will become of me? or, How shall I be ready? feeling thy unreadiness and unfitness thereunto.

Shepard's literary production ranges from religious treatises such as *The Sincere Convert* (1640) and *The Sound Believer* (1649) to life-writing, a most representative Puritan genre. As a typical Puritan, Shepard believed in the correlation between his soul and the outer world which produced an elaborate sign system conveying God's will.

Educated at Harvard College, Samuel Danforth (1626–1674) was the author of the sermon that became the model for the classic New England jeremiad, "A Brief Recognition of New England's Errand into the Wilderness" (1670). This form of the sermon, which adverse historical conditions such as religious declension, King Philip's War, and the loss of the Massachusetts charter made particularly popular, still stressed the destiny of New Englanders as God's chosen people. Yet, at the same time, it criticized them for their sinful lives and urged them to follow the road to redemption: "The hardships, difficulties, and sufferings which you have exposed yourselves unto that you might dwell in the house of the Lord . . . And shall we now . . . lose that full reward which the Lord hath in his heart and hand to bestow upon us? . . . And do we now repent of our choice and prefer the honors, pleasures, and profits of the world before it? . . . How sadly hath the Lord testified against us because of our loss of our first love." According to Danforth, the Lord was punishing his chosen people for their lapses with "severe drought, . . . great tempests, floods, and sweeping rains that leave no food behind."

A similar providential interpretation of natural occurrences appeared in "captivity narratives." In the *Narrative of the Captivity and Restoration of Mrs. Mary Rowlandson* (1682), Mary Rowlandson (1635–1678) described the eleven weeks she spent as a Native American prisoner. Her narrative displays a broad use of biblical imagery which guides the reader to interpret Rowlandson's experience as part of a providential design. Her captivity is defined as a story of redemption through absolute dependence on God and fittingly ends with the explicit exposition of the teachings Rowlandson derived from her experience: "That we must rely on God Himself, and our own dependence must be upon Him . . . I have learned to look beyond present and smaller troubles and to be quieter under them. As Moses said, 'Stand still and see the salvation of the Lord.'" Rowlandson paralleled her biblical learning with elements of adventure and heroism, a mix that made her narrative one of the most popular pieces during prose of the seventeenth century and the initiator of the genre of "Indian captivities." This genre has proved influential in American literature and has been adapted to fictional form by writers as diverse as James Fenimore Cooper (*The Last of the Mohicans*) and William Faulkner (*Sanctuary*).

When the years of the Founding Fathers began to fade in the memory of the settlers, second- and third-generation Puritans found it necessary to remind their contemporaries of the saintliness of New England's founders. Cotton Mather (1663–1728), who had helped found Yale to contrast Harvard's increasing heterodoxy, best captured the yearning for the glorious beginnings of New England with the epic narrative *Magnalia Christi Americana* (1702). Adopting several literary styles which ranged from church history to sermon, from biography to verse, Mather assigned New England a prominent place in the unfolding of world history. Through his reconstructions of the lives of New England's early saints, such as Winthrop and Bradford, Mather chose not to focus on the increasing dissolution of the Puritan theocracy and orthodoxy. His strategy, on the contrary, was to offer exemplary lives of the potential within each American believer. These saintly lives would serve as models of behavior against the threat of increasing heterodoxy. Often indicted for his self-indulgence and the victim of famous parodies (such as Benjamin Franklin's character Silence Dogood), Mather has been assigned a key role in the formation of American ideology, given his focus on exemplary individuals. Sacvan Bercovitch has defined Mather as the model for what was to become a typical "American self" who unites sacred and secular history and turns private trials into public triumph. The chapter on Bradford in *Magnalia*, for example, presents a series of difficulties against which Bradford emerges triumphant: "Here was Mr. Bradford, in the year 1621, unanimously chosen the governor of the plantation, the difficulties whereof were such, that if he had not been a person of more than ordinary piety, wisdom and courage, he must have sunk under them."

The stereotypical image of austere Puritans suspicious of culture and art is at odds with the abundant production of poetry in seventeenth-century New England. Poetry was conceived as a genre for personal moral uplift. In addition, when poems were made public, they had a didactic function and were instrumental to commemorate notable events. They could also be composed to explain theological doctrines or mourn the death of dear departed ones through elegies. These early pieces of poetry were forgotten throughout the centuries and only became widely available during the nineteenth century. For example, the poems of Edward Taylor (1644–1729) were only partially published in 1939, and a complete edition only became available in 1960. A Harvard graduate, Taylor spent his entire life working as a pastor and a physician in the frontier town of Westfield, Massachusetts. His interest for poetry was lifelong and his production encompassed all poetic genres, including elegies, epic poems (*God's Determination*), and a voluminous book of martyrs (*Metrical History of Christianity*). His most famous poems, however, are the two hundred *Preparatory Meditations*, composed while Taylor was preparing his weekly sermons and celebrating his wonder of the union between man and God. The style of the *Meditations* with its attention to puns and paradoxes reflects Taylor's acquaintance with English metaphysical poetry of John Donne and George Herbert.

The poetry of Anne Bradstreet (1612–1672), which was more appreciated by her contemporaries, included long meditative and philosophical poems, yet modern readers have focused their attention on Bradstreet's unusually realistic portrayals of domestic and family life. Her volume *The Tenth Muse Lately Sprung Up in America* (1650) was the first collection of verse by an American resident to be published and widely read. Bradstreet received an education superior to that of most women of her times and was married to an important magistrate who would also serve as governor of the Massachusetts Bay Colony. Although she shared her father's and her husband's Puritan faith, Bradstreet's relationship with religion was often controversial and she admitted that she was troubled about the truthfulness of the Scriptures. Although she did not overtly challenge male superiority, Bradstreet also argued for the rights of women to pursue their vocations and talents.

The minister Michael Wigglesworth (1631–1705) captured the Puritan imagination with his long poem *The Day of Doom* (1662) which sold eighteen hundred copies the same year of its publication. Composed of 224 eight-line stanzas, the text is as frightening as it is comforting, because it reassures the reader that order will eventually prevail

> ## Puritan Poets
>
> Many New Englanders wrote poetry besides Edward Taylor, Anne Bradstreet, and Michael Wigglesworth. The typical Puritan dichotomy of enthusiasm for the theocratic experiment and warning for its possible failure is expressed in the poems of Thomas Tillam (?–1676), who spent several years in New England, returned to the mother country, and, after the Restoration, moved to Heidelberg in Germany. John Wilson (1588–1667), who was prolific but circulated his poems mainly in manuscript form without publishing them, is particularly known for his funeral elegies. These are based on anagrams of the dead person's name. John Saffin (1626–1710), a merchant also involved in the slave trade, collected about fifty poems in his *Notebook* which vary greatly in theme and style. In the last years of his life, he engaged in a bitter debate with Samuel Sewall over the legitimacy of slavery and the slave trade. Benjamin Tompson (1642–1714) was Cotton Mather's teacher and the author of the epic poems *New England Crisis* (1676) and *New England Tears* (1676), which portrayed the conflict with the Algonquian confederation as a challenge for the devotion of New England's colonists. Settling first in Connecticut and then in Rhode Island in the 1680s, Richard Steere (c. 1643–1721) is the author of *The Daniel Catcher* (1713), an anti-Catholic reply to John Dryden's *Absalom and Achitophel.* Roger Walcott (1679–1767), who rose from humble origins to the role of governor of Connecticut, composed *Poetical Meditations, Being the Improvement of Some Vacant Hours* (1725), an epic poem on the founding of the colony, which is given a mythic character.

in all things with the coming of Christ. The reign of Christ will be eternal and his chosen will reign with him: "there the saints are perfect saints, / and holy ones indeed, / From all the sins that dwelt within / their mortal bodies freed: / Made kings and priests to God through Christ's / dear love transcendency, / There to remain, and there to reign with Him eternally." Wigglesworth's success as a poet compensated his inability to preach and his scarce popularity with his congregation in Malden, Massachusetts, where he lived for fifty years of his life.

During the seventeenth century, New England developed as a Puritan experiment, and its Puritan roots remained firmly established well after orthodox Calvinism came to an end. Its impact can be detected in the works of such diverse writers as Nathaniel Hawthorne and Norman Mailer. Still, as John Conforti has pointed out, "the Puritan era too often has functioned as a New England ur-civilization, invoked across time to explain everything from the region's low homicide rate to the fatalism of its Boston Red Sox fans."[2] The historical and cultural developments of New England hint at both continuities and discontinuities with its Puritan beginnings. Thanks to the original commitment to culture remarked on earlier, New England developed through the centuries important cultural institutions such as universities, newspapers, and lyceums. In addition to the founding of Harvard and Yale, New England had the first newspapers published in colonial America: the *Boston Weekly News-Letter* (1704) and the *New England Courant* (1721). At the end of the eighteenth century, more than a hundred newspapers were published in America, and New England was home to half of them. The Puritan interest in the past also provoked a constant production of historical writings which contributed to make the region reflect on its complex identity. Yet, outlining these Puritan influences on New England cultural history should not blind us to the fact that Puritanism itself was not a single and unified cultural and religious system.

THE EIGHTEENTH CENTURY

The culture of the eighteenth century was marked by the Enlightenment values of rationality and scientific inquiry which tested and challenged the religious dogmas of the previous century. In addition, the political form of representative democracy began to take shape and to replace the Puritan theocracy. Enlightenment writers were committed to these ideals as inherent rights of humankind, and this commitment generated the new literary genre of the political pamphlet, which should communicate the author's idea in a clear and concise manner. Contrary to the new genre, the poetry of this century adopted pompous neoclassical models and tried to apply the rigid conventions of the epic, the satire, and the mock-heroic to American events.

The journey of Benjamin Franklin (1706–1790), a key personality of the American eighteenth century and of the Revolution, from Boston to Philadelphia has been defined as symbolic of the transition of American culture and society from Puritanism to the Enlightenment. Franklin gave material grounding to the rhetoric of Puritanism, sharing its emphasis on regeneration while adopting a crucially different perspective. According to the Puritans, only God's grace could purge the self from evil, but Franklin believed that humankind was perfectly able to make itself good. His *Autobiography* is the applied illustration of the "bold and arduous project of arriving at moral perfection," documented by the famous charts of weeks and days. Franklin starts and ends each day with a self-questioning and an introspection typical of Puritans: "What good shall I do this day?" "What good have I done today?" Franklin turns the fervent Puritan hope for self-transformation into a more secular and quintessentially American form of self-improvement.

Franklin's *Autobiography* and his proverbs in *Poor Richard's Almanack* celebrate the strength of the American middle-class, its quest for progress and scientific knowledge, and its unashamed search for personal wealth. Franklin's own story and maxims honor economic individualism and upward mobility. His autobiography traces Franklin's progress from his low beginnings and his obscure family to his international reputation through his strict work ethic: "I was seen at no places of idle diversion. I never went out a-fishing or shooting; a book, indeed, sometimes debauched me from my work; but that was seldom, snug and gave no scandal." The text provided American literature with its classic statement of the American dream of material success.

The eighteenth century was not only the era of the Enlightenment, but also that of a conservative reaction against its secularized society. The name of Jonathan Edwards (1703–1758), minister of Northampton, Massachusetts, has become synonymous with the movement of the "Great Awakening." Educated at Yale, Edwards served in Northampton until he was dismissed by his congregation and spent the last eight years of his life in the mission church at Stockbridge, where he composed most of his writings. He produced a number of important and complex philosophical treatises and is considered the greatest American theologian and one of the few meaningful American philosophers of the colonial period. Edwards' religious outlook is based on Calvinist doctrine, but takes on personal nuances. His *Personal Narrative* (1739) follows the model of Augustine's *Confessions* but complicates its sequencing of sin, repentance, and peace, presenting a narrator who is always challenging his accomplishments. *A Treatise Concerning the Religious Affections* (1746) analyzes the religious revivals of the Great Awakening. The book had a limited influence at the time of its publication but became a key text for modern philosophers and psychologists of religion, such as William James. More influential was Edwards' *Freedom of the Will* (1754), which was used as a theology textbook at Yale for several decades. In his works, Edwards tried to recapture the original sense of religious commitment, which he considered his contemporaries had lost. To do this, he wanted to act upon the reactions of his congregation, whose members should not only understand his preaching but also be moved by it. In this last aspect, Edwards followed closely the ideas of the English philosopher John Locke (1632–1704), who argued that religious ideas should be apprehended experientially.

A number of New England writers responded to the events of the American Revolution using literature as a medium for political expression. Mercy Otis Warren (1728–1814), who married a member of the Massachusetts House of Representatives, covered in her writings genres as diverse as poetry, drama, history, journalism, and propaganda. She put her literary skills to the service of the American Revolution and was the first female author to produce plays. The three political plays that have been attributed to Warren—*The Adulateur* (1772), *The Defeat* (1773), and *The Group* (1775)—were not performed and therefore were not subject to the Massachusetts law against theater performances. They expose the political corruption of the Royalist administration of Massachusetts and identify the source of all evil in the figure of Governor Thomas Hutchinson, nicknamed "Rapatio." After the Revolution, the Warrens felt progressively uneasy with the politics of the new republican government and retired from active political life, though Mercy continued her political writings with two more plays, *The Sack of Rome* and *The Ladies of Castille*. Included in her volume *Poems, Dramatic and Miscellaneous* (1790), both plays are historical in nature and draw parallels between the historical events they dramatize and the American Revolution. In particular, they reflect on the role of women as writers and political agitators. Warren was also one of the first women to venture in the field of history with her three-volume *History of the Rise, Progress and Termination of the American Revolution* (1805). The work had a long genesis of over twenty-five years and argued that women had a crucial role in obtaining and maintaining liberty.

John Adams (1735–1826), one of the Founding Fathers of the American Republic, was an important Boston revolutionary leader. His political career continued after the Revolution when he became America's first vice-president for two terms (1788 and 1792) and the country's second president in 1796. Adams' political views and career were influenced by the daughter of a wealthy Congregationalist minister, Abigail (1744–1818), whom he married in 1764. Their dynasty would continue to hold a crucial role in American political and intellectual life until the twentieth century. John Adams has been characterized as "impelled by a frantic desire for affluence and fame."[3] His *Diary and Autobiography* recorded his early years as a practicing lawyer. These reveal his contemptuous attitude toward his political opponents, whom he dismissed as forces of ignorance or as inept aristocrats. Adams expressed his discomfort for the unpopular Stamp Act with his *Dissertation on the Canon and Feudal Law*, a collection of letters addressed to fellow lawyers. He exposed the Act as an effort to introduce "feudal inequalities" in America. These letters, together with those included in *Novanglus* (1775), established the heart of American revolutionary theory, arguing for the rights of the people to be taxed only with their consent.

Adams' postrevolutionary writings such as *Defence of the Constitution of Government of the United States* (1787–1789) and *Discourses on Davila* (1790) were sometimes received with less enthusiasm than his prerevolutionary works and showed problematic aspects of Adams' conservatism. Adams' vision of a system based on the separation of powers and on checks and balances was eventually incorporated in the American republic. Yet, his assertion that social and economic inequalities were an inevitable result of human nature and private property seemed to counter the typical American faith in upward social mobility. His failure to be reelected in 1800 frustrated Adams and persuaded him that Americans had not given him credit for his commitment to the country. From his retirement in Massachusetts, Adams composed his *Autobiography* but also exchanged interesting letters with Thomas Jefferson, the man who had defeated him in the presidential election and who died the very same day that Adams did.

In the dialogue between the two politicians, one can observe how New England and the South gave rise to two different types of republicanism. The Jeffersonian variant was more secular and individually oriented, thus valuing personal opportunity and individual rights. On the other hand, New England republicanism was more religious and communal in character. Its roots must be looked for not only in Roman and Greek culture, but also in Puritanism:

> the "classical" republicanism of the Revolutionary era was . . . imbued with Puritanism, the righteous rhetoric of the jeremiad, for example, audible in the morally charged vocabulary of virtue. New England's moralistic republicanism installed religious piety as the taproot of virtue. In short, New Englanders Puritanized republicanism, espousing an ideology that was morally accented by the pieties of their religious heritage. But New England's Revolutionary leaders also republicanized Puritan history. They reimagined the founders of the region as the new nation's preeminent proto-republicans who had resisted an earlier English assault on civil liberty. Moreover, Revolutionary New Englanders projected their region's sense of chosenness onto the new nation. Independence from the corrupt mother country confirmed *America's* covenanted relationship with God as a republican New Israel, a redoubt of liberty and virtue in a fallen world that now embraced England.[4]

The Revolution and the process of building a nation projected New Englanders into the national arena, making them increasingly aware of their regional difference. John Adams summarized this feeling of difference and superiority when he remarked in 1775: "The characters of gentlemen in the four New England colonies, differ as much from those in others, as that of the common people differs; that is, as much as several distinct nations almost. . . . Gentlemen, men of sense or any kind of education, in the other colonies, are much fewer in proportion than in New England."

This feeling of superiority and strong sense of regional belonging is also echoed in the geographical writings of Jedidiah Morse (1761–1826), often described as the "father of American geography." Morse was a minister well read in Puritanism and thus constituted an important link between the earlier founders of regional identity and the republican thought of the eighteenth century. His geography textbooks represent New England as the only homogeneous cultural region in the newly independent America: "A nation within a nation, New England's cultural coherence derived from the homogeneity of its people, a sacred history, and shared habits, customs, and institutions broadly diffused across the region from their original hearths in Connecticut and Massachusetts. Morse's texts exalted New England as the republic's republic, a model for the rest of the Union."[5] In widely read books such as *The American Geography* (1789), *The American Universal Geography* (1793), *The American Gazeteer* (1797), and *A Compendious History of New England* (1804), New England emerged as the guide to the nation, as the land of industry, temperance, and frugality, immune to the temptations of luxury. Morse idealized the small towns that made up New England and appointed Boston as the capital of the whole region, although, because its historical record was unblemished by witch-hunt trials, he preferred Connecticut to Massachusetts as the center of republican virtue.

Timothy Dwight (1752–1817) came from a Puritan background, being the grandson of Jonathan Edwards. Born in Northampton, Massachusetts, Dwight became a prominent cultural leader, both because of his production covering fictional and nonfictional genres and because of the institutional roles he had during his lifetime. He became president of Yale College in 1795, where he had previously studied for a B.A. and an M.A., and held office for twenty-two years. Because of his autocratic ways, he was nicknamed "Pope Dwight." During his time as a student, Dwight was a member of the literary group of the "Connecticut Wits" (or "Hartford Wits") which included Joel Barlow (1754–1812), John Trumbull (1750–1831), and David Humphreys (1752–1818), along with Noah Webster (1758–1843) and Lemuel Hopkins (1750–1801). Conservative at heart, these poets criticized liberal personalities and attitudes in their satirical verses modeled after Samuel Butler's *Hudibras* and Alexander Pope's *Dunciad*. Their most ambitious work was *The Anarchiad: A Poem on the Restoration of Chaos and Substantial Night* (1786), a mock epic targeting the states that were too slow in ratifying the Constitution. Dwight's early poems comprised the biblical epic "The Conquest of Canaan" (1785) and the satirical narrative "The Triumph of Infidelity" (1788). "The Triumph" is ironically dedicated to the French *philosophe* Voltaire and stages a confrontation between Satan and Jonathan Edwards. In 1794, Dwight published "Greenfield Hill," dedicated to Vice President John Adams, a long pastoral poem which celebrated the virtues of Connecticut. Dwight's descriptions of the beautiful scenery also have a moral and social significance. The region is presented as an American utopia, which is favorably compared to European corruption: "America's bright realms arose to view, / And the old world rejoic'd to see the new."

Dwight also documented his extensive travels with the collection of notebooks *Travels in New England and New York* (1821–1822), which offer the same vision of "Greenfield Hill." John Conforti has aptly described *Travels* as "a promotional tract" where "Dwight labors to persuade his readers, and himself, that New England will extend its republican ways and abide, as he announces at the beginning of the book, as 'that part of the American republic in which its strength is principally found.'"[6]

Just like Dwight, Joel Barlow aspired to write the great American epic and wrote in that mode such poems as *Prospect of Peace* (1778), *The Vision of Columbus* (1787), and *The Columbiad* (1807). Barlow combined his literary work with his political and diplomatic career which, because of his acquaintance with Thomas Paine, Mary Wollstonecraft, and Thomas Jefferson, progressively shifted from the conservatism of his Yale years to the religious liberalism typical of the century: "The United States is not a Christian nation any more than it is a Jewish or a Mohammedan nation." Barlow was the founder of the weekly *American Mercury* in 1784 and assisted the publication of Paine's *The Age of Reason* (1794). He supported the French Revolution, but condemned the Reign of Terror and was American consul to Algiers from 1795 to 1797. In 1811, President James Madison sent Barlow to France as minister plenipotentiary to negotiate a treaty with Napoleon. Barlow's final poem, *Advice to a Raven in Russia* (1812), was written after witnessing Napoleon's disastrous Russian campaign.

After graduating from Yale, John Trumbull became a lawyer and, after practicing in Boston, moved to Connecticut where he became state attorney and judge of the superior court. His most famous poem was "M Fingal," from the name of its central character, a satire which describes the conflict between loyalists and patriots during the Revolution:

> When Yankies, skill'd in martial rule,
> First put the British troops to school;
> Instructed them in warlike trade,
> And new maneuvers of parade,
> The true war-dance of Yankee reels,
> And manual exercise of heels;
> Made them give up, like saints complete,
> The arm of flesh, and trust the feet,
> And work, like Christians undissembling,
> Salvation out, by fear and trembling;
> Taught Percy fashionable races,
> And modern modes of Chevy-Chases:
> From Boston, in his best array,
> Great 'Squire M'Fingal took his way,
> And graced with ensigns of renown,
> Steer'd homeward to his native town.

First appearing in 1775, the poem had three editions during the war and was extremely successful for decades afterward.

Born in Derby, Massachusetts, David Humphreys graduated from Yale and joined the army at the beginning of the Revolutionary War in 1776, becoming a colonel and aide-de-camp to General Washington four years later. After the war, he pursued a diplomatic career, traveling abroad with Franklin, Adams, and Jefferson, and was then appointed minister to Lisbon and Madrid. He was a prolific poet as well, producing patriotic and didactic texts as the very titles show: "Elegy on the Burning of Fairfield in Connecticut," written a few months after the British had burned the town of Fairfield in 1779. He also wrote "A Poem on the Future Glory of the United States of America," "A Poem on the Happiness of America," "A Poem on Industry," and "Ode to Washington."

Lemuel Hopkins was one of the most influential physicians of his time and the founder of the Medical Society of Connecticut. After his association with the "Hartford Wits" and the composition of *The Anarchiad*, Hopkins wrote parts of the series of satirical papers called "The Echo" and "The Political Greenhouse," and contributed also to "The Guillotine." He was also a satirical journalist and wrote the poem "The Hypocrite's Hope" and the elegy "The Victim of a Cancer Quack."

Eighteenth-century women poets were often hampered by rigidly defined gender roles, confining them to the domestic sphere, and those who contravened such roles were viewed with suspicion. Though mainly written by wealthy and middle-class white women, these poems add an important dimension to our understanding of colonial life. Jane Coleman Turell (1708–1735) of Boston, for example, was a prolific writer of poems, letters, and diaries. Yet, like many eighteenth-century women, she could not publish her manuscripts during her lifetime and the only surviving ones are those published in the posthumous *Some Memoirs of the Life and Death of Mrs. Jane Turell*.

Sarah Wentworth Morton (1759–1846) was part of a wealthy Boston merchant family and received an unusually complete education. Her house became an important literary circle, where Morton initially circulated her manuscripts without publishing them until 1790. In that year, she published the epic poem *Ouâbi: or the Virtues of Nature. An Indian Tale in Four Cantos*, about an interracial romance on the Illinois frontier. Yet, as her career developed, she was struck by tragedy. Her sister had an affair with Sarah's husband and committed suicide. The scandal was the basis for what is considered the first American novel, *The Power of Sympathy* (1789) by William Hill Brown. Morton successively lost three of her five children and only published another book, *My Mind and Its Thoughts* (1823).

Born in Gloucester, Massachusetts, in a respected family, Judith Sargent Murray (1751–1820) was the author of poems, essays, plays, and even a brief novel, *The Story of Margaretta*. Her works addressed the most discussed and controversial American topics of her era such as female equality, literary nationalism, the federalist system of government, and religious universalism. Murray held that American literature should focus on American scenes and events and break away from British traditions. Her essays mainly came out in two parallel series: *The Repository* (religious themes) and *The Gleaner* which appeared in the *Massachusetts Magazine* from 1792 to 1794. Murray indissolubly linked the independence of America to the independence of women: the new republic should grant equal opportunity to all its citizens. In the appendix to her work *The Equality of the Sexes* (1792) she wrote:

Yes, ye lordly, ye haughty sex, our souls are by nature equal to yours; the same breath of God animates, enlivens, and invigorates us; and that we are not fallen lower than yourselves, let those witness who have greatly towered above the various discouragements by which they have been so heavily oppressed; and though I an unacquainted with the list of celebrated characters on either side, yet from the observations I have made in the contracted circle in which I have moved, I dare confidently believe, that from the commencement of time to the present day, there hath been as many females, as males, who, by the mere force of natural powers, have merited the crown of applause; who thus unassisted, have seized the wreath of fame.

Hannah Webster Foster (1758–1840), the daughter of a wealthy Massachusetts merchant, was the author of the successful epistolary novel *The Coquette; or, The History of Eliza Wharton* (1797), which described the seduction and consequent doom of the title character by the rake Peter Sanford. In spite of its success, the book failed to make Foster famous because it was published anonymously. A year later, Foster published *The Boarding School; or, Lessons of a Preceptress to Her Pupils* (1798), a didactic work on female education. After these two books, she devoted herself full-time to journalism. Like Foster, Susanna Haswell Rowson (1762–1824) was the author of one of the most successful novels of the 1790s, *Charlotte Temple*, which was first published in London in 1791 as *Charlotte, A Tale of Truth* and had its first American edition in 1794. The book went through over two hundred editions and was widely read. As in *The Coquette*, the story depicts the seduction and the following fall of its female heroine. Rowson was also an actress, but she eventually gave up this profession and established a very successful school, Mrs. Rowson's Young Ladies' Academy, in Boston. She became a celebrated educator and a regular columnist for *Boston Weekly Magazine*.

The African Americans Lucy Terry (1730–1821) and Phillis Wheatley (1753–1784) represent important exceptions in the literary panorama of eighteenth-century women writers. Terry was born in Africa and was taken by slave traders to Rhode Island at a very young age. She lived in Deerfield, Massachusetts, where she was a slave until her marriage with a free black in 1756. In 1764, the couple settled in Vermont. Terry's only surviving poem, "Bars Fight" (1746), is the earliest existing poem by an African American and commemorates the death of white pioneers in a fight with natives in 1746. Sold as a slave at the South Boston market, Wheatley received her education from the family who owned her. The treatment she was given differed greatly from that reserved to other slaves. Wheatley was very precocious: in 1767, when she was only thirteen or fourteen years old, she published her first verses in a Newport newspaper. Wheatley was the first African American to publish a volume of poems. Rejected in America on racial grounds, her poems appeared in London in 1773 with the title *Poems on Various Subjects, Religious and Moral*. The poem "On Being Brought from Africa to America" clearly indicts racism: "Some view our sable race with scornful eye. / Their color is a diabolic dye. / Remember, Christians, Negroes, black as Cain, / May be refined, and join the angelic train." Yet, Wheatley's career could not fulfill its early promise: she died in poverty and was buried in an unmarked grave. She is best known for her religious texts, but her production covered different themes, and in her posthumously published letters, she displayed a deep sense of her African roots. Wheatley was rejected by the white literary establishment, although she followed the neoclassical standards of the times and her verses were forgotten until Massachusetts abolitionists reprinted them in the 1830s.

Jupiter Hammon (1711–1806?), too, was born into slavery on Long Island, and was later taken to Stamford and then to Hartford, Connecticut. There Hammon published verses as well as "An Essay on Ten Virgins," advertised in *The Connecticut Courant* in 1779. Hammon's seven surviving works are four poems and three prose tracts. His most widely circulated work is "An Address to the Negroes in the State of New York" (1787), which condemned slavery. Hammon's works show consciousness of the increasing political significance of blacks in the period and argue for black moral and social autonomy, though his key theme was Christian redemption.

Samson Occom (1723–1792) was the son of Joshua Tomacham and Sarah, thought to be a descendant of the famous Mohegan chief, Uncas. He studied in Lebanon, Connecticut, for four years under the supervision of Reverend Eleazar Wheelock and subsequently worked as a preacher with the Native Americans in New England. Beset by financial trouble throughout his life, Occom published only two works: the extremely successful *Sermon Preached by Samson Occom, . . . at the Execution of Moses Paul* (1772) and *Collection of Hymns and Spiritual Songs* (1774).

Until the American Revolution, drama did not enjoy popularity in New England. As we have seen, some New England authors wrote plays, but they were never represented and were only intended for reading. Both Puritanism and Quakerism openly disapproved of theaters. Yet, after Independence from Britain, the development of an American dramatic tradition became another way to affirm national identity so that antidrama bans were lifted. Royall Tyler (1757–1826) was one of the first playwrights to emerge with his comedy *The Contrast*, which was represented in 1787 and was an immediate hit. The Bostonian Tyler earned degrees from both Harvard and Yale and, after a career as a lawyer, he was a lecturer of law at the University of Vermont and became chief justice of the Supreme Court of Vermont. *The Contrast* was modeled after Richard Brinsley Sheridan's *The School for Scandal* (1777) and contrasts the honest ways of Captain Manly, a revolutionary hero, and Jonathan, his humble servant, with the aping of British customs on the part of fashionable but corrupt members of New York's high society. Jonathan stands as the first American dramatic representation of the Yankee. After the success of *The Contrast*, Tyler continued to write plays, satires, and also a picaresque novel, *The Algerine Captive* (1797).

THE NINETEENTH CENTURY

The nineteenth century witnessed an increase in the appeals for the development of a national literature, and the appearance of such literary masterpieces as Nathaniel Hawthorne's *The Scarlet Letter* (1850) and *The House of the Seven Gables* (1851), Herman Melville's *Moby Dick* (1851) and *Pierre* (1852), and Walt Whitman's *Leaves of Grass* (1855) prompted critics to talk about an American Renaissance. As F. O. Mathiessen writes at the beginning of his famous critical study *American Renaissance*, although "it may not seem precisely accurate to refer to our mid-nineteenth century as a *re-birth*," this was how the writers themselves perceived what was happening. "Not," Mathiessen continues, "as a rebirth of values that had existed previously in America, but as America's way of producing a renaissance, by

Mark Twain (Samuel Clemens, 1835–1910) made Hartford, Connecticut, his home from the 1870s to the 1890s. Courtesy Library of Congress.

coming to its first maturity and affirming its rightful heritage in the whole expanse of art and culture."[7] Nineteenth-century writers "felt that it was incumbent upon their generation to give fulfillment to the potentialities freed by the Revolution, to provide a culture commensurate with America's political opportunity."[8]

Although born in Missouri, Mark Twain (Samuel Clemens, 1835–1910) lived in Hartford, Connecticut, from the 1870s to the 1890s, which were central years both in his writing career and in his involvement with the infamous Paige Typesetter, the project that caused his bankruptcy in 1894. During these years Twain abandoned his early successful career as a journalist to become a full-time fiction writer. His prolific New England production included the satire *The Gilded Age* and the extremely successful *The Adventures of Tom Sawyer* (1876), *The Prince and the Pauper* (1882), and *Adventures of Huckleberry Finn* (1884), the story of Huck, a teenaged misfit who rejects the oppressive teachings of the Widow Douglas and floats on a raft down the Mississippi River with an escaping slave, Jim: "After supper she got out her book and learned me about Moses and the Bulrushers, and I was in a sweat to find out all about him; but by and by she let it out that Moses had been dead a considerable long time; so then I didn't care no more about him, because I don't take no stock in dead people." According to Hemingway, the publication of *Huck Finn* marked the beginning of modern American literature, but the book has also raised endless controversies on Twain's representation of race. These New England works further established Twain's international reputation, which led him to the then unusual move to copyright his pseudonym and his face. After the failure of the Paige Typesetter, Twain left New England to settle down in Europe. In 1907 he returned to Connecticut, where he died in 1910.

Transcendentalism

The most prominent New England cultural movement of the nineteenth century was certainly Transcendentalism. Roughly corresponding to European Romanticism and sharing the same reaction against the Enlightenment, the movement had among its leading intellectuals Ralph Waldo Emerson (1803–1882), Henry David Thoreau (1817–1862), Margaret Fuller (1810–1850), the educator Bronson Alcott (1799–1888), the preachers Theodore Parker (1810–1860) and William Henry Channing (1780–1842), and the journalist and editor George Ripley (1802–1880). Although deeply rooted in New England and particularly in

Boston, these figures were also cosmopolitan and acquainted with both Western and non-Western sources. Their influence can be traced in various artistic and philosophical fields and their ideas were disseminated through their works as well as their magazine *The Dial*. The term Transcendentalism derived from Immanuel Kant's philosophy and refers to his concept that what we know about God and the world does not come from our senses, but from the transcendental and intuitive categories in our minds. Although not primarily philosophers themselves, Transcendentalists also borrowed from other idealistic philosophical traditions, such as Platonism and Neoplatonism, and from Romantic authors such as Carlyle and Coleridge. In particular, they opposed Coleridge's view of the human mind as creative to Locke's theory of the mind as a passive receiver of impressions. The birth of Transcendentalism was stimulated by a quarrel in the Unitarian churches of Boston, and Transcendentalist texts always reveal a polemical edge. While Unitarian ministers claimed that God's divinity can be proven empirically by the miracles recorded in the Gospels, Transcendentalists argued that Christian faith depended on the believer's inner experience of Christ's teachings. It would be wrong, however, to assume that the movement was homogeneous and only confined to the religious sphere. Actually, the most enduring legacy of Transcendentalism can be detected in literature and in the Transcendentalist portrayal of the poet as a genius dismissive of traditional rules and conventions. Transcendentalists conceived the figure of the poet as favoring personal expressions, organic forms as well as metaphorical and evocative language and imagery.

Born in Boston, Ralph Waldo Emerson lost his father at a very early age. Although his childhood was marked by poverty, he was encouraged in pursuing his studies by his aunt Mary Moody. He first attended Boston Public Latin School and then Harvard on a scholarship from 1817 to 1821. After graduating, he started a career as a teacher, but he soon changed his mind and turned to the study of theology. In 1829, he became junior pastor of Boston's Second Church. Yet, Emerson became so skeptical about religious dogmas and sacraments that he left the ministry in 1832. Because of his literary appeal to exploit unexplored American materials and themes ("We have listened too long to the courtly muses of Europe," he wrote in *The American Scholar*), Emerson is widely considered the founding father of American literature.

Emerson's intellectual efforts were initially aimed at reaching freedom of thought in the areas of philosophy, culture, and religion. This is clear in Emerson's three important declarations of the 1830s: *Nature*, published anonymously in 1836, *The American Scholar* (1837), often described as "the American intellectual declaration of independence," and *The Divinity School Address* (1838), which caused him to be barred from speaking at Harvard until after the Civil War. In 1841, Emerson published the collection *Essays, First Series*, which was followed by *Essays, Second Series* (1844). These two volumes contain his most famous essays such as "Self-Reliance" and "Experience." As he became a celebrated prose writer, Emerson shifted from philosophical prose to social observation with the volumes *Representative Men* (1850), *English Traits* (1856), and *The Conduct of Life* (1860). The main concern of these works was to illustrate the lives of important men in democratic society, offering them as a model of behavior.

Henry David Thoreau lived in Concord all his life except for brief periods of time. He became part of the American literary canon only posthumously in the

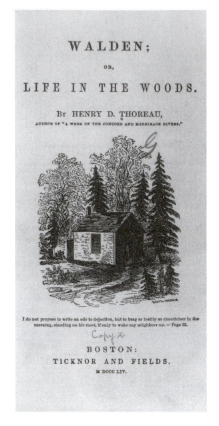

WALDEN;

OR,

LIFE IN THE WOODS.

By HENRY D. THOREAU,

AUTHOR OF "A WEEK ON THE CONCORD AND MERRIMACK RIVERS."

I do not propose to write an ode to dejection, but to brag as lustily as chanticleer in the morning, standing on his roost, if only to wake my neighbours up. — Page 92.

BOSTON:

TICKNOR AND FIELDS.

M DCCC LIV.

Title page of Henry D. Thoreau's *Walden; or, Life in the Woods*, 1854, showing Thoreau's hut at Walden Pond, Massachusetts. Courtesy Library of Congress.

first decades of the twentieth century: during his lifetime, he was considered little more than a minor disciple of Emerson. Thoreau's name represents for many the ultimate embodiment of American individualism, often conceived as a reaction against modernity and a plea for a return to simple living. He has been hailed as an icon from such different currents of thought as laissez faire capitalism (for his critique of state's intervention), pacifism, civil rights, and environmentalism. Queer theorists have also started to detect homoerotic themes and situations in his prose.

After graduating from Harvard in 1837, Thoreau followed an unusual self-education for the rest of his life, including the reading of material not so well-known in America at the time, such as Asian philosophies and religions. However, Thoreau was not the recluse that the legend has passed on to us. He was deeply involved with the activities of the Transcendentalists who had one of their main centers in Concord. His first essay, "Resistance to Civil Government" (1848), or "Civil Disobedience," as it was called after his premature death at forty-four years of age, remains his best-known and most widely disseminated work. It influenced thinkers such as Mahatma Gandhi and Martin Luther King. "Civil Disobedience," like "Slavery in Massachusetts" (1854) and three essays on John Brown, critiques slavery and adopts a radical abolitionist perspective, influenced by William Lloyd Garrison. Refusing to pay taxes to a government complicit with slavery, Thoreau argued, was just. In addition to several other essays, Thoreau wrote two books, *A Week on the Concord and Merrimack Rivers* (1849), an account of a boating trip taken with his brother, and *Walden* (1854), a report of one year spent by the author in a cabin by Walden Pond. *Walden* does not argue that everyone should live as a hermit in the woods, but leads readers to reflect on their way of living and to challenge it.

Margaret Fuller was a leading figure in the Transcendentalist group, and her example was crucial for many women writers from Lydia Maria Child to Emily Dickinson, from Louisa May Alcott to Edith Wharton. Fuller's career began with the translations of German texts and continued with the editorship of *The Dial*. On the Transcendentalist journal she published the controversial protofeminist essay "The Great Lawsuit; Man vs. Men, Woman vs. Women," which she then expanded into the book *Woman in the Nineteenth Century* (1844). She also wrote important articles for Horace Greeley's *New York Daily Tribune*. Through her book and her articles, Fuller gained the reputation of being an outspoken and daring intellectual who, had she not died in a shipwreck while returning to the United States from Italy, would have challenged many literary and social orthodoxies of the era. There seems to be an obsession with Fuller in many male writers of the nineteenth century, such as in the writings of Nathaniel Hawthorne, Herman Melville, Walt Whitman, Edgar Allan Poe, and Henry James.

Nathaniel Hawthorne (1804–1864) was linked to the Transcendentalist movement through the Brook Farm experiment in which he took part for half a year in 1841. The utopian community of Brook Farm, led by George Ripley, was an effort to translate the Transcendentalists' ideas into practice and was located in West Roxbury, Massachusetts. Hawthorne would later dramatize this experience in his third novel, *The Blithedale Romance* (1852). A descendant of Puritan immigrants and a Salem judge at the infamous witchcraft trials, Hawthorne has been considered one of the most important American writers by different generations of scholars in spite of their different critical agendas. He continues to hold a central position in the American literary canon. His career was split between literature and politics because Hawthorne found it difficult to support himself by writing alone. He was forced to take on institutional roles such as those of measurer in the Boston customhouse, surveyor of the Salem customhouse, consul to Liverpool (1853–1857), and Pierce's biographer. He never liked the routine and the constraints that these political appointments put on his life and literary production. He disliked the materialism of his own society and was besieged by self-doubt that ultimately silenced him. Both in his romances and in his short-stories, Hawthorne dealt with psychological themes such as the consequences of pride and guilt, the influence of the Puritan past on the present, the ineffectiveness of social reform, and the perpetual presence of sin in human lives.

Through *The Scarlet Letter* (1850), his first novel, Hawthorne confronts both America's Puritan past and its present. The preface to the novel, "The Custom-House," is a biographical account of Hawthorne's experience as surveyor and condemns officials who plotted against the author leading to his dismissal. Against the drab and bureaucratic background of the customhouse, Hawthorne presents himself as a superior artist endowed with integrity and honesty. This draws a clear parallel with the experience of Hester, the heroine of the novel, and her conflict with Puritan hypocrisy. The introductory piece also codifies the main characteristic of the romance genre in which Hawthorne would excel. Dealing with ancestral guilt is also the theme of Hawthorne's second novel, *The House of the Seven Gables* (1851), written during his period of friendship with Herman Melville (1819–1891), who would praise "Hawthorne's power of blackness" and dedicate to him his literary masterpiece, *Moby Dick*. The preface of this second work too returns to the difference between novel and romance, assigning to the romance writer "a right to present that truth under circumstances, to a great extent, of the writer's own choosing or creation. If he think fit, also, he may so manage his atmospherical medium as to bring out or mellow the lights and deepen and enrich the shadows of the picture. He will be wise, no doubt, to make a very moderate use of the privileges here stated, and, especially, to mingle the Marvelous rather as a slight, delicate, and evanescent flavor, than as any portion of the actual substance of the dish offered to the public. He can hardly be said, however, to commit a literary crime even if he disregard this caution." *The Marble Faun* (1860) was the last of Hawthorne's romances, composed while he was living in Italy. He was never able to finish the other several literary projects he was working on and, in his later years, held political views on slavery and the South that ran counter to the prevailing sentiment in Northern states.

Critics have increasingly become interested in how Hawthorne dramatized gender conflicts of his own times and represented life within the domestic sphere. Hawthorne responded to his own anxieties over powerful women through stories such as "Rapaccini's Daughter" (1844), where the need to control women's sexuality and imagination becomes an obsession for the male characters. Such psychological tensions are the result of the division between male and female spheres in nineteenth-century American society. In his four novels, women, and particularly Zenobia in *The Blithedale Romance*, loosely based on Margaret Fuller, are described as unfeminine due to their commitment to art or politics. On the other hand, Hawthorne also challenged the norm of femininity that he seemed to propose as a model. In *The House of Seven Gables*, the innocent Phoebe leads the radical Holgrave to give up his reformist intents, while in *The Marble Faun* it is the unconventional Miriam who takes center-stage.

While nineteenth-century authors like Louisa May Alcott wrote of the concerns of the middle class, working-class women in Lowell, Massachusetts, created an outlet for their own literary productions in *The Lowell Offering*, "a repository of original articles, written by 'factory girls.'" Courtesy Lowell National Historical Park.

Women Writers

The domestic sphere was also at the center of the writings of many women writers from New England. Louisa May Alcott (1832–1888), the daughter of the educator and philosopher Bronson Alcott, grew up in Concord, Massachusetts, where her family was part of the Transcendentalist circle. Until the 1970s feminist revival, Alcott's unyielding fame was largely due to the *Little Women* trilogy. Yet, the growth of the women's movement led to the publication of material that she had published anonymously in sensational weekly magazines and of previously little-known works by her, such as the adult novels *Moods* (1864) and *Work* (1873). These texts balance and complement the image of Alcott from *Little Women* as a domestic feminist who thought it the mission of cultured women to encourage the renewal of society through their roles of mothers and wives. Focusing on *Moods*, which candidly treats the theme of infidelity and exposes social constraints that force women to choose marriage as the only possible career, literary critics have shed light on a different Alcott, one who was critical of the gender restrictions of Victorian America.

Lydia Maria Child (1802–1880) was born in Medford, Massachusetts, and was praised in 1833 by the *North American Review* as America's most distinguished female writer. That same year, Child also published *An Appeal in Favor of That Class of Americans Called Africans* which put her at the vanguard of the American abolitionist movement. In her prolific career, Child published fifty-eight books ranging from adult and children's fiction to domestic manuals, from treatises on women's and Native Americans' rights to slavery. She also edited the *National Antislavery Standard* from 1841 to 1843. Child's domestic manuals responded to the myth of the male Yankee that was pervasive in New England culture of the nineteenth century. As Conforti points out, "Child popularized the image of the matriarchal Yankee, who assumed the burden of safeguarding the American character from its anti-republican excesses. She insisted that . . . the national character would be formed in the home, not simply . . . in the marketplace."[9]

Child was not, however, exempt from criticism. Her first novel, *Hobomok* (1824), was attacked for its portrayal of a relationship between a Puritan woman and a Native American man. Her active abolitionism initially prompted her to discourage antislavery organizations campaigning also for women's rights: their only goal should be the abolition of slavery, and advocating other causes could harm their main purpose. Yet, as she grew older, she increasingly resented women's inferior role in society and she once complained in a letter that hers was a man's heart trapped within a woman's fate.

Like Child, Harriet Beecher Stowe (1811–1896), born in Connecticut, produced an incredibly varied body of texts: historical romances, novels of manners, regional sketches, household manuals, children's stories, poetry, and essays on women's rights and religion. She is most controversially remembered for her abolitionist writings, in particular for the novel *Uncle Tom's Cabin* (1852), which contrasts an orderly New England with an exotic and disorienting South. Over the decades, a number of debates have characterized Stowe as a racist (the contemporary description of a subservient African American as an Uncle Tom derives from imprecise popular adaptations of her novel), as a passionate abolitionist, as an advocate of domesticity, as a sentimental writer. We should probably reconsider her works not as offering a single perspective but as embodying their century's ambivalences toward the burning issues of class, race, and gender. While Stowe was able to challenge through her sentimental style the distance between whites and blacks that was one of the very assumptions that made slavery possible, she also pushed her predominantly white readers to consider their own values as universal, thus dismissing the importance of the black experience. In addition, her radical claims for emancipation were based partly on racialist theories.

New England abolitionism was also called into question by African American writers. The African American writer Harriet Wilson (1808–c. 1870) has finally surfaced from decades of neglect and her novel *Our Nig, or Sketches from the Life of a Free Black, In a Two-Story White House, North. Showing that Slavery's*

Harriet Beecher Stowe (1811–1896) was born in Connecticut and produced an extremely varied body of texts. Courtesy Thoemmes.

311

Shadow Fall Even There (1859), originally published anonymously, offers an extremely rare insight into the treatment of African American women in the Antebellum North and into their precarious existences, constantly endangered by the Fugitive Slave Act (1850). Probably born in New Hampshire in the 1820s, Harriet, whose maiden name was Adams, spent her childhood working as an indentured servant for the Haywards, a farming family living near Milford, who, according to historical research, had strong abolitionist connections and may have considered themselves to be abolitionists. This experience is at the base of the plot of *Our Nig*, the first novel to be written by an African American woman, set in the slave-free state of Massachussetts, where the main character Frado (diminutive for Alfrado, also referred to as "Our Nig") is deserted by her white mother after the death of her black father and becomes an indentured servant for the Bellomonts who treat her cruelly. At eighteen, in a turn which again closely parallels Wilson's own life, Frado leaves the Bellomonts and marries a young African American who deserts her after she has given birth to a child. Her following impoverishment forces her to be separated from the child. The writing of the book is Frado's attempt to regain her child by earning enough money to recover him from charitable maintenance.

The ending of the story sees Frado concentrated "on her steadfast purpose of elevating herself," always threatened by slave-hunting kidnappers and "maltreated by professed abolitionists, who didn't want slaves at the South nor niggers in their own houses, North." Coming at the end of the novel, this sentence is a powerful indictment both of the Fugitive Slave Act, which gave the pretext to unscrupulous slave hunters to capture any African American found in the North accusing them to be fugitives, and of Northern hypocrisy. It points to how deep-rooted the phenomenon of racism really was even in the North, compromising the conduct of supposed abolitionists. The sufferance Frado has to endure with the Bellomonts exposes African American oppression in the Antebellum North, where domestic service was the main form of employment for free blacks, and in particular for women. The very fact that Wilson states in her preface that she has "purposely omitted what would most provoke shame in our good anti-slavery friends at home" may signify that she has omitted any reference to possible abolitionist sympathies of the Bellomonts, modeled on the abolitionist Haywards. *Our Nig* focuses on the growing awareness of a girl made into a servant who turns into a woman, throwing light on the different situation of African American women in a racist context. New England and the South, so distant in the abolitionist narratives of Child and Stowe, are suddenly linked by Wilson's novel.

The other powerful contesting voice of New England's civilizing mission is that of the Native American William Apess (1798–?), who was born near Colrain, Massachusetts, a descendant of the Pequot tribe. Apess rewrote the history of the region adopting a Native American point of view that subverted the standard roles usually assigned to whites and Native Americans in New England narratives. Paralleling Wilson's experience, Apess' autobiography *A Son of the Forest* (1829) documents his indenture to white families, where he was forced to internalize the whites' stereotypical views of Native Americans as deceitful and violent, and was thus terrified by his own people. Apess charges that all past accounts of New England's providential mission in American history do not acknowledge the role of whites as aggressors and destroyers of Native American life. The text timely appeared during the debate over the Indian Removal Act (1830), which allowed the government to confiscate Native Americans' lands east of the Mississippi, in Indian Territory and other areas that were advantageous for white settlement. The same commitment for Native American rights prompted Apess to describe the Mashpee struggle to retain self-government in *Indian Nullification of the Unconstitutional Laws of Massachusetts, Relative to the Marshpee [sic] Tribe* (1835), one of the most powerful pieces of Native American protest literature. Apess' contact with this tribe, which being a mixture of Native American, white, and black was subjected to considerable white prejudice, and their fight for civil and political rights made him an advocate of their cause. Apess became a spokesman for the tribe and publicized their case in the Boston press. His efforts, which persuaded the abolitionist William Lloyd Garrison (1805–1879) to advocate Mashpee rights in his Boston newspaper *The Liberator*, led to one of the few Native American victories in the 1830s. Apess' final work, *Eulogy on King Philip* (1836), originally delivered as a series of lectures in Boston, is a study of white-native relations in seventeenth- and eighteenth-century New England. Apess' works, like Wilson's, eventually faded into obscurity and were not recovered and republished until the 1990s.

Emily Dickinson (1830–1886) is the nineteenth-century New England poet who left the most enduring legacy on American literature, modernizing the literary conventions of the poetic genre. Born in Amherst, Massachusetts, into a wealthy family, Dickinson lived most of her life in her parents' house, although the image of recluse that is conventionally attached to her is far from reality. Her family was a prominent and influential one both at town and state levels, so that the house where Emily lived was constantly visited by people. Only ten of her numerous poems were published during Dickinson's lifetime and her complete poems were not published until the 1950s.

According to Delbanco, Dickinson was endowed with limitless imagination. According to the same critic, she had a crucial role in the revision of the cultural and religious heritage of New England:

> [N]o poet surpassed the precision and power with which she expressed what is conventionally called the nineteenth century "loss of faith"—as a vast gap opened between the old religious platitudes New Englanders still heard in their churches and the new universe of impersonal forces that science was beginning to disclose.[10]

In her poetry as well as in her life, Dickinson refused to accept orthodox religious beliefs. She did not accept pain as the just consequence of original sin or as a reality to be transcended, but she defined it as an inescapable factor of human life: "For each ecstatic instant / We must an anguish pay / In keen and quivering ratio / To the ecstasy." Some of her poems and her letters were also explicitly addressed to women and, though in a veiled and metaphorical way, expressed same-sex desire. In addition to her thematic innovations, Dickinson radically experimented with poetic diction and revolutionized poetic conventions: she often omitted punctuation except for her characteristic dashes, she altered conventional word order, and she did not employ consistent rhyme schemes through her poems. These features make her poetry a constant source of interest for readers.

Contrary to Dickinson, the most celebrated New England poets of the nine-

In addition to her thematic innovations, Emily Dickinson (1830–1886) radically experimented with poetic diction and revolutionized poetic conventions. Courtesy Library of Congress.

teenth century such as William Cullen Bryant (1794–1878), Henry Wadsworth Longfellow (1807–1882), John Greenleaf Whittier (1807–1892), and James Russell Lowell (1819–1891) have failed to excite contemporary readers. Their poetry is certainly more conventional than Dickinson's, although at the time it was important because it established American events and landscapes as adequate poetic subjects. They thus answered Emerson's call for a distinctive American literature. Yet, their diction was clearly marked by the influence of European classics, such as Dante and Homer, or romantics, such as Wordsworth. Longfellow was certainly one of the most important New England poets of the century. His oeuvre celebrated American past and legends, often through European poetic structures. For example, *Hiawatha* (1855) adapted Native American legends to Finnish folk metre. In *Evangeline* (1847) and *The Courtship of Miles Standish* (1856), Longfellow tried to create a distinctively American epic poetry, modeled on the poems of Homer and Virgil. Both texts follow their characters throughout American historical events and landscapes, as the beginning of Canto V from the second part of *Evangeline* makes clear: "In that delightful land which is washed by the Delaware's waters, / Guarding in sylvan shades the name of Penn the apostle, / Stands on the banks of its beautiful stream the city he founded. / There all the air is balm, and the peach is the emblem of beauty, / And the streets still re-echo the names of the trees of the forest, / As if they fain would appease the Dryads whose haunts they molested." Through his work as a translator, which included the entire version of Dante's *Divine Comedy*, Longfellow introduced many Americans to European literature.

THE TWENTIETH CENTURY

The literary works of the twentieth century, the century of modernism and postmodernism, constitute a radical break with previous traditions, "living amidst the tools of modern relativism, skepticism, and hope for secular change."[11] The main cultural movements of the twentieth century share a vision of "history or human life not as a sequence, or history not as an evolving logic" so that their works are not ordered chronologically or sequentially. They tend instead to "work spatially or through layers of consciousness, working towards a logic of metaphor or form."[12] As Marshall Berman has put it, the experience of modernity is contradictory:

To be modern is to find ourselves in an environment that promises us adventure, power, joy, growth, transformation of ourselves and the world—and, at the same time, that threatens to destroy everything we have, everything we know, everything we are. Modern environments and experiences cut across all boundaries of geography and ethnicity, of class and nationality, of religion and ideology: in this sense, modernity can be said to unite all mankind. But it is a paradoxical unity, a unity of disunity: it pours us all in a maelstrom of perpetual disintegration and renewal, of struggle and contradiction, of ambiguity and anguish. To be modern is to be part of a universe in which, as Marx said, "all that is solid melts into air."[13]

In the United States, the years at the turn of the century witnessed important changes, usually linked with the processes of industrialization, immigration, and urbanization, which challenged traditional values and systems of behavior. As Brian Lee and Robert Reinders have observed, "these changes . . . required new disciplines, new goals and a kind of new consciousness from a predominantly rural folk. The value system based on the existential realities of an agrarian society had to be adapted and partly transformed to meet the new realities."[14] These national changes affected the cultural geographies of New England.

American public life after the turn of the century was shaped by the power of print media. Technological innovations coupled with the expansion of the urban market encouraged the flourishing of journalism. New England contributed to the history of American journalism with important publications. The *Boston Globe* was founded in 1872 by six Boston businessmen, led by Eben Jordan. However, Jordan soon remained the only financial supporter of the paper and appointed General Charles H. Taylor, a Civil War veteran and a journalist, as temporary business manager to solve the economic problems that were plaguing the *Globe*. As a result of his success, Taylor became Jordan's partner and the Taylor family published the paper until 1993, when the *Globe* merged with the New York Times Company in the largest single newspaper acquisition in U.S. history. The event marked the alliance of two important families of American journalism: the Taylors of the *Globe* and the Sulzbergers of the *Times*. The *Globe* positions itself to the center-left of American politics, supporting Democratic candidates and agendas.

The *Hartford Courant* started as a daily publication in 1837, although it had already been in print as a weekly since 1764. This makes the *Courant* the oldest newspaper in continuous publication in the history of American journalism. In 1979, the paper was acquired by the Times Mirror corporation, whose other publications include the *Los Angeles Times*, and in 2000 it became part of the Chicago-based Tribune Company. The *Courant* has an average circulation of two hundred thousand copies which rises to three hundred thousand for its Sunday edition. Like the *Boston Globe*, it espouses center-left policies. The *Christian Science Monitor* was founded in 1908 by Mary Baker Eddy and has been published ever since by Eddy's First Church of Christ, Scientist, in Boston. The church of Christian Science claims that everything associated with the physical world is an illusion and devotes itself to the rediscovery of primitive Christianity and the practice of healing, the recognition of the error of believing in the flesh. The church has had a major influence in American media history: in addition to the *Christian Science Monitor*, which has become a respected international daily during the twentieth century,

Christian Science has also published journals such as *The Christian Science Journal*, *Christian Science Sentinel*, and *Christian Science Quarterly*. In the late 1980s, the group also started their own cable TV station, a radio station, and a public affairs magazine, though all three were short-lived.

The cultural and social changes affecting America as the country was entering the twentieth century were often criticized by the literary establishment. William Dean Howells (1837–1920) was born in Ohio, but settled down in Boston in 1866, after being American consul in Venice. In Boston, Howells was first assistant editor and then editor of the *Atlantic Monthly*. Thanks to this position, he became one of the most prominent intellectuals of his time and continued to champion literary realism as the best form to express American democratic values. His novel *The Rise of Silas Lapham* (1885) looks nostalgically to the past: his protagonist, a self-made Boston businessman, is defeated by the increasing corruption of the post–Civil War world of expanding industrialization. Yet, in spite of his financial ruin, he emerges as the moral winner of the story. From his preeminent position of "the Dean of the American letters," Howells endorsed the careers of several African American and women writers.

While Howells espoused progressive causes, Henry James (1843–1916) produced sharp critiques of democracy and reform from a conservative standpoint, particularly in *The Bostonians*. Set in Boston, where James attended Harvard Law School before moving to Europe in 1866, the novel depicted the conflict between the idealistic and commercial strains of post–Civil War America. James focused chiefly on the movement for women's suffrage and expressed his unease for what he perceived as declining gender differences. James' relationship to New England cultural heritage was controversial as he rejected Transcendentalism, whose optimism he found naïve, preferring Hawthorne's exploration of evil in the present world. *The Bostonians* is one of the few novels by James to be set entirely in America; mirroring his own situation as an expatriate in Europe, the majority of his works, such as the short-story *Daisy Miller* (1858) and the novel *The Portrait of a Lady* (1880), centered on contrasts between European and American traditions. His late novels *The Wings of the Dove* (1902), *The Ambassadors* (1903), and *The Golden Bowl* (1904) are usually grouped under the heading of "major phase" and, with their psychological focus, played an influential role in the development of Modernism.

The same dialectics between past and present and between order and chaos are found in the works of Henry Adams (1838–1918), a descendent of the American presidents John Adams and John Quincy Adams. Born in Boston and educated at Harvard, Adams first started a career as a politician in Washington in 1860, but returned to Harvard disillusioned ten years later and became the editor of the *North American Review*. Throughout his complex and interdisciplinary inquiries, Adams explored and ironically challenged the supposed coherence of human experience, history, and the natural phenomena which made them manageable by human intelligence. In spite of irony and his challenges, Adams, who defined himself as a "conservative Christian anarchist," tried to recover the unity that underlined the chaos of the natural and social worlds. His volume *The Education of Henry Adams* won the Pulitzer Prize in 1919 and is an unconventional type of autobiography as it adopts a mocking third-person narrator and defined Adams as a "manikin." Adams conceives his life as a failure typical of his times that gave little or no control to individuals to shape their own experiences. For his skepticism on human agency, Adams has been praised as proto-postmodern. Adams' academic research focused on the role women had played in different civilizations, a subject to which he also devoted two novels, *Democracy* (1880) and *Esther* (1884), which explored the condition of women in American society.

Born in Connecticut, Charlotte Perkins Gilman (1860–1935) also studied the role of women in society and became a leading figure in the woman's movement from the 1890s to 1920. Gilman's works span several genres, as she was a prolific writer of short-stories, romances, articles, speeches, essays, and poems. In spite of all their shortcomings which have caused Gilman to be charged with racism, ethnocentrism, and anti-Semitism, her oeuvre is still considered relevant in the twenty-first century. It deals with issues relating to gender difference such as the origins of women's subjugation, the struggle for self-support and for fulfilling personal relationships, the central role of work in the definition of one's identity, and the need for new educational strategies to create a world of equal rights for both men and women. All these themes are well summarized by a passage at the end of Gilman's first book-length volume, *Women and Economics* (1989):

> The economically independent mother, widened and freed, strengthened and developed, by her social service, will do better service as a mother than it has been possible for her before. No one thing could do more to advance the interests of humanity than the wiser care and wider love of organized human motherhood around babies. This nobler mother, bearing nobler children, and rearing them in nobler ways, would go far toward making possible the world which we want to see.

One of Gilman's most celebrated shorter pieces is "The Yellow Wallpaper," published in the *New England Magazine* in January 1892, which was based on her own struggle with neurasthenia and the "rest cure" that had been prescribed to her and to many other late nineteenth-century women.

Sarah Orne Jewett (1849–1904) was an acute observer of New England regional life. Born in South Berwick, Maine, Jewett divided her life between her natal village and the house she shared in Boston with her lifelong companion Annie Fields, the widow of the founder of the *Atlantic Monthly*, James Fields. In her fiction, which often has been described as belonging to the "local color" movement, Jewett presented New England village life as under threat from the forces of industrialization and praised the resilience of country women. Jewett dramatized most effectively the encounter and subsequent clash between rural life and the forces of modernity in her short story "A White Heron" (1886), in which the heroine Sylvia refuses to tell a passing hunter the location of the nest of a white heron. Thus, Jewett also explored the opposition of masculine and feminine, and the ending of the story clearly points to the hunter as the destroyer of country life and to Sylvia's refusal as a way to refuse a heterosexual romance:

> Dear loyalty, that suffered a sharp pang as the guest went away disappointed later in the day, that could have served and followed him and loved him as a dog loves! . . . She forgot even her sorrow at the sharp report of his gun and the piteous sight of thrushes and sparrows dropping silent to the ground, their songs hushed and their pretty feathers stained and wet with blood.

At the turn of the century, ethnic voices became increasingly prominent in New England literature. Mary Antin (1881–1949) was a Jewish immigrant from Polotzk, Russia, and the author of *The Promised Land*, which was published in the *Atlantic Monthly* between 1911 and 1912 and as a book in 1912. The book is considered the classic immigrant autobiography documenting the transformation from immigrant to American citizen. The book constituted a powerful rejection of the growing "American nativist hostility to immigration by presenting the inwardness of a consciousness that underwent the transformation from foreign immigrant to American citizen successfully."[15] Tellingly, Antin's initial remarks precisely point to her present self as other from her immigrant identity:

> I was born, I have lived and I have been made over. . . . I am absolutely other than the person whose story I have to tell. . . . I could speak in the third person and not feel that I was masquerading. I can analyze my subject, I can reveal everything; for *she*, and not *I* is my real heroine. My life I still have to live; her life ended when my began.

Born in the New England town of Great Barrington, Massachusetts, William Edward Burghardt (W.E.B.) DuBois (1868–1963) became the most outspoken civil rights activist at the turn of the century and was the first African American to obtain a Ph.D. degree at Harvard University. Thus DuBois' career encompassed different areas: political activism, academic teaching and research, and literary writing. His written production included books of sociology, history, fiction, and poetry and contributions to journals and newspapers. His politics became increasingly radical as DuBois witnessed growing racial violence against African Americans. DuBois' decision to end his life in Ghana mirrors his own wavering between calls for complete racial integration and the suggestion that black Americans and Africans should forge an alliance that would permit them to be independent from whites.

DuBois' most famous formulations were contained in his collection of essays *The Souls of Black Folk* (1903). He declared that "the problem of the twentieth century is the problem of the color line,—the relation of the darker to the lighter races of men in Asia and Africa, in America and the islands of the sea." These lines should be read together with those on the "double consciousness" with which African Americans are both blessed and cursed, a formulation that scholars have traced to William James' influence: "It is a peculiar sensation, this double consciousness, this sense of always looking at oneself through the eyes of others, of measuring one's soul by the tape of a world that looks on in amused contempt and pity. One ever feels this twoness—an American, a Negro; two warring souls, two thoughts, two unreconcilable strivings, two warring ideals in one dark body, whose dogged strength alone keeps it from being torn asunder." Therefore, the problem of the color line is the problem of understanding racial difference in a world shaped by the heritage of slavery and colonialism.

Angelina Weld Grimké (1880–1956) was born in Boston and became one of the leading figures of the New Negro Movement of the 1920s. Her poetry was included in the three most important anthologies of the period: Alain Locke's *The New Negro* (1925), Charles S. Johnson's *Ebony and Topaz* (1927), and Countee Cullen's *Caroling Dusk* (1927). Grimké's poems are less concerned with race than the rest of her writings, and they have been often criticized for their adoption of a white male voice.

This was a common strategy, however, for women poets of the early twentieth century and allowed Grimké to express freely her love of women at a time when lesbianism was still a taboo. In contrast to her poetry, her play *Rachel* (1920) as well as the majority of her short stories focus on lynching and aggressions against African Americans. Their depiction of violence is often compared with that of Richard Wright's fiction.

The relationship of New England poets to the modernism of T. S. Eliot, Pound, and Yates was often controversial. Although born in San Francisco, Robert Frost (1874–1963) moved to Lawrence, Massachusetts, and became the most celebrated New England poet of the period. Both a literary and a political conservative, he rejected the use of free verse and employed traditional rhyme and metrical schemes in his poetry. Like his contemporary Edward Arlington Robinson (1869–1935), many of Frost's texts can be read as dramatic narratives with a logical and consequential plot development which defied the poetic rules of Anglo-American

The poetry of Robert Frost (1874–1963) depicted the countryside and rural scenes of northern New England. Photofest.

modernism. His poems depicted the countryside and rural scenes of northern New England and were collected in several volumes such as *A Boy's Will* (1913), *North of Boston* (1914), *Mountain Interval* (1916), and *New Hampshire* (1923). Frost focused on the lives of common people, adopting their language and tone, and exploring tragedy and the thrust toward transcendence implied in ordinary events. In the poem "Out, Out—" (1915), for example, Frost inserts tragedy in a pastoral setting and relates a farmyard incident in which a boy bleeds to death when he loses control of the saw he is using: "He lay and puffed his lips out with his breath. / And then—the watcher at his pulse took fright. / No one believed. They listened at his heart. / Little—less—nothing!—and that ended it. / No more to build on there. And they, since they / Were not the one dead, turned to their affairs."

The same celebration of New England regional culture and of its common people was found on the pages of one of the most successful American regional magazines, the New Hampshire-based *Yankee*. Launched by Robb Sagendorph (1901–1970) in 1935, the magazine constantly presented a resourceful New England courageously facing the Depression, but which was, however, under constant threat from the centralizing policies of Roosevelt's New Deal. The magazine, which still enjoys a wide circulation today, examined New England customs and traditions and its aim, as Sagendorph himself put it, was "the expression and perhaps, indirectly, the preservation of that great culture in which every Yank was born and by which every real Yank must live." This purpose was all the more urgent in the face of the impending "sea of chain stores, national releases, and nation wide hookups," which, together with "mass production, mass distribution, mass advertising, and mass almost-everything-you-can-think-of," were destroying the New England Yankee's typical "individuality, initiative, and natural ingenuity." Sagendorph's legacy is still influential to this day as the *Yankee* Web site makes clear: "Yankee Publishing Inc. remains a family-owned business, one of the few independent publishing companies of its size. The company's employees and shareholders are determined to keep Robb Sagendorph's dream alive by publishing a magazine that 'expresses our great New England culture' and reflects the New England way of life today."

The more literary *Atlantic Monthly* followed an opposite strategy to the *Yankee* magazine, trying to maintain its nineteenth-century reputation throughout the twentieth by giving up its New England roots. Founded in 1857, the magazine soon became the expression of the nation's high culture, publishing pieces by Ralph Waldo Emerson, Henry Wadsworth Longfellow, Nathaniel Hawthorne, William Dean Howells, and Henry James as well as by women writers such as Harriet Beecher Stowe and Sarah Orne Jewett. Yet, the magazine became increasingly associated with the American literary canon. At the turn of the century, it was branded as a reactionary and elitist review which was outdated in a nation that was facing important social upheavals such as industrialization, massive immigration, and urbanization. Because of its steadily declining sales, which reached their lowest level in the 1900s, *The Atlantic Monthly* changed editorial strategy and enlarged its literary scope from New England high culture to more fashionable writers, whom it often prided itself in discovering. These included Ernest Hemingway, Philip Roth, Eudora Welty, Louise Erdrich, James Dickey, Joyce Carol Oates, and Bobbie Ann Mason. Also, contrary to its beginnings, the magazine has not eschewed the discussion of problematic political topics, publishing, for example, a defense of Sacco and Vanzetti shortly before their execution, critiques of the atom bomb, and Martin Luther King's "Letter from a Birmingham Jail." Its editor Cullen Murphy claimed in the mid-1990s that "the *Atlantic Monthly* is not an antiquarian enterprise, a museum piece."

Contrary to Frost, Boston poet Amy Lowell (1874–1925) was a self-proclaimed imagist. In her poetic collections *Sword Blade and Poppy Seeds* (1914), *Men, Women, and Ghosts* (1916), and *What's O'Clock* (1925), as well as in her theoretical works such as *Tendencies in Modern American Poetry* (1917), Lowell rejected poetic conventions. Like the imagists, Lowell believed that poetry should aim for the creation of precise images rather than vague abstractions. The reception of her prolific poetic production suffered, particularly after her death, because of her lesbianism, and several scholars have even declared that Lowell had nothing to offer to non-lesbian readers. Yet, in the 1990s, a new generation of scholars has rediscovered her work, relating it to camp aesthetics.

Wallace Stevens (1879–1955) too wrote modernist poetry, though he started his literary career after becoming the executive of an insurance company in Hartford, Connecticut, and continued to be an executive even after winning the Pulitzer and the National Book Award in 1955. His first collection, *Harmonium*, was published in 1923 when he was over forty years old. Stevens' poetry was influenced by the philosophy of William James and Friedrich Nietzsche as well as by his mentor at Harvard University, George Santayana. The result of these influences was an attempt to join European traditions with American experiences. Although his poetry is philosophical in content and tone, with long meditative lines, Steven grounded his philosophical observations in material objects and he expressed his preference for "The poem of pure reality, untouched / By trope or deviation, straight to the word, / Straight to the transfixing object, to the object / At the exactest point at which it is itself, / Transfixed by being purely what it is."

e.e. cummings (1894–1962) grew up in Cambridge, Massachusetts, and was educated at Harvard University where he became interested in modernist poetry. His interest in cubism and imagism soon brought him to rebel against both social and literary orthodoxies which he found embodied in Cambridge society: "the Cambridge ladies who live in furnished souls / are unbeautiful and have comfortable minds / (also, with the church's protestant blessings / daughters, unscented shapeless spirited) / they believe in Christ and Longfellow, both dead." His earlier poems are literary equivalents of pictorial cubism, as the layout of the text on the page was supposed to

e.e. cummings' (1894–1962) earlier poems are literary equivalents of pictorial cubism, as the layout of the text on the page was supposed to lead the reader to the meaning. Courtesy Library of Congress.

lead the reader to the meaning. Because of their significant break with conventions, their sharp satire, and their criticism of the lingering Puritanism in New England culture, cummings' collections *Tulips and Chimneys* (1923), *&* (1925), and *XLI Poems* (1925) received hostile critical reviews. *No, Thanks* (1935) signals a turning point in cummings' career as he became increasingly more conservative after a trip to Soviet Russia had acquainted him with the crimes of Stalinism. By the 1950s, cummings was considered an essential part of the American poetic canon.

The same modernist vein can be found in the verses of Charles Olson (1917–1970), who was born in Worcester, Massachusetts, and enrolled in the first program of American Studies at Harvard in 1936. From his studies on Melville to his poetic works and theoretical statements, Olson took part in the vast effort to redefine the United States as a civilization with a culture of its own. Tellingly, one of Olson's first poems, "The Kingfishers," rejects an identity linked to the classical past and embraces the cultures of the New World: "I am no Greek, hath not th'advantage. / And of course, no Roman: he can take no risk that matters, the risk of beauty least of all." In the 1950s, Olson formulated his own idea of postmodernism which he saw as a continuation of the modernist project, but also as a critique of the modernists' ethnocentrism. Olson's poetic imagination remained tied to New England, where he set *The Maximus Poems* (1960–1975), an epic account of America's birth and development. Olson was the mentor of a new generation of poets, the New Englander Robert Creeley (1926–) among them. Born in Arlington, Massachusetts, Creeley grew up in West Acton and, after studying in a New Hampshire secondary school, went to Harvard, where, however, he did not earn a degree. Creeley corresponded with Ezra Pound and William Carlos Williams, but it was Olson who helped him to publish his first collection of poems. Although Creeley published several books of poetry in the 1950s, he only attained literary fame in 1962 with the volume *For Love: Poems, 1950–1960*, which was followed by other acclaimed works such as *Words* (1967), *A Day Book* (1972), *Dreams* (1989), and *Life and Death* (1998). In his poetry, Creeley embraced Olson's theory of the projective verse which rejected fixed poetic structures based on meter or stanzas in favor of free verse. His poems are constantly concerned with the subject of love and human relationships.

Born in Manhattan and raised in New Jersey, Richard Wilbur (1921–) has adopted New England as his place of residence ever since his university days at Amherst College in the 1940s. In his poetry Wilbur tried to absorb both the experimental modernism of Pound and Eliot and the confessional vein of Lowell and Plath. His first collection, *The Beautiful Changes, and Other Poems* (1947), employed a highly metaphorical language to record Wilbur's experiences in World War II, illustrating his statement on the oblique relationship existing between the poet and reality. His two following books *Ceremony, and Other Poems* (1950) and *Things of This World* (1957) led him to win the Pulitzer in 1957 and continued his ironic and oblique exploration of reality through regular formal structures. His most recent collections *New and Collected Poems* (1988) and *Mayflies: New Poems and Translations* (2000) confirmed his vision of poetry as a rational act focusing on daily objects which are then transposed in a spiritual dimension. His recent "Mayflies," for example, starts with the concrete observation of "a mist of flies" and "a crowd of stars" to conclude on the observer's spiritual quest for a supplementary meaning in nature: "Watching those lifelong dancers of a day / As night closed in, I felt myself alone / In a life too much my own, / More mortal in my separateness than they— / Unless, I thought, I had been called to be / Not fly or star / But one whose task is joyfully to see / How fair the fiats of the caller are."

Elwyn Brooks White (1899–1985) was an influential literary stylist and essayist as well as the author of the children's classics *Stuart Little* (1945), *Charlotte's Web* (1952), and *The Trumpet of the Swan* (1970). White grew up in New York, where he also worked as a journalist for the *New Yorker* in the 1920s before moving to North Brooklin, Maine, where he remained until his death. White's essays and books dealt both with contemporary political issues such as the founding of the United Nations (*The Wild Flag*, 1946) and stylistic matters. His *Elements of Style* (1956) became the standard manual for high school and college students taking English courses.

New England is also home to authors of successful best sellers. John Updike (1932–) was born in Pennsylvania, but has long settled down in Massachusetts. His more than fifty books have managed to attract both a vast readership and a massive body of scholarly work. They have also earned him prestigious literary awards including the National Book Award and the Pulitzer Prize. Although his production encompasses numerous genres, Updike is mostly celebrated as a fiction writer whose novels mainly address the moral responsibility of the individual coupled with a nostalgic quest for a simpler American way of life in the face of contemporary social collapse. His fiction has generated three main series. The first one, which includes *The Centaur* (1963), centers on the fictive town of Olinger, Pennsylvania. The Rabbit sequence, *Rabbit, Run* (1960), *Rabbit Redux* (1971), *Rabbit Is Rich* (1981), and *Rabbit at Rest* (1990), portray the life of Harry "Rabbit" Angstrom, a star athlete, from his youth through the social and sexual turmoil of the 1960s, to later periods of his life, and to final decline. Finally, several of Updike's works such as *Couples* (1968) focus on American suburbia, whose surface of respectability hides inner failures and feelings of guilt, a theme Updike shares with another contemporary New England writer, John Cheever (1912–1982).

Stephen King (1947–) was born in Maine where he still lives. He is one of the most successful contemporary American writers, and his best-selling books have helped to revive the horror genre, through which he has addressed the fundamental issues of our contemporary society. King's first novel, *Carrie* (1974), was initially only a moderate success, but its paperback edition and Brian DePalma's film adaptation, together with the author's second novel *Salem's Lot* (1976), made King a literary star. His following books *The Shining* (1977), *Misery* (1987), *The Dark Half* (1989), and *Bag of Bones* (1998) confirmed his reputation as a horror writer who is also capable of exploring the darkest areas of the human mind.

Born in New Hampshire, John Irving (1943–) attained literary success and the status of cultural icon thanks to his fourth novel, *The World According to Garp* (1978), which centered on an eccentric feminist writer and her son. His following books which include *The Hotel New Hampshire* (1981), *The Cider House Rules* (1985), and *A Prayer for Owen Meany* (1989) have all become international best sellers and have often been adapted for the screen. Irving's distinguishing trait is his preference for elaborate comical plots which often reach a dramatic and violent ending; not surprisingly, one of the models for Irving's fiction is Charles Dickens. Although he denies that his books are concerned with social or political issues, Irving has often dealt with controversial subjects such as abortion, sexism, AIDS, and racism. His comments on *The Cider House Rules* well illustrate this dichotomy:

> [It] is never the social or political message that interests me in a novel. I begin with an interest in a relationship, a situation, a character. Before I began *The Cider House Rules*, I thought I wanted to write about a father-son relationship that was closer, more conflicted, and ultimately more loving, than most. Then I began to think of a relationship between an old orphanage director and an unadoptable orphan—a kid who goes out into the world and fails and keeps coming back, so that the old guy ends up with someone he's got to keep. In my research I suddenly saw that the doctors in those orphanage hospitals were far more likely to perform abortions than other legitimate doctors, because they knew firsthand what happened to the kids who were left behind. Who else would be sympathetic? Who else would risk his profession to perform this illegal procedure? Not some moron like Newt Gingrich asking for the return of orphanages, but someone who really knew what orphanages were like and how sad the stories involving the kids were.

Anita Shreve (1946–) first wrote nonfiction studies linked to women's issues and only started to write mainstream romantic fiction in 1989 with her first novel, *Eden*

Close, whose success allowed her to give up journalism and devote her life to fiction. Shreve's subsequent books, *Fortune's Rocks* (2000), *Sea Glass* (2002), and *All He Ever Wanted* (2003), combine a fluid narration with a depth of characterization and historical accuracy that is not usually associated with romantic novels.

Given the importance of media in twentieth-century American political life, it is not surprising that many nonfiction authors achieved an increasingly national visibility. Joseph Alsop (1910–1989) was born in Avon, Connecticut, and graduated from Harvard University in 1932. That same year Alsop was employed by the *New York Herald Tribune*, thus starting a successful career as a journalist which declined after his controversial Vietnam War writings. Though Alsop had been a supporter of Roosevelt's New Deal, Alsop grew more conservative with the years, and his pieces on the Southeast Asia situation from the 1950s to the 1970s were characterized by an increasing anticommunist stance and by a staunch support of American intervention. Alsop, who is credited with the invention of the modern political column, also wrote nonfiction books such as *The 168 Days* (1938) and *FDR—1882–1945: A Centenary Remembrance* (1982), both on Roosevelt; *The Reporter's Trade* (1958), a collection of his articles and views on journalism; and the autobiographical *I've Seen the Best of It: A Memoir* (1992).

Born in California, the film critic Pauline Kael (1919–2001) eventually settled down in Great Barrington, Massachusetts. From the 1960s to the 1990s, Kael was the leading film critic for the *New Yorker*, where she acquired a reputation for her controversial and iconoclastic reviews written in a conversational and brash style. Kael was not afraid of the movie establishment: she dismissed films such as *The Sound of Music* in favor of the more controversial *Bonnie and Clyde*, *The Godfather*, *Last Tango in Paris*, and *Nashville*. She was often accused of preferring trash to more self-consciously artistic films, yet she became a model either to be adopted or rejected for a whole generation of film critics. Her reviews also helped to launch the New Hollywood films by Peckinpah, Altman, Bogdanovich, and DePalma. Kael published her reviews in several successful volumes such as *I Lost It at the Movies* (1965), *Going Steady* (1970), *Deeper into Movies* (1973), which won the National Book Award, *When the Lights Go Down* (1980), and *For Keeps* (1994). Her *Citizen Kane Book: Raising Kane* (1971) argued that the contribution of screenplay writer Herman Mankiewicz to *Citizen Kane* was as important as that of the director Orson Welles, a thesis which continues to generate debate.

A native of Newburyport, Massachusetts, James Parton (1912–2001) was a journalist, an editor, and the president and publisher of *American Heritage* magazine from 1954 to 1970. The aim of the magazine, which Parton cofounded after serving in the U.S. Army Air Forces during World War II, was to acquaint Americans with their own history in an entertaining way and with the use of copious illustrations. Under Parton's leadership, the magazine became a remarkable editorial success with subscription peaking in the 1960s at more than 350,000. The magazine also started to produce books on American history, though the increasing costs of their production led to the selling of the publication to McGraw-Hill in 1969. Parton continued his career as president of the Encyclopedia Britannica Educational Corporation from 1970 to 1973 and as assistant Librarian of Congress from 1976 to 1977.

In the course of the twentieth century, voices contesting the literary and social establishment as well as those from marginalized groups such as women, gays and lesbians, African Americans, and immigrants began to enter forcefully in the New England literary heritage. Born in Boston, Robert Lowell (1917–1977), a descendant of Amy Lowell and James Russell Lowell, devoted his life to composing and teaching poetry, but also took controversial political stances that led him to become a conscientious objector during World War II and to criticize the Vietnam War. He was imprisoned for his first choice in 1943, and two years after his release, he produced his first major volume, *Lord Weary's Castle* (1946). Lowell rejected the Boston Brahmin milieu into which he was born, forever trying to escape "this planned / Babel of Boston where our money talks." His poetry addressed both public and private spheres, often with linguistic innovations. After this first volume, Lowell suffered personal setbacks and did not regain his poetic fame until 1959 with the publication of his autobiographical *Life Studies*, which portrays the poet from his condition of a young boy suffering for his parents' conflicts to his own maturity and crises. Lowell continued his autobiography in verse with the volume *Notebook 1967–1968* (1969) and also wrote political plays such as *The Old Glory* (1964) and *Prometheus Bound* (1967).

Emotional disturbances also plagued the life of another New England poet, Anne Sexton (1928–1974). Born in Newton, Massachusetts, Sexton began writing poetry after a suicide attempt in 1956 and the poetry seminar led by Robert Lowell in 1959 where she met Sylvia Plath (1932–1963). Her first collection *To Bedlam and Part Way Back* (1960) established her reputation as a confessional poet, a definition which, like Robert Lowell, she always rejected. Her following collections, including *All My Pretty Ones* (1962), *Live or Die* (1966), and *Transformations* (1971), won international praise and prestigious awards. In her poems, Sexton focused on families and family relationships, yet it is reductive to assume that Sexton was always talking about *her* family and *her* relationships. Her texts opposed male and female identities. In particular, those concerned with doctors and analysts celebrated the power of women's voices to escape male authority and authentication. In "The Abortion," Sexton wrote that the girl's "case history / stays blank" as the poem's female character refuses to answer the questions of male doctors who are simply interested in cold facts rather than in her emotional condition. Plath too was a central figure of confessional poetry. Born in Boston to parents of German descent who taught at Boston University, she was a successful student whose academic achievements paradoxically led her to recurrent depression. She realized that she would never fit the roles of wife and mother that women were expected to embrace in the American society of the 1950s. In 1960, Plath published her first collection of poetry, *The Colossus and Other Poems*. Three years later, she wrote the novel *The Bell Jar* about her suicide attempt in the late 1950s. After only a month from the publication of her novel, Plath committed suicide, and her death triggered interest in her poetry which challenges standard poetic forms and themes.

Francis Otto Mathiessen (1902–1950) was the leading scholar of American literature in the first half of the twentieth century. Because of his strong left-wing leanings and his homosexuality, Mathiessen found it difficult to conform to the social norms of Harvard University, where he taught from 1929 to 1950, the year of his suicide. Mathiessen's critical works include *Sarah Orne Jewett* (1929), the influential *American Renaissance* (1941), *Henry James: The Major Phase* (1944), and *Theodore Dreiser* (1951). Mathiessen was particularly interested in the relationship between literature and society. Since Mathiessen was gay, some critics have been disappointed by his covert discussions of homosexuality, bordering at times on homophobia, in artists such as Jewett, James, Whitman, and Melville. Others point out instead that more careful readings can reveal a celebration of sexual difference in his critical studies.

Jack Kerouac (1922–1969) is mostly known as the author of the novels *On the Road* (1957) and *The Dharma Bums* (1958), where he preached nonconformity and self-expression as a way of life. Yet, he also wrote books about his childhood in his native mill town of Lowell, Massachusetts, such as *The Town and the City* (1950) and *Visions of Gerard* (1963) about his brother's premature death. Kerouac, whose parents were French Canadian immigrants, was part of the Beat Generation movement and, like other members of the group, complemented his prose production with poetry. Kerouac's poems hark back to Whitman and struggled to make poetic form and content free from academic orthodoxies. His poems often focused on urban themes and marginal characters such as prostitutes and criminals, and their form likens them to performative acts. Accordingly, Kerouac called many of them "blues," linking his poetry to the revolutionary form of jazz and, at the same time, to the increasing interest in Eastern religions. For example, *Mexico City Blues* (1959) ends with a meditation on "Buddhist Saints" and Kerouac includes the jazz myth Charlie Parker on his list. Parker, the poem claims, "looked like Buddha." For all his rebellious posture and his travels throughout America, Kerouac's imagination, as well as that of the Beats in general, can be linked to the New England tradition, embodied by Emerson and Thoreau, which places the individual above social norms and envisions literary composition as a sacred task.

Galway Kinnell (1927–) was born to Irish and Scottish immigrant parents in Providence, Rhode Island. He is the author of several books of poems as well as the novel *Black Light* (1966), set in Iran. His *Selected Poems* (1983) won him the Pulitzer Prize and the American Book Award. In spite of these institutional awards, Kinnell often took part in protest campaigns which led him to demonstrate against the Vietnam War and to hold antinuclear poetic readings. His political concerns are apparent in poems such as "The Last River" and "Vapor Trail Reflected in the Frog Pond" in the collection *Body Rags* (1968), and "The Dead Shall Be Raised Incorruptible" in *The Book of Nightmares* (1971). "The Fundamental Project of Technology" in the collection *The Past* (1985) exposes the nuclear threat to humankind and is set in a Japanese museum commemorating the American bombing of Nagasaki. The museum displays objects which have been forever changed by the nuclear bomb: "glass dishes which changed / in color; pieces of transformed beer bottles; / a household iron; bundles of wire become solid / lumps of iron; a pair of pliers; a ring of skull- / bone fused to the inside of a helmet; a pair of eyeglasses / taken off the eyes of an eyewitness, without glass, / which vanished, when a white flash sparkled." Tellingly, human characters are introduced only in the second stanza to emphasize the deadly landscape left by the bomb. The poem ends with a circular structure with the prophecy of a world when "no one lives / to look back and say, a flash, a white flash sparkled." Kinnell's confrontation with death constitutes the thematic link between his political texts and his more intimate ones such as the elegies he wrote for the death of his brother. While his earliest poems had adopted traditional rhyme schemes and meters, from the 1960s, Kinnell adopted less rigid structures that combined free verse with more colloquial register.

Sadly neglected today, Edwin O'Connor (1918–1968) was born in Providence, Rhode Island, from Irish immigrants. He is the author of the award-winning novels such as *The Last Hurrah* (1956), loosely based on the career of the four-time Boston mayor James Michael Curley and adapted for the screen by John Ford, and *The Edge of Sadness* (1961). O'Connor wrote about the Irish immigrant experience, combining social realism with an allegory of the American immigrant experience. Delbanco has summarized his contribution to American immigrant literature as showing the immigrants' struggle "not only for political power but for the dignity of full citizenship" and the loss of ethnic identity that their victory entailed.[16]

The Italian roots of John Ciardi (1916–1986), born in Medford, Massachusetts, were evident in his literary interests, which climaxed with his translation of Dante's *Divina Commedia* (1977). Ciardi's career was split between his own writing of poetry and that of a literary instructor and editor. He was the poetry editor of the *Saturday Review*, where his reviews often sparked controversy.

Nobel Prize winner Joseph Brodsky (1940–1996) was born in Leningrad, the Soviet Union, but became an American citizen in 1977 following his expulsion from his mother country. He established close links with New England as he taught at Mount Holyoke College, Massachusetts, from 1981 until his death. Brodsky composed poetry in both Russian and English. His main sources of inspiration were Western art and cultural conventions, hence the label of classicist that is often attached to him. Brodsky used a series of events and characters of Western tradition to ponder on timeless questions of moral and social responsibility.

Another Russian exile who eventually settled down in New England was the Russian novelist, playwright, and memoirist Aleksandr Solzhenitsyn (1918–). After his expulsion from the Soviet Union due to the publication in Western countries of *The Gulag Archipelago* (1973), a collection of sketches from the lives of individual victims of the Soviet prison camps, Solzhenitsyn lived in Germany and Switzerland before moving to Cavendish, Vermont, where he stayed from 1976 to 1994. During his American years, Solzhenitsyn wrote *Nevidimki* (*Invisible Allies*, 1991), which portrays the author's activities as well as those of his collaborators as dissident activists against the Soviet regime. The book completes the narrative of his earlier volume *Bodalsia telenok s dubom* (*The Oak and the Calf*, 1975). *The Mortal Danger: Misconceptions about Soviet Russia and the Threat to America* (1980) reveals from its very title the writer's view of Russian socialism as irreconcilable with American culture and also his conviction that the United States seemed unwilling to confront the harsher truths of the Soviet regime. While in the United States, Solzhenitsyn also planned a series of novels about the Russian Revolution with the collective title *The Red Wheel*. He returned to Russia in the mid-1990s, where he was received with great honors by President Boris Yeltsin.

The son of Russian Jewish parents who had emigrated to the Roxbury ghetto of Boston, Nathan Hentoff (1925–) became a prominent journalist as well as a fiction and nonfiction writer in the 1960s when he became involved in the civil rights movement. Hentoff wrote on such diverse subjects as the jazz scene, civil rights issues (*The New Equality*, 1964), children's novels (*Jazz Country*, 1965, and *I'm Really Dragged but Nothing Gets Me Down*, 1967), and adult novels focusing on race and the left (*Call the Keeper*, 1966, and *Onwards*, 1967). Hentoff devoted several of his nonfiction books to topical social and political issues. In *A Doctor Among the Addicts* (1967), he documented the effective action of a methadone clinic in

Harlem, and in *A Political Life* (1969) he portrayed the life of New York City mayor John V. Lindsay. Hentoff also wrote two autobiographical volumes: *Boston Boy* (1986) and *Speaking Freely: A Memoir* (1997). In 1995 he was awarded the National Press Foundation Award for distinguished contribution to journalism, and in 2000 he received a Lifetime Achievement Award from the National Society of News-paper Editors.

Dorothy West (1907–1998), a leading figure in the Harlem Renaissance, grew up within the Bostonian black middle class. In addition to two novels, memoirs, and short-stories, in the 1930s West founded the journal *Challenge* which gave voice to many African American writers. *The Living Is Easy* (1948), West's first novel, is a semibiographical account of her childhood, satirizing her own social class and exposing the elitism and racial denial of Boston's society. Such themes also inform West's later production. One of the chapters from the collection *The Richer, the Poorer* (1995) depicts middle-class African Americans on vacation on Martha's Vineyard with characteristic irony: "The early blacks were all Bostoni-ans . . . in today's connotation they were 'cool'. It was a common condition of black Bostonians. They were taught very young to take the white man in stride or drown in their own despair. Their survival was proved by their presence on the Island in pursuit of the same goal of happiness. . . . They made a point of not bunching together. They did not want the whites to think they knew their place." West's concern with race and gender is always complemented with her interest in class which illustrates her involvement in the proletarian movement of the 1930s.

Jumpa Lahiri (1965–   ) was born in London to Indian parents, but grew up in Rhode Island. Her first collection of short stories *Interpreter of Maladies* (1999), which was followed by the novel *The Namesakes* (2003), won her the Pulitzer Prize in 2000. Her stories have both American and Indian settings, and Lahiri drama-tizes the complex negotiation between two sets of values and two generations. The same negotiation of two cultural heritages is conveyed by the poetry and the two successful novels (*How the Garcia Girls Lost Their Accents*, 1991, and *In the Time of the Butterflies*, 1994) of the Latina author Julia Alvarez (1950–   ). Alvarez was born in New York City to Dominican parents, but attended college in Connecticut and Vermont, where she currently lives. Alvarez defines herself as "Dominican, hy-phen, American," refusing to adhere to one or the other cultural paradigm. This hyphenated identity is theorized at length in the second and expanded version of her first collection of poems *Homecoming* (1984) which was published in 1998 as *Homecoming: New and Collected Poems. Something to Declare.* Her works interweave questions of race, gender, and class, making it impossible for the reader to disen-tangle these categories from the texts. In a poem from the second version of *Home-coming*, Alvarez declares, "Who touches this poem touches a woman," while in "Bookmaking" from her collection *The Other Side/El Otro Lado* (1995), she pow-erfully links textuality and sexuality claiming that "the words become flesh": "the seam of the spine / centered in the jacket of the shoulders, / the ligaments tooled in the plates / of the clavicles, the legible bones / of the wrists and the ankles."

The different voices that have strongly emerged in the course of the nineteenth and twentieth centuries and that still continue to be heard in the twenty-first cen-tury have progressively called into question the definition of New England cul-tural and literary heritage solely through references to its Puritan and Yankee past.

As John Conforti has stressed at the end of his study of New England regional identities, "we need a new narrative of how New England developed not only as a Puritan-Yankee city on a hill but also as an ethnic city by the mill."[17]

RESOURCE GUIDE

Printed Sources

Berman, Marshall. *All that Is Solid Melts into Air: The Experience of Modernity*. London: Verso, 1982.

Bradbury, Malcolm, and James McFarlane. "The Name and Nature of Modernism." In Malcolm Bradbury and James McFarlane, eds., *Modernism*. London: Penguin Books, 1976. 19–55.

Conforti, John. *Imagining New England: Explorations of Regional Identity from the Pilgrims to the Mid-Twentieth Century*. Chapel Hill: University of North Carolina Press, 2001.

Delbanco, Andrew, ed. *Writing New England: An Anthology from the Puritans to the Present*. Cambridge, MA: Harvard University Press, 2001.

Lee, Brian, and Robert Reinders. "The Loss of Innocence: 1880–1914." In Malcolm Bradbury and Howard Temperley, eds., *Introduction to American Studies*. London: Longman, 1989. 211–232.

Mathiessen, F. O. *American Renaissance: Art and Expression in the Age of Emerson and Whitman*. New York: Oxford University Press, 1941.

Sollors, Werner. Introduction to *The Promised Land*, by Mary Antin. New York: Penguin Books, 1997.

Web Sites

American Transcendentalism Web. 2004.
Psymon. February 19, 2004.
http://www.vcu.edu/engweb/transcendentalism/

The Transcendentalist movement and its writers and thinkers.

Colonial and Revolutionary Literature: Early National Literature.
Volume 15 of W. P. Trent, J. Erskine, S. P. Sherman, and C. Van Doren, eds., *The Cambridge History of English and American Literature: An Encyclopedia in Eighteen Volumes*. New York: G. P. Putnam's Sons, 1907–1921; New York: Bartleby.com, 2000. January 11, 2004.
http://www.bartleby.com/225/index.html#2

Vanspanckeren, Kathryn. *Outline of American Literature*. 2004.
U.S. Department of State's Bureau of International Information Programs. January 17, 2004.
http://usinfo.state.gov/products/pubs/oal/oaltoc.htm

Videos/Films

The Crucible. Dir. Nicholas Hytner. Per. Daniel Day-Lewis, Winona Ryder. Twentieth Century Fox, 1996.

Emily Dickinson. Instructional Media Services (AIMS), 2002.

The New England Transcendentalists. Films for the Humanites and Sciences, 1997.

Poets of New England: An Introduction with William Moebius. Academic Instructional Media Services (AIMS), 2002.

Robert Frost. Instructional Media Services (AIMS), 2002.

Organizations

Connecticut Center for the Book
Hartford Public Library
500 Main St.
Hartford, CT 06103-3075
phone: 860-695-6320 / fax: 860-722-6870
http://www.hplct.org/cfb.htm

Maine Center for the Book
Maine Humanities Council
P.O. Box 7202
Portland, ME 04112
phone: 207-773-5051 / fax: 207-773-2416
e-mail: info@mainehumanities.org
http://www.mainehumanities.org/about/center.html

Massachusetts Center for the Book
Main Office
Hampshire College—MCD
893 West St.
Amherst, MA 01002
phone: 413-559-5678
e-mail: massbook@hampshire.edu
http://www.massbook.org

Massachusetts Historical Society
1154 Boylston Street
Boston, MA 02215-3695
phone: 617-536-1608
http://www.masshist.org/welcome/

New England Archivist
220 Morrissey Boulevard
Boston, MA 02125h
http://nils.lib.tufts.edu/newengarch/index.html

Special Collections.

New England Young Writers' Conference
Gifford Hall
Middlebury College
Middlebury, VT 05753
http://cat.middlebury.edu/~neywc/index.html

Annual conference for high school students and professional writers.

New Hampshire Center for the Book
New Hampshire State Library
20 Park St.
Concord, NH 03301
phone: 603-271-8520 or 1-800-499-1232, ext. 4
http://www.state.nh.us/nhsl/bookcenter/index.html

Rhode Island Center for the Book
Providence Public Library
225 Washington St.

Providence, RI 02903
phone: 401-455-8134 / fax: 401-455-8134
http://www.provlib.org/ricfb/

Vermont Center for the Book
256 Haywood Dr., Ste. B
Chester, VT 05143
phone: 802-875-2751 / fax: 802-875-2790
e-mail: postmaster@vermontbook.org
http://www.vermontbook.org/

MUSIC

*Barry Marshall and
Suzanne Cope*

New England's music history has been influenced by many factors. The region was one of the first inhabited by immigrants from Europe, and the Old World was a major influence on New England's early musical development. The region also is home to many tribes of Native Americans and borders French Canada to the north, creating an influx of varied cultures. From the beginning, Boston was the main center of culture in the region and led the nation in many areas of music through the seventeenth, eighteenth, and nineteenth centuries, but lost its cultural hegemony—to New York City, and a continued shift of population westward—by the beginning of the twentieth century. The city, however, has regained some of its influence and prestige in several genres of popular music—including folk, Americana, jazz, and classical—through a confluence of factors that enables it to maintain its status in the music world. Other cities such as Portland, Maine; Burlington, Vermont; and Providence, Rhode Island, have also increasingly come into their own as cultural centers in this part of the country.

NATIVE AMERICANS

The history of New England's music began with its first inhabitants, the Native Americans, who used music as an integral part of their lives. It was not recorded in written form and was passed along as part of an oral tradition. The Native American groups of New England, like the Mohegan and Pequot (both in present-day Connecticut), Narragansett (Rhode Island), Wampanoag (Southeastern Massachusetts), Massachusett (Massachusetts Bay), Pawtucket or Pennacook (New Hampshire), and Penobscot (Maine), used music primarily in spiritual rituals to communicate with higher powers and create unity with the world around them. The subjects ranged from tales of ancient heroes to the daily work of hunting, fishing, or agriculture. Drums and flutes were the two main instruments, although the drum was by far the most important. Native Americans likened the

333

Both dance and music were performed at powwows to honor Mother Earth and to bring unity to the tribe. Photo by Nancy Walker.

beat of the drum to the heartbeat of "Mother Earth" and felt that the drumbeat was necessary to connect all living things. The use of varied drumbeats and the call and response method of singing—the revered "Head Singer" would often choose the song, and many times his response singers as well—was as important as the numerous native dances. Both dance and music were performed at the pow-wow to honor Mother Earth and bring unity to the tribe, and for centuries Native American music was performed solely within a community for religious and social purposes.

It is only in the last few decades that Native Americans have brought their music outside their respective tribes. Now as much a vehicle for personal expression, modern Native American musicians still draw greatly from the tradition of their ancestors. Heavy drumbeats and traditional flutes still figure heavily in recordings today. But today's Native American artists take the music of their heritage and meld it with blues, folk, new age, rock, and even rap to create an entirely new genre, distinctive enough to merit their own awards ceremony—the Native American Music Awards, or "the NAMMYs." Sounds of America Records, or SOAR, is a major Native American music label, and has over three hundred titles of contemporary and traditional albums in print from groups from the New England area and around the country, and boasts numerous NAMMY winners among its catalog.

PURITANS AND RELIGIOUS MUSIC

The first settlers to join the Native Americans in New England were the Pilgrims and the Puritans. Both groups left the Old World in search of religious freedom and landed in New England around 1620. Religion was a major influence in nearly every aspect of their lives in the New World, and their music reflected that.

The religious music was psalms, songs, and even latter-day versions of Gregorian chants, mostly brought over from England and adapted from older hymns. Much of what was sung were adaptations of older songs, and many of the hymnals did not use musical notation at all; they merely printed the words and referenced older known melodies. As for secular music, the colonists brought guitars, fiddles, drums, trumpets, and flutes from England and used them to make informal music at home or even on the town green.

The control of the clergy over all aspects of life in much of New England started to decline somewhat in the latter half of the seventeenth century. This decline was partly because of the demographic changes caused by immigration, and partly because of the dilution of the religious fervor that had brought many over from England a generation or two earlier. Music began to be played and sung more often in contexts other than religious ones.

The *Bay Psalm Book* (1640), the first music book printed in New England, became the standard text in its many editions and replaced Ainsworth's psalter and Ravenscroft's *The Whole Book of Psalms*, which had been brought over from England. The book contained only thirteen melodies from familiar songs to be used for 150 psalms. By the early eighteenth century when the *Bay Psalm Book* had become widely adopted throughout New England, the current style of singing, which grew mainly from an oral tradition, had shifted so far away from the original melodies, because most Congregationalists were not able to read music, that the Puritan ministers were horrified. A musical reform movement began as ministers devised music instruction books and singing schools mainly to improve church music by teaching sight-reading. Out of this grew the singing schools and singing societies.

SINGING SOCIETIES

The Society for Promoting Regular Singing started in Boston in 1722, and before long these singing schools and singing societies emerged throughout New England. They soon developed into secular social clubs as well, and students began singing more than just psalms. They would learn three- and four-part harmonies without instrumental accompaniment, and would often give a public performance—or concert—at the end of a set of classes. By the late eighteenth century these singing schools and societies had spread throughout the colonies. In New England there were the Psallion Society of Providence, Rhode Island; the Beethoven Society of Portland, Maine; the Essex Music Association of Massachusetts; and the Concord Musical Society of Concord, New Hampshire. Not long thereafter, composers began to write specifically for the societies and singing schools.

Because the popularity of the public performances of these singing schools and societies had grown, the first official concert in America was held in Boston in 1729. By the 1740s, concerts were being held in Boston's Faneuil Hall, and other parts of the region soon followed suit. Providence, Rhode Island, had its first concert in 1768, Newport, Rhode Island, in 1772, and Salem, Massachusetts, by 1798.

By 1800, cities like Portland, Maine, and Portsmouth, New Hampshire, also had their first concerts.

The Handel and Haydn Society, established in Boston in 1815 by Gottlieb Graupner (1767–1836), directly grew out of the popularity of these singing societies. Its original mission was to "cultivate and improve a correct taste in the performance of sacred music, and also to introduce into more general practice the works of Handel, Haydn, and other eminent composers." Influenced by this, other New England cities sought to emulate this thriving society, the most successful being Portland, Maine, which started a Beethoven Society in 1819, and then the Portland Sacred Music Society succeeded it in 1837. Today the society is still going strong and is comprised of both professional and amateur singers and musicians as it has been for over two hundred years.

NEW ENGLAND COMPOSERS

Early Composers

One of the first truly American composers was a singing-school master named William Billings (1746–1800). Billings' first two tune-books, *The New-England Psalm-Singer* (1770) and *The Singing Master's Assistant* (1778), dealt with patriotism and regional settings and subjects; the lyrics were very popular at the time, including one song, "Chester," which was adopted as a theme song by the colonial Minutemen.

Billings' style of vocal writing became known as "fuging" tunes. These compositions, less complex than the real fugues being written in Europe, had as many as four parts, and used simple counterpoint. Billings' influence spread throughout the new nation and is still felt in some American religious singing.

Other composers from the singing-school era were Supply Belcher (1752–1836) of Farmington, Maine, Daniel Read (1757–1836) of New Haven, Connecticut, and Andrew Law (1749–1821) of Milford, Connecticut. Belcher published an anthology, *The Harmony of Maine*, in 1794 and became known as the "Handel of Maine." Read's contribution to American music is that he published the second tune-book (after Billings) that consisted of the music of one composer, called *American Singing Book* (1785). Law was influential as a minister who organized several singing-schools and distributed his tune-books far beyond New England.

Lowell Mason (1792–1872) was a major figure in both the history of American music and the history of education. He was a sacred music composer, a compiler of classic collections of sacred tunes, a leader of Boston's most important musical institutions of the mid-nineteenth century, and musical director of numerous church choirs. Perhaps most important, he introduced music into public education in the United States.

Mason was born in Medfield, Massachusetts, and played several instruments and even composed hymns while still in his teens. He continued to write hundreds of hymns and guided many others in that pursuit as well. Mason's suggestion of an old German tune to Francis Smith to set to words that he wrote called "America" (aka "My County 'Tis of Thee"), which also became the tune of "God Save the King," and was first sung at the Park St. Church in Boston on July 4, 1831, was among his most famous composition credits. He also cowrote, with Thomas Hastings, *Spiritual Songs for Social Worship*, which contained Hastings' still sung "Rock of Ages" and Mason's perennial "Nearer My God to Thee."

As part of Mason's efforts to reform church music and music education, he helped start the seminal Boston Academy of Music, whose primary mission was to promote music education for the public and to train music teachers. Through the academy, Mason began a push to include music education in the public schools. He started by donating his services locally at the Hawes School, and by the 1850s much of the country had adopted music education as part of the curriculum thanks to Mason's efforts.

Later New England Composers

John Knowles Paine (1839–1906) was from Portland, Maine, and became Harvard's first professor of music in 1876, helping to make the college an important center of music as resident composer for thirty years. A composer as well as a teacher, Paine is considered by many to be America's first celebrated symphonist. His contribution to the developer of college music curriculum and his influence as a role model and educator to later musicians and composers are perhaps his most important legacy.

One of the first recognized female composers, Amy Beach is also notable for her use of American folk influences in her compositions. Born Amy Cheney in Henniker, New Hampshire, she married a prominent Boston doctor who helped her gain acceptance in the male-dominated music world. Her talent as a pianist, her determination to succeed, and the favorable climate of Boston toward the newly emerging woman's movement were also factors in her emergence as a trenchant composer of the early twentieth century, but her eclectic embrace of folk melodies and her fervent synthesis of Romantic influences were equally important. Her most significant output included art songs and piano works, but she also was the first American woman to compose a symphony, the *Gaelic Symphony in E Minor* (1894), and a piano concerto, the *Piano Concerto in C-sharp Minor* (1899).

Charles Ives (1874–1954) was certainly the most important New England composer of the latter half of the nineteenth century and early part of the twentieth century. Ives was born in Danbury, Connecticut, and wrote very modern sym-

---

Boston Symphony Orchestra

Henry Lee Higginson (1834–1919), a wealthy banker and amateur musician, founded the Boston Symphony Orchestra (BSO) in 1881, the same year that Georg Henschel directed the first BSO concert in Old Boston Music Hall, where concerts were held for almost twenty years. On October 15, 1900, Symphony Hall was inaugurated, and the Boston Symphony Orchestra continues to call it home. James Levine, who was named to replace the venerable Seiji Ozawa as music director in 2001, was the fourteenth to hold that position, and the first American-born.

In all the BSO has introduced or commissioned over 250 works since its inception, including works by Aaron Copland, Igor Stravinsky, Leonard Bernstein, Serge Koussevitsky (director of the BSO for over 25 years), J. S. Bach, and Bela Bartok. The BSO was also one of the first orchestras to celebrate the work of female composers, such as Amy Beach (1867–1944) and Mabel Wheeler Daniels (1878–1971).

The Boston Pops, originally called "Promenade Concerts," is officially under the tutelage of the Boston Symphony Orchestra. The first concerts were in the summertime in the late 1800s as an offering of a "lighter kind of music" (so described by founder Henry Lee Higginson). In 1900 the name was officially changed to the Boston Pops and "The Stars and Stripes Forever" became the official finale of each concert, a tradition that continues today.

In what many later critics discerned as a precursor to modernism, Charles Ives combined classical music with popular "marching band" qualities and even juxtaposed early psalms with sounds that intimated the disorder of the modern world. Courtesy Library of Congress.

phonic and choral music for that period. In what many later critics discerned as a precursor to modernism, Ives combined the bedrock conservative basics of classical music with popular "marching band" qualities and even early psalms juxtaposed with sounds that intimated the disorder of the modern world. He wrote often in essays about his music, and he compared his compositions to an unstructured New England town meeting, which still has its own order amid the wide-ranging discussions. Not afraid of trying new composition techniques, Ives used quotations from well-known hymns and marches, incorporated mistakes, and sometimes included out-of-tune playing purposefully in his pieces.

Ives tried to promote his work during the later years of his life, and it started to gain some fame when other composers like Aaron Copland and Elliott Carter praised his work. He was awarded the Pulitzer Prize for his *Symphony No. 3*, a composition that conductor Leonard Bernstein later made part of his standard repertoire.

One of the most important musicians and composers of this time period is Gunther Schuller (1925–). Although he was born in New York, Schuller spent much of his life in New England playing a profound role in the shaping of this region's musical landscape. His contributions span genres at a time when popular music was moving beyond classical to jazz and swing, making Schuller one of the few individuals to have such an influence as a musician, composer, and educator.

An accomplished French horn player, Schuller played for the Metropolitan Opera in 1945 and on Miles Davis' seminal *Birth of the Cool* album in 1949–1950. Besides playing with Miles Davis, Schuller also collaborated with Charles Mingus, Eric Dolphy, Dizzy Gillespie, and Gil Evans. During this period he began to develop ideas about combining elements of jazz improvisation and arranging it with classical composition, which later led to his "Third Stream" theories of music. By the 1960s he changed his musical focus from playing the French horn to concentrating on other musical pursuits, like composing and conducting.

Schuller taught at the Manhattan School of Music and the Yale Music School before becoming president of the New England Conservatory of Music in Boston (1967–1977), where he instituted the first degree program in jazz. He was also head of composition and then artistic director of the Tanglewood Berkshire Music Center from 1963 to 1984.

Gunther Schuller established himself as a prolific composer in classical as well as jazz and won the Pulitzer Prize in 1994 for his classical piece *Of Reminiscences and Reflections.* Schuller established the company GM Recordings in 1981 and has released over 120 albums of jazz, classical, and multigenre music, featuring such distinguished artists as Ran Blake, Joe Lovano, Dave Douglas, Russell Sherman, and the Kronos Quartet, as well as the works of challenging composers like Milton Babbit, Elliott Carter, and even himself. His record company has also revived works by highly regarded traditional composers like Scott Joplin and John Knowles Paine, more as a public service than a commercially viable endeavor. Because he contributed to the New England musical landscape in so many ways, Schuller's vision and knowledge of various genres of music have been primary influences on the region's musical history since the mid-1900s.

Among Gunther Schuller's accomplishments is his tenure as artistic director of the Tanglewood Berkshire Music Center. Many composers of the 1900s saw the performance of their work at the Tanglewood Music Festival as a goal, and when Schuller was in residence he was one of the first to support the new popular jazz and swing music. Established in 1936, Tanglewood is the Boston Symphony Orchestra's summer home and is located in the Berkshire hills of western Massachusetts. Drawing more than 350,000 visitors annually, this rural destination now offers jazz and popular offerings besides its original repertoire of classical performances by the Boston Symphony Orchestra.

JAZZ IN NEW ENGLAND

New England has a rich history of jazz music, and many accomplished jazz musicians were born in this region or later chose to call it home. One reason for this is Boston's early reputation for supporting racially mixed jazz bands.

Sea Chanteys

Between 1820 and the early 1900s chanteys were sung by New England sailors on oceangoing voyages. They were often simple, witty, lyrical songs about seafaring life that kept the sailors' spirits up while performing mundane tasks on board the vessel or during idle periods at sea. A crewman would begin with a line or verse, followed by the rest of the crew singing a chorus or response. One of the most popular chanteys, sung by New England sailors on their return voyage, was "Rolling Home," which included the following lyrics:

> Call all hands, to man the capstan, see the cables running clear.
> Heave away, and with a will boys, for New England we will steer.
> Rolling home, rolling home, rolling home, across the sea
> Rolling home, to old New England, rolling home, dear land to thee
> Off Cape Horn, one frosty morning, and our sails were full of snow.
> Clear the sheets and sway the halyards, swing her off and let her go.
> Rolling home, rolling home, rolling home, across the sea
> Rolling home, to old New England, rolling home, dear land to thee . . .

Sailors often improvised while singing chanteys and adapted new lyrics to suit their own situation. In another version of "Rolling Home," we find an English variation of the song:

> Now, it takes all hands to man the capstan,
> Mister see your cables clear!
> Soon you'll be sailing homeward bound sir,
> And for the channel you will steer.
> See your sheets and crew lines free sir,
> All your buntlines overhauled;
> Are the sheerpoles and gear all ready?
> Soon for England we will steer.
> Rolling home, rolling home,
> Rolling home across the sea,
> Rolling home to dear old England
> Rolling home, dear land to thee . . .

Other versions of the homeward-bound chantey include the line "Rolling home to dear old Ireland," making it a transatlantic song that was sung in various forms according to country or region.

The first place in the country to have a public jazz performance of a racially integrated group was at the Brunswick Hotel in 1928 with Leo Riesman, a black violinist. And in 1935 at the Boston Ritz Carlton, the great Duke Ellington became the first black musician to lead an orchestra.

Ellington, originally from New York, spent considerable time in the New England region, in part because its acceptance of African American musicians. He played numerous summer residencies at large venues like Symphony Hall and RKO Theatre (now the Wang Center) as well as shows at smaller clubs like Starlight Lounge in Peabody, Massachusetts, and the Roseland State Ballroom in Boston. Ellington also inspired and employed some of the best jazz musicians of the era. Johnny Hodges (1907–1970), born in Cambridge, played for decades with Ellington as lead alto saxophonist and is recognized worldwide as one of the greatest solo instrumentalists ever.

Harry Carney (1910–1974), born in Boston, joined Duke Ellington's band when he was sixteen years old and played with him for over forty-six years. A baritone saxophonist, Carney is considered to possess one of the most distinctive sounds in the history of jazz and was known for his colorful palette of sounds. Paul Gonsalves (1920–1974), born in Boston, also spent decades with Ellington, and his extended solo with the Ellington band at the Newport Jazz Festival in 1956 made

Born in Cambridge, Johnny Hodges played for decades with Duke Ellington as lead alto saxophonist and is recognized worldwide as one of the greatest solo instrumentalists ever. Courtesy Library of Congress.

him a legend. All three of these musicians were recently elected to the newly established New England Jazz Hall of Fame.

Duke Ellington's presence in New England helped keep jazz popular, and a number of jazz clubs and ballrooms featured other talented musicians from the region. The High Hat, Savoy Ballroom, Paul's Mall, and Wally's Paradise all were popular clubs that played a large role in introducing and nurturing jazz and swing music to oft-conservative New Englanders.

Another important Boston jazz club during the sixties and seventies was the Jazz Workshop, which started in 1964 and was coupled with the larger Paul's Mall club. Both were owned by Fred Taylor and presented some of the finest acts in jazz and pop six nights a week, featuring two shows a night. Countless amazing jazz acts performed at the workshop, including Miles Davis, Larry Coryell, Herbie Hancock, Keith Jarrett, and even Patti Smith. Paul's Mall saw the Boston debuts of many acts, including the American debut of the Wailers (featuring reggae legend Bob Marley) in 1973. The clubs lasted until 1979, and Fred Taylor is still active in promoting and booking concerts at Sculler's, one of the premier jazz clubs in Boston.

Newton, Massachusetts, native George Wein (1925–) made his living as a jazz musician when he was a young man in the 1940s, playing some of these rooms with great Boston-bred musicians like Vic Dickenson (trombone), Ruby Braff (trumpet), Edmond Hall (clarinet), and Frankie Newton (trumpet). In 1950 Wein opened the premier jazz club of the era, Storyville. Originally located in the Copley Square Hotel, Storyville hosted many of the greatest acts in jazz, and was especially proud of featuring cutting-edge bebop acts like Charlie Parker, Clifford Brown, Dizzy Gillespie, and Miles Davis, while giving respect to the older heritage of jazz with bookings like Louis Armstrong and Count Basie as well as the ubiquitous Duke Ellington. He also spotlighted many of the important appearances by great jazz divas like Sarah Vaughn, Ella Fitzgerald, Lee Wiley, Dinah Washington, and Billie Holiday.

The experience of running Storyville led to George Wein's next project: starting the Newport Jazz Festival, in Newport, Rhode Island. Until this time, there was only one other music festival in New England, the Tanglewood Festival, a mostly classical music event in the western Massachusetts town of Lenox. With the financial backing of Newport society figures Lois and Elaine Lorillard, Wein launched a festival that would have a profound effect on not only the world of jazz, but on all genres of music.

New England Jazz Clubs

Boston had many jazz and swing clubs dotting Massachusetts Avenue in the South End from the 1930s through the 1950s. Perhaps the most influential club was opened in 1947 by Joseph L. Walcott (1897–1998), who was the first black nightclub owner in New England. Named after Walcott himself, Wally's Paradise became known for featuring the hottest national acts as well as offering local students at the Berklee School of Music, the New England Conservatory of Music, and the Boston Conservatory a chance to play with some of their idols. Wally's has hosted such jazz greats as Roy Hargrove, Branford Marsalis, Sam Newsome, Mark Whitfield, and Joshua Redman, many while they were still quite young. It is no coincidence that many of these inspired musicians went on to international success. The exciting mix of young and proven talent made for legendary shows at Wally's, and was so popular that Wally's is still open—now located across the street and renamed Wally's Café—and continues to offer a nightly mix of talented student and professional live jazz.

The Newport Festivals

The Jazz Festival started in 1954 in the blue-blooded town of Newport, Rhode Island, and soon blossomed into the most important jazz, folk, and rock festival. It also served the purpose of furthering racial integration years before similarly situated affluent resort towns allowed blacks the social and economic amenities of white America. Throughout the 1950s and 1960s the festival showcased, and in many instances discovered or revived, many of the greatest acts in jazz from Duke Ellington to Miles Davis. George Wein also booked innovative artists like Charles Mingus, John Coltrane, Sonny Rollins, and Thelonius Monk when few large venues would have them. Wein extended his influence to acts outside of the jazz genre by booking rhythm-and-blues singer Ray Charles, gospel singer Mahalia Jackson, blues shouter Big Maybelle, and rock 'n' roller Chuck Berry at the Newport Jazz Festival in 1958. Wein branched out into other genres with his inauguration of the Newport Folk Festival, which started in 1960.

The Newport Folk Festival, along with many of the folk clubs of Boston and Cambridge, like Club 47 and the Unicorn, played a major part in the rediscovery of many great blues artists who had slipped into obscurity in recent years. In the late 1960s, Wein was the first to book rock and pop acts alongside legendary jazz musicians, exposing generations of young listeners who had come to hear the likes of Janis Joplin, Sly and the Family Stone, James Brown, or Bob Dylan to their first taste of jazz, blues, or folk artists. Although this eclectic booking policy ultimately led to problems that caused Wein and the festivals to abandon Newport for over a decade, this early experiment in diverse booking is one of Wein's lasting legacies.

In 1971, Wein left Newport and moved his festival to New York City. Although he had much success in New York and his jazz festival continues there to this day, still it was never quite the same as the magical festivals in Newport. In the 1980s, Wein came back to Newport and revived both the folk and jazz festivals with a slightly scaled-down approach (usually with crowds between 10,000 and 15,000 as opposed to the crowds of over 100,000 in 1969).

George Wein continues to be a major figure in the music business, and his innovative programming has taken his Festival Productions all over the world. He is the most important promoter for jazz and blues festivals throughout Europe and the United States, and has arguably done more to further the appreciation of those genres than anyone else in the business.

THE RISE OF POPULAR MUSIC IN NEW ENGLAND

New England is historically a place of firsts, and its record of musical accomplishments is no different. One explanation for this is demographic: the Boston area has more college students than any other urban area in the United States and boasts prestigious music schools such as Berklee College of Music, New England Conservatory, Boston Conservatory, and the Longey School. There are also a number of influential universities outside the Boston area, such as Yale in New Haven, Connecticut, Amherst College in western Massachusetts, and the University of Vermont in Burlington. For years, the music industry has viewed these college towns as a ready-made market for music, especially as a place to introduce new and developing artists to radio, television, the retail sector, and live venues.

One of the cultural and historical factors that created a downside to the Boston music scene is the continuing influence of its Puritan legacy. Boston actually had a city censor until the 1980s, although he (there never was a female censor) was usually more concerned with books, theater, and film than with the music industry. Also, many of the so-called blue laws that control alcohol licensing and hours of operation are part of this legacy and have a direct effect on the success or failure of a music venue. Boston and Cambridge's nightclubs usually have to close by 1 a.m., leaving less time for bands to perform and less money for the venue to make on alcohol and ticket sales. This, in turn, often results in lower pay for musicians, while increasing competition for performance opportunities. Even today you will find world-class musicians playing local pubs for $30 a night just for the chance to perform while on break from national tours. In addition, many musicians have used Boston's culturally rich scene as a stepping-stone for more lucrative opportunities in larger cities like New York.

Another major issue for the New England music scene is the region's racial and ethnic composition. New England has a history of neighborhoods and towns made up of tight ethnic enclaves, which can be culturally rich and interesting but also can manifest attitudes and prejudices that are insular and parochial. This has resulted in the nurturing of ethnic music—the continuing interest and growth in traditional Irish music is a good example—but can also keep scenes very localized and sometimes inhibits growth.

Due in part to these factors, Boston never developed the infrastructure of record companies, managers, booking agents, and necessary coverage of the entertainment media to be a music industry center like New York, Los Angeles, or Nashville. Nonetheless, because many thousands of exuberant young people, rich ethnic influences, and scores of talented musicians make this area their home, New England has become, and remains, an important center for developing shows and musicians and a key market center for the music industry.

The 1950s and the Birth of Rock 'n' Roll

A boom in popular music—specifically the controversial rock 'n' roll—came of age in American culture in the mid-1950s through a combination of social, economic, and historical factors. The United States was in the midst of an economic upswing that allowed for a huge expansion of the middle class. Many families started moving from cities to the suburbs, and teenagers had an influx of expendable income and the desire to spend it in ways that expressed their newfound quest for freedom. Combined with a new awareness of international events, this new self-awareness corresponded with, and gave expression to, the rise of rock 'n' roll.

Rock 'n' roll first became popular with these trend-setting teenagers through radio airplay. Boston's first popular radio disk jockey (D.J.) to play rock 'n' roll on the radio was Joe Smith. He played records at WILD and WCOP in the mid-1950s, and later went on to become a major recording executive at Warner Brothers. But perhaps the most important D.J. of the decade spanning 1956–1966 was

Arnie "WooWoo" Ginsberg, who started at WBOS in 1956, the same year that Elvis Presley's success ensured the cross-over of rhythm and blues to rock 'n' roll and the mass embrace of the genre by teenagers. Ginsberg, who grew up in Maine, started at WMEX in 1958 and inspired teenagers all over New England with his *Night Train* show. His antics included the use of sound effects like a taxi horn, train whistle, bone rattles, New Year's noisemakers, animal sound effects, and a manic adenoidal delivery that mimicked a live party on the radio. More important, he was one of the few D.J.s in New England to have total control over what they played on the radio. Not only was he able to "break" (to be the first one to play and give momentum to a record) many of the classic hits of the late 1950s through the mid-1960s, he also debuted some of the best local bands and introduced them to a national audience.

Besides the burgeoning popularity of rock 'n' roll, doo-wop was also a style that had many fans during the 1950s and became popular with the help of supportive D.J.s. Mirroring other regions in the nation, New England had its share of doo-wop acts to gain national fame. The Tune Weavers were a black vocal group from Boston whose "Happy, Happy Birthday" not only rose to number five on the charts but also became a standard birthday alternative to the more traditional version. Another group that received national attention was the G-Clefs, a group of brothers who hit the national charts in 1957 with "Ka Ding Dong." The most successful musician in this period, however, was Freddie "Boom Boom" Cannon, born Freddie Picariello in Revere, Massachusetts, in 1940. He began playing in a house band at the Surf ballrooms in New England seaside towns such as Revere Beach, Nantasket Beach (Hull), and Salisbury Beach. His first big hit, "Tallahassee Lassie," reached number six on the charts nationally in 1959, again with help from WMEX D.J. Arnie Ginsberg's airplay. Subsequent top-ten hits like "Way Down Yonder in New Orleans" (1960), "Palisades Park" (1962), "Abigail Beecher" (1963), and "Action" (1964) helped define the sound of summer for a generation of young Americans.

Freddie Cannon's boost to national stardom was also helped by an important factor in the development of original homegrown rock 'n' roll in this period in New England: the "teen club" phenomenon. This was a "scene" that developed mostly in suburban former big band ballrooms and was an outgrowth of the 1950s "sock hop," wherein local church groups or schools would hire a radio personality to play the latest rock 'n' roll records to crowds of teenagers (they were called "sock hops" because the events were often held in gymnasiums and students had to remove their shoes so as not to ruin the floor). Occasionally these hops would have live bands, usually made up of local high school kids. Bill Spence was an owner of Boston Harbor and suburban ferryboats who seized on the hop idea and applied it to an old big band ballroom on the South Shore of Boston in Nantasket Beach, called the Surf. Starting in the late 1950s, Spence used Arnie Ginsburg as emcee and would import major recording stars like Frankie Avalon or Gene Pitney and would feature local acts.

The Rockin' Ramrods (later renamed the Ramrods) was a popular rock band who received its start from The Surf and parlayed it into national success. They were one of the first rock bands, and covered early Beatles and Little Richard songs as well as performing some originals. Their popularity reached its pinnacle in 1966 when they toured the country opening for the Rolling Stones.

Barry and the Remains made an even greater impact on the regional and national rock 'n' roll scene. Both guitarist/singer Barry Tashian and pianist Billy Briggs from Westport, Connecticut, met Waterbury, Connecticut, drummer Chip Damiani and New Jersey bassist Vern Miller at Boston University in 1963. They were the first rock 'n' roll bands to play the Kenmore Square club the Rathskeller—also known as "the Rat"—building up a solid local following in the pre-Beatles rock era. They went on to national success in 1966 while touring with the Beatles and promoting their classic album *The Remains*, which included such garage classics as "Diddy Wah Diddy" and "Don't Look Back."

The 1960s and the Emergence of Folk Music

The number of college students increased in the 1960s with many of them painfully aware of their narrow escape from the horrors of the war in Vietnam. This increasing awareness of the outside world and the newfound freedom of many young people on their own for the first time created a hotbed of activism in the 1960s, which used music and social gatherings as one way of expressing this unrest. One of the most influential havens for folk music in the 1960s was Club 47 in the heart of Harvard Square in Cambridge.

Joan Baez lived in Belmont, Massachusetts, with Mimi Farina. Joan was a student at Boston University when she started performing at Club 47 in 1958. She quickly became a star of this budding scene, and in 1959 she recorded her first album for the national label Vanguard Records. She performed a breakout set at the first Newport Folk Festival in 1959 at the age of eighteen, which led to her becoming the first major female star of this growing interest in folk music. A breakout article in *Time* magazine in 1962 characterized the burgeoning folk scene as represented by Joan Baez. "She wears no makeup. . . . In performance she comes on, walks straight to the microphone, and begins to sing. No patter. No show business. . . . She is only 21 and palpably nubile. But there is little sex in that clear flow of sound." This new sound was not flashy rock 'n' roll, but a simple return to the roots of music as well as values of peace and simplicity and acceptance, and Joan was one of the first to make this style popular and was also one of the first of the younger folk singers to become involved in civil rights and antiwar demonstrations.

Joan Baez also was a great influence on perhaps the most popular and groundbreaking folk singer of the time. She helped and encouraged Bob Dylan when he came to the Boston-Cambridge nexus in 1961–1962. She let the lesser-known Dylan share her stage as an opening act, or they performed as a duet. By 1965, Dylan's career had eclipsed Baez's in popularity, and he had scandalized the traditional folk world with both his "electrified" musical approach—performing with a full band including electric guitars and drums—and his turn to personal subjects and away from political protest in his songwriting.

From an impeccable folk-singing pedigree comes Arlo Guthrie (1947–), son of the truly legendary folk troubadour Woody Guthrie. Arlo was born in New York and went to high school in western Massachusetts. Honing his craft locally at folk venues like Club 47, he exemplified the politics of folk singing in its heyday as well as reinforcing the conservative attitudes in many parts of New England during the 1960s. Arlo Guthrie's most famous song, "Alice's Restaurant," is an eighteen-minute epic about a humorous encounter with the police chief of Stockbridge,

Bob Dylan at Newport

Bob Dylan's appearance at the Newport Folk Festival during the summer of 1965 became a story of legend and is recounted in scores of memoirs and books as a turning point in the development of the sixties "counter-culture." Dylan played his set with an electric guitar and fellow musicians blues guitarist Mike Bloomfield, Sam Lay on drums (both of the Paul Butterfield Blues Band), Harvey Brooks on electric bass, and Al Kooper (later of the Blues Project and Blood, Sweat and Tears) on organ. As some of the audience booed and some clamored for the volume to be turned up, Eric von Schmidt describes the chaotic scene in *Baby, Let Me Follow You Down*:

> Almost as soon as it got to the point where you could begin to hear Dylan's voice over the band, he stopped and left the stage. The audience was in a total uproar by this time. . . . he had only intended to do the two songs [the band] had rehearsed— "Maggie's Farm" and "Like a Rolling Stone"—and had gone to get his acoustic guitar and pull himself together for the rest of his set.

He took a few minutes to find an acoustic and came back on to play "It's All Over Now, Baby Blue" while many fans "cheered, thinking that they had forced him to give in and play acoustic," but the "tone of the evening had been shattered."[1]

A new generation of young folk fans showed little loyalty to the values and concerns of the old guard folkies like Pete Seeger and Alan Lomax. Some thought that with his more personal lyrics and electric guitar, he was selling out and bowing to commercialism. Others did not want to accept that folk music as they knew it was changing. Whatever the reason, that summer afternoon in 1965 changed the folk music scene forever.

which resulted in Guthrie's arrest for littering and enabled Guthrie—at least in the song—to get out of the military draft for the war in Vietnam. "Alice's Restaurant" launched his career when he performed it at the Newport Folk Festival in 1967 and he made a memorable appearance at the Woodstock Festival that same year. Arlo is still based in western Massachusetts. In 1991, he purchased the Trinity Church in Stockbridge, Massachusetts—the inspiration for "Alice's Restaurant"—where he has set up the Guthrie Foundation (a nonprofit organization that addresses social issues) and the Guthrie Center (a nonprofit interfaith church that provides community outreach services).

While Joan Baez and Bob Dylan were two of the most famous musicians to pass through Club 47 and other venues such as the Unicorn and the Sword in the Stone, New England provided a nurturing and creative environment for many of the greatest American folk talents of the 1960s and 1970s. Other folk musicians such as Mimi Farina (Joan's sister who made influential recordings as part of a duo with her husband, Richard Farina), Tom Rush, Maria Muldaur and, a little later, Arlo Guthrie, James Taylor, and Bonnie Raitt spent at least their formative years in New England. Many of these artists were strongly influenced by the social activism of the Boston-Cambridge scene—especially in the civil rights and antiwar movements—and became involved in the political and social movements of the sixties and beyond.

The infamous Club 47 changed its name to Club Passim in 1969 and has been in Harvard Square in Cambridge for over forty years where it remains today. Now a nonprofit entity, it continues to be an influential performance space and continue its mission of promoting folk and acoustic music by nurturing new and influential artists.

Rediscovering the Blues

One of the most important achievements of both the Boston-Cambridge folk scene and the Newport Folk and Jazz Festivals was the role that each played in the rediscovery of some the country's greatest blues artists and in the subsequent reintroduction of blues as a popular music genre. One of the highlights of the Newport Folk Festival in 1963 was a performance by Mississippi John Hurt, who had previously been living in obscurity in Mississippi for thirty-five years until a local blues fan sought him out. His performance inspired a rash of interest in once-popular blues musicians from the 1950s. Within a year Skip James, Son House, and Muddy Waters, among others, were featured at the Newport Folk Festival, Club 47, and the Unicorn. This resurgence in popularity of this musical genre led to a major blues revival and influenced countless young artists and musicians who went on to form important acts like Peter Wolf (the J. Geils Band), Al Wilson (Canned Heat), Taj Mahal (from Springfield, Massachusetts), and Chris Smithers.

Tom Rush (1942–), from Portsmouth, New Hampshire, was key in the refocus on blues in the late 1960s and early 1970s. Originally moving to Cambridge to go to Harvard in 1961, Rush began performing in the area coffeehouses and clubs soon after and started recording in 1962. His early style was folk-blues, and was heavily influenced by the blues greats he had been gigging with at Club 47 and the Unicorn. By the mid-1960s he was well known for finding songs by unknown musicians and rerecording them himself in his signature style, while bringing attention to the orginal artist as well. He recorded the first versions of Joni Mitchell, James Taylor, or Jackson Browne songs, before any of them had even made a record, and many artists cite him as a major influence. He was one of the first popular performers of the 1960s to infuse folk music with heavy blues influences and in many ways was instrumental in the rediscovery of the blues.

Paul Rishell (1950–) was very much on the cutting edge of musical styles during this time period as well. Born in Brooklyn, New York, Rishell started his musical career playing in the rock and surf bands of the late 1950s and early 1960s while becoming a talented and in-demand guitar player. Proficient in both electric and acoustic, Rishell got studio and accompanying work playing with such masters as Son House, Johnny Shines, Sonny Terry, Brownie McGhee, and Howlin' Wolf, among others. His first album was half acoustic and half electric, clearly reflecting this pivotal time in the merging of folk and blues.

Another derivative of the folk and blues styles to come out in the late 1960s and 1970s was the singer-songwriter genre. One of the most prolific and talented artists in this style is Boston-born James Taylor (1948–). After going to Milton Academy, James started both on the folk circuit in Boston-Cambridge and in a rock band called the Flying Machine in New York City. He was too late for the golden era of Club 47, but did perform in coffeehouses like the Sword in the Stone on Charles Street and the Unicorn. This style is exemplified by the plaintive narrative singing inspired by the folk movement, as well as the rhythmic and emotive musical styles of the blues.

James Taylor's breakout album was *Sweet Baby James* (1970), which contained three massive hits: "Fire and Rain," "Country Road," and "Sweet Baby James." The success of this album not only launched James' career, it also caused the explosion of the singer-songwriter genre, which dominated much of music in the seventies. James Taylor has toured incessantly over the years, and still enjoys commercial success as epitomized by his recent Grammy-winning album, *October Road* (2002).

One of the most influential bands of the late 1960s to be influenced by the blues

Boston-born James Taylor's breakout album *Sweet Baby James* (1970) caused the explosion of the singer-songwriter genre, which dominated much of music in the 1970s. Photofest.

was the J. Geils Band. Started in 1968 by the charismatic local singer and D.J. Peter Wolf (1946–) and drummer Stephen Jo Bladd, who played together in the Hallucinations, they recruited guitarist Jay Geils, bassist Danny Klein, harpist Magic Dick, and organist Seth Justman in what was originally called the J. Geils Blues Band. Influenced by classic rhythm and blues as well as rock 'n' roll, the J. Geils Band perfected their unique sound playing frequently around the New England area at clubs such as the Boston Tea Party.

Four years later they were signed by Atlantic Records, a label with a reputation for supporting blues artists. The band stood out because of both their new take on blues-inspired rock and their high-energy live shows, where they dressed more like classic blues musicians of the 1920s than in the hippie style that was so popular in the late 1960s and early 1970s. The J. Geils Band flourished throughout the 1970s, becoming one of the most popular bands in the country until their breakup in 1983. They are still regarded for their stellar songwriting and their role in popularizing blues-rock.

In part influenced by the blues-rock sound that the J. Geils Band was popularizing in New England and across the country, Aerosmith got its start in Sunapee, New Hampshire, where lead singer Steven Tyler (1948–) had grown up and played drums in teen bands. He was joined by Berklee College dropouts Joe Perry and Brad Whitford, both on guitar, New Hampshire native Tom Hamilton on bass, and New Yorker Joey Kramer on drums. After playing clubs around New England, Aerosmith's reputation for high-energy shows and driving rock and blues caught the attention of Columbia Records in 1973. The band went on to create their own brand of glamour-tinged rock 'n' roll and became a huge commercial success, with several major hits and large concert draws throughout the 1990s.

Punk and the Birth of New Wave

While Aerosmith was captivating stadiums of fans with radio-friendly hits and the J. Geils Band was bringing their unique brand of blues-rock to the masses, the Modern Lovers were playing a whole new brand of music that was never as commercially successful but perhaps even more influential in the history of modern music.

Jonathan Richman (1951–), born in Natick, Massachusetts, was a true original. In the late 1960s and early 1970s when pot-smoking hippies played long psychedelic solos, he stood out with his deadpan, witty lyrics—some about how he *doesn't* smoke pot—and traditional song structures. After hearing the Velvet Underground in 1970, Jonathan was so inspired by this original sound—the beginnings of punk rock—that he began the Modern Lovers with his high school neighbor, guitarist John Felice. They recruited drummer David Robinson, bassist Rolf Anderson, keyboardist Jerry Harrison, and bassist Ernie Brooks and were soon signed by manager David Geffen. Producer John Cale, who worked with their idols the Velvet Underground, helped them create their monumental first LP soon thereafter.

The Modern Lovers went on to moderate commercial success, touring the United States and Europe, but they leave a rich and lasting legacy. Their confluence of talent and unique sounds inspired an era of punk rock: driving rhythms, heavy bass, and witty lyrics. Bands such as the Sex Pistols cite them as an influence, and the members of the Modern Lovers went on to front other, more commercially successful groups: Jonathan Richman is well known as a solo artist and was featured in the box-office movie hit *There's Something About Mary*, Jerry Harrison's keyboard playing helped define the Talking Heads' sounds, original member John Felice began the punk rock band the Real Kids, and David Robinson found fame with the Cars.

The Mighty Mighty Bosstones took the hard-edged punk sensibilities of the Modern Lovers and other garage rock bands and added a heavy dose of ska—brass section and all—to create a whole new sound in 1985, coining the term "ska-core." Their music had a definite edge, and Dicky Barrett's scratchy vocals and the band's in-your-face name exemplified their Boston attitude. The Bosstones' on-stage uniform of full suits—often bright plaid—belied their Boston Irish roots, and their infectious energy at their live shows made them popular draws. They were the first American ska band signed to a major label in 1993 when they contracted with Mercury Records. The Mighty Mighty Bosstones had moderate commercial success, including a cameo in the box-office hit movie *Clueless*. They have never forgotten their Boston roots, however, and their local shows are highly anticipated and sell out quickly. Their unique brand of ska-core has inspired a number of bands to add ska or other seemingly disparate musical genre influences to their music.

The Boston club the Rathskellar, known as the Rat, was a major supporter of the punk rock and new wave scene in the 1970s and early 1980s. In 1974 the band Mickey Clean and the Mezz—Michael Cleanthes, Asa Brebner, who toured with the Modern Lovers, Jeffrey Wilkinson, and Scott Baerenwald—approached colorful owner Jimmy Harrold and begged him to give their band a show. Harrold acquiesced, and the night was a huge success during a time when most of the other clubs in town were converting to the more popular disco music or booking mindless "boogie" bands—a sort of watered-down version of blues-rock. Dark, dank, and dirty, the Rat had the trappings of a quintessential rock club and began booking original hard edged rock 'n' roll seven nights a week. The Rat scene heated up in 1975–1976, around the same time that CBGB's Club in New York City became popular for its cutting-edge music. The Rat was influential for giving a home and identity to many punk and garage rock bands of this era.

In 1977, the local band the Cars was gaining a following among the music fans who frequented the Rat and other clubs such as Cantone's that showcased punk and garage rock bands. Most of the members of the Cars were seasoned musicians:

leader Ric Ocasek had played with lead singer and bassist Ben Orr back in the 1960s in their hometown of Cleveland, Ohio, before moving to Cambridge. Greg Hawkes began playing with the pair in 1973, and in 1975 Elliot Easton, the youngest of the group and a Berklee College of Music graduate, joined them. The group was complete in 1977 when they added David Robinson from the Modern Lovers and debuted as the Cars on New Year's Eve. Almost from their inception, they garnered popular and critical acclaim. Ocasek's songs simplified and focused both musical and thematic approaches of past acts like the Velvet Underground and the Modern Lovers, and yet the band utilized many of the newer sounds and images of the emerging punk aesthetic in a fresh way. The Cars featured the two contrasting lead singing styles of Orr, a crooner and melodic belter, and Ocasek, who sang in a cool and detached monotone. Hawkes' variety of keyboard and synthesizer textures, Easton's dynamic yet succinct solos, and Robinson's minimalist genius on drums made the Cars into an amalgam of everything catchy, cool, and artsy about the new music. With several big hits including "Drive" and "Hello Again," they had commercial success and even MTV airtime. Alongside bands like Blondie and the Talking Heads from New York City, the Cars came to define what became known as new wave.

During new wave's heyday in the 1980s, a pair of brothers from Boston, Maurice Starr (Lawrence Johnson, 1950–) and Michael Jonzun (Johnson, 1955–), took the most commercial aspects of that genre, mixed in watered-down rock and rhythm and blues, and applied it to create the entirely new mass market "boy-band" genre. Their first big successes were the bands New Edition and Jonzun Crew, both catering to the teen demographic with each band's trendy yet wholesome good looks and commercial and accessible style.

In the early 1980s recording technology had developed to the point of using sequencing, drum machines, and synthesizers instead of or in addition to live musicians. Even with relatively primitive eight-track recording technology, Maurice and Michael were able to record pop hits, playing and singing nearly everything themselves. This pair of producers was one of the first to utilize this approach in "teen pop" recordings. Maurice later fine-tuned the concept in his hugely successful New Kids on the Block records of the late 1980s and early 1990s, paving the way for numerous subsequent immensely popular boy bands. Once again the relatively young demographic of the Boston area, with its high concentration of colleges and universities, was a perfect starting ground to introduce such commercial bands to the youth market.

In the early 1980s, instruments more associated with the new wave genre were also influencing bands other than bubblegum boy bands. Punk and garage rock bands were beginning to use prerecorded music and sounds (early versions of what we now know as "samples"), feedback, and electric instruments like keyboards and drum machines in their music. Mission of Burma was an influential front leader in this new genre known as post punk. Starting in Boston in 1979, Mission of Burma consisted of Clint Conley, Peter Prescott, and Roger Miller on bass, drums, and guitar, respectively; as well as Martin Swope on "tape loops" and sound treatments—this new form of instrumentalization. As Michael Azerrad writes in *Our Band Could Be Your Life* (2001), they "took elements of free jazz, psychedelia and experimental music and injected them into often anthemic punk rock."[2] What they came up with was a unique amalgam of screeching dynamics and occasional melody.

Together for only four years, the band broke up due to guitarist Miller's worsening tinnitus condition; most likely the incredible on-stage volume at which they usually performed exacerbated it. Despite their short tenure, this groundbreaking band introduced the world to a new brand of jagged, restless punk music. Mission of Burma influenced numerous rock and punk bands that saw their high-energy shows locally at the Rat, or studied their few feedback-laden recordings.

Phish and Jam Bands

Many historians and fans credit the Grateful Dead with creating the jam band aesthetic. Starting in San Francisco in the mid-sixties, the band created its own musical and touring concept, comparable to a traveling carnival. Hoards of fans who called themselves "deadheads" followed the band on its tours and developed a lifestyle to go with the shows. Their music took influence from the impromptu, meandering solos and instrumentals of jazz

Phish. Photofest.

combined with the musical feel of blues-rock. The first band to pick up this aesthetic and take it several steps further was Phish. Although removed from the Dead by nearly two decades, Phish developed the jam band approach to the point where they can be said to have reinvented the genre, while providing a role model for millions of fans and scores of jam bands. The band started in Burlington, Vermont, in 1983. Guitarists Trey Anastasio (1964–) and Jeff Holdsworth (1964–), bassist Mike Gordon (1965–), and drummer Jon Fishman (1965–) met at the University of Vermont, where most of them were students, and started playing semiprofessional college gigs there in 1984. Page McConnell (1963–) joined on keyboards in 1985, and Holdsworth left in 1986 after he graduated from the University of Vermont.

They began playing college and club shows around Burlington, building up a large local following. In 1988 they began playing shows outside Vermont and saw the enormous potential for their music among the new hippies of the late 1980s—those who were against the excess, greed, and gentrification that seemed to characterize the 1980. Phish encouraged fans to tape shows, as the Dead had done, and strove to create a community among fans instead of trying to squeeze every last dollar from touring and record sales. They began building their audience gig by gig with word of mouth and through their huge mailing list—becoming one of the first bands with an e-mail list in 1990.

The band has released successful albums, but the records are almost tangential to Phish's success. Their theatrical live show, which began to incorporate innovative sound and light systems and worked in community-building, audience-pleasing elements, was unique among the major-label–sponsored tours. Phish's popularity has continued to grow through their grassroots and atypical marketing efforts. The group has proven that an act does not have to live in a major music city to become nationally successful, and that a band does not have to adhere to the typical touring and promotional framework to become popular or influential. This, more than the music itself, may be their most important legacy.

THE RETURN TO TRADITIONALISM, FROM THE 1980s TO THE PRESENT

Despite the influx of new instruments and dissonance during the 1980s, the traditional blues and folk scenes were still going strong. New England had never ceased being a region that supported these genres with its ongoing Newport Folk Festival and clubs like Cambridge's Joe's Place and the Speakeasy, and Providence's Roomful of Blues.

This adherence to traditional influences has made the Boston-Cambridge-Somerville area one of the mainstays in modern folk and Americana music to the present day. With Club Passim—the renamed Club 47—as its center, folk musicians have gravitated to the New England region. Folk music as it was in the 1960s—mainly a singer/songwriter playing with an acoustic guitar—was a common attraction both in clubs around the area and among street musicians, often seen in Harvard Square. Despite the sometimes inclement weather, many musicians have started their careers playing for tips in the Square and attending one of the many weekly open mike nights, eventually garnering enough recognition to get booked at a local folk club. Attracting forward-thinking people since then, Cambridge became known as an open-minded city where unseasoned folk singers could get a start and liberal ideals were embraced. Other modern bluegrass and folk-inspired bands grew out of this scene and from the traditional music migrating to the cities from smaller communities in the mountains of northern New England.

Treat Her Right was a country-blues band that broke away from the increasingly electric and modern sound of the mid-1980s with a return to the Cambridge folk and blues tradition. Begun in 1986 by David Champagne, Mark Sandman (1952–1999), Billy Conway, and Jim Fitting, Treat Her Right had strong blues and country influences—most evident in Sandman's unique style of slide bass playing. This new take on classic rhythm and blues and old-time rock 'n' roll was a wake-up call in the midst of the new wave craze, and Treat Her Right received high acclaim and fame for their unique musical direction.

Mark Sandman refined his bluesy bass drawl and went on to form one of the most influential bands of the 1990s. Morphine had a unique minimalist sound that grew out of their unusual instrumentation: Sandman played slide bass (starting out on one string and later graduating to two so "he could play chords," as he liked to joke), Dana Colley played baritone saxophone, and drummer Billy Conway—replacing founding member Jerome Dupree—often played a stripped-down kit without cymbals. Sandman referred to the band's low-fi sound as "a light-hearted experiment in darkness" and they were noted for creating stripped-down rock with heavy bass and the unique and moody quality of Colley's saxophone. The band was touring Europe in the summer of 1999 when leader Sandman collapsed on stage in Italy and died of a heart attack.

The Blood Oranges formed in the late 1980s as an outlet for mandolin player Jimmy Ryan (1957–) to fuse his love of traditional music with his interest in rock 'n' roll. With bassist/vocalist Cheri Knight, guitarist Mark Spencer, and drummer Ron Ward, the Blood Oranges were influenced greatly by the traditional bluegrass and fiddle music that Jimmy grew up with. Combining folk, bluegrass, and rock elements, the band exemplified the new Americana or alt-country genre that was just beginning in areas across the country. This amalgam of modern rock infused with traditional folk found fans across the demographics. Students were attracted to its modern sensibilities, thirty- and forty-somethings liked the more mellow feel and top-notch musicianship required, and even older fans began coming out to the clubs to hear reinterpretations of the traditional music they grew up with. The Blood Oranges broke up in 1995, but their long tenure was an inspiration to many musicians struggling to reconcile the traditional music they grew up loving with more modern influences.

The Benders, started in 2000 by Bow Thayer, Steve Mayone, Jabe Beyer, Nolan McKelvey, and Tim Kelly, drew even more heavily on traditional music. Combining seemingly disparate influences—bluegrass, folk, and modern rock sensibilities—they helped shape the new genre of bluegrass rock, or new Americana music. The Benders exemplified this new traditional music taking hold and played across New England, from Boston to Burlington. Consisting of banjo, mandolin, acoustic guitar, upright bass, and dobro, the instrumentation appeared very traditional, but the music they produced was obviously influenced by rock 'n' roll. They were all stellar musicians and all contributing songwriters, their arrangements were tight, and their songs and lyrics had a northern edge that southern bluegrass lacked. The Benders broke up in 2003, but Thayer, Mayone, Beyer, and McKelvey all have successful solo careers with a similar Americana feel.

The Benders and subsequent new Americana groups demonstrated a return to New England roots. This new genre is unique to the region and is greatly influenced by the harshness of the mountains of Vermont, New Hampshire, or Maine, as well as traditional French Canadian fiddle music found in small towns around the area. The lyrics and mood of the music express the extreme weather, change of seasons, and winter loneliness felt by northerners who have traditionally toiled to subsist in a difficult landscape, and the music has an edge that its southern bluegrass cousin doesn't.

French Canadian Music in New England

The new Americana sound coming out of New England today would not exist if it weren't for the influence of French Canadian music on the region. The French Canadian province of Quebec to the north has exerted a strong influence through the countless émigrés who settled in northern Rhode Island and southern Maine and in towns near the border in northern New Hampshire and Vermont.

Originally performed for special occasions and holidays, French Canadian musical events most often centered around the *quadrille* or French square dance, which consisted of couples dancing while "callers" indicated the steps. The musical accompaniment always included one or more fiddlers, and often guitars, accordions, harmonicas, and spoons, and was soon expanded to include the piano and any number of wind instruments. Members of the community would bring instruments and entertainment at these events, which were truly social occasions to which the entire community was often invited. The French *quadrille* dances are closely associated with American square dancing and English contra dancing, and the French were the first to employ this style of dance.

Quadrilles are still quite popular today in communities with strong French Canadian ties and have even made their way into the cities of Providence, Boston, Portland, and Burlington, where young people are rediscovering this centuries-old form of dance and socializing.

Besides the social aspect, however, the musical accompaniment to *quadrille* dancing influenced the country and bluegrass sound that was cultivated in the mountains of Vermont, New Hampshire, and Maine. Long winters and limited social opportunities bred accomplished musicians—especially fiddlers—who practiced their craft for personal and family entertainment and in preparation for community dance events. This music had been played for generations as entertainment within these close-knit communities, but it wasn't until the mid-1900s, when young people began moving to the cities, that bands began forming with commercial success in mind, drawing inspiration from these traditional musical influences. As discussed earlier, this had a direct influence on the new Americana sound popular today in New England.

Contra dancing is a close cousin to the French Canadian *quadrilles*. Although English in origin, it is generally accepted that the European French influences this style of dance, and it was eventually brought to America by the first English settlers. Like the *quadrilles*, contra dancing involves couples dancing to fiddle, accordion, or woodwind music to dances indicated by a caller, and the occasion for such events was social or a holiday. Contra dancing lost popularity in the mid-twentieth century, but it has seen a comeback in the past decade or so, with college and dance students and other young people becoming interested in this traditional form of dance as a means to connect with their heritage or as an alternative social event.

Celtic Music in New England

The city of Boston has been home to Irish and Scottish immigrants for centuries, and there has always been a community to support traditional dance parties called *ceilidhs* and pub jams called *seisiuns*. Often these are instrumental performances where the fiddle is the main—or only—instrument. Like the French Canadian *quadrilles*, Celtic music was performed as a community social event at people's houses or public buildings, often with Celtic jig dancing for entertainment or special occasions. The pub scene, where generations of mostly Irish Americans have gathered, and the ubiquitous Scottish bagpipe groups at every city parade have been part of Boston's very identity for years. The history of having live *seisiuns* in pubs has given the Boston area a reputation as an excellent place to see live music, and performances of expert fiddling have paved the way for the emergence of other music genres.

Seisiuns are lively fiddle performances where a number of musicians play known variations on a traditional melody. These have been traditional events one night or more a week at many Irish pubs for decades, but the Celtic scene has seen quite a revival in the past ten years. A new generation of both Irish and Scottish Americans as well as musicians from other backgrounds have discovered an interest in Celtic fiddling. Strong teachers are found at the top music schools in the area, and fiddling camps are becoming popular in New England and around the country.

With Celtic music's growing popularity, traditional *seisiuns* can be found any night of the week, most often in pubs such as the Burren in Somerville, the Skellig in Waltham, and Matt Murphy's in Brookline. Modern Celtic music has also become its own genre, with bands such as the Chieftains from Ireland, who perform often in the United States, and Old Blind Dog taking traditional influences and adding rock or country influences to create a new and even more accessible genre of Celtic-inspired music.

Portuguese Music in New England

New England's history as a shipping and whaling region has brought generations of Portuguese immigrants to the area to share their expertise in towns and cities that rely heavily on such industries. With them comes their musical influence as well. An early form of Portuguese musical performance was resonant with people of all cultures who relied on whaling or fishing to support their families. The *fado* is a solo reflecting on pain and uncertainty, often associated with sorrow over those who did not come back from boating disasters. A widow wearing black who sings accompanied by a Portuguese guitarra or viola while gazing toward the sea traditionally performs the *fado*. This traditional Portuguese form of singing influenced classical American compositions and is still performed much as it was centuries ago.

Popular Portuguese-influenced dances and the music that accompanied them were influenced in part by the Iberian Peninsula's proximity to Africa, as well as the Portuguese occupation of Brazil. Heavy drumming and an infectious beat characterize both the samba and the tango, two of the more popular dance forms, and their accompanying music brought to the United States by Portuguese immigrants.

New Bedford, Massachusetts' Feast of the Blessed Sacrament is the largest Portuguese feast in the world and the largest ethnic festival in New England. Started in 1915 by four Madeiran immigrant men who wanted to re-create the religious festivals that were so common in the villages of their home island and to commemorate their safe passage to America, this food and music festival attracts hundreds of thousands of visitors yearly from all over the globe. Important for its mix of traditional and modern Portuguese music as well as for showcasing regional acts representing various musical genres, the feast is an important ethnic tradition that brings attention to the large Portuguese community in New Bedford as well as those on Cape Cod and the islands. Modern Portuguese acts who have played at the feast in recent years include Climax, a group of talented and established New England musicians whose style still draws heavily from traditional roots, and Entrain, a dance-rock band with heavy reliance on percussion.

Cape Verdean Music in New England

A close musical relative to the *fado* is the Cape Verdean *morna*. Also accompanied by stringed instruments, the *morna* reflects the difficulties of life on Cape Verde: centuries of Portuguese occupation, drought, and famine. These challenges of life on Cape Verde led to many immigrants finding their way to American shores, often to work as fishermen or boat builders. The sorrowful tone and minor keys of the Cape Verdean *morna* made the voyage with scores of immigrants, many who settled around New Bedford, northern Rhode Island, and Cape Cod. This music is still performed within the diverse Cape Verdean communities in these areas.

While the popular *morna* is an important musical tradition to Cape Verdeans, the more upbeat *coladeira* is faster calypso-like dance music. Dancing and music have always been an important part of the Cape Verdean social community, and the *coladeira* has been the central style. Different groups have drawn heavily upon this tradition and have adapted the faster, infectious rhythms and heavy thumping beat of the *coladeira* and combined it with popular music of the day. Some of the first electric versions of songs were recorded in the 1960s, and in the 1980s the band Santiago popularized the dance club version, creating club hits in New England and beyond. Rarely notated, both the *morna* and the *coladeira* are traditions that have been passed down by the elders of each generation. Interest in Cape Verdean music has continued to grow, with New England bands like Toi Grace & the Verdatones and the Alberto "Kinzinhu" Rodrigues Band leading the way.

Brazilian Music in New England

Brazilian music has similarities to Portuguese music, most likely from the lingering influence of the mixing of cultures during Portugal's occupation of Brazil. New England's larger Brazilian communities are in New Bedford, northern Rhode Island, and the cities of Dorchester and Somerville adjacent to Boston. There are strong community centers and churches in these areas which offer traditional Brazilian music and dance performances and social activities, and most dance schools in these areas offer traditional Brazilian lessons and socials as well.

Brazil also has the traditional *fado* style of singing, which is similar in its slow and mournful tone. The Brazilian *fado* is sometimes accompanied by the *fado* dance which consists of a hop, skip, and a kick, with the soul of the dance being of despair. Dancing is very popular in Brazilian culture, with the samba and tango both being popular. Also popular is the martial art capoeira, which was developed by Brazilian slaves of African descent, and is often accompanied by drumming. This style of combat was disguised as a dance so that the slaveholders would not know the slaves were training themselves to revolt. The newly formed Brazilian Cultural Center of New England offers numerous music and dance classes and events, and many of the region's dance clubs have nights that feature Latin dancing.

CONCLUSION

New England has a rich cultural history marked by its long tradition of new immigrants as well as its deep traditionalism. It is no surprise that New England's richest musical legacies are as diverse as the century-old Boston Symphony Orchestra and the ever-evolving Cambridge folk scene, as well as the traditional fiddling finding its way into popular music and the revival of contra dancing among New England's youth. This is a region that will continue to influence music for centuries to come.

RESOURCE GUIDE

Printed Sources

Azerad, Michael. *Our Band Could Be Your Life: Scenes from the American Indie Underground, 1981–1991*. Boston: Little, Brown, 2001.

Gehr, Richard, and Phish. *The Phish Book*. New York: Villard, 1998.

Goodman, Fred. *The Mansion on the Hill: Dylan, Young, Springsteen, and the Head-on Collision of Rock and Commerce*. New York: Random House, 1997.

Hitchcock, H. Wiley. *Music in the United States*. 3rd ed. Upper Saddle River, NJ: Prentice-Hall, 2000.

Schuller, Gunther. *Musings: The Musical Worlds of Gunther Schuller: A Collection of His Writings*. New York: Oxford University Press, 1986.

Tawa, Nicholas E. *From Psalm to Symphony: A History of Music in New England*. Boston: Northeastern University Press, 2001.

Von Schmidt, Eric, and Jim Rooney. *Baby Let Me Follow You Down: The Illustrated Story of the Cambridge Folk Years*. Garden City, NY: Anchor Books, 1979.

Wein, George, with Nate Chinen. *Myself Among Others: A Life in Music*. Cambridge, MA: Da Capo Press, 2003.

Web Sites

Boston Rock Storybook. 2004.
Little Big Horn Productions and Joe Harvard. January 15, 2004.
http://www.rockinboston.com

A collection of interviews, features, and articles on popular music in New England.

Crooked Root Records. 2004.
Crooked Root Records. January 23, 2004.
http://crookedroot.com/

Vermont record label for folk, rock, bluegrass, and American roots music. The site also includes information about New England musicians.

Dirtywater: The Boston Rock & Roll Museum. 2004.
BerkshireNet. January 17, 2004.
http://www.dirtywater.com

Extensive articles and timelines about popular music in New England.

Jazzhouse.org. 2004.
Howard Mandel, ed. The Jazz Journalists Association. January 20, 2004.
http://www.jazzhouse.org/

Information on the history of jazz music.

New England Jazz Alliance. January 8, 2004.
New England Jazz Alliance (NEJA). January 23, 2004.
http://www.nejazz.org

An Internet resource for the promotion of jazz in New England.

Rock & Roll Library. 2004.
Rock & Roll Library Company. January 23, 2004.
http://www.rocklibrary.com/

An Internet resource for the promotion and preservation of popular music, including artists and music from New England.

Recordings/Albums

Aerosmith. *Aerosmith*. Columbia, 1973.
Aerosmith. *Toys in the Attic*. Columbia, 1975.
Baez, Joan. *Joan Baez*. Vanguard, 1959.
Boston. *Boston*. Epic, 1976.
Cannon, Freddy. *14 Booming Hits*. Rhino Records, 1982.
The Cars. *The Cars*. Elektra, 1978.
The Cars. *Shake It Up*. Elektra, 1982.
Curless, Dick. *Traveling Through*. Rounder, 1995.
Ellington, Duke. *Ellington at Newport*. Columbia, 1956.
Farina, Richard, and Mimi Farina. *Reflections, Memories*. Vanguard, 1967.
Ives, Charles. *Symphony No. 4*. London Philharmonic Orchestra. Serebrier. RCA, 1973.
Ives, Charles. *Three Places in New England*. Boston Symphony Orchestra, Michael Tilson Thomas, conductor. Deutsche Grammophon, 1970.
J. Geils Band. *The Morning After*. Atlantic, 1971.
J. Geils Band. *Freeze Frame*. EMI, 1982.
Guthrie, Arlo. *Alice's Restaurant*. Warner Brothers, 1967.
Jonzun Crew. *Lost in Space*. Tommy Boy, 1983.
The Life Magazine History of the United States. *The Sounds of History*. Time Inc., 1963.
Mann, Aimee. *Magnolia Soundtrack*. Warner Brothers, 1999.
Mission of Burma. *Signals, Calls and Marches*. Ace of Hearts, 1981.
The Modern Lovers. *The Modern Lovers*. Beserkley, 1976.
Morphine. *Cure for Pain*. Rykodisc, 1993.
Muldaur, Maria. *Maria Muldaur*. Warner/Reprise, 1973.
New England Ragtime Ensemble. *The Art of Scott Joplin*. Ginther Schuller, Conductor. Angel, 1974.
Orpheus. *Orpheus*. MGM, 1968.
Phish. *Slip Stitch and Pass*. Elektra, 1997.
Pratt, Andy. *Andy Pratt*. Columbia, 1973.
Raitt, Bonnie. *Nick of Time*. Capitol, 1989.
The Remains. *The Remains*. Epic, 1966.
Rush, Tom. *The Circle Game*. Elektra, 1968.
Schuller, Gunther, with the Cincinnati Symphony. *Three Concertos*. GM, 1985.
Schuller, Gunther/Orange Then Blue. *Jumpin' in the Future*. GM, 1988.
The Sidewinders. *The Sidewinders*. RCA, 1972.
Summer, Donna. *The Journey: The Very Best of Donna Summer*. UTV/Mercury Records, 2003.
Tavares. *Best of Tavares*. Capitol Records, 1977.
Taylor, James. *Sweet Baby James*. Warner Brothers, 1970.
Taylor, James. *October Road*. Columbia, 2002.
'Til Tuesday. *Voices Carry*. Epic, 1985.
Various artists. *Bay State Rock: Vol. 1: The Sixties*. Star Rhythm, 1978.

Various artists. *Dick Tracy Soundtrack* (soundtrack album produced by Andy Paley features many Boston area artists and musicians). Sire, 1990.

Wolf, Peter. *Lights Out*. EMI, 1984.

Festivals and Organizations

Berklee College of Music
1140 Boylston Street
Boston, MA 02215
http://www.berklee.edu

Berkshire Choral Festivals
245 North Undermountain Road
Sheffield, MA 01257
http://www.choralfest.org/

Boston Blues Festival
Blues Trust Productions
75 Altamont Avenue
Melrose, MA 02176
http://www.bluestrust.com/

Boston Early Music Festival & Exhibition
P.O. Box 1286
Cambridge, MA 02238
http://www.bemf.org/

Boston Folk Festival
University of Massachusetts Boston
100 Morrissey Boulevard
Boston, MA 02125
http://www.bostonfolkfestival.org/

Boston Pops
Symphony Hall, 301 Massachusetts Avenue
Boston, MA 02115
http://www.bostonpops.org/

Boston Symphony Orchestra
Symphony Hall, 301 Massachusetts Avenue
Boston, MA 02115
http://www.bso.org/

Country Dance and Song Society
132 Main Street/P.O. Box 338
Haydenville, MA 01039-0338
http://www.cdss.org/

Dirtywater: The Boston Rock & Roll Museum
P.O. Box 5276
Wayland, MA 01778
http://www.dirtywater.com

Glasgow Lands Scottish Festival
P.O. Box 86
Blandford, MA 01008
http://www.glasgowlands.org/

Includes Scottish Celtic music.

Greater New Bedford Summer Fest
State Pier and in the New Bedford
Whaling National Historical Park
New Bedford, MA
http://users.rcn.com/koro.ma.ultranet/summfest.htm

Music festival.

Jenny Brook Bluegrass Festival
164 Church Avenue
Bellows Falls, VT 05101
http://www.jennybrookfestival.com/

Manchester Music Festival
42 Dillingham Avenue
Manchester, VT 05254
http://www.mmfvt.org/

New England Conservatory of Music
290 Huntington Avenue
Boston, MA 02115
http://www.newenglandconservatory.edu

New England Folk Festival
PMB 282
1770 Massachusetts Ave.
Cambridge, MA 02140
http://www.neffa.org/

New England Jazz Alliance
33 Morris Street
East Boston, MA 02128
http://www.nejazz.org/

Newport Waterfront Irish Festival
Waterfront
Newport, RI
http://www.newportfestivals.com/

Includes Celtic Irish music.

North Atlantic Blues Festival
Harbor Park
Rockland, ME
http://www.northatlanticbluesfestival.com/

Sunset Music Festival
Waterfront
Newport, RI
http://www.newportfestivals.com/

Tanglewood
297 West Street
Lenox, MA 01240
http://www.bso.org/

Music festival in the Berkshires, Massachusetts.

Vermont Jazz Center
72 Cotton Mill Hill
Studio 222
Brattleboro, VT 05301
http://www.vtjazz.org/

Center for the promotion and preservation of jazz.

RELIGION

Jeremy Bonner with Anthony George

New England has contributed greatly to the shaping of many facets of the life of the American republic, not the least in religion. From a handful of Puritan colonies, whose purpose was to create a "separate" and godly religious culture, the region matured into a commercial economy centered on Boston that helped power the British Empire but ultimately rejected it. Although New England's contribution to the Revolution was undeniable, it had ceased to lead the nation by the 1790s, with the political initiative falling to Virginia and the mid-Atlantic states. In religious terms, the Congregationalists who dominated the New England scene were overtaken nationally by the Methodists and Baptists who championed greater religious pluralism in the early nineteenth century, although they did "seed" the belt of New England settlement in western New York, northern Ohio, and upstate Michigan that would drive the cause of abolitionism in the 1840s and 1850s. New England Protestantism in the early nineteenth century, though no longer possessed of the same national prestige, was second to none in religiously inspired campaigns against slavery and in favor of temperance and penal reform. In modified form, then, the Puritan obsession with creating a purified social order persisted. In 1861, some of the most enthusiastic recruits for the Union Army were drawn from graduates of the small New England colleges established under religious auspices a century before.

The Civil War confirmed the final transfer of economic hegemony from New England to the more industrial states of the Mid-Atlantic and Midwest, although the region remained a center of textile production. While Protestant numbers showed no rapid rate of increase, the immigration boom that had begun during Ireland's great famine and continued into the 1890s served to utterly transform the religious complexion of southern New England, making Boston the archetypical Irish metropolis. The arrival of Catholics in the region was anything but welcome to many in the Protestant community, but they proved unable to stem either the tide of newcomers or their high birth rates, and by the early twentieth century Catholic majorities in Massachusetts and Rhode Island promised a new outlook for New England. Catholic New England continued to nurse grievances against the Protestant ascendancy that were only fully assuaged with the election of John F. Kennedy as president in 1960. It was an immigrant society, caught between its attachments to its countries of origin and a rapidly Americanizing second generation.

With the coming of the 1960s, New England entered a third phase of existence, that of religious pluralism, but this was a pluralism that operated within the limits of Catholic cultural identity. Even today, almost three-quarters of New England church goers (73.4 percent) claim to be Catholic, a figure thirty points above the national average and which exceeds that of both the Mid-Atlantic (63.0 percent) and the Pacific (59.3 percent). Certainly there is a significant Jewish presence, as well as newer communities of Buddhists, Muslims, and Hindus, but the non-Christian churches do not seem to have found much of New England appealing. Significantly, the two strongest non-Catholic Christian groups are the United Church of Christ and the Episcopal Church, historically significant, but also among the most liberal in mainstream Protestantism today. Non-Catholic conservative Christians are conspicuous by their absence, and many New England Catholics appear to regard the most conservative cultural pronouncements of their church as open to interpretation. Some might argue that, while Unitarianism has never gained a large body of followers, even in its birthplace, its perspectives govern much of the religious life in New England at the beginning of the twenty-first century.

NATIVE AMERICANS

Precolonial Native American religion was represented by the New England tribes of Housatonic, Narraganset, Mohawk, Mohegan, Wampanoag, Delaware, and Massachusetts, all of which spoke an Algonquian dialect. They lived a simple hunter-gatherer existence in seasonal villages, but following the great epidemic of 1616, which killed nine-tenths of the region's inhabitants, the native population of New England dwindled to perhaps twenty-five thousand by the time of the arrival of the first settlers in 1620. In 1631, the Puritans counted fewer than five hundred natives in villages around Boston Bay. New England Native Americans believed that spirits were everywhere and in everything and respected the elements and forces of nature. They communicated with a wide variety of spirits, but also believed in a Great Spirit—a supreme creator who gave the world to humanity as a gift. Every tribe had its own creation stories, handed down from generation to generation. The conduct of religious life was in the hands of tribal shamans, who would undertake specific ceremonies involving dances, sacrifices, smoking tobacco, chants, and songs, when requested by a member of the tribe to exercise influence over the weather, personal health, or success in courtship, hunting, or war. There were also seasonal ceremonies to influence the weather and the seasons of sowing and harvesting, and to give thanks at the appropriate times of the year. One ceremony with known Algonquian antecedents is the "Shaking Tent Ceremony," in which tribal members seeking enlightenment would go to the shaman and prepare themselves by fasting, praying, making an offering, and purifying themselves in a sweat lodge. The shaman might sing while accompanying himself with a drum or rattle, and then enter into a trance or dream state, waiting for a spirit to enter his tent and shake the tent violently as it did so. Some shamans claimed to be able to enter the spirit world of the dead or to see over long distances. New England Native Americans were also acquainted with the sweat lodge—an area of ground lined with heated stones and covered by a small structure of wood or skins, within which participants lay, while water was poured over the stones to produce steam. The sweat lodge was used to purify the bodies of those who wished to communicate with the spirits, and to prevent or cure ailments caused by spirits. It also served to initiate adolescents of the tribe into adulthood.

THE CITY ON THE HILL: 1620–1660

Puritans

While the settlers who began to arrive in the 1620s had little time for Native American "paganism," their first concern was the stability of their own communities. Hailing from East Anglia, Lincolnshire, the West Riding, the Midlands, and the Southwest, as well as London, the English Puritans represented those who increasingly questioned the long-term commitment of the English crown to the Protestant Reformation, particularly after the accession of James VI of Scotland to the English throne in 1603 and his subsequent refusal to tolerate Protestant religious dissent. Some Puritans withdrew to Protestant Holland, where they received the sympathetic backing of the state's rulers, but the challenge presented by James' son, Charles, whose wife was a practicing Catholic, and Archbishop William Laud of Canterbury persuaded many who had chosen to remain in England that the English Church was a lost cause.

The two earliest colonies in America believed in differing Puritan perspectives, although they shared a common Calvinist theology. The first Puritans under William Bradford arrived on the *Mayflower* in 1620, establishing the first religious colony in New England. From such small beginnings emerged the Plymouth Plantation, a "separatist" community that had fled Holland because of dislike of its religious pluralism and had no desire to reform the Church of England. Ten years later, however, John Winthrop (1588–1649), a wealthy English landowner and dedicated Puritan, led a group of one thousand organized Puritans from England to found the Massachusetts Bay Colony, which sought to create a Bible Commonwealth in the New World to provoke reform at home. It was this community that would have the greatest impact on New England's first hundred years of religious life. Having rejected the option of armed rebellion against the Stuart monarchy, Winthrop and his supporters formed a compact that would govern life in the New World and included a congregational style of church government and a political franchise based on church membership. John Winthrop (who was elected governor by the settlers) and his officers believed that they had a commission from God to form a government for the new colony and that this government should be organized on biblical principles. All colonists were required to read and discuss the Bible, and the first public schools were set up to teach children to read the Bible for themselves, as well as to write. The first college in America was opened at Harvard, in Cambridge, in 1636, to educate men for the ministry. Education was a central concern of the Puritans. All the colonies passed laws requiring children to attend school at an early age, while towns with over fifty families were required to

Pilgrims Praying, a painting by Henry Mosler. Courtesy Library of Congress.

have a grammar school, and New England enjoyed a high rate of literacy, among females as well as males.

The cultural practices and institutions of the first settlers helped shape much of New England's subsequent development. Protestant forms of worship, strongly disciplined and conservative social habits, and the concept of the town hall meeting all derived from the struggles of the first pioneers. Most Puritans considered that government should exist to uphold religious ideals and that all citizens should obey strictly the dictates of religious leaders. While all were considered equal before God, exercise of the franchise was a privilege reserved for free men. Limited democracy was a basic principle for the Puritans in America, very far from the ideas of universal manhood suffrage in vogue 150 years later. To receive the franchise, a citizen had first to go through a "conversion experience" and become a church member. Although no formal procedure for this process has been recorded, the common standard involved testimony by the individual about a personal religious experience in which the sinner became aware of his *humiliation*, a sense of sorrow for his sins; *justification*, an awareness of God's forgiveness of those sins; and *sanctification*, an enduring ability to lead a godly life. The clergy wielded enormous power and social control over the populace, although they were never allowed to hold public office during the time of Governor Winthrop, and were elected to serve as ministers for as long as they or their congregation desired. Church officers, on the other hand, were elected annually and could be removed for failure to do their duties. Church and state were closely intertwined, but they were never one and the same.

As Calvinists, New England Puritans believed both in original sin—that all human beings had become depraved and corrupt since Adam's Fall—and predestination—that salvation was predetermined and "good works" on earth would have no effect on that outcome. Such notions did not result in a licentious society, since most Puritans held that while salvation could not be earned, if one was saved by grace, that condition should be evidenced in sober living and serious comportment. Having witnessed the collapse of the social and moral order in England, they wished to create a more just and peaceful society in New England, whose social regulations reflected a concern with the health of the body politic. Sexual relations outside of marriage were condemned as a danger to everyone involved, including children, but large families were encouraged. Dancing was considered too stimulating to be condoned, and while alcohol might be tolerated as a gift from God when used in moderation, drunkenness was never tolerated because it showed a dangerous carelessness for one's own life and the life of the community. Fancy clothes were condemned because they indicated a lack of seriousness, and while games were common, little time was allowed for them or for music, except in the context of worship. Everyone was required to work hard at all times, both as a sign of gratitude to God for salvation and, more practically, to ward off starvation and death. With New England's harsh winters, rocky soils, new diseases, and periodically hostile natives, the settlers were well aware of their precarious situation and the need for a disciplined life.

As good land became harder to find around Boston, ministers led congregations south into the Connecticut River valley, where they founded towns like Wethersfield and Windsor in 1635 and Hartford in 1636. The government of Connecticut Colony, established in 1639, was modeled on the Massachusetts Bay model of a Bible commonwealth, but it lacked a royal charter until 1662. As a result, both its political and religious structures proved much more flexible than those of Massachusetts Bay, with the franchise open to non–church members and many congregations modifying the requirements for admission to membership. A very different order prevailed in John Davenport's New Haven, established in 1638 under the Plantation Covenant, which sought to base church and state on the "Seven Pillars"—leading figures in the community who constituted "the Court." New Haven was far more authoritarian than the Massachusetts Bay Colony until it was absorbed into Connecticut in the 1660s. The year 1638 also witnessed the establishment of a town at Exeter, in what would later become New Hampshire.

Religious Challenges to the Puritans

In 1642, the outbreak of the English civil war led many Puritans to return to England, largely stopped the migration of English people to Massachusetts, and caused the economy in New England to slow down. With the triumph of Parliament over the king, however, better communications between Puritan New England and Puritan England became possible and immigration resumed. As more and more people arrived who were not in close agreement with the first settlers, however, the initial consensus was shattered. In the face of demands that they conform to existing regulations, many chose to organize their own communities. Some were extreme separatists, so zealous for religion that they had no tolerance for anything less than perfection, while others were members in good standing who, over time, developed new ideas and were unwilling to remain in allegiance. Puritans argued a great deal over the Bible and its correct interpretation, but they also encouraged church order and discipline and had little tolerance for heterodox opinions and behavior. Governor Winthrop was a moderate who understood the weaknesses and sinfulness of all people and institutions and believed in leniency and charity in the new commonwealth, but for him and his successors the dilemma would be how to ensure freedom of conscience and control over moral infringements at the same time. In 1648, the challenge of the Baptists prompted the ministers of New England to issue the Cambridge Platform, which defended limited church membership, gave ministers the sole authority to preach and administer the sacraments of baptism and communion, affirmed the principle that local churches be formed from the visible saints, who in turn selected the ministers, and emphasized that church synods existed for the purposes of advice and did not supersede the autonomy of the congregation.

An early portent of religious divisions was the theological dispute that led to the establishment of a colony in Providence, Rhode Island. In 1632, a young man named Roger Williams (1603–1683) arrived in the New World. An extreme separatist who had studied for the ministry, Williams rejected offers of pulpits of congregations in Boston and Salem because they had refused to renounce all links with the Church of England. His views caused increasing disquiet within the settled Massachusetts Bay Colony. He argued that the royal grant that had established the community lacked legitimacy, given the abhorrence in which the Puritans held the theological views of the Stuart monarchy, and that the only godly solution was to give up their lands and return to England. Equally unsettling, Williams believed that the natives should be better compensated for the loss of their lands. Insisting on a clear division between the godly and the godless, he argued that, in the public sphere, residents who were not freemen—and hence unregenerate—should not be obliged to take a religious oath to support the colony, and that a regenerate person should not pray with unregenerate persons, even members of their own family. Finally, Williams significantly departed from prevailing notions of church governance in arguing that the secular authorities had no right to determine the beliefs and practices of a church, to punish breaches of religious laws, or to compel attendance of the people at church services, views that struck at the heart of civil governance as it had been conceived by Winthrop and his supporters.

After the more sympathetic Plymouth Colony offered him a pulpit, Williams proceeded to denounce all the other congregations of New England for their lack of fidelity to Christian principles. In 1635, the General Court enacted a sentence of banishment, but at Winthrop's suggestion Williams went instead to Narragansett Bay, where, with some of his Plymouth parishioners, he founded Providence Colony. In later life, Williams came to realize the impossibility of his earlier ideals and shifted from a belief in the segregation of the godly elect to a belief that he should preach to and pray with *all* people. Williams permitted no laws in his colony governing worship in churches or allowing government influence there, and Rhode Island became one of the most open and tolerant of all the early colonies. It attracted many who were unable to worship freely and remain in the Massachusetts Bay Colony, including Baptists, Quakers, and even Jews.

Anne Hutchinson (1591–1643) presented another challenge to the Puritan establishment after she came to the Massachusetts Bay Colony. In 1636, she attacked the Puritan minister John Wilson for preaching that good deeds helped a sinner *prepare* for the reception of God's saving grace, instead of this resulting from an unanticipated event. Her antinomianism (the belief that the moral law was of no relevance in the plan of salvation) led her to elevate the condition of the converted above the limitations imposed by their human condition. She argued that the Holy Spirit communicated directly with the converted from the moment of their sanctification and that the latter were able to communicate with God directly. In this scheme, even the Bible, which was held by all to be the common basis of their Protestant faith, took second place to personal revelation. Hutchinson's attacks on the New England clergy and her belief that most of the ministers and leaders of Massachusetts were not saved provoked a sharp reaction, but she proved a much more able disputant than Winthrop and was able to convince many people to agree with her. Put on trial for "traducing the ministers" and trying to change the makeup of the colony, she was found guilty only of sedition and banished from the colony. At the invitation of Roger Williams, she and her followers settled in Providence Colony, but many soon abandoned her, as she came to rely more and more on her own private revelations from God for her guidance and behavior.

THE NEW ENGLAND MIND: 1660–1776

The restoration of the monarchy in England in 1660 provoked a profound reassessment in New England society. In 1662, a "half-way covenant" was proposed that would have allowed the children and grandchildren of the first settlers who had not enjoyed a conversion experience to join their local churches, but the New England community was divided and many congregations refused to adopt it.

Greater attention was also lavished on the Native American community, with the first complete Bible printed in America being a 1663 translation into the Algonquian language published in Cambridge by John Eliot and some of his Native American converts. Eliot went on to establish many towns for "Praying Indians" in Massachusetts, the first of which was Natick. Other dissenting groups came on the scene in the mid-seventeenth century. The Baptists came to Rhode Island in the 1640s and to Boston in 1665. Baptists were separatists who were opposed to infant baptism, considering only those of sufficient age and reasoning ability to be eligible for church membership. They were more strictly congregational and were strongly opposed to relations between church and state. A small number of Quakers came to Massachusetts in the 1650s, although most settled in the Middle Colonies, especially Pennsylvania. At first, the Quakers refused to go to any church or follow any clergyman. They refused to pay taxes for the upkeep of churches or clergy, to take oaths in courts, or to take up arms for any cause; many suffered imprisonment—and some were executed—for their beliefs.

Early Judaism in New England

Of equal interest is the arrival of the first non-Christian tradition in this period, namely Judaism. The first New England Jew of record was Solomon Franco, a Sephardic trader who visited Boston in 1649, but most Jewish traders tended to favor the more tolerant Dutch colonies. The New England Puritans were deeply interested in the Hebrew language and culture (Hebrew was a prerequisite for entry to Harvard), and in 1722 Harvard hired the Jewish scholar Judah Monis to teach the students, only to experience the shock of having Monis convert to Christianity and join the First Church in Cambridge. In general, though, the Puritan colonies did not welcome Jewish immigrants. The great exception was Rhode Island where Roger Williams himself guaranteed absolute toleration. In 1658, Sephardic Jews established Congregation Jesuit Israel in Newport. It was also here that the Touro Synagogue designed by Peter Harrison—the first Jewish synagogue in America—was erected in 1763.

The Church of England in New England

Perhaps the most direct threat to Congregationalism came from the Church of England. Until 1684, most practicing Anglicans had been expelled from the area, as Massachusetts wrote its own laws, called them the king's, and organized its churches to exclude other forms of worship, ignoring Charles II's injunction in 1660 to use the Book of Prayer. In that year, however, James II revoked the charter of the Massachusetts Bay Colony. Two years later, he appointed Sir Edmund Andros as the first royal governor of New England and the King's Chapel was organized in Boston. The new charter of 1691 made property rather than church membership the basis of the franchise, provoking a widespread fear among the Puritans that the imposition of the king's religion would not be far off. Although James was a Roman Catholic, he actually sought general toleration, which benefited New England Puritans as well as the Catholic minority. In 1688, however, the Glorious Revolution ushered in a new king, the Protestant William of Orange, and a year later the people of Boston rose up against Governor Andros and imprisoned him and restored the elected assembly. Many Anglicans were jailed or forced to flee, but the King's Chapel survived.

In 1717, the Church of England opened a new front in Connecticut with extensive missionary work undertaken by the Society for the Propagation of the Gospel (SPG). In 1722, they achieved a great coup when Yale's president, Timothy Cutler, and two of the college's tutors and four other clergymen announced their conversion to Anglicanism. From then on, Anglicanism was a serious intellectual rival in New England. The following year, Christ Church, Boston, was organized and Cutler took Holy Orders and was appointed its rector, where he served until 1756. While many Massachusetts Episcopalians represented an intellectual elite educated at Harvard and Yale, there were also men of moderate means, like John Checkley, an apothecary and layman at King's Chapel. An eloquent pamphleteer, Checkley was the first person to publish tracts denouncing New England Puritanism for its complicity in regicide. His attacks on Calvinism enabled him to place Anglicanism midway between the Roman Church and the Reformed tradition, insisting that the sacraments, the liturgy and the apostolic succession were all great evidence of Christian truth. By 1775, there were twenty-five Anglican congregations in Massachusetts alone.

For many Puritans, the Half-Way Covenant of 1662 constituted a watering down of the true church, and from the 1670s onward there were increasing calls for reform of the depraved lives of New Englanders by such preachers as Solomon Stoddard (1643–1729) and a steady increase in sermons and literature calling for the strengthening of the national covenant and the tightening of discipline. The founding of Yale College in Connecticut in 1701 was due in part to a desire to counteract the loosening of standards at Harvard or, rather, to provide those who favored experiential religion with a place of education of their own. "New Schoolism" became a catch-phrase for those who believed in perpetuating revivals, establishing Sunday schools for the teaching of religion, promoting temperance, and organizing domestic and foreign evangelical missions. Complementing this was a professionalization of the status of the minister—ordinations were increasingly carried out by other ministers rather than church elders—that downplayed the notion of the priesthood of all believers. Into the void created by this distance between pastor and people came the open-air revival meeting, which achieved full force with the first visit of the Anglican preacher George Whitefield (1714–1770) to Boston in 1740. A year later, the young Jonathan Edwards (1703–1758) preached his famous "Sinners in the Hands of an Angry God" sermon at Enfield, Connecticut. This was the Great Awakening, an eighteenth-century phenomenon that broke denominational boundaries and bound together the proponents of emotional religion across the American colonies. People were called to repent their sins, to pray for their salvation, and to join the established churches.

Whitefield's tactics were increasingly the subject of controversy. He argued that "new birth" experience that came during revivals helped create a new understanding and new affections in the minds of Christians. He rejected the focus on baptism and the Eucharist that was central to Anglicanism and significant in Congregational thought. Generally, Whitefield would arrive in a town and ask to preach in the Anglican church. If admitted he would deliver a sermon attacking Anglican doctrine, and if refused he would claim persecution and preach to a large outdoor crowd or in other Protestant churches. Although he established ties with Jonathan Edwards, Whitefield was repudiated by New England's Anglican clergy for using extemporaneous prayer and denying the need for apostolic succession for an ordained clergy. In Boston, Timothy Cutler expressed concern about Whitefield's "enthusiasm," his lack of concern for church order, and alliances with dissenters. By 1744, however, opposition to Whitefield had begun to appear even in Congregationalist ranks. His opponents, dubbed the "Old Lights" in contrast to the "New Light" revivalists, favored a greater emphasis on works, righteousness, and gradual conversion (an issue that had been raised during the Antinomian Controversy of the seventeenth century), and were led by Charles Chauncey (1705–1787) of First Congregational Church, Boston, who would later be a leading Unitarian. The faculties of Harvard and Yale also criticized Whitefield's methods when he returned in 1744. In New England, opposition to Whitefield helped the Church of England expand. Growing numbers of Harvard and Yale graduates entered the Anglican ministry during the 1760s and an Anglican chaplain was designated for Yale during the 1770s.

One final issue that the Great Awakening brought into plain relief was the issue of a colonial episcopate. The absence of American bishops was acknowledged to place a severe strain on the efficiency of colonial Anglicanism, since any American candidates for ordination were obliged to travel to England for this purpose. During the 1760s, the bishop of London, Thomas Sherlock, put forward the Butler Plan, calling for nonpolitical, non–tax-supported bishops. Opposition immediately arose from Congregationalists and Presbyterians, who saw it as an Anglican plot to root out the New England establishments and insisted that such a move would threaten toleration. Although the issue of bishops might seem comparatively mundane, it carried with it a host of implications and historical memories for New England Congregationalists that would not lightly be born.

FROM ESTABLISHMENT TO ABOLITIONISM: 1776–1865

The Shakers

As the American colonies prepared for war with England in 1774, a remarkable communal religious organization, the United Society of Believers in Christ's Second Appearing, was headed for New England. Popularly known as the Shakers, they were a group of Quakers committed to celibacy and who practiced a form of ecstatic dance and were led by a psychic mystic Mother Ann Lee (1736–1787), whom they believed to be a new manifestation of Christ. After her death and the accession of Joseph Meacham as leader in 1787, the Shakers experienced dramatic growth, with six thousand members in nineteen communities across the United States by 1830, but they had largely faded away by the end of the nineteenth century.

Congregationalists and Episcopalians

The American Revolution affected the two main Protestant groups in New England very differently. Congregationalist ministers were dubbed the "Black Regiment" by the British and were certainly fearful of attempts to impose Anglican bishops upon America, yet despite the belief often expressed in sermons that God was on the side of the Revolution, ministerial support was never wholehearted. The legacy of the Great Awakening prompted them to continue to urge New Englanders to live righteous lives, and they were not convinced that the triumphalism of the Revolution was inculcating a proper concern for social stability, which may help to explain their postwar adhesion to the Federalist Party.

For American Anglicans, by contrast, the Revolution was a disaster, since they ultimately picked the losing side. In New England, most clergymen, especially the SPG missionaries who received their salaries from England, were Loyalists. Many were forced to flee, abandoning their church buildings, and membership experienced a dramatic decline. The New England clerical establishment was decimated, with only four active clergymen in Massachusetts and one in New Hampshire by the end of the war. By the same token, New England Anglicans avoided the fate of their counterparts in the South, whose churches had been established before 1776 and their buildings remained their own, although they did lose the financial aid that had previously come from the SPG.

In the aftermath of the war, Anglicans throughout America turned to the question of how they were to exist in the absence of the Church of England. Without any bishops of their own, their position was precarious, since they could not ordain future clergy. Early attempts to obtain ordinations for Americans in England foundered over the issue of an oath of loyalty to the crown that all priests were obliged to make. In the South, and to a lesser extent the Middle States, enthusiasm for episcopacy was, in any case, weak. In 1782, William White, rector of Christ Church, Philadelphia, stressed in his *The Case of the Episcopal Churches in the United States Considered* the need to build from the parish up and not from the diocese down as had been the case with the Church of England, reflecting the civic idea that the people's interest and good government were identical. White insisted that there should be no differentiation between the power of the clergy and that of the laity at church conventions or such gatherings and no area of church government should be beyond the scope of such gatherings, and he defended the notion of a Presbyterian type of ordination as a temporary expedient until bishops could be consecrated.

In New England, however, there were strong objections to the rejection of the authority of the historical episcopate in favor of a congregational polity. In 1783, ten Connecticut clergy met in secret, fearing lay opposition, and elected two candidates as bishop, one of whom, Samuel Seabury, accepted. Seabury had been part of the Loyalist circle in New York before the Revolution and chaplain to the King's American Regiment and had been imprisoned in Connecticut. In 1784, Seabury traveled to England, where he warned that bishops needed to be introduced quickly and asked for financial support for an American bishop from the SPG. When the archbishop of Canterbury resisted Seabury's appeal, for fear of upsetting peace negotiations, Seabury traveled to Scotland where he was consecrated by three nonjuring bishops and signed a concordat agreeing to use the prayer of consecration from the 1549 Book of Common Prayer, which asserted episcopal independence from lay control. By September 1785, Seabury had held two conventions, ordained twelve priests, and informed Episcopalians outside New England about his plans for church union. His conventions were solely clerical affairs and he developed an active covenant theology that stressed the role of bishops in the rites of ordination and confirmation. Such activities roused resentment in the Middle States and the South, particularly after Seabury attacked the proposed general constitution of the Episcopal Church in 1785 for circumscribing the power of bishops.

Trinity Church, Newport, Rhode Island. Photo by Anne Marie McLaughlin, courtesy of Newport, Rhode Island Convention and Visitors Bureau.

Before the General Convention of 1786, several states elected bishops, a move seen as a response to Seabury and his authoritarianism. William White did not question the validity of Seabury's ordination, but he also recognized that the English church was legally forbidden from acknowledging the nonjurors. After the English Parliament passed legislation rescinding the requirement for loyalty oaths, William White and Samuel Provoost were consecrated in England as bishops in 1787. Efforts by the Connecticut clergy to get more bishops ordained in Scotland proved fruitless, but their opponents were also unable to establish the canonically required bloc of three bishops. By 1788, some Connecticut clergy were pressing

Rt. Rev. Samuel Seabury, D.D. (1726–1796), first Episcopal bishop of Connecticut. Courtesy Library of Congress.

for a merger, believing Seabury an obstacle to union, but at the General Convention of 1789, the validity of Seabury's orders was affirmed and three clergymen he had ordained were seated as delegates. In 1792, Seabury joined his rivals to make Thomas Claggett the first bishop consecrated in America.

A good example of the postwar climate can be seen in the Episcopal Diocese of Massachusetts, whose first bishop, Edward Bass, helped to reconcile Samuel Seabury with his detractors. Unlike Episcopalians in Connecticut or New York, Massachusetts' Episcopalians were mostly disgruntled Congregationalists and Baptists who, in the light of the disarray of their own denominations, sought the reassurance of corporate worship. Such a constituency helped create a generally low church diocese, although parishes bordering Connecticut tended to be high and those near Rhode Island tended to adopt the charismatic style of that community. The clergy of the diocese proved very active in funding missions, establishing the Massachusetts Episcopal Missionary Society in 1815 and the Board of Missions in 1836. Not all the ordinaries proved to be tactful in dealing with the diversity of their diocese, however. Bishop Manton Eastburn, a strong Evangelical, kept up a persistent feud with the Church of the Advent, Boston—a high church parish—throughout his time in office.

While Episcopalians consolidated their gains, Congregationalists found themselves forced to grapple with both a loss of status and the secession of their left wing into Unitarianism. Established Congregationalism was the rule in Connecticut, Massachusetts, and New Hampshire throughout the eighteenth century. In Massachusetts, Anglicans were exempted from church taxes in 1727 and Quakers and Baptists a year later, but the constitution of 1780 still allowed the state to regulate worship and church attendance and levy taxes for the maintenance of church buildings, and a similar situation prevailed in Connecticut. After 1800, however, New England Congregationalism was increasingly associated with the Federalist Party, leading President Thomas Jefferson and Democratic-Republicans in New England to favor disestablishment. In 1816, a Fusion (Toleration) Party was organized in Connecticut and within a year had captured the governorship, leading to disestablishment in 1818, with New Hampshire following suit a year later. Resistance was stronger in Massachusetts, where a Religious Freedom Act was approved in 1811 but repealed by the Federalists after they won the next election. During the 1820s, however, divisions emerged among Massachusetts Congregationalists over the establishment issue and finally, in 1833, an amendment to disestablish the church was ratified by the people by a margin of ten to one.

Unitarianism

One reason for the shift in outlook was the emergence of Unitarianism within New England Congregationalism. This was triggered by the appointment of Henry Ware as Professor of Divinity at Harvard in 1803. As Harvard became a stronghold of liberal churchmanship, disgusted conservatives organized Andover Seminary in 1808, with a declared commitment to Calvinism, and Boston's Pond Street Church in 1809, dedicated to conservative churchmanship and revivalism. In 1815, Jedidiah Morse went further when he called for formal separation from liberal churches, to which William Ellery Channing (1780–1842) responded in 1819 with the address "Unitarian Christianity," which helped define the principles of the movement. Channing objected to Trinitarianism because, he claimed, it denied divine unity and also to what he regarded as two-being Christology, which implied that Jesus was two persons rather than one. Furthermore, Channing insisted that the doctrine of the atonement was wrong. Since God the Father was necessarily merciful, it was clear that Christ had been sent to deliver humankind from sin, not merely from the punishment for it.

By the 1820s, it was said that all the most prominent people in Boston were Unitarians. Their first gain came at the formerly Anglican King's Chapel, in Boston, but the movement expanded rapidly among the Congregationalists in New England. As it did so, it provoked numerous conflicts over church property and in 1820, the Con-

Methodism

With immigration in the late seventeenth and early eighteenth centuries, the Episcopal Church grew and spread to all the cities of New England. By the end of the revolutionary period, however, Methodism, an offshoot of the Episcopal Church, became the fastest-growing denomination in the United States, especially in the South and the backcountry. Although the movement did not gain a strong foothold in New England, its numbers continued to grow at a rapid rate in other states, making it the largest American denomination by the early nineteenth century. In 1774 its membership had been about two thousand; in 1792, about sixty-six thousand; and thereafter its numbers doubled every decade. Yet, according to a survey of churches in New England (see table below), only one Methodist church existed in the region by 1776, and the denomination did not grow at the same rate in the North as in the South, the mid-Atlantic states, and the backcountry.

Denomination	Number of churches, by state					
	ME	NH	VT	MA	CT	RI
Congregational	26	78	13	310	222	9
Separatist-Congregation	—	1	1	7	14	1
Presbyterian	11	27	2	7	4	1
Episcopal	6	2	2	17	46	5
Baptist	3	13	2	51	25	26
Methodist	—	—	—	1	—	—

Source: Thomas L. Purvis and Richard Balkin, eds., *Revolutionary America, 1763 to 1800* (New York: Facts on File, 1995), 198, 201.

gregationalists were shocked when the Massachusetts Supreme Court sided with the parish of First Church, Dedham, which wished to call a Unitarian minister, rather than the church authorities. Ultimately, about 120 churches, mostly in the Boston area, joined the American Unitarian Association when it was formed in 1825. Universalism also gained a footing during this period, advanced by John Murray (1741–1815), who believed that Christ had made full payment for the sins of all people and blessedness awaited everyone on Judgment Day. Murray's followers formed a new denomination in Boston and New Hampshire, which slowly spread throughout New England, often uniting with Unitarians to form Unitarian-Universalist churches.

Transcendentalism

The case of the New England Transcendentalists provides evidence of the convergence of philosophy and religion. Many Americans in the early 1800s felt constrained by Old World traditions and beliefs and sought to apply the New World experience to the life of the mind and spirit. Some ministers even left their church to pursue more purely intellectual pursuits. New England religious figures were at the forefront of the movement, although many of them studied in Europe and absorbed ideas from all over the world. They included Bronson Alcott, Theodore Parker, and Henry David Thoreau, but the most famous was undoubtedly Ralph Waldo Emerson (1803–1882), who resigned from the ministry of Boston's Second Church (Unitarian) in 1832 and embarked on a writing and lecturing career. His essays and lectures have become classics of American literature. Included in his iconoclastic, free-thinking and imaginative writings were ideas from Hindu and Buddhist texts, then being translated into English for the first time. The Transcendentalists sought to go beyond their inherited traditions to get a larger view of the human situation and its potentialities. They felt there were intuitive powers not yet tapped by the human mind, well beyond the mundane interests of mere reason. They believed that moral and spiritual progress was still in its early stage and were the first people in America to talk seriously about non-Christian religions. Another influential voice was that of the Connecticut clergyman Horace Bushnell who in his *God in Christ* (1849) rejected the ideas of inherent human depravity and distance between God and Man. Bushnell took a positive view of human development and stressed the "freeness" of God and the "ease of approach" to Him, for which he was ostracized by many in Connecticut but praised in Massachusetts, and he helped lay the foundations for the Social Gospel tradition in American Congregationalism.

The Presbyterian Church

In 1801, the Congregational Church entered upon the Plan of Union with the Presbyterian Church, which aimed to simplify missionary work and avoid duplication of effort by allowing pastors of both denominations to serve their churches and congregations to opt to join either a local general association or a local presbytery. The plan ultimately worked much more to the advantage of the missionary-minded Presbyterians, and when the Second Great Awakening swept across the United States during the 1830s and Presbyterain revivalists like Charles Grandison Finney (1792–1875) proved a little too Arminian (advocating salvation though works) for Congregationalist taste, the plan was brought to an end in 1837. The impact of the Unitarian debacle had nevertheless made the Congregationalists more conscious of themselves as a denomination. Slowly but surely they developed an apparatus of voluntary societies designed to impose the New England vision on American society. Such bodies included the American Board of Commissioners for Foreign Missions (1810), the American Education Society (1815), the American Colonization Society (1817), and the American Temperance Society (1826). Above all, the Congregationalists turned to the great moral cause of the early nineteenth century—slavery. In this respect, they were better off than their Methodist and Presbyterian counterparts, who had a large constituency in the South. Congregationalism risked no possibility of a split on the slavery issue, and a plethora of antislavery societies was the result. In 1811, Harriet Beecher Stowe was born in Fairfield, Connecticut, the daughter of a prominent Congregational minister. Her *Uncle Tom's Cabin* (1851) would ultimately become the classic antislavery novel.

RELIGIONS IN NEW ENGLAND: 1865 TO THE EARLY TWENTIETH CENTURY

The Catholic Influx, 1865–1918

Writing of nineteenth-century Boston, James O'Toole makes the following observations:

> At first, the most significant immigration to Boston had come from famine-devastated Ireland, and thus, for most of its first century, Boston Catholicism had meant Irish Catholicism. New parishes and institutions came into existence to serve overwhelmingly Irish populations. Every bishop from the 1840s onwards was of Irish stock, and the clergy and religious who assisted them had similar backgrounds. In this way Boston was different from many other emerging centers of American Catholicism because it lacked broad ethnic diversity.[1]

The Catholic influx changed New England as a whole, though perhaps on a lesser scale than Boston. Following the creation of the dioceses of Boston (1808) and Hartford (1843), six additional jurisdictions emerged over the next sixty years, elevating the four smaller states to independent dioceses by 1884 and establishing the new dioceses of Springfield (1870) and Fall River (1904) in Massachusetts. Rural parishes in northern New England often encompassed huge areas, however, so although there were fewer Catholics per priest, the priests had to cover great distances to care for their flock. In parts of Maine, some parishes were even cared for by priests from Quebec. In the face of hostility from the Protestant establishment, many Catholics turned inward seeking to secure for themselves an enclave centered on the parish and a weekly round of liturgy and devotional exercises. Three masses every Sunday was the rule in urban areas and two in more rural settings, with sung vespers on Sunday evenings and monthly recitation of the rosary after Mass. New England Catholics made frequent use of the sacrament of confession, but often received Communion only once or twice a year, and only about 40 per cent were regular attendees at Mass. During the 1850s, Marian devotions during the month of May and Eucharistic processions both became more common. In the later part of the nineteenth century and into the twentieth, the range of liturgical options continued to swell with the addition of the stations of the cross to Lenten devotions and the greater incidence of Holy Hours of Adoration and confraternities of the Rosary. Mass schedules also increased, particularly as churches were built with upper and lower levels, allowing for simultaneous celebrations of the Eucharist.

Liturgy was an important part of the glue of parish life, but equally important were voluntary associations and parochial education. In the first category, the Irish parishes enjoyed the usual complement of altar and rosary societies (for women) and Holy Name societies (for men), which maintained the physical structure of their churches. Equally important were the benevolent and building and loan societies, which provided the penniless immigrant with sickness and death benefits and helped give him or her access to credit. Education was an equally important issue, given Protestant control of the public school system, since most Catholics desired an education for their children that emphasized the sacramental life of the Church, the European heritage of the immigrants, and training for marriage or religious vocation. Here, however, New England fell behind other centers of Catholic immigration. Although there was a steady increase in the number of parochial schools in New England, the dioceses of Boston and Springfield had some of the smallest proportions of parishes with schools and Catholic children in such schools in the whole of the Northeast. The range of organizations increased after 1890, with the establishment of Catholic clubs (for male recreation), Boy Scout and Girl Scout units, and parish athletic teams. Popular education classes, modeled on the national Chautauqua, were added to the roster of parish activities and parish conferences of the St. Vincent de Paul Society (the organization devoted to charitable work) also increased. Such infrastructural investment inevitably brought with it higher levels of church debt, necessitating constant fund-raising and the establishment of building fund societies to try to keep pace with the spending of many parishes.

After 1880, there was both a marked increase in Catholic immigration and a change in its composition. The new immigrants hailed from Italy and Poland and evidenced a less American sense of identity and soon sought national parishes of their own. The attitude of Archbishop William O'Connell was that national parishes could only be created when a critical mass of one nationality had been reached and if the community had the means to financially support a parish. Nevertheless, the number of national parishes in Massachusetts increased from seventeen in 1900 to forty-one in 1910 and fifty-seven in 1920.[2] The Poles in Pittsfield, Massachusetts, who initially attended St. Charles Church, where the priest allowed a Polish mass in the basement every Sunday and brought in a Polish missionary twice a year for confessions, had their own church by 1913—Immaculate Conception Chapel of the Mother of God—built with their own labor and in which, during the 1920s, they spent much time teaching Polish language and history to their offspring. Italian immigrants, by contrast, arrived with a much less developed sense of national identity and often hardened anticlerical attitudes. They were more willing to attend Irish parishes, and while such parishes often became largely Italian, they were not necessarily national parishes. A third group of Catholic immigrants were the French Canadians who migrated from Quebec to the textile factories of southern New England. In 1900, French-speakers at St. Mary's, Uxbridge, and St. Patrick's, Whitinsville, in Massachusetts, started to request a church of their own. Four years later they formed *La Société des Artisans*, a lay-inspired group that worshipped separately, and in 1907 a church building was erected, with a convent and school added in 1921. In Springfield, Massachusetts, where French Canadians had begun to arrive in the 1870s, St. Thomas Aquinas Church was another French parish formed in 1907 to propitiate an increasingly vocal Catholic minority.

Irish Catholics and New England Politics

While the newer Catholics were building their ethnic enclaves, the Irish had begun to enter the political sphere in increasing numbers. Such figures as John J. Fitzgerald (the grandfather of John F. Kennedy) and David I. Walsh, the first Catholic to be elected governor of Massachusetts in 1914 and U.S. Senator in 1918, tapped the Catholic vote to its fullest extent. Their relationship with church leaders was ambiguous, however. Archbishop O'Connell had many Republican friends and was often critical of the boss-centered politics of Boston and its hinterland. Over the initiative and referendum and women's suffrage, he was at odds with Governor Walsh, and he also entered the field in 1917 to oppose a constitutional amendment supported by many Catholic politicians that would have ended state aid to all private educational and charitable institutions. The political argument was that it would level the playing field, since Protestant hospitals and colleges received the bulk of state appropriations, but O'Connell considered that, in the light of increased public acceptance of Catholicism, the possibility of state aid to Catholic institutions would not be long delayed. By 1918, the Catholic majority had begun to show its full potential in New England politics, heralding Al Smith's consoling victories in Massachusetts and Rhode Island in his otherwise crushing defeat in the presidential election of 1928.

Protestant Denominations and Judaism

Although Catholicism dominated the religious life of New England during the late nineteenth century, the age of industrialism had an effect on other denominations. Within Congregationalism, there was a renewed desire for some sort of confessional statement that would help define what the denomination had become, and in 1865 representatives met at Plymouth to draft the Burial Hill Declaration (the first official statement since the Cambridge Platform of 1648), which modified the strict Calvinism of the past, reiterated the importance of local autonomy, and stressed the need for greater ecumenical dialogue with other Christian traditions. Increasingly, too, Congregationalists took an interest in the Social Gospel. Andover Seminary opened its journal to social commentary and Washington Gladden, who was to become the denomination's great authority on social issues, began his career as a pastor in Massachusetts in the 1860s and 1870s.

Episcopalians manifested a similar interest in organizational restructuring and social reform. In 1893, Bishop William Lawrence of Massachusetts restructured his diocese to create functioning archdeaconries, through which the voice of the ordinary parishioner could be heard (since they included lay as well as clerical representatives) and by which the affairs of the diocese could be administered. During the 1920s, diocesan offices for education, social service, finance, and stewardship were

The Jewish Quarter, Boston, c. 1899. Courtesy Library of Congress.

established as the principles of scientific management began to be applied to even religious institutions. As far as social reform was concerned, Episcopal advocates in New England included Vida Scudder, a professor at Wellesley College, and William Dwight Porter Bliss, rector of the Church of the Carpenter in Boston. Bliss founded the Church Association for the Advancement of Labor and the Christian Social Union. The Church Association, which had many bishops as members, investigated sweatshops and tenements, mediated strikes, and encouraged observance of Labor Sunday (before Labor Day). It also required its members to take at least one journal devoted to the interests of labor and study social questions in the light of the Incarnation.

The condition of the Jewish community also drew attention after the marked increase in immigration from Russia. The small community from Prussian Poland that had settled in Boston's South End during the 1840s had founded Boston's first Jewish congregation, Ohabei Shalom, in 1843 and erected its first synagogue in 1852. Two other synagogues were erected by the German Jewish community before 1870. All three showed great susceptibility to adapt to their new environment. Discovering that they could not avoid working on the Sabbath, these synagogues introduced Sunday services, and in 1865, they further broke with Jewish tradition by joining the Christian churches in holding mourning services for the assassinated President Lincoln. Such Jews were ready recruits for the Reform movement led by Rabbi Solomon Schindler, who founded Temple Israel in 1885. They also provided the milieu that fostered the rise of Zionism in the early twentieth century and the emergence of prominent Jews like Louis Brandeis and Horace Kallen. By contrast, the Russian Jews who arrived in Boston after 1880 strongly resisted Americanization and sought to preserve in toto the religious traditions they had observed in Europe.

The Church of Christ, Scientist and the Church of the Living God

New England also gave birth to two more esoteric sects during this period, one of which endures to this day. This is the Church of Christ, Scientist founded by Mary Baker Eddy (1821–1910) in 1879 and reorganized in Boston in 1892, after her healing from an illness in 1866 while reading the account in the Gospel of

Matthew where Jesus healed a paralytic. Eddy embarked upon an extended period of Bible study, which ultimately led to her abandonment of the Congregational Church to promote a system of divine healing based on the teachings of the Bible. Unlike other metaphysical churches, the Church of Christ, Scientist defines itself as Christian and affirms its allegiance to the inspired Word of the Bible, while Jesus is acknowledged as the "Way-Shower." While holding Eddy in high regard, the Church of Christ, Scientist does not elevate her to prophetic status, nor does it consider her *Science and Health with Key to the Scriptures* (1875) a second revelation, but rather a tool for understanding the Bible. Christian Science holds that everyone should study to understand the world and their lives as being connected to the divine, properly or improperly. Sin, sickness, death, and hell are not considered real, but rather as states of mind to be overcome. Human beings suffer simply because they give those states of mind too much influence. God saves and forgives people from these errors by stripping them away and revealing a better path, so healing is not a medical process but a "divinely natural" one. One comes to understand that pain is a mental concept that can be dispelled by following the Holy Spirit. Heaven, for the Christian Scientist, is less a place than the reign of the Spirit, while hell is error, hatred, lust, remorse, sickness, and death.

Leadership of the Church is vested in the Mother Church based in Boston, whose rules are contained in the *Church Manual*. While local branches are democratically run by their members, worship is conducted by elected readers who must be members in good standing of the Mother Church. Services consist of readings from the Bible and *Science and Health*, and branch churches also maintain public reading rooms where the public can come in and peruse the Bible, *Science and Health*, and other literature and talk with a member. Practitioners—members advanced in the

Christian Science Church, Boston. © The Christian Science Publishing Society. All rights reserved.

art of Christian Science healing and prayer—are also available to help people to achieve full health. The church runs its own newspaper, the Pulitzer Prize–winning *Christian Science Monitor*, and the Mother Church complex is a major architectural landmark in Boston and one of the city's most visited tourist stops.

While Christian Science has endured for over a century, more fleeting was the Church of the Living God, a Holiness sect founded by Frank Sandford in Brunswick, Maine, in 1894, which stressed a second experience of the Holy Spirit after conversion, which produced "entire sanctification." Sandford stressed evangelism and was one of the first to include divine healing, as well as baptism, the Lord's Supper, and worship among the movement's ordinances. It also practiced Saturday worship and closed communion. In 1901, it was announced that Sandford was the Prophet Elijah who had returned to announce the reign of Christ, and the movement grew rapidly until 1904 when Sandford was convicted of manslaughter over the death of several missionaries in Greenland. After his release from prison in 1920, he was forced to decentralize his group to avoid legal action by the state of Maine, but he remained its unofficial leader until his death in 1947.

A NEW MAJORITY: 1918–1970

Roman Catholics

The New England Catholic community of the 1920s and 1930s enjoyed a new sense of self-worth that came with political power. Escaping the constraints imposed by the middle-class Republican minority, New England's Catholics looked to take full advantage of their numerical dominance not only in Boston but also in Providence, Rhode Island, Hartford, Connecticut, and Manchester, New Hampshire. This did not immediately translate into political liberalism, however. Archbishop O'Connell of Boston took upon himself the mantle of a guardian of public morals, harking back, as he did so, to a New England tradition established by the Puritans. Applauding the Catholic National Legion of Decency's activities, O'Connell turned his guns on immoral literature and theater performances, opposed Sunday baseball, and attacked "crooners" (singers of slow love songs). He organized campaigns, directed by priests of his archdiocese, to repudiate the national Child Labor Amendment to the Constitution and to oppose Governor James Curley's plans for a state lottery in 1935 and an attempt to liberalize Massachusetts laws on birth control in 1941. The coming of the Great Depression, however, saw a steady change in political outlook as even the most culturally conservative of all Catholics—the French Canadians—lined up behind the New Deal coalition. In Connecticut, Massachusetts, and Rhode Island, the steady unionization of the working-class Catholics pushed the community to the political left and kept those states solidly behind Franklin Roosevelt's New Deal coalition. Northern New England, with its enduring Yankee Protestant community, proved more resistant, however, and both Maine and Vermont voted for Republican Alfred Landon in the presidential election of 1936.

The Catholic community witnessed increased Americanization during the 1920s and 1930s, after the Immigration Act of 1924 cut off the flow of migrants from the Old World. Although the birth rate remained high, the rate of population increase was considerably down in the beginning of the century. Nevertheless, interwar growth was acknowledged in the creation of the Diocese of Worcester in Massachusetts in 1950 and the dioceses of Bridgeport and Norwich in Connecticut in 1953. Catholic organizations such as sodalities and the Legion of Mary came on the scene and there was a new interest in miraculous medal novenas. After 1940, there was a considerable interest in the problem of juvenile delinquency in the Catholic community, which led to the establishment of Catholic Youth Organizations that sponsored games, dances, and plays. The 1940s and early 1950s were a time of optimism for the Catholic Church. Catholics were moving steadily into the middle class, and applications to seminaries and religious orders were at an all-time high. Yet this success was bought at a price. Ethnic Catholicism suffered a severe loss of appeal among the second generation. At Holy Family Church in Pittsfield, Massachusetts, there was a steady decline in membership and knowledge of the Polish language during the 1940s, while younger members at the French Canadian St. Aloysius Church in Springfield, Massachusetts, had begun to ask for services in English. More problematic were heightened rates of failed Easter Duty and a considerable increase in the number of mixed marriages. In an early sign that the parochial school system might not survive indefinitely, churches like St. Thomas Aquinas in Springfield began to experiment with the Confraternity of Christian Doctrine program, under which Catholic parents were given the training to instill the faith, a task which had, in previous generations, been entrusted to clergy and others with religious vocations.

The 1960s witnessed a steady decline in authority wielded by church leaders, a decline compounded by John F. Kennedy's public assurances in seeking the presidency that he would not be subject to the papal dictates and Pope John XXIII's admonitions to Catholic laity during the Second Vatican Council (1962–1965) to free themselves from the priestly authoritarianism of the past. Among the council's innovations was an assertion that everyone enjoyed *charism* and was obliged to participate actively in the life of the church. In liturgy, private devotions to Mary and the saying of the rosary experienced a marked decline, while numerous varieties of the Mass appeared following the decision to adopt an entirely vernacular liturgy. Despite the desire to renew the church, the 1970s witnessed a marked decline in regular Mass attendance and in men entering the seminary. Meanwhile, many priests and nuns abandoned their pastoral duties (and in some cases their orders) to embark upon a life of social action. Between 1970 and 1980, for example, the Jesuit Father Robert Drinan won election to Congress, representing the Boston suburbs of Brookline and Newton.

Parish life was enhanced by the addition of such programs as Cursillo and Marriage Encounter and the establishment of new lay ministries and parish councils, as evidenced in St. Paul's Church, Hingham, Massachusetts, which took up the message of the council with a strong parochial school and parish council, an adult enrichment program, and numerous support groups. In many other parishes, however, the old ethnic Catholicism was not replaced with anything new, but merely slowly eroded as younger Catholics abandoned such communities. The church was also obliged to cope with a new influx of immigrants from Puerto Rico and Central America. Spanish apostolates and a greater incidence of Spanish masses both became commonplace, and parishes like St. Mary's Church, Lawrence, Massachusetts, were transformed from Irish to Spanish almost overnight. Between 1970 and 1980, St. Thomas Aquinas Church in Springfield, Massachusetts, gained 4,409

Puerto Ricans and lost 1,418 French Canadians. It is not unusual today to observe celebrations for the Day of the Dead or the Virgin of Guadalupe in many New England cities and towns.[3]

Not all Catholics viewed the changes implemented by the Second Vatican Council with enthusiasm. As early as the 1940s, Boston had been the site of protests by traditionalist Catholics led by the Jesuit Father Leonard Feeney who taught at Weston College in Cambridge. Although his initial target was secularism at Harvard, Feeney went on to attack church leaders for watering down the doctrine that there was no salvation outside the Roman Catholic Church. A group of his followers started a religious order pledged to Feeney at the Thomas Moore Bookstore in Harvard Square. When Feeney defended four professors at Boston College who had been sacked for accusing their colleagues of heresy, he was silenced by Archbishop Richard Cushing and ultimately excommunicated in 1953. His followers then declared themselves the Slaves of the Immaculate Heart of Mary, which moved to Still River, Massachusetts, in 1958 and established an ascetic celibate community. In 1974, however, Feeney led twenty-nine members back into communion with Rome, and in 1988 the order was regularized as a lay order of the Roman Catholic Church. Still separated is the Orthodox Roman Catholic Movement, founded by Father Francis Fenton in Monroe, Connecticut, in 1970, when he began to celebrate Latin masses at his home. Joined by four other priests in 1975, Fenton's group spread to Florida and California as well as other parts of the Northeast, but other traditionalist Catholics disapproved of his membership in the John Birch Society, and when he left the movement in 1978, it collapsed. A single parish endures in Monroe, which continues to publish the newsletter *Catholics Forever*.

Jews

The American Jewish community also experienced a change of pace after 1918. While the 1920s and 1930s were devoted to the building of colleges and hospitals, the 1940s and 1950s saw a dramatic shift in favor of ecumenical dialogue with Christians, especially African Americans. Many Boston rabbis participated in the March on Selma, and Martin Luther King Jr. addressed a Passover service at Temple Israel in 1965. Better relations were also established with the Roman Catholic Church. At the same time, the Cambridge-Lexington area of Massachusetts drew many young professional Jews into the area for graduate school, who demanded a different sort of religious community, which led to the creation of *Havurat Shalom* in Somerville in 1968 as a place for alternative expressions of religious sensibilities. Many younger Jews felt increasingly cut off from their religious roots and find the established synagogues of little use in giving them a sense of religious purpose.

The United Church of Christ

For the Congregationalists, the years after 1918 marked a further retreat from historic Calvinism and an ever greater commitment to social mission. They also experienced a profound shift toward church federation. In 1923 and 1927, negotiations were held with the Episcopal and Presbyterian churches, respectively, although they led to no great breakthrough. In 1927, they absorbed the Evangelical

Protestant Church and in 1931 the Christian Church, while in 1940 they began negotiations with the historically German Evangelical and Reformed Church, which had produced two influential Neo-orthodox theologians, Paul Tillich and Reinhold Neibuhr. Finally, in 1957, the two denominations agreed on a merger that would create the United Church of Christ, although a minority of Congregationalists (including thirty-nine of the 454 Massachusetts synods) declined to participate. The new denomination has acquired a strong reputation for social liberalism on such as issues as abortion, homosexuality, affirmative action, and war, and was the first mainline Protestant denomination to ordain women and practicing homosexuals.

POSTETHNIC NEW ENGLAND: 1950–2000

If we examine the statistical returns for New England (see Table 3), several things become clear. Regional participation in religious organizations attains 57.4 percent, but with great variation between northern and southern New England. On the one hand are the states of Massachusetts (64.1 percent) and Rhode Island (63.5 percent) with Connecticut (57.9 percent) only a little way behind. New Hampshire (47.7 percent) is a borderline case, while Vermont (39.1 percent) and Maine (36.4 percent) are increasingly secular, with rates comparable to those of states in the Pacific Northwest.[4] Although the Roman Catholic Church enjoys the backing of over 60 percent of the church-going population in every state, there is a twenty-point difference between the overwhelming Catholicism of Rhode Island (81.5 percent) and the more modest showings in Maine (61.1 percent) and Vermont (62.1 percent), while Jews are concentrated in the urban states of Massachusetts (6.8 percent) and Connecticut (5.5 percent). As for the various strands of American Protestantism, in no state does a single denomination exceed 10 percent. The United Church of Christ heads the list in Connecticut, New Hampshire, and Vermont, the United Methodists in Maine, and the Episcopal Church in Rhode Island, while in Massachusetts, once the cradle of Congregationalism, the United Methodists are level with the Congregationalists. The United Church of Christ ranges from a high of 9.1 percent in Vermont to a low of 1.3 percent in Rhode Island; the Episcopal Church from a high of 4.0 percent in Rhode Island to a low of 2.4 percent in Massachusetts; the United Methodists from a high of 8.0 percent in Vermont to a low of 1.3 percent in Rhode Island; and the American Baptists from a high of 5.7 percent in Maine to a low of 1.3 percent in Massachusetts. If anywhere in New England is contested ground, it is the small northern states. In southern New England, there really is no contest. The Lutheran Church, particularly prominent in the Midwest, the mid-Atlantic, and Great Plains regions, is a small force in the Northeastern United States.

Religion once drove education, but in New England the religious legacy is a small one. There are eighteen Catholic colleges and universities operating in New England today, nine of them in Massachusetts and three in Connecticut, including such institutions as Assumption College, Boston College, and College of the Holy Cross in Massachusetts, Fairfield University in Connecticut, Providence College in Rhode Island, and St. Anselm's College in New Hampshire. No Protestant colleges remain in a region where faith and education were once inseparably linked, except for Trinity College in Hartford, Connecticut, which is associated with the Episcopal Church. The Episcopal Church also has two seminaries: Berkeley Di-

Table 3. Religious adhesion in New England, 2000

Denomination	Number	Percentage of Total Adherents
Roman Catholic	5,869,303	73.4
Jewish congregations	423,500	5.3
United Church of Christ	340,476	4.3
Episcopal Church in the United States of America	240,374	3.0
United Methodist	193,419	2.4
American Baptists, U.S.A.	169,908	2.1
Muslim	77,662	1.0
Evangelical Lutheran Church in America	76,145	1.0
Other	605,905	7.5
TOTAL	7,996,692	100.0

Source: Dale E. Jones, Sherri Doty, Clifford Grammich, James E. Horsch, Richard Houseal, Mac Lynn, John P. Marcum, Kenneth M. Sanchagrin, and Richard H. Taylor, *Religious Congregations and Membership in the United States, 2000: An Enumeration by Region, State and County Based on Data Reported for 149 Religious Bodies* (Nashville, TN: Glenmary Research Center, 2002).

vinity School at Yale and Episcopal Divinity School in Cambridge, Massachusetts. The United Church of Christ, in addition to Harvard University School of Divinity and Yale Divinity School, maintains Andover Newton Theological Seminary in Massachusetts, Hartford Seminary in Connecticut, and Bangor Theological Seminary in Maine.

Fundamentalist Churches

While most of the new religious phenomena in New England have been non-Christian, some fundamentalist churches have made gains. Island Pond, Vermont, is the home of the Messianic Communities of New England, which began in Chattanooga, Tennessee, in 1972 as part of the Jesus people movement, led by Gene and Marsha Spriggs. In 1979, the community moved to Vermont, where it initially encountered local hostility and was raided on false allegations of child abuse. It is evangelical, operates on the New Testament model, upholds an authoritative and inerrant Bible, salvation by grace, and justification by faith, and is hostile to homosexuality. During the 1980s, it sent workers to France, Canada, New Zealand, and Brazil. If the Messianic Communities are an example of rural fundamentalism, then the Boston Church of Christ is its urban counterpart. Organized by Kip McKean in 1979, it grew from 50 to 3,200 members over a ten-year period—a megachurch with daughter churches in Atlanta, Chicago, Denver, Los Angeles, Miami, Orlando, San Francisco, and San Diego. It represented a movement to revitalize the Churches of Christ—a denomination centered in Tennessee and Texas—which younger members felt was stagnating. It broke with its parent by using instrumental music, requiring rebaptism of all new members, and emphasizing good works, and it is also intensely hierarchical rather than congregational.

Eastern Religions

New Englanders were well informed about Eastern religions from comparatively early in their history, but the presence of Buddhist and Hindu communities is a largely postwar phenomenon, although Boston had a Chinatown district during the nineteenth century and Harvard appointed its first Chinese faculty member in 1879. One of the earliest postwar developments was the Cambridge Buddhist Association in Massachusetts organized at the request of faculty and students by two visiting Buddhist scholars in 1957. For many years, it was the only Zen Buddhist center in the Boston area and a popular location for dialogue between Buddhists and Christians, which contributed to Aelred Graham's *Conversations: Buddhist and Christian* (1968). Today the association maintains an extensive library and a daily meditation session open to the public, as well as retreats and lectures. Another Western group is the England-based Friends of the Western Buddhist Order, which maintains an American outpost in Newmarket, Rhode Island. Founded by an English convert, the order is devoted to preaching Buddhism in a way that is relevant to the West and is composed of a lay order of men and women who commit to following the Buddhist path to enlightenment (in contrast with much of Eastern Buddhism which emphasizes the monastic life).

Several other Buddhist groups have more overtly Eastern origins. The Khmer Buddhist Society of New England was organized by Ven. Maha Gosananda in 1981 to assist Cambodian refugee communities fleeing the Khmer Rouge regime and between 1983 and 1986, eighty monks helped establish forty-one temples. The Kwan Um Zen School in Cumberland, Rhode Island, was founded in 1983 by Seung Sahn of the Chogye Order, who came to Providence in 1972 with the aim of planting a new Buddhist tradition in the West. Sahn argued that the purpose of Zen Buddhism was to find one's true self and then assist others in the same process. In addition to a temple in Rhode Island, he organized branch centers in Cambridge, Massachusetts, and New Haven, Connecticut, and in the 1990s carried his work into Europe. Finally, Satya Narayn Goenka was responsible for Vipassana Meditation Centers, based in Shelburne Falls, Massachusetts, in 1982, which operated thirty centers in the United States and Canada by 1997.

In the early 1990s, Tibetan Buddhism obtained a foothold in New England initially through the Dzogchen Foundation in Cambridge, Massachusetts, established in 1991 by Lama Surya Das (born Jeffrey Miller) who had traveled in India and Nepal in the 1970s and studied in Tibetan monasteries. The foundation seeks to promote dialogue between the various strands of Buddhism, holds an annual month-long retreat, and translates and publishes texts and teachings. In 1994, it was joined by the Center for Dzogchen Studies in New Haven, Connecticut, headed by Lama Padma Karma Rinpoche (a convert from Christianity), which is devoted to the teachings and practices of the Heart Tradition of Tibetan Buddhism. The center stresses the practice of resting in awareness as a means of bringing one into contact with the flux of one's thought patterns, something which they believe can be learned even by non-Buddhists.

The high-tech environment of southern New England has also brought significant numbers of Hindu migrants to the area. The Vishwa Hindu Parishad (founded in New York in 1970) is now based in Berlin, Connecticut, from which it organizes fellowship for Hindus of different ethnic traditions, cultural programs for children, celebrations of Indian festivals, and promotion of understanding of Hinduism by Americans. Amrit Desai's Kirpalu Center for Yoga and Health, founded in Pennsylvania in 1971, moved to Lenox, Massachusetts in 1983, where it offered a full range of yoga programs and trained two thousand yoga instructors. It was the largest yoga center in North America in the early 1990s, with 220 residents, but came under a cloud in 1994 when Desai was accused of sexual improprieties and had to resign. The Hindu community also received a boost when the Sri Lakshmi Temple (New England's largest Hindu temple) was consecrated in Hopkinton, Massachusetts, in 1990.

Islam

Since the 1960s, the number of Muslims has also grown rapidly, though they are not as numerous here as in some places. In New England, the first mosque was built in Quincy, Massachusetts, in 1963 by a small group of families from the Middle East who were working at the shipyards. Today, mosques are becoming more and more a part of the New England landscape, often with additions in the form of libraries, schools, community rooms, museums, and apartments. The Islamic Society of New England reports twenty mosques on its registry and the Islamic Center of New England, in Sharon, Massachusetts, has over thirty countries represented in its membership.

New Age and Magick Religions

In addition to Eastern religions, some New Englanders have been drawn to New Age and Magick cults. Perhaps the most prominent of the former is Universal Life, based in Woodbridge, Connecticut, but founded in Germany in 1975, which teaches that the spirit of God teaches the path to experience God in one's inner being based on prophetic revelations given to the present generation which clarify divine laws and their application to daily life. While Universal Life still makes some claim to be Christian, the Magick groups are overtly neo-Pagan. They include the Abbey of Thelema in Old Greenwich, Connecticut, a secret order founded by Aleister Crowley in the early 1900s, and the Temple of Isis in Salem, Massachusetts, founded by Laurie Cabot in the 1970s. Cabot moved to Salem in the 1960s, taught "Witchcraft as a Science" in adult education classes, opened the Witch Shop, and helped found the Witches' League for Public Awareness. She was later ordained and her temple dedicated by the National Alliance of Pantheists. Nashua, New Hampshire, boasts Lady Sabrina's Our Lady of Enchantment: Church of the Old Religion, which moved there from California in 1982. Seeing religion, art, science, and magic as an integral whole, it provides public classes, worship services, and degreed training programs in Wicca and is recognized by state and federal governments as a church and educational institution.

Native American Religions Today

Since the 1970s, there has also been a resurgence of interest in Native American religious customs. The Wampanoag tribe, based on Martha's Vineyard, elects a governing council, but the chief and medicine men are chosen by other tradi-

A Narragansett Indian powwow. Courtesy of Rhode Island Tourism Division.

tional means. The Penobscot in Maine now conduct an annual one-hundred-mile trek up Mount Katahdin, their ancestral "Greatest Mountain." Native American powwows are also becoming more common in New England, as places for tribes to learn each other's ways, trade, find mates, and bond with the spirits of nature and as a way for non–Native Americans to learn first-hand about Native American culture. Sweat lodges are sometimes conducted and drumming and other forms of music are almost constant from beginning to end. Dancing demonstrations and competitions always carry a sense of sacred symbolism. There are also hunting dances, rain dances, and mating dances, which include prayers and occasional rituals. Shelburne Powwow and Schemitzun Powwow are the two largest in New England, with thousands of people in attendance.

CONCLUSION

It is all too evident that New England has come a considerable distance from its origins as a religious colony dedicated to perfectionist religion. As we have seen, even New England Puritanism was never wholly monolithic, and life in early New Haven, Massachusetts Bay, or Providence exposed the English migrants to very different structures of religious life. Nevertheless, they all had a common inheritance: a legacy of religious persecution, a well-defined Calvinist preoccupation with experiencing the presence of God, and a belief in the need for citizens to respect the existing temporal and spiritual authorities. All this changed with the arrival of Church of England missionaries backed by the full force of the state. Suddenly, Puritan New England was confronted by a credible theological rival that threatened to undermine the Godly Commonwealth. The picture was further complicated by the arrival of George Whitefield, whose revivalist campaigns split the

Congregationalist community into competing factions. It might be argued that despite great figures like Jonathan Edwards, Congregationalism never really recovered from the chaos of the Great Awakening. Overtaken by more evangelistic Methodists, Baptists, and Presbyterians and seriously depleted by the Unitarian controversy, Congregationalism was ill-prepared to defend its heartland against the Catholic influx of the 1840s.

The advent of significant Catholic immigration changed the rules of the game in New England. As Boston became an Irish metropolis, New England ceased to be the shaper of America's Protestant worldview. Protestants still dominated the professions and the executive class, but the region's religious culture would become Catholic to a degree found in few other metropolitan settings. Liturgy and personal devotions rather than theological inquiry would characterize New England's religious life from the 1880s until the 1940s. This is not to say that the old Puritan notions of regulation of public morality were abandoned. It is clear that Bishop O'Connell was all too willing to apply the same sort of standards to his flock that the Puritan elders had upheld for their own congregations. New England Catholicism in the early twentieth century was as subject to regulation as the earlier tradition had been.

Simply to judge by statistics, it is hard to see how things have changed to any great extent since 1970. Religious participation seems high and most New Englanders claim to be Catholic. These appearances, however, are deceptive. To identify oneself as a Catholic is often a far cry from living an intense religious life, and it is clear from opinion polls and election results that many New England Catholics do not regard their religious identity as affecting their activities in the world. In New England, as on the West Coast, many educated professionals have tended to abandon their religious faith. The steady erosion of mainstream Protestantism in this part of the world bears testimony to the fact that religion is merely a form of social justice that can be accomplished without setting foot inside a church. It is perhaps significant that New England was in the religious headlines in 2003, after the Episcopal Diocese of New Hampshire chose a practicing homosexual as its bishop, with long-term consequences for the whole Anglican Communion. With a few notable exceptions, there has been no great appearance of the nondenominational conservative evangelical churches that exist in other regions of the United States. New England long ago ceased to be the Godly Commonwealth, and whether she is still the Catholic Commonwealth must surely be open to question.

RESOURCE GUIDE

Printed Sources

Casino, Joseph J. "From Sanctuary to Involvement: A History of the Catholic Parish in the Northeast." In Jay P. Dolan, ed., *The American Catholic Parish: A History from 1850 to the Present*. Vol. 1. Mahwah, NJ: Paulist Press, 1987. 7–116.

Conley, Patrick T. *Catholicism in Rhode Island: The Formative Era*. Providence, RI: Diocese of Providence, 1976.

Duffy, Mark J., ed. *The Episcopal Diocese of Massachusetts: A Mission to Remember, Proclaim and Fulfill*. Boston: Episcopal Diocese of Massachusetts, 1984.

Liptak, Dolores. *European Immigrants and the Catholic Church in Connecticut, 1870–1920*. New York: Center for Migration Studies, 1987.

Miller, Perry. *The New England Mind: The Seventeenth Century*. Cambridge, MA: Harvard University Press, 1939.

O'Toole, James M. *Militant and Triumphant: William Henry O'Connell and the Catholic Church in Boston, 1859–1944*. Notre Dame, IN: University of Notre Dame Press, 1992.

Paradis, Wilfrid H. *Upon This Granite: Catholics in New Hampshire, 1768–1988*. Portsmouth, NH: Phoenix Publishing, 1988.

Pestani, Carla G. *Quakers and Baptists in Colonial Massachusetts*. New York: Cambridge University Press, 1991.

Potash, P. Jeffrey. *Vermont's Burned-Over District: Patterns of Community Development and Religion, 1761–1850*. Brooklyn, NY: Carlson Publishing, 1991.

Sarna, Jonathan D., and Ellen Smith, eds. *The Jews of Boston: Essays on the Occasion of the Centenary (1895–1995) of the Combined Jewish Philanthropies of Greater Boston*. Boston: Combined Jewish Philanthropies of Greater Boston, 1995.

Web Sites

Church of Christ, Scientist. 2004.
The First Church of Christ, Scientist. January 22, 2004.
http://www.tfccs.com

Official site for Church of Christ.

Episcopal Divinity School, Cambridge, Massachusetts. 2000.
Episcopal Divinity School. January 21, 2004.
http://www.episdivschool.edu

Episcopal seminary in Cambridge, Massachusetts.

Roman Catholic Archdiocese of Boston. 2004.
Archdiocesan Office of Communications. January 25, 2004.
http://www.rcab.org

Official publication of the Archdiocesan Office of Communications.

United Church of Christ. 2004.
United Church of Christ. January 25, 2004.
http://www.ucc.org

Official site for the United Church of Christ.

Organizations and Museums

Cathedral of St. Joseph
140 Farmington Avenue
Hartford, CT 06105
http://www.cathedralofsaintjoseph.com/

King's Chapel
58 Tremont Street
Boston, MA 02148
http://www.kings-chapel.org/

Old First Church
Monument Avenue
Bennington, VT 05201
http://www.neinfo.net/New_England/Vermont/Bennington/attractions/Old_First_Church/

Pilgrim Hall Museum
75 Court Street
Plymouth, MA 02360
http://www.pilgrimhall.org

St. John's Church
101 Chapel Street
Portsmouth, NH 03801
http://www.stjohnsnh.org/

St. Patrick's Catholic Church
32 Pond Road
P.O. Box 598
Newcastle, ME 04553
http://www.stpatricksnewcastle.org/

Touro Synagogue National Historic Site
85 Touro Street
Newport, RI 02840
http://www.tourosynagogue.org

SPORTS AND RECREATION

Martin J. Manning

INTRODUCTION

Since the beginning, New England has been a region of sports and recreational activities. The Native Americans were the first to introduce stick-and-ball games to the region. They played lacrosse and engaged in a variety of recreational activities, such as hunting and fishing. When the Puritans arrived, they were suspicious of leisurely pursuits but kept up the tradition of sports, introducing English games like stick ball and "ninepins and bowle" (both earlier versions of American baseball and bowling). They also introduced English recreations like cards and dancing. For Puritans, sports and recreations were informal events, tolerated if they did not infringe upon the mores of the Bible commonwealth. For much of the colonial period and part of the nineteenth century, this tradition of amateur or gentlemanly sports and recreations was commonplace in New England. Baseball, football, and later basketball and hockey were played by nonprofessional athletes, while recreations were simply for the sake of enjoyment or for gambling. By the second half of the nineteenth century, however, a body of professional American sports evolved from these informal activities, resulting in the professionalization of New England sports and recreations and their association with an American identity. The process of this evolution is the subject matter of the following chapter.

EARLY NEW ENGLAND SPORTS

Sports and recreations played a more prominent role in the lives of Native American peoples than any other inhabitants of colonial North America. Universality amid diversity best characterizes the recreations of Native Americans. Physical, competitive recreations were integral parts of virtually every phase of their existence. Although Native Americans frequently engaged in recreations purely for pleasure, the activities termed *sports* were actively related to tribal ceremonials and

Lacrosse

Lacrosse, or baggataway, as the Native Americans called it, is a ball-and-goal field game played with a netted stick by teams of ten on a side. The French gave lacrosse its name, derived from the primitive form of racket which vaguely resembled a bishop's crozier (crosse). The New England natives used a crosse three to four feet (914 mm.–1.219 m.) in length, with a stick that was curved at one end to form a loop or rough circle some four inches (102 mm.) in diameter. The game, which would last two to three days with goals marked by trees and set about five hundred yards (457 m.) apart, had a religious significance but was also played to train tribal warriors. After the Civil War, lacrosse became popular in the United States with several exhibition games staged in areas around Boston and New York. The National Lacrosse Association, which adopted Canadian rules, was established in 1849 with Boston University as one of its members, while Harvard, Princeton, and New York University in 1882 created the Intercollegiate Lacrosse Association, which soon included Boston University. Harvard was also a member of the Intercollegiate Lacrosse League, founded in 1905, which in turn became the U.S. Intercollegiate Lacrosse Association in 1929. In 1939, the U.S. Women's Lacrosse Association was formed by clubs from Baltimore, Boston, New York, and Philadelphia. In 1933, Frances Elizabeth "Betty" Richey (1912–) from Brookline, Massachusetts, was named to the first national women's lacrosse team and was a member of the team for the next twenty-one years. Richey was also a successful field hockey and squash player.

rites: to cure illness, prepare for war, ensure the fertility of plants and animals, or produce rain. Native American sports and recreations blurred the distinction between work and play. Children's games were a preparation for adulthood roles, while women transformed utilitarian crafts into artistic creations. Dancing brought all age groups and both sexes together in an activity that was frequently both ceremonial and recreational. In addition to deriving pleasure and provisions from hunting and fishing, adolescent and adult males participated in contests of strength and dexterity, such as archery, wrestling, and foot racing, that honed survival skills. Although individual sports were important in conferring personal status and tribal leadership roles, group games played the most important role in Native American cultures.

Games between or among New England tribes, villages, or clans were often violent, and group sports were approached and executed with a seriousness that reflected their important political, social, and economic functions in Native American culture. They played them for a variety of reasons, including resolving disputes short of war, allocating or reallocating economic resources, and exchanging goods and services. With their tribal cohesion and ceremonial play, Native American recreations in New England resembled the popular village pastimes of Europe. There were no animal blood sports, however, which clearly expressed their respect for and reliance upon wildlife.

Native Ball Games

New England native recreations and sports extended to different regions in North America. Despite regional and tribal variations, ball games were part of the North American native community and variations of the game baggataway (lacrosse) extended from Canada to the Gulf of Mexico and to the Great Plains. Stickball, considered one of the oldest North American sports, originated in the southeast region of North America and was played by New England natives as well. Games involving kicking and throwing a ball were universal in North America. Kickball games, like stickball, generally involved a competition between tribes, villages, or clans and were played over great distances, sometimes from one village to the next. Other ball games, such as handball, sans net (volleyball), dodgeball, and juggling, generally were played as intravillage activities.

Although the New England settlers had little influence on Native American sports and recreations during the colonial period, native techniques used in hunting and fishing and in native sports like lacrosse influenced New Englanders. New England native games generally involved a religious or political dimension that was absent in European sport. The one exception was gambling. A gambling culture, Native Americans found French and British frontiersmen eager to bet on contests.

Colonial Games and Amusements

The Protestant reformers who fled to America abolished the traditional ecclesiastical calendar of feast days and legislated against the popular communal games associated with them, while the isolation of rural towns precluded significant intercommunity recreations. The lone occasion for communal sport was training day, when local militiamen gathered for a little military drill and more raucous pursuits such as wrestling, running, jumping, target shooting, and sometimes drinking and gambling while a number of New Englanders pursued private recreations that they avoided in public, such as cards, dancing, and bowling.

Despite popular belief, Puritans did not reject pleasurable activities; they played sports and participated in recreations, yet the nature of the activity and the age of the participant were critical considerations. Children participated freely in playtime activities, including ball games on the town commons or village green, while adolescents and adults were encouraged to exercise and to participate in selected recreations appropriate to one's calling. However, Puritans condemned activities that might arouse physical and emotional passions, promote immorality, divert attention from one's familial and work responsibilities, or become pleasurable ends in themselves, to the detriment of one's commitment to God. Upon reaching majority, adults abandoned childish pastimes and publicly pursued recreations and exercises designed to promote physical and emotional well-being. Privately, they engaged in table games of chance or intellectual skill.

In 1670, the Massachusetts General Court, responding to what it saw as an increase in card playing, made the mere possession of cards or dice a crime because it was assumed that the playing of cards necessarily involved gambling. Horse racing was also made illegal near towns and major roadways in 1677 because it involved gambling and misspending time, "drawing of many persons from the duty of their particular Callings."[1]

Field sports, favored by church and state authorities, remained the most popular activities. Cockfights, bowling, and a host of like sports flourished in and around taverns while student-initiated sports flourished at primary schools as well as at Harvard and Yale. The growing participation and acceptance of sports and recreation formed part of an increasingly diversified and cosmopolitan social order. If New England recreations were increasingly less restrained religiously by the mid-eighteenth century, the Puritan legacy had an unmistakably inhibiting effect on the development of sport in the region.

The sports that amused the populace in England, such as bowling, card playing, dice throwing, billiards, shuffleboard, angling, hunting, and horse racing, were familiar to seventeenth-century New Englanders. These are mentioned in official documents, diaries, and letters. The New England poet Edward Taylor (1642–1729) used English games in his religious metaphors, suggesting that games were commonplace in colonial days. The ambiguous attitude of many settlers toward games is illustrated in the diary of Samuel Sewall (1652–1730).[2] In May 1689, when Sewall was a young man, he made the rounds of a number of taverns, and usually ended up playing ninepins at one of them. In August 1715, some twenty-six years later, he helped break up a game of ninepins on what was officially referred to as Mount-Whoredom, near what is now Louisburg Square on Beacon Hill in Boston.

New England Puritans opposed "unlawful" recreations, like cards, dice, shuffleboard, or any game associated with gambling and drinking at taverns and inns. As early as 1637, the Massachusetts General Court complained about such profane recreations: "[I]t hath appeared unto this court, upon many sad complaints, that much drunkenness, wast of the good creatures of God, mispence of precious time, & other disorders have frequently fallen out in the inns . . . whereby God is much dishonored, the p[ro]fession of religion rep[r]oached, & the welfare of this com[m]onwealth greatly impaired, & the true vse of such houses (being the necessary releefe of travellers) subverted."[3]

To counter this, in 1647, the court passed a law making it illegal to play such games at taverns. In the eighteenth century, English games were commonplace in New England. Printed ads announced horse races, hog racing, and bear baiting, a bowling green was established in Boston in 1700 on a tract of land (now the Boston Common), and residents played billiards and nine pins. Seventeenth-century New Englanders did not disapprove of sports and recreations as long as they were "lawful" recreations, and did not interfere with godly observances like the Sabbath. As Increase Mather (1639–1723) explained in *A Testimony Against Several Prophane and Superstitious Customs, Now Practised by Some in New-England: the evil whereof is evinced from the Holy Scriptures, and from the writings both of ancient and modern divines*, "Foer A Christian to use recreation is very lawful, and in some cases a great duty." Or as the Reverend John Downame told his congregation before migrating to New England, "Wee must constantly and continually, in everything, and at everytime, performe service unto God in all our actions and throughout our whole course and conver-sation . . . in the meanest duties of the basest calling, yea even in our eating and drinking, lawful sports and recreations, when as wee doth them in faith."[4]

POPULAR NEW ENGLAND SPORTS

Ever since football was introduced into the United States on Boston Common (1862) and basketballs were first stuffed into baskets in Springfield, Massachusetts (1881), New England has been a sports trailblazer. Games similar to baseball were played in the early nineteenth century. The region's colleges have fostered sports rivalries, and New Englanders are avid fans of sports at all levels of play.

Baseball

The sport that evokes more nostalgia in the United States than any other is baseball. Played by both children and adults, it has become known as "the national pastime." A more diverse and inclusive game than football and basketball, it can be played by athletes of average height and size. Early champions of the game fine-tuned it to include the kind of skills and mental judgment that had made cricket respectable in England. In particular, scoring and record-keeping gave baseball gravity. Baseball's ancestors consisted of various stick-and-ball games played by generations of Englishmen and American colonists, for example, "old cat" games, rounders, and town ball. Printed references to "base ball" appeared as early as 1700 in America. Robin Carver, in his *Book of Sports* (1827), noted that Americans called their form of rounders "base ball" because they used bases instead of stakes as in cricket.

The "Massachusetts Game," also known as "town ball," was an early form of baseball popular throughout New England during the first half of the nineteenth century. The game used stakes for bases and had sixty-foot base paths. The hitter stood halfway between home plate and first base, with the pitcher thirty feet away. Rules varied somewhat from town to town, generally with ten to fourteen players on a team; runners were put out by being hit with a thrown ball while between the bases. In one version of the game, the first team to score one hundred runs was the winner. Eventually, the game disappeared, and it was supplanted by the New York Knickerbocker Club's modern game in 1860.[5]

In 1858, amateur baseball clubs in the Northeast region of the United States organized themselves into the National Association of Professional Base Ball Players (NAPBBP). At the time, the most dominant club was Henry Wrigley's Bostonians, who had a record win of 227 out of 287 games between 1871 and 1875. By March 1871, ten clubs formed the National Association of Professional Base Ball Players and established a series of games leading to a championship. One of the original teams was the Boston Red Stockings. After they were barred from professional baseball by the BAPBBP, which maintained that only whites could uphold baseball's "gentlemanly character," African Americans organized themselves into the League of Colored Baseball Clubs in 1887, with teams in Boston and in other major cities outside New England. Although owners of professional teams had signed contracts with skilled African American players, this ended in 1887 after a series of racial incidents; the most prominent occurred when a white player for Syracuse (International League) refused to stand in a team picture with an African American teammate. After incidents such as this, International League owners stopped signing African Americans while allowing existing players of African American descent to remain in the league.

By the beginning of the next decade, the Players' (Brotherhood) League, with eight teams, including Boston, had formed to protest the low salaries paid by the National League and American Association of Base Ball Clubs, but this did not seem to affect the consistent excellence of the playing; in 1894, Hugh Duffy of the Boston Nationals had the highest batting average for a season ever compiled by a major league baseball player (.438).

Although the Civil War caused a lull in the baseball boom, the postwar years kindled a new surge of nationalism, and baseball became the athletic expression of this unifying force. The growing professionalism proved to be the prime force behind this new phase, which culminated in the founding of the National League in 1876. The Providence Greys were in the National League from 1878 through 1885; they won pennants in 1879 and 1884. On September 25, 1882, the Providence and Worcester teams played major league baseball's first double-header. The league entered a "Golden Age" in the 1890s and, along with the institution of the American League in 1901 which led to the establishment of the World Series in 1903, it assured baseball's continued recognition as "the national game."

For the first half of the twentieth century, Boston was a two-baseball-team town. The two teams were the American League's Boston Red Sox and the National League's Boston Braves, which formed in 1900 and which played its home games in a stadium in Allston that is now part of the Boston University complex. The Braves won the World Series in 1914, when they defeated the Philadelphia Athletics (American League) 4–0, but lost it in 1948 to the Cleveland Indians. They were considered Boston's blue-collar team with working-class heroes on its roster, such as Sibby "Super Sub" Sisti, Bob "Mr. Team" Elliott, and Chuck Workman. In March 1953, the Braves moved to Milwaukee. Devotion to the Braves continues to this day, however, with the Boston Braves Historical Association, with an annual reunion, newsletter, hall of fame, and over five hundred devoted fans.[6]

Professional baseball outside Boston is healthy. The Pawtucket Paw Sox, a Triple-A (minor league) farm team of the Boston Red Sox in Pawtucket, Rhode Island, plays all spring and summer. Its home field is McCoy Stadium in Pawtucket, just north of Providence. Paw Sox games at McCoy Stadium offer baseball fans a night out at a ballgame without the hassle and expense of driving to Fenway Park. The Pittsfield-based Berkshire Black Bears and the Lynn-based North Shore Spirit are members of the independent Northeast League. The Pittsfield team plays its home games at Wahconah Park in Pittsfield. The Brockton Rox, and their member of the Northeast League, is a Triple-A team based in Burlington, Vermont.

The Cape Cod Baseball League

The Cape Cod Baseball League (CCBL) is the nation's oldest amateur league. It was founded in 1885. It is also the country's most competitive summertime college proving ground ("Where the stars of tomorrow shine tonight," according to its Web site). CCBL players who went on to the major leagues include Hall of Famer Red Sox catcher Carlton Fisk, the late Thurman Munson (Yankees catcher), and Chicago Cubs shortstop Nomar Garciaparra, who played for the Red Sox for many years. The CCBL has teams in Brewster, Chatham, Falmouth, Harwich, Orleans, and Yarmouth-Dennis. In Concord, New Hampshire, Red Eastman Field is the site of the Sunset League, also known as the "oldest after supper amateur baseball league in the United States." It was organized in 1909. Today the Sunset League consists of five teams, four from Concord and one from Manchester. Players are at least seventeen years old, teams are locally sponsored, and a sixteen-game schedule is played.

The Red Sox Nation

Founded in 1901 as one of the original teams of the American League, the Boston Red Sox are as much a part of the geography of New England as the autumn foliage and the coastline beaches. The Red Sox Nation, to give the fan base its proper designation, includes most of New England. These fans have "lived and

The 1946 Boston Red Sox, American League pennant winners. Courtesy Boston Red Sox.

died and avidly supported their teams through trauma, tragedy, pathos, festering boils, and swarms of locust," to quote Derek Catsam.[7] No matter what kind of season they have, fans hold their loyalty and affection during numerous heartbreaking pennant races and postseason series, especially against the archrival New York Yankees.

Fenway Park

The Red Sox originally played at the Huntington Avenue Grounds, a wooden ballpark that opened in 1901, when the team came into existence as the Boston Americans. The team was renamed the Red Sox in 1908. The Red Sox moved to Fenway Park on April 20, 1912, in Boston's Kenmore Square, next to Boston University. This park was extensively renovated in 1934 when the wooden left-field wall was replaced with the present "Green Monster," which is thirty-seven feet high. Distances from home plate are 315 feet down the left-field line, 420 feet to center, and 302 feet to right field. Seating capacity is approximately 33,583. In 1999, the Red Sox proposed building a new Fenway Park with the same basic layout but about 10,000 additional seats. Under this plan, portions of the present field would be preserved as a museum and the team would spend about $65 million for

"The Curse of the Bambino" and "Game Six" Lore

Until their 2004 victory over the St. Louis Cardinals, the Red Sox had not won a World Series since 1918, and many fans pointed to the mythical "Curse of the Bambino" as the reason. All-time great Babe Ruth (also known as "the Bambino," 1895–1948) was a star of the 1918 team. But in 1920, Red Sox owner Harry Frazee sold Ruth to the New York Yankees so that he could fund a Broadway musical entitled *No, No, Nanette.* Since then, the Red Sox have suffered many pennant-race losses to the Yankees, who have won twenty-six world championships since 1923.

The phrase "Game Six" also has endured as a memorable one in the bittersweet lore of the Red Sox. In the sixth game of the 1975 World Series, Boston catcher Carlton Fisk hit a famous, game-winning home run over Fenway Park's "Green Monster." (Fisk's home run is alluded to in a scene in the film *Good Will Hunting*, which is set in Boston.) Boston lost the series to the Cincinnati Reds in seven games, however.

In Game Six of the 1986 World Series, the Red Sox were one strike away from winning their first modern-day championship, but the New York Mets staged a historic comeback and won both Game Six and Game Seven to take the series.

Ted Williams

Red Sox left fielder Ted Williams (1918–2002), considered by many to be the best hitter of all time, won six American League batting titles despite missing five seasons to serve as a pilot in World War II and Korea. Williams signed with the Red Sox in 1939. In his rookie year, "the Splendid Splinter," as he was quickly nicknamed, hit .327 with 31 home runs and led the American League in runs batted in with 145. His subsequent career was one of the best in major league baseball. In 1942, Williams won the Triple Crown with a .356 average, 36 home runs, and 137 runs batted in. When he returned after World War II, he hit .342 and won the league's Most Valuable Player award in 1946; the next year, he won his second Triple Crown, batting .343 with 32 home runs and 142 runs batted in and collected his fourth batting title. Williams' last season with the Red Sox was in 1960, when he batted 0.318 and hit a dramatic home run in his final at-bat. Boston's third harbor tunnel, which opened in 1995, was named the Ted Williams Tunnel to honor the Red Sox Hall of Famer. It connects South Boston to East Boston and Logan Airport.[8]

land and $350 million on design and construction, while the city and the commonwealth (the state) would be expected to pay about $50 million on infrastructure improvements and $80 million on two parking garages. No public money has been allocated to this plan, however. Fenway Park continues to be a cherished part of the Red Sox lore.

Basketball

On December 21, 1891, James Naismith (1861–1939), a physical-education instructor at the Young Men's Christian Association Training School in Springfield, Massachusetts, introduced the game of basketball to his students to replace gymnastics and calisthenics routinely practiced during the winter months. Basketball is the only popular American game that does not have English origins. After studying the attributes of lacrosse, football, rugby, and soccer, Naismith created a game in which players would bounce and pass a soccer ball to one another and score points by tossing the ball into a suspended goal. The fundamental concept came to Naismith, a native Canadian, from watching rugby players spend the winter months throwing rugby balls into boxes. Instead of boxes, Naismith used bottomless peach baskets hung at opposite ends of the railing surrounding the YMCA gymnasium, ten feet above the floor. Some students wanted to call the game "Naismith Ball," but the inventor refused, so they started calling it "basket ball."

Boston Celtics

The Boston Celtics—one of two National Basketball Association (NBA) teams who have played in the same city under the same name throughout their history—are "the Franchise," Celtics Green is "the Color," and the winking leprechaun that serves as the team's logo symbolizes five decades of NBA tradition. The club was founded in 1946 as a charter member of the Basketball Association of America, which evolved into the NBA. Boston flies more title banners from the rafters of its home arena than any other franchise. Although the Celtics have known some tough years, no other professional sports team has ever dominated a league the way Boston did from 1957 to 1969, when the club won eleven NBA Championships. For those thirteen years, the team was "the Dynasty."

The Celtics came into being on June 6, 1946, when eleven men, all of whom owned either professional hockey teams, large arenas in major cities, or both, met to discuss the formation of a new professional basketball league. They christened the new league the Basketball Association of America (BAA) and modeled its season, which featured a sixty-game schedule and a series of playoffs, after the National Hockey League's. The game itself was based on college basketball, but with the contests lengthened to forty-eight minutes rather than the forty minutes played in college. A driving force behind the BAA was Celtics owner Walter Brown, who ran the Boston Garden and was part of the NHL's Boston Bruins organization. Brown hired John "Honey" Russell as his first coach, and the Celtics' maiden home game was played on November 5, 1946.

Since then, the NBA has seen the Celtics take home the league championship banner sixteen times, including a run from 1959 to 1966 in which the Celtics won the championship every year. Coach Red Auerbach, a fixture with the organization, turned the team into a dynasty under the strength of players such as Bill Russell, Bob Cousy, Tommy Heinsohn, and John Havlicek. In the late 1970s Auerbach again assembled a Celtic dynasty around a new collection of basketball legends including Larry Bird, Robert Parrish, and Kevin McHale. Twenty-nine members of the Boston Celtics organization had been elected to the Naismith Memorial Basketball Hall of Fame as of 2004.

Boston Celtics center Bill Russell. Courtesy Library of Congress.

The UConn Lady Huskies

The University of Connecticut women's basketball team has developed a strong following while emerging as an NCAA dynasty. Under coach Geno Auriemma, the Lady Huskies have won five national championships since 1995, including an undefeated season in 2001–2002. UConn has a proud legacy of players such as Rebecca Lobo, Sue Bird, Jennifer Rizzotti, and Diana Taurasi.

Football

Football was introduced to the nation in 1862 when it was first played by students on the Boston Common, but the game received a big boost when it was played on the college level, especially in what is considered the oldest college football rivalry, Harvard v. Yale, which began in 1873. In 1883, Yale University won the first national college football championship with Yale's record at eight wins, no losses, and no ties. From 1908 to 1916, Harvard University, coached by Percy Haughton, dominated the Ivy League, posting a record of seventy-one wins, seven losses, and five ties. At the professional level, the Hartford Blues played in the National Football League, but only for one season, in 1926. The Providence Steamroller lasted longer; they were in the National Football League from 1925 through 1931 and won the 1928 NFL championship.

Yale and Harvard first played each other on November 13, 1875, and remain rivals to this day. This picture was taken c. 1905. Courtesy Library of Congress.

New England Patriots

The region's only modern-day NFL team, the New England Patriots, began play as the Boston Patriots in the fledgling American Football League in 1960. In 1970, after a decade of playing at different sites including Boston University Field, Harvard Stadium, Fenway Park, and Boston College Alumni Stadium, the Patriots selected Foxboro as the team's new home, and the team changed its name to the New England Patriots in 1971. During the 1976 season, the Patriots earned a wild-card playoff berth but lost to the eventual Super Bowl Champion Oakland Raiders. In 1985, the Patriots gained a wild-card berth in the playoffs and went on to win their first American Football Conference Championship and a trip to Super Bowl XX. The team returned to the Super Bowl after the 1996 season. While the Patriots lost in their first two trips to the Super Bowl, they finally won the NFL title in Super Bowl XXV in 2002 behind MVP quarterback Tom Brady. Brady again won MVP honors in Super Bowl XXXVIII, which the Patriots also won.

WINTER SPORTS

Figure Skating

Figure skating is one of the most popular winter sports, natural to New

Walter Camp

The "Father of American Football," Walter Camp (1859–1925), was associated with football at Yale University from 1876 to 1910. From 1877 to 1880, Camp developed rule changes that cast the foundation of modern American football. Among Camp's innovations were the scrimmage and the downs system. Camp also served as secretary of the Intercollegiate Football Rules Committee from 1877 to 1906. Camp vigorously promoted the commercialization of college football through the application of marketing techniques to boost spectator interest and promote the game to the public. His most successful device in generating broad spectator appeal was the selection of the All-American Team, which he first instituted in 1889. In the 1890s, Camp led a crusade to reform the brutal, and even deadly, game of college football and spearheaded an investigation of its brutality.

England because of its cold weather, abundant lakes and rivers, and hundreds of indoor community skating rinks. On March 21, 1914, in the first U.S. Figure Skating Championship, Norman N. Scott of Montreal, Canada, won the men's division and Theresa Weld Blanchard (1893–1978), from Brookline, Massachusetts, won the women's division. Four years later, in the same competition, Nathaniel W. Niles (1887–1932) of Boston won the men's singles division and the pairs division with Weld Blanchard, his longtime skating partner. As the first woman competitor for the United States in the Olympics, Weld Blanchard won the bronze medal at the 1920 Games. Another important figure skater was Maribel Y. Vinson Owen (1911–1961) from Winchester, Massachusetts, who won the North American championship in 1937 but placed fourth in the 1928 Olympics, won the bronze at the 1932 Games, and placed fifth in 1936. Owen and her two daughters, also skaters, were killed in a plane crash, along with fifteen other members of the U.S. figure skating team, while en route to the world championships in Prague. The first great homegrown skater (1935, Newton, Massachusetts) was Tenley Albright, who won the women's world figure skating championship in 1953 and an Olympic gold medal in 1956. In 1976, Dorothy Hamill (b. 1956) of Riverside, Connecticut, won gold medals at the Winter Olympics and world championships. Nancy Kerrigan, born in Woburn, Massachusetts, won a silver medal at the 1996 Winter Olympics.

Hockey

Amateur-level hockey is a perfect sport for the cold New England winters. Its young players get their start on ice rinks, frozen roads, and playgrounds, natural arenas for children in a region with very cold weather from October to March. Whether on a frozen lake or pond or one of the many Massachusetts Transportation Authority skating rinks in the greater Boston area, hockey draws both male and female skaters. A common picture is watching small children, two and three years old, held up by parents or other relatives as they wobble on their first hockey skates. Amateur teams are organized from Pee Wee leagues to the college level. Many of these teams have been the training ground for talented players who have won college scholarships and even gone to the pros. The most famous example is probably Bobby Orr, who was spotted by the Boston Bruins scouts playing midget hockey in Ontario, Canada, and placed on their protected list, the only steps that were necessary at that time to obtain the rights to an amateur player.

When the Boston Arena, later renamed Matthews Arena and home to the Northeastern Huskies, first opened in 1910, it was home to all hockey at the amateur level in the Greater Boston area and to all four of the major college hockey teams: Boston College, Boston University, Harvard University, and Northeastern University. Since these four teams competed with each other, an idea developed for doubleheader tournaments in which each college had the chance to play each of the other three in successive years, and to allow other New England hockey powers, such as Dartmouth, to compete as well. This tournament became the Beanpot, officially the New England Invitational Tournament. The first games began on December 26 and 27, 1952; Boston University defeated Northeastern 4–1 and Harvard beat Boston College 3–2.[9]

Bobby Orr

Robert G. "Bobby" Orr (1948–) in his prime was considered the greatest hockey player ever. The Bruins first spotted Orr when he was only twelve and playing midget hockey; he was put on their protected list and he joined the team in 1966. Beginning in his first season, Orr picked up awards for his brilliant on-ice maneuvers, sometimes winning several in one season. In the 1969–1970 season, for example, Orr collected the Conn Smythe Trophy as playoff MVP, as well as the Hart, the Ross (a first for a defenseman), and the Norris Trophy, which he won consecutively from 1968 through 1975. In 1970, Orr became the only defenseman ever to lead the NHL in scoring and the second player to score more than one hundred points in a season, a feat he repeated in 1975. On January 9, 1979, Orr's Number 4 jersey was retired before a January 9 exhibition game against the Soviet Wings. During his career, Orr totaled 270 goals and 645 assists for 915 points while his average of 1.393 points per game was the fifth best ever and by far the highest for any defenseman.[10]

Boston Bruins

The Boston Bruins of the National Hockey League have won the coveted Stanley Cup five times, most recently in 1972. When the team was founded in 1924, it became the first U.S. professional team in the National Hockey League. The Bruins have had a number of players who attained a significant following in Boston and throughout New England, including Cam Neely, Ray Bourque, and Bobby Orr.

The Providence Bruins is a farm team for the Boston Bruins that plays a regular schedule of games at the Civic Center in Rhode Island's capital city in the fall and winter. The New England Whalers of the World Hockey Association (WHA), originally based in Boston, moved to Springfield, Massachusetts, in 1974 and then to Hartford, Connecticut, in 1975. The Whalers joined the National Hockey League in 1979 when the WHA and NHL merged but dropped "New England" from their name because the Boston Bruins objected to it. The franchise moved to Greensboro, North Carolina, in 1997 and became the Carolina Hurricanes.

Massport Jets Girls' Ice Hockey Team

The Massport Jets was a ground-breaking girls' ice hockey team, founded in 1970 by Anthony Marmo, who was well known in East Boston, Massachusetts, for his advocacy of youth ice hockey programs. The Massport Jets were partially supported by the Massachusetts Transportation Authority, which is where the team derived its name. As word of girls' ice hockey spread, over a dozen new teams formed in Massachusetts, and Marmo founded the American Girls Hockey Association (AGHA). The teams were coached first by Marmo and then by Robert E. Travaglini, who became majority whip of the Massachusetts Senate. The Massport Jets were champions of the first Girls' Invitational Hockey Tournament in 1975. Two years later, they were enshrined in the International Hockey Hall of Fame in Kingston, Ontario. In 1988, Marmo was inducted into the New England Sports Museum as founder of the AGHA.[11]

The Fleet Center

Both the Bruins and the Celtics now play their home games at the Fleet Center, New England's premier sports and entertainment facility. Although it is best recognized as home to two of the most storied franchises in all of sports (the NHL's Boston Bruins and NBA's Boston Celtics), the Fleet Center prides itself on its wide variety of events. The Fleet Center hosts ice shows, the circus, gymnastics, concerts, Disney shows, professional wrestling, the Beanpot, and many more events. The arena opened on September 30, 1995, and it features numerous modern amenities. New England sports and entertainment fans can enjoy the luxuries of a year-round, 19,500-seat facility, fully equipped with two restaurants, a private club, air conditioning, 104 executive suites, 4 promenade suites, more than 2,500 club seats and a multimillion-dollar video scoreboard. The arena's impressive facilities and Boston's appeal have helped the Fleet Center attract several national profile events, including the first and second rounds of the 1999 NCAA Men's Basketball Tournament, the 1999 NHL Draft, the 2000 U.S. Olympic Gymnastics Trials, and the 2001 U.S. Figure Skating Championships.

Skiing

With its mountains and snow, New England is a skier's paradise, a region that can hold its own with the Pacific Northwest. All levels of slopes await the skier, whether beginner or champion. Skiing vacations are popular tourist attractions especially in Maine, New Hampshire, and Vermont, and ski lodges and inns that cater to the skiing enthusiast offer many types of package deals.

Scandinavian immigrants introduced skiing in New Hampshire's logging camps in the 1870s. The Norwegian-speaking Nansen Ski Club was founded in Norway Village near Berlin, New Hampshire, about 1872; with six other clubs it founded the U.S. Eastern Amateur Ski Association in 1922 and survives to this day. Ski fever spread to the college circuit after Dartmouth's Outing Club was founded in 1909. Just five years later, Dartmouth College librarian Nathaniel Goodrich was the first to descend Vermont's highest peak, Mount Mansfield in Stowe. This was all without trails, of course, much less the "up-ski" devices—rope tows, J-bars, and ultimately aerial trams, gondolas, and high-speed quads—that came decades later. The sport was essentially confined to "touring" (comparable to today's cross-country), jumping off wooden chutes, and the odd foray into the woods. In 1926, Appalachian Mountain Club hutmaster Joe Dodge was the first to hurtle down Mount Washington's Tuckerman Ravine. By then, skiing was well on its way to popularity. In 1929, fresh from a Switzerland ski trip, Katharine Peckett opened the country's first organized ski school at her family's resort in Sugar Hill, New Hampshire. Soon, the Boston and Maine Railroad began running ski trains to New Hampshire. Then, in 1934, New England's first rope tow was constructed at Gilbert's Hill in Woodstock, Vermont.

Skiing was dormant during the gas-rationing of the early 1940s, but numerous ski areas sprouted up in the late 1940s and 1950s, among them Vermont's Mount Snow, Smugglers Notch,

Downhill skiing remains a popular winter pastime in New England.

Stratton, Sugarbush, and Killington. At Killington, in the mid-1960s, the Graduated Length Method was introduced, easing the way for the general public to approach this often intimidating sport: tyros would start on short skis, gradually increasing the length as their prowess improved.

A notable Olympic ski champion is Barbara Cochran (b. 1951) of New Hampshire and later Vermont, who won the gold medal (Alpine skiing-women's slalom) at the Winter Olympic Games in 1972. Cochran was the only medalist from her family (brother Bobby, two sisters Marilyn and Lindy) who competed at those games, but in the media buildup, the family was highly promoted. Their father, Mickey Cochran, was a U.S. coach, and his grandchildren include Jim Cochran and Jessica Kelley, current members of the U.S. ski team. Another international champion, who competed but never won an Olympic medal, was Andrea Mead (1932–) from Rutland, Vermont.

Snowboarding

Just to keep the challenge on the slopes fresh, Jake Burton Carpenter, a bartender in Stratton, Vermont, had come up with an innovation in the mid-1960s that changed the landscape of skiing. Carpenter had started experimenting with "snurfing" (as the underground sport of snowboarding was then called) at night. It would take years, but his Burton Snowboards company in Londonderry, founded in 1977, would become a leader in the field and, in the process, create a "rad" new skiing subculture.

When no major ski resort would allow snowboards, Carpenter approached Stratton Mountain manager Paul Johnston, who allowed the snowboarders to take a few runs with the ski patrol to show they knew what they were doing. In return, Carpenter and his Burton Snowboards staff had to give lessons and certify all snowboarders. The U.S. Open Snowboarding Championships started in 1982 on a hill called Suicide Six, outside Woodstock, Vermont, but moved to Stratton Mountain in 1985.[12]

Every March, at about the time the smoke starts to billow from the sugarhouses, the U.S. Open Snowboarding Championships return to southern Vermont, the state that launched the sport into the mainstream. This event draws the world's best riders as participants in one of three formats (rail jam, half-pipe and slopestyle); they compete before some thirty-five thousand spectators.

SUMMER SPORTS

Golf

In 1888, the St. Andrews Club, a prestigious golf club, was established in Yonkers, New York. Other clubs soon opened in the Boston area (Brookline Country Club) and in Philadelphia. The Brookline Country Club was one of the five charter members of the U.S. Golf Association (USGA), a successor to the Amateur Golf Association, which was formed in 1894 to administer and to standardize the game. On October 4, 1895, USGA held the first U.S. Open golf tournament in Newport, Rhode Island. It was won by Horace Rawlins, an English immigrant working at the Newport Golf Club. At the college level, Yale defeated Columbia by a margin of thirty-five strokes in the first intercollegiate golf tournament on November 7, 1896.

Rowing, Sailing, and Fishing

On July 2, 1914, eight men from Harvard won the Grand Challenge Cup at the Henley Royal Regatta in England, marking the first victory of an American crew in the event. The Union Boat Club of Boston took second place. This was the beginning of the local and college rivalries that have become annual events, most notably, the annual Harvard-Yale Regatta held every June in New London, Connecticut. In late June, Windjammer Days are held in Boothbay Harbor, Maine; shoreside events there complement a parade of graceful sailboats. At the same time, on Block Island, Rhode Island, the Storm Trysail Club Block Island Race Week, a week-long event, the largest sailing event on the coast, is held. Another annual event, Schooner Days, is a maritime festival in mid-July that includes boat races and a parade of classic windjammers; it is held in Rockland, Maine. The Newport Regatta, a classic event and one of the highlights of the Newport, Rhode Island, summer season, attracts over 300 boats annually. In early September, Camden, Maine, hosts Windjammer Weekend, a celebration of the state's fleet of classic sailing ships. The prestigious Head of the Charles Regatta meets in Cambridge, Massachusetts, each October.

Fishing was at first a means of survival for the Native Americans and the Puritans. With its thousands of natural lakes as well as the Atlantic Ocean (which touches all its states except Vermont), New England is considered a fisherman's paradise. Fishing was one of the first Native American activities that the Pilgrims witnessed, as the Native Americans fished for their livelihood. It was fishing that allowed the Puritans to survive their very difficult first year in Massachusetts Bay Colony, but it was a livelihood for the Native Americans well before the Pilgrims arrived in 1620.

Francis Ouimet

Francis D. Ouimet (1893–1967) was a caddy at the Brookline Country Club who practiced at the public course at Franklin Park in Boston. While a student at Brookline High School, he won the Boston Interscholastic Championship (1909) but failed to qualify for the U.S. Amateur Championship three times (1910–1912). At the state level, Ouimet made the final round of the Massachusetts State Amateur Championship (1912) and won the state amateur title the next year. That same year, Ouimet qualified and then won the U.S. Open in an eighteen-hole play-off round with British champions Ted Ray and Harry Vardon. In the play-off round, Ouimet shot a one-over-par 72 to win the title, the first amateur to capture the tournament, in an upset victory that remains one of the most significant in the development of golf in the United States. Ouimet never won the U.S. Open again. In 1914, he finally won the U.S. Amateur Championship; he won his second one in 1931. Ouimet retired from golf in 1949 and established the Francis Ouimet Caddy Scholarship Fund, which provided caddies with the funds to seek a college education. In 1955, Ouimet was awarded the Bob Jones Trophy for distinguished sportsmanship by the U.S. Golf Association. He authored three books: *Golf Facts for Young People* (1921), *A Game of Golf* (1932), and *The Rules of Golf* (1948).

Yale varsity crew members practice for a race with Harvard, c. 1915. Courtesy Library of Congress.

Running and the Boston Marathon

The Boston Marathon, one of the oldest footraces in North America, was inspired by the 1896 Olympic marathon, conceived by Michel Breal, a French classicist and historian, who insisted that the athletic program of the first modern Olympic Games must include an endurance foot race. Breal suggested a 40-km race to celebrate the feat of Pheidippides, a Greek soldier who ran that distance from Marathon to Athens to announce the Greek triumph over Persia in 490 B.C.E. Spiridon Louis, a Greek shepherd, won the 1896 Olympic marathon in less than three hours. After the Olympic Games, the Boston Athletic Association decided to hold a similar race to commemorate Paul Revere's famous ride on the eve of the American Revolution. At the first race, April 19, 1897, John J. McDermott, a Canadian, won with a time of 2:55:10, against fourteen other runners. The race followed a 24.7-mile course from Ashland to Boston. Since then, the race has become an annual Patriot's Day sporting event. John C. Lorden, of Cambridge, Massachusetts, became the first local runner to win the Boston Marathon in 1903, but a more consistent winner was Clarence Demar (1888–1958), born in Reading, Massachusetts, who won the race in 1911, 1922, 1923, 1924, 1927, 1928, and 1930. The Boston Marathon is held the third Monday in April.[13]

Boxing and Other Sports Activities

Along with major team sports, New England has offered other leisure activities that suit the New England character and climate. Boxing in New England is better known for its giants in the sport than for any regional significance. John L. Sullivan (1858–1918), the last bare-knuckle prizefighting champion, was one of the first American sports heroes and contributed to the development of boxing, transforming it from an illicit and reprobate activity to a publicly accepted professional sport. In his first recorded fight, Sullivan defeated John "Cockey" Woods in five rounds in Boston (1879). By 1881, Sullivan was known in prizefighting circles as the "strong boy of Boston" because of his many victories in knockouts. He captured the bare-knuckle heavyweight championship in 1882. Over the next five years, he finished thirty-two matches, winning each time, and he participated in exhibitions. Many exhibitions had to be cancelled because Sullivan was too drunk to perform, but he remained a big hero in Boston. He continued his championship win in 1888 against British champion Charlie Mitchell in Chantilly, France, and won his last bare-knuckle contest in 1889 in Richburg, Mississippi, but lack of training and a change in fighting rules cost Sullivan his title on September 7, 1892, when James J. Corbett knocked Sullivan out in the twenty-first round. After this, Sullivan fought one more time, then officially retired. He continued in stage exhibitions, wrote his autobiography (*Life and Remembrances of a 19th Century Gladiator*) and toured the United States giving speeches on the evils of liquor.

The second great boxer from New England was probably Rocky Marciano (born Rocco F. Marchegiano, 1923–1969) from working-class Brockton, Massachusetts, the heavyweight boxer who, when he retired in 1956 was the only world champion to have won every fight (490) of his professional career. Paul Newman portrayed the boxer in a Hollywood film of Marciano's life, *Somebody Up There Likes Me* (MGM, 1956; directed by Robert Wise). Another boxer out of Brockton was

Marvin Hagler. Other great New England boxers are Paul Pender and Johnny Ruiz, from Chelsea, one of the first Hispanic boxers in the pro ranks.

SCHOOL COMPETITIONS

New England college teams have developed a rich history of rivalry. The oldest colleges, Harvard and Yale, have developed the longest, most intense rivalry with their annual football game. Some colleges like the University of Massachusetts, Amherst, and the University of New Hampshire, have become state school rivals. Boston College (football and basketball) used to be the traditional rival of Holy Cross. The Amherst versus Williams rivalry (mostly football), grew out of the fact that Williams was once part of Amherst. The University of Connecticut's men's and women's basketball teams have become nationally competitive, overshadowing regional rivalries. The University of Vermont's most heated rivalries are with the universities of Maine and of New Hampshire. Needham-Wellesley is one of the oldest high school rivalries in the country, and the Medford-Malden rivalry was started by soldiers in World War II. Another is Boston English v. Boston Latin, the oldest public school in the country, but public school football rivalries are a tradition throughout the region. Every Thanksgiving, local newspapers devote coverage to the athletes and the schools, and promote the rivalries.

AMUSEMENT PARKS AND RECREATIONAL FACILITIES

Amusement parks were man-made environments that duplicated and very often distorted the urban experience. The earliest ones, in the late nineteenth century, began as wooded parks at the end of trolley lines and noisy avenues on the outskirts of cities, the direct result of the development of streetcar and railway lines and, later, subway systems. Since electric power companies charged transit firms a flat monthly rate regardless of the amount of electricity used, city railway owners needed to increase the number of riders during slow weekends and evenings. Their solution was pleasure parks located at the end of the line, often picnic groves near bodies of water. Soon, the owner started regular entertainments, mechanical amusements, dance halls, sports fields, boat rides, and restaurants. By 1929, there were approximately 1,500 to 2,000 amusement parks in the United States that provided these entertainments. The first one in New England was at Revere Beach, outside Boston.

The New England states have a variety of amusement parks and outdoor rinks that are available for recreation, but a select group have been designated by the National Park Service as historic landmarks. Along with Fenway Park, New England boasts the Yale Bowl in New Haven, Connecticut, built in 1914 to accommodate sixty-one thousand spectators and now the second oldest active college stadium in the United States. Harvard Stadium in Boston was erected in 1903 and is highly significant in the history of stadium design for the technology used in its construction and for its associations with Harvard football coaches and teams, who played a major role in the early development of intercollegiate football in the United States. Newport Casino in Newport, Rhode Island, with its expanses of grass tennis courts, some of the only grass courts in the United States now available for public use, was started in 1880–1881 as America's answer to Wimbledon. Boston Common, which comprises fifty acres of open space in the heart of Boston right below the State House with its notable golden Bulfinch Dome, actually began in 1634 in what were tidal marshlands. Boston Public Garden occupies land that was dedicated to that purpose in 1859. Flying Horses Carousel at Oak Bluffs on Martha's Vineyard, which measures thirty-six feet in diameter, was constructed between 1876 and 1878 and has been operated by electricity since 1900. Crescent Park Looff Carousel and Shelter Building in East Providence, Rhode Island, was almost certainly designed and built shortly after its manufacturer Charles Looff signed a lease with the park's owner in April 1895. Flying Horse Carousel, also called the Watch Hill Carousel, Westerly, Rhode Island, for its location in the summer resort town, was almost certainly built in 1876, although there is evidence it was built a few years earlier. The Flying Horse Carousel in Oak Bluffs and the Watch Hill Carousel represent the two oldest extant carousels in the United States.

The Circus

The circus was not strictly an American, let alone a New England, invention, but it owes its popularity to Phineas Taylor Barnum (1810–1891), a Bethel, Connecticut, native, a circus promoter who considered himself "the great American showman" with an uncanny knack for knowing what the public wanted and how to promote it. In 1881, Barnum staged the first three-ring circus that he transported by railroad. Combining Barnum's resources with those of his keenest rival, James Anthony Bailey (now the Ringling Bros. and Barnum and Bailey Circus), Barnum's circus featured exotic animals, including "the only mastodon on earth," Jumbo the elephant, the pride of the Royal Zoological Society in London. The British press protested this "American vandalism," but Barnum encouraged it for its publicity value and avoided customs duties on Jumbo by importing him "for breeding purposes." The animal earned its keep; it could feed from third-story windows as it walked the circus parade. Barnum later served in the Connecticut legislature and was mayor of Bridgeport, Connecticut, but he is best remembered as a circus promoter who knew the value of advertising and the effect it had on American marketing. Every year, there is a Barnum Circus Festival in Bridgeport that honors one of the state's most famous citizens. There is also a Circus Smirkus, an international youth circus, that stages shows around New England between early June and the middle of August. The major circus troupe, Ringling Bros. Barnum and Bailey Circus, tours the country, with stops in New England at arenas in Boston, Hartford, Connecticut, and Providence, Rhode Island.

RECREATION AND TOURISM

During the last half of the twentieth century, tourism reversed the decline of New England and changed its relationship with the rest of the country. Tourism benefited from the discovery that a beautiful and intrinsically varied region, steeped in rich human history, was attractive to a wide variety of visitors. In the nineteenth century, palatial hotels along the seashore (e.g., Newport, Rhode Island) and at various points in the New Hampshire mountains catered to a wealthy clientele, but after World War II, tourism in New England included the growing middle class, and ski resorts appeared in the mountainous regions of Vermont and New Hampshire.

Sports and recreation activities in New England depend heavily upon the travel and tourism industry to strengthen their local economy, especially when the Red Sox, Celtics, or Bruins or the college teams manage to make it to the championship playoffs. Location has a lot to do with this state of mind. New England is geographically located on the Atlantic Ocean; all of New England's states except Vermont have a border on the ocean—but the Green Mountain State compen-

Kayakers. Courtesy Maine Office of Tourism.

sates with thousands of lakes. Like most of the major cities and resorts in the United States that depend on tourism and travel as a major part of the region's economy, however, New England has suffered from the effects of the post-9/11 downbeat as more Americans choose to stay closer to home rather than risk longer trips by plane and train.

What attracts tourists to New England? There is a persistent localism, owing to the region's topography and temperament.[14] There are four seasons but no single rhythm or pattern to the weather. Snow in April and hot weather in November are not unheard of. New England does have a climate suitable for many outdoor activities that visitors can engage in throughout much of the year includ-

Acadia National Park, Maine. Courtesy Maine Office of Tourism.

Cape Cod National Seashore Courtesy National Park Service.

ing bicycling, hiking, camping, mountain climbing, and beach recreations. New England offers bike and walking trails, mountain ranges, fresh and salt water lakes, state parks, national forests, wilderness areas, and hundreds of campgrounds. Acadia National Park, on Mount Desert Island, Maine, is an area of great natural beauty and the only national park in New England. Cape Cod Rail Trail, on the Cape's north coast, is a totally flat but popular bike path on the site of the former Old Colony Railroad, and Cape Cod National Seashore, which President Kennedy saved from development because of his fondness for it, extends along much of the Cape's Atlantic side, stretching forty miles from Chatham to Provincetown. The rugged White Mountains of New Hampshire, a year-round destination popular with winter skiers and summer hikers, attract some 6 million annual visitors. Less harsh are the Green Mountains, which form the backbone of Vermont; these are most accessible in the summer when they offer perfect opportunities for hiking, camping, fishing, canoeing, and swimming.

CONCLUSION

New England sports and recreation have a long and diverse history. From informal activities involving Native Americans and colonials to the professionalization of sports and recreation in the late nineteenth and twentieth centuries, there has been an evolution of sports and recreation in New England that has spread throughout America. From lacrosse to ice hockey and from earlier European sports to the rise of baseball, football, and basketball in the nineteenth century, New England has played a pivotal role in the development of professional American sports and recreations.

RESOURCE GUIDE

Printed Sources

Abbott, John, ed. *Oxford Companion to Sports and Games*. London: Oxford University, 1975.

Carruth, Gorton, and Eugene Ehrlich. *Facts and Dates of American Sports*. New York: Harper and Row, 1988.

Charleton, James H. *Recreation in the United States: National Historic Landmark Theme Study*. Washington, DC: National Park Service, U.S. Dept. of the Interior, 1986.

Glenroy, John H. *Ins and Outs of Circus Life*. Boston: M.M. Wing, 1885.

Hickok, Ralph. *Encyclopedia of North American Sports History*. 2nd ed. New York: Facts on File, 2002.

Johnson, Richard A. *A Century of Boston Sports*. Boston: Northeastern University Press, 2000.

McFarlane, Brian. *The Bruins: Brian McFarlane's Original Six*. Toronto: Stoddart Publishing, 1999.

Rielly, Edward J., ed. *Baseball and American Culture: Across the Diamond*. New York: Haworth, 2003.

Rousmaniere, John. *America's Cup Book, 1851–1983*. New York: Norton, 1983.

Ryan, Bob, and Dick Raphael. *The Boston Celtics: The History, Legends, and Images of America's Most Celebrated Team*. Reading, MA: Addison-Wesley, 1989.

Shaughnessy, Dan. *The Curse of the Bambino*. New York: Penguin Books, 1991.

Smith, Curt. *Our House: A Tribute to Fenway Park*. Lincolnwood, IL: Masters Press, 1999.

Web Sites

Boston.com Sports. 2004.
The New York Times Company. February 2, 2004.
http://media3.travelzoo.com/banner/

Boston Globe and New England Sports Network (NESN) sports pages.

New England Ballparks. 2003.
Paul Healey, Project Ballpark. January 16, 2004.
http://projectballpark.org/ne/

Ballparks in New England.

New England SportsLine.com. March 30, 2000.
New England SportsLine.com.
January 21, 2004.
http://newenglandsportsline.com

Links to professional, collegiate, and high school sports in New England.

New England Sports Online. February 4, 2004.
Scholastic Tools, Inc. February 15, 2004.
http://www.newenglandsports.com

Information on New England High School Championships.

New England Sports Portal. 2004.
New England Sports Portal.
January 16, 2004.
http://www.riinteractive.net/nesp/

Professional, collegiate, high school, and community sports in New England.

Sports Temples of Boston. 2003.
Boston Public Library. January 4, 2004.
http://www.bpl.org/sportstemples

Images of historic ballparks, arenas, and stadiums in Boston, 1872–1972.

Yankee Magazine. 2004.
Yankee Publishing, Inc. January 4, 2004.
http://www.YankeeMagazine.com

New England leisure and recreation.

Videos/Films

Baseball. Dir. Ken Burns. Public Broadcasting Service (PBS), 1994.
Celtic Pride. Dir. Tom De Cerchio. Perf. Dan Aykroyd, Daniel Stern, Damon Wynans. Hollywood Pictures/Caravan Pictures, 1996.
The Curse of the Bambino. HBO Sports, 2003.
Field of Dreams. Dir. Phil Alden Robinson. Perf. Kevin Costner, James Earl Jones. Universal Pictures, 1989.
Summer Catch. Dir. Michael Tolin. Perf. Freddy Prinze Jr., Jessica Biel. Warner Brothers, 2001.

Events and Festivals

Block Island Race Week
Block Island, RI
http://www.blockislandraceweek.com

Annual sailing regatta on Block Island Sound, Rhode Island.

Fishermen's Festival
Boothbay Harbor, ME
http://www.boothbayharbor.com

Annual fishing festival at Boothbay Harbor, Maine.

International Tennis Hall of Fame Grass Court Championships
Newport, RI
http://www.tennisfame.com

Annual tennis tournament held at Newport, Rhode Island, and the only professional one to be played on grass in the United States.

Jackson Ski Festival
Jackson, NH
http://www.jacksonnh.com

Annual ski festival held in New Hampshire.

New England Regional Sled Dog Championships
Mad River Valley, VT
http://www.madrivervalley.com

Regional sled dog race held in February.

U.S. Open Snowboarding Championships
Stratton Mountain, VT
http://www.usopen-snowboarding.com

Annual snowboarding tournament held at Stratton Mountain, Vermont.

Yale-Harvard Regatta
New London, CT
http://www.yale.edu

Annual rowing tournament and the oldest collegiate competition in the United States.

Museums

American Museum of Fly Fishing
P.O. Box 42
Manchester, VT 05254
http://www.amff.com

The Barnum Museum
820 Main Street
Bridgeport, CT 06604
http://www.barnum-museum.org

Green Mountain Club, Inc.
4711 Waterbury Stowe Road
Waterbury Center, VT 05677
http://greenmountainclub.org

Herreshoff Marine Museum/America's Cup Hall of Fame
One Burnside Street
Bristol, RI 02809
Mailing address:
P.O. Box 450
Bristol, RI 02809-0450
http://www.herreshoff.org

International Tennis Hall of Fame and Museum
194 Bellevue Avenue
Newport, RI 02840
http://www.tennisfame.com

Maine Sports Hall of Fame
University of Maine
5747 Memorial Gymnasium
Orono, ME 04469-5747
http://www.goblackbears.com/hof

Museum of Yachting
Fort Adams State Park
Newport, RI 02840
Mailing address:
P.O. Box 129
Fort Adams State Park
Newport, RI 02840
http://www.moy.org

Naismith Memorial Basketball Hall of Fame
100 W. Columbus Avenue
Springfield, MA 01105-2532
http://www.hoophall.com

New England Ski Museum
Cannon Mountain Tramway

Interstate 93
Parkway Exit 2
P.O. Box 267
Franconia, NH 03580-0267
http://www.skimuseum.org

Sports Museum of New England
One Fleet Center Place
Suite 200
Boston, MA 02114-1303
http://www.sportsmuseum.org

Volleyball Hall of Fame
444 Dwight Street
Holyoke, MA 01040
Mailing address:
P.O. Box 1895
Holyoke, MA 01041
http://www.volleyhall.org

Teams

Boston Bruins
One Fleet Center
Suite 250
Boston, MA 02114
http://www.bostonbruins.com

Boston Celtics
151 Merrimac Street
Boston, MA 02114-4714
http://www.nba.com/celtics

Boston Red Sox
4 Yawkey Way
Boston, MA 02215
http://www.redsox.com

Cape Cod Baseball League
449 Braggs Lane
Barnstable Village, MA 02630
http://www.capecodbaseball.org

New England Patriots
One Patriot Place
Foxborough, MA 02035
http://www.patriots.com

Pawtucket Paw Sox
Ben Mendor Way
Pawtucket, RI 02860
http://www.pawsox.com

Providence Bruins
One Lasalle Square
Providence, RI 02903
http://www.providencebruins.com

TIMELINE

1600	Founding of the East India Company.
1602	Bartholomew Gosnold explores the coast of New England from southern Maine to Buzzards Bay.
1603	James I (James VI of Scotland) becomes king of England, Scotland, and Ireland.
1617–1619	English and Dutch fishermen introduce smallpox epidemic that kills about 90 percent of the Massachusetts Bay's Native American population.
1620	The Pilgrims land at Plymouth Rock and establish Plymouth Colony along the eastern coast of Massachusetts.
1621	William Bradford becomes governor of the Plymouth Colony.
1622	Sir Ferdinando Gorges and Captain John Mason receive royal charter for the province of Maine.
1623	First permanent settlement in New Hampshire.
1625	Charles I becomes king of England, Scotland, and Ireland.
1629	A group of English Puritans form the Cambridge Agreement and receive a charter for the Massachusetts Bay Colony.
1630	John Winthrop and a group of English Puritans sail to New England and establish the Massachusetts Bay Colony.
1633–1635	First settlers arrive in Connecticut.
1634	Dutch transmit smallpox epidemic that kills about 95 percent of the Native American population living along the Connecticut River, prompting further settlement by the English.
1635	Roger Williams is banished from the Massachusetts Bay Colony, and the following year establishes Providence, Rhode Island.

A great hurricane passes between Boston and Plymouth, Massachusetts.

The Boston Latin School, British North America's first public school in America, is founded in Boston.

1636	Harvard College, British North America's first institution of higher learning, is founded in Newetowne (later called Cambridge).
	Thomas Hooker founds a settlement at Hartford, Connecticut.
1636–1637	The Massachusetts Bay Colony and Connecticut Colony defeat the Pequot tribe.
1637	The trial of Anne Hutchinson. She is removed to Aquidneck Island, Rhode Island, and later to Long Island.
1638	Three hurricanes pass through the Boston and Rhode Island area.
	Anne Hutchinson is banished from Massachusetts and moves to Rhode Island.
	Theophilus Eaton and John Davenport establish the New Haven Colony in Connecticut.
1639	The first American printing press is set up in Cambridge, Massachusetts; the first volume published is the *Bay Psalm Book*.
1641	Massachusetts Bay Colony recognizes slavery.
	New Hampshire falls under the jurisdiction of the Massachusetts Bay Colony.
1642	First school act of Massachusetts, requiring parents and masters to teach children to read.
1645	New Englanders sign a peace treaty with the Narragansett Native Americans.
1648	Margaret Jones of Charlestown, Massachusetts, becomes the first New Englander to be executed for witchcraft.
1648–1649	Smallpox and whooping cough spread from Scituate to Cape Cod and north to Boston and Roxbury.
1652	John Hull establishes a mint in Boston, Massachusetts.
1659	Puritans ban Christmas.
1660	Mary Dyer, a Quaker, is hanged on the Boston Common.
1666	First major smallpox epidemic kills about forty of four thousand inhabitants in Boston.
1675–1676	King Philip's War.
1675	A New England hurricane causes extensive damage in Connecticut, Rhode Island, and Massachusetts.
1677–1678	Smallpox breaks out, killing more people than the 1666 epidemic.
1679	New Hampshire becomes a separate royal colony.
1684	The Massachusetts Bay Charter is revoked and Massachusetts becomes a royal colony.

1690	First paper money issued.
1692	The Salem witch trials begin in Massachusetts, resulting in nineteen executions.
1699	The pirate Captain Kidd is captured in Boston and later extradited to England for trial.
1701	Yale University is founded in Connecticut.
1702–1703	Smallpox and scarlet fever break out and 4 percent of the New England's population die.
1704	Massachusetts newspapers begin publishing notices of deaths and marriages.
1705	Copper discovered in Simsbury, Connecticut.
1719	New Englanders plant their first potato at Londonderry Common Field, New Hampshire.
1728	The first American steel mill begins to operate in Simsbury, Connecticut.
1737	Doctor Samuel Higley of Simsbury, Connecticut, begins the first copper coinage in America.
1752	Britain and the British colonies switch from the Julian to the Gregorian calendar.
1756	First publication of the *New Hampshire Gazette*, one of the oldest newspapers of continuous publication in the United States.
1763	The Touro Synagogue, the oldest synagogue in the United States, is built in Rhode Island.
1764	First publication of the *Hartford Courant*, the United States' oldest newspaper still in circulation.
1769	Founding of Dartmouth College in New Hampshire.
1771	Richard Smith of Salisbury, Connecticut, uses community contributions to buy two hundred books from London, launching the Scoville Memorial Library.
1773	Boston Tea Party protesting the British tea tax.
1774	The first circus in the United States is held at Newport, Rhode Island.
1775–1783	American Revolution, beginning with the battles of Lexington and Concord, Massachusetts, in April 1775, and ending with the signing of the Treaty of Paris in September 1783.
1777	Vermont declares independence from England and from the colonial governments of New York and New Hampshire.
1786	Shays' Rebellion in western Massachusetts.
1788	Connecticut is admitted the fifth state of the Union.
	Massachusetts is admitted the sixth state of the Union.
	New Hampshire is admitted the ninth state of the Union.

1790	Rhode Island is admitted the thirteenth state of the Union.
1791	Vermont is admitted the fourteenth state of the Union.
1793	Pottery manufacture begins in Bennington, Vermont.
1794	Repeal of theater prohibition in Massachusetts; theater is founded in Boston.
	Massachusetts Historical Society is the first historical society founded in the United States.
1797	John Adams of Massachusetts becomes second president of the United States.
1799	Charles Bulfinch completes the Massachusetts State House in Boston.
1800	Middlebury College is founded in Vermont.
1802	First canal is built in the United States at Bellows Falls, Vermont.
	Bowdoin College opens in Brunswick, Maine.
1808	Paul Revere opens the first U.S. copper rolling mill in Canton, Massachusetts.
1809	Mary Kies of South Killingly, Connecticut, becomes the first woman to receive a U.S. patent for a method of weaving straw with silk.
1810	The Scoville Memorial Library in Salisbury, Connecticut, receives public support at town meeting.
1812	War of 1812 begins and New Englanders defend Fort Cassin in Vermont against the British.
1813	Colby College is founded in Maine.
1814	First complete mechanized cotton fabric production from raw cotton to cloth begins in Waltham, Massachusetts.
1818	Boston Handel and Haydn Society, founded in 1815, performs first *Messiah* concert.
1820	Maine is admitted the twenty-third state of the Union.
1821	Amherst College is founded in Massachusetts.
1822	African American poet James M. Whitfield is born in Exeter, New Hampshire.
1825	John Quincy Adams of Massachusetts becomes the sixth president of United States.
1826	First rail line in the United States is laid down from Neponset River to the granite quarries in Quincy, Massachusetts.
1827	Massachusetts is the first state to use tax money for public education.
1828	Noah Webster of West Hartford and New Haven, Connecticut, publishes the first American dictionary.
	Four hundred women working at the Dover Cotton factory in New Hampshire walk out, initiating the first women's strike in the United States.

1829	William Apess publishes *A Son of the Forest*, the first autobiography of a Native American to be published in the United States.
1831	Wesleyan College is founded in Middletown, Connecticut.
	William Lloyd Garrison launches *The Liberator*, an abolitionist newspaper, in Boston.
1832	Perkins Institute, the first school for the blind in the United States, opens in south Boston.
	Samuel Francis Smith composes hymn "America" at Andover Seminary in Boston.
1833	A public library is founded in Peterborough, New Hampshire.
1835	First American music school is established in Salem, Connecticut; Oramel Whittlesey establishes Music Vale Seminary.
1836	Ralph Waldo Emerson of Boston helps to launch the movement known as Transcendentalism.
	Ralph Waldo Emerson publishes *Nature*; first meeting of the Transcendentalist Club.
1839	Boston Academy of Music performs the city's first instrumental concerts.
1841	George Ripley establishes Brook Farm, a communal farm, in West Roxbury, Massachusetts.
1844	Amos Bronson Alcott establishes Fruitlands, a communal farm, at Harvard, Massachusetts.
1845	First sewing machine is invented in Boston by Elias Howe.
	Henry David Thoreau moves to Walden Pond, Massachusetts.
1847	First publication of the *New England Historical and Genealogical Register*.
1850	Nathaniel Hawthorne publishes *The Scarlet Letter*.
1851	Herman Melville publishes *Moby Dick*.
1853	Franklin Pierce of New Hampshire becomes the fourteenth president of the United States.
1855	Boston public schools are racially integrated.
1861	Massachusetts Institute of Technology (MIT) is founded in Cambridge, Massachusetts.
1866	The University of New Hampshire is founded in Durham, New Hampshire.
1867	New England Conservatory of Music is founded in Boston.
1868	Louisa May Alcott publishes *Little Women*.
1869	Last whaling voyage from Nantucket.
1870	Founding of the Boston Museum of Fine Art.
1875	First Harvard-Yale football game.
1876	Polo is played for the first time in the United States near Newport, Rhode Island.

	Mark Twain publishes *Tom Sawyer* while living in Hartford.
	Alexander Graham Bell invents the telephone in Boston.
1881	Founding of Boston Symphony Orchestra.
	University of Connecticut is founded in Storrs, Connecticut.
	Chester Arthur of Vermont and later New York becomes the twenty-first president of the United States.
1883	Winslow Homer moves to Prouts Neck, Maine, and begins painting the sea.
1885	The sculptor Augustus Saint-Gaudens moves to Cornish, New Hampshire, where he dies in 1907.
1890	Emily Dickinson's poems published posthumously.
1891	First basketball game played in Springfield, Massachusetts.
1894	Founding of Boston Immigration Restriction League.
1895	W.E.B. DuBois of Great Barrington, Massachusetts, receives Ph.D. from Harvard University.
	The first American hamburger is cooked in New Haven, Connecticut.
	The game volleyball is played for the first time in Holyoke, Massachusetts.
1896	The Boston *Transcript* publishes a genealogical query column (until 1941).
1897	Boston builds the first subway system in the United States.
1899	The first National Lawn Tennis Championship is held at Newport, Rhode Island.
	Biggest banquet in the country's history is held in Boston to celebrate the U.S. Senate's ratification of peace treaty with Spain.
1900	Electric trolleys replace horse-drawn trolleys in Boston.
1901	Boston Red Sox established.
1902	Fannie Farmer opens a cooking school in Boston.
1903	Boston Red Sox win first World Series, defeating Pittsburgh.
1907	William James publishes *Pragmatism*; Henry Adams publishes *The Education of Henry Adams*.
1908	First publication of *Christian Science Monitor* in Boston.
1909	New Hampshire adopts direct primary law.
1910	Hartford *Times* begins a genealogical query column (until 1967).
1912–1918	Boston Red Sox win four World Series, their last victories until 2004.
1914	Yale University builds Yale Bowl, a 64,000-seat stadium, in New Haven, Connecticut.
	Robert Frost's poetry anthology, *North of Boston*, becomes a best seller.
1920	Plymouth Rock is moved back to water's edge from town square.

1922	e. e. cummings publishes *The Enormous Room*.
1923	Calvin Coolidge of Vermont and later Massachusetts becomes thirtieth president of the United States.
1928	Massachusetts votes for Alfred Smith, a Roman Catholic, for president.
1929	Massachusetts establishes its own unemployment program before federal government offers Depression relief.
1932	Bennington College is founded in Vermont.
1933	Woodstock, Vermont, operates the first ski-tow in the United States.
1936	First Berkshire Music Festival at Tanglewood in Lenox, Massachusetts.
1938	First New England hurricane in 100 years.
1939	First helicopter built in Connecticut.
1941	Vermont declares war on Germany before the official declaration of war by the United States.
1942	Fire in Cocoanut Grove, a Boston nightclub, kills 487 people.
1946	John F. Kennedy of Massachusetts is elected to Congress.
	Rhode Island passes law requiring employers to pay women equal wages with men.
1947	Composer Charles Ives, a resident of Connecticut, receives Pulitzer Prize for his Third Symphony.
	Horror writer Stephen King is born in Portland, Maine.
1948	MIT builds first chess computer.
	Brandeis University is founded in Waltham, Massachusetts.
1954	*Nautilus*, first American nuclear submarine, launched in Groton, Connecticut.
	Connecticut elects Abraham Ribicoff, the state's first Jewish governor.
1959	Boston Celtics win the first of eight consecutive championships.
1961	John Fitzgerald Kennedy of Massachusetts becomes thirty-fifth president of the United States.
1962	Massachusetts elects Edward Brooke, the first African American U.S. Senator since Reconstruction.
1969	Race riots in Hartford, Connecticut.
1970	Boston Bruins win Stanley Cup.
	Hampshire College is founded in Massachusetts.
	Cartoonist Garry Trudeau graduates from Yale and launches "Doonesbury."
1972	Massachusetts is only state to vote for McGovern over Nixon in presidential election.
1975	Mob violence in Boston after judicial decision to impose school desegregation busing plan.

1977	Justice Department supports Maine Indians in their lawsuit against the state to recover aboriginal lands.
1979	Massachusetts is the first state to establish a lottery specifically for the arts.
1980	The state of Maine reaches a compromise in the legal battle between Penobscot and Passamaquoddy tribes to recover land in northern Maine.
1982–1983	The federal government recognizes the Pequot tribe and its land claims.
1988	Rhode Island is the only remaining state to celebrate VJ Day, commemorating victory over Japan in World War II.
1989	George H. W. Bush of Massachusetts and later Texas becomes the forty-first president of the United States.
1990	68 percent of Vermont's population is rural, the highest in the United States.
	Uninsured paintings worth $100 million are stolen from the Isabella Stewart Gardner Museum in Boston.
1992	Ethel Hudson, the last surviving member of the New Hampshire Shaker community, dies at the age of ninety-six.
1993	Boston elects Thomas Menino, its first mayor of Italian descent.
1990s	The Big Dig, the largest publicly funded construction project in the United States, begins in Boston.
2000	The film *The Perfect Storm* memorializes the lives of members of the fishing community of Gloucester, Massachusetts.
	State of Vermont approves same-sex unions.
2001	George W. Bush of Connecticut and later Texas becomes the forty-third president of the United States.
2002	New England Patriots win Super Bowl.
2003	Episcopal Church in the United States elects and consecrates first gay bishop: Gene Robinson of New Hampshire.
	Massachusetts Supreme Court rules in favor of gay marriage.
2004	New England Patriots win Super Bowl.
	Boston Red Sox win their first World Series since 1918.

NOTES

Introduction

1. Edward L. Ayers and Peter S. Onuf, eds., *All Over the Map: Rethinking American Regions* (Baltimore: Johns Hopkins University Press, 1996), 4.

2. John Conforti, *Imagining New England: Explorations of Regional Identity from the Pilgrims to the Mid-Twentieth Century* (Chapel Hill: University of North Carolina Press, 2001), 15.

3. William Cronon, *Changes in the Land: Indians, Colonists, and the Ecology of New England* (New York: Hill and Wang, 1983), 36.

4. David Hackett Fischer, *Albion's Seed: Four British Folkways in America* (New York: Oxford University Press, 1989), 122–124.

5. Quoted in Cronon, *Changes*, 122.

6. Constance Rourke, *American Humor* (New York: Harcourt, Brace, 1931), 16–17.

7. Conforti, *Imagining New England*, 167–168.

8. Stephen Nissenbaum, "New England as Region and Nation," in Ayers and Onuf, *All Over the Map*, 40.

9. Andrew Delbanco, ed., *Writing New England: An Anthology from the Puritans to the Present* (Cambridge, MA: Harvard University Press, 2001), x.

Art

1. Laurel Thatcher Ulrich, *The Age of Homespun: Objects and Stories in the Creation of an American Myth* (New York: Alfred A. Knopf, 2001), 42, 47, 72–73.

2. Ralph Waldo Emerson, "Nature," in Alfred R. Ferguson, ed., *The Collected Works of Ralph Waldo Emerson*, vol. 1 (Cambridge, MA: Belknap Press, 1971), 9–10.

3. Impressionism originated and first thrived in France, particularly in and around Paris, in the late 1860s and 1870s. For more on the history of Impressionism, consult John Rewald, *History of Impressionism* (New York: Museum of Modern Art, 1973), for a thorough chronological overview; Phoebe Pool, *Impressionism* (reprint, New York: Thames & Hudson, 1988), for an introduction organized according to individual artists; and Robert Herbert, *Impressionism* (New Haven: Yale University Press, 1991), for social and historical context.

4. Hassam's given first name was Frederick. When he was young he was encouraged to abandon the use of it because his more unusual middle name Childe (pronounced "child") would attract more attention for an aspiring artist. His family is supposed to have come from a long-standing Anglo-Saxon family whose name had originally been "Horsham." It has recently been suggested that Hassam's family history was partly Arab, and that the name "Hassam" may have been derived from something like "Hassan." For more on Hassam's youth and family history, see Ulrich W. Hiesinger, *Childe Hassam: American Impressionist* (New York: Prestel USA, 1999).

5. The best introductory survey of the Bauhaus is Frank Whitford, *Bauhaus* (New York: Thames & Hudson, 1984).

Ecology and Environment

1. Neil Jorgensen, *A Guide to New England's Landscape* (Barre, MA: Barre Publishers, 1971), 26–44, 161; John Kricher, *Eastern Forests: A Field Guide to Birds, Mammals, Trees, Flowers, and More* (Boston: Houghton Mifflin, 1998), 75–77.

2. Jorgensen, *Guide to New England's Landscape*, 62–71.

3. "More Salt, Less Phosphate Found in Three Rivers," *Worcester Telegram*, July 25, 2003; "Woonsocket," at www.woonsocket.org; "Connecticut River," *Encyclopedia Britannica Online*; "Blackstone River and Canal Heritage State Park," at www.state.ma.us.

4. William Cronon, *Changes in the Land: Indians, Colonists, and the Ecology of New England* (New York: Hill and Wang, 1983), 12, 22, 36, 86, 120–126, 150–169; Diana Muir, *Reflections in Bullough's Pond: Economy and Ecosystem in New England* (Hanover, NH: University Press of New England, 2000), 5; and Peter Marchand, *North Woods: An Inside Look at the Nature of Forests in the Northeast* (Boston: Appalachian Mountain Club Books, 1987), 13.

5. Marchand, *North Woods*, 3–8, 12; Jorgensen, *Guide to New England's Landscape*, 98, 140–154; Kricher, *Eastern Forests*, 12–13, 60, 73, 155; Jennifer Lucarelli, "Moose Crash Kills Woman," *Worcester Telegram*, July 25, 2003.

6. Marchand, *North Woods*, 3–15, 23–31; Muir, *Reflections*, 58; John Cumbler, *Reasonable Use: The People, the Environment, and the State, New England, 1790–1930* (New York: Oxford University Press, 2001), 39–40, 125.

7. Kenneth Lockridge, *A New England Town: The First Hundred Years* (New York: W. W. Norton, 1971), x, 8–12, 31, 34, 64–67, 94–102.

8. J. John Palen, *The Urban World* (Boston: McGraw-Hill, 1997), 65–66; Howard P. Chudacoff and Judith E. Smith, *The Evolution of American Urban Society* (Upper Saddle River, NJ: Prentice Hall, 2000), 5–7.

9. Chudacoff and Smith, *Evolution of American Urban Society*, 11.

10. Cumbler, *Reasonable Use*, 4–5, 8–10, 20–24, 34–35, 53; Marchand, *North Woods*, 16–17; Muir, *Reflections*, 63, 70, 137.

11. Muir, *Reflections*, 104–112, 160–161.

12. Theodore Steinberg, *Nature Incoporated: Industrialization and the Waters of New England* (Amherst: University of Massachusetts Press, 1991), 206–207; Muir, *Reflections*, 93–97.

13. Cumbler, *Reasonable Use*, 54–56, 77–100.

14. N. S. Shaler, "Environment and Man in New England," *The North American Review*, vol. 162 (June 1896), 725–740 (courtesy of Cornell University Library, Making of America Digital Collection).

15. Cumbler, *Reasonable Use*, 3, 103–107, 158.

16. Ibid., 3, 51, 103–107, 132–136, 138–140.

17. Joel Garreau, *Edge City: Life on the New Frontier* (New York: Anchor Press, 1992), 6–7, 74–89.

18. John J. Monahan, "Tainted Soil May Give Life to Old Dump," *Worcester Telegram*, July 27, 2003.

19. Marchand, *North Woods*, 135–136; Environmental Protection Agency, "2002 State of the Environment Report—New England," accessed at www.epa.gov.

20. J.R. Greene, *The Creation of Quabbin Reservoir: The Death of the Swift River Valley* (N.p.: J&R Printers, 2001), vi–94.

21. Environmental Protection Agency, "2002 State of the Environment Report"; Muir, *Reflections* 222–226; "The Sorry Story of George's Bank," BIOBULLETIN, American Museum of Natural History, accessed at http://sciencebulletins.amnh.org; "More Salt, Less Phosphate."

Ethnicity

1. Quoted in James Axtell, *Native and Newcomers: The Cultural Origins of North America* (New York: Oxford University Press, 2001), 18.

2. Thomas Hylland Eriksen, "Ethnicity, Race and Nation," in *The Ethnicity Reader: Nationalism, Multiculturalism and Migration*, ed. M. Guibernau and J. Rex (Oxford: Blackwell Press, 1999).

3. Max Weber, *Economy and Society* (Los Angeles: University of California Press, [1922] 1978).

4. Ibid.

5. Eduardo Bonilla-Silva, "Rethinking Racism: Towards a Structural Interpretation," *American Sociological Review* 62 (1999): 465–480; Michael Omi and Howard Winant, *Racial Formations in the United States: From the 1960s to the 1980s* (New York: Routledge Press, 1994).

6. Barry Pritzker, *Native Americans: An Encyclopedia of History, Culture, and Peoples*, vol. 2 (Santa Barbara, CA: ABC-CLIO, 1998), 577.

7. Leonard Dinnerstein, Roger L. Nichols, and David M. Reimers, *Native and Strangers: A Multicultural History of Americans* (New York: Oxford University Press, 2003), 4.

8. Axtell, *Native and Newcomers*, 47.

9. Ibid.

10. Barry T. Klein, *Reference Encyclopedia of the American Indian*, 9th ed (New York: Todd Publications, 2000), 1.

11. Carl Waldman, *Atlas of the North American Indian* (New York: Facts on File, 1988), 31.

12. Alden T. Vaughan, *New England Frontier: Puritans and Indians 1620–1675* (Norman: University of Oklahoma Press, 1995), 28.

13. Sharon Malinowski and Anna Sheets, eds., *The Gale Encyclopedia of Native American Tribes*, vol. 1 (New York: Gale, 1998).

14. Vaughan, *New England Frontier*, 29.

15. Margo Burns, "Native American Indians," *17th Century New England (with special emphasis on the Salem Witchcraft Trials of 1692)*, April 25, 2003, http://www.ogram.org/17thc/natives.shtml (July 9, 2003).

16. Gordon Day, "English-Indian Contacts in New England," in *In Search of New England's Native Past: Selected Essays by Gordon M. Day*, ed. Michael K. Foster and William Cowan (Amherst: University of Massachusetts Press, 1998), 65.

17. Dinnerstein, Nichols, and Reimers, *Native and Strangers*, 4.

18. Claudia Durst Johnson, *Daily Life in Colonial New England* (Westport, CT: Greenwood Press, 2002), 133.

19. Kathleen J. Bragdon, *Native People of Southern New England, 1500–1650* (Norman: University of Oklahoma Press, 1996), 25.

20. Klein, *Reference Encyclopedia*, 11–12, 18.

21. Bragdon, *Native People*, 25.

22. David Cressy, *Coming Over: Migration and Communication Between England and New England in the Seventeenth Century* (New York: Cambridge University Press, 1987), 4.

23. Ibid., 1.

24. Bruce J. Bourque, *Twelve Thousand Years: American Indians in Maine* (Lincoln: University of Nebraska Press, 2001), 118.

25. Cressy, *Coming Over*, 4.

26. Ibid., 3.

27. Ibid., 6.

28. Vaughan, *New England Frontier*, 3–4.

29. Louis Martin Sears, "The Puritan and His Indian Ward," *American Journal of Sociology* 22, no. 1 (July 1916): 80–93.

30. Ibid., 83.

31. Ibid., 80.

32. William S. Simmons, "Cultural Bias in the New England Puritans' Perception of Indians," *William and Mary Quarterly*, Third Series 38, no. 1 (January 1981): 56–72.

33. Axtell, *Native and Newcomers*, 41.

34. Dinnerstein, Nichols, and Reimers, *Native and Strangers*, 3.

35. Ibid.

36. Daniel R. Mandell, *Behind the Frontier: Indians in Eighteenth-Century Eastern Massachusetts* (Lincoln: University of Nebraska Press, 1996), 10.

37. Axtell, *Native and Newcomers*, 16.

38. Bragdon, *Native People*, 6.

39. Vaughan, *New England Frontier*, 59.

40. Jan Nederveen Pieterse, "White Negroes," in *Gender, Race, and Class in Media: A Text-Reader*, 2nd ed., ed. Gail Dines and Jean M. Humez (Thousand Oaks: Sage Publications, [1992] 2003), 113.

41. Ibid., 114.

42. Ibid.

43. Enrique Morales-Diaz, "Resistance and Counter-Discourse in Reinaldo Arenas' Writing," *Journal of Caribbean Literatures* (forthcoming).

44. Bragdon, *Native People*, 4.

45. Dennis Walder, *Post-Colonial Literatures in English: History, Language, Theory* (Oxford: Blackwell Publishers, 1998), 40.

46. Vaughan, *New England Frontier*, 58.

47. Cressy, *Coming Over*, 20.

48. Quoted in Bragdon, *Native People*, 3–4.

49. Norman R. Yetman, ed., *Majority and Minority: The Dynamics of Race and Ethnicity in American Life*, 6th ed. (Boston: Allyn and Bacon, 1999), 91.

50. Bourque, *Twelve Thousand Years*, 120.

51. Mandell, *Behind the Frontier*, 9.

52. Frederick Matthew Wiseman, *The Voice of the Dawn: An Autohistory of the Abenaki Nation* (Hanover, NH: University Press of New England, 2001), 69.

53. Ibid.

54. Ibid., 70.

55. Mandell, *Behind the Frontier*, 14–15.

56. Donna Keith Barron, J. Edward Hood, and Holly V. Izard, "They Were Here All Along: The Native American Presence in Lower-Central New England in the Eighteenth and Nineteenth Centuries." *William and Mary Quarterly*, Third Series 53, no. 3 (July 1996): 561–586.

57. Ibid., 564.

58. Mandell, *Behind the Frontier*, 10.

59. Vaughan, *New England Frontier*, 30.

60. Johnson, *Daily Life*, 134–135.

61. Virginia DeJohn Anderson, *New England's Generation: The Great Migration and the Formation of Society and Culture in the Seventeenth Century* (New York: Cambridge University Press, 1991), 16.

62. Cressy, *Coming Over*, 74.

63. Quoted in DeJohn Anderson, *New England's Generation*, 18.

64. Vaughan, *New England Frontier*, 94.

65. Mandell, *Behind the Frontier*, 13.

66. Ibid., 14.

67. DeJohn Anderson, *New England's Generation*, 19.

68. Ibid., 39–40.

69. Juan González, *Harvest of Empire: A History of Latinos in America* (New York: Viking, 2000), 13.

70. Johnson, *Daily Life*, 156.

71. Ibid., 147.

72. Winthrop D. Jordan, *White over Black: American Attitudes Toward the Negro, 1550–1812* (New York: W. W. Norton, 1977), 243.

73. Ibid., 247.

74. Lorenzo Johnston Greene, *The Negro in Colonial New England* (New York: Atheneum, 1968), 18–19.

75. Ibid., 19.

76. Louis Ruchames, "The Sources of Racial Thought in Colonial America," *Journal of Negro History* 52, no. 4 (October 1967): 251–272.

77. Dinnerstein, Nichols, and Reimers, *Native and Strangers*, 11.

78. Ruchames, "Sources," 253.

79. Jordan, *White over Black*, 67–68.

80. Ibid., 68.

81. Yetman, "Majority and Minority," 103.

82. Ibid.

83. Ruchames, "Sources of Racial Thought," 251.

84. Yetman, "Majority and Minority," 103.

85. Johnson, *Daily Life*, 148.

86. Ibid.

87. Kerby A. Miller, "'Scotch-Irish' Myths and 'Irish' Identities in Eighteenth- and Nineteenth-Century America," in *New Perspectives on the Irish Diaspora*, ed. C. Fanning (Carbondale Illinois: Southern Illinois University Press, 2000).

88. Miller, 80–83.

89. Ibid.

90. Hasia Diner, "Erin's Children in America: Three Centuries of Irish Immigration to the United States," in *Origin and Destinies: Immigration, Race, and Ethnicity in America*, ed. Susan Pedraza and Ruben G. Rumbaut (Albany: Wadsworth Publishing Group, 1996), 161–171.

91. Ibid.

92. Ibid.

93. United States Historical Census Data Browser (2003).

94. Duncan Social Economic Index Score or 24.33 (*28.47*).

95. Ramón Borgas-Mendez, "Migration, Social Networks, Poverty and Regionalization of Puerto Rican Settlement: Barrio Formation in Lowell, Lawrence, and Holyoke, Massachusetts," *Latino Studies Journal* 4 (1993): 3–21; Jose E. Cruz, *Identity and Power: Puerto Rican Politics and the Challenge of Ethnicity* (Philadelphia: Temple University Press, 1998), 15–19; Ruth Glasser, *Aquí me quedo: Puerto Ricans in Connecticut* (Hartford: Connecticut Humanities Council, 1997), 35; Julio Morales, *Puerto Rican Poverty and Migration: We Just Had to Try Elsewhere* (Westport, CT: Praeger Publishers, 1986), 56.

96. Ibid., 30–36.

97. Jorge Duany, *The Puerto Rican Nation on the Move: Identities on the Island and in the United States* (Chapel Hill: University of North Carolina Press, 2002), 102–105; Adalberto Lopez, *Puerto Rico and Puerto Ricans: Studies in History and Society* (New Jersey: John Wiley & Sons, 1974), 96–100; Morales, *Puerto Rican Poverty*, 56–60.

98. Arturo Morales-Carrion, *Puerto Rico: A Political and Cultural History* (New York: W.W. Norton, 1984), 89–94; Francisco Rivera-Batiz and Carlos Santiago, *Island Paradox* (New York: Russell Sage Foundation, 1996), 110–115.

99. Pedro A. Caban, "The Colonizing Mission of the United States in Puerto Rico, 1898–1930," in *Transnational Latina/o Communities: Politics, Process, and Cultures* ed. C.G. Velez-Ibanez and A. Sampaio (Lanham, MD: Rowman and Littlefield, 2002), 31–33; Lopez, *Puerto Rico*, 96–100.

100. Borgas-Mendez, "Migration," 3–21; Cruz, *Identity and Power*, 15–19; Glasser, *Aquí me quedo*, 35; Morales, *Puerto Rican Poverty*, 56.

101. Rivera-Batiz and Santiago, *Island Paradox*, 25.

102. Enrico Marcelli, "Latinos in Massachusetts: Legal Immigration to New England During the 1990s," *Mauricio Gastón Institute for Latino Community Development and Public Policy* (University of Massachusetts—Boston, April 2002), 2.

103. Ibid.

104. Armand Chartier, *The Franco-Americans of New England: A History*, trans. Robert J. Lemieux and Claire Quintal (Worcester, MA: ACA Assurance; Institut Français of Assumption College, [1999] 2000), 45–53.

105. Claude Bélanger, "French Canadian Emigration to the United States, 1840–1930," vol. 2003, Department of History, Marianopolis College, 2–4.

106. Chartier, *Franco-Americans*, 45–53.

107. Bélanger, "French Canadian Emigration," 2–4.

108. Ibid.; Richard S. Sorrell, "The Survivance of French Canadians in New England (1865–1930)," *Ethnic and Racial Studies* 4, no. 1 (January 1981): 91–109.

109. Bélanger, "French Canadian Emigration," 3–5.

110. Ibid.

111. U.S. Census, 2001.

Fashion

1. Teri Agins, *The End of Fashion: The Mass Marketing of the Clothing Business* (New York: William Morrow, 1999).

2. Laurel Thatcher Ulrich, *Good Wives: Image and Reality in the Lives of Women in Northern New England, 1650–1750* (New York: Vintage Books, 1980), 80–81.

3. Jane C. Nylander, *Our Own Snug Fireside: Images of the New England Home, 1760–1860* (New York: Alfred A. Knopf, 1993), 80.

4. Laurel Thatcher Ulrich, *A Midwife's Tale: The Life of Martha Ballard Based on Her Diary, 1785–1812* (New York: Alfred A. Knopf, 1991), 202.

5. Sarah Gooll Putnam Journals, July 25, 1868, vol. 10, Massachusetts Historical Society.

6. Paul J. Lindholdt, ed., *John Josselyn, Colonial Traveler* (Hanover, NH: University Press of New England, 1988), 92–93.

7. Alexander Young, *Chronicles of the First Planters of the Colony of Massachusetts Bay, from 1623 to 1636* (Boston: Charles C. Little and James Brown, 1856), 266.

8. Nylander, *Our Own Snug Fireside*, 264.

9. Linda Baumgarten, *What Clothes Reveal: The Language of Clothing in Colonial and Federal America* (Williamsburg, VA: Colonial Williamsburg Foundation, 2002), 95.

10. Ibid., 82.

11. William R. Bagnall, *The Textile Industries of the United States*, vol. 1, 1639–1810 (Cambridge, MA: Riverside Press, 1893), 12.

12. Baumgarten, *What Clothes Reveal*, 97.

13. Nylander, *Our Own Snug Fireside*, 155.

14. Arthur Harrison Cole, ed., *Industrial and Commercial Correspondence of Alexander Hamilton Anticipating His Report on Manufactures* (Chicago: A. W. Shaw Company, 1928; reprint, New York: Augustus M. Kelley, 1968), 4.

15. Alice Morse Earle, *Two Centuries of Costume in America 1620–1820*, 2 vols. (1903; reprint, New York: Dover, 1970), 738–739.

16. Ibid., 600.

17. Hannah Fisher Diaries, Newport Historical Society.

18. Thomas Dublin, ed., *Farm to Factory: Women's Letters, 1830–1860* (New York: Columbia University Press, 1981), 19.

19. Jeffrey A. Butterworth, "Forming the Past," *Historical Archaeology* 32 no. 3 (1998): 91–98.

20. Linda Welters, "From Moccasins to Frock Coats and Back Again: Ethic Identity and Native American Dress in Southern New England," in *Dress in American Culture*, ed. Patricia C. Cunningham and Susan Voso Lab (Bowling Green, OH: Bowling Green State University Popular Press, 1993), 28.

21. Henry David Thoreau, *The Portable Thoreau*, ed. by Carl Bode (New York: Penguin Books, 1977), 276–277.

22. Ibid., 318–319.

23. Sarah Gooll Putnam Journals, December 2, 1869, vol. 10, Massachusetts Historical Society.

24. Gerard J. Brault, *The French-Canadian Heritage in New England* (Hanover: University Press of New England, 1986), 58.

Film and Theater

1. Richard Ruland and Malcolm Bradbury, *From Puritanism to Postmodernism: A History of American Literature* (New York: Viking, 1991), 17.

2. Margot Heinemann, *Puritanism and Theatre: Thomas Middleton and Opposition Drama under the Early Stuarts* (Cambridge: Cambridge University Press, 1980), 23.

3. Ibid., 31.

4. Ruland and Bradbury, *From Puritanism to Postmodernism*, 32.

5. Ibid., 17.

6. Bruce McConachie, "American Theatre in Context, from the Beginnings to 1870," in *The Cambridge History of American Theatre*, ed. Don B. Wilmeth and Christopher Bigsby, vol. 1 (Cambridge: Cambridge University Press, 1998), 116–117.

7. Quoted in Perry D. Westbrook, *A Literary History of New England* (Bethelehem, PA: Lehigh University Press, 1988), 96.

8. George O. Seilhamer, *History of the American Theatre: Before the Revolution* (Philadelphia: Globe Printing House, 1888), 96–97.

9. Mary C. Henderson, "Scenography, Stagecraft, and Architecture in the American Theatre," in *The Cambridge History of American Theatre*, ed. Don B. Wilmeth and Christopher Bigsby, vol. 1 (Cambridge: Cambridge University Press, 1998), 391.

10. McConachie, "American Theatre in Context," 136.

11. Ibid., 113.

12. Christopher Bigsby and Don B. Wilmeth, "Introduction," *The Cambridge History of American Theatre*, ed. Don B. Wilmeth and Christopher Bigsby, vol. 1 (Cambridge: Cambridge University Press, 1998), 19.

13. Thornton Wilder, "Preface" to *Three Plays* (New York: Harper & Row, 1957), x.

14. Harriet Beecher Stowe, letter, 1852.

15. Marvin Carlson, "Ernesto Rossi in America," in *Theatrical Touring and Founding in North America*, ed. L. W. Connolly (Westport, CT: Greenwood Press, 1982), 7.

16. Howard Taubman, *The Making of the American Theatre* (New York: Coward McCann, 1965), 95.

17. Correspondence with author.

18. Quoted in Bigsby and Wilmeth, "Introduction," 1.

19. Eugene O'Neill, *Complete Plays* (New York: Library of America, 1988), 219.

20. Thomas Postlewait, "The Hieroglyphic Stage," in *The Cambridge History of American Theatre*, ed. Don B. Wilmeth and Christopher Bigsby, vol. 2 (Cambridge, England: Cambridge University Press, 1998), 113.

Folklore

1. Elizabeth Reynard, *The Narrow Land* (Boston: Houghton Mifflin, 1978), 24–25.

2. Marge Bruchac, "Deep Presence: Abenaki History and Influence (2002 Conference Summary)," http://www.fpc.edu/monadnockinstitute/conf2002.html, Monadnock Institute of Nature, Place and Culture.

3. http://www.kstrom.net/isk/stories/cinder3.html.

4. Richard Dorson, *America in Legend* (New York: Pantheon, 1975), 20.

5. Ibid.

6. Ibid., 21.

7. Edward Rowe Snow, *Ghosts, Gales and Gold* (Cornwall, NY: Cornwall Press, 1972), 8.

8. Ibid., 8–9.

9. Jill Lepore, *The Name of War: King Philip's War and the Origin of American Identity* (New York: Vintage, 1998), 102.

10. Ibid., 103.

11. Dorson, *America*, 41.

12. Ibid., 42–43.

13. Reynard, *Narrow Land*, 163.

14. Richard Dorson, *Buying the Wind: Regional Folklore in the United States* (Chicago: University of Chicago Press, 1964), 55–56.

15. Julien Olivier, *D'la Boucane*, trans. Michael Hoberman (Cambridge, MA: Lesley College, 1979), 25–26.

16. Constance Rourke, *American Humor* (New York: Harcourt, Brace, 1931), 16–17.

17. Richard Dorson, *Jonathan Draws the Long Bow* (Cambridge, MA: Harvard University Press, 1946), 128–129.

18. Dorson, *Buying*, 32–33.

19. S. E. Schlosser, "Old Man Moses," www.americanfolklore.net/folktales/nh.html.

20. Michael Hoberman, *Yankee Moderns: Folk Regional Identity in the Sawmill Valley of Western Massachusetts, 1890–1920* (Knoxville: University of Tennessee Press, 2000), 41.

21. George Carey, "It's Home I Want to Be: Joanna Colcord's Maritime Legacy," *Northeast Folklore* 35 (2000): 46.

22. B. A. Botkin, *A Treasury of American Folklore* (1944) (New York: Bonanza Books, 1983), 831.

23. Hoberman, *Yankee*, 57.

24. Pamela Wood, ed., *The Salt Book* (Garden City, NY: Anchor, 1977), 417–419.

25. Ibid., 419.

26. Ibid., 416.

27. Stephen Nissenbaum, "New England as Region and Nation," in *All Over the Map: Rethinking American Regions*, ed. Edward Ayers and Peter Onuf (Baltimore: Johns Hopkins University Press, 1996), 39–40.

28. "Manchester and the Amoskeag," New Hampshire Public Television, www.nhptv.org/kn/itv/ournhtg10.htm.

29. Donald Deschenes, "The Dream of a Better Life in the Songs of Departure to the United States," in *Steeples and Smokestacks*, ed. Claire Quintal (Worcester, MA: Institut Français, 1996), 439.

30. Gerard Brault, *The French Canadian Presence in New England* (Hanover, NH and Montreal, Canada: University Press of New England and McGill Queens University Press, 1986).

31. Michael Hoberman, "High Crimes and Falling Factories: Nostalgic Utopianism in an Eclipsed New England Industrial Town," *Oral History Review* 28, no. 1 (Winter–Spring 2001): 32.

32. Josee Vachon, personal interview, June 4, 1994.

33. Doris Kirkpatrick, *Around the World in Fitchburg* (Fitchburg, MA: Fitchburg Historical Society, 1975), 25.

34. Olivier, *D'la Boucane*, 91.

35. Dick Sweterlitsch, "Sophia Bielli: A Story Teller," *Northeast Folklore* 30 (1995): 47.

36. Ibid., 49.

37. Anna Sevigny and Julia Moore, "Anna May," *Northeast Folklore* 20 (1979): 17.

38. Mary Doyle Curran, *The Parish and the Hill* (1948; New York: Feminist Press, 1978), 6–7.

39. Howard Russell, *A Long and Deep Furrow* (Hanover, NH: University Press of New England, 1982), 257.

40. Hoberman, *Yankee*, 39.

41. Pauleena MacDougall, "Edward Dawson Ives: Folklorist, Biographer, Professor: A Biographical Sketch," *Northeast Folklore* 35 (2000): 3–28.

42. Dorson, *America*, 153.

43. Ibid.

44. Hoberman, *Yankee*, 76–77.

45. Ibid., 47.

46. Barre Toelken, *The Dynamics of Folklore* (Boston: Houghton Mifflin, 1979), 137.

47. Ibid.

48. Linda Silka, "The Southeast Asian Environmental Justice Partnership: Citizens Revive a New England Mill Town River," *New Village Journal*, no. 3 (2003), http://newvillage.net/Journal/Issue3/3silka.html.

49. William Cumpiano, "Cultural Translations," *Newsletter of the Pioneer Valley Folklore Society* 15, no. 6 (November–December 1991): 6–7.

50. Ibid.

51. Hoberman, "High Crimes," 36.

52. Sebastian Junger, *A Perfect Storm* (New York: Harper Perennial, 1997), 87.

53. Jill Linzee and Michael P. Chaney, *Deeply Rooted: New Hampshire Traditions in Wood* (Durham, NH: Art Gallery, University of New Hampshire, 1997), 34.

54. Kathy Neustadt, *Clambake* (Amherst: University of Massachusetts Press, 1992), 69.

55. Michael Hoberman, "Teenage Folklore in the Pioneer Valley," *Folk Life: A Publication of the Pioneer Valley Folklore Society*, Spring 1993, 26.

Food

1. Excerpt from a letter by Edward Winslow, December 11, 1621, from *Mourt's Relation: A Journal of the Pilgrims at Plymouth* (1622).

2. *Godey's Lady's Book*, November 1865, 466.

3. Harriet Beecher Stowe, *Oldtown Folks* (Boston: Fields, Osgood, 1869), 2.

Language

1. Quoted in Jacob Bennett, "George Savary Wasson and the Dialect of Kittery Point, Maine," *American Speech* (Spring/Summer 1974): 54.

2. Walt Wolfram and Natalie Schilling-Estes, *American English* (Malden, MA: Blackwell, 1998), 103.

3. J. L. Dillard, *A History of American English* (London: Longman, 1992), 6.

4. H. L. Mencken, *The American Language*, 4th ed. (New York: Alfred A. Knopf, 1936), 106.

5. Quoted in Raoul Smith, *The Language of Jonathan Fisher (1768–1847)*, Publication No. 72 of the American Dialect Society (Tuscaloosa: University of Alabama Press for the Society, 1985), 9.

6. David Hackett Fischer, *Albion's Seed: Four British Folkways in America* (New York: Oxford University Press, 1989), 59.

7. Sarah Orne Jewett, *The Country of the Pointed Firs and Other Stories* (New York: Doubleday, 1989), 50.

8. Harriet Beecher Stowe, *Three Novels* (New York: Library of America, 1982), 1214–1215.

9. Robert E. Abrams, "Charles Farrar Browne," *Dictionary of Literary Biography*, vol. 11: *American Humorists, 1800–1950* (Farmington, MI: Gale Group, 1982), 64.

10. John Gould, *Maine Lingo* (Camden, ME: Down East Magazine, 1975), xiii.

11. R. E. Gould, *Yankee Drummer* (New York: McGraw-Hill, 1947), 38.

12. Craig M. Carver, *American Regional Dialects* (Ann Arbor: University of Michigan Press, 1987), 25.

13. Ibid., 17.

14. Correspondence with the author, March 19, 2004.

15. Walt Wolfram, *Dialects and American English* (Englewood Cliffs, NJ: Prentice-Hall, 1991), 76, 19.

16. Carver, *American Regional Dialects*, 21.

17. Crawford Feagin, "Entering the Community: Fieldwork," in *The Handbook of Language Variation and Change*, ed. J. K. Chambers, Peter Trudgill, and Natalie Schilling-Estes (Malden, MA: Blackwell, 2002), 27.

18. Carver, *American Regional Dialects*, 9.

19. Marcella Bombardieri, "It's Still a Mahk of Distinction: The Accent Sets Bostonians Apart," *Boston Globe*, September 23, 1999, B1.

20. Ibid., 8.

21. Mary R. Miller, "Bilingualism in Northern New England," *Publication of the American Dialect Society*, no. 52 (November 1969): 11.

22. Jane S. Smith, "Maine-ly English," *Language Magazine*, forthcoming.

Literature

1. Andrew Delbanco, ed., *Writing New England: An Anthology from the Puritans to the Present* (Cambridge, MA: Harvard University Press, 2001), xiii.

2. John Conforti, *Imagining New England: Explorations of Regional Identity from the Pilgrims to the Mid-Twentieth Century* (Chapel Hill: University of North Carolina Press, 2001), 3.

3. Bernard Bailyn, "Butterfield's Adams: Notes for a Sketch," *William and Mary Quarterly*, 3rd Ser., 19 (1962): 243.

4. Ibid., 80.

5. Ibid., 82–83.

6. Ibid., 111.

7. F. O. Mathiessen, *American Renaissance: Art and Expression in the Age of Emerson and Whitman* (New York: Oxford University Press, 1941), vii.

8. Ibid., xv.

9. Conforti, *Imagining New England*, 165.

10. Delbanco, *Writing New England*, 60.

11. Malcolm Bradbury and James McFarlane, "The Name and Nature of Modernism," in *Modernism*, ed. Malcolm Bradbury and James McFarlane (London: Penguin Books, 1976), 49.

12. Ibid., 50.

13. Marshall Berman, *All that Is Solid Melts into Air: The Experience of Modernity* (London: Verso, 1982), 15.

14. Brian Lee and Robert Reinders, "The Loss of Innocence: 1880–1914," in *Introduction to American Studies*, ed. Malcolm Bradbury and Howard Temperley (London: Longman, 1989), 211.

15. Werner Sollors, introduction to *The Promised Land*, by Mary Antin (New York: Penguin Books, 1997), xv.

16. Delbanco, *Writing New England*, 181.

17. Conforti, *Imagining New England*, 316.

Music

1. Eric von Schmidt and Jim Rooney, *Baby, Let Me Follow You Down: The Illustrated Story of the Cambridge Folk Years*, 2nd ed. (Amherst: University of Massachusetts Press, 1994), 262.

2. Michael Azerard, *Our Band Could Be Your Life: Scenes from the American Indie Underground, 1981–1991* (Boston: Little, Brown, 2001), 95.

Religion

1. James M. O'Toole, *Militant and Triumphant: William Henry O'Connell and the Catholic Church in Boston, 1859–1944* (Notre Dame, IN: University of Notre Dame Press, 1992), 144.

2. Ibid., 146.

3. Joseph J. Casino, "From Sanctuary to Involvement: A History of the Catholic Parish in the Northeast," in Jay P. Dolan, ed., *The American Catholic Parish: A History from 1850 to the Present*, vol. 1 (Mahwah, NJ: Paulist Press, 1987), 87.

4. All percentages are derived from Dale E. Jones, Sherri Doty, Clifford Grammich, James E. Horsch, Richard Houseal, Mac Lynn, John P. Marcum, Kenneth M. Sanchagrin, and Richard H. Taylor, *Religious Congregations and Membership in the United States, 2000: An Enumeration by Region, State and County Based on Data Reported for 149 Religious Bodies* (Nashville, TN: Glenmary Research Center, 2002).

Sports and Recreation

1. *General Laws and Liberties of the Massachuset[t]ts Callings*. Revised and re-printed by order of the General Court holden at Boston, May 15th, 1672: Edward Rawson, secr. (Cambridge, MA: Printed by Samuel Green, for John Usher of Boston, 1672), 347; also see "Arts and Amusements," in Claudia Durst Johnson, *Daily Life in Colonial New England* (Westport, CT: Greenwood Press, 2002).

2. Samuel Sewall, *The Diary of Samuel Sewall, 1674–1729*, newly edited from the manuscript at the Massachusetts Historical Society by M. Halsey Thomas (New York: Farrar, Straus and Giroux, 1973), vol. 1, 1674–1708; vol. 2, 1709–1729.

3. *Massachusetts. Records of the Governor and the Company of Massachusetts Bay* [Massa-

chusetts Records], I, November 30, 1631; printed by order of the legislature, ed. Nathanial B. Shurtleff (Boston: William White Press, 1853), 5 vols. S, I, November 30, 1637, 213.

4. Increase Mather, *A Testimony Against Several Prophane and Superstitious Customs* (London, 1687); John Downname, *A Guide to Godlynesse: or, a Treatise of a Christian Life* . . . (London: Printed by Felix Kingstone for Ed. Weuer and W. Bladen, 1622), 164.

5. Ralph Hickok, *Encyclopedia of North American Sports History*, 2nd ed. (New York: Facts on File, 2002), 293.

6. Nathan Cobb, "Remembering the Braves and Having a Ball," *Boston Globe*, March 8, 2003, G1, G8.

7. Derek Carsam, "On Fenway, Faith, and Fandom: A Red Sox Fan Reflects," in *Baseball and American Culture: Across the Diamond*, ed. Edward J. Rielly (New York: Haworth, 2003), 21.

8. Hickok, *Encyclopedia*, 536.

9. Bernard Corbett, *The Beanpot: Fifty Years of Thrills, Spills, and Chills* (Boston: Northeastern University, 2002), 2–3.

10. Hickok, *Encyclopedia*, 373–374.

11. Description from records held in the Arthur and Elizabeth Schlesinger Library, Radcliffe Institute for Advanced Study, Harvard University, Cambridge, Massachusetts.

12. E. M. Swift, "Vermont Made," *Sports Illustrated*, March 29, 2004, 33–34.

13. Hickok, *Encyclopedia*, 84–85.

14. Richard Higgins, "Their Quest: Capturing New England's Character," *Boston Globe*, May 6, 2001, B6.

BIBLIOGRAPHY

Ayers, Edward L., and Peter S. Onuf, eds. *All Over the Map: Rethinking American Regions*. Baltimore: Johns Hopkins University Press, 1996.

Beales, Carleton. *Our Yankee Heritage: New England's Contribution to American Civilization*. Freeport, NY: Books for Libraries Press, 1955.

Benes, Peter, and Jane Montague Benes, eds. *The Bay and the River, 1600–1900*. Boston: Boston University, 1982.

————. *Foodways in the Northeast*. Boston: Boston University, 1984.

————. *New England Prospect: Maps, Place Names, and the Historical Landscape*. Boston: Boston University, 1980.

Benes, Peter, Jane Montague Benes, and Ross W. Beales, Jr., eds. *New England/New France, 1600–1850*. Boston: Boston University, 1992.

Bercovitch, Sacvan, ed. *The American Puritan Imagination: Essays in Reevaluation*. New York: Cambridge University Press, 1974.

Bragdon, Kathleen J. *Native People of Southern New England, 1500–1650*. Norman: University of Oklahoma Press, 1996.

Brault, Gerard J. *The French-Canadian Heritage in New England*. Hanover, NH: University Press of New England, 1986.

Buell, Lawrence. *New England Literary Culture from Revolution Through Renaissance*. New York: Cambridge University Press, 1986.

Carroll, Peter N. *Puritanism and the Wilderness: The Intellectual Significance of the New England Frontier, 1629–1700*. New York: Columbia University Press, 1969.

Chartier, Armand. *The Franco-Americans of New England: A History*. Trans. Robert J. Lemieux and Claire Quintal. Worcester, MA: ACA Assurance; Institut Français of Assumption College, 2000.

Conforti, John. *Imagining New England: Explorations of Regional Identity from the Pilgrims to the Mid-Twentieth Century*. Chapel Hill: University of North Carolina Press, 2001.

Cressy, David. *Coming Over: Migration and Communication Between England and New England in the Seventeenth Century*. New York: Cambridge University Press, 1987.

Cronon, William. *Changes in the Land: Indians, Colonists, and the Ecology of New England*. New York: Hill and Wang, 1983.

DeJohn Anderson, Virginia. *New England's Generation: The Great Migration and the Formation of Society and Culture in the Seventeenth Century*. New York: Cambridge University Press, 1991.

Delbanco, Andrew, ed. *Writing New England: An Anthology from the Puritans to the Present*. Cambridge: Harvard University Press, 2001.

Fischer, David Hackett. *Albion's Seed: Four British Folkways in America*. New York: Oxford University Press, 1989.

Foster, Michael K., and William Cowan, eds. *In Search of New England's Native Past: Selected Essays by Gordon M. Day*. Amherst: University of Massachusetts Press, 1998.

Hale, Judson D. *Inside New England*. New York: Harper and Row, 1982.

Hall, Joan Houston, ed. *The Dictionary of American Regional English*. Vol. 4. Cambridge: Belknap Press, 2002.

Johnson, Claudia Durst. *Daily Life in Colonial New England*. Westport, CT: Greenwood Press, 2002.

Johnston Greene, Lorenzo. *The Negro in Colonial New England*. New York: Atheneum, 1968.

Jones, Dale E., Sherri Doty, et al. *Religious Congregations and Membership in the United States 2000: An Enumeration by Region, State and County Based on Data Reported for 149 Religious Bodies*. Nashville, TN: Glenmary Research Center, 2002.

Kurath, Hans. *A Word Geography of the Eastern United States*. Ann Arbor: University of Michigan Press, 1949.

La Voie, Ronald. *New England, 1790 to 1970: A Graphic Presentation of Population Data by State and County*. Hartford: Northeast Utilities Service Co., 1976.

Leonard, Justin. *American Cooking: New England*. New York: Time-Life, 1970.

McManis, Douglas R. *Colonial New England: A Historical Geography*. New York: Oxford University Press, 1975.

Miller, Perry. *The New England Mind: From Colony to Province*. Cambridge: Harvard University Press, 1953.

————. *The New England Mind: The Seventeenth Century*. Cambridge: Harvard University Press, 1954.

Nissenbaum, Stephen, "New England as Region and Nation." In Edward Ayers and Peter Onuf, eds., *All Over the Map: Rethinking American Regions*. Baltimore: Johns Hopkins University Press, 1996.

Nylander, Jane. *Our Own Snug Fireside: Images of the New England Home, 1760–1860*. New York: Knopf, 1994.

O'Brien, Robert, and Richard D. Brown, eds. *The Encyclopedia of New England*. New York: Facts on File, 1985.

Snow, Dean R. *The Archaeology of New England*. New York: Academic Press, 1980.

Sorrell, Richard S. "The Survivance of French Canadians in New England (1865–1930)." *Ethnic and Racial Studies* 4 (1981): 91–109.

Starbuck, David R., and Charles E. Bolian, eds. *Early and Middle Archaic Cultures in the Northeast*. Rindge, NH: Department of Anthropology, Franklin Pierce College, 1980.

Ulrich, Laurel Thatcher. *Good Wives: Image and Reality in the Lives of Women in Northern New England, 1650–1750*. New York: Vintage Books, 1980.

Vaughan, Alden T. *New England Frontier: Puritans and Indians 1620–1675*. Norman: University of Oklahoma Press, 1995.

Vaughan, Alden T., and Francis J. Bremer, eds. *Puritan New England: Essays on Religion, Society, and Culture*. New York: St. Martin's Press, 1977.

Westbrook, Perry D. *A Literary History of New England*. Bethlehem: Lehigh University Press, 1988.

Whitehill, Jane. *Food, Drink, and Recipes of Early New England*. Sturbridge, MA: Old Sturbridge Village, 1963.

Whiting, Edward Elwell. *Changing New England*. New York: The Century Co., 1929.
————. *The New England Town in Fact and Fiction*. Rutherford, NJ: Fairleigh Dickinson University Press, 1982.
Wilson, Harold F. *The Hill Country of Northern New England: Its Social and Economic History, 1790–1930*. New York: AMS Press, 1967.
Zeigler, Joseph Wesley. *Regional Theatre: The Revolutionary Stage*. New York: Da Capo Press, 1973.

INDEX

Note: Page numbers in *italic* type refer to illustrations.

ABOUT THE
EDITOR AND
CONTRIBUTORS

MICHAEL SLETCHER holds a Ph.D. in history from the University of Cambridge, where he has taught colonial American history. He is Assistant Editor of the Benjamin Franklin Papers at Yale University and has published articles on colonial America and early modern Britain. He is the author of *New Haven: From Puritanism to the Age of Terrorism* (2004).

GABRIEL AQUINO is a Ph.D. candidate at the University at Albany and a visiting lecturer at Skidmore College, Department of Sociology, Anthropology, and Social Work. He has held a variety of research positions, including statistician at the Stratton Virginia Medical Center and Research Scientist II at the New York State Office of Mental Health. He has published reports for the New York State Office of Mental Health and an article for *Phoebe: A Journal of Feminist Scholarship, Theory, and Aesthetics*. His areas of specialization include race and ethnicity, work, inequality, Latin America and the Caribbean, demography, and urbanization.

LISA KRISSOFF BOEHM is Assistant Professor of Urban Studies at Worcester State College. She holds a Ph.D. in American history from Indiana University. She is the author of *Popular Culture and the Enduring Myth of Chicago 1871–1968* (2004) and the forthcoming *"Making a Way Out of No Way": African American Domestic Workers in the Industrial North 1940–1970*, a work based on newly collected oral histories of women who took part in the Second Great Migration.

JEREMY BONNER holds a Ph.D. in American history from the Catholic University of America in Washington, D.C., and is currently an independent scholar in Baltimore, Maryland. He has published on political and religious history in such journals as the *Journal of Mormon History* and *Anglican and Episcopal History*. He is currently working on a biography of Victor J. Reed, Catholic Bishop of Oklahoma City and Tulsa, 1958–1971.

SUZANNE COPE is a freelance writer in the Boston area. A recurring columnist and feature writer for *Citizen Culture* magazine, she also works in book and music promotion.

ANTHONY GEORGE holds a Master's of Divinity from the University of Edinburgh and a Ph.D. in Humanities, with a concentration in Philosophy of Religion, from Florida State University. He teaches humanities at the New England Institute of Art, Boston.

HERBERT R. HARTEL, JR., holds a Ph.D. in modern and American art history from the Graduate School of the City University of New York. He has taught at John Jay College of Criminal Justice, Baruch College, York College, Fordham University, and Pratt Institute. He has published studies on the American landscape painter John F. Kensett and his research interests include American landscape painting and the influence of Emersonian Transcendentalism on American visual culture.

MICHAEL HOBERMAN is Assistant Professor of English and Folklore at Fitchburg State College. He is the author of *Yankee Moderns: Folk Regional Identity in the Sawmill Valley of Western Massachusetts, 1890–1920* (2000). He is currently working on a book about the cultural lives of Jews in rural New England.

BLANCHE LINDEN holds a Ph.D. in History of American Civilization from Harvard University. She has published a variety of articles and books, most recently *Boston Freedom Trail* (1996) and *Spring Grove: Celebrating 150 Years* (1995). She is also one of the editors of the forthcoming *Encyclopedia of New England Culture*.

MARTIN J. MANNING is a research librarian in the Bureau of International Information Programs, U.S. Department of State, Washington, DC, on the Economic Security Team and archivist of the Public Diplomacy Historical Collection. He has just completed *Historical Dictionary of American Propaganda*, to be published with Herbert Romerstein by Greenwood Publishing Group (2004). He and Dr. Frank Hoffman co-edit *Contemporary Sports Series* for Haworth Press (1999–   ) and both are collaborating on a book on the globalization of American popular culture for the same publisher.

BARRY MARSHALL is an Assistant Professor at the Berklee College of Music and the New England Institute of Art. He is the producer of over thirty albums, working with artists like Lavern Baker and Peter Wolf, and a songwriter for feature films like *Dick Tracy* and Broadway shows like *Wild Women Blues*.

ENRIQUE MORALES-DÍAZ is Assistant Professor of Spanish at Hartwick College in Oneonta, New York, where he also teaches courses in Latino Studies Gender/Sexuality and Queer Theory. He has published articles on Esmeralda Santiago and Reinaldo Arenas, and serves as the co-editor of *Phoebe: A Journal of Feminist Scholarship, Theory and Aesthetics* published by the Department of Women's & Gender Studies at SUNY Oneonta.

ROBERT F. MOSS received a Ph.D. in English from the University of South Carolina. His recent publications include books and articles on food history and on the detective fiction of Raymond Chandler and Ross Macdonald. He lives in Charleston, South Carolina.

BRUCE F. MURPHY is the author of *The Encyclopedia of Murder and Mystery* (2001) and the editor of the fourth edition of *Benét's Reader's Encyclopedia* (1996). His first collection of poems won the Bobst Award. His poetry, fiction, and essays have appeared in *Critical Inquiry, Paris Review, Poetry, TriQuarterly*, and other journals.

LUCA PRONO holds a Ph.D. in American Studies from the University of Nottingham, United Kingdom. He has published articles on Italian, British, and American literature, Film Studies, and Critical Theory. He lives in Bologna, Italy, where he teaches English as a foreign language.

LINDA WELTERS, Ph.D., is Professor of Textiles, Fashion Merchandising and Design at the University of Rhode Island. She has published widely on the material culture of New England and the folk dress of Europe. She currently is under contract for a book on twentieth-century American fashion. She also edits *Dress*, the scholarly journal of the Costume Society of America.

The Greenwood Encyclopedia of American Regional Cultures

The Great Plains Region, *edited by Amanda Rees*

The Mid-Atlantic Region, *edited by Robert P. Marzec*

The Midwest, *edited by Joseph W. Slade and Judith Yaross Lee*

New England, *edited by Michael Sletcher*

The Pacific Region, *edited by Jan Goggans with Aaron DiFranco*

The Rocky Mountain Region, *edited by Rick Newby*

The South, *edited by Rebecca Mark and Rob Vaughan*

The Southwest, *edited by Mark Busby*